D0567224

REVIEW OF RESEARCH

CONTRIBUTORS

JANET BIXBY
SHARON CONLEY
PETER T. EWELL
JOHN GLENN III
HOWARD GARDNER
EDWARD H. HAERTEL
JANNA HERMAN
THOMAS JAMES
SUSAN KLEIN
N. DICKON REPPUCCI
DAVID SADKER
MYRA SADKER
JANET WARD SCHOFIELD
KENNETH A. STRIKE
DENNIE WOLF

IN EDUCATION

17

1991

GERALD GRANT
EDITOR
SYRACUSE UNIVERSITY

PUBLISHED BY THE
AMERICAN EDUCATIONAL RESEARCH ASSOCIATION
1230 Seventeenth Street, NW
Washington, DC 20036-3078

Library of Congress
Catalog Card No.—72-89719
Printed in the United States of America
ISBN 0-935302-12-3
ISSN 0091-732-X

Contents

Introduction

The position of editor of the *Review of Research in Education* is one of the most interesting and pleasurable jobs in academe. Because the *RRE* publishes only commissioned essays, the editor avoids the disagreeable duties entailed with preparing letters of rejection. And because the scope of the journal is broad, many interests can be explored. These interests are explored in meetings with members of the editorial board who sit or walk about in Palo Alto or Cambridge (to mention the last two places we met) with no other responsibility than to have a good conversation about ideas worth publishing. What you hold in your hands is the outcome of such a conversation.

While our mandate is broad, it was also intelligently framed by the first board of editors and published in Volume 1 in 1973 by Fred N. Kerlinger. Although the *RRE* should have a bias toward "empirical evidence in the scientific tradition," the original board also wisely provided for reviews of philosophy, such as Kenneth Strike's magisterial review of the problems of moral education in this volume, where the word *empirical* may be misplaced. They also felt a place should be reserved for discussion of developments "that may substantially affect educational policy and practice for good or ill." Perhaps none of the reviews published herein is without policy implications, but several splendid reviews, especially those by Thomas James on state politics and Janet Ward Schofield on intergroup relations, will have a significant impact on how we frame policy, as well as plan research.

The volume opens with a policy-laden discussion of new forms of assessment at all levels of education. The reviews of evolving forms of teacher assessment by Edward Haertel and of recent developments in assessment of students by Dennie Wolf and colleagues both discuss the origins of current testing practices in the development of modern bureaucratic systems of education. The emerging consensus, says Haertel, is that these practices, developed in a system of sorting and selecting, are doomed to failure. The assessments that are envisaged are intimately bound up with the improvement of teaching and of the profession itself. The assessment of teaching needs to reflect the complexity of the task—such as making decisions under conditions where it is impossible to specify a single correct answer or acceptable instructional procedure. New evaluation methods must take account of broader professional responsibilities that teachers are now assuming for curriculum development, policy-making, and new roles of mentoring and peer evaluation. The challenge is to develop forms of assessment that reach beyond traditional stereotypes of classroom teaching and address examinees' qualifications for some roles that do not yet exist. This has driven developers to look anew at definitions of the knowledge base of teaching and to experiment with forms of assessment that model the complexities of the teaching act. Haertel describes the range of new strategies being developed, including simulated lessons, interviews that probe a prospective teacher's process of pedagogical reasoning, portfolios and work samples, and classroom observations. He concludes, however, that although these developments are promising, reliability and validity have yet to be demonstrated. He believes the goal should be to develop assessments that "credit the full range of . . . solutions to pedagogical problems" and to move to criterion-referenced standards for certification of teachers. That is, candidates should show that they "have met established standards of professional practice, not merely that they have outperformed a specified fraction of their peers" (p. 25).

Part of our current problem in student assessment is that teachers themselves are so poorly prepared as assessors in their own training. If the examination of teachers must be modeled on good teaching practice, Dennie Wolf, Janet Bixby, John Glenn, and Howard Gardner argue analogously in their chapter that new assessments of students must examine what is meant by "being able to think." The authors ask us to consider thinking as a "performance" involving risk and humility, something that requires interpretations of information and beliefs and is sustained over time and across obstacles. Current testing practices have grown out of a set of beliefs about the nature of intelligence that has had pervasive effects."Chief among these practices are the emphasis on relative ranking above actual accomplishment; the privileging of easily quantifiable, rather than messy and complex, displays of knowledge; the assumption that individual performances, rather than collaborative forms of cognition, are the most powerful indicators of educational progress; and an image of evaluating educational progress as a matter of scientific measurement" (pp. 43–44). The new culture of assessment should focus on documenting accomplishments rather than relative position on an intelligence scale. The notion of unitary intelligence should give way to a view "that the human ability to process and understand is the result of the interaction of multiple intelligences such as an acute understanding of verbal, spatial, or kinesthetic information on differing kinds of aptitudes such as 'street smarts,' creativity, or the capacity for academic inquiry" (p. 49). New assessment instruments must focus on what students can do with resources and engage students in dialogue about what they know and how they can apply it. "At its heart are reflection, judgment, and discussion, in addition to quantification and reliability" (p. 57). Wolf and her colleagues conclude with recognition of the enormousness of the task confronting those who wish to join in developing the new psychometrics they advocate. They foresee a fierce contest between those, like themselves, who are "opening up the possibility of multiple paths to excellence" and those who hold to "idealized, universal descriptions of progress." They argue that those who value clinical judgment and diversity of opinions will need to revise their notions of high-agreement reliability, finding "a previously uncharted course between insisting on uniform judgments and mayhem." Differentiated portraits of student performance mean that we recognize that some students can arrive at an idea but may not be able to express it "in any but the most conventional and boring ways," while others may be lively authors but limp critics (p. 63).

In chapter 3, Peter Ewell portrays the effort to impose new forms of assessment in higher education as a social movement—not unlike what we have just been hearing—driven by political forces while being rooted in measurement practice. Ewell proposes a new taxonomy to distinguish among the purposes of assessment (improvement or demonstration of attainment) and the units of analysis (individuals or groups). Within the individual/improvement cell of his taxonomy, he sees the major new development as "performance assessment designed to document individual mastery of complex, integrated abilities" (p. 83). It is the group/demonstration cell that has kicked off the most heated debate in higher education, however, with increased federal and state demands for colleges and universities to provide more data on outcomes achieved for dollars spent. This has resulted in some highly questionable practices. In Tennessee, for example, the allocation of thousands of dollars in aid "ride[s] on what may in essence be a random process" of discriminating among institutions (p. 114).

The final chapter in the assessment section grapples with the sensitive issues of assessing the effectiveness of sexuality education programs and efforts to educate children so as to prevent or detect child sexual abuse. Millions of children have been exposed to these programs, but the authors of chapter 4, N. Dickon Reppucci and Janna Herman, do not believe that the research justifies their widespread use. At the least, they should be labeled "use with caution." Many existing programs to prevent child abuse seem to be based on the simplistic idea that they can teach children enough information during one or two presentations to enable them to understand the issues and protect themselves. While Reppucci and Herman cite examples of a few programs that have merit, the effectiveness of most remains unproven. In both sexuality education and child sexual abuse prevention programs, "evaluation is much discussed but seldom implemented with sophisticated research designs. . . . Most past evaluations have been flawed in that they have failed to use comparable control groups, to make comparisons of programs, or to report findings of ineffectiveness. . . . Poorly designed and executed evaluations have therefore hindered the improvement of programs and the reduction of health and social problems that could accompany effective education'' (p. 158).

Thomas James opens the next section of the volume with a review of the politics of educational change. Chapter 5 explores the tension between increased emphasis on the need for local initiative and ``an accelerating tilt'' toward more commanding policy controls at the state level. These divergent tendencies will be difficult to reconcile, he believes. Teachers are demanding more say in educational reform. Major changes in governance such as those recently enacted in Chicago give parents more say in the running of individual schools. Governors will become increasingly active participants in setting the educational agenda, and legislatures will do battle with them in attempting to assert control over educational policy. A high priority for researchers now is to sort out the changes ``in the highly interactive roles of policy formulation'' (p. 173). These disputes will lead us to reexamine fundamental questions about what constitutes democratic political community and what purposes the schools should serve. James predicts that the prospect of venturing into such discussions ``will be unsettling for many researchers, especially policy researchers, for it suggests that they can no longer rely on specialized, disciplined, technical control of knowledge about educational change. They must strip away the framework of state intentions that implicitly shapes so much of social-scientific inquiry, and they must start back at the beginning with ethical, risky questions about the democratic reasoning that brings states into the morass of education in the first place'' (p. 175).

Whereas James looks at these tensions primarily through the lens of history and the role of the state, Sharon Conley is at the other end of the telescope with an examination of the role of teachers in decision making within schools. In chapter 6, she finds that much of the research has been poorly conceptualized. For example, earlier research distinguishing among types of participation structures is rarely consulted by those doing new work on specific forms of participation. And too much of what exists has been written from a managerial perspective: there is a dearth of research about teacher participation in decision making that is grounded in the daily internal work of schools. Conley argues that we need research that will tell us why some experiments labeled as participative are not actually increasing teachers' involvement in decision making. She also suggests that researchers should pay more attention to dimensions and domains of decision-making power, and to which actors' interests are being served under different versions of supposedly shared decision making.

In chapters 7 and 8, we turn to issues of gender and race. In both domains, reviewers find that research shows remarkable progress has been made toward achieving more equity but society falls far short of the goals we should achieve. With respect to gender, Myra Sadker, David Sadker, and Susan Klein review four areas of research on equity: curriculum, instruction, administration, and educational outcomes. They find that sex-role stereotyping in textbooks has been markedly reduced, although studies of the stories grade school teachers actually read to their children are much more likely to feature male heroes and masculine themes. By the 1980s, elementary school science series had as many illustrations of females as males, and women were involved in a wide variety of science career roles. Gains in history texts were less impressive, with contributions of women minimized. Children's literature, especially prize-winning books such as the Caldecott medal winners, have become more fair and inclusive. Gains have been especially slow in the field of educational administration, and in some areas declines have occurred. For example, whereas over half of all principals in 1928 were women, today women account for only a quarter of public schools principalships. Women with similar degree qualifications are also paid less than men in like positions. The authors' review of educational outcomes shows that males have approached parity with females on verbal achievement and that females have shown gains on mathematical ability but do not yet equal male performance. They conclude that more research should be undertaken on the causes of intellectual differences between boys and girls and on possible gender bias in assessment instruments. There is a great need, they argue, to identify factors that lower achievement and self-esteem for girls, to assess effective interventions, and to reexamine the impacts of coeducation and single-sex education at different stages of development.

In chapter 8, Janet Ward Schofield provides both a painstaking and sweeping review of the research on race relations—painstaking in that it is a close analysis of the shortcomings of research, and sweeping in that she surveys 50 years. Schofield divides the research on desegregation into six periods. In the first, before the Supreme Court struck down segregation in 1954, few studies were done because there were few integrated schools, but it was important that social scientists did arrive at a consensus about the harm that segregation had done and that they so testified before the Court. In the decade after Brown, the major findings were established by the U.S. Civil Rights Commission report. It was not until the third period (1968–1975), which Schofield calls the active empirical years, that widespread studies were undertaken. These studies were seriously flawed because they focused on outcomes rather than process, gave limited cross-sectional snapshots of complex events, and rarely were able to incorporate adequate control groups. This inaugurated a period of review, disillusionment, and redirection (1975–1983) as it was realized that desegregation alone was not an answer to negative intergroup relations. It also produced an emphasis on qualitative studies in order to understand the complexities of the desegregation process and a focus on what works, on what it would take to make desegregation succeed. Experimental studies were funded to reduce tension and increase positive group interaction, which led to an emphasis on cooperative learning. Schofield sees the last 6 years as a period of theory building. The purposes of desegregation needed rethinking—whether, for instance, the social purpose should be the maintenance of group identities or the establishment of color-blind policies and institutions. Researchers have also been attending to contact theory, which has generated new work on contact between Arab and Israeli youth, between Germans and immigrant populations, between Catholics and Protestants in Northern Ireland, and between Blacks and Whites in South Africa. Writers on intergroup relations have also been absorbing new work on the formation and change of stereotypes. Schofield pleads, however, that while cognitive approaches are important, "it is [also] important to recognize the fundamental role that preexisting affect plays in intergroup situations and to find acceptable, effective, and constructive ways to study conflicted intergroup situations." Without abandoning ethical concerns about exacerbating problems, researchers must have the courage to venture into potentially explosive situations to study "the difficult cases in which affect is strong and negative" (p. 386).

The exceptional essay by Kenneth Strike that concludes the volume provides a vivid example of the public philosophy that Strike finds sadly lacking in current debates about schooling. "A society that conducts its policy debates in academic journals and its politics on Madison Avenue is unlikely to be both intelligent and democratic at the same time," he warns us (p. 414). Strike believes that the academy bears part of the responsibility for creating the appetite for public philosophy and that if we in the academy fail, the result is not trivial.

In examining the moral role of schooling in a liberal democratic society, Strike asserts that the central question is this: How do we constitute the *e pluribus unum* of our society? How do we understand "both what should unite the citizens of a democratic society and the ways in which they permissibly differ" (p. 418). In the liberal view, the state exists to protect individual rights and freedoms and not to establish a moral community or to make people virtuous. "In such a state there is allowed no claim of moral superiority of one citizen over the other," and schools should allow children to explore widely and choose freely among cultural goods. This leads to some ambivalence about the autonomy children should enjoy when they differ with their parents on important moral choices. And there is a question of what role the schools would have in a liberal state in inculcating a sense of justice necessary for a democracy to function. The liberal view is also unacceptable to those who are sympathetic to the Aristotelian ideal that individuals "cannot become fully human apart from associations with others" and that "those goods that constitute human flourishing . . . cannot be achieved" apart from participation in a community (pp. 422, 424). On the other hand, liberals are quick to see the tendency to repression in such communities.

Strike reviews three major responses to these dilemmas, the first of which he captions as versions of "strong democracy" offered by John Dewey and, more recently, by Amy Gutmann, as well as, in a different vein, by some neo-Marxists. Under the label of "democratic traditionalism," he discusses the writings of Mortimer Adler, R. F. Butts, Alan Bloom, E. D. Hirsch, and others who argue in various ways that democratic practice must be rooted in a tradition of democratic thought. That is, children must be instructed about the cultural tradition in which democracy developed. Under "civic republicanism," Strike groups Robert Bellah, Thomas Green, and writers who combine various strands of both Aristotelian and Deweyan traditions. He concludes with a synthesis of his own, arguing that liberal and democratic hopes for education must be based on three considerations: Children must be initiated into communities where "some human goods" are valued and pursued; these communities should exemplify a sustained moral tradition that "contains adquately sophisticated cognitive resources to make moral reflection possible"; and that reflection should proceed in critical interaction with others who hold alternative views. In such settings children will "form the attachments that are the substratum of a sense of justice," which would be greatly different from "the morally chaotic and purposeless institutions that currently dominate the lives of children" (pp. 475–476).

Let me conclude this introduction by offering my thanks to the Editorial Board. They are acknowledged at the beginning of the volume by name, and I want to include here as well an unofficial board composed of graduate students and faculty who joined a seminar I offered at Syracuse University in the fall of 1989 on editing the *RRE*. Their advice was invaluable. I especially want to thank John Covaleskie, Christine Murray, and Rajeswari Swaminathan for their editorial assistance. Consulting editors who offer constructive criticism to authors are also acknowledged in the front of the book, but let me add my special thanks to Maxine Greene of Teachers College at Columbia University and C. W. Bowers of the University of Oregon. I am also grateful to the Center for Advanced Study in the Behavioral Sciences at Stanford University for its award of a Spencer Fellowship that enabled me to spend the 1988–1989 academic year there and for hosting the Editorial Board in the spring of 1989 as part of the planning of this volume.

January 6, 1991
Syracuse University

Gerald Grant
Editor

I.
ASSESSMENT

Chapter 1

New Forms of Teacher Assessment

EDWARD H. HAERTEL
Stanford University

Beginning in the 1970s and continuing through the 1980s, teacher testing initiatives swept virtually all of the 50 states. The tests mandated by the different states for entry into teacher education programs, exit from such programs, initial teacher certification, regular or permanent certification, or occasionally even for continuation of tenured teachers generally comprise little more than multiple-choice questions testing basic literacy and numeracy, "professional knowledge," and, sometimes, subject matter knowledge. For teachers already in the classroom, low-inference observation checklists are sometimes used as well.

The 1990s may see fundamentally new forms of teacher tests, implemented for new purposes and reflecting new views of the teaching profession and of teaching and learning processes. The prospects are exciting, the promises as yet unfulfilled. The new assessment methods described in this chapter are, for the most part, only now being developed. Little can be said, as yet, about their psychometric properties, let alone their eventual impacts on the educational system, teachers and teaching, or schooling outcomes. Nonetheless, given the rapid emergence of new methods and applications for teacher testing, it is a propitious time for this review.

The teacher tests now in common use have been strenuously and justifiably criticized for their content, their format, and their impacts, as well as the virtual absence of criterion-related validity evidence supporting their use. More fundamentally, the justification for these tests is bound up with a "bureaucratic" model of the educational system and the work of teaching. Movements toward teacher professionalization and school restructuring are creating both the possibility and the demand for new forms of teacher assessments.

After summarizing criticisms of the objective teacher tests now in wide use, this chapter contrasts the bureaucratic and professional models of teaching and describes how professional examinations might differ from the teacher tests in use today. It then takes up the question of the knowledge base of teaching: What are these new forms of teacher assessment supposed to measure? Next, some current research and development efforts are described, and examples of prototype teacher performance exercises are presented. Finally, the chapter raises some of the persistent issues that will need to be addressed as these new assessment procedures are refined and implemented, including matters of reliability and validity, the generalizability of teaching proficiency, and problems of standardization and of standard setting.

TESTING UNDER BUREAUCRATIC VERSUS PROFESSIONAL MODELS OF TEACHING

There has been a dramatic rise in teacher testing over the past 10 years (Baker & Ogle, 1989, pp. 70–71, 127–128; Harris & Harris, 1988, pp. 129–130; Rudner, 1988; Sandefur, 1986), but the tests in use have been strenuously criticized. They generally employ multiple-choice questions and sometimes brief writing samples to assess basic literacy and numeracy skills, and they use more multiple-choice questions to measure subject matter knowledge in particular areas, mostly recognition of facts; however, they do little to measure pedagogical expertise. There are questions about the laws and regulations teachers should be familiar with, and about bureaucratic procedures, but questions about teaching itself are usually limited to descriptions of brief scenarios for which the examinee must select the "correct" teacher action (Darling-Hammond, 1986b).

These tests have been criticized for treating pedagogy as generic rather than subject-matter specific (Madaus & Pullin, 1987; Shulman, 1986, 1987a), for showing poor criterion-related validity (Ayers & Qualls, 1979; Haney, Madaus, & Kreitzer, 1987; Nelsen, 1985; Quirk, Witten, & Weinberg, 1973) or failing to address criterion-related validity altogether (Oppenheim, 1985), for failing to measure many critical teaching skills (Darling-Hammond, 1986b; Madaus & Pullin, 1987), and for their adverse impact on minority representation in the teaching profession (Goertz & Pitcher, 1985; Haney et al., 1987; Smith, 1987; Smith, Miller, & Joy, 1988). Although many of these criticisms have been directed at the National Teacher Examinations (NTE), these tests are probably no worse than others of the same genre. The NTE tests have tended to be singled out for criticism because they are most widely used and have been studied most extensively, and because, to its credit, the Educational Testing Service (ETS) has been more willing than some other test developers to make information from validity studies available to researchers. In their broad review and analysis of current teacher testing practices, Haney et al. (1987, p. 209) conclude that "it is . . . a sad delusion to think that current teacher tests hold promise for improving education in the United States."

Classroom observations have also been used for teacher evaluation, especially at the district level, both in reaching tenure decisions and for periodic evaluation of practicing teachers. Except in a few districts where teachers are evaluated by their peers, these classroom observations are generally conducted by administrators, usually building principals. Relatively unstructured, global judgments have often been used, although there seems to be a trend toward more systematic evaluation procedures in recent years (Stodolsky, 1990). Even systematic procedures based on brief classroom observations are notoriously unreliable, however, especially when the same observation scheme is employed across content areas and grade levels (Medley & Coker, 1987; Stodolsky, 1984, 1990). Results from low-inference observation schedules tend to have very limited generalizability (Shavelson & Dempsey-Atwood, 1976).

Like the current written examinations, these observational methods have been strongly criticized. Wise, Darling-Hammond, McLaughlin, and Bernstein (1984, p. vi) characterize district-level teacher evaluation as "an underconceptualized and underdeveloped activity" and cite as problems the limited competence and resolve of principals, teacher resistance and apathy, lack of uniformity within school systems, and inadequate training of evaluators (Wise et al., 1984, p. 22). Principals often experience role conflict as they try to serve as both evaluators and instructional leaders. They also tend to lack expertise in specialized subject matter areas, especially at the secondary school level.

In addition to district-level teacher evaluation systems, a few states supplement written tests for teachers with classroom observations using behavior checklists such as the Florida Performance Measurement System (FPMS). These instruments may provide satisfactory levels of interrater reliability (Peterson, Micceri, & Smith, 1985), but they have been criticized for trivializing teaching proficiency (Macmillan & Pendlebury, 1985) and for reinforcing a single, narrow conception of effective teaching as fast-paced, teacher-centered direct instruction (Haertel, 1988; Stodolsky, 1990). This may be a highly effective model of teaching for attaining some learning objectives with some learners, but it trivializes the work of teaching to assert that all classroom instruction, across grade levels, content areas, and educational goals, should be carried out in the same way. The best teachers command a broad repertoire of instructional approaches and vary their teaching in complex ways (Shulman, 1987b). Simplistic prescriptions for "effective teaching" usurp the teacher's professional role and responsibility.

As Sykes (1986, p. 365) has observed, "the current reform wave rightfully places the teacher at the heart of what is known as 'educational excellence.'" These reforms have little chance of succeeding, however, unless the work of teaching itself is restructured to give teachers more control over their own work (Darling-Hammond, 1985). There is little, if any, evidence that all the testing and classroom observation now being required has materially improved the quality of the teaching force. Indeed, the virtual absence of criterion-related validity evidence in support of these practices casts serious doubt upon their value. There is an emerging consensus that testing efforts rooted in the current bureaucratic conception of teaching are doomed to failure; significant reform and improvement can only come through the *professionalization* of teaching. Darling-Hammond (1986a) succinctly contrasts these two perspectives:

> The bureaucratic conception of teaching implies that administrators and specialists plan curriculum, and teachers implement a curriculum planned for them. Teachers' work is supervised by superiors whose job it is to make sure that teachers implement the curriculum and procedures of the school district. In the pure bureaucratic conception, teachers do not plan or inspect their work; they merely perform it.
>
> In a more professional conception of teaching, teachers plan, conduct, and evaluate their work both individually and collectively. Teachers analyze the needs of their students, assess the resources available, take the school district's goals into account, and decide on their instructional strategies. . . . Evaluation of teaching is conducted largely to ensure that proper standards of practice are being employed. (p. 532)

Most significantly for assessment, professionalization of teaching implies the adoption of control mechanisms like those employed in such established professions as medicine and law. This may mean the establishment of more rigorous formal education requirements for entry into the profession, the creation of state professional practice boards intended to ensure that teachers have the knowledge and skills required to practice independently, changes in school governance to permit greater teacher participation in planning and decision making, new roles for professional organizations such as the National Education Association (NEA) and the American Federation of Teachers (AFT), and new forms of assessment of both student work and teacher performance. So long as teacher evaluation is thought of as something done to teachers by administrators, it will continue to reinforce a model of teaching that discourages teachers' initiative in exercising their own critical, professional judgment. Evaluation under a bureaucratic model is unlikely to improve either teachers or teaching (Wise & Gendler, 1990).

New forms of assessment and evaluation figure prominently in initiatives for the professionalization of teaching. The Holmes Group (1986) envisioned a three-tiered structure for a new teaching profession, with different entrance requirements and assessment procedures at each level. In addition to rigorous subject matter examinations, candidates aspiring to the second level, "professional teacher," would be subjected to "a balanced, rigorous scrutiny of [their] practice with a variety of learning groups," which might be based on portfolios of teaching, planned exhibitions of teaching, and unannounced observations (Holmes Group, 1986,

p. 12). Under the Holmes Group's proposal, multiple forms of assessment would be used to evaluate teachers as professional practitioners, not merely as students of their subject area specialties.

In the same year that the Holmes Group issued their report, the Carnegie Task Force on Teaching as a Profession issued a report called *A Nation Prepared: Teachers for the 21st Century*. One of their key recommendations was the creation of a national board for professional teaching standards "to establish standards for high levels of competence in the teaching profession, to assess the qualifications of those seeking board certification, and to grant certificates to those who meet the standards" (Task Force on Teaching as a Profession, 1986, p. 62). The National Board for Professional Teaching Standards (NBPTS) has now been established, and has requested proposals to establish assessment development laboratories (ADLs) to develop assessment instruments and supporting materials for the certification of teachers in various content areas for specific age/grade ranges.

Teacher assessments under a professional model would be very different from the tests and observation systems described above. Professional teacher assessments would be designed to ensure a high standard of professional practice, not to elicit an approved canon of answers to multiple-choice questions that trivialize teaching's complexities (cf. Darling-Hammond, 1986b) or to monitor conformity to a checklist of approved classroom behaviors. Because professionals are expected to exercise judgment and discernment in their work, there are many areas of professional practice where it is impossible in principle to specify a single correct answer or a single acceptable instructional procedure. Thus, professional teacher assessments would necessarily be more complex and open-ended than current examinations and observation systems.

Emergent forms of teacher assessment are also expected to be far more specific to different subject matters and age/grade levels than are present tests. Although there is probably a common core of professional knowledge that is important across the entire K–12 curriculum, the specific knowledge of learners, of subject matter, and of pedagogy required of the second-grade reading teacher versus the high school biology teacher are so different that it is an insult to either to suggest that their respective professional competences be judged by the same measure (Madaus & Pullin, 1987; Stodolsky, 1984).

Even today, a teacher's responsibilities extend well beyond classroom teaching itself. Teachers must plan lessons; interact with parents, staff, administrators, and one another; and, to a limited extent, share in the governance of their profession. In the future, the responsibilities of professional teachers may be even broader, embracing instructional planning at the classroom and school levels, participation in school governance, and, possibly, mentorship of less experienced teachers and participation in peer evaluation and other collegial interactions. It is unlikely that a valid and comprehensive professional examination could be limited to classroom performance alone.

Finally, the governance and control of teacher assessments under a professional model would be more largely in the hands of teachers themselves. At the state level, professional teachers would participate in articulating and enforcing performance standards. At the school and district level, they would share responsibility for their peers' adherence to high standards of professional practice (Wise & Gendler, 1990). It is noteworthy that the bylaws of the NBPTS assure that a majority of its members are drawn from the ranks of practicing teachers.

THE KNOWLEDGE BASE OF TEACHING

Comparisons of teaching to learned professions such as law or medicine can shed some light on the deficiencies in the organization and control mechanisms of teacher testing, but are not very helpful in establishing just what knowledge, skills, or dispositions a new generation of teacher tests should measure or in suggesting the particular measurement approaches that might be used. Clearly, new teacher assessments must be grounded in some conception of the knowledge base of teaching. Two obvious starting points in defining that knowledge base would be teacher education curricula or job analyses of classroom teaching. Unfortunately, both have been tried and found wanting. The National Teacher Examinations were, in fact, originally designed to reflect the content of typical teacher education programs (Educational Testing Service, 1984; Haney et al., 1987), and one of the methods by which state licensure examinations are commonly "validated" is by asking a panel of teacher educators to judge whether graduates of their programs would have had an opportunity to learn the content of each item (Cross, 1985). Thus, it might be argued that present tests are already more or less aligned with present teacher education curricula. Moreover, the same Holmes Group report that called for prospective teachers "to demonstrate mastery of important knowledge and skill through multiple evaluations across multiple domains of competence" (Holmes Group, 1986, p. 65) also called for sweeping changes in the content and organization of teacher education programs.

Current state certification tests have also been "validated" by comparing them to the reported activities of classroom teachers. For example, Rosenfeld, Thornton, and Skurnik (1986) present an extensive study of the reported relationships between the work of teaching and the functions assessed by the NTE Core Battery, based on a survey of nearly 150 administrators and 2,000 teachers in sites chosen to represent a range of demographic characteristics. The study did not involve any direct observation of actual teaching, but the participating teachers and administrators did rate each of 34 knowledge areas assessed by the three core battery tests as significantly related to at least one of six core job functions that teachers must perform.

One reason that such validations against teacher education curricula and the day-to-day activities of teaching have failed to yield more valid tests is the manner in which these validations have been conducted. Ensuring that each item on the test is relevant to the preparation teachers have received or the work they do merely establishes that the test addresses a subset of the work of teaching. It fails to address the importance of that subset relative to the part left untested. To be sure, in validations against teacher education curricula, panels of teacher educators may be asked to "list any major content areas in the teacher-education curriculum that are not shown on the test specifications" (Cross, 1985, p. 8), but, in practice, such instructions are quite unlikely to ensure the comprehensiveness of the examination. In a validation of the NTE for use by New York State, for example, Faggen (1983) reports that panelists were given an opportunity to list any additional topics that, in their opinion, could be assessed reliably using a paper-and-pencil format and were of sufficient importance to be included on the test. Their responses did not lead to any augmentation of the NTE.

There is a more fundamental reason why current teacher education curricula and current teaching practices are of limited value in deriving a conception of the knowledge base of teaching to guide the development of professional examinations. Like present testing practices, present teaching training and even the work of teaching are grounded in a model that holds teachers responsible primarily for implementing prescribed procedures, as opposed to relying on their own professional judgment to select or formulate, and then implement, effective instructional approaches tailored to particular situations. The new, professional teaching tests must address examinees' qualifications for some roles that do not now exist, and must reach beyond traditional stereotypes of classroom teaching:

> Self-contained classrooms, whole-group, textbook-centered instruction, teaching as telling, learning as the passive acquisition of facts, standardized testing—these patterns of schooling are as familiar as chalk dust. They constitute an unintended national curriculum that, as an unrelieved diet, does not adequately serve the educational needs of a diverse and dynamic society. Good teachers, of course, depart in many ways from these routines. (NBPTS, 1989, p. 27)

Thus, rather than beginning from some empirical distillation of common teaching practice, it seems more promising to set forth a theory about the underlying knowledge and skills teaching requires, informed by studies not of the typical classroom routine but of outstanding, exemplary teaching (e.g., Shulman, 1986, 1987b). Assessment approaches may then be developed in light of that theory.

One of the first formulations of the knowledge base of teaching for purposes of professional teacher assessment appeared in a paper prepared by Lee S. Shulman and Gary Sykes for the Task Force on Teaching as a Profession, a task force of the Carnegie Forum on Education and the Economy:

> Teaching has a substantial and growing knowledge base that incorporates but is distinct from the general norms of civility, from the general ethics of childrearing, from the disciplines that are dealt with as subject matters in the school curriculum, and from the social sciences employed in educational research and practice. A large core of that knowledge base is amenable to the formation of persuasive and testable standards that, in part, define a profession. (Shulman & Sykes, 1986, pp. i–ii)

As a starting point for deliberations about the knowledge base of teaching, Shulman and Sykes discussed eight categories that might be included. In addition to a general liberal education (including basic literacy and numeracy skills), content knowledge in the domains where teaching was to occur, and general knowledge of pedagogical principles and practice, these included the important category of content-specific pedagogical knowledge, later called *pedagogical content knowledge*. Their preliminary list of eight categories was completed by understanding of student diversity and individual differences, curricular knowledge (i.e., knowledge of curriculum materials, topics, and alternatives), performance skills (voice, manner, poise, etc.), and educational foundations.

The most distinctive of these categories, content-specific pedagogical knowledge, represents an integration of subject matter knowledge, knowledge of general pedagogical principles, and knowledge of learners. It is perhaps nearest the core of the special knowledge teachers must possess, capturing the distinction between "those who know how to teach [a] subject [and] those who merely know it as a student" (Holmes Group, 1986, p. 14). Shulman and Sykes (1986) described it as follows:

> Content specific pedagogical knowledge includes understanding the central topics in each subject matter as it is generally taught to children . . . [and addresses such questions as] What are the core concepts, skills and attitudes which this topic has the potential for conveying to students? How are these related to prior and later opportunities for achieving those goals in the curriculum? What are the aspects of this topic that are most difficult to understand for students? What is of greatest intrinsic interest? What analogies, metaphors, examples, similes, demonstrations, simulations, manipulations, or the like are most effective in communicating the appropriate understandings or attitudes of *this topic* to students of particular backgrounds and prerequisites? What student preconceptions are likely to get in the way of learning? What "cases" of instruction for this topic can the [teacher] cite and

describe that document the experiences of others with this topic? . . . and many more questions of this ilk. (Shulman & Sykes, 1986, pp. 8–9)

In later writings, Shulman (1987b, p. 8) has used slightly different categories and has added "knowledge of educational contexts" from the classroom through district levels and outward to communities and cultures, but pedagogical content knowledge has remained central. It is closest to the actual practice of teaching; highly specific to different subject areas, grade levels, and teaching contexts; and, as yet, poorly codified. For these reasons, pedagogical content knowledge may be the aspect of professional teacher knowledge that is both most difficult and most important to assess.

The NBPTS has formulated a description of a professional knowledge base for teaching, which appears in the Board's position paper, *Toward High and Rigorous Standards for the Teaching Profession* (NBPTS, 1989). This statement is important in that the NBPTS, with its explicit recognition of teachers as professionals, its strong representation of practicing teachers among its members, and its endorsements from professional teaching organizations, has some warrant to speak for the teaching profession itself. The Board sets forth a set of ideals to guide development of assessment methods and certification standards, organized under five key propositions: (a) Teachers are commited to students and their learning; (b) teachers know the subjects they teach and how to teach those subjects to students; (c) teachers are responsible for managing and monitoring student learning; (d) teachers think systematically about their practice and learn from experience; and (e) teachers are members of learning communities. These propositions, as elaborated in the NBPTS document, go far beyond the domains of knowledge, skills, and dispositions that could be addressed using existing tests or any tests on the horizon. They emphasize the role of professional judgment and commitment; express the importance of teachers' lifelong learning; acknowledge the extensive, detailed, contextually bound knowledge that teachers must possess; and set forth an ethical stance as well as a conception of professional capabilities. Aspects of pedagogical content knowledge are woven through several of the propositions. The importance of teachers' knowledge of student preconceptions and the points at which they are likely to have difficulty, specific instructional strategies and materials, alternative instructional approaches and when to try them, and other aspects of subject-specific teaching knowledge are included. The Board's vision of the professional teacher is complex and demanding. It "acknowledges that even state-of-the-art assessments probably can not fully capture teaching's complexities, and the standards it eventually will ask candidates to meet may not be as rich as the portrait of a Board-certified teacher sketched above" (NBPTS, 1989, p. 43).

Although a great deal is known from educational research and teachers' collective experience about sound and unsound classroom practices, there is as yet no well-established and generally accepted canon of acceptable and unacceptable solutions to pedagogical problems and no definitive textbooks setting forth the pedagogical content knowledge of the different subject matters. The NBPTS position paper provides a compelling description of kinds of knowledge professional teachers must possess, but does not really indicate the *sources* of that knowledge.

Shulman (1987b) suggests that there are at least four major sources from which the content of the knowledge base of teaching may be derived. First, teaching in each subject area must be informed by scholarship in the cognate discipline, including both its accumulated literature and studies and its own epistemology. Teachers must understand not only the important ideas and skills in a domain, but also the rules and procedures of sound scholarship in that domain. A second major source is the corpus of instructional materials and institutional structures and settings created to further the aims of organized schooling. This includes knowledge not only of curricula, textbooks, testing materials, and so forth, but also of the organization of educational institutions, professional educational organizations, relevant governmental agencies at different levels, and other elements of the complex social and institutional matrix within which teachers must function. A third source for a knowledge base of teaching is, of course, formal educational scholarship. The work of teaching must be informed by research on teaching and learning, on human diversity and development, on schooling and school organizations, and on the communities and cultures within which schooling occurs. Shulman (1987b, p. 10) calls attention especially to scholarship on the normative and theoretical aspects of teaching, which can enrich our visions of the possible. Empirical research, including research on teacher effectiveness, is important but incomplete. The last of the four sources is the wisdom of practice itself—"the practical pedagogical wisdom of able teachers" (Shulman, 1987b, p. 11). This is the least well codified of the four, a mixture of valid generalizations, habit, and folklore. It may be that in order to capitalize on this practical wisdom, educational researchers and teachers themselves will need to develop some kind of case literature of teaching to establish a history of practice from which valid principles can be derived (Shulman, 1986, 1987b).

TOWARD NEW METHODS FOR TEACHER ASSESSMENT

Clearly, current multiple-choice tests and generic classroom observation checklists cannot yield valid and comprehensive measures of the knowledge base of teaching. Although some aspects of teacher knowledge, such as factual knowledge of content, may be adequately assessed with multiple-choice questions, the assessment of critical understanding is likely to require tests on which examinees produce extended responses rather than selecting among prespecified phrases. The assessment of teacher judgment and decision making will require testing formats in which a richer context can be presented for the decision to be taken. If classroom observations are used, allowance will have to be made for the complexity of teachers' decision making and the fact that different acts are called for in different situations. Educational researchers in colleges and universities, state departments of education, and elsewhere are actively investigating alternative assessment approaches, but most of this work has begun quite recently. In another 2 to 5 years, much more should be known about the reliability, validity, and utility of different assessment methods now under development.

The Teacher Assessment Project

In 1986, at the same time the Carnegie Task Force on Teaching as a Profession began moving toward the establishment of the NBPTS, the Carnegie Corporation of New York also began funding the Teacher Assessment Project (TAP) at Stanford University, under the direction of Professor Lee S. Shulman. The TAP was conceived as a research project independent of the work of the NBPTS but intended to generate research on teacher assessment approaches that might later help to inform the Board's deliberations.

The TAP continued from June 1986 through July 1990. Over the course of its existence, the faculty, staff, and graduate students involved with TAP authored over 100 theoretical papers, technical reports, book chapters, and journal articles as well as several dissertations on specific assessment exercises, alternative assessment methods, assessing teachers representing or working with different cultures, scoring performance exercises, and other topics.[1]

In the first phase of its work, roughly the first 2 years of its existence, the TAP developed and piloted prototype exercises in the areas of upper elementary mathematics instruction, especially the teaching of the equivalence of fractions and related topics, and 11th-grade U.S. history, especially the American Revolution and the formation of the new government. Fairly specific topics were chosen in light of the presumed specificity of pedagogical content knowledge. For the most part, the exercises in math and history were designed around the idea of an assessment center, where experienced teachers might spend from 1 to 3 days in such activities as critiquing a textbook, developing a lesson plan using materials provided, demonstrating an exemplary lesson of their own choosing (prepared in advance), answering simulated student questions, or viewing and discussing a videotape of another teacher presenting a lesson (Shulman, Haertel, & Bird, 1988).

The second phase of the TAP's work focused on elementary literacy instruction, especially the use of children's literature in integrated language arts instruction, and on high school biology. The TAP's work in these areas combined the assessment center approach with an exploration of portfolios of teacher work, constructed by teacher examinees over a period of time, in their own classrooms. Because biology teachers sequence topics differently, the project's timeline and logistics precluded any topical focus for biology teacher portfolios beyond introductory biology.

In addition to stand-alone assessment center exercises and portfolio entries that were simply evaluated as submitted, some exercises were piloted in which examinees at an "assessment center" discussed their portfolio entries or answered questions tailored to the portfolio they had submitted. Among other assessment activities, biology teachers discussed the use of specific instructional software as a teaching tool, analyzed the use of alternative materials for accomplishing particular instructional objectives, completed a laboratory monitoring entry, and discussed ways of using a particular (flawed) textbook. In the elementary literacy assessment, a variety of specific exercises and portfolio entries were organized under the three areas of creating a literate environment in the classroom, planning and teaching of integrated language arts, and assessment of student learning.

NBPTS-Sponsored Assessment Development Laboratories

Even as the TAP is ending, the NBPTS has begun issuing requests for proposals (RFPs) for the establishment of ADLs to develop assessment instruments, materials, and procedures for Board certification in particular content areas. These assessments are to attest to excellence in teaching, not minimum competence, and are to employ a variety of innovative assessment methods. The first RFP, for example, for an ADL on early adolescence/English language arts instruction, calls for documentation from the candidate's (i.e., examinee's) school site, assessment of knowledge of both early adolescent development and English language arts, and assessment of ability to analyze and respond to various teaching problems and situations. The assessments developed are likely to rely on videotapes of the examinee's own classroom performance, portfolios documenting classroom teaching, or both; written examinations requiring extended responses; and assessment center exercises. To the extent possible, teacher knowledge is to be assessed in the context of teaching situations. The NBPTS is also sponsoring "cross-cutting research" on the use of videoportfolios to document current teaching practice, the quality and potential of existing subject matter examinations, assessment of a teacher's ability to work with diverse students, and issues raised by the use of student work products in the course of the NBPTS assessment process.

State Education Agencies

A number of state departments of education have also begun developing new forms of teacher tests for both initial licensure and permanent certification. In October 1987, the Connecticut and California departments of education and the California Commission on Teacher Credentialing became charter members of the Interstate New Teacher Assessment and Support Consortium (originally under a slightly different name), funded by a grant from the National Governor's Association. The Consortium is presently administered as a project of the Council of Chief State School Officers (CCSSO), with over a dozen states as paying members. Its primary purposes are, first, to develop a network for sharing information among state agencies, colleges and universities, professional associations, and researchers concerned with teacher assessment, and, second, to foster collaboration in the development of assessments for teacher licensure that may be compatible with the vision of the NBPTS. To further these aims, the Consortium has established a clearinghouse[2] and has conducted periodic seminars to discuss issues and ongoing work in beginning teacher assessment.

Colleges and Universities

In addition to the work of the TAP and work sponsored by the NBPTS on new forms of assessment for experienced teachers, and the work of the Consortium on beginning teacher assessment, the Holmes Group (1989, p. 19) reports that many of its member institutions are exploring new assessment methods in teacher education, including "review of teaching episodes on video, preparation of portfolios of lesson plans, curricular materials, and student work, and development of original instruments to measure change in attitudes, values, and knowledge." ETS has also initiated a major project to rethink and redesign the NTE.

EXAMPLES OF TEACHER PERFORMANCE EXERCISES

It is not possible in the space of this chapter to describe all of the teacher assessment exercises being developed, but descriptions of a few prototypes from TAP and elsewhere will serve to illustrate the kinds of materials, questions, and scoring approaches under consideration. It must be emphasized that most of these prototypes represent no more than preliminary investigations of possible exercise formats and activities. They may or may not resemble the exercises eventually used by the

NBPTS or by the states. Moreover, although all of the prototypes described have been piloted, most have yet to be implemented in a context with real consequences for examinees.

Lesson Planning in Elementary Mathematics

A lesson planning exercise in elementary mathematics was developed by the TAP (Mitchell & Tyson, 1989), and was also incorporated, with modifications, into one of several exercises piloted in 1989 by the California New Teacher Project (CNTP) (Estes, Stansbury, Long, Wheeler, & Quellmalz, 1990). Examinees are given a recent fifth-grade mathematics textbook, and their attention is directed to two pages covering the simplification of fractions. They are informed that they will have 30 minutes to plan a lesson on that topic, to be taught in a single class period, and that they are free to follow the approach in the text or to introduce other materials and approaches that they would normally include. They are to plan the lesson as if for their own class, assuming that the topics normally covered prior to "simplifying fractions" have been covered but that the textbook provided is the one their students actually use. Examinees are also asked to prepare a brief outline of critical points in the lessons from the day before and the day after, and may indicate the homework assignment they would give, if desired.

After 30 minutes, the examinee is interviewed about the lesson. The interview is audiotaped, and the interviewer also takes notes. The examinee is asked to give a 2-minute overview, and then is asked (a) to explain what makes the lesson difficult; (b) what specific points are most difficult and how students would be helped to understand them; (c) whether questions would be asked of students in the course of the lesson and, if so, what they would be; (d) about the significance or importance of the lesson in the fifth-grade math curriculum; (e) about specific other topics in the curriculum that this topic relates to; and (f) about the importance of the topic in the "real world." Examinees are also asked to indicate under what circumstances they might deviate from their lesson plan, what they would do if students seemed not to understand, and how they would know whether students were understanding the lesson. Finally, they are given three specific vignettes to respond to, for example, "You have the students simplifying $8/18$, at their seats. While circulating around the room, you discover that a student has tried to divide both numerator and denominator by 4."

The protocol resulting from this exercise includes the examiner's notes on an examinee's responses to each (scripted) question, as well as the audiotape. A scoring scheme was developed with guidelines for rating the protocol with respect to five characteristics: connects topic to math curriculum, shows insight into important concepts and what is hard and easy, shows flexibility in anticipating deviations, shows insight in use of problems and/or examples, and shows insight in dealing with student difficulties. Ratings in these areas were weighted differentially and combined to arrive at an overall score.

In the modification of this exercise by the CNTP, a simplified scoring scheme was used, with holistic ratings of pass/fail for each of a series of specific components of teacher performance. Raters also had the option of indicating "unable to score," and checklists of major points were provided for responses in some categories. Teachers were required to pass 75% of the components to receive an overall pass on lesson planning (Estes et al., 1990, p. 5.6).

Documentary History in High School History/Social Studies

This TAP exercise prototype was conceived for use at an assessment center. Prior to arriving at the center, examinees are given a list of potential topics for this exercise, including the actual topic, the Battle of Lexington, April 19, 1775. At the assessment center, the examinee is presented with a textbook summary of the battle, facsimiles of depositions taken at the time of the battle, and facsimiles of three paintings of the event, one painted shortly thereafter, one about 50 years later, and one about a century later. There is also a map of Lexington Green as it appeared at the time of the battle.

Examinees are, first of all, given 5 minutes to review these materials. With the exception of the pictures, these may be marked up (underlined, annotated) as desired. Examinees then spend the next 30 minutes planning how these materials might be used in teaching and preparing to answer questions not only about how the materials might be used in the classroom, but also about the story they tell and their bearing on the nation's history. This preparation period is following by an audiotaped interview lasting close to an hour. The examiner also takes notes on answers to scripted questions.

During the interview, the examinee is asked about some of the ways the materials could be used in teaching, the purposes they could serve and which would be most important, which particular documents would be used if time were short, and how they might organize a 3- or 4-day unit during which students would analyze the documents and come to some agreement about what happened on Lexington Green. They are also asked about the ways in which differences among the three pictures might be exploited to teach something about history and about their relative accuracy. Finally, examinees explain how they would respond to vignettes in which students make specific statements raising issues or indicating confusion (McGreevy & Hyink, 1989).

The documentary history exercise was scored separately for subject matter knowledge and pedagogical content knowledge. For each of these dimensions, a series of four or five paragraphs was written describing different performance levels. The examinee's performance was compared to these holistic descriptions, and a rating was assigned according to the paragraph providing the closest match. Scores might also be assigned that were intermediate between the documented proficiency levels.

For "subject matter knowledge," the description at the lowest level is as follows: "Candidate is befuddled by the documents and sees only a mass of details; shows little awareness of the different types of evidence presented and draws few distinctions in sizing up the evidence . . . provides little evidence of understanding . . . makes inferences not rooted in the evidence or arrives at interpretations that cannot be defended . . . provides little evidence of . . . a broad background in history . . . [violates] spirit of historical method." At the high end, the description refers to skillful use of internal evidence, checking documents against one another, differentiating types of evidence, seeing themes and trends, evaluating trustworthiness of sources, drawing analogies to other historical events, and other evidences of sophisticated understanding.

With regard to pedagogical content knowledge, the description at the high end states that "candidate articulates multiple purposes for which documents can be used, stressing motivational as well as cognitive goals . . . [considers] different types of learners . . . draws relevant analogies [to] help convey major learning objectives. Candidate shows awareness of student misconceptions . . . formulates strategies for dealing with these misconceptions . . . [exploits] learning opportunities . . . anticipates problems students would have . . . possesses overarching goals for the use of documents and can articulate to students why study of documents is important." The low end of this continuum is indicated by little or no awareness of why documents might be useful in teaching history or of the ways in which they can be used (McGreevy & Hyink, 1989).

Teacher Portfolio Entries in Elementary-Level Integrated Language Arts

Teachers assisting the TAP in the role of "candidates" (examinees) for purposes of exercise development in elementary literacy were asked to assemble portfolios documenting their work. Each teacher was provided with a detailed handbook, including worksheets, instructions, and limited suggestions for the creation of the portfolio entries requested. The content of the portfolio was summarized by Athanases (1990, p. 12) as follows:

1. A prose or graphic overview of 3 to 5 weeks of instruction.
2. Details of two to three consecutive lessons.

3. A roster of literary works and other resources selected for use.
4. Copies of handouts to students.
5. Samples of student work.
6. Photos or written records of blackboard and bulletin board work (optional).
7. Videotape of teaching: (a) large-group lesson on literature, (b) small-group discussion of literature (4–8 participants, 10 to 15 minutes in length), and (c) one-to-one writing conferences with students of two different skill levels.
8. Audiotape of teaching (optional).
9. Notes by observer of teaching (administrator, mentor, resource person) (optional).

In addition to these artifacts of teaching, candidates were asked to keep a journal logging their lesson plans, any adaptations to those plans, and their reasons for such adaptations. Candidates also were asked to provide statements of rationales for the videotaped segments and some additional contextual information to accompany the other materials. Finally, after the portfolio was completed and submitted, the candidate was asked to discuss it in an interview at a mock assessment center.

A complex scoring scheme was developed, in which each part of the portfolio was rated with respect to roughly 5 to 10 specific criteria, and these ratings, together with ratings of assessment center exercises, were aggregated to the level of three areas: assessment of students, creating a literate environment, and planning and teaching language arts.

Teacher Portfolios in Introductory High School Biology

The final area in which TAP developed exercise prototypes was high school biology. Each candidate in biology was asked to complete five of seven portfolio entries, some required and some optional. A *background* entry (required) summarized the candidate's academic and occupational history and present teaching context. A *unit planning* entry (required) provided general information on the planning and execution of a 2- to 4-week sequence of instruction. A *student evaluation* entry (required) comprised a log of evaluative procedures used over a 6-week period, together with samples of student work chosen to illustrate a range of assessment approaches and student ability levels. These were generally accompanied by copies of assignments, quizzes, and tests, and candidates were also encouraged to find ways to document assessment procedures that were not based on students' written work. In the *alternative materials* entry (optional), candidates submitted a videotape, instructional materials, and a plan and rationale for a lesson in which they relied primarily on media or materials other than the students' textbook. Those teachers who did not complete alternative materials instead completed the closely parallel *laboratory lesson* entry, which also called for a videotape. This entry documented a lesson in which students worked with biological equipment or materials. For both the alternative materials and the laboratory lesson entries, TAP project staff were available to assist in videotaping. The *professional exchange* entry (optional) included a 6-week log of professional interactions with other teachers, school and district staff, teacher organization members, and so forth. Teachers also wrote a general discussion addressing a series of questions about their professional exchanges, and wrote in somewhat more detail about one or two interactions of their own choosing. Finally, the *community exchange* entry (optional) was completed by those teachers who elected not to complete the professional exchange entry. It focused on professional interactions with parents, guest speakers, social workers or probation officers, or other representatives of the community at large (Bird & King, 1990).

In response to feedback from candidates, fairly specific instructions and worksheets were developed for completing each of these exercises, setting forth a specific "set of tasks to do, paragraphs to write, and suggested documentation to insert after the instruction sheet" (Bird & King, 1990, p. 8).

Scoring and rating procedures for the biology portfolio entries and assessment center exercises were developed with an eye toward efficiency. The rating was done by the examiners, and largely completed at the conclusion of the mock assessment center. The intent was to arrive at ratings in five categories corresponding to the key propositions set forth by the NBPTS (1989), plus a sixth "overall" category. Raters were provided summaries of the discussion in the NBPTS document and were instructed to arrive at global judgments, for each category, first of the *relevance* of that rating category to the performance being evaluated and the adequacy of the *evidence* the performance provided with respect to that category. They then rated the *difficulty* the performance presented to the candidate and, finally, the *goodness* of the performance.

Relevance and evidence ratings were intended to establish how much importance should be attached to the goodness rating, and the difficulty rating was intended to help raters disentangle the quality of the performance from the degree of challenge in the task attempted (Bird, 1990). Analysis of these ratings is ongoing.

The Connecticut Competency Instrument

The State of Connecticut has developed a high-inference classroom observation system for use with beginning teachers, the Connecticut Competency Instrument (CCI). This instrument has been piloted extensively in Connecticut and is now in use there. With minor variations, it has also been piloted in California (Estes et al., 1990). The CCI focuses on 10 indicators, grouped as follows:

- Management of the Classroom Environment
    1. Promoting a positive learning environment.
    2. Maintaining appropriate standards of behavior.
    3. Engaging students in activities of the lesson.
    4. Effectively managing routines and transitions.
- Instruction
    5. Creating a structure for learning.
    6. Presenting appropriate lesson content.
    7. Developing a lesson to promote achievement of lesson objectives.
    8. Using appropriate questioning techniques.
    9. Communicating clearly.
- Assessment
    10. Monitoring student understanding and adjusting teaching.

There are several defining attributes for each of these indicators, but it is explicitly recognized that competence may be manifested in diverse ways, and trained assessors are expected to exercise their professional judgment.

In completing the CCI, an assessor first conducts a preobservation interview and completes a preassessment information form, next observes a 45–60-minute lesson, and then conducts a brief postobservation interview to discuss any deviations from the lesson plan. Finally, working from notes taken during the classroom observation, the assessor completes one-page forms for each of the 10 indicators, summarizing relevant positive and negative evidence, and then arrives at a judgment of "acceptable" or "unacceptable." Indications of "cannot rate" or "not applicable" are also allowed in some cases. Connecticut requires acceptable ratings on at least 7 of the 10 areas for an overall pass, and also requires that the CCI be administered six times, twice each near the beginning, middle, and end of the school year. The two ratings at each time are conducted independently by two different observers.

PSYCHOMETRIC AND TECHNICAL ISSUES

As Linn (1986) has observed, there are compelling reasons for the persistence of objective multiple-choice tests in spite of all the criticisms leveled against them. Written teacher tests using objective formats are amenable to standardized administration, highly reliable, and inexpensive to use and score. Although there is little or no direct evidence that they can predict effective classroom performance, they correlate well with other test scores and are moderately predictive of performance in academic settings, including teacher education programs. Moreover, current multiple-choice examinations for teachers have proven legally defensible, despite the lack of direct evidence that they predict teaching quality.

New forms of teacher assessment are being developed in response to dissatisfactions with both the content and the format of current tests. In order to assess pedagogical content knowledge, many provide richer descriptions of teaching problems or situations and call for more elaborated responses. State-of-the-art classroom observations acknowledge that the same behavior may be appropriate in one situation and inappropriate in another, and depend on the professional judgment of an assessor who may accept different specific evidence for the same indicator, depending on the situation. These new assessment approaches may have higher face validity than conventional tests, but obviously their use cannot be justified on that basis alone (Popham, 1990). The reliability of each alternative assessment approach must be demonstrated, and the validity of score-based inferences must be investigated for each intended application.

Eventually, issues of legal defensibility will have to be addressed as well. Teacher tests, primarily but not exclusively basic competency tests for beginning teachers, have been challenged on various legal grounds (Madaus, 1990; Rebell, 1986, 1990), and concerns over legal defensibility have probably contributed to the uniformity of state tests and validation procedures (Haney et al., 1987). Once a validation method has survived legal scrutiny, it is likely to be copied elsewhere. As new contexts, forms, and purposes for teacher testing evolve, higher standards for test validation must be established. Rather than trying to work within the narrow confines of present testing formats and validation procedures, scholars and practitioners involved with teacher testing must strive to create the very best measures possible and subject them to the most rigorous scrutiny, trusting that the resulting instruments as well as the distinctions they confer will not only be found legally defensible but will command the respect of professionals and lay persons alike.

Replicability and Generalizability

In recognition of the complexity and context specificity of teaching, the new forms of teacher assessment discussed in this chapter all permit variation from one examinee to another in the responses they provide. The content and even the form of teacher portfolios, classroom videotapes, interview responses, or written essays may vary, even among teachers of the same content area at the same grade level. In this sense, the new forms of teacher assessment are less standardized than either multiple-choice tests or low-inference classroom observations. This flexibility necessitates reliance on human judgment in scoring, which may make it more difficult to derive reliable scores (Haertel, 1990).

Probably the first psychometric issue to be addressed in developing new teacher assessments is the consistency of the scoring procedure itself. A commitment to interpreting teacher performance in context probably precludes scoring based on simple keys or checklists, but with careful selection and training, independent raters should nonetheless be able to agree reasonably closely on the score(s) that should be assigned to a specific protocol. In the prototype teacher performance exercises developed to date, scoring has relied on the judgment of knowledgeable raters as to the appropriateness of candidate responses to a given situation, as well as their factual accuracy and conformity to generally accepted pedagogical principles. The CCI, as implemented in Connecticut, must be scored by the same person who conducts the classroom observation, but reliability is monitored and improved by conducting independent replications of the entire assessment procedure.

Reliabilities reported for observations of teacher performance have often failed to account for variability from one occasion of measurement to another (Shavelson, Webb, & Burstein, 1986). After establishing that a specific performance sample could be rated consistently, the next issues to be addressed might include test-retest and parallel forms reliability. If performances on an assessment are not stable across occasions, or if scores on one exercise are not predictive of scores on similar exercises, there is little hope that they will be valid for teacher licensure or certification. (Although it may be valuable for research purposes to disentangle unreliability due to rater and unreliability due to the sampling of occasions of measurement, it is the overall consistency of scoring that matters in practice. Note that the implementation of the CCI in Connecticut confounds variance due to rater and occasion.)

It may not be obvious how to define "parallel" or "similar" exercises. The extensive stimulus materials and complex instructions used in performance exercises or portfolio entries might be altered in any number of ways to create alternative forms, and as yet there are few rules of thumb to suggest how different variations would be likely to influence the scores obtained. Teachers highly knowledgeable about one topic, proficient in one pedagogical technique, or effective with one student population or within one school context might perform quite differently teaching different materials or in different settings. Does the teacher who has practiced teaching *The Adventures of Huckleberry Finn* year after year possess generalized knowledge of how to teach literature, or knowledge specific to that one literary work? If one exercise were based on *Huckleberry Finn*, what might be the basis of a parallel exercise? The answers to such questions await further research, although descriptions of the versatility and consistency of superior teachers give reason for optimism that teaching excellence is indeed generalizable across settings and teaching approaches (Shulman, 1987b).

Criterion-Related Validity

To be useful, new teacher assessments must not only be reliable, but must be relevant to the decisions they are to inform. The fact that present teacher tests have survived legal challenge despite the virtual absence of criterion-related validity evidence by no means obviates the requirement for responsible validation of new assessments.

The difficulty in criterion-related validation, of course, is to formulate reliable and valid criterion measures. Unstructured or low-inference classroom observations are clearly unsuitable as criterion measures, for the same reasons that they are unsuitable as teacher examinations. Direct use of measured student learning outcomes for teacher evaluation is also problematical (Haertel, 1986). Emergent models of teacher induction and beginning teacher support may employ mentors who work systematically with beginning teachers (Wise et al., 1984). Such arrangements may provide opportunities to develop new kinds of criterion measures based on systematic classroom observation and in-depth discussions of teaching between a candidate and a more expert or experienced teacher, conducted over a period of weeks or months.

Evidence supporting the validity of new teacher assessments may also be sought in the pattern of relationships among different forms of exercises. Portfolio entries can serve as criteria for validating performance assessments, for example. If multiple, diverse forms of evidence converge in identifying the same candidates as high or low in particular areas of teaching expertise, the case for the validity of all of them is strengthened.

Bias and Adverse Impact

The fact that, on average, some racial/ethnic, gender, or other identifiable groups outperform others on an examination does not in itself imply that the examination is biased, but should nonetheless trigger a careful scrutiny of the test itself, the conditions of its use, and the prior preparation of examinees to ensure, to the extent humanly possible, that test bias is not present. Group differences (calculated, for example, in standard deviation units) may be just as large on new forms of examinations as on existing tests. It may well happen that using new forms of assessment reduces the adverse impact of teacher testing, and if so, that is all to the good. But the magnitude of group differences does not in itself inform the validity of an examination.

Regardless of group differences, development and use of more valid forms of teacher assessment should help in understanding the reasons for performance differences among groups. Analysis of portfolios, exercise protocols, or other materials may highlight areas where stronger preparation is needed, or may reveal biases or unwarranted assumptions that have crept into the assessments themselves, as when teachers are found to use acceptable procedures that are not recognized in scoring keys. The goal must be to develop assessments and scoring schemes that credit the full range of effective and appropriate solutions to pedagogical problems.

Standard Setting

In general, the standards for teacher licensure or certification established by the states, the NBPTS, or other responsible institutions must be criterion referenced, not norm referenced; that is, licensure or certification must attest that candidates have met established standards of professional practice, not merely that they have outperformed some specified fraction of their peers. Clearly, establishing defensible performance standards is critical to the success of any application in which tests are used for teacher licensure or certification.

The judgmental methods most widely used for standard setting on present teacher tests have been severely criticized as arbitrary and even irrational (e.g., Glass, 1978; Haney et al., 1987; Madaus, 1986; Shepard, 1980, 1984), but I believe there is room for cautious optimism that judgmental methods, suitably tailored for use with performance tests and then carefully implemented, can yield reasonable and defensible standards. A fundamental difficulty with judgmental standard setting on multiple-choice tests for teachers arises because the performances being judged, usually the darkening of circles on a piece of paper, are so unlike the performances being predicted, usually the management of a complex classroom environment and the structuring of experiences through which children can learn. Regardless of classroom teachers' wisdom or experience, it may be impossible for them to say what percentage of minimally competent teachers should be able to answer a particular multiple-choice question correctly, especially when they are given no information whatsoever about the correlations of that item with any relevant criteria.

If those same teachers are instead asked to judge the adequacy of a lesson plan, the appropriateness of comments written in the margins of a student's paper, or the level of student engagement shown in a classroom videotape, they can bring their own teaching knowledge and experience to bear much more directly. Careful selection of judges, use of a sufficient number of judges, appropriate specification of the judgment task and training of judges, and other procedural matters are also critical (Haertel, 1990; Jaeger, 1990).

Once standards are established, of course, validation efforts should continue, and periodic adjustments should be made as warranted. The implementation of new forms of teacher tests may spur rapid growth in the knowledge base of teaching and may bring significant changes in teacher education. As the profession evolves, both the content and the level of expectations of teacher examinations will need to evolve as well.

NOTES

[1] Publications are available at cost from the Teacher Assessment Project, School of Education, Stanford University, Stanford, CA 94305-3096. An annotated bibliography may be obtained free of charge by writing to that address.

[2] Information about Consortium clearinghouse materials may be obtained from Jean Miller, CCSSO, 139 Hall of the States, 400 North Capitol Street NW, Washington, DC 20001.

REFERENCES

Athanases, S. Z. (1990, March). *Assessing the planning and teaching of integrated language arts in the elementary grades* (Technical Report No. L3). Stanford, CA: Stanford University, School of Education, Teacher Assessment Project.

Ayers, J. B., & Qualls, G. S. (1979). Concurrent and predictive validity of the National Teacher Examinations. *Journal of Educational Research, 73*, 86–91.

Baker, C. O., & Ogle, L. T. (1989). *The condition of education 1989. Vol. 1: Elementary and secondary education* (Publication No. CS 89-650). Washington, DC: U.S. Government Printing Office.

Bird, T. (1990, March). *Report on the rating procedures used to assess portfolios and assessment center exercises for high school biology teachers* (Technical Report No. B3). Stanford, CA: Stanford University, School of Education, Teacher Assessment Project.

Bird, T., & King, B. (1990, March). *Report on the use of portfolios to assess biology teachers* (Technical Report No. B1). Stanford, CA: Stanford University, School of Education, Teacher Assessment Project.

Cross, L. H. (1985). Validation of the NTE tests for certification decisions. *Educational Measurement: Issues and Practice, 4*(3), 7–10.

Darling-Hammond, L. (1985). Valuing teachers: The making of a profession. *Teachers College Record, 87*, 205–218.

Darling-Hammond, L. (1986a). A proposal for evaluation in the teaching profession. *Elementary School Journal, 86*, 531–551.

Darling-Hammond, L. (1986b). Teaching knowledge: How do we test it? *American Educator, 10*(3), 18–21, 46.

Educational Testing Service. (1984). *A guide to the NTE Core Battery tests: Communication Skills, General Knowledge, Professional Knowledge*. Princeton, NJ: Author.

Estes, G. D., Stansbury, K., Long, C., Wheeler, P., & Quellmalz, E. (1990, March). *Assessment component of the California New Teacher Project: First year report*. San Francisco: Far West Laboratory for Educational Research and Development.

Faggen, J. (1983). *Report on a study of the NTE Core Battery tests by the State of New York*. Princeton, NJ: Educational Testing Service.

Glass, G. V. (1978). Standards and criteria. *Journal of Educational Measurement, 15*, 237–261.

Goertz, M. E., & Pitcher, B. (1985). *The impact of NTE use by states on teacher selection* (Research Report No. 85-1). Princeton, NJ: Educational Testing Service.

Haertel, E. H. (1986). The valid use of student performance measures for teacher evaluation. *Educational Evaluation and Policy Analysis, 8*, 45–60.

Haertel, E. H. (1988). Assessing the teaching function. *Applied Measurement in Education, 1*, 99–107.

Haertel, E. H. (1990, April). *From expert opinions to reliable scores: Psychometrics for judgment-based teacher assessment.* Paper presented at the meeting of the American Educational Research Association, Boston.

Haney, W., Madaus, G., & Kreitzer, A. (1987). Charms talismanic: Testing teachers for the improvement of American education. *Review of Research in Education, 14*, 169–238.

Harris, S., & Harris, L. B. (1988). *The teacher's almanac 1988–89*. New York: Facts on File.

Holmes Group. (1986). *Tomorrow's teachers*. East Lansing, MI: Author.

Holmes Group. (1989, January). *Work in progress: The Holmes Group one year on*. East Lansing, MI: Author.

Jaeger, R. M. (1990). Setting standards on teacher certification tests. In J. Millman & L. Darling-Hammond (Eds.), *The new handbook of teacher evaluation* (pp. 295–321). Newbury Park, CA: Sage.

Linn, R. L. (1986). Barriers to new test designs. In Educational Testing Service, *The redesign of testing for the 21st century: Proceedings of the 1985 ETS Invitational Conference* (pp. 69–79). Princeton, NJ: Educational Testing Service.

Macmillan, C. J. B., & Pendlebury, S. (1985). The Florida Performance Measurement System: A consideration. *Teachers College Record, 87*, 67–78.

Madaus, G. F. (1986). Measurement specialists: Testing the faith—A reply to Mehrens. *Educational Measurement: Issues and Practice, 5*(4), 11–14.

Madaus, G. F. (1990). Legal and professional issues in teacher-certification testing: A psychometric snark hunt. In J. V. Mitchell, Jr., S. L. Wise, & B. S. Plake (Eds.), *Assessment of teaching: Purposes, practices, and implications for the profession* (pp. 209–259). Hillsdale, NJ: Erlbaum.

Madaus, G. F., & Pullin, D. (1987). Teacher certification tests: Do they really measure what we need to know? *Phi Delta Kappan, 69*, 31–38.

McGreevy, J., & Hyink, L. (1989, June). *Documentary history* (Technical Report No. H1). Stanford, CA: Stanford University, School of Education, Teacher Assessment Project.

Medley, D. M., & Coker, H. (1987). How valid are principals' judgments of teacher effectiveness? *Phi Delta Kappan, 69*, 138–140.

Mitchell, J., & Tyson, P. (1989, June). *Lesson planning (mathematics)* (Technical Report No. M1). Stanford, CA: Stanford University, School of Education, Teacher Assessment Project.

National Board for Professional Teaching Standards. (1989). *Toward high and rigorous standards for the teaching profession*. Washington, DC: Author.

Nelsen, E. A. (1985). Review of NTE programs. In J. V. Mitchell, Jr. (Ed.), *Ninth mental measurements yearbook* (Vol. 2, pp. 1063–1066). Lincoln: University of Nebraska Press.

Oppenheim, D. B. (1985). Review of pre-professional skills tests. In J. V. Mitchell, Jr. (Ed.), *Ninth mental measurements yearbook* (Vol. 2, pp. 1187–1188). Lincoln: University of Nebraska Press.

Peterson, D., Micceri, T., & Smith, B. O. (1985). Measurement of teacher performance: A study in instrument development. *Teaching and Teacher Education, 1*, 63–77.

Popham, W. J. (1990). Face validity: Siren song for teacher testers. In J. V. Mitchell, Jr., S. L. Wise, & B. S. Plake (Eds.), *Assessment of teaching: Purposes, practices, and implications for the profession* (pp. 1–14). Hillsdale, NJ: Erlbaum.

Quirk, T. J., Witten, B. J., & Weinberg, S. F. (1973). Review of studies of the concurrent and predictive validity of the National Teacher Examinations. *Review of Educational Research, 43*, 89–113.

Rebell, M. A. (1986). Disparate impact of teacher competency testing on minorities: Don't blame the test-takers—or the tests. *Yale Law and Policy Review, 4*, 375–403.

Rebell, M. A. (1990). Legal issues concerning teacher evaluation. In J. Millman & L. Darling-Hammond (Eds.), *The new handbook of teacher evaluation* (pp. 337–355). Newbury Park, CA: Sage.

Rosenfeld, M., Thornton, R. F., & Skurnik, L. S. (1986). *Analysis of the professional functions of teachers. Relationships between job functions and the NTE Core Battery* (Research Report No. 86-8). Princeton, NJ: Educational Testing Service, Center for Occupational and Professional Assessment. (ERIC Document Reproduction Service No. ED 275 693)

Rudner, L. M. (1988). Teacher testing: An update. *Educational Measurement: Issues and Practice, 7*(1), 16–19.

Sandefur, J. T. (1986). State assessment trends. *AACTE Briefs, 7*(6), 12–14.

Shavelson, R. J., & Dempsey-Atwood, N. (1976). Generalizability of measures of teaching behavior. *Review of Educational Research, 46*, 553–611.

Shavelson, R. J., Webb, N. M., & Burstein, L. (1986). Measurement of teaching. In M. C. Wittrock (Ed.), *Handbook of research on teaching* (3rd ed., pp. 50–91). New York: Macmillan.

Shepard, L. A. (1980). Standard setting issues and methods. *Applied Psychological Measurement, 4*, 447–467.

Shepard, L. A. (1984). Setting performance standards. In R. A. Berk (Ed.), *A guide to criterion-referenced test construction* (pp. 169–198). Baltimore: Johns Hopkins University Press.

Shulman, L. S. (1986). Those who understand: Knowledge growth in teaching. *Educational Researcher, 15*(2), 4–14.

Shulman, L. S. (1987a). Assessment for teaching: An initiative for the profession. *Phi Delta Kappan, 69*, 38–44.

Shulman, L. S. (1987b). Knowledge and teaching: Foundations of the new reform. *Harvard Educational Review, 57*, 1–22.

Shulman, L. S., Haertel, E., & Bird, T. (1988). *Toward alternative assessments of teaching: A report of work in progress*. Stanford, CA: Stanford University, School of Education, Teacher Assessment Project.

Shulman, L. S., & Sykes, G. (1986, May). *A national board for teaching? In search of a bold standard* (Paper prepared for the Task Force on Teaching as a Profession). Hyattsville, MD: Carnegie Forum on Education and the Economy.

Smith, G. P. (1987). The impact of competency tests on teacher education: Ethical and legal issues in selecting and certifying teachers. In M. Haberman & J. M. Backus (Eds.), *Advances in teacher education: Volume 3* (pp. 218–249). Norwood, NJ: Ablex.

Smith, G. P., Miller, M. C., & Joy, J. (1988). A case study of the impact of performance-based testing on the supply of minority teachers. *Journal of Teacher Education, 39*(4), 45–53.

Stodolsky, S. S. (1984). Teacher evaluation: The limits of looking. *Educational Researcher, 13*(9), 11–18.

Stodolsky, S. S. (1990). Classroom observation. In J. Millman & L. Darling-Hammond (Eds.), *The new handbook of teacher evaluation* (pp. 175–190). Newbury Park, CA: Sage.

Sykes, G. (1986). Introduction. *Elementary School Journal, 86*, 365–367.

Task Force on Teaching as a Profession. (1986, May). *A nation prepared: Teachers for the 21st century*. Hyattsville, MD: Carnegie Forum on Education and the Economy.

Wise, A. E., Darling-Hammond, L., McLaughlin, M. W., & Bernstein, H. T. (1984, June). *Teacher evaluation: A study of effective practices* (Report No. R-3139-NIE). Santa Monica, CA: The Rand Corporation.

Wise, A. E., & Gendler, T. (1990). Governance issues in the evaluation of elementary and secondary schoolteachers. In J. Millman & L. Darling-Hammond (Eds.), *The new handbook of teacher evaluation* (pp. 374–389). Newbury Park, CA: Sage.

Chapter 2

To Use Their Minds Well: Investigating New Forms of Student Assessment

DENNIE WOLF, JANET BIXBY, JOHN GLENN III, and HOWARD GARDNER
Project Zero
Harvard University

The irony of social inventions is that one-time innovations turn to habit. There is perhaps no better illustration of how insight turns to reflex than what has happened to the practice of educational testing in American schools. Currently, American educators, the most determined designers, advocates, and consumers of standardized testing, are confronting the limits of the testing technologies they perfected between 1900 and 1950—at least in instances like the College Board examinations—as a way of providing more equal access to higher education. In the face of demands to teach thinking to all students and to open the curriculum to more than recall and simple rules, the shortcomings of multiple-choice formats as a model or as a singular probe for thought have become stunningly clear. There is growing, if far from universal, impatience with student assessment that addresses chiefly facts and basic skills, leaving thoughtfulness, imagination, and pursuit untapped. There is equal impatience with testing treated as a matter of pure measurement rather than an evolving discussion of what versions of excellence will be encouraged. Researchers and educators, families and students want assessment that offers rigorous and wise diagnostic information rather than the rankings of normal curves. In this climate, the possibilities of performance assessments borrowed from fields as disparate as business and the arts have become increasingly, perhaps even romantically, attractive.

This discussion of how we will measure educational progress cannot afford to be sheerly contemplative. In the spring of 1990, the president

This chapter was supported by grants from the Rockefeller, Mellon, and Panasonic Foundations. The ideas in it were substantially refined in the context of editing a series of essays on thinking, supported by the Office of Academic Affairs at the College Examination Board. We would like to thank several readers for their comments and critiques: Lawrence Frase, Ross Traub, and Kate Wilson. The opinions are solely those of the authors.

of the United States met with state governors to put forth a set of national education goals—broad, even sweeping, pointers to change in the educational success of a nation. The third, and longest, of these goals reads:

> By the year 2000, American students will leave grades four, eight, and twelve having demonstrated competency in challenging subject matter including English, mathematics, science, history, and geography; and every school in America will ensure that all students learn to use their minds well, so that they may be prepared for responsible citizenship, further learning, and productive employment in our modern economy. (cited in Walker, 1990, p. 16)

The word *ensure* should not be missed. Although the words *testing* and *assessment* never surface explicitly in this statement or any of the other six points, undoubtedly both will have a major role in defining and documenting what it is to use a mind well (DeLoughry, 1990; Goodlad & Keating, 1990; Wolf, in press). Moreover, the search for these forms of insurance will occur at an urgent speed: Only 6 months after the presidential goals appeared, there were already proposals for national examinations (Rothman, 1990c).

But we are in no sense ready to "ensure" student learning. Teachers, alone in their classrooms, observe, comment on, and grade students' actions, homework, and projects almost largely without professional training in assessment or ongoing critique by colleagues (Stiggins, 1988, 1989a, 1989b). They work off of solitary intuitions and received traditions; they are frequently conflicted about whether assessments should index behavior, effort, or achievement. Outside of classrooms, we have just the opposite—technically elegant testing systems designed to focus clearly on the achievement of overspecified and particular learner outcomes measured with respect to national norms. However, if we scrutinize the practices and results of this technically elegant system, we find that it distorts instruction (Raizen et al., 1989; Romberg, Zarinnia, & Williams, 1989; Zessoules & Gardner, in press), underscores inequities in access to education (Chachkin, 1989; Hilliard, 1990; O'Connor, 1989), and forecloses on students and teachers becoming active participants in signal debates over the standards that will be applied to their work (Schwartz & Viator, 1990; Wolf, in press). In effect, many current tests are psychometrically accurate and efficient means of data collection—at a high price. Multiple-choice items are, at least in their average and widely used forms, exercises in detection and selection rather than generation. They often enforce a view of single correct answers at the expense of recognizing culturally variegated forms of excellence or contrasting approaches to displaying understanding (Cummins, 1986). Finally, the technical demands of item construction, test design, and psychometrics discourage, if not outright prevent, vigorous discussions of what will count as evidence that all students are able to use their minds well (Schwartz & Viator, 1990).

To counter this technically elegant but demonstrably distorting testing system, educators are beginning to examine and experiment with alternative forms of assessment. If nurtured and made rigorous, these alternatives might permit the assessment of thinking rather than the possession of information. They might also enable teachers to develop sophisticated clinical judgments about students' understanding of significant ideas and processes and encourage educators to discuss, rather than simply measure, educational progress. However, the design and implementation of these new forms of assessments will entail nothing less than a wholesale transition from what we call a *testing culture* to an *assessment culture*. This transition will have to be wholesale because the observable differences in the form, the data, and the conduct of standardized testing and its alternatives are in no way superficial matters or mere surface features. They derive from radical differences in underlying conceptions of mind and of the evaluation process itself. Until we understand these differences and their network of consequences, we cannot develop new tools that will allow us to ensure that a wide range of students use their minds well.

In this chapter, we sketch out two major dimensions of what is involved in such a shift. These include changes in the basic epistemology of learning and equally far-reaching alterations in our approach to monitoring and evaluating educational progress. In so doing, we discuss the design of several approaches to assessment that seem promising as productive means of not only monitoring but also promoting student learning, including developmental assessments, performance tasks, exhibitions, and portfolio-like processes. But in closing, we apply the demand for mindfulness to those who would move beyond testing to assessment, insisting that they face a number of difficult questions that stand between promise and realization (Rothman, 1990b).

A VIEW OF LEARNING AND ASSESSMENT

Any discussion of changing views of student assessment has to be situated in the larger framework of views on learning and education. At present, we have a national curriculum—a course of study that yields low-level basic skills for a large and diverse population of students (Smith, 1990). But we simply cannot afford schools that train only a very few students in more than decoding level reading, calculation arithmetic, or the kind of writing required for filling out unemployment forms. Everything we know about early literacy learning stresses the power of families (chiefly mothers) to convey early lessons in the pleasures and powers of language for invention and inquiry (Heath, 1983; Snow & Chall, 1982). Therefore, we cannot think that young girls who will "only" be wives and mothers need nothing more than meager survival skills; if enabled, they first become teachers, passing along curiosity and belief (Comer, 1988). Nor can we think about young minority males who fail in school as falling into a safety net of jobs as manual laborers. As Berryman (1990) points out:

> In machining, computerized numerical control (CNC) machiners radically alter the processes of set-up, control, and operation, replacing manual set-up and control by skilled hand and skilled eye, with set-up by symbolic command. Such systems depart in significant ways from the traditional systems of knowledge that reflect accumulated production wisdom. They are content-free, formal, closed conceptual systems that have many of the characteristics of school subjects, such as mathematics or grammar. Individuals who elected traditional machining were usually, while in school, not thought to have to function within such systems. Now they do. (p. 37)

But if we are determined to teach all students more than decoding or calculation, there remains the hard work of determining just what constitutes "being able to think." Many of the aspects of what we need to teach beyond basic skills can be captured if we imagine thinking as a *performance* (Wolf, in press). First, serious thinking, like any performance, is a combination of humility and risk: It takes on noisy, ill-defined problems, alternately collecting data, observing, and hazarding guesses (Holt, 1990; Lakotas, 1976; Lampert, 1990; Polya, 1954). It involves large projects that combine invention and investigation with craft and insight and embedded accuracy. Second, like other performers, someone engaged in thought sustains a long arc of work over time and across obstacles. Thinking involves rehearsals, revisions, criticisms, and new attempts arranged in nothing like the straightforward orderings we offer in discussions of the scientific method or the directions for writing a term paper (Greeno, 1988; Perkins, 1982, 1986; Schoenfeld, 1988). Finally, thought, like performance, involves interpretation. Like an actor or a musician, a historian or a scientist has to decide how to make sense of information and beliefs.

The difference between a performance of thought and school learning as we currently teach and test it is evident in what a 17-year-old biology student says about two episodes in his biology class: what amounts to a rote verification of an "experiment" and a final field project in which he had to formulate and sustain an investigation. His accounts of these two experiences are shown in Appendix 1.

Courtesy of the respirometer experiment (see Appendix 1), this student would certainly be able to match the word *respirometer* to a definition. He would be able to write a short essay stating what "happens" when you test for oxygen with dried and living material. He might be able to use the equipment to measure oxygen in another task. But he would know very little about acting on the critical verbs of science: *wonder*, *experiment*, and *infer*. The results of the field project are promisingly different. To begin, the student learns the facts concerning the history of earlier approaches to forest fires as a part of understanding the larger question of the shifting nature of ecological theory building. He also learns about sustaining work over time—zigzagging from an original notion of fire as damage to a revised conception of fire as a necessity in a healthy ecosystem. He acquires skill in provoking information from diverse sources, including books, interviews, and on-site observations. In this way, he learns about the social construction of knowledge: His formulations emerge from talks with the ranger, from reading, and from sharing early drafts with his family and his teacher. Not incidentally, he confronts the diversity of opinions about fire damage that emerge across time and among different commentators. If only implicitly, he realizes that human knowledge has kinds and varieties rather than solitary correct answers.

To assess this kind of performance demands both a conception of learning and an assessment quite different from what standardized testing currently offers. First, a useful assessment of this student's performance would have to be multidimensional; it ought to capture his craft (his control of relevant information and his skills such as interviewing, researching, and writing) as it is exercised *in the context* of his larger undertaking. It should be longitudinal enough to inquire into the processes through which he developed his understanding. It should offer information about his ability to amplify his own thought by connecting it to tools, resources, and other thinkers. Moreover, it ought to be keen enough to index the student's depth of understanding: whether he acts only as a correct summarizer or whether he develops a point of view—with all the risk of having to meld values and experience with information and data. Second, any district, state, or national assessment of this student's learning should be complemented and supported by classroom practices in which students reflect on the quality of their own work and in which teachers and students openly discuss the standards for good work (Schwartz & Viator, 1990; Wiggins, 1989a, 1989b). Third, any powerful assessment should provide a response to the student, offering both a critique and the possibility of returning to improve the work. Finally, any worthwhile assessment would ask teachers to consider this and other students' work, engaging them in a discussion of what that work suggests to them about science learning and asking them to debate where it stands in their vision of excellence, and what its implications are for changing what is taught.

BETWEEN TWO EPISTEMOLOGIES

But currently any educator who would raise, never mind answer, questions about how we would use testing or assessment to "ensure" that students think hears two competing messages. The first is that salvation lies in shoring up and pushing harder on familiar and well-articulated forms of testing: refining the tools we have, such as commercially available achievement tests, state tests, and the National Assessment of Educational Progress, and testing more frequently with higher stakes for success and for failure. This is the message of the president's recent educational summit, many state education reform acts of the early 1980s, and numerous business roundtables. The second message is that we must turn away from these well-rehearsed measures and practices, in part reclaiming and in part inventing quite different modes of assessment: observations, performances, and portfolios (Collins, 1988; Frederikson, 1990; Resnick & Resnick, in press). In this second view, we must also redraft, if not invent, the assumptions and procedures of traditional psychometrics. This debate is often phrased as if it were a matter of turning away from some dark chapter in earlier learning theories and models of measurement. But perhaps it is more a matter of standing on the shoulders rather than the faces of another generation. We can never know what we should demand of the design of alternative modes of assessment without grasping what we have learned about the limitations of the earlier epistemology of intelligence and the testing practices to which it gave rise.

The Epistemology of Intelligence

> Preliminary investigations indicate that an I.Q. below 70 rarely permits anything better than unskilled labor; that the range of 70–80 is pre-eminently that of semi-skilled labor; from 80–100 that of skilled or ordinary clerical labor; from 100–110 or 115 that of the semi-professional pursuits; and that above all these are the grades of intelligence which permit one to enter the professions or the large fields of business. Intelligence tests can tell us whether a child's native brightness corresponds more nearly to the median (or one or another of these classes). This information will be of great value in planning the education of a particular child and also in planning the differentiated curriculum. (Terman, 1922)

The epistemology that informs Terman's views has deep roots going back as far as the Renaissance conception of the great chain of being and early-19th-century notions of progress (Nisbet, 1980). But it took definitive shape between 1850 and 1900 in the wake of developing evolutionary theory and the design of comprehensive public schooling for what many educators experienced as an abruptly multiplied and heterogeneous population. The view that emerged had several linked components. First, intelligence was a unitary and immutable trait. It had no kinds or varieties, only ranks. Intellect was also envisioned as rare, predictably located (varying with race, class, and gender), and fixed. Therefore, as Terman so confidently described, individuals could be ranked in stable ways according to their mental capacities. Second, education should be organized in a scalar fashion so as to prepare individuals for their inevitable lot in later life. Consequently, the curriculum should be a ladder: Entry-level learning, and schooling for the less than talented student, should be simple; only at later levels or in classes for those headed toward the "larger fields" could complex skills be introduced. Finally, as a major marker of individual difference and the chief metric for sorting students, it was imperative to assess learning in the most individualistic fashion, apart from collaboration, resources, or tools. No one unfit should slip into the pool of the average or the gifted. These were not a random trio of beliefs. They were a formidable, mutually reinforcing network of presuppositions. To appreciate the almost seamless and unquestionable justification they offered for who could learn what, they must be examined in closer detail.

Intelligence as Ranked, Fixed, and Predictably Located

Evolutionists were fascinated by what set man apart from beast and, by extension, what distinguished "primitive" from civilized society and worker from manager. As these questions were taken up, particularly by Americans, three putatively scientific but highly debatable stances about intelligence appeared. The first, and perhaps most pernicious, proposed to treat intelligence as a matter of relative position on a normal curve, not as a matter of criterion-referenced achievement. But that is only an ordinal description—one that carries no necessary predictions about anything but relative capacity. Yet both early studies of brain size and later studies of intelligence assumed that to be below the mean was to be stupid, and to be above average was to be bright. The result has been an enduring confusion between rank and accomplishment. In a second equally dangerous stance, intelligence was likened to other heritable characteristics such as skin pigmentation and, thus, was taken to be immutable. The final stance concerned predictable associations between levels of intellect and group membership. If race and gender are regularly associated with certain heritable physical features, why shouldn't there be a genetically mediated tie between the pattern or amount of intellect and group membership? In an effort to get at these associations, mid- and late-19th-century evolutionary scientists developed comparative studies in which children, retardates, and women, as well as different races and classes, were used as proxies for "less-developed" individuals based on a profound error in which naturally occurring within-group variation was used as a model for across-group differences (Fallows, 1989; Gould, 1981). In this way, social access and familiarity with the knowledge valued in Western, middle-class culture became fundamentally confused with ability. This stance provided the basis for the conflation of difference and deficit that has dogged the comparative study of intelligence ever since (Cole & Means, 1981).

In the late 19th and early 20th centuries, as the school population swelled with visibly different immigrants from southern and eastern Europe, as students were being pulled from the work force by emerging child labor laws, and as many African-American families migrated northward, these notions of a ranked, fixed, and predictably located intellect filled a critical need in American public schooling (Callahan, 1962; Katz, 1987; Tyack, 1967). Under these conditions, the conceptions of ranking, fixedness, and predictability provided the "scientific" basis for two enduring institutional responses to the diversity of styles, cultures, and academic backgrounds of students: universal testing and the systems of tracking students.

Prior to compulsory schooling, educators relied on sheer numbers of years in a common curriculum to carry educational distinctions. Once the school-leaving age became 16, however, educators armed with the notion of fixed cohorts of differentially skilled students designed different kinds of instruction and distinct sorts of educational materials for the students who tested at what they interpreted as different levels. This solution was so appealing and so singular that even progressive educators called for sorting, ranking, and the consequent implementation of different courses of study for different students (Fass, 1989). By the period of the Depression, the notions of individual differences in intellect and equal educational opportunity were dangerously linked in a pattern of differential access to the curriculum:

> The two concepts were intended to describe a school system that was at once pedagogically enlightened, progressively democratic, and protected the individual from the tyranny of sameness threatened by mass education. The linking of these two concepts was seriously misleading . . . it . . . provided the foundations for systematic differentiations in curricula, in performance, in expectations, and ultimately in school rewards. (Fass, 1989, pp. 69–71)

But particularly in the face of democratic beliefs, there had to be a strong rational basis for sorting students. Test developers like Terman and Thorndike, eager for just such a tool, borrowed and transformed Binet's fundamentally clinical procedure for diagnosing retardation into paper-and-pencil batteries that could be cheaply reproduced and efficiently administered to entire school populations. With this change, intelligence testing became virtually universal, providing scores that were to domineer the work of distinguishing different types of students and virtually creating the language of ranks we still live with: "gifted," "academically talented," and "low-achieving" (Fass, 1989; Oakes & Lipton, 1990; Rose, 1988). Although the rhetoric surrounding IQ has had to soften, the practices it enables remain largely intact. Entry into most gifted and talented or special education classes is set by test scores. Similarly, access to classes in general math or algebra is typically established via scores on achievement tests that are descendants from Terman and Thorndike's tests in impulse and form.

These tracking practices are not antique: They still keep the majority of American students cordoned off from the best teachers, resources, and instructional practices. (In 1982, for instance, 62% of students fell below the highest tracks and, of that majority, a disproportionate number were females or poor and minority children [Oakes, 1985; Oakes & Lipton, 1990].) This remains so even though we have widespread evidence concerning the destructive rather than remedial character of tracking (Esposito, 1973; Good & Marshall, 1984; Noland, 1985; Persell, 1977; Rosenbaum, 1980; Slavin, 1986). We know that the longer students stay in lower tracks, the more their performances decay. We also know that tracking prevents both less prepared and academically skilled students from making improvements that occur when they participate in heterogeneously grouped classrooms. But the underlying beliefs about intelligence and resulting possibilities for learning bind us still to these destructive practices (Rand Corporation, 1990; Rothman, 1990a).

A Scalar View of Learning

The epistemology of intelligence not only ranks students, but exhibits a privileging of orders over kinds of knowledge as well. This is evident in several ways—in an evaluative weighing of kinds of knowledge, in the conviction that there is a fixed progression linking simple entry-level skills through a long chain of hard-earned but molecular steps leading to mastery, in the view of literature as "soft" and physics as "hard," and in the displays of knowledge deemed appropriate to different gradations of learning (e.g., multiple-choice formats for special education classification and essays for advanced placement candidates).

As far back as Aristotle, philosophers have drawn a sharp distinction between the superior work of thinkers who ask "why" and the inferior work of artisans who make and do. Subsequent theories of knowledge in Western culture have continued to privilege acts of pure thought in this way. According to this view, theory building, the acquisition of concepts, and symbolic manipulations are more worthy and valuable than practical, situated, or commonplace problem solving (Resnick, 1987b). In this view, learning is the acquisition of information or skills that generate decontextualized knowledge (Resnick, 1987a; Resnick & Resnick, in press; Scribner, 1984). Translated into school terms, individuals know nothing until—or unless—they take up the particular brand of formal knowing prescribed by school. For instance, children who can merely *say* "he runs" or "I run" do not understand the concept of subject-verb agreement. Only those who can state the rule and define the terms grasp the concept. In short, those who have the competence, but not the terms, the definitions, the algorithms, and the orthodox procedures, cannot be viewed as knowledgeable. Thus, there is clearly a distinct hierarchy of knowledges: At the bottom is practical problem solving and at the upper reaches is theoretical speculation.

This hierarchy of kinds of knowledge was complemented by the scalar view of learning that envisioned a fixed and long chain of small steps that separated entry-level skills from expertise. This view of learning was evident in the very structure of the first generation of intelligence tests developed by Binet, Terman, and Yerkes; all began with simple questions and led gradually to more complex ones in a highly ordered progression. Once conjoined with strict age rather than ability grading, educators had what has since become the bread and butter of public school curricula: a scope and sequence organization that purveys information and low-level algorithms not as concomitants but as prerequisites to concepts, powerful strategies, or independent thinking. In the textbooks of the early 20th century, beginning reading became phonics practiced on single words rather than the attempt to match sounds with remembered texts taken from familiar books. Early mathematics instruction was translated into the deductive application of rules to closely controlled instances (such as "doing the three's tables"). Moreover, successful performance on these kinds of simple and rote tasks became the gatekeeper to more complex and demanding work.

As the curriculum for comprehensive schools was formed, educators sought new ways to convey the requisite skills to large numbers of average students seen by educators as headed for semiskilled labor (Cuban, 1984). The models they drew on included application forms, shipping invoices, and business letters rather than experiments, essays, or journals. Out of these choices have come the media of most public education: fill-in-the-blank exercises, multiple-choice items, sets of preestablished chapter-end questions, five-paragraph essays, book reports, and science labs that entail no more than verification of someone else's hypotheses and procedures in a highly specified order. The verbs that dominate directions for seat work, class instruction, or tests are *complete*, *choose*, and *match*, not *ask*, *analyze*, *investigate*, or *revise* (McNeil, 1986; Olson & Astington, in press).

This parceled approach to cognition was taken up and ratified first by the efficiency movement within schools (Callahan, 1962) and then later by the appearance of explicit psychologies of learning that stressed the molecular and incremental nature of cognition. In these frameworks, learning was formally and explicitly envisioned as a linear sequence of acquisitions in which complex understandings are the result of "the accretion of elemental, prerequisite learnings" (Shepard, 1990, p. 15) that, *it is assumed*, eventually add up to larger achievement. Thus, Thorndike explained the learning of arithmetic as the formation of local bonds between elements. Later, B. F. Skinner described learning in this way:

> The whole process of becoming competent in any field must be divided into what is not a very large number of small steps, and reinforcement must be contingent upon the accomplishment of each step. (Skinner, cited in Shepard, 1990, p. 15)

The conviction was that the answer to efficient and successful teaching was identical—dissolve all learning "all the way back to chains and simple discriminations" (Gagné, cited in Shepard, 1990). Again, these scalar views of learning are not antique: Benjamin Bloom's (1956) taxonomy describes learning as progressing in linear fashion from basic forms of recognition and imitation to higher activities such as analysis and synthesis. Moreover, the bulk of instructional and assessment materials proceed as if this description held, despite abundant evidence, that even sophisticated thought follows a "zigzag" course between craft and vision (Lakotas, 1976; Polya, 1954).

This stratification of learning became and remains pervasive, even in fields like the visual arts where one would least expect it. For example, the following excerpt comes from the section on teaching and evaluating student artwork in a state curriculum framework. In it, the writers struggle, but essentially fail, to break out of the language of small behavioral objectives:

> As suggested . . . the instructor can specify [the] product or outcome for a particular lesson: visible easily read and indentifiable art work where certain criteria is [*sic*] evident. It is important that a specific idea is measurable. An example would be: With appropriate instruction, students will be taught information about body movement, specifically, the bending of joints; the outcome would be that the student will show evidence that the figure which they are asked to produce will demonstrate bent joints; the measurement or evaluation will be clear and simple . . . bent joints. But evaluation can go further. An expressive component can be added. By asking the students to demonstrate bent joints and adding that the figure should be doing an activity, the teacher can get expressive artwork. (Arizona Department of Education, 1988, p. 69)

The distortion is large: In the course of making drawings, the skill of rendering bent joints is not an end in itself; rather, it is a kind of accuracy that is embedded in a much larger endeavor of making meaning. Moreover, expression is no more something you add on to rendition than a point of view is something you tack onto an essay. Here an 18-year-old and her teacher reflect on the integral relation between rendition and expression in the context of portraying a relationship between herself and her father.

> *Student:* This (portrait) is of my dad and myself . . . I drew it pretty much as his likeness, his high cheekbones, the Indian part of him, and I like that. I felt (at first) that I didn't draw

the arm right. (She looks at a later version of the earlier portrait.) It's the same arm. I guess what changed my opinion of it was the fact that, hey, it's not too bad. Because I have pictures in art magazines where the arms are somewhat distorted. . . .

Teacher: I never thought about it . . . but the significance of the arm really encompassing, wrapping around . . . does it add something to the drawing for you?

Student: My dad is just like that arm. I mean, he's really protective. . . . Yeah, I think that arm wrapping around shows his personality, his character a lot. (Wolf & Pistone, in press)

The Assumed Autonomy of Intelligence

Nineteenth-century scientists and educators embraced still a third set of values—one that claimed increasing autonomy and individuality of thought as one went from laborer to thinker. Wage earners had to operate in conjunction with others, and their work depended on tools. By contrast, a philosopher, an artist, or a scientist was an isolated individual—Descartes alone in his bed, Rodin's *The Thinker* lost in contemplation, Eve Curie alone at midnight in her laboratory. Moreover, these individuals used tools, but were not limited to them, dealing primarily in the probes of inspiration, insight, and imagination. Consider how the French mathematician Poincaré framed his struggle to prove that a particular variety of mathematical phenomena, Fuchsian functions, could not exist. As he reports it, he worked for more than 2 weeks steadily, in long bouts, on the proof without success. Yet, one day while climbing aboard a bus, he was struck by the realization that Fuchsian functions were identical to another set of well-known functions, the transformations of non-Euclidean geometry. At this point he recalls:

> The incidents of travel made me forget my mathematical work. Having reached Coutances, we entered an omnibus to go some place or other. At the moment when I put my foot on the step, the idea came to me, without anything in my former thoughts seeming to have paved the way for it. . . . I did not verify the idea; I should not have had time, as, upon taking my seat in the omnibus, I went on with a conversation already commenced, but I felt a perfect certainty. (Poincaré, 1955, p. 37)

What Poincaré offers us is a picture of an unheralded revelation discontinuous with his own or others' earlier framing of the problem. Yet we know from his own account that the solution came in the wake of deep involvement in the domain. The account also stresses the private and isolated nature of creative work. Even though it was a time of rapid exploration in abstract mathematics in Europe, we get no mention of colleagues whose views he took to be wrong or insufficient, articles he had read, or debates he had been a part of. Even his account of his insightful interior monologue and his apparently ordinary exterior dialogue underscores the essentially private, and untooled, nature of his mathematical creativity. It ends by privileging individual processes such as meditation or writing to the exclusion of group processes such as collaborative research or debate. To this tradition, the epistemology of intelligence has added the conviction that individual intellect is one of the major dimensions of individual difference, a characteristic that distinguishes one person from another, just as names or fingerprints do. Thus, it has taken cognitive research from Soviet and Asian cultures to suggest that a critical determinant of cognitive growth may reside in the individual's ability to imitate, eavesdrop, borrow, or seek help (Hatano & Inagaki, 1987; Vygotsky, 1978).

Such is the epistemology of intelligence: It is tightly woven around the fundamental image of a unified scale of worth, ratified in biology, and verified in the search for enduring group differences. Intellect, like height, is a trait. Individuals arrive and die in this world with fixed amounts of intelligence. Where this epistemology reigns, the only hope for public schooling is to organize and be informed by those realities and to develop tracks and instructional sequences in which the acquisition of conventions and basic skills acts as a gatekeeping mechanism. And the only reasonable way to make the system rational is for each student to take the same scientifically designed tests and to be educated according to the results.

The Culture of Testing

In the earliest investigations of intelligence, certain physical characteristics such as brain weight, head circumference, stature, and limb length were taken as clues to an individual's intellectual development, just as gills, circulatory systems, or skeletal patterns were taken as evidence for an animal's position in the evolutionary order (Gould, 1981). Later, in the work of psychologists like Terman and Thorndike, calipers and scales gave way to a series of test items that were believed to measure not the brain itself, but the individual's capacity for intellectual work. In this way, the *concept* of intelligence was reified, and testing became the instrumental realization of the many presuppositions endemic to the epistemology of intelligence. Although the effects of this epistemology on the form of standardized tests are well documented (Collins, 1988; Gardner, in press; Resnick & Resnick, in press; Wiggins, 1989a, 1989b), the culture of testing extends far beyond the specifics of item design and test construction. It involves a network of activities that extend to the conduct of testing, the forms of reporting data, and the uses to which those data are put. Chief among these practices are the emphasis on relative ranking above actual accomplishment; the privileging of easily quantifiable, rather than messy and complex, displays of skill and knowledge; the assumption that individual performances, rather than collaborative forms of cognition, are the most powerful indicators of educational progress; and an image of evaluating educational progress as a matter of scientific measurement.

The Dominance of Ranking

The view of intelligence as rare, fixed, and predictably associated with group membership has meant that we have designed tests to yield data that will rank students' performances rather than describe their level of learning against some fixed and external criteria. Thus, the dominant tool or image for testing is the normal curve, which presumes some poor performers, a bulge in the middle, and a few high performers. This tool also assumes that the most useful form of information is the comparison of students or cohorts. Hence, in major tests, there are many items composed of only those types and contents that distinguish between students. Consequently, the vast majority of test results are reported in terms of percentiles or ranks that describe where a student stands with respect to other comparable students (by age, grade, type of school, etc.). The resulting pressure is to move up in rank rather than in accomplishment.

But if closely examined, this is a troublesome legacy. Given our history of ranking and tracking, the mathematical necessity of a bottom quartile translates into a readiness to believe that there must be a group of students who cannot learn. Moreover, information about where a student actually stands with respect to achieving the standards for good work in a domain is obscured. A student may be calculating better than 50% of a national sample of sixth graders and still be much less than halfway toward the kinds of mathematical knowledge that will allow him or her to function in a job that technology may change three times in his or her working life (Berryman, 1990; Cannell, 1988, 1989). Conversely, a student may consistently score in the 30th percentile across 3 years and still have acquired significant understandings in mathematics or reading—news that the student, her or his family, and teachers might use to fuel belief and further efforts (Comer, 1980, 1988; Dweck, 1986). In essence, for all the sophistication of our testing system, the concern for ranking and classifying has led to the acceptance of a significant proportion of failure or poor performance as "natural." The attention to such relative information overshadows the responsibility to see that all students learn and the necessity to provide explicit information about students' current levels of achievement.

Testing Artifacts

Current forms of standardized testing are largely paper-and-pencil collections of individual items with single correct answers, requiring chiefly the detection of errors or selection among alternatives. Given this structure, many tests are without analogues in the actual conduct of problem solving, writing, or experimentation. Consider a sample item that a classroom teacher modeled on one that appears in the language arts section of the standardized test her children take:

> Find and correct the error in each section of the sentence.
> /the old dog/goed home/slow/
>   A.   B.   C.
>
> A should be:
>
> a. the Old Dog
> b. The old dog
> c. The Old Dog
> d. it is correct

In writing or speaking, one is guided by a sense for the intent and meaning that develops over the long run of the previous discourse. The above item is a single sentence with no surrounding context. To write or speak is to produce—to have ideas, to map them into chosen words, and to reflect on the power and accuracy of what you have produced. To pick out and to correct is only to detect. At its best, this item might be a model for the skill of copyediting or paper correcting. At its narrowest, it is a predictor of how a student will do on other such items. It is as incoherent a sample of a student's ability to generate or understand written English discourse as a written test for the administration of cardiopulmonary respiration would be. Because they are based on these kinds of items, standard achievement tests inquire only into answers as end products. They offer no way to sample the wondering, investigation, data collection, or reflection that are essential to serious work well done (Collins, 1988; Frederikson, 1990; Resnick & Resnick, in press). Moreover, tests are timed collections of first-draft responses. In this way, tests promote a model of knowing that privileges speed and efficiency above contemplation and accuracy above risk (Callahan, 1962). Thus, as a result of this kind of testing and the instruction that flows from it, students who can do quite well on the items may, in fact, be unable to perform in the domain those items are meant to sample (Schoenfeld, 1987).

In this way, we have yoked the high stakes and publicity of testing to the strange work of teaching students how to engage in cold-start, often artifactual forms of learning and to understand that speed and correctness outweigh overall quality and risk. Not surprisingly, these messages overspill the boundaries of standardized testing. Teachers' own tests frequently mimic these structures and underlying values. Textbook exercises customarily use the item types that appear on tests, and in many schools where districtwide end-of-course exams are required, there are often explicit rules that the exam must contain at least one half to one third multiple-choice questions.

Tests as a Portrait of Solo Learning

Many tests also enforce a view of cognition as individual and isolated, insisting that the correct measure of achievement is the most naked: No collaboration and no tools are to be present. The instructions that any teacher reads to students before they break the seal on their California Test of Basic Skills or Metropolitan test booklets are indicative. They bid the teacher to respond to questions only by rereading or paraphrasing the original test instructions. Those same directions also bid students to do their own work, not to converse or look at another student's paper. Those same test directions often insist that students put away all books, papers, and calculators. It is the absolutely individual, solo performance that is sought—not what a student can accomplish in concert with others or with the tools or resources of a domain or his or her own preparations based on those tools. So deep do these beliefs run that it was front page news when, in the fall of 1990, the College Board announced that students might use calculators in the SAT. Moreover, we have been so convinced of the notion that intellect is an isolated, individual quality that we utterly lack the procedures or the psychometrics to study students' performances in group situations. We regularly assay the quality of a school or a district via aggregated individual student scores, never imagining that perhaps we ought to be examining the quality of what occurs in classroom discussion or the range of performances in groups of students working together. In this way, our belief in the individuality of intelligence is peculiarly out of touch with the nature of most serious adult work, occurring as it does in the context of co-workers and tools designed to amplify human performances (Resnick, 1987b).

Tests as Scientific Instruments

Finally, we presume that standardized tests are instances of scientific measurement acting like thermometers, fathometers, or scales. They are meant to slip into an educational setting (e.g., for a brief period), collect relevant data, and silently withdraw, causing no perturbation. They are presumed to be neutral, treating students just like the ocean bottom or any substance to be weighed—as if the students who tick off items were inert matter to be assayed and as if all the agency and inquiry belongs to those doing the measurement. The same might be said for teachers: The tests they administer are frequently manufactured by outside experts on the grounds that only these outsiders have the expertise to make such precision instruments. Tests arrive sealed in plastic pouches and, when completed, must be resealed and signed—unread by teachers. Ahead of time it is difficult to examine entire tests, to question them, or to get access to sample performances that were scored as passing, failing, or superior. In most cases, neither students nor teachers will see test results, or at best they will see *only* results without the opportunity to look at errors and successes. Consequently, there is little opportunity to contest, discuss, or learn from their students' performances. Through these routines, we teach students and teachers not to value their past performances as a source of learning.

The nature of scores on standardized achievement tests is equally revealing. The number of items correct, not the overall quality of response, determines the score. This accretion model obscures precisely those dimensions and qualities that inhere in no one answer but characterize larger performances of thought: pursuit, research, imagination, and point of view. It is as if the number of completed sentences in an editorial mattered more than the overall power of its argument or the integrity of its perspective. In this way, the technology of scoring has become one of the most powerful realizations of behaviorist views of learning and performance.

Thus, the epistemology of intelligence, realized in the culture of testing, has given us an efficient and highly quantifiable way of assaying student learning. The difficult discovery has been that both what is assessed and the manner of assessment are problematic. Standardized tests, the chief technology of this epistemology, are constructed so that only a few can score high; they have yielded artifacts rather than authentic samples, promoted an isolated view of learning, and treated assessment as a matter of pure measurement. Out of these realizations has developed a growing conviction that we must find alternatives: first, an epistemology that is concerned with accomplishment rather than rank and, second, modes of assessment that sample what it is we want students to know rather than what it is possible to score cleanly.

Epistemology of Mind

From its earliest applications, the epistemology associated with measuring intelligence and the ensuing culture of testing galvanized an opposing point of view. Its proponents argued against the rare and fixed nature of intelligence, and perhaps no one spoke out more vigorously or more elegantly than Charles Eliot, at least during his tenure as the chairman of the Committee of Ten on Secondary Schools at the close of the 19th century. During those years, his was a deep-running belief in the potential of virtually all learners, and consequently his opposition to a tracked and segregated curriculum based on teachers' intuitions or on test scores was heated:

> It is a curious fact that we Americans habitually underestimate the capacity of pupils at almost every stage of education from the primary school through the university. . . . It seems

to me probable that the proportion of grammar school children incapable of pursuing geometry, algebra, and a foreign language would turn out to be much smaller than we imagine. (cited in Madaus, 1990)

In recent years, Eliot's early values and hunches have gathered empirical support with the emergence of quite a different view of learning, what we term the *epistemology of mind*. In this epistemology, the capacity for thoughtfulness is widespread, rather than the exclusive property of those who rank high, and our views of students' abilities are susceptible to change. Not only may students' capacities leapfrog our predictions, but our cultural conceptions of skill and learning inevitably develop (or at least change). In this alternative theory, learning at all levels involves sustained performances of thought and collaborative interactions of multiple minds and tools as much as the individual possession of information.

The Widespread Presence of Mind

Eliot spoke out of a long tradition reaching back to Jefferson that envisioned a broadly educated populace, regardless of whether they worked as farmers and cabinetmakers or physicians and scholars. The underlying tenet is that the capacity for thoughtfulness is widespread: To make the best use of expensive mahogany requires knowledge of geometry. Currently, both developmental and cognitive psychology offer empirical and philosophical grounds for entertaining this more generous view of the distribution of thoughtfulness (Gardner, 1989; B. Rogoff, 1989; Scribner, 1984). Together, these perspectives emphasize a notion of mindfulness as an essential human quality that looks much the same across infants and adults, blue-collar workers and professors. Across ages and classes, all learners construct (rather than merely absorb) knowledge, because inference, observation, rule generation, and theory building are open to all. Studies of young children learning their native languages indicate that even 15-month-old children are able to generate powerful grammatical rules based on the diverse input they receive (R. Brown, 1973). Young children reinvent the categories that underlie their uses of male and female pronouns and the cognitive architecture that makes counting such a powerful way to organize and compare phenomena as different as pennies and number of teeth lost (Armstrong, 1980; Beth & Piaget, 1966; Carey, 1985; Paley, 1986). Similarly, if we acknowledge rather than denigrate the everyday forms of thought, we find that it is not just engineers and mathematicians who solve problems in sophisticated ways. If we look, for example, at the arithmetic practiced by members of Weightwatchers and by workers loading dairy cases (Lave, 1988; Scribner, 1984), or at the rhetorical and linguistic skills of oral narrative and personal arguments (Cummins, 1983, 1986), we find that individuals who perform poorly on academic tasks can recognize and resolve problems where the situation is motivating, the materials concrete, and the stakes high and clear.

If mind is not rare, neither is it as fixed as Terman and his colleagues would have had us believe. Researchers working with retarded and at-risk children, for example, have demonstrated that it is possible to teach what were at one time construed to be immutable and inaccessible constituents of intelligence, such as basic strategies for problem solving and reading comprehension (Feuerstein, 1979; Hilliard, 1990). Moreover, these same teaching efforts have led not to temporary or memorized strategies, but to the lasting and apparently generative acquisition of more demanding standards for questioning, comprehension, and remembering (A. Brown, 1988; Palinscar & Brown, 1984). Research of this kind upsets the usual presumption that only achievement, not underlying ability, can be modulated by experience and instruction. Instead, these studies suggest that the apparent immutability of intelligence may have more to do with what we have been willing or able to *treat* as capable of being taught.

At the same time, it is clear that intelligence cannot be fixed in at least one other sense: Our cultural concept of what counts as thoughtfulness inevitably evolves. At one time, to be literate was to be able to read out of highly familiar texts, whereas we now expect readers to decode anything at first glance (Wolf, 1988). At an even more pervasive level, a number of theorists have called into question the most basic presuppositions underlying the epistemology of intelligence. Although there remains debate (Lohman, 1989), many researchers doubt that intelligence is the unitary dimension of human mental functioning that Binet and Terman proposed. They argue instead that the human ability to process and understand is the result of the interaction of multiple intelligences such as an acute understanding of verbal, spatial, or kinesthetic information or differing kinds of aptitudes such as "street smarts," creativity, or the capacity for academic inquiry (Gardner, 1982; Sternberg & Wagner, 1985).

Performances of Thought

Long before Skinner and Gagné gave us visions of student learning as a matter of gradually accruing basic skills, educators raised questions about the image of understanding as a linear sequence of small skills. Again, in writing for the Committee of Ten in 1892, Eliot insisted that it was not enough for students to possess what he called "the furniture of the mind." Students must also have "the discipline" of the mind, that is, the capacity to generate and apply that information in thoughtful ways (Eliot, 1961).

Like Eliot's earlier reservations about a stratified curriculum, this view has been borne out a century later by the research of developmental and cognitive scientists. If that work makes a major point, it is that learning does not take place in small, linear increments but is better described as occurring in qualitative and uneven shifts in understanding. A 5- and a 10-year-old, therefore, are dramatically different thinkers not only because of the amount of information they control, but also because the older child understands how to organize a task, how to think in conventional categories, and how to take directions. However, whereas the 10-year-old may be able to organize a game or a narrative, she may have a hard time setting up a rigorous experiment where she isolates a cause. Similarly, the differences in a novice and an expert photographer, or an introductory and an experienced chess player, do not reside so much in the information they control as in their ability to organize that information all at once, in a vision of the finished work or the projected game. Thus, learning might be better described as passing major milestones in the nature and organization of knowledge and skills (Chall, 1983; Fischer & Bullock, 1984). Learning is the individual's understanding of how to apply what she or he knows (e.g., when to estimate and when to count, when to make a drawing and when a map is more to the point, when to use standard English and when to speak in a home dialect). As Messick (1984) puts it:

> At issue is not merely the amount of knowledge accumulated but its organization or structure as a functional system for productive thinking, problem solving, and creative invention in the subject area as well as for further learning. (p. 1)

If developmental research has a second point, it is that there is intelligent activity at all levels. A dyslexic student who invents alternative routes to spelling and reading exhibits high levels of cognition, despite what appear to be low levels of literacy. Young children, who lack conventional world knowledge or certain structures of logical thought, nevertheless display ardent forms of questioning and investigation (Tizard & Hughes, 1984).

Mind as Extending Beyond the Skin

Thinking, like other performances, is also profoundly social—it faces outward. It occurs often at the instigation of others (B. Rogoff, 1989). Understanding becomes deeper or more complex with the opportunity to witness other minds at work and under the pressure of intrusions, challenges, and differing versions of others (Collins, Brown, & Newman, 1989; Hatano & Inagaki, 1987; Palinscar & Brown, 1984; B. Rogoff, 1989; R. Rogoff & Lave, 1984; Vygotsky, 1978; Siever, Kilpatrick, & Schlesinger, 1990; Stenmark, 1990). Thinking occurs in conjunction with resources and tools: pencils, resource books, or computer programs that contain both data and algorithms that will organize and manipulate that data (National Council of Teachers of Mathematics, 1989; Pea, 1987). Moreover, it is with the use of such tools that people with limited education or novice-level skills are able to participate in cognitively complex activities that turn out to be powerful learning environments. For instance, keyboards and word processing permit dyslexic students to write. Audiotapes accompanying children's books permit 3-year-olds to "read." To invent or to use cognitive prostheses, whether they are diagrams or software programs, is to understand how to overcome the limits of one mind and one memory. This leads to a radically different view of ability; any individual has a range of knowledge and competence rather than some fixed level of performance. Depending on how much support and familiarity with the materials at hand she or he has, an individual's performance will be greatly affected. It may be just as crucial to measure the quality of that supported performance—or the gap between solo and supported thought.

The Culture of Assessment

Even in its earliest formulations, the culture of testing, like the epistemology of intelligence, provoked dissenting responses. No one was a more articulate doubter of the technology of tests and their underlying presuppositions than William James in his *Talks to Teachers*:

> No elementary measurement, capable of being performed in a laboratory, can throw light on the actual efficiency of the subject; for the vital thing about him, his emotional and moral energy and doggedness, can be measured by no single experiment, and becomes known only by the total results in the long run. . . . Be patient, then, and sympathetic with the type of mind that cuts a poor figure in examination. It may, in the long examination which life sets us, come out in the end in better shape than the glib and ready reproducer, its passions being deeper, its purposes more worthy, its combining power less commonplace, and its total mental output consequently more important. (James, 1915, pp. 135–143)

Implicit in what James wrote were key critiques of the practices that were to amplify and deepen the effects of testing. James worried that assessment would become solely a matter of one-time measurement. He argued instead that if we want rigorous evidence concerning educational progress, we must describe large-scale accomplishments and we have to think developmentally, collecting longitudinal data that follow the growth of a student "in the long run" against the background of major accomplishments in a field or subject. But James went further still. In his use of words such as *passion* and *purpose*, James also points at another characteristic of assessment. As compared to measurement, assessment is inevitably involved with questions of what is of value, rather than simple correctness. Questions of value require entry and discussion. In this light, assessment is not a matter for outside experts to design; rather, it is an episode in which students and teachers might learn, through reflection and debate, about the standards of good work and the rules of evidence.

From Relative Ranks to Developmental Assessments

If William James was right, then assessment ought to document *accomplishment* rather than the relative positions of Terman's "normal" distribution of individuals within a population concept of intelligence. Key in this change is a move from norm-referenced to criterion-referenced evaluations of student learning in which what students can and cannot do is clearly stated. These descriptions have to be anchored at one end in the capacities most children bring to school and at the other end in the capacities all high school graduates should possess. Between these end-points, moments of major conceptual reorganization have to be cited and described. The point of these developmental sequences is that a student's real, rather than relative, skills can be assessed both for the adequacy and the fullness of his or her learning. The materials in Appendix 2, taken from the current national assessments in Great Britain, sketch out what adequate or expected levels of accomplishment are for young adolescents in the domain of design and technology. They also suggest directions and extent of progress, and, in this way, indicate explicit educational goals and standards.

To document accomplishment, we must also, as James hinted, design assessments that are longitudinal, sampling the baseline, the increment, and the preserved levels of change that follow from instruction. Building on notions quite close to those suggested by James, Ralph Tyler has long argued for the power of plotting such growth curves:

> One is not able to evaluate an instructional program by testing students only at the end. . . . Without knowing where the students were at the beginning, it is not possible to tell how far changes have taken place. . . . However, it is not enough to have only two appraisals in making an educational evaluation because some of the objectives aimed at may be acquired during an educational program and then be rapidly dissipated or forgotten. In order to have some estimate of the permanence of the learning, it is necessary to have still another point of evaluation which is made sometime after the instruction has been completed. (Tyler, 1949, pp. 106–107)

Many teachers working in primary school classrooms engage in this kind of developmental and longitudinal assessment of emerging literacy. On the basis of extensive naturalistic research on early reading and writing, the major steps to independent literacy have become clear. Using checklists, teachers observe children at work, keeping "running records" of students' current level of writing skill as evidenced by both independent and group work. They index these skills at a number of points during the year, monitoring whether children have passed the milestones that would allow them to change the level of their current reading and writing activities. A sample of one teachers' checklist generated for kindergarten children in a school assessment in Madison, Wisconsin, is shown in Figure 1.

Even though it is simple, this approach to assessment provides concerete descriptions of what children can and cannot do posed within a full range of accomplishments characteristic for the earliest phase of literacy development. Also, through its columns for repeated observations, this approach permits a look at whether or not the child's literacy skills are changing substantially or only marginally during a period of time when reading and writing are key school tasks. In accompanying comments, a teacher can index the robust or thin nature of these acquisitions by including comments, observational notes, and samples. As simple as this approach appears, along with regional and national standard-setting and adjudication sessions, it forms the basis of some aspects of national assessments in countries as large and as diverse as New Zealand and Great Britain and states as diverse as California and Connecticut (Baron, 1990; California Assessment Program, 1990a, 1990b).

Although such assessments are a beginning, they are only a beginning. For instance, they fail to capture the depth or richness of student learning: Is it accomplished with simple and meager forms of understanding, or is it done in a way that exhibits invention, transfer, and further inquiry? Appendix 3 describes how teachers working for the Northern Examining Board in England have tried to capture the leanness versus richness of student work. Quite possibly, then, we need to break step with the usual two-dimensional models of charting student progress that simply map age against level. In addition, we have to find ways to index newer dimensions such as the "thickness" or richness of accomplishment (Traub, personal communication, October 15, 1990).

There are significant consequences here for how achievement data are reported and educational goals are set. Major questions become ones of levels of accomplishment, longitudinal change, and depth of understanding. In thinking about accomplishment, we have to do away with the ranking and the relativity carried by the technology associated with normal curves. The real point is, How many children, and at what ages, are there at each milestone? In thinking longitudinally, we have to ask, How much genuine movement does a child (or a group of children) make in a given period? That is, how steep is the learning curve from baseline to year-end for middle- and working-class children or African-American and Caucasian children? In thinking about depth of understanding, we have to ask whether we are getting small or large numbers of children to un-

FIGURE 1
Teachers' Checklist of Early Steps in Literacy

Writing Development Record

for ______________________

yr. ——— teacher ______________________

Forms of Writing — Occasions for Observation

Conventional Spelling

Invented Spelling - transitional

Invented Spelling - beginning

Copying Environmental Print

Letters - random

Letter-like symbols

Scribble

Drawing

Forms of Rereading

Conventional

Attempt to decode/read sight words

Retells intended content:
written language-like

oral language-like

Label/Describe/Expand

Dialogue with Teacher

Refusal

Eyes on Print?

Yes

Occasionally

No

Note. Adapted by permission from working materials of the Madison Metropolitan School District, 1989. The first page of that text was, in turn, adapted from "Developmentally Appropriate Assessment of Reading and Writing in the Early Childhood Classroom" by William H. Teale, 1988, *Elementary School Journal, 89* (2).

derstand what they are learning in generative ways. The point is simple: The purpose of assessment must be to demonstrate where students are in their educations, not where they are with respect to a constantly changing population of peers (Cannell, 1988, 1989). Within this framework, the index of educational success becomes not the will-o'-the-wisp chase for all students and schools to clamber above normal, but the demonstration that with each successive class of first or fifth graders increasing numbers of students from all segments of the population attain later milestones, exhibit steeper growth curves, and acquire and hold on to a deeper understanding. To do so, we have to replace the hegemony of normal curve and two-dimensional statistics with longitudinal and criterion-referenced measures of more than age and level.

Sampling Performances of Thought

At the Waterford crystal workshops, in order to graduate from apprenticeship, an individual has to cut the "apprentice bowl"—one that bears samples of each kind of cut a master would have to produce (Madaus, 1990). Similarly, auditions, driving tests, foreign language proficiency exams, and athletic competitions all directly sample the behaviors valued (Hirsch, 1989; Wiggins, 1989a, 1989b). Thus, if we care about the performance of thought, that is what we have to sample and assess.

Increasingly, in an effort to break free of the artifactual knowledge evaluated in many standardized tests, schools, districts, and states are instituting what is often termed *performance assessment*. In these evaluations, students are asked to write, to read, and to solve problems in genuine rather than artificial ways. The example of a performance assessment shown in Appendix 4 is taken from the Pittsburgh Public Schools Syllabus Examination Project and was designed as the final exam for individual students in a required high school course in Shakespeare based on *A Midsummer Night's Dream*. A centerpiece of this course is the work of viewing and interpreting three distinctive filmed versions of the one scene as part of the larger effort to understand that plays are essentially scores with many interpretations. The essay portion of that exam is presented in Appendix 4.

The assessment pushes beyond what might well be considered a familiar aim of traditional literature exams by acknowledging the place of film and performance as much as text. It insists explicitly that students are to take a point of view and support that stance with examples from vision, audition, and memory. It stresses the possibility of a range of possible answers. In these ways it models hunches and analyses of avid film viewers and readers.

Assessments of Distributed Cognition

If we want to acknowledge and understand what students know about the profoundly social character of mind, we have to alter the forms of assessment we design in major ways. For instance, if we take assessment events like graduate thesis orals or the review of scholarly papers as serious models, we would see that assessment, not just learning, can and perhaps ought to be a highly social experience. In thesis orals, students quite literally defend their research to a diverse audience that includes professors and often other students. They take on-line questions, and part of the assessment touches on their ability to present themselves as knowledgeable, alert, and able to think *in situ*. In the case of the journal review, the author's work is reviewed by more than a single reader and a range of opinions is returned. The expectation is that the spectrum of opinions faces the writer with making good use of criticism—understanding where reviewers all converge in their recommendations and where they offer divergent opinions that are a matter of point of view and taste.

These same qualities can be extended to many levels of education through what Sizer (1984) has referred to as exhibitions. Clear examples of such exhibitions include entry into athletic competitions, graduation recitals at a performing arts conservatory, and science fair displays. They share many of the qualities of performance assessments (attention to large issues, sustained work, etc.). However, they can be set off by an additional characteristic. Exhibitions demand intense attention to the social and public nature of understanding. The designers of the International Baccalaureate exams in foreign language, in order to inquire into students' competence as readers, listeners, and speakers in a second language, ask them to read a book or a series of books in a foreign language and to prepare a 20-minute talk on the author or a subject of interest. Furthermore, this talk must be delivered using only note cards. Following the talk, the student is asked questions by fellow students and by a panel of examiners. The student is graded not only on the prepared portion of the talk, but on the flexibility with which she or he entertained the inquiries from the floor—as someone traveling in a foreign country certainly would have to do.

It is equally clear that we need assessments that focus on what students can do with resources: Do they know how and when to call on texts, colleagues, or documents? The work of the national assessment center (CITO) in Holland provides a remarkable illustration of this kind of assessment. Each year in the fall, the committee of teachers who design the yearly and school-leaving exams announces the organizing theme or central problems for the national end-of-year examinations. In art history, for example, the committee selects a theme that will be the unifying subject for the exams, such as "the supernatural" or "revolution" as exemplified in the art of a diverse range of periods and cultures. In order to support the best possible performances by students, the government funds the development and distribution of packets of background materials (readings, slides, study questions, and lists of Dutch museums where relevant works can be found). Teachers are encouraged to use these materials and to work intensely with their students on the selected theme, modeling the process of visiting works, discussing them, and developing a point of view. Here, the occasion of year-end assessment is used, quite deliberately, to help students synthesize and extend their current knowledge through models, conversations, and demonstration of how to use cultural resources (Hermans, 1988).

Assessment as an Episode of Learning

Growing out of the epistemology of mind is quite a different conception of evaluating student learning. It presumes that all learners have minds that develop with experience and teaching; it underscores thinking rather than the possession of information; and it recognizes that minds function in concert with other minds and the tools their culture makes available (Baron, 1990). But, in addition, if testing is modeled on the measurement of learning with a neutral instrument, assessment practices are modeled on something closer to the workings of a visiting committee or the debate that goes on among film critics. At its heart are reflection, judgment, and discussion, in addition to quantification and reliability.

In the culture of testing, we presume that a week of Stanford Achievement Tests can slip in unnoticed, like a thermometer. But if we look at the letters, journals, and notebooks of productive and inventive individuals, it is clear that these individuals use occasions of both internal and external assessment to reflect on their own cognitive and creative footprints. These reflections are a way of deriving lessons and possibilities for future work (John-Steiner, 1987; Perkins, 1982). Thus, in assessments, we ought to recognize the perturbations caused by any evaluation and attempt to use them productively for both students and teachers. In this context, the point of collecting samples of student performances extends beyond the derivation of indicators of educational progress. Assessment then becomes an occasion for learning.

Portfolio-based assessment can provide a context where students can learn to regard assessment as an occasion for learning. Typically, portfolios include not only earlier and later works, but also a structured sampling of different kinds of works characteristic of the domain (e.g., writing in multiple genres or math problems taken from different topics). The result of keeping portfolios is that teachers and students have access to a continuous body of work in which to discern acquisitions, characteristic patterns of interest and style, or remaining difficulties. As work with portfolios has been pursued in greater depth in recent years, however, this traditional conception has begun to evolve. For example, in the context of Arts Propel, an assessment project in the arts and humanities conducted in the Pittsburgh public schools, students, teachers, and researchers have been developing what are called *process-folios*. These collections of work differ from familiar portfolios in a number of ways. The generation of these process-folios is embedded in a much larger classroom context where teachers and students frequently discuss what goes into creating worthwhile work, what makes for helpful critique, and how to plow comments back into ongoing work. In addition to finished works, these collections contain sample "biographies of work"—documentation of the various stages of a project. When collected at diverse points, these biographies permit a longitudinal look at a student's changing control of the processes for shaping a final piece. Students often keep journals and write reflections about their work (Seidel & Zessoules, 1990). Finally, the collections of work students build are anything but archival. They regularly return to earlier works to revise or make comparisons with later ones. At the close of the year, students reenter their collections to make a final selection of biographies, reflections, and final pieces that can serve as the basis for a course grade and/or part of a permanent record of their development (Camp, 1990a, 1990b; Howard, 1990; Wolf, 1989). In this sort of work, students have the opportunity to see samples of different levels of work and to discuss the criteria that distinguish strong performances. They also witness the multidimensional nature of such work (i.e., that it involves the ability to pose an interesting problem, to learn from and comment on someone else's work, or to revise an earlier draft). Finally, if students are permitted to reenter the assessment process by making new selections or improving earlier ones, they learn something about how to make use of criticism and reflection to improve their skills and understandings (Brewer, 1990; California Assessment Program, 1990a, 1990b).

If students benefit from being included rather than excluded from assessments, so do teachers. Although most teachers receive little or no training in assessment, based on experiences in district-level competency exams, advanced placement programs, and International Baccalaureate programs, we know that with the requisite training teachers can become skilled and reliable appraisers of student work (Berliner, 1989; Clark, 1988; Elbaz, 1983). Thus, when teachers have to set the questions for end-of-year exams, they must grapple with what is worth remembering and carrying forward. When they read district-level exams or portfolios, they have to confront very difficult questions concerning competency and excellence. One group of high school teachers reading writing tests, for example, came across a well-written but highly racist essay. For several hours, they debated whether the paper was to be scored purely on the grounds of craft or whether the politics of the writer could enter into its rating. For the participating teachers, this was an important moment in working out the criteria on which they would judge the writing of students in their district.

At this juncture, the point of assessment becomes much more complex. Yes, it is a part of holding educators accountable to an outside community for good work well done. However, it is also designed to promote intense discussion of standards and evidence among all of the parties who are affected. This involves a move away from the presumptions of pure measurement to a model of clinical judgment (LeMahieu, personal communication, September 26, 1990). If teachers are going to take charge of instructional and diagnostic work, and if they are to grow and develop as professionals, they need the opportunity to debate standards and dimensions of performance (National Board for Professional Teaching Standards, 1990). Moreover, if students are going to leave school as competent assessors of their own work, they deserve sustained opportunities to internalize standards and ways of questioning and improving the quality of their work. This should and will have deep repercussions for how we think about traditional approaches to scoring and reliability.

CONCLUSION

As our conceptions of students, our definition of intelligence, and our sense for the point of assessment have changed, there has been a growing awareness that we need expanded and diversified models of assessment that offer alternatives to both epistemology and the practices associated with standardized testing. In particular, we need assessments that can illuminate the capacities of a wide range of students, model sustained thoughtfulness, and offer useful information about teaching and learning (Wiggins, 1989a, 1989b).

As the earlier quotes from Eliot, James, and Tyler suggest, the search for good measures of understanding is not a contemporary concern. Nearly a hundred years ago, observers wondered how testing would distort the curriculum. Teachers working in progressive schools as far back as the 1920s relied heavily on running records, projects, and folders of student work (Kilpatrick, 1918; Tyler & Smith, 1942). Many of the innovative science, mathematics, and social studies curricula of the 1960s collected ongoing samples of student work rather than imposing separate tests. Since its inception during the Cold War period, language proficiency testing has made thoughtful use of on-line student performances in conversation, impromptu translation, and realistic writing tasks rather than multiple-choice items (Hirsch, 1989). Therefore, what are often heralded as "new modes of assessment" are much more accurately described as "rediscovered" modes of assessment. There is a critical lesson here: If the current interest in alternatives to standardized testing is to be anything but this decade's flurry, we have to be as tough-minded in designing new options as we are in critiquing available testing. Unless we analyze the workings of these alternatives and design them carefully, we may end up with a different, but perhaps no less blunt, set of assessment instruments (Linn, 1990). As with any form of assessment, the familiar, difficult, and nasty issues of efficiency, equity, and evidence persist. Whereas there is considerable criticism of the approaches taken by standardized tests, as yet we have no such critical tradition for new modes of assessment. And we cannot be without one.

Efficiency

New modes of assessment will inevitably take shape against the demand for accountability in schools, states, and the nation. The relationship between these multiple levels of assessment could easily become schizophrenic with local forms of student assessment taking the form of intensive sampling of performances, and other levels of assessment adhering to the proven efficiency, low costs, and familiarity of standardized testing. This could be disastrous. On one hand, it creates obvious discontinuities in putting together an articulated view of educational progress. On the other hand, such a situation would undercut students and teachers taking part in the discussion of the evidence and standards entering into high-stakes decisions. Even though exhibitions or portfolio readings are undoubtedly more expensive and unruly than standardized tests, we have to find the means to ensure that such forms of assessment become a part of district- and state-level assessments. We can call on matrix sampling (the selective reading of representative sets of portfolios), involve members of the community as readers, or argue in union negotiations that acting as readers is a part of teachers' professional training and responsibility.

Equity

There is considerable hope that new modes of assessment of the kind outlined above will provide one means for exposing the abilities of less traditionally skilled students by giving a place to world knowledge, social processes, and a great variety of excellence. This may eventually be the case, particularly if assessments are used to unify, rather than stratify, access to knowledge and strong educational practice. For example, teachers writing Pittsburgh's Shakespeare exam are insisting that all students, not only the best and the brightest, be enrolled in a literature course that permits them to think about and interpret what they read. And clearly the hope is that it draws instruction in its wake, so that the exam is not the first occasion when students are asked to read and think like actors and directors.

There is a second dimension to the work of using performance assessments to expose mindfulness in a wide rather than a constricted range of students. We can deliberately honor real-world knowledge, expressly scaffold the relevant steps or questions in the process, permit students the stimulation of collaborative work (Brown, 1988; Hatano, 1982; Hatano & Inagaki, 1987), allow for a range of forms and formats in responses (e.g., graphs, essays), and provide for revision (Frederikson, 1990). The following example, taken from the Connecticut Core of Common Learning, demonstrates what this kind of assessment might look like (Baron, 1990):

> Many local supermarkets claim to have the lowest prices. But what does this really mean? Does it mean that every item in their store is priced lower, or just some of them? How can you really tell which supermarket will save you the most money? Your assignment is to design and carry out a study to answer this question. What items and prices will you compare and why? How will you justify the choice of your "sample"? How reliable is the sample, etc.?

Here students are being asked to apply their understanding of basic mathematical operations (such as averaging, units, and comparing quantities) to a familiar situation in which the goal of the construction of a sample, the scope of inferences to be drawn from the sample, and the applicability of the model have evident consequences. Its designers have effectively broken through the presumption that only calculus students can or should practice demanding mathematics.

However, new modes of assessment such as writing samples or mathematics portfolios could demonstrate equal or greater gaps between the performances of minority and majority children. If so, we have to be prepared to investigate why, rather than cursing or abandoning the project. Is it because the tasks and scoring systems entail subtle presumptions about single, correct approaches (Chachkin, 1989; O'Connor, 1989)? For instance, will a scoring rubric designed to rate the essays of white, middle-class students be able to distinguish what is remarkable, albeit different, about this African-American student's writing?

> It was a phrase by Woodrow Wilson, former president of the United States that surprisingly gave the "negro race" hope in 1917. It was the beginning of World War I. The reason given by this president for the American involvement in the war was "to make the world safe for democracy". This phrase had special meaning for the "Old Negro" because for so many long, incredibly long years they were deprived the promised, documented, and signed freedom rights for "man". So when the white president of that time came right out and said safe for democracy most Black Americans of that time thought the president meant them

also. In fact he did not. I say surprisingly gave hope because Black Americans and women are people too and when the constitutions and amendment and bills said ". . . for all" they found out that these excluded them. So after years of knowing that, some white man said "world democracy," and again this statement excluded them. (Woodard, 1990)

Alternatively, new modes of assessment could reflect the fact that some students have been taught how to enter into and make use of new modes of assessment, whereas others have been left to flounder. Like any measure of student learning, performance assessments entail a number of presuppositions. They assume a student who knows that it is all right to collaborate, that revision is likely to be helpful, or that the test is not calling for a regurgitation of what was done in class. Access to these presuppositions has to be widely available or alternative assessments will reproduce, rather than challenge, old patterns of performance across boys and girls and majority and minority children. Finally, if, in our best judgment, valid and reliable forms of performance and portfolio assessment index gaps in the learning of more demanding thought processes, we have to be willing to examine such pernicious habits as tracking and differential resources for poor schools.

Evidence

If we want to pursue these new modes of assessment, we cannot do so on the mere conviction that they are better. We cannot use the notion of developmental accomplishments or holistic scores to excuse us from developing rigorous standards and thoughtful rules of evidence that will offer candid pictures of what students are learning. We have to establish clear expectations about what a high school student should be able to do in a field like mathematics or history, and equally explicit descriptions of what portion of that should be accomplished by the end of middle school: If we move to developmentally based scoring, are we going to acknowledge that students in the fifth year of school will range in their abilities from those characteristic of second grade to those characteristic of eighth grade? We must think through whether it is enough for students to pass performance assessments with lean, rather than generous, understandings. When we insist that all students be able to engage in performances of thought, what do we actually mean? What do we take as evidence that a student grasps concepts such as "friction" or "heat"? Is the traditional essay or problem set enough, or do we need evidence from experiments, demonstrations, and diagrams? If we are going to look at student performances, we have to learn to design tasks that actually tap the skills in question. If we want teachers as clinical judges and want to honor multiple opinions, are we going to demand averaged scores, or do we want to preserve the diversity of opinions by means of a range of scores or the collection of comments?

A New Psychometrics

If we are able to design tasks and modes of data collection that permit us to change the data we collect about student performance, we will have still another task in front of us. This is the redesign or the invention of educational psychometrics capable of answering the much-changed questions of educational achievement. In place of ranks, we will want to establish a developmentally ordered series of accomplishments. However, this will entail hard questions in two directions. First, in stepping away from the 19th-century notion of a single chain of being, we are opening up the possibility of multiple paths to excellence. Yet, the vast majority of scoring rubrics for performance assessments, exhibitions, or portfolios still presume a single progression from novice to expert. We live in an increasingly multicultural society, learning-disabled students are more frequently mainstreamed, and students enter school with widely varying backgrounds in literacy and numeracy. In this setting, as we move to different modes of assessment, the contest between idealized, universal descriptions of progress and differentiated but potentially divisive rubrics will be fierce.

Second, if we indeed value clinical judgment and a diversity of opinions among appraisers (such as certainly occurs in professional settings or postsecondary education), we will have to revise our notions of high-agreement reliability as a cardinal symptom of a useful and viable approach to scoring student performance. We will have to find a previously uncharted course between insisting on uniform judgments and mayhem. Possibly, we will have to seek other sorts of evidence that responsible judgment is unfolding—that participants agree on the relevant categories for describing performance, that scores fall with a certain range, or that recipients can make thoughtful use of the range of opinions offered to them.

Third, we will have to break step with the drive to arrive at single, summary statistics for student performance. In line with more diversified notions of intelligence, it is critical to develop ways of looking at student profiles, both across and within domains. After all, it is critical to know that a student can arrive at an idea but cannot organize her or his writing or cannot use the resources of language in any but the most conventional and boring ways. It is equally important to know whether students can be authors but cannot read the writings of others critically. Unless we develop these kinds of differentiated portraits of student performance within a domain, it is difficult to envision student assessment ever informing, rather than merely measuring, the educational process.

Finally, we have to consider different units of analysis. At present, we deal in single students or aggregates of individual performances. However, because so much of learning occurs either in social situations or in conjunction with tools and resources, we need to consider what performance looks like in those more complex units. For instance, we need measures of the quality of classroom discussion or the functioning of a heterogeneous group of students working out a problem in economics or history. We also need to understand the kind of scientific modeling students can accomplish given computer support or the kind of writing a student can do given word-processing training and support.

A Reconceptualization of Assessment

Assessments of student learning are exceptionally human documents. Our conceptions of learning and what is worth being learned evolve at the high speed of culture rather than the gradual speed of biology. Only a century ago, to be literate was to be able to sign your name or read a highly familiar text, but neither of these definitions is sufficient today. Similarly, if we are to ensure student learning, we will have to conduct ourselves as learners in developing alternatives to standardized testing. We have to push beyond generating engaging alternatives by listening to critiques and revising and improving our own portfolio of approaches. It will take what the painter Ben Shawn saw as the heart of good artistry: "the capacity to be the spontaneous imaginer and the inexorable critic"—not once, but iteratively—as our culture shifts and our understanding deepens.

REFERENCES

Arizona State Department of Education. (1988). *Arizona visual arts essential skills*. Tucson, AZ: Author.

Armstrong, M. (1980). *Closely observed children*. London: Writers and Readers.

Baron, J. (1990, July). *Blurring the edges of assessment, curriculum, and instruction*. Paper presented at the Institute on New Modes of Assessment, Cambridge, MA.

Berliner, D. (1989). Implications of studies of expertise in pedagogy for teacher education and evaluation. In *New directions for teacher assessment: Proceedings of the 1988 ETS International Conference* (pp. 39–78). Princeton, NJ: Educational Testing Service.

Berryman, S. (1990). Sending clear signals to school and labor markets. In J. Schwartz & K. Viator (Eds.), *The prices of secrecy: The social, intellectual, and psychological cost of current assessment practice* (pp. 35–46). Cambridge, MA: Educational Technology Center, Harvard Graduate School of Education.

Beth, E. W., & Piaget, J. (1966). *Mathematical epistemology and psychology*. Dordrecht, Holland: Reidel.

Bloom, B. (Ed.). (1956). *Taxonomy of educational objectives. Handbook I: Cognitive domain*. New York: McKay.

Brewer, R. (1990, July). *The development of portfolios in writing and mathematics for state-wide assessment in Vermont.* Paper presented at the Institute on New Modes of Assessment, Cambridge, MA.

Brown, A. (1988). Motivation to learn and understand: On taking charge of one's own learning. *Cognition and Instruction, 5,* 311–321.

Brown, R. (1973). *A first language.* Cambridge, MA: Harvard University Press.

California Assessment Program. (1990a). *The California Assessment Program: A position paper on testing and instruction.* Sacramento, CA: Author.

California Assessment Program. (1990b). *Guidelines for the mathematics portfolios.* Sacramento, CA: Author.

Callahan, E. (1962). *Education and the cult of efficiency.* Chicago: University of Chicago Press.

Camp, R. (1990a). *Arts Propel: Ideas for stimulating reflection.* Unpublished manuscript, Educational Testing Service.

Camp, R. (1990b, Spring). Thinking together about portfolios. *The Quarterly of the National Writing Project,* pp. 8–14, 27.

Cannell, J. J. (1988). Nationally normed elementary achievement testing in America's public schools: How all 50 states are above the national average. *Educational Measurement: Issues and Practice, 7,* 2, 5–9.

Cannell, J. J. (1989). *The "Lake Woebegone" report: How public educators cheat on standardized achievement tests.* Albuquerque, NM: Friends for Education.

Carey, S. (1985). Are children fundamentally different kinds of thinkers and learners than adults? In S. F. Chipman, J. W. Segal, & R. Glaser (Eds.), *Thinking and learning skills* (Vol. 2, pp. 487–517).

Chachkin, N. (1989). Testing in elementary and secondary schools: Can misuse be avoided? In B. Gifford (Ed.), *Test policy and the politics of opportunity allocation: The workplace and the law* (pp. 163–187). Boston: Kluwer Academic Publishers.

Chall, J. (1983). *Stages of reading development.* New York: McGraw-Hill.

Clark, C. M. (1988). Asking the right questions about teacher preparation: Contributions of research on teacher thinking. *Educational Researcher, 17*(2), 5–12.

Cole, M., & Means, B. (1981). *Comparative studies of how people think.* Cambridge, MA: Harvard University Press.

Collins, A. (1988). Reformulating testing to measure learning and thinking. In N. Frederiksen, R. Glaser, A. Lesgold, & M. Shafto (Eds.), *Diagnostic monitoring of skills and knowledge acquisition* (pp. 75–87). Hillsdale, NJ: Erlbaum.

Collins, A., Brown, J. S., & Newman, D. (1989). Cognitive apprenticeship: Teaching the crafts of reading, writing and mathematics. In L. B. Resnick (Ed.), *Knowing, learning, and instruction: Essays in honor of Robert Glaser* (pp. 453–494). Hillsdale, NJ: Erlbaum.

Comer, J. (1980). *School power: Implications of an intervention project.* New York: Free Press.

Comer, J. (1988). *Maggie's American dream: The life and times of a black family.* New York: New American Library.

Cuban, L. (1984). *How teachers taught.* New York: Longmans.

Cummins, J. (1983). Functional language proficiency in context: Classroom participation as an interactive process. In W. J. Tikunoff (Ed.), *Compatibility of the SBIS features with other research on instruction for LEP students* (pp. 109–131). San Francisco: Far West Laboratory.

Cummins, J. (1986). Empowering minority students: A framework for intervention. *Harvard Educational Review, 56*(1), 18–36.

DeLoughry, T. (1990, March 7). Governors approve education goals with little mention of colleges. *Chronicles of Higher Education,* p. A-24.

Department of Education and Science and the Welsh Office. (n.d.). *National curriculum: Task group on assessment and testing.*

Dweck, C. S. (1986). Motivational processes affecting learning. *American Psychologist, 41,* 1040–1048.

Elbaz, F. (1983). *Teacher thinking: A study of practical knowledge.* London: Croom Helm.

Eliot, C. W. (1961). *Charles W. Eliot and popular education* (E. A. Krug, Ed.). New York: Teachers College Press.

Esposito, D. (1973). Homogenous and heterogenous ability grouping: Principal findings and implications for evaluating and designing more effective educational environments. *Review of Educational Research, 43,* 163–179.

Fallows, J. (1989, May). What's wrong with testing? *The Washington Monthly,* pp. 12–24.

Fass, P. (1989). *Outside in: Minorities and the transformation of American education.* New York: Oxford University Press.

Feuerstein, R. (1979). *The dynamic assessment of retarded performers: The learning potential assessment device.* Baltimore: University Park Press.

Fischer, F., & Bullock, D. (1984). Cognitive development in school-age children: Conclusions and new directions. In W. A. Collins (Ed.), *Development during middle childhood: The years six to twelve* (pp. 70–146). Washington, DC: National Academy Press.

Frederikson, J. (1990, August). *New approaches to assessment.* Paper presented at the annual meeting of the American Psychological Association, Boston.

Gardner, H. (1982). *Frames of mind: The theory of multiple intelligences.* New York: Basic Books.

Gardner, H. (1989). Zero-based arts education: An introduction to Arts Propel. *Studies in Art Education, 30*(2), 71–83.

Gardner, H. (in press). Assessment in context: The alternative to standardized testing. In B. Gifford (Ed.), *Report of the commission on testing and public policy.* Boston: Kluwer Academic Publishers.

Good, T. L., & Marshall, S. (1984). Do students learn more in heterogenous or homogenous groups? In P. Peterson, L. Wilkinson, & M. Hallinan (Eds.), *The social context of instruction* (pp. 15–28). New York: Academic Press.

Goodlad, J., & Keating, P. (1990). *Access to knowledge.* New York: The College Entrance Examination Board.

Gould, S. J. (1981). *The mismeasure of man.* New York: Norton.

Greeno, J. (1988). *Situations, mental models, and generative knowledge* (IRL Report No. 5). Palo Alto, CA: Institute for Research in Learning.

Hatano, G. (1982). Cognitive consequences of practice in culture specific procedural skills. *Quarterly Newsletter of the Laboratory of Comparative Human Cognition, 4,* 15–18.

Hatano, G., & Inagaki, K. (1987). A theory of motivation for comprehension and its application to mathematics instruction. In T. A. Romberg & D. M. Stewart (Eds.), *The monitoring of school mathematics: Background papers, Volume 2. Implications from psychology, outcomes for instruction* (Program Report No. 87-2, pp. 27–66). Madison: Wisconsin Center for Educational Research.

Heath, S. B. (1983). *Ways with words: Language, life, and work in communities and classrooms.* New York: Cambridge University Press.

Hermans, P. (1988, July). *The development of art history exams in Holland.* Paper presented at the AICA Institute in Art Education, New York.

Hilliard, A. G. (1990). Misunderstanding and testing intelligence. In J. Goodlad & P. Keating (Eds.), *Access to knowledge: An agenda for our nation's schools* (pp. 145–157). New York: The College Entrance Examination Board.
Hirsch, B. (1989). *Languages of thought*. New York: The College Entrance Examination Board.
Holt, T. (1990). *Thinking historically: Narrative and imagination in history*. New York: The College Entrance Examination Board.
Howard, K. (1990, Spring). Making the writing portfolio real. *The Quarterly of the National Writing Project,* pp. 4–8, 27.
James, W. (1915). *Talks to teachers*. Boston: Riverside Press.
John-Steiner, V. (1987). *Notebooks of the mind*. Albuquerque: University of New Mexico.
Katz, M. (1987). *Reconstructuring American education*. Cambridge, MA: Harvard University Press.
Kilpatrick, P. (1918). The project method. *Teachers College Record, 19,* 319–335.
Lakotas, I. (1976). *Proofs and refutations: The logic of mathematical discovery*. New York: Cambridge University Press.
Lampert, M. (1990). When the problem is not the question and the solution is not the answer: Mathematical knowing and teaching. *American Educational Research Journal, 27,* 29–64.
Lave, J. (1988). *Cognition in practice: Mind, mathematics, and culture in everyday life*. New York: Cambridge University Press.
Linn, R. (1990, June). *Cautions about performance assessments*. Paper presented at the Education Commission of the States, Boulder, CO.
Lohman, D. (1989). Human intelligence: An introduction to advances in theory and research. *Review of Educational Research, 59,* 333–373.
Madaus, G. (1990, July). *The history of testing in American schools*. Paper presented at the Institute on New Modes of Assessment, Cambridge, MA.
McNeil, L. (1986). *The contradictions of control: School structure and school knowledge*. New York: Routledge & Kegan Paul.
Messick, S. (1984). Abilities and knowledge in educational achievement testing: An assessment of dynamic cognitive structures. In B. S. Plake (Ed.), *Social and technical issues in testing: Implications for test construction and usage* (pp. 155–172). Hillsdale, NJ: Erlbaum.
National Board for Professional Teaching Standards. (1990). *Request for proposals for cross-cutting research to develop instruments for assessing accomplished teaching*. Washington, DC: Author.
National Council of Teachers of Mathematics, Commission for Standards on School Mathematics. (1989). *Curriculum and evaluation standards for school mathematics*. Reston, VA: Author.
Nisbet, J. D. (1980). *The impact of research on policy and practice in education*. Aberdeen: Aberdeen University Press.
Noland, T. (1985). *The effects of ability grouping: A meta-analysis of research findings*. Unpublished doctoral disseration, University of Colorado, Boulder.
Northern Examining Association. (1988). *Standards for English literature*. Sheffield, UK: Author.
Oakes, J. (1985). *Keeping track: How schools structure inequality*. New Haven, CT: Yale University Press.
Oakes, J., & Lipton, M. (1990). Tracking and ability grouping: A structural barrier to access and achievement. In J. Goodlad & P. Keating (Eds.), *Access to knowl-*

edge: An agenda for our nation's schools (pp. 187–204). New York: The College Entrance Examination Board.

O'Connor, M. C. (1989). Aspects of differential performance by minorities on standardized tests: Linguistic and socio-cultural factors. In B. Gifford (Ed.), *Test policy and the politics of opportunity allocation: The workplace and the law* (pp. 129–181). Boston: Kluwer Academic Publishers.

Olson, D., & Astington, J. (in press). Talking about text: How literacy contributes to thought. *Journal of Pragmatics*.

Paley, V. (1986). *Molly is three: Stories of growing up in school*. Chicago: University of Chicago Press.

Palinscar, A., & Brown, A. (1984). Reciprocal teaching of comprehension-fostering and comprehension monitoring activities. *Cognition and Instruction, 1*(2), 117–175.

Pea, R. D. (1987). Cognitive technologies for mathematics education. In A. H. Schoenfeld (Ed.), *Cognitive science and mathematics education*. Hillsdale, NJ: Erlbaum.

Perkins, D. (1982). *The mind's best work*. Cambridge, MA: Harvard University Press.

Perkins, D. (1986). *Knowledge as design*. Hillsdale, NJ: Erlbaum.

Persell, C. (1977). *Education and inequality: The roots and results of stratification in America's schools*. New York: Free Press.

Pittsburgh Public Schools. (1990). *"Midsummer night's dream": Tenth grade drama unit of the Syllabus Examination Project*. Pittsburgh: Author.

Poincaré, H. (1955). Mathematical creation. In B. Gheslin (Ed.), *The creative process* (pp. 33–42). Berkeley, CA: University of California Press.

Polya, G. (1954). *Induction and analogy in mathematics*. Princeton, NJ: Princeton University Press.

Raizin, S., et. al. (1989). *Assessment in elementary school science: Publication No. 303*. Andover, MA: National Center for Improving Science Instruction.

Rand Corporation. (1990). *Multiplying inequalities: The effects of race, social class, and tracking opportunities to learn mathematics and science*. Santa Monica, CA: Rand Publications, Inc.

Resnick, L. B. (1987a). *Education and learning to think*. Washington, DC: National Academy Press.

Resnick, L. B. (1987b). Learning in school and out. *Educational Researcher, 16*(9), 13–20.

Resnick, L. B., & Resnick, D. (in press). Assessing the thinking curriculum: New tools for educational reform. In B. R. Gifford & M. C. O'Connor (Eds.), *Future assessments: Changing views of aptitude, achievement, and instruction*. Boston: Kluwer Publishers.

Rogoff, B. (1989). *Apprenticeship in thinking*. New York: Cambridge University Press.

Rogoff, R., & Lave, J. (Eds.). (1984). *Everyday cognition*. Cambridge, MA: Harvard University Press.

Romberg, T. A., Zarinnia, E. A., & Williams, S. R. (1989). *The influence of mandated testing in mathematics instruction: Grade 8 teacher perceptions*. Madison: National Center for Research in Mathematical Science Education, University of Wisconsin, Madison.

Rose, M. (1988). *Lives on the boundary: The struggles and achievements of America's unprepared*. New York: Free Press.

Rosenbaum, J. (1980). Social implications of educational grouping. In D. Berliner

(Ed.), *Review of research in education* (Vol. 8, pp. 361–401). Washington, DC: American Educational Research Association.

Rothman, R. (1990a, May 30). Ford study urges new test system to "open gates of opportunity." *Education Week,* pp. 1, 12.

Rothman, R. (1990b, September 12). New tests based on performance raise questions. *Education Week,* pp. 1, 10, 12.

Rothman, R. (1990c, September 26). Two groups laying plans to develop national exams. *Education Week,* pp. 1, 14.

Schoenfield, A. (1985). *Mathematical problem solving.* New York: Academic Press.

Schoenfeld, A. (1987). When good teaching leads to bad results: The disasters of "well taught" mathematics courses. In P. L. Peterson & R. L. Carpenter (Eds.), *Educational psychology: Learning through instructions.* Hillsdale, NJ: Erlbaum.

Schwartz, J., & Viator, K. (Eds.). (1990). *The prices of secrecy: The social, intellectual, and psychological costs of current assessment practices.* Cambridge, MA: Educational Technology Center.

Scribner, S. (1984). Studying working intelligence. In B. Rogoff & J. Lave (Eds.), *Everyday cognition.* Cambridge, MA: Harvard University Press.

Seidel, S., & Zessoules, R. (1990, July). *Through the looking glass: The place of reflections in student learning.* Paper presented at the Institute of New Modes of Assessment, Cambridge, MA.

Shepard, L. (1990, April). *Psychometricians' beliefs about learning.* Paper presented at the annual meeting of the American Educational Research Association, Boston.

Silver, E., Kilpatrick, J., & Schlesinger, B. (1990). *Thinking through mathematics.* New York: The College Entrance Examination Board.

Sizer, T. (1984). *Horace's compromise.* Boston: Houghton Mifflin.

Slavin, R. (1986). *Ability grouping and student achievement in elementary schools: A best evidence synthesis* (Report of the National Center for Effective Elementary Schools). Baltimore: Johns Hopkins University.

Smith, M. (1990, September). *State roles in improving instruction.* Paper presented at the meeting of the Commission of Chief State School Officers, Clearwater, FL.

Snow, C., & Chall, J. (1982). *Families and literacy: The contribution of out-of-school experiences to children's acquisition of literacy.* Cambridge, MA: Harvard University, Graduate School of Education.

Stenmark, D. (1990). *Assessment alternatives in mathematics.* Berkeley, CA: EQUALS Publications.

Sternberg, R., & Wagner, R. (1985). *Practical intelligence.* New York: Cambridge University Press.

Stiggins, R. (1988). Revitalizing classroom assessment. *Phi Delta Kappan, 69*(5), 363–368.

Stiggins, R. (1989a). *Assessment literacy.* Unpublished manuscript, Northwest Educational Laboratory, Portland, OR.

Stiggins, R. (1989b). *Teacher training in assessment.* Unpublished manuscript, Northwest Educational Laboratory, Portland, OR.

Terman, L. M. (1922). *Intelligence tests and school reorganization.* Yonkers-on-Hudson, NY: World Book Co.

Tizard, B., & Hughs, M. (1984). *Young children learning.* Cambridge, MA: Harvard University Press.

Tyack, D. B. (1967). *The one best system: A history of American urban education.* Cambridge, MA: Harvard University Press.
Tyler, R. (1949). *Basic principles of curriculum and instruction.* Chicago: University of Chicago Press.
Tyler, R., & Smith, E. (1942). *Appraising and recording student progress.* New York: Harper Bros.
Vygotsky, L. (1978). *Mind in soociety.* Cambridge, MA: Harvard University Press.
Walker, R. (1990, February 28). Governors set to adopt national education goals. *Education Week,* p. 16.
Wiggins, G. (1989a). A true test: Toward more authentic and equitable assessment. *Phi Delta Kappan, 70,* 703–713.
Wiggins, G. (1989b, October). *Questions and answers on authentic assessment.* Paper presented at Beyond the Bubble: Curriculum Assessment/Alignment Conference, Sacramento, CA.
Wolf, D. (1988). *Reading reconsidered: Literature and literacy in high school.* New York: The College Board.
Wolf, D. (1989). Portfolio assessment: Sampling student work. *Educational Leadership, 46*(7), 35–39.
Wolf, D. (1990, Spring). Toward a theory of creativity. *Newsletter for the Society for Research in Child Development,* pp. 1–2.
Wolf, D. (in press). *Presence of minds, performances of thought.* New York: College Entrance Examination Board.
Wolf, D., & Pistone, N. (in press). *Taking full measure.* New York: The College Entrance Examination Board.
Woodard, T. (1990). *Harlem renaissance.* Unpublished high school essay.
Zessoules, R., & Gardner, H. (in press). Authentic assessment: Beyond the buzzword and into the classroom. In V. Perrone (Ed.), *Assessment in schools: Issues and possibilities.* Washington, DC: The Association for Supervision and Curriculum Development.

APPENDIX 1*
A 17-Year-Old's Description of Two Biology Experiences

An In-Class Biology Experiment

Once we were doing an experiment with a respirometer to measure how much oxygen was being used by germinating peas and dry peas. And we knew that the germinating peas should be using more oxygen because they are conducting cellular respiration, and the dry peas are dormant. So we spent about 45 minutes trying to get numbers that would show that. The respirometers were leaking, so we were having trouble getting the kinds of numbers we knew we should. So we just used someone else's data that was right.

An Independent Biology Project

Once I was in a state park and saw these people standing around *watching* a fire burn. Someone from the park told me it was a "controlled burning." I couldn't get it: "Let the forest burn?" So I began asking questions.

---

*From *Presence of Minds, Performances of Thought* by D. Wolf, in press, New York: College Entrance Examination Board. Adapted by permission.

See, originally forest fires were seen as bad. You can see how that happens: You look at all the black trunks and the black ground and think about all animals without a place to live. So everyone tried to protect the forests from fire—Smokey the Bear and rules against campfires and all that.

Then what people came to understand is just the opposite. When you suppress fires, it leads to the build-up of fuels. In a way it makes for something like a traffic jam in the forest. So when a fire does happen, it's giant.

If you look at trees in a healthy forest, you find fire scars. The burns allow for an old forest to give up to a new generation of forest. The old one is just a plateau. The fire changes the forest into a new environment. It allows for new species or more species of plants and animals to emerge and survive.

So in the 1960s, biologists and state park people began to argue that conditions should be restored to what they were before the white man came. They wanted to let fires burn as a part of the natural way things work. That was really tested in 1988 when there were giant fires in places like Yosemite. People were raging that the park service was letting the park burn. But it was really much more of a political fire than a real disaster. What you see is that it took people a hundred years to figure out that part of what they ought to be conserving was fire.

APPENDIX 2*
Developmental Descriptions from a Design and Technology Assessment

Statements of Attainment

Level 4 (Average 11-year-old)

Pupils should be able to:

1. Use hand tools and simple equipment appropriate to the materials to be worked, safely, and with a broad degree of accuracy (for example, use scissors to cut cardboard, a saw to cut wood, a computer keyboard to enter data);
2. Use under supervision making and assembling procedures appropriate to the range of tools and materials;
3. Use simple plans, drawings, and diagrams to assist making (for example, use their working sketches and diagrams to make a vehicle that moves); and
4. Suggest a possible solution to a problem that arises during making (for example, suggest different means of dealing with wheel spin in a vehicle they have designed).

Level 5/6 (Average 14-year-old)

Pupils should be able to:

1. Use a range of hand and powered tools and equipment (for example, plane, air-brush, cooker, database and spreadsheet software package, sewing machine) with due regard to function, safety, and the need to leave them in a fit condition for future use;
2. Prepare tools and equipment for use (for example, checking routines for powered tools and equipment, setting tension on a sewing machine, and setting for depth of cut);
3. Use these tools and equipment to a level of precision and finish appropriate to the working characteristics of the materials and the function of the artifact or system justifying any departure from the design brief (for example, setting hinges to a box lid, inserting a concealed zip);
4. Use an increased range of making and assembling procedures required by the range of tools and materials, including techniques such as preparing and marking out timber, preparing and cutting out a fabric to a pattern, and assembling several components (for example, an electrical circuit, using a spreadsheet and database together in an IT system);

---

*From *National Curriculum: Task Group on Assessment and Testing* by the Department of Education and Science and the Welsh Office.

5. Interpret plans, drawings, and diagrams (for example, a switching circuit, a working drawing, a dress pattern) in order to achieve the outcome described; and
6. Alter planned procedures to cope with unforeseen problems arising from the materials or tools being used (for example, power failure, component breakage).

APPENDIX 3*
Northern Examining Board Draft Criteria To Be Used as Grade Indicators in the Process of Assessing English Literature

3.18 In describing the process of reading and engaging with literature, we have tried to emphasize the degree to which it is a creative task (i.e., the reader's individual construction of the text). Accordingly, any attempt to describe performance and specific levels must take account of the range of factors that may influence that performance (e.g., the text, the task set, the stage in the process of reading the text reached by the candidate, supplementary information offered to the candidate, and the candidate's previous reading experiences). In the descriptions that follow, we attempt to define the qualities that we think are characteristic of the work of candidates who will achieve grades F and A. We do not wish to suggest that all these qualities will be present in the work of an individual candidate. Equally, we recognize that there are many other qualities that may be present but that we have not described.

The Work of Candidates Achieving Grade F

3.19 F grade candidates show glimpses of autonomy as readers, in relation to chosen appropriate texts. They identify the main contents of texts, following narrative threads, seeing the main issues and themes. They describe characters, their motives, and their relationships, and recognize similarities and differences between them. They begin to show awareness of particular effects and uses of languages. In reading and rereading texts they can give personal reactions and select elements they like or dislike and relate the issues and characters in texts to their own experience. They empathize with characters who are facing choices and problems and for whom they have sympathy. During the process of reading or rereading they modify their views in the light of new evidence that bears on previous meanings and judgments. They make use of personal knowledge and experience to inform their reading. In their work, written or oral, these candidates convey their ideas and feelings directly and use evidence to support their views showing some awareness of the nature of the task specified.

The Work of Candidates Achieving Grade A

3.20 A grade candidates convey a sense of autonomy, as readers and as writers, about their reading. Whether work is speculative, creative, or expository, they have a confident grasp of the text as a whole, tracing developments in the plot, appreciating crucial moments, and connections between various strands of the text, particularly between central and peripheral issues. These candidates recognize that the world created and conveyed by the text is shaped by the ways it is constructed, and so they comment on such matters as characterization, plot, theme and intention, layers of meaning, effects, and the functions of these in the text. They are aware of the viability of alternative interpretations of particular language use and of overall structures in texts. In responding to particular tasks A grade candidates draw on a wide reading experience, both explicitly and implicitly using their views of what they have read.

3.21 For these candidates, feeling "at home" with a text suggests that they can give personal reactions to what they read, selecting elements that they like or dislike, and that they can reflect upon these reactions. They recognize clues to meanings and speculate on their significance during the process of reading and rereading; they tol-

*From *Standards for English Literature* by Northern Examining Association, 1988, Sheffield, U.K. Updated materials are available from the Joint Matriculation Board, Manchester, U.K., M15 6EU.

erate ambiguities, exploring possible alternative meanings; and when considering alternative interpretations of texts, they construct viewpoints and versions of events for a range of characters and situations, whether these are sympathetic or antipathetic to the reader.

3.22 In their work, both written and oral, these candidates convey a sense of coherence and in work of various kinds they are forceful and convincing in using evidence and in conveying their ideas and feelings.

Intermediate Grades

3.23 In the grade indicators for F and A there are elements that are clearly connected and that indicate areas of progress and development for candidates. The incremental progression that we envisage will be an individual process, so that there will be unevenness of achievement across these elements. Candidates achieving the same grade between F and A are likely to present quite different profiles of performance, and the grade awarded to them must be a recogniton of what each has done. When we analyzed candidates' work within this range, we found that elements within the work were similar, and so the profiles of individual candidates seemed inevitably to be expressed in terms of quantity—"more" or "less," "often" or "on occasion." Such quantities cannot be readily defined, and we did not feel able at this point to develop distinctive statements of the performance of candidates achieving particular grades between F and A. It may be that the analysis of individual candidates' work could in time lead to agreement as to how some such candidates' grades can be indicated, but our work did not reveal such methods.

3.24 We noted, however, that between grades F and A candidates become increasingly able to use narrative of plot, comments about character, and explanations of meaning to support an argument, rather than to act as a substitute for one. Their ability to discriminate between key events, issues, and features of a text can also be seen to improve.

3.25 With more reading experience, they develop familiarity with their chosen material, or with genres, and with the ways in which the literature works, and are able to make comparisons between texts or references to other relevant material that they have read.

3.26 They develop the confidence and willingness to persist with the interpretation of literature, and the explanation of what it means to them, moving from glossing the surface (of a story or poem) to more probing exploration of the text, and making better use of evidence from it to illustrate their comments.

3.27 There is an increasing sense of themselves as readers, and writers about their reading, and of their ability to convey their knowledge, understanding, and enjoyment of literature.

APPENDIX 4*
SEP English 10, Drama Unit Examination, Essay Section: *A Midsummer Night's Dream*

General directions: Read the assignment carefully. Then take a few minutes to plan your essay. Write your essay on pages 3 and 4.

From your study of this drama unit you have developed an awareness of the choices a director has when he or she is staging a play. As you viewed three different interpretations of the Pyramis and Thisby scene from *A Midsummer Night's Dream*, you watched carefully for the various choices the director made and took notes that you later transferred to a graphic organizer. In a discussion that followed, you shared per-

---

* From "*Midsummer Night's Dream*": *Tenth Grade Drama Unit of the Syllabus Examination Project* by the Pittsburgh Public Schools, 1990. Adapted by permission.

ceptions and information with other students. Use this knowledge and the information on your graphic organizer to write a composition on the following topic:

> Choose the interpretation of the Pyramis and Thisby play in which you feel the director has made the most effective staging choices. In a multiparagraph essay, explain, using details from your graphic organizer, why the interpretation you chose is effective.
>
> Remember to include the following elements in your composition:
>
> - Develop a *focus* for the essay.
> - Use *details from the selected scene* to develop your focus.
> - Provide an *appropriate conclusion.*

Chapter 3

To Capture the Ineffable: New Forms of Assessment in Higher Education

PETER T. EWELL
National Center for Higher Education Management Systems

Assessment in higher education has become, by any estimate, a curious phenomenon. Begun modestly as a series of isolated institutional experiments in the late 1970s, assessment has become, for many institutions, a condition of doing business. A concomitant result has been the conversion of a scholarly measurement technology into a major and controversial tool of public policy. Thus, on one hand, assessment in higher education has the characteristics of a social movement—driven by political forces and constrained by societal demands (Ewell, 1989). On the other hand, through its language, symbolism, and technology, it is equally rooted in measurement practice. Any attempt to come to terms with it, therefore, must equally partake of both.

In this review, I attempt to do so in the following manner. First, in order to fully understand current assessment practice, it is critical to establish its historical and political context. Regardless of its technical guise, assessment in higher education cannot be divorced from a visible reform agenda. I begin by laying out this background with particular emphasis on the evolution and origins of assessment's contradictory imperatives: academic improvement and external accountability. Interaction between these two imperatives has produced a bewilderingly complex pattern of "assessment" activities on college and university campuses. Indeed, the term itself has rapidly acquired multiple meanings, each of which carries with it a particular referent and history. In the second portion of the review's initial section, therefore, I attempt to sort out some of these complexities in terms of a commonly applied taxonomy of assessment approaches.

This preliminary discussion sets the stage for the second section: a critical review of current practice. Like many other areas of applied research, assessment in higher education has rapidly moved from a sophisticated measurement technology emphasizing prediction and precision toward a field approach centered on robustness and utility. Three recent developments, in particular, demand attention. First, demands for better information about group performance have led to important (and controversial) new approaches to test making. Not only are these developments in measurement technology important in their own right, but they rekindle ongoing debates about the existence and nature of such claimed generic cognitive outcomes of college as critical thinking, creativity, and problem solving. Second, notable changes have taken place in the conceptual basis of assessment measurement, particularly in the model of student learning and development grounding inquiry. Early linear developmental conceptions (e.g., the popular notion of "value-added") have been replaced by more complex formulations demanding truly longitudinal research designs and a theoretical foundation based on complex integrated abilities. One result has been a growing number of institutional studies that, although intended as action research, can provide useful field verification for more carefully designed studies of collegiate learning and development. Third, as in evaluation more generally, the practice of assessment is increasingly naturalistic. Single-purpose research tools applied under carefully controlled conditions are rapidly being discarded in favor of multimethod approaches embedded in existing classroom or campus settings. Like naturalistic inquiry in other settings, assessments of this kind raise important issues about whether the authenticity gained in such settings is worth the apparent sacrifice of methodological rigor. I treat each of these trends in turn as the review's central core.

Beyond their immediate interest, these trends raise important epistemological issues about research on collegiate learning. Are traditional concepts of validity and reliability fundamentally altered, as some assessment practitioners are claiming, when the unit of analysis becomes an individual performance rather than an estimated group trait? Should the distribution of stakeholders and the size of the stakes associated with the use of any assessment become an integral part of the research effort itself? As assessment practitioners debate such critical questions, they echo earlier voices in the wider testing and evaluation communities (e.g., Guba & Lincoln, 1981; Messick, 1988b). In a final section, I summarize these emerging issues in terms of three general questions that must be posed of any assessment: "What's the construct?" "What's the context?" and "What's the use?" Although assessment practitioners have yet to reach consensus on their answers, the issues raised by these questions are capable of informing all aspects of research on cognitive development.

As a prominent feature of higher education's landscape, assessment appears here to stay. But beyond the attention that comes from emerging prominence, a critical examination seems compelling in at least three ways. First, assessment is by no means the first reform movement of its kind to affect higher education. Examining its origins, dynamics, and probable future can potentially add to our more general understanding of such phenomena. Second, as a technology in use, the evolution of assessment has much in common with other fields of action research—raising familiar issues of method, politics, and ethics. Treatment of their latest manifestation may provide new insights into how such issues can arise, develop, and possibly be resolved. Finally, the techniques of assessment, though intended to inform practice, are breaking new ground for research on student learning and development. As a clinical counterpart to more formal inquiry, both its methods and its findings are of scholarly interest. A review of this kind, of course, is never complete, and I freely acknowledge the inevitable errors of omission or conclusion that infect the activities of a participant observer. If trends and issues are clear, however, my central purpose is attained.

HIGHER EDUCATION ASSESSMENT: DEFINING THE GROUND

Assessment's Roots: Two Agendas for Reform

Any appraisal of the current assessment movement in higher education requires recognition of both its recent history and its two quite different origins. One ancestral theme, signaled by a series of prominent reports on undergraduate education in the mid-1980s, lies firmly within the academy. A second, marked by steadily growing state interest in accountability in the same period, is rooted externally. Both involve a multifaceted reform agenda in which assessment plays a key role and without which its current practice cannot be fully understood. Interaction between them, moreover, yields a bewildering array of activities that, despite a common label, are different in both technology and intent.

The Internal Agenda: The Undergraduate Reform Reports of 1984–1985

The internal agenda for reform, many observers claim, is grounded in a periodic swing of fashion regarding the structure and content of the undergraduate curriculum (e.g., Edgerton, 1987). Much as the discipline-based "germanic" curricula of the emerging 20th century spawned in reaction a rediscovery of general education in the 1930s, a curricular swing toward greater coherence in the early 1980s arose in part in opposition to the unstructured, choice-based curricula of the 1960s (Grant & Riesman, 1978). Student assessment is an integral part of this dynamic of curricular reaction. Resnick and Goulden (1987), for example, argue that an "assessment movement" was similarly present with the reemergence of general education in the 1930s, and ascribe this phenomenon historically to a natural period of consolidation following the end of enrollment growth.

The emergence of assessment as an explicit ingredient of reform was clearly signaled by four major reports on undergraduate education, all published in 1984–1985 and all stimulated in part by prior inquiries into national deficiencies in elementary and secondary education (U.S. Department of Education, 1983). Each report, in its own way, made a basic connection between assessment and undergraduate reform. For one of the first of these reports, *Access to Quality Undergraduate Education* (Southern Regional Education Board, 1985), a key linkage lies in the need to identify and address growing basic skills deficiencies among incoming college freshmen. Rather than an exclusionary view of admissions testing, entering basic skills assessment is coupled with improved remediation and directed placement in a comprehensive strategy aimed at recapturing a lost generation of college students let down by the failures of earlier schooling. More than any other, this report signaled the reemergence of widespread basic skills testing in higher education, foreshadowed by New Jersey's statewide program and by a range of integrated testing/placement programs in community colleges (Richardson, Fisk, & Okun, 1983).

For perhaps the most comprehensive of the four reports, *Involvement in Learning* (National Institute of Education, 1984), the linkage lies in the last of its three major themes—high standards, active student involvement in the learning process, and explicit feedback on performance. Notions of feedback through assessment contained in this report strongly echo the views of two of its major authors (Astin, 1977; Bowen, 1977) and contain two quite different propositions. The first, supported by substantial research, is that individual student learning can be significantly enhanced through frequent communication about performance (Astin, 1985). The second, advanced despite the apparent prior failure of large-scale program evaluation based on the methods of social science to effect significant organizational change throughout the 1960s and 1970s (Shapiro, 1986), is that institutions can also "learn" through information about results and can make continuous improvements in response (Ewell, 1984). Themes apparent in the two remaining reports—*Integrity in the College Curriculum* (Association of American Colleges, 1985) and *To Reclaim a Legacy* (Bennett, 1984)—are similar, though both are more traditionally focused on curricular content and structure. Here, the curricular connection to assessment lies largely in the felt need for intensive, integrative demonstrations of student knowledge and capacities (similar in structure to the comprehensive examinations typical of earlier undergraduate liberal arts curricula) to complete and certify the process of undergraduate instruction. In addition, both reports sounded a new note by insisting that higher education institutions were substantially (and unhealthily) unaccountable to their major constituents for their educational product. A primary target here was not, however, the kind of public mandate for outcomes testing then emerging in K–12 education. Rather, the intent was to move such existing accountability mechanisms as institutional accreditation away from their traditional reliance on input as the sole hallmark of quality.

Although the actual kinds of assessment called for in these reports remained relatively unspecified, their general requirements were clear. First, for institutional feedback, the results of assessment must be immediately useful in guiding intervention. One implication is that results be provided in sufficiently disaggregated form that distinct dimensions of performance can be identified or clear differences among types of students can be adequately diagnosed. At minimum, the framers of these reports recognized, this required different forms of testing than those then available: Most postsecondary assessment instruments at that time existed only in the form of standrdized instruments used for college and graduate school admissions, advanced placement, or certification, for which no subscores or item profiles were typically available. For individual feedback, an equal requirement was for developmental measures—usually involving integrative or simulated performance—using expert assessor judgments (Gamson & Associates, 1984; Grant & Kohli, 1979). In both cases, however, a substantially new (though equally rigorous) technology was required. Indeed, what made these reports different from similar curricular reexaminations in prior decades was that developing such new technologies was *itself* a major premise of reform.

The Accountability Movement in State Governance

Comprehensive though it was, the internal stimulus for higher education assessment did not function long in isolation. By late 1986, responding to state government had clearly supplanted internally sponsored academic reform as the primary reason for most institutional action (El-Khawas, 1987). What was responsible for this major shift of attention? One component is an escalating public policy concern with the effectiveness of funds invested. This is, in part, a function of rising costs and increasing complexity. Both legislators and governors have become unusually sensitive (especially in tight budget years) to the fact that they know very little about the actual impacts of investments in postsecondary education that can consume from a quarter to a third of state general fund revenues each year. At the same time, state higher education leaders have become more sophisticated in their claims about public benefit (Folger & Berdahl, 1987). As a result, explicit links between proposed investments in public higher education and return on investment through economic development—particularly visible in areas such as high technology—have become more salient recently than in prior decades. Both trends have fused in a markedly new pattern of accountability for public higher education (Ewell, 1990): Like their counterparts in business and industry, state leaders appear willing to trade off as the substance of accountability detailed auditing and reporting requirements in such areas as expenditures and personnel decision making in return for much broader performance information. The champions of such reforms, moreover, are not those in legislatures and statehouses that wish to cut higher education funding, but those instead who constitute higher education's traditional political allies.

In the mid-1980s, shifting public policy concerns also spawned a series of national reform reports—prominent among them *Transforming the State Role in Undergraduate Education: Time for a Different View* (Education Commission of the States, 1986) and *Time for Results* (National Governors' Association, 1986). Consistent with prior academic improvement reports, these documents highlighted the use of assessment as a tool of reform. Like the public K–12 assessment tradition that informed them, however, these reports also had a strong accountability flavor: Both maintained that information on college student performance should be publicly available and comparable across institutions, should be used to inform policy and resource allocation decisions at the state level, and should be appropriate to inform consumer choice on the part of students and their parents in the decision of which college to attend.

Like their academic counterparts, these reports also unmistakably signaled what kinds of assessments were required. First, to be maximally credible, assessment techniques should be easily understood and should, if possible, result in quantitative indicators of institutional or program performance. Although academic improvement remains a goal, it is to be achieved primarily through the action of external market forces informed by assessment results and through the unilateral responses of institutions to incentives or sanctions applied through their appointed governing or regulatory bodies. Above all, the process should emphasize demonstrable return on investment in the form of aggregate student performance (Kean, 1987). A popular policy alternative, prominent in state discussions at the time, was "performance funding" as practiced in Tennessee (Banta, 1986): Those institutions best demonstrating their effectiveness through assessment should derive commensurate rewards in the form of additional resources. An alternative available policy choice was directed investment, as practiced in New Jersey, Florida, and Virginia (Berdahl & Studds, 1989): Here the imperative is that marginal resources be directed toward particular institutions and programs specifically to address designated problems or deficiencies that assessment might help to reveal.

Action in response to these reports was unusually prompt. In 1982 there were only 3 or 4 states with recognizable state policy initiatives in higher education assessment; by 1986, however, the number had grown to 15 (Boyer, Ewell, Finney, & Mingle, 1987). Currently, some 27 states have established such programs through board resolution, executive directive, or statute (Ewell, Finney, & Lenth, 1990; Paulson, 1990). Further initiatives are expected or planned in an additional dozen states over the next 5 years. Current state approaches vary widely because of differing resource climates, structures of governance, and political circumstances (Ewell & Boyer, 1988). A few include common statewide testing of the basic skills of incoming college freshmen; a much smaller number require periodic statewide testing of college students (usually at the sophomore or senior years) to determine program effectiveness. But by far the majority of current state initiatives require that each institution submit and receive approval for a local assessment plan consistent with institutional mission. Here, in some cases, only one institutional sector is involved; however, in many cases plan approval by a state governing or coordinating board is in some way linked to institutional funding. States also have exhibited widely varying levels of investment in such programs. Frequently, no new dollars are associated with the mandate, as legislators argue that this is an activity that colleges and universities should have been involved in all along. In other states, categorical grant programs have been used to support demonstration projects at individual institutions. Finally, in a few cases substantial new dollars have been invested in direct support of the initiative.

Defining Assessment Practice

Interactions among these internal and external reform agendas yield a complex pattern of activities now undertaken in the name of assessment. Before 1984, the number of institutions possessing identifiable assessment programs was extremely small. Best current estimates, however, indicate that up to 70% of American colleges and universities are establishing such programs, most of them in the last 2 or 3 years (El-Khawas, 1989; Hyman, Jamison, Woodard, & von Destinen, 1988). At the same time, continuing developments in individualized testing, performance assessment, and program evaluation consistent with the academic reform tradition have generated additional activities also grouped under the terminological rubric of assessment.

Faced with such escalating diversity, some observers have claimed that the term *assessment* itself in current higher education usage is insufficiently discriminating to be of descriptive value (Edgerton, 1987). More common have been attempts to systematically classify diverse assessment activities in terms of their visible attributes, for example, by the methods

TABLE 1
A Taxonomy of Assessment Activities in Higher Education

	Purpose of assessment	
Unit of analysis	Improvement (formative)	Demonstration (summative)
Individual level	diagnosis/feedback	certification/"gatekeeping"
Group level	evaluation/self-study	Accountability/quality assurance

Note. From "Assessment with Open Eyes" by P. T. Terenzini, 1989, *Journal of Higher Education, 60,* p. 648. Adapted by permission.

and standards of evidence used, by their basic purposes or applications, or by the disciplinary traditions that provide their theoretical grounding.

A Basic Taxonomy

Perhaps the most useful such classification (Erwin, in press; Ewell, 1987; Terenzini, 1989) combines two quite different criteria (see Table 1). A first taxonomic dimension is basic purpose, founded upon the classic distinction between formative and summative evaluation design. Here the primary object of analysis varies from information-based improvement to an unambiguous demonstration of attainment against previously defined performance standards. A second dimension is based on primary unit of analysis. Performance information can be gathered and reported for individuals—the most commonly understood traditional notion of assessment—or it can be compiled across analytic aggregations of individuals, most commonly programs, curricula, institutions, and geographic or demographic groupings. (A third dimension, sometimes added, is the domain of assessment, which encompasses traditional college outcomes categories such as knowledge, skills, and attitudes/values [Ewell, 1984; Terenzini, 1989].) Cells within this matrix enable important distinctions among assessment activities to be drawn. At the same time, the classification allows location of the many existing assessment activities that occur routinely (though in uncoordinated fashion) on most college and university campuses. Finally, the taxonomy allows the current state of the art in higher education assessment, including those areas where most of the new approaches have emerged, to be described in an efficient manner.

Most obviously included in the *individual/improvement* cell, for example, is the diagnostic basic skills placement testing that frequently occurs on entry into college. Testing of this kind on a statewide basis is currently in place in Texas, Tennessee, and New Jersey, and is often accompanied by mandatory course placement and/or remediation. More commonly, institutions engage in placement testing on an individual basis, using a range of commercially available standardized instruments. Less commonly, noncognitive instruments (e.g., the Myers-Briggs type indicator or the Strong-Campbell personal interest inventory) are used for individual counseling or advising (G. Hanson, 1982). Rarely, however, are assessments of this kind conducted beyond the freshman year. The major *new* development within this cell is performance assessment designed to document individual mastery of complex, integrated abilities. The best current examples of this practice in higher education are at Alverno College (Alverno College Faculty, 1979), although the method is now being extended to a wide range of settings—particularly medical education (Stone & Meyer, 1989) and teacher education (Shulman, 1987a). At the same time, the practice has much in common with the way individual student work is routinely evaluated in the fine or performing arts through portfolio review or audition. Typically, this method involves placing individuals in actual or in carefully simulated performance settings that demand the simultaneous deployment of judgment and a range of integrated abilities. Individual performances are rated by multiple expert judges (termed *assessors*) who can both certify the ability at a given proficiency level and provide detailed feedback to the learner. Consistent with the curricular reform agenda, frequent and active feedback on performance is a hallmark of the method; indeed, a major objective is for students to become continuous "self-assessors" (Mentkowski & Doherty, 1984).

Established activities within the *individual/demonstration* cell of this taxonomy include credentialing and gatekeeping, both of which may entail substantial consequences for the individual student. The former is best exemplified by the vast range of professional certification or licensure examinations required for practice in professions such as medicine, accountancy, engineering, nursing, and, in many states, K–12 teaching. An additional variant embraces graduate or professional school admissions examinations (e.g., Medical College Admissions Test [MCAT], Law School Admissions Test [LSAT], or Pre-Professional Skills Test [PPST]) used to select or screen potential students. Gatekeeping examinations, in contrast, are intended to directly regulate student progress by requiring explicit demonstration of established proficiency as a condition for advancement. Florida's College Level Academic Skills Test (CLAST), for example, is a basic skills examination that all public college students must pass to achieve full standing as juniors. Similarly, upper-level writing requirements at institutions as diverse as the University of Arizona, the University of Northern Colorado, Wayne State University, Bethany College, and the California State University system consist of locally designed and administered essay examinations to certify writing proficiency; these are expected to be taken at the end of a student's sophomore year, but all must be passed before a degree is conferred. A more traditional gatekeeping practice, senior comprehensive examinations in the major field, was once a common feature of undergraduate liberal arts college curricula; currently, such end-of-program examinations are reemerging in response to external assessment mandates. Consistent with traditional practice, many senior comprehensives require more than one reader, whereas some use external examiners recruited from other institutions (Fong, 1987). Although the current assessment movement has yielded few new activities within this cell, performance-based assessment methods are finding their way into professional certification, most notably, at present, in the proposed assessment of teachers (Shulman, 1987b).

Activities within the *group/improvement* cell have probably seen the greatest development as a result of an explicit national assessment movement. Partly in response to emerging state mandates—most of which assign responsibility for designing and carrying out assessment activities to individual institutions—and partly in response to the internal imperatives of curricular reform, many institutions are now undertaking identifiable assessment efforts. Within these programs, many existing institutional data-collection activities are subsumed (Ewell, 1983). Generally lacking, however, are an explicit coordination function and information on the effectiveness of the curriculum as a whole, particularly in general education. Although details of emerging institutional assessment programs vary widely, most contain a number of common features. This is, in part, because many such programs have been modeled on a few widely quoted examples. The following are the most prominent: for public research universities, the University of Tennessee, Knoxville (Banta, 1985); for public state colleges, Northeast Missouri State University (McClain & Krueger, 1985) and Kean College of New Jersey (Boyer, 1989); for private institutions, Alverno College (Mentkowski & Loacker, 1985) and Kings College (Farmer, 1988); and for public community colleges, Miami-Dade Community College (McCabe, 1983). Another reason for this uniformity is that the majority of recently established programs have been developed in response to state guidelines, which strongly resemble one another.

Among the most common features of such programs are (a) an identified office or individual assigned explicit responsibility for coordinating the assessment function, for advising individual academic units in the design of assessment procedures, and for helping to interpret obtained results; (b) systematic basic skills testing in reading, writing, and computation; (c) evaluation of the effectiveness of general education through examining the development over time of such integrative skills as critical thinking and problem solving; (d) evaluation of the effectiveness of instruction in the student's major field; and (e) determination of current and former student satisfaction and behavior through periodic follow-up surveys (Ewell, 1987). Often, such programs involve reorganization of existing information functions on campus, and responsibility is assigned to an established testing office or office of institutional research rather than to a free-standing assessment office (Nichols, 1990).

Finally, the *group/demonstration* cell of the matrix contains some of the most debated assessment proposals in higher education. Here, relevant practices and discussions are largely colored by the perceived experience of lare-scale accountability testing in K–12 education (Darling-Hammond, 1988). For the most part, higher education has not experienced assessment activities of this kind in the past. Institutional accreditors, though their actions are summative, have only recently recognized learning outcomes as indicative of quality (Thrash, 1988; Wolff, 1990). Professional program accreditors are also moving in this direction, but none as yet requires administration of a particular outcomes instrument to demonstrate program effectiveness. Some state-based assessment mandates, consistent with the thrust of the National Governors' Association (NGA) report, have come closer to this summative ideal; they include Tennessee's performance funding program, South Dakota's 3-year experiment with commonly administered institutional outcomes testing, and New Jersey's current statewide program to assess "general intellectual skills." In each of these cases, a primary motivation was to provide the public with comparative performance information as a form of accountability or consumer protection. Both motivations have been given additional impetus by recent actions of the federal government. Regulations promulgated in the fall of 1987 require all federally approved accreditation organizations to collect outcomes information as a part of the accreditation process (U.S. Department of Education, 1987); new "track record disclosure" regulations passed for 2-year occupational/technical programs and currently under consideration for 4-year programs also require institutions to provide potential students with such statistics as program completion and job placement rates (D. Hanson, 1990).

Some Implied Methodological Imperatives

Not only do these two taxonomic dimensions delineate distinct kinds of assessment activities, but they also help to highlight some profoundly different approaches to measurement. Within the primary purpose dimension, for example, demonstration requires, above all, measurement precision with respect to an obtained estimate of performance. The dominant requirement is for instruments and techniques that can, as fully as possible, *determine* whether or not a given performance standard has been achieved. Information-based improvement, in contrast, demands a different kind of optimization. Here, the dominant requirement is to chart a process of change and to determine what in the curriculum or environment is responsible for it. This fundamental difference underlies much recent debate regarding the appropriateness of so-called value-added assessment (e.g., Baird, 1988; G. Hanson, 1988; Pascarella, 1987; Terenzini, 1989). Beyond the technical properties of difference scores in this discussion lie profound differences in analytical requirements.

Similarly, shifting the unit of analysis may entail significant changes in measurement assumptions and opportunities. Traditional testing and measurement practice in higher education, reflecting the customary applications of tests, has been overwhelmingly concentrated on obtaining usable individual scores. Here, embodied in such instruments as collegiate or graduate admissions examinations and basic skills placement examinations, the dominant requirements of individual reliability and predictive value have largely determined what constitutes adequate practice. Estimating *group* properties and performance, however, allows the application of new techniques and poses additional conceptual challenges. First, of course, reliable group-level estimates can be established without assessing all individuals. But any sample-based strategy may raise profound questions not only about representativeness, but also about the political credibility of obtained results (Ewell, 1988b). Second, not all items in a given domain need be given to every individual. As a result, item spiraling techniques have become a common feature of emerging group-level assessment techniques. But using these techniques means accepting some critical assumptions about uniform item functioning across individuals and about the appropriate interpretation of composite scores compiled from the individual performances of different test takers on quite different tasks (Mislevy, 1990).

Methodological tensions such as these have been visible throughout the practice of higher education assessment. A well-known instance is the use of Graduate Record Examination (GRE) scores as an aggregate comparative indicator of higher education effectiveness (Adelman, 1985, 1989). Although a proven device for use in individual/summative decision making, the form and content of the GRE general examinations reflect little of the domains most observers see as important cross-disciplinary college outcomes. Using such scores effectively for group/improvement purposes, moreover, requires the release of item scores, but releasing items may severely compromise the examination's original purpose as a secure selection device.

More subtle methodological tensions are illustrated for institutions and states by the respective cases of Northeast Missouri State University and the statewide General Intellectual Skills assessment in New Jersey. At Northeast Missouri, the original motivation for assessment was clearly demonstrative—to provide credible evidence that the institution was producing "degrees with integrity" (McClain, 1984). Within this context, the choice of nationally normed standardized instruments including the American College Testing Program (ACT) Assessment and GRE subject examinations as the major vehicle for assessment was not merely a matter of convenience; it was entirely consistent with the program's intent. Charges of inappropriateness since directed at these methods miss this primary purpose, assuming instead that the principal goal was formative. Similarly, an announced policy intent of New Jersey's new General Intellectual Skills examination was to provide a statewide accountability benchmark with regard to collegiate skills—a goal quite similar in essence to that of the National Assessment of Educational Progress (NAEP) in K–12 education (College Outcomes Evaluation Program [COEP] Council, 1990). The choice of a nontraditional, performance-based format for the examination, using extended intellectual tasks instead of multiple-choice items, was based as much on the need to build credibility for the instrument within the academic community as it was on the technical grounds of improved validity that an actual production measure might yield. Ironically, the resulting task-based instrument now in use may be far better suited to local diagnostic applications than to producing a stable, easily interpretable summative snapshot of collegiate abilities in New Jersey.

So long as assessment is undertaken for different purposes, such tensions will inevitably be present. As a consequence, any methodological comment and criticism must rest on a clear understanding of what a given assessment initiative is ultimately *for*, and how its results will be applied in decision making.

THREE EMERGING TRENDS IN HIGHER EDUCATION ASSESSMENT

Even though the extent and diversity of assessment activities in higher education have rapidly expanded, and even though only a partial consensus has been achieved about the dimensions underlying these assessment activities, some clear patterns in the technical practice of such assessments have nonetheless emerged. Although far from settled, these patterns suggest an emerging consensus regarding "meta-methodology," regardless of purpose or unit of analysis. More important, the direction of these tendencies suggests an eventual outcome far different from the current practice of assessment in K–12 settings.

In brief, three major trends in assessment technology can be noted. The first is the development of new, special-purpose instruments to replace the available off-the-shelf testing technology used in most pioneering institutional assessment efforts. More significant, there is an emerging shift in the model of student development underlying assessment—from an additive "production process" view of education to one that recognizes complex, often nonlinear paths of development. Finally, there has been a clear trend toward more naturalistic approaches—on one hand, taking greater advantage of existing settings as vehicles for assessment, and, on the other hand, stressing actual task performance rather than indicative item performance as its primary vehicle. Each trend can be used both to succinctly summarize current practices and to briefly suggest the most probable future developments.

New Kinds of Tests

At the beginning of the assessment movement in 1985, numerous commerically available examinations already existed for purposes of individual placement, admissions, and certification. But little technology was available in higher education to compare with NAEP in K–12, capable of supporting more general evaluation. Ironically, by 1982, the Educational Testing Service (ETS) had allowed its Undergraduate Assessment Program (UAP), founded upon both general and discipline-based examinations, to lapse. Normed at the college senior level and intended to provide evidence of overall curricular effectiveness, these examinations were built on items derived from parallel GRE exams and were fairly widely used in the 1950s. Simultaneously, ETS abandoned work on a new general education assessment instrument intended primarily to provide group-level results.

With a resurgence of interest in group-level results, the response of the standardized testing community followed two lines of development. A first response was to reengineer existing placement and disciplinary knowledge examinations for newer purposes. Although this filled an immediate need, it did little to change existing test-making technology. A more far-reaching result was development by the major testing companies of a second generation of general purpose instruments that emphasized production of group-level results, particularly in general education.

Old Wine in New Bottles

Given an escalating interest in assessing group-level performance after 1985, an obvious first approximation was to use off-the-shelf technology. Thus, several pioneering institutional, curricular, and state-mandated assessment programs used the ACT Assessment—designed to generate individual scores for collegiate admissions decision making—in a test-retest design (Lenning, Munday, & Maxey, 1969; McClain & Krueger, 1985). At the same time, available discipline-based tests such as the GRE field examinations and the College Level Examination Program (CLEP) area examinations were used to assess group-level knowledge outcomes, particularly in the student's major field. Obvious drawbacks to extending such examinations beyond their designed purposes, however, quickly emerged. Off-the-shelf examinations rarely covered the curricular domain actually taught by the institution, and the few obtained scores provided by the test makers were often ill-suited to formative use in guiding curriculum improvement (Banta & Pike, 1989; Heffernan, Hutchings, & Marchese, 1988). At the same time, because of self-selection, the norm bases of most of these examinations were of little value in judging the performance of representative college-going populations (Adelman, 1989).

To address many of these deficiencies, existing content-based examinations could fairly easily be reconfigured for the production of group-level results, using shorter forms and a recalculated norm base. By 1990, ETS had in place over a dozen new "major field achievement tests" of approximately an hour in length, drawing heavily on prior experience with equivalent GRE field examinations. At the same time, some professional fields moved to construct model content assessments of their own. For example, by 1987 the American Association of Collegiate Schools of Business (AACSB), working with ACT, had piloted several specially constructed examinations designed to assess the content of the basic business core (Blood, 1987). Other content-specified designs followed particular curricular presecriptions—for example, a cultural literacy examination (Hirsch, 1989), drawn from the controversial work of the same name (Hirsch, 1987), and the content-based Survey of College Seniors' Knowledge of History and Literature (The Gallup Organization, 1989) based on the "Fifty Hours" curriculum proposed by the National Endowment for the Humanities (Cheney, 1989).

The many new basic skills tests emerging during the same period also entailed few departures from traditional testing practice. Development of instruments to support the Texas Academic Skills Program (National Evaluation Systems, 1987) in 1987–1988, for example, followed a path similar to that of the New Jersey Collegiate Basic Skills Placement Test and Florida's College Level Academic Skills Test (CLAST) almost a decade before (Postsecondary Education Planning Commission, 1988), and resulted in comparable instruments. Similar commercial offerings such as ACT's ASSET are designed to be multipurpose and to be more compatible with other instruments in supporting longitudinal research, but are otherwise familiar. For placement testing, however, new developments in computerized test administration offer considerable potential for the future. Here, computer-adaptive techniques that allow test takers to be given items whose difficulty levels are tailored to prior performance promise enormous savings in test-taking time. The latest "computerized placement tests" offered by ETS, for example, can be administered in approximately a third of the time required by conventional paper-and-pencil alternatives (The College Board, 1987). Field evidence also indicates that computerized test administration is more satisfying to students because it provides immediate scoring and feedback, avoids the frustrations associated with inappropriate difficulty levels, and reduces test anxiety (League for Innovation, 1988).

New Tests for General Education

Although such developments were promising, they did little to address the pressing need to gather group-level information about general education. This was a far more serious enterprise partly because, for many observers, such claimed results of general education as critical thinking or solving problems remained definitionally elusive. By 1989, however, four second-generation examinations were available for use in assessing general education outcomes (Pike, 1989b), only one of which was in place before 1985. They include the ACT College Outcomes Measures Project (COMP), the ETS Academic Profile, the ACT Collegiate Assessment of Academic Proficiencies (CAAP), and the College Basic Subjects Examination (College-BASE) developed by the University of Missouri. For most institutions, these four examinations remain the universe of standardized alternatives for assessing the effectiveness of general education. Although each is distinct in architecture, all four have characteristics in common.

The earliest of the four, the ACT COMP, was ground breaking in several respects when it was introduced in 1976 (Forrest & Steele, 1978). First, its domain is defined by a matrix of three process and three content areas, with each test item contributing to two or more subscores depending on its position in the matrix. Second, COMP's design emphasizes knowledge and skills *use*, with most items confronting test takers with a multifaceted problem-solving situation; in the long-form "composite examination," for example, students write and speak in response to questions, and stimulus material is presented across a range of media both visually and aurally. Content areas are primarily applications based rather than knowledge based (e.g., "functioning within social institutions" and "using the arts"). Third, the examination's design optimizes estimation of group-level results through a shorter testing form (the "objective test") that requires 2½ hours of testing time rather than the 4½ hours needed for the composite. Scores derived from the objective test are not individually reliable and must be used in aggregated form. Finally, COMP's approach emphasizes examining curricular impact through the use of test-retest difference scores; in cases where pretests are not available, the instrument's design allows estimation of imputed COMP scores from existing ACT Assessment scores. COMP's ready availability in the mid-1980s resulted in its substantial use as state assessment mandates began to emerge and no alternative standardized examinations were available. Current estimates suggest that at least 500 institutions have used the examination

(Steele, 1988), and it remains a key common component of such approaches as Tennessee's widely publicized performance funding program (Levy, 1986).

Other more recently developed second-generation general education instruments share many features of COMP's basic design. Although a far more traditional examination, the ETS Academic Profile is equally founded on a matrix of domains (four skills and three content areas), and also uses a short form optimized around the need to estimate group scores (Educational Testing Service, 1989b). In its short form, however, required testing time has been cut to less than 50 minutes through the use of item spiraling and design based on item response theory (IRT). The latest version of the Academic Profile provides criterion-based performance information in the form of the percentage of test takers attaining each of three hierarchical proficiency levels within each skill area, in addition to traditional norm-referenced scores. This feature meets a growing assessment demand for information about curricular goal achievement.

College-BASE, in contrast, was designed from the outset around criterion-referenced reporting (Osterlind, 1988). Also founded on a matrix design (four skills and four content areas), its architecture is more complex. Content areas, for example, are organized into levels of increasing specificity, with two to six "enabling subskills" successively defining skills, aggregate skill clusters, and, finally, entire subject domains. Similarly, the four tested skills areas ("competencies") are not independent, but are organized hierarchically. The result is an examination that is unusually theory driven, though also theory bound if individuals do not fit the test's implied models of cognitive functioning. As is the case with the COMP and the Academic Profile, moreover, short and long forms are available for College-BASE, with an "institutional matrix" form allowing group-level results to be estimated in approximately an hour of testing time.

Easily the most traditional examination of the four, the ACT CAAP is the only one not founded on a matrix design (American College Testing Program, 1988). Instead, the CAAP is intended to fit comfortably into ACT's traditional array of instruments (e.g., the ACT Assessment and the ASSET) as a collegiate midpoint examination. A modular design consisting of five self-contained, 40-minute multiple-choice tests (writing skills, mathematics, reading, critical thinking, and science reasoning) and a writing sample of equivalent length allows flexible administration in any combination. All score reporting for CAAP is on a norm-referenced basis, with pilot norming data being compiled through the end of 1990. Although the newest of the four, CAAP's design signals a return to more traditional purposes. Modular scores are individually reliable so that they can be used independently or can be combined to yield group results for institutional assessment. At the same time, the test's reversion to easily understandable, free-standing content domains reflects some of the difficulties encountered in meaningfully interpreting and applying the more analytic subscores produced by the COMP.

Standardized Testing: The Face of the Future?

Three features of these second-generation instruments appear to point strongly toward future test development: (a) further concentration on underlying integrative and analytic skills as a proper domain of assessment, (b) increased focus on group performance with consequent use of item or form spiraling and IRT to produce shorter testing times, and (c) further experimentation with produced response as an alternative to classic multiple-choice items. All three trends are visible in perhaps the most innovative current instance of large-scale assessment in higher education: the New Jersey General Intellectual Skills (GIS) Assessment, first administered in 1990 (COEP Council, 1990).

The GIS is an integral part of a much larger state-based assessment effort, the College Outcomes Evaluation Program (COEP), initiated in 1986. After a year of statewide discussion, a task force charged with developing appropriate approaches to determine student cognitive development concluded that although assessable outcomes might differ in many areas from institution to institution, "students' general intellectual skills are developed and refined at all of New Jersey's institutions of higher education . . . no matter which program or department students major in, or what degree or certificate they ultimately attain" (College Outcomes Evaluation Program, State of New Jersey Department of Higher Education, 1987, p. 7). Intended to define and provide benchmark performance information on the development of such skills in college students across the state, initial requirements for the GIS were thus for an instrument that could be administered at several points in a typical college career and that could adequately encompass the complexity of college-level work.

With the assistance of ETS, a highly innovative large-scale assessment approach was designed. First, following ETS experience with the Academic Profile and other matrix-based examinations, faculty drawn from across the state developed a taxonomy consisting of three kinds of skills: gathering information, analyzing information, and presenting information. After pilot testing, an additional quantitative analysis skill was identified and added to the taxonomy (COEP Council, 1990). Each skill, though a general outcome of college, might be manifested in one of three basic disciplinary groupings—the humanities, social sciences, and sciences—with scores for each skill combined across all three groupings.

More radically, the entire GIS examination would be performance based, engineered around extended 90-minute "tasks" with required performance components carefully designed to cover one or more cells of the skills/content matrix. Each student would complete only one task, and results would be combined to yield reliable group-level estimates. Pilot testing confirmed that at least seven tasks would be required to adequately cover the taxonomy's domain and that approximately 200 students per institution would suffice to produce usable group-level results. Task scoring would be accomplished by teams of faculty members using a "core scoring" technique recently developed at ETS (Conlin, 1987). According to this method, a minimally adequate core score is determined for each task element, with additional scores above and below this point assigned on the basis of specific response characteristics defined by a scoring guide.

Pilot tested twice in 1988–1989, the GIS was first administered on a statewide basis in the spring of 1990. Results of both the pilots and the operational program suggest that task-based technology is feasible for large-scale assessments and is significantly more likely than standard multiple-choice testing to be acceptable to faculty and students as representing college-level work (COEP Council, 1990). Statistical analyses using parallel forms of assessment based on tasks and standard multiple-choice items, moreover, clearly suggest that different skills are being tapped (Educational Testing Service, 1989a). Statistical properties of the scores obtained, however, are still being explored, as the combined effects of a spiraled matrix design in which different parts of the domain are taken by different students, a new task-based testing technology based on judgmental core scoring, and an intact classroom sampling strategy at the institutional level render issues of statistical confidence exceedingly complex. Nevertheless, the GIS is a path-breaking effort, perhaps nothing less than the prototype for a "third generation" of standardized general purpose assessment instruments in higher education.

Generic Instruments: Enduring Issues, Uncertain Future

Fulfilling the strong promise of these new testing technologies, however, will demand resolution of a number of persisting questions. First, can common skills dimensions appropriate to higher education settings really be identified and estimated across disciplinary contexts? One difficulty encountered by developers of the ETS Academic Profile in its pilot year, for example, involved extremely high intercorrelations among taxonomic skills scores—a phenomenon also reported by other general skills test developers (Pike, 1989c). In a major exploratory research effort in Washington that cross tested students on the ACT COMP, the ACT CAAP, and the Academic Profile, moreover, results strongly indicated that despite differing testing architecture and conceptual foundations, obtained results on the three examinations were very similar (Council of Presidents and State Board for Community College Education, 1989; Thorndike, 1990). These results were sustained by large-sample studies at the University of Tennessee, Knoxville, in which students were cross tested on the COMP and the Academic Profile (Banta & Pike, 1989). At the same time, persistent reports of age/performance correlations on the ACT COMP suggest that some general skill elements may be a product of social maturation and that the COMP remains a better measure of individual differences than an indicator of program effects (Pike, 1989a). These findings echo earlier debates about whether or not such attributes as critical thinking are true generalizable abilities (e.g., Campione & Armbruster, 1985) and raise doubts about the ultimate utility of instruments that seek to assess them.

Second, if general abilities do exist, can they be connected to anything? Initial research and development findings on the ACT COMP reported detectable curricular impacts, but also noted more significant relationships with such general adult functioning indicators as employer ratings of employee performance (Forrest, 1982). More significantly, on the basis of a substantial multiyear sample of students, researchers at the University of Tennessee, Knoxville, were unable to identify interpretable linkages between student experiences and positive difference scores obtained on the COMP using a freshman-senior test-retest design (Banta, Lambert, Pike, Schmidhammer, & Schneider, 1987), although later work at the University of Tennessee using a differential coursework pattern methodology did identify clusters of courses associated with greater than expected performance on some COMP dimensions (Pike & Phillipi, 1989). No similar studies have as yet been executed using CAAP, the Academic Profile, or College-BASE. At minimum, therefore, given the often limited correspondence between the domains typically assessed by general purpose instruments and what college faculty say they teach (Banta & Pike, 1989), the effectiveness of such instruments in guiding curricular improvement remains uncertain.

Overall, these two factors leave the future potential of commercial general-purpose assessment instruments in some doubt. Clearly, there is strong faculty affect against any kind of standardized testing as an appropriate vehicle for assessing collegiate outcomes, and using such instruments is likely to entail considerable political opposition. Emerging experience with the logistics of these examinations also suggests that problems of student motivation for an exercise involving few stakes for the learner, although possible to overcome, are substantial and often unpredictable. Experience indicates that once students sit down to take such an examination, they either take it seriously or their response patterns are easily detectable. But in initial attempts to use such examinations without sufficient time for preparation, many institutions have experienced no-show rates in excess of 50%, largely obviating a valid sample. Although material inducements such as cash payments or gift certificates have some effect, more successful have been clear and repeated explanations of assessment's purpose, the promise of individual feedback on results, and making participation a curricular requirement (Erwin, in press). Nevertheless, concerns about motivation are real and are increasingly dominating discussions of test administration using standardized instruments.

On the other hand, ease of procurement means that such instruments are often an institution's first encounter with assessment. In this respect, their use can raise important process questions about curricular goals, and their results can stimulate a range of productive faculty discussions (e.g., Banta & Moffett, 1987). At the same time, the perceived unambiguity of obtained scores may be the only basis on which to found such statewide summative applications of testing as performance funding (Banta, 1988; Ewell, 1986). Finally, the promise of such performance-based approaches as the GIS in addressing state and system-level assessment needs in a manner parallel to the role of NAEP in K–12 education remains alluring. These implications yield a conclusion that new test technology will play a strong but controversial role in higher education assessment for the foreseeable future.

New Models of Student Development

In 1985, the rhetoric of the national assessment movement in higher education centered almost completely on measuring discrete cognitive outcomes. This, after all, was what was missing in most practice-oriented investigations of student experience in college, and was the arena in which new instrumentation was most in demand. Five years of evolution, however, has brought assessment practice to the brink of rediscovering two elements of traditional wisdom embodied in decades of scholarly research on collegiate learning and development: Outcomes cannot be understood independently of the processes that preceded them, and student learning and development is a complex, multifaceted phenomenon unusually resistant to single-factor explanations (Ewell, 1988a; Pascarella, 1985). The result for emerging assessment practice has been twofold. First, both individual and group-level efforts are increasingly being based on truly longitudinal rather than one-shot or test-retest research designs. Second, the outcomes to be assessed are increasingly being modeled holistically, as complex combinations of cognitive and noncognitive attributes. Neither trend, it must be stressed, is currently typical, as most institutional efforts are in an initial stage dominated by the short-term need to respond to state accountability mandates. But both are strongly present in a growing body of more mature institutional initiatives, begun some 4 to 5 years ago.

Longitudinal Designs: The New Face of Value-Added

Considerable stimulus for the operational use of true longitudinal research designs derived in part from ongoing debates about the merits and interpretation of gain scores. Popular and much-discussed early models of assessment based on the concept of value-added (Astin, 1977) emphasized the repeated administration of comparable instruments in a test-retest design as the optimal core of an assessment strategy aimed at isolating real institutional impacts (Jacobi, Astin, & Ayala, 1987; McClain & Krueger, 1985). At the same time, test designers at ACT were designing the COMP largely around a test-retest design, and the state of Tennessee had made the decision to incorporate the concept as a key component of statewide performance evaluation. But objections to the value-added concept were legion. One such objection was philosophic—that the term's implied identification of student learning with an industrial production process was inappropriately mechanistic. Others were more practical; for example, little of importance could be learned from pretesting students on material to which they had not yet been exposed (Pace, 1979; Warren, 1984). But some of the most important objections to value-added were technical—that the use of difference scores themselves (particularly if based on estimated gain) entailed multiplicative sources of error and could lead to critical misinterpretations regarding actual patterns of development (Baird, 1988; G. Hanson, 1988; McMillan, 1988; Pascarella, 1987).

Defenders of value-added as a useful metaphor for institutional quality quickly realized the need to distance the concept from a particular measurement technique (Astin & Ewell, 1985). Resulting reformulations of the basic notion in the form of "talent development" (Astin, 1985) not only proved more acceptable philosophically but also entailed a quite different methodological core for assessment. Within a single longitudinal database, information on student input characteristics, environmental experiences, and learning outcomes might be combined to support complex multivariate studies of talent development in different settings (Astin, 1990). This reformulation of the basic value-added concept, however, had major implications for both institutional assessment practice and the analytic paradigm used to make sense of its results.

In terms of practice, this new conceptual foundation for institutional assessment was already being piloted in the field. Indeed, by 1989 several institutions were embarking on complex, multifaceted longitudinal studies of student impact as a cornerstone for institutional assessment. One much-imitated study involving 320 students was begun at Stanford in 1977 (Katchadourian & Boli, 1985). Through a combination of quantitative questionnaire-based techniques and qualitative interviewing techniques, students in the sample were followed up each year of their college careers, with results providing a rich array of insights into both differential patterns of development and the ways in which the college environment was perceived and experienced. Similar studies under way at the University of Arizona (Dinham, 1988) and the University of Virginia (Kellams, 1989), both undertaken largely in response to state mandates on assessment, also are attempting to integrate survey questionnaire and face-to-face annual interviews. Advances in computer technology, moreover, allow considerably more background and experience information about students in the study population to be compiled from existing student records data. Early results of these studies, partly because of their richness and immediacy, have proven particularly easy to communicate to a campus community (University of Virginia, 1990).

Longitudinal research designs of this kind have considerable research potential in their own right and enjoy growing popularity as a foundation for institutional assessment. But they have many problems. One is the sheer level of resources involved, particularly if face-to-face interviewing is used and if sample sizes are large enough to sustain reasonable generalizations. Costs for the 4-year University of Virginia panel study, for example, are substantial, and resource limitations have confined the University of Arizona project to perilously small sample sizes. Another challenge is panel attrition and the resulting representativeness of a survivor population; in this respect, it is no coincidence that the institutions most interested in pursuing such studies have graduation rates that are well above average. Most challenging, however, are potential experimenter effects induced by the repeated interview design itself. Despite these difficulties, ongoing longitudinal studies of varying complexity, founded on an explicit database, will probably become the design of choice for most institutional practitioners.

More subtly, reformulation of the value-added concept and its embodiment in longitudinal research designs has profound implications for the analytic paradigm for assessment. Although test-retest designs clearly reflect the methodological imprint of controlled experiments drawn from cognitive psychology, making sense of longitudinal databases requires an analytic model based on multivariate statistical control more akin to the disciplines of sociology and econometrics. Statistical techniques pioneered by Astin (1977) that use the residuals obtained from regressing outcomes variables on a range of input controls as the primary criterion variable for environmental effect studies have thus become accepted practice in recent attempts to document curricular impact (Pike & Philippi, 1989; Ratcliffe & Associates, 1990). This approach, of course, reflects a methodological tradition already established in the scholarly literature of college student development (e.g., Pascarella, 1985), but its effective practice requires a level of statistical sophistication in assessment practitioners that is not often attained. One result, and clearly a trend for the future, is a growing demand for formal practitioner training in assessment emphasizing statistical analysis (Astin, 1990).

Holistic and Hierarchical Learning Models: The New Face of Student Development

A second emerging conceptual rediscovery in assessment practice is the value of a holistic model of student development. This, too, arose partly in reaction to proposed test-retest methodologies. Not only did the production process analogy embedded in value-added imply linear development, but it also suggested that developmental attributes could be examined one at a time. As a result, although many early assessment efforts were appropriately founded on multiple methods, they made little attempt to incorporate separate investigations of discrete student attributes into an integrated developmental pattern. More recent and sophisticated assessment approaches reject this notion and, like the reformulation of value-added, the resulting change has implications for both practice and analysis.

By 1985, the practical application of an integrated model of student learning and development to ongoing institutional assessment had already been demonstrated at a handful of institutions, most effectively, perhaps, at Alverno College (Mentkowski & Loacker, 1985). Beginning in the early 1970s, Alverno faculty not only pioneered the practice of individual performance assessment in higher education, but they also made integrated developmental abilities the primary foundation of their instructional program. Indeed, the two were intimately related—a linkage often lost on those who later attempted to imitate Alverno's approach to assessment without having previously thought through what was meant by developmental abilities and how they might be taught. Alverno's curriculum is currently founded on eight well-defined abilities—communication, analysis, problem solving, valuing, social interaction, taking environmental responsibility, involvement in the contemporary world, and aesthetic response—each of which is a complex combination of cognitive, affective, and behavioral traits (Alverno College Faculty, 1976; Ewens, 1979). As they progress through the curriculum, students are successively certified at each of six levels within each ability through a performance assessment process involving both self-assessment and feedback from multiple trained assessors (Alverno College Faculty, 1979). At the same time, the individual assessment process is periodically validated externally through a group-level evaluation process that employs a range of external cognitive and affective instruments and an ongoing longitudinal follow-up design (Mentkowski & Doherty, 1984). At the heart of Alverno's assessment concept is the proposition that integrated abilities are not simply additive trait combinations, observable in isolation, but are undifferentiable learned performance capabilities that can neither be defined nor observed in the absence of actual performance settings (Mentkowski & Rogers, 1988).

As in the case of longitudinal research designs, the conceptual foundations for integrated developmental approaches were already well established in the literature of student development. On the basis of extensive student interviewing over time, Perry's (1970) model of staged development combining traditional cognitive and noncognitive traits had substantial impact on student development practice (e.g., Mentkowski, Moeser, & Straight, 1981). These and other holistic developmental conceptions, such as Chickering's "vectors of identity" (Chickering, 1969) and Kohlberg's "scale of moral development" (Kohlberg, 1981), were actively used in assessment at Alverno and are being increasingly discussed in the assessment approaches of other institutions. By 1985, all had also been embodied in more tractable formats for use in large-scale assessment through paper-and-pencil techniques (Erwin, 1983; Erwin & Delworth, 1980; Rest, 1986, 1987).

Currently, the effects of these concepts are visible in assessment practice in at least two ways. One is a growing breakdown in the classic cognitive/noncognitive distinction underlying much early institutional assessment work. To some extent this is due to increased recognition on the part of faculty—who ground and direct most current institutional assessment efforts—that much of the impact of college is not strictly cognitive. At the same time, many faculty now recognize that such distinctions can leave important things out. Intellectual "habits of mind" such as intellectual integrity, openness to different points of view, and intellectual curiosity and commitment to continued learning are thus emerging as salient assessable general curricular objectives within a growing number of proposed institutional assessment plans (e.g., College of William and Mary, 1989; Conrad, Jamison, Kroc, MacCorquodale, & Summers, 1987). Similarly, the most recent overall treatments of assessment practice (e.g., Erwin, in press) feature developmental objectives as equivalent in status to classic knowledge and skills objectives in the design of assessment programs, and intentionally blur classic divisions between cognitive and affective outcomes.

A second impact of holistic developmental conceptions is to highlight the importance of individual differences in the assessment process (Knefelkamp, 1989). Particularly important here have been gender differences in both outcomes and perceptions of the collegiate experience (e.g., Light, 1990), and outcomes differences based on learning style and personality type. Assessment practitioners now recognize that conclusions based only on the high levels of aggregation typically used in sample-based institutional assessment can be extremely vulnerable to misinterpretation if such differences are not taken into account. As a result, most now emphasize substantial disaggregation of obtained results (Astin, in press; Erwin, in press).

Three Implications for Practice

Beyond their conceptual impacts, emerging developmental models have more specific methodological consequences for assessment practice. First, the need to identify "environmental" or "treatment" effects in complex longitudinal research designs has led to considerably greater attention to documenting student behavior. Because most of the data required are already available in computerized student record systems, the greatest recent progress has been the ability to efficiently extract such information in a format suitable for supporting studies of longitudinal student development (Ewell, Parker, & Jones, 1988). Using such techniques, for example, institutions have been able to determine the overall effectiveness of remediation efforts (Adelman, Ewell, & Grable, 1989) or the relative effects of different general education core course sequences. Methodologically more sophisticated course-taking pattern studies have established not only the general existence of "behavioral curricula" within typical distribution-based requirements (Boyer & Algren, 1987; Zemsky, 1989), but also the relationships of specific course clusters to selected outcomes measures (Pike & Philippi, 1989; Ratcliffe & Associates, 1990). Unfortunately, no such ready data source as registrar's records currently exists for documenting other forms of student experience, particularly in the co-curriculum, and most practitioners continue to rely on survey self-reports of such activities for inclusion in longitudinal databases.

A second implication for practice is the need to more fully ascertain student motivations and goals—particularly among nontraditional students. Community college populations, for example, may attend college-level classes for many reasons other than to earn a degree or transfer to a 4-year institution. Among the reasons are job or skills upgrades, retraining, or simple personal interest. Yet students with quite different goals may inhabit the same classrooms and enroll for the same programs as students with more traditional objectives. As a result, emerging assessment practices focused on nontraditional college populations increasingly stress early goal assessment of incoming students (e.g., Walleri & Japely, 1986). In more sophisticated applications, results of goal assessments are used to develop student typologies based on clusters of related characteristics (Aquino, 1989; Sheldon, 1981). In others, changes in student goals are tracked over time or compared to later self-reports of goal fulfillment. In the ultimate extension of this logic, goal assessment can be extended to the individual course or curriculum as an ingredient of "classroom research" (Stark, Shaw, & Lowther, 1989). Given anticipated increases in student diversity, whatever the mechanism used, periodic goal assessments of this kind will remain important in making sense of longitudinal student behavior.

A third ingredient, partially related to goals, is the student's own investment in the learning process. Part of this investment is time on task, an often cited factor in learning research (Astin, 1985; Pascarella, 1985). As a result, items tapping student out-of-class time spent studying and preparing for class are sometimes now included in regularly administered student assessment questionnaires or course evaluations (e.g., Krueger & Heisserer, 1987). A parallel but more intensive technique is the use of time diaries (Astin, 1979) for selected bodies of students—an ingredient in several current longitudinal interview studies (e.g., Angelo, 1988). Its most extensive variant is the concept of "quality of student effort" embodied in the now widely administered College Student Experiences Questionnaire (CSEQ), which contains 14 involvement scales that tap levels of student use of or participation in a range of campus resources, services, and activities (Pace, 1984). Quality of effort as assessed by the CSEQ has been related to persistence and performance across a range of college settings (Pace, 1990), and the instrument is increasingly in demand as a key ingredient in institutional assessment.

Overall, recent evolution in assessment's core model of student learning toward continuous and holistic development raises important issues regarding future practice. One implication is the level of investment required to do good work. The increased sophistication required for longitudinal data collection and analysis not only demands technical sophistication, but also requires an administration with a long attention span. Political support may not persist as long as students do, and there may be little long-term constituency for activities such as assessment that seem to take so long to show results (Ewell, 1990). More disturbingly, unless assessment is made integral to teaching practice, faculty also may lose interest. Indeed, a real danger inherent in assessment approaches founded largely on integrated developmental concepts in the absence of real curricular transformation is that faculty may come to see assessment as the province of specialists. Fortunately, for different reasons, a strong countervailing trend is moving assessment practice more extensively into the classroom and curriculum. But the threat of bureaucratic isolation—already partly induced by the fact that assessment is, for most institutions, seen initially as an external reporting requirement—can potentially be exacerbated by increasing methodological sophistication. In most institutions, faculty ownership and involvement in assessment remains strong, and there is an appropriate balance between technical evolution and grass-roots applicability. Recently characterized as "happy amateurs" (Hutchings & Marchese, 1990), assessment practitioners retain their faculty roots as they refine their methods. As a result, the slow evolution of a relatively simple technique will probably be the dominant pattern for the future.

A "Naturalistic" Mode of Inquiry

When assessment first emerged as a major topic of college and university discussion, it was clearly seen as a new activity, quite different from anything already in place. This was, in part, in response to accountability demands that appeared to require a distinctly identifiable bureaucratic process. Also, it was due to the language of academic reform that in the same period appeared to require technically proven, externally credible measurement devices. Whatever the stimulus, initial concern with assessment at most institutions tended to focus on creating a visible capability, located perhaps in a professionally staffed and adequately funded assessment center and founded upon periodic large-scale data-gathering efforts. The most prominent prototype, of course, was mass testing (often on a designated "assessment day") using a specially designed, nationally normed standardized assessment instrument.

Currently, this methodological center of gravity appears to be shifting. Imitating the history of more general program evaluation efforts in the 1970s, the primary mode of inquiry for assessment has become increasingly naturalistic, relying less heavily on distinct special-purpose instruments and data-collection opportunities and conforming instead to the existing rhythms of college and university life. Partly, the reasons are similar to those that drove practitioners of program evaluation to a more naturalistic approach (Shapiro, 1986). Complex research designs involving carefully selected samples and special-purpose instruments often broke down under the practical demands of field settings. In many cases, moreover, student motivation problems proved intractable, particularly where testing was implemented quickly or its purposes were not made plain. More significantly, it was often difficult for assessment practitioners to gain political support among faculty for an activity that seemed an add-on to existing classroom instruction, requiring additional resources and having only a small chance of local benefit. Indeed, experiences were sufficiently similar for members of the evaluation community to quite rightly, and somewhat smugly, point them out (e.g., Davis, 1989).

At the same time, it was becoming clear that, as in program evaluation, some of the greatest benefits of assessment occurred in its early stages, when faculty were forced to actively wrestle with questions of curriculumwide instructional goals and how they might be recognized. Also, such benefits occurred particularly in situations where faculty, by choice or circumstance, designed their own assessments (Banta & Moffett, 1987). For most institutions, this initially took place in the major field. But by 1988, significant numbers of institutions had also begun to experiment with locally designed techniques in general education (e.g., Hutchings, 1987; Paskow, 1988). Although in many cases methodologically problematic, these approaches had the major virtue of engagement, and if, as many claimed, the primary goal of assessment was to get faculty to think more critically about what they were doing, increased engagement was well worth a sacrifice in measurement precision. In general, this shift toward more naturalistic methods is visible in two main arenas. First, there is a strong trend toward exploiting existing points of contact with students rather than developing large numbers of new special-purpose data-collection methods. Second, reflecting the fact that most existing points of contact lie within the curriculum itself, there is an emerging trend toward curriculum-embedded techniques and classroom research conducted independently by individual faculty members.

Using What You Have: Curriculum-Embedded Assessment

Exploiting existing data-collection opportunities as occasions for assessment began with recognition that much that might be called "assessment" was already taking place on most college campuses (Ewell, 1983). Community colleges, for example, are increasingly building on initial orientation and placement testing as settings for collecting additional information on student goals, perceptions, and anticipated difficulties (Adelman et al., 1989; Vorhees & Hart, 1989). Common data-collection opportunities are less frequent at later points in most college curricula, but they are not unknown and, if available, they can be used in alternative ways. Upper level writing requirement examinations at Bethany College (West Virginia), for example, are now used to examine not only individual writing proficiency, but are also used at the group level to tap student perceptions of the campus environment (Ewell & Lisensky, 1988). Where formal opportunities involving all students do not exist, individual curricular requirements may already be structured in such a way that many students pass through a particular course at about the same time. Assessment guidelines at Kean College, for example, suggest that departments might use "key courses" of this kind as occasions for broader inquiry (Kean College of New Jersey, 1986). Existing student surveys often present an additional opportunity. Inventories of such instruments undertaken as a first step in assessment generally identify dozens of such instruments of uncertain quality, administered on a one-shot basis; a first step in many emerging institutional assessment plans, therefore, is to consolidate such efforts into a few carefully designed comprehensive survey instruments. Similarly, some institutions now include items on self-reported gain or quality of effort on the course evaluation forms traditionally used to rate faculty (Ewell & Lisensky, 1988).

A more important naturalistic line of development involves incorporating assessment techniques directly into the classroom or curriculum. Because of the enormous diversity of such efforts, it is useful to classify them along two descriptive dimensions. One is *domain*, as most institutions make a clear distinction between assessment in the major field—which is generally the responsibility of each individual department—and assessment processes intended to determine the broader outcomes of general education. Initial experiments with curriculum-embedded techniques first took place in the major field, where clear course progressions often existed and where faculty were better able to identify appropriate opportunities. Only recently have such techniques begun to emerge in general education, usually after extensive consideration of or a disappointing experience with standardized general education instruments.

A second distinction addresses the *level of intervention* involved. In its most active form, curriculum-embedded assessment may involve explicitly designed performances, exercises, or examinations that are carefully crafted to provide group-level as well as individual-level information and intended to be inserted into classroom or field settings. Primary examples here include integrated performance assessments as pioneered by Alverno, as well as more traditional devices such as senior seminars and comprehensive examinations. In its least obtrusive form, curriculum-embedded assessment may include systematically collecting existing student products, generated as a natural result of the curriculum as currently taught, for later evaluation as evidence of overall curricular goal attainment. Most salient examples here involve extensions of the portfolio approach traditionally used for evaluating writing or performance in the fine arts. Between these two extremes lies a continually expanding range of practice.

Curriculum-embedded assessment in the major field. Within the major field, curriculum-embedded assessment takes a variety of forms. Perhaps the most popular alternative, though highly obtrusive, is a faculty-designed examination. Traditional comprehensive examinations that must be passed in order to graduate, and that require students to demonstrate both broad disciplinary knowledge and its application to typical problems or settings, are enjoying a significant revival on many college campuses. Like their standardized counterparts, however, such examinations have severe limitations in producing group-level assessment information. Carefully designed multidimensional rating schemes are required to render these examintions useful in providing program-level information (Erwin, in press), and multiple readers may be needed to ensure adequate reliability. Faculty-designed major field examinations intended from the outset to produce group-level results about the attainment of curricular goals are also visible in growing numbers. Among the best current examples are a range of major field examinations at the University of Tennessee, Knoxville, and James Madison University, developed in response to state mandate. Here, examination items typically are first designed by faculty themselves, with substantial assistance from campus assessment professionals (Banta & Schneider, 1988). For the most part these examinations are based on multiple-choice items, though more recently, faculty are being encouraged to include performance-based items or tasks. An extensive literature of practice has grown up around the construction of such instruments (e.g., Appelbaum, 1988; Erwin, in press; Pike, 1989b). Not surprisingly, the bulk of this advice follows the logic of standard instrument development methods, beginning with a clear specification of objectives, the costs and benefits of different testing modalities and formats, establishment of item and obtained score validity and reliability, and interpretation of results. Instruments constructed in this fashion, with domains carefully matched to local curricular coverage, have proven powerful departmental tools for curricular review and improvement (Boyer, 1989; Farmer, 1988). But because performances are not generally of consequence for individual students, such examinations can also suffer from the high nonparticipation rates and uncertain student motivation experienced by their standardized counterparts.

An alternative to stand-alone examinations is to embed assessment exercises in an existing capstone experience (e.g., a senior seminar, project, internship, or field placement). Less obtrusive, this approach is also less likely to provide complete coverage of any particular curricular goal domain. Existing individual student evaluation procedures in some disciplines are particularly amenable to curriculum evaluation purposes and can be modified with relatively little difficulty. At Glassboro State College in music, for example, consistent numeric rating schemes are incorporated into existing auditions and performances, and tapes of the performances are archived for comparison over time (Keith, 1989). In other professional or practice disciplines, a senior project or common experience is either already present in the curriculum or can appropriately be created. Examples include marketing at Kings College (Farmer, 1988), where seniors take a capstone course that involves team development and presentation of a complete marketing plan, or social work at Kean College of New Jersey (Boyer, 1989), where departmental assessment is grounded partly on ratings of student journals kept during field practice placements.

The success of such ventures in producing usable group-level assessment information depends heavily on three factors. First, the capstone exercise must truly be comprehensive (i.e., effective performance must depend on knowledge and skills learned throughout the curriculum); the more limited the domain of the performance (e.g., a senior thesis on a specialized topic), the less useful it is for evaluation. Second, judgment of the performance must involve multiple raters who can achieve reasonable consensus about what they see; typical senior capstone courses taught by single faculty members without cross-grading or external validation do not achieve this standard. Finally, rating scales must contain a sufficient number of dimensions that group-level diagnostic information can be obtained by aggregating obtained ratings on a single dimension across individuals; capstone experiences, senior seminars, or projects in which only a single summative grade is awarded do not meet this criterion. As in the case of faculty-designed major field examinations, substantial advice on practices that embody such principles is now available (Alverno College Faculty, 1979; Erwin, in press), and institutional use of this approach will undoubtedly accelerate.

The least obtrusive approaches to major field assessment rely entirely on a review of existing products. Appelbaum (1987), for example, suggests an "audit" procedure consisting of intensive reviews of course syllabi and required exercises, together with sample student products at different stages to roughly determine curricular goal achievement. Somewhat similar are portfolio techniques that collect systematic examples of student work over time for later collective review. An emerging vehicle for such exercises is program review. For example, in its most recent history review, the University of Virginia requested visiting scholars serving as external reviewers not only to inspect the undergraduate curriculum but also to read and comment on a selection of student theses (Moomaw, 1989).

Curriculum-embedded assessment in general education. Parallel assessment approaches in general education also span the continuum of active to unobtrusive. Although faculty-designed general examinations are rare, occasional well-grounded attempts to provide local, tailored alternatives to available standardized instruments such as the ACT COMP, CAAP, and Academic Profile have emerged (e.g., at James Madison University; Erwin, in press). These examinations have the substantial advantage of being carefully configured to fit local curricular requirements, but they are expensive to produce and validate and are equallly subject to problems of student motivation. An interesting variant is the "sophomore-junior project" at Kings College: Before entry into the major, students are required to complete a transition exercise that emphasizes the use of general skills in the context of the discipline they are about to enter (Farmer, 1988).

A more common approach is course-embedded assessment, in which specifically designed questions addressing cross-curricular abilities are included in the final examinations of existing general education courses (Warren, 1988). Faculty read and grade examinations in the usual way, but the answers to the specially constructed items are also read collectively and rated against curricular goals using defined scoring criteria. This approach effectively obviates the student motivation problem often encountered by more obtrusive assessment techniques. In six core general education courses at Kean College of New Jersey, for example, faculty worked with ETS to develop special essay questions designed to tap carefully specified analytic abilities; responses are scored by teams of faculty readers using ETS core scoring methods (O'Day & Kelly, 1987). At Kings College (Farmer, 1988), "pretest" and "posttest" essays are used in interdisciplinary core course sequences, both to assess skills development within each course and to determine the degree to which analytical skills learned in one context can be effectively transferred to another (e.g., one such question asks students to apply previously learned economic concepts of profit, capital, interest, loans, principal, and assets to the physical arena of energy, currently being covered by an interdisciplinary science course).

Major challenges to widespread use of this technique are domain specificity and the degree of faculty agreement required. Most institutional definitions of general education goals, in themselves, provide an insufficient basis for developing the kinds of specific scoring guides required—partly because they are designed to politically accommodate courses drawn from many disciplines and departments and partly because they are rarely stated in outcomes terms. At the same time, unless courses offered for general education credit are designed and taught consistently, faculty will see the inclusion of general purpose questions in their own examinations as intrusive. Promising though it is, therefore, this approach has yet to be applied successfully outside curricula that lack a common core.

Less obtrusive approaches, as in the major field, rely heavily on secondary analysis of naturally occurring student products. The most popular emerging technique is the portfolio, in which representative samples of student work are compiled across courses and assembled for secondary reading according to defined criteria (Hutchings, 1990). This is a well-known technique in the evaluation of writing, and, not unnaturally, it has been most fruitfully applied in writing. A carefully executed recent experiment with sample portfolios at the College of William and Mary illustrates both the pitfalls and potential of this approach as a prime ingredient of general education assessment (College of William and Mary, 1988). An initial sample of 50 students was selected for the project, and their current courses were determined. Faculty were asked to duplicate selected students' work for combination into portfolios, which were then read by multiple readers using defined rating criteria. Reviewers believed that writing and critical thinking capability could be meaningfully assessed; however, they felt that additional general abilities could not be assessed because they were insufficiently delineated and, more important, because the class assignments associated with most of the instances of student work collected did not actually require the relevant skill.

Other general education portfolio review projects have foundered on sheer volume and confusion of purpose. Because portfolios undoubtedly have benefits for individual students when used to anchor feedback and self-assessment (Elbow & Belanoff, 1986), many institutions initially propose to apply the portfolio technique universally to achieve both group-level and individual assessment purposes. This is rarely successful, as maximum individual benefit requires the portfolios to be compiled and held by the students themselves, whereas collective review is a time-intensive exercise that can only be effectively accomplished on a sample basis. These drawbacks will probably temper the current heavy interest in portfolio evaluation techniques. As a result, future applications of portfolio methods in general education will probably be confined, appropriately, to the evaluation of student writing and critical argument.

A promising alternative to longitudinal portfolios, related to curricular audit techniques, is to systematically sample and analyze median performance. Essentially, this technique involves sampling the classroom products of the median earned-grade performer in each class and evaluating the results collectively as a work sample of a composite average performer. Although this technique, by definition, reveals nothing about the distribution of performance, it does allow central performance patterns to be readily identified across a range of general education dimensions. Because the maximum number of work samples collected is equivalent to the number of course sections offered, moreover, the process is fairly manageable logistically. It is interesting to note that median performance samples of this kind have occasionally been collected over time by individual faculty members who teach the same course year after year to determine trends in ability and as a hedge against unconscious shifts in personal grading standards (H. Friedman, personal communication, June 1988).

Fusing Assessment and Teaching Practice: Classroom Research

Simple techniques such as median performance sampling also emphasize the ultimate possibility for naturalistic practice—the use of assessment by individual faculty members in their own classrooms as an integral part of teaching. Dubbed "classroom research," such techniques enjoy increasing popularity as an approach to assessment because of their extreme flexibility and because their coverage and employment remain within the control of individual faculty members. In contrast to more formal assessment approaches that rely on an external proactive research strategy to effect instructional change, proponents of classroom research maintain that widespread innovative activities across hundreds of classrooms, though diverse and uncoordinated, will eventually induce a set of far more fundamental (and effective) changes in instructional practice (Cross, 1990).

In essence, classroom research consists of a diverse body of techniques intended to be flexibly used by individual faculty members to (a) directly assess student learning of class content and taught developmental skills, (b) assess and provide feedback to students about the ways they learn and their own self-consciousness as learners, and (c) obtain immediate feedback about how delivered instruction is being received (e.g., which concepts are being understood and which are not) in order to immediately adjust what is taught and how. Emphasis is placed on straightforward techniques that provide immediate information on student perceptions or levels of comprehension. Cross and Angelo (1988), for example, classify and fully describe such techniques in three general areas—assessing academic skills and intellectual development, assessing students' self-awareness as learners and self-assessments of learning skills, and assessing student reactions to teachers and teaching methods or materials. Among the latter, perhaps the most widely cited and employed is the "one-minute paper" that students are requested to complete after every class, documenting the most important thing they learned and the most important unanswered questions remaining (e.g., Light, 1990). More sophisticated techniques include "focused dialectical notes," in which students actively create a critical dialogue around statements encountered in assigned reading in order to practice critical thinking skills, and "one-sentence summaries," in which students are asked to concisely reorganize the essence of a particular concept in a single grammatical sentence. Such techniques have been extensively field tested, particularly in community college settings, and have proven powerful tools for focusing faculty attention on what constitutes good teaching.

Classroom research of this kind enjoys strong advantages as a general approach to assessment. Because its unit of analysis is the individual classroom, results can be applied directly in an arena in which faculty are directly invested and over which they, in fact, have control. More significantly, classroom research appropriately refocuses analytical attention on the *process* of instruction, in contrast to merely documenting outcomes. This shift is critical and is visible in a growing variety of assessment settings. Widely cited findings from the Harvard Assessment Seminar on the value of group study or the characteristics of highly respected courses (Light, 1990) provide a salient example of this critical redirection. At the same time, recent studies on the physical attributes of effective teaching practice (e.g., Chickering & Gamson, 1987; Gamson & Poulsen, 1989) are beginning to directly influence institutional assessment design, particularly in their demands for better information about classroom process and out-of-class student behavior (e.g., Minnesota State University System, 1989; Winona State University, 1990). Both developments, partly stimulated by the classroom research movement, promise a return of assessment's attention to neglected process and environmental concerns.

Emerging Issues of Naturalistic Assessment

Taken together, recent shifts in assessment technique toward a more naturalistic approach raise important practical issues. One is a concern about technical quality. At its extreme, the impetus toward more naturalistic designs can be seen as sanctioning a methodological philosophy of "anything goes"—an opinion that measurement advocates in assessment are quick to point out (Adelman, 1986, 1988). If formal assessment practices result in the same kinds of impressionistic evidence about educational effects as does traditional wisdom, the entire impetus of assessment's development since 1985 may be in jeopardy (Ewell, 1989). At minimum, if appropriate technical rigor is to be maintained, a major faculty development effort is required, guided by clear standards and principles of good practice (e.g., Light, Singer, & Willett, 1990).

Another emerging dilemma is the appropriateness of data aggregation across successively more inclusive units of analysis. By definition, naturalistic studies produce greater volumes of information in less compatible forms than do more intrusive and standardized measurement techniques. Already, in states that have mandated assessment while allowing considerable diversity in institutional data-gathering practices, there is growing concern about how to summarize and communicate results. Institutional leaders recognize and voice similar concerns. An emerging demand may be for layered instead of cumulative assessment designs, in which the results of assessment studies undertaken at different levels of analysis are neither aggregated nor directly compared because fundamentally different questions are being investigated in each. Despite these issues, current trends toward naturalistic inquiry in higher education assessment are unlikely to be reversed. The challenge for the future is to develop more rigorous measurement metrics and concepts better suited to such designs without doing violence to their intent or authenticity.

EMERGING ISSUES AND FUTURE DIRECTIONS

As assessment in higher education continues to evolve, its practitioners cannot avoid some fundamental questions of meta-methodology. Most now recognize that the movement's early promise, rooted in a simple linkage between measurement technology and academic reform, will be hard to fulfill without seriously rethinking some basic assumptions of measurement theory. Most are also vexed by the question of use, and in practice are finding the application of obtained results to decision making a difficult business. Like everything else in assessment, these questions are not new. Indeed, they are a limited replay of recent rethinking in the educational measurement and evaluation communities.

The majority of these questions can be treated through the recent conceptual development of the term *validity* (Messick, 1975, 1988a) traced by the testing and measurement community. Initially conceived of as a narrowly technical property of the measurement device, validity is now proposed as a unitary but "faceted" concept that embraces, at minimum, the intent and design of the instrument, the nature of the results obtained, the interpretation of these results, and the uses to which the findings are put. Conceptual discussions among assessment practitioners are currently centering on validity in these terms for at least two reasons. First, as the enterprise becomes increasingly localized through the use of faculty-designed instruments and naturalistic techniques, there is an urgent need for credible local validation procedures (Mentkowski & Doherty, 1980), both to ensure sound intervention and to engender external confidence. Second, as policymakers increasingly consider assessment results in making high-stakes decisions, there is an urgent need to ensure that the instruments and techniques used are sound enough to support these applications (e.g., Banta, 1988). Central concerns in these discussions can be effectively summarized in terms of three major questions embedded in the concept of validity that each attempt at assessment must pose and answer.

What's the Construct?

The growing use of performance measures in higher education assessment raises important questions about both the nature of the phenomenon being investigated and the epistemology underlying the investigation. Most assessment practitioners now agree that the kinds of cognitive properties claimed as collegiate outcomes are complex, and far more so than those addressed by traditional educational measurement practice. But do they require, as some now claim, completely rethinking the model of inquiry? Critics of current measurement practice point out that traditional assessment technology is wedded to a model of discrete trait estimation founded on the use of large numbers of independent compensatory items (e.g., Rogers, 1988). Although this approach may suffice for estimating basic skills or cognitive content, they claim, it is ill-suited for investigating complex, integrated abilities. The choice of demonstrated performance as the primary mode of inquiry, moreover, is not simply a question of face validity or authenticity but involves a radically different concept of the trait itself. Is the intent to estimate how much of a defined something an individual *has*, or to determine, in particular, what that individual can and cannot *do*? In the first case, the individual becomes one among many instances of the trait; in the second, the trait is inseparable from the individual.

The answer to this question matters for future assessment practice in at least three ways. First, if complex abilities are integrated and developmental, obtained trait estimates may mean different things for the same individual at different points in time. Measurement theorists increasingly recognize this proposition as they experiment with the kinds of hierarchically staged developmental models embodied in item response theory, with "inference networks" in which evidence from a wide variety of sources can be used to iteratively obtain probability estimates about an individual's current characteristics, and with more sophisticated "tectonic plate," "latent class," and "componential" models of test theory founded upon examining the response patterns typical of different states and stages rather than upon estimating overall proficiency (Mislevy, 1990). Advocates of performance assessment, moreover, argue that quite different kinds of tasks are appropriate at different points in a developmental sequence and that a repeated measures design tells little about the actual development of a complex ability.

Second, if complex abilities are not abstractly present but are properties of a given individual, obtained response patterns may legitimately differ from individual to individual regardless of any underlying proficiency. Not only does this raise questions about interpreting individual assessment results for purposes of feedback, it poses major challenges to the common use of analyses based on central tendency for grounding valid group-level inferences. The use of IRT-based techniques in test development, for example, allows much more sophisticated theory-based conclusions about group functioning to be drawn from a particular item response pattern but also demands identification of those (sometimes significant in number) for whom the theory-based response pattern does not hold (Mislevy, 1990). At the same time, in group-level work on student affective development using questionnaires and interviews, G. Hanson (1988) cautions against the unexamined use of central tendency methods and instead argues for response interpretations based primarily on the identification of "themes and patterns" in the data.

A final implication involves the nature and treatment of measurement error. Classical theory based on discrete trait estimation conceives of measurement error as an obtained deviation from a hypothetical true result, occurring because of imperfections in instruments, administration procedures, scoring procedures, and testing conditions. In the use of multiple-judgment rating scales, for example, interrater reliability calculations are needed to establish the range of judgmental variation that typically occurs around repeated observations of a presumed trait or ability across individuals. Evaluators of writing (and increasingly other advocates of complex performance assessment) disagree, maintaining that the different judgments of independent, professional raters may legitimately diverge and that such differences should not be lightly averaged to approximate a single hypothesized "true score" (White, 1990).

All three implications converge on a single admonition for future assessment practice: the need to be much more precise up front about the nature of the ability being investigated and how it might be recognized at different stages of development. If assessment is to prosper, currently predominant "menu-driven" practices of method selection will need to be replaced by choices based on an explicit theory of instruction.

What's the Context?

The emerging naturalistic paradigm for assessment allows for a vast range of possibilities for practice, but at the same time raises fundamental questions about the confidence that can be placed in obtained results. Lacking validation, critics maintain, admittedly innovative local practices are no more sound a basis for making inferences and decisions than the course grades and accumulated credit hours that they were intended to supplant. The resulting dilemma leads assessment practitioners to two current concerns—the nature of contextual validity and the contents of appropriate validation procedures for locally developed techniques.

The notion of contextual validity (Mentkowski & Rogers, 1988; Rogers, 1988) parallels that of authenticity recently called for in K–12 assessment (e.g., Wiggins, 1989), and the procedures it requires have much in common with established guidelines for naturalistic evaluation practice (Lincoln & Guba, 1986). In essence, its proponents argue, contextual validation requires establishing appropriate congruence among three elements: (a) the elicited performance itself and particularly its depth and complexity, (b) the typical contexts in which performances requiring the ability actually occur, and (c) the ways in which obtained results will be used to provide feedback or to make decisions. Validation in this sense becomes less a process of statistical confidence building than one of iterative negotiation among a variety of stakeholders in an attempt to establish common ground. As described, the proposed process resembles that which naturally occurs in the development of many assessments. Design of the GIS in New Jersey, for example, extended over a 2-year period and involved extensive consultation with faculty drawn from different disciplines and types of institutions as well as members of the business and professional communities (COEP Council, 1990). Throughout the pilot process, contextual validation was constantly sought in the form of faculty comments on the depth and appropriateness of the tasks required given what students were typically asked to produce in college classrooms.

But far too many local assessment decisions are currently made without such a process. As a result, they are vulnerable to charges of inappropriateness or inapplicability only after the results are in. To address this situation, proposals for local validation of faculty-designed instruments and assessment procedures are beginning to emerge in greater numbers (e.g., Erwin, in press; Mentkowski & Rogers, 1988). Their intent is not to supplant existing technical components of a validation—such as interjudge agreement, comparisons between obtained results and those produced by other similar instruments and techniques, and demonstrable linkages to the curriculum or other environmental effects. But they typically add to the validation process such components as practitioner judgments about the appropriateness of posed problems and limits regarding how obtained results should be used or not used. In the future, much will depend on the ability and willingness of faculty to rigorously apply such processes to their own instruments and procedures. Absent them, obtained results will be neither used inside the institution nor believed outside it.

What's the Use?

Probably the most often voiced current concern about assessment is the inappropriate use of its results. For the most part, moreover, concerns about use turn on the presumed technical limits of a given instrument or approach in providing information of sufficient quality to ground a reasonable decision. This is particularly the case where the decision in question involves high stakes (e.g., preventing a student from graduating, terminating a program, or denying significant levels of funding to an institution). Where high-stakes decisions are based on instruments with wide error ranges, this situation is extreme. Tennessee's performance funding program, for example, has been criticized for allowing the allocation of many thousands of dollars to ride on what may in essence be a random process, because current allocational decision points lie well within the standard error range of the procedure used (Banta, 1988). Similar concerns arise where an instrument designed for one high-stakes purpose is used for another. Comparative aggregate pass rates on Florida's CLAST examination, for example, occasionally have been used to evaluate institutional performance without taking into account either differences in test-taker characteristics across institutions or the technical capability of the CLAST instrument, designed to assess individuals, to support inferences about curricular impact (Ewell, 1990). Both situations, although rare so far in higher education assessment, raise additional validity issues with which testing and measurement professionals are familiar. Messick, for example, argues cogently for a comprehensive definition of validity that prominently includes considering the consequences of use (Messick, 1975, 1988a). Instruments and techniques are not "valid" in this construction, but rather interpretations and uses. Each time the use context changes, the question of validity must be raised and addressed anew.

Growing recognition of this insight, in conclusion, brings the assessment movement in higher education face to face with its initial roots and values. Conceived as an integral part of an explicit reform agenda, assessment first arose as a technology in use. The promise of outcomes measurement appeared bright because its powerfully perceived technical merits seemed deployable in the service of improved undergraduate teaching and learning. Lurking within a technical approach to reform, however, was always a danger of reification: Assessment might easily become an end in itself, the exclusive province of an isolated professional measurement cadre little concerned with how its results were applied. That this has not occurred is due to the unwillingness of both faculty and public policymakers to let go of assessment's initially motivating question—how to better understand and improve collegiate learning. Evolution of a predominant method toward naturalistic inquiry, ultimately rooted in the individual classroom, signals not only methodological maturation but also a determination to keep that question vital. Equally important for the long run, it may help keep measurement honest.

REFERENCES

Adelman, C. (1985). *The standardized test scores of college graduates, 1964–82.* Washington, DC: U.S. Government Printing Office.

Adelman, C. (1986). To imagine an adverb: Concluding notes to adversaries and enthusiasts. In *Assessment in American higher education: Issues and contexts* (pp. 73–82). Washington, DC: U.S. Government Printing Office.

Adelman, C. (1988). Metaphors and other guidances in higher education assessment. In C. Adelman (Ed.), *Performance and judgment: Essays on principles and practice in the assessment of college student learning* (pp. 279–293). Washington, DC: U.S. Government Printing Office.

Adelman, C. (1989). Indicators and their discontents. In C. Adelman (Ed.), *Signs and traces: Model indicators of student learning in the disciplines* (pp. 1–10). Washington, DC: U.S. Government Printing Office.

Adelman, S. I., Ewell, P. T., & Grable, J. R. (1989). LONESTAR: Texas's voluntary tracking and developmental education evaluation system. In T. H. Bers (Ed.), *Using student tracking systems effectively* (New Directions for Community Colleges No. 66, pp. 75–82). San Francisco: Jossey-Bass.

Alverno College Faculty. (1976). *Liberal learning at Alverno College.* Milwaukee, WI: Alverno Productions.

Alverno College Faculty. (1979). *Assessments at Alverno College*. Milwaukee, WI: Alverno Publications.

American College Testing Program. (1988). *Collegiate assessment of academic proficiency (CAAP): Guidelines*. Iowa City: ACT.

Angelo, T. A. (1988). *Assessing what matters: How participation in work, athletics and extracurriculars relates to the academic success and personal satisfaction of Harvard undergraduates* (A First Report on the Harvard Assessment Seminar's 1987–88 Interview Study). Cambridge, MA: Harvard Graduate School of Education.

Appelbaum, M. I. (1987). Assessment through the major. In C. Adelman (Ed.), *Performance and judgment: Essays on principles and practice in the assessment of college student learning* (pp. 117–138). Washington, DC: U.S. Government Printing Office.

Aquino, F. J. (1989, April). *A five year longitudinal study of community college student behaviors: Toward a definition of student success and student failure*. Paper presented at the Association for Institutional Research Annual Forum, Baltimore.

Association of American Colleges. (1985). *Integrity in the college curriculum: A report to the academic community*. Washington, DC: Association for American Colleges.

Astin, A. W. (1977). *Four critical years: Effects of college on beliefs, values and knowledge*. San Francisco: Jossey-Bass.

Astin, A. W. (1979). Student-oriented management: A proposal for change. In *Evaluating educational quality: A conference summary* (pp. 3–18). Washington, DC: Council on Postsecondary Accreditation.

Astin, A. W. (1985). *Achieving educational excellence: A critical assessment of priorities and practices in higher education*. San Francisco: Jossey-Bass.

Astin, A. W. (1990, June). *Proposed assessment curriculum*. Paper presented at the Fifth National Conference on Assessment, Washington, DC.

Astin, A. W. (in press). *Assessment for excellence*. New York: Macmillan.

Astin, A. W., & Ewell, P. T. (1985). The value-added debate . . . continued. *AAHE Bulletin, 37*(8), 11–13.

Baird, L. L. (1988). Value added: Using student gains as yardsticks of learning. In C. Adelman (Ed.), *Performance and judgment: Essays on principles and practice in the assessment of college student learning* (pp. 205–216). Washington, DC: U.S. Government Printing Office.

Banta, T. W. (1985). Use of outcomes information at the University of Tennessee, Knoxville. In P. T. Ewell (Ed.), *Assessing educational outcomes* (New Directions for Institutional Research No. 47, pp. 19–32). San Francisco: Jossey-Bass.

Banta, T. W. (1986). *Performance funding in higher education: A critical analysis of Tennessee's experience*. Boulder, CO: National Center for Higher Education Management Systems.

Banta, T. W. (1988). Assessment as an instrument of state funding policy. In T. W. Banta (Ed.), *Implementing outcomes assessment: Promise and perils* (New Directions in Institutional Research No. 59, pp. 81–94). San Francisco: Jossey-Bass.

Banta, T. W., Lambert, E. W., Pike, G. R., Schmidhammer, J. L., & Schneider, J. A. (1987). Estimated score gain on the ACT COMP exam: Valid tool for institutional assessment? *Research in Higher Education, 27*, 195–217.

Banta, T. W., & Moffett, M. S. (1987). Performance funding in Tennessee: Stimulus for program improvement. In D. F. Halpern (Ed.), *Student outcomes as-*

sessment: What institutions stand to gain (New Directions in Higher Education No. 59, pp. 35–44). San Francisco: Jossey-Bass.

Banta, T. W., & Pike, G. R. (1989). Methods for comparing outcomes assessment instruments. *Research in Higher Education, 30*, 455–470.

Banta, T. W., & Schneider, J. A. (1988). Using faculty-developed exit examinations to evaluate academic programs. *Journal of Higher Education, 59*, 69–83.

Bennett, W. J. (1984). *To reclaim a legacy: A report on the humanities in higher education*. Washington, DC: National Endowment for the Humanities.

Berdahl, R. O., & Studds, S. M. (1989). *The tension of excellence and equity: The Florida enhancement programs*. College Park, MD: National Center for Postsecondary Governance and Finance, University of Maryland.

Blood, M. R. (1987). *Outcome Measurement Project, Phase III Report, May 1987*. St. Louis: American Assembly of Collegiate Schools of Business.

Bowen, H. R. (1977). *Investment in learning: The individual and social value of American higher education*. San Francisco: Jossey-Bass.

Boyer, C. M. (1989). *Improving student learning: The Outcomes Assessment Program at Kean College of New Jersey*. Union, NJ: Kean College of New Jersey.

Boyer, C., & Algren, A. (1987). Assessing undergraduates' patterns of credit distribution: Amount and specialization. *Journal of Higher Education, 58*, 430–442.

Boyer, C. M., Ewell, P. T., Finney, J. E., & Mingle, J. R. (1987). Assessment and outcomes measurement: A view from the states. *AAHE Bulletin, 39*(7), 8–12.

Campione, J. C., & Armbruster, B. B. (1985). Acquiring information from texts: An analysis of four approaches. In J. W. Segal, S. F. Chipman, & R. Glaser (Eds.), *Thinking and learning skills* (Vol. VI, pp. 317–362). Hillsdale, NJ: Erlbaum.

Cheney, L. W. (1989). *50 Hours: A core curriculum for college students*. Washington, DC: National Endowment for the Humanities.

Chickering, A. W. (1969). *Education and identity*. San Francisco: Jossey-Bass.

Chickering, A. W., & Gamson, Z. F. (1987). Seven principles for good practice in undergraduate education. *AAHE Bulletin, 39*(7), 3–7.

The College Board. (1987). *Computerized placement texts: An exciting and innovative placement tool*. New York: The College Entrance Examination Board.

College Outcomes Evaluation Program Council, New Jersey Department of Higher Education. (1990). *Report to the Board of Higher Education on the first administration of the General Intellectual Skills (GIS) Assessment*. Trenton: Department of Higher Education, State of New Jersey.

College Outcomes Evaluation Program, State of New Jersey Department of Higher Education. (1987). *Report to the New Jersey Board of Higher Education from the Advisory Committee to the College Outcomes Evaluation Program*. Trenton: Department of Higher Education, State of New Jersey.

College of William and Mary, Office of the Associate Provost. (1988). *Portfolio assessment: A pilot project*. Williamsburg, VA: Author.

College of William and Mary, Office of the Associate Provost. (1989). *Assessment of undergraduate liberal education: A report to the State Council of Higher Education for Virginia*. Williamsburg, VA: Author.

Conlin, G. (1987, April). *Core scoring: A method of evaluating written free responses*. Paper presented at the annual meeting of the American Educational Research Association, Washington, DC.

Conrad, C. F., Jamison, A., Kroc, R., MacCorquodal, P., & Summers, G. (1987). *Plan for assessing undergraduate education at the University of Arizona* (Report of the Task Force on Assessment of the Quality and Outcomes of Undergraduate Education). Tucson: The University of Arizona.

Council of Presidents and State Board for Community College Education. (1989). *The validity and usefulness of three nationally standardized tests for Washington college sophomores: General report*. Bellingham, WA: Western Washington University Office of Publications.

Cross, K. P. (1990, June). *Collaborative classroom assessment*. Paper presented at the Fifth National Conference on Assessment in Higher Education, Washington, DC.

Cross, K. P., & Angelo, T. A. (1988). *Classroom assessment techniques: A handbook for faculty*. Ann Arbor: National Center for Research to Improve Postsecondary Teaching and Learning, University of Michigan.

Darling-Hammond, L. (1988). Assessment and incentives: The medium is the message. In *Three presentations: From the Third National Conference on Assessment in Higher Education*. Washington, DC: American Association of Higher Education Assessment Forum.

Davis, B. G. (1989). Demystifying assessment: Learning from the field of evaluation. In P. J. Gray (Ed.), *Achieving assessment goals using evaluation techniques*. (New Directions for Higher Education No. 67, pp. 5–20). San Francisco: Jossey-Bass.

Dinham, S. M. (1988). *Summary of assessment activities at the University of Arizona* (Report No. 4). Tucson: Center for Research on Undergraduate Education, University of Arizona.

Edgerton, R. (1987). An assessment of assessment. In *Assessing the outcomes of higher education, Proceedings of the 1986 ETS Invitational Conference* (pp. 93–110). Princeton, NJ: Educational Testing Service.

Education Commission of the States. (1986). *Transforming the state role in undergraduate education: Time for a different view*. Denver: Author.

Educational Testing Service. (1989a). *New Jersey College Outcomes Evaluation Program: A report on the development of the General Intellectual Skills Assessment*. Princeton, NJ: Author.

Educational Testing Service. (1989b). *The new academic profile: Assessing the outcomes of general education*. Princeton, NJ: Author.

Elbow, P., & Belanoff, P. (1986, October). Portfolios as a substitute for proficiency examinations. *College Composition and Communication*.

El-Khawas, E. (1987). *1987 campus trends survey*. Washington, DC: American Council on Education.

El-Khawas, E. (1989). *1989 campus trends survey*. Washington, DC: American Council on Education.

Erwin, T. D. (1983). The Scale of Intellectual Development: Measuring Perry's scheme. *Journal of College Student Personnel, 24*, 6–12.

Erwin, T. D. (in press). *Assessing student learning and development in college*. San Francisco: Jossey-Bass.

Erwin, T. D., & Delworth, U. (1980). An instrument to measure Chickering's vector of identity. *National Association of Student Personnel Administrators Journal, 17*, 19–24.

Ewell, P. T. (1983). *Information on student outcomes: How to get it and how to use it*. Boulder, CO: National Center for Higher Education Management Systems.

Ewell, P. T. (1984). *The self-regarding institution: Information for excellence*. Boulder, CO: National Center for Higher Education Management Systems.

Ewell, P. T. (1986). Performance funding and institutional response: Lessons from the Tennessee experience. In T. W. Banta (Ed.), *Performance funding in higher education: A critical analysis of Tennessee's experience* (pp. 105–120). Boulder, CO: National Center for Higher Education Management Systems.

Ewell, P. T. (1987). Establishing a campus-based assessment program: A framework for choice. In D. Halpern (Ed.), *Student outcomes assessment: A tool for improving teaching and learning* (New Directions for Higher Education No. 59, pp. 9–24). San Francisco: Jossey-Bass.

Ewell, P. T. (1988a). Outcomes, assessment, and academic improvement: In search of usable knowledge. In J. C. Smart (Ed.), *Higher education: Handbook of theory and research* (Vol. IV, pp. 53–108). New York: Agathon Press.

Ewell, P. T. (1988b). Implementing assessment: Some organizational issues. In T. W. Banta (Ed.), *Implementing outcomes assessment: Promise and perils* (New Directions for Institutional Research No. 59, pp. 15–28). San Francisco: Jossey-Bass.

Ewell, P. T. (1989). Hearts and minds: Some reflections on the ideologies of assessment. In *Three presentations from the Fourth National Conference on Assessment in Higher Education* (pp. 1–26). Washington, DC: American Association of Higher Education.

Ewell, P. T. (1990). *Assessment and the "new accountability": A challenge for higher education's leadership*. Denver: Education Commission of the States.

Ewell, P. T., & Boyer, C. M. (1988). Acting out state-mandated assessment: Evidence from five states. *Change, 20*, 40–47.

Ewell, P. T., Finney, J. E., & Lenth, C. (1990). Filling in the mosiac: The emerging pattern of state-based assessment. *AAHE Bulletin, 42*, 3–7.

Ewell, P. T., & Lisensky, R. P. (1988). *Assessing institutional effectiveness: Redirecting the self-study process*. Washington, DC: Consortium for the Advancement of Private Higher Education.

Ewell, P. T., Parker, R., & Jones, D. P. (1988). *Establishing a longitudinal student tracking system: An implementation handbook*. Boulder, CO: National Center for Higher Education Management Systems.

Ewens, T. (1979). Transforming a liberal arts curriculum: Alverno College. In G. Grant & Associates (Eds.), *On competence: A critical analysis of competence-based reforms in higher education* (pp. 259–298). San Francisco: Jossey-Bass.

Farmer, D. W. (1988). *Enhancing student learning: Emphasizing essential student competencies in academic programs*. Wilkes-Barre, PA: Kings College.

Folger, J., & Berdahl, R. O. (1987). *Patterns in evaluating state higher education systems: Making a virtue out of necessity*. College Park: National Center for Postsecondary Governance and Finance, University of Maryland.

Fong, B. (1987). *The external examiner approach to assessment*. Washington, DC: American Association for Higher Education.

Forrest, A. W. (1982). *Increasing student competence and persistence: The best case for general education*. Iowa City: American College Testing Program.

Forrest, A. W., & Steele, J. M. (1978). *College Outcomes Measures Project*. Iowa City: American College Testing Program.

The Gallup Organization. (1989). *A survey of college seniors' knowledge of history and literature, conducted for the National Endowment for the Humanities*. Princeton, NJ: Author.

Gamson, Z. F., & Associates. (1984). *Liberating education*. San Francisco: Jossey-Bass.

Gamson, Z. F., & Poulsen, S. J. (1989). Inventories of good practice: The next step for the seven principles for good practice in undergraduate education. *AAHE Bulletin, 42*, 7–8.

Grant, G., & Kohli, W. (1979). Contributing to learning by assessing student performance. In G. Grant & Associates (Eds.), *On competence: A critical analysis of competence-based reforms in higher education* (pp. 138–159). San Francisco: Jossey-Bass.

Grant, G., & Riesman, D. (1978). *The perceptual dream: Reform and experiment in the American college*. Chicago: University of Chicago Press.

Guba, E. G., & Lincoln, Y. S. (1981). *Effective evaluation: Improving the usefulness of evaluation results through responsive and naturalistic approaches*. San Francisco: Jossey-Bass.

Hanson, D. C. (1990). Federal disclosure regulations: The "worst case" scenario for outcomes assessment. *AAHE Bulletin, 42*, 9–10.

Hanson, G. R. (1982). Critical issues in the assessment of student development. In G. R. Hanson (Ed.), *Measuring student development* (New Directions for Student Services No. 20). San Francisco: Jossey-Bass.

Hanson, G. R. (1988). Critical issues in the assessment of value added in education. In T. W. Banta (Ed.), *Implementing outcomes assessment: Promise and perils* (New Directions for Institutional Research No. 59, pp. 53–68). San Francisco: Jossey-Bass.

Heffernan, J. M., Hutchings, P., & Marchese, T. J. (1988). *Standardized tests and the purposes of assessment*. Washington, DC: American Association of Higher Education.

Hirsch, E. D. (1987). *Cultural literacy: What every American needs to know*. New York: Houghton Mifflin.

Hirsch, E. D. (1989). *Cultural literacy: Form A, standardized edition*. Chicago: Riverside.

Hutchings, P. (1987). *Six stories: Implementing successful assessment* (Paper prepared for the Second National Conference on Assessment in Higher Education). Washington, DC: American Association for Higher Education Assessment Forum.

Hutchings, P. (1990). Learning over time: Portfolio assessment. *AAHE Bulletin, 42*, 6–8.

Hutchings, P., & Marchese, T. W. (1990). Watching assessment: Questions, stories, prospects. *Change, 22*(5), 12–38.

Hyman, R., Jamison, A., Woodard, D., & von Destinon, M. (1988). *Student outcomes assessment survey, 1987–88*. Washington, DC: National Association of Student Personnel Administrators.

Jacobi, M., Astin, A. W., & Ayala, F. (1987). *College student outcomes assessment: A talent development perspective* (ASHE-ERIC Higher Education Report No. 7). Washington, DC: ERIC Clearinghouse on Higher Education, The George Washington University.

Katchadourian, H. A., & Boli, J. (1985). *Careerism and intellectualism among college students*. San Francisco: Jossey-Bass.

Kean College of New Jersey. (1986). *A proposal for program assessment at Kean College of New Jersey: Final report of the Presidental Task Force on Student Learning and Development*. Union, NJ: Author.

Kean, T. H. (1987, September/October). Time to deliver before we forget the promises we made. *Change*, pp. 10–11.

Keith, N. (1989). *Report on student learning and development assessment at*

Glassboro State College (Prepared for the College Outcomes Evaluation Program, State of New Jersey Department of Higher Education). Glassboro, NJ: Learning Assessment Center, Glassboro State College.

Kellams, S. (1989). *University of Virginia longitudinal study of undergraduate education: Interview program methods and results.* Charlottesville: Student Assessment Program, Office of the Provost of the University, University of Virginia.

Knefelkamp, L. L. (1989). Assessment as transformation. In *Three presentations from the Fourth National Conference on Assessment in Higher Education, June 1989, Atlanta.* Washington, DC: American Association for Higher Education Assessment Forum.

Kohlberg, L. (1981). *The meaning and measure of moral development.* Worcester, MA: Clark University Press.

Krueger, D. W., & Heisserer, M. L. (1987). Assessment and involvement: Investments to enhance learning. In D. F. Halpern (Ed.), *Student outcomes assessment: What institutions stand to gain* (New Directions in Higher Education No. 59, pp. 45–56). San Francisco: Jossey-Bass.

League for Innovation. (1988). *Computerized adaptive testing: The state of the art in assessment at three community colleges.* Laguna Hills, CA: Author.

Lenning, O. T., Munday, L., & Maxey, J. (1969). Student educational growth during the first two years of college. *College and University, 44*, 145–153.

Levy, R. A. (1986). Development of performance funding criteria by the Tennessee Higher Education Commission: A chronology and evaluation. In T. W. Banta (Ed.), *Performance funding in higher education: A critical analysis of Tennessee's experience* (pp. 13–26). Boulder, CO: National Center for Higher Education Management Systems.

Light, R. J. (1990). *The Harvard assessment seminars: Explorations with students and faculty about teaching, learning, and student life* (First Report, 1990). Cambridge, MA: Harvard Graduate School of Education and Kennedy School of Government.

Light, R. J., Singer, J. D., & Willett, J. B. (1990). *By design: Planning research on higher education.* Cambridge, MA: Harvard University Press.

Lincoln, Y. S., & Guba, E. G. (1986). But is it rigorous? Trustworthiness and authenticity in naturalistic evaluation. In D. D. Williams (Ed.), *Naturalistic evaluation* (New Directions for Program Evaluation No. 30, pp. 73–84). San Francisco: Jossey-Bass.

McCabe, R. H. (1983). *A status report on the comprehensive educational reform of Miami-Dade Community College.* Miami, FL: Office of the President, Miami-Dade Community College.

McClain, C. W. (1984). *In pursuit of degrees with integrity: A value-added approach to undergraduate assessment.* Washington, DC: American Association of State Colleges and Universities.

McClain, C. J., & Krueger, D. W. (1985). Using outcomes assessment: A case study in institutional change. In P. T. Ewell (Ed.), *Assessing educational outcomes* (New Directions for Institutional Research No. 47, pp. 33–46). San Francisco: Jossey-Bass.

McMillan, J. H. (1988). Beyond value-added education. *Journal of Higher Education, 59*, 564–579.

Mentkowski, M., & Doherty, A. (1980). *Validating assessment techniques in an outcome-centered liberal arts curriculum: Insights from the evaluation and revision process.* Milwaukee, WI: Office of Research and Evaluation, Alverno College.

Mentkowski, M., & Doherty, A. (1984). *Careering after college: Establishing the validity of abilities learned in college for later careering and performance.* Milwaukee, WI: Alverno Publications.

Mentkowski, M., & Loacker, G. (1985). Assessing and validating the outcomes of college. In P. T. Ewell (Ed.), *Assessing educational outcomes* (New Directions for Institutional Research No. 47, pp. 47–64). San Francisco: Jossey-Bass.

Mentkowski, M., Moeser, M., & Straight, M. J. (1981). *Using the Perry scheme of intellectual and ethical development as a college outcome measure: A process and criteria for assessing student performance.* Milwaukee, WI: Office of Research and Evaluation, Alverno College.

Mentkowski, M., & Rogers, G. P. (1988). *Establishing the validity of measures of college student outcomes.* Milwaukee, WI: Office of Research and Evaluation, Alverno College.

Messick, S. (1975). The standard problem: Meaning and values in measurement and evaluation. *American Psychologist, 30*, 955–966.

Messick, S. (1988a). The once and future issue of validity: Assessing the meaning and consequence of measurement. In H. Wainer & H. I. Braun (Eds.), *Test validity* (pp. 33–48). Hillside, NJ: Erlbaum.

Messick, S. (1988b). *Meaning and values in test validation: The science and ethics of assessment.* Princeton, NJ: Educational Testing Service.

Minnesota State University System. (1989). *A proposed quality indicators process.* St. Paul: Author.

Mislevy, R. J. (1990). Foundations of a new test theory. In N. Frederiksen, R. J. Mislevy, & I. Bejar (Eds.), *Test theory for a new generation of tests* (pp. 3–40). Hillsdale, NJ: Erlbaum.

Moomaw, W. E. (1989). *First annual report on the Student Learning Assessment Program at the University of Virginia.* Charlottesville: Student Assessment Program, Office of the Provost of the University, University of Virginia.

National Evaluation Systems. (1987). *Texas Academic Skills Program (TASP).* Amherst, MA: National Evaluation Systems, Inc.

National Governors' Association. (1986). *Time for results: The governors' 1991 report on education.* Washington, DC: National Governors' Association.

National Institute of Education, Study Group on the Conditions of Excellence in American Higher Education. (1984). *Involvement in learning: Realizing the potential of American higher education.* Washington, DC: U.S. Government Printing Office.

Nichols, J. O. (1990). *The role of institutional research in implementing institutional effectiveness or outcomes assessment* (AIR Professional File No. 37). Tallahassee, FL: Association of Institutional Research.

O'Day, D., & Kelly, M. (1987). *Kean College General Education Program: Report on assessment activities, 1986–87.* Union, NJ: General Education Program, Kean College of New Jersey.

Osterlind, S. J. (1988). *College Basic Academic Subjects Examination: Guide to test content.* Columbia: Center for Educational Assessment, University of Missouri—Columbia.

Pace, C. R. (1979). *Measuring the outcomes of college: Fifty years of findings and recommendations for the future.* San Francisco: Jossey-Bass.

Pace, C. R. (1984). *Measuring the quality of college student experiences.* Los Angeles: Higher Education Research Institute, University of California, Los Angeles.

Pace, C. R. (1990). *The undergraduates: A report of their activities and progress*

in college in the 1980's. Los Angeles: Center for the Study of Evaluation, University of California, Los Angeles.
Pascarella, E. T. (1985). College environmental influences on learning and cognitive development: A critical review and synthesis. In J. C. Smart (Ed.), *Higher education: Handbook of theory and research* (Vol. I, pp. 1–61). New York: Agathon Press.
Pascarella, E. T. (1987). Are value-added assessments valuable? In *Assessing the outcomes of higher education, Proceedings of the 1986 ETS Invitational Conference* (pp. 71–92). Princeton, NJ: Educational Testing Service.
Paskow, J. (Ed.). (1988). *Assessment programs and projects: A directory*. Washington, DC: American Association for Higher Education Assessment Forum.
Paulson, C. P. (1990). *State initiatives in assessment and outcome measurement: Tools for teaching and learning in the 1990's*. Denver: Education Commission of the States.
Perry, W. G. (1970). *Forms of intellectual and ethical development in the college years*. New York: Holt, Rinehart and Winston.
Pike, G. R. (1989a). Background, college experiences, and the ACT-COMP exam: Using construct validity to evaluate assessment instruments. *Review of Higher Education, 13*, 91–117.
Pike, G. R. (1989b). Assessment measures. *Assessment Update, 1*(2), 8–9.
Pike, G. R. (1989c). Assessment measures. *Assessment Update, 1*(1), 10–12.
Pike, G. R., & Phillipi, R. H. (1989). Generalizability of the differential coursework methodology: Relationships between self-reported coursework and performance on the ACT-COMP exam. *Research in Higher Education, 30*, 245–260.
Postsecondary Education Planning Commission. (1988). *College level academic skills test review: Prepared in response to specific appropriation 537A of the 1987 General Appropriations Act*. Tallahassee: Postsecondary Education Planning Commission, State of Florida.
Ratcliffe, J. L., & Associates. (1990). *Determining the effect of different coursework patterns on the general learned abilities of college students* (Working Paper OR 90-524). Research Institute for Studies in Education at Iowa State University and Center for the Study of Higher Education at The Pennsylvania State University.
Resnick, D., & Goulden, M. (1987). Assessment, curriculum and expansion in American higher education: A historical perspective. In D. Halpern (Ed.), *Student assessment: A tool for improving teaching and learning* (New Directions for Higher Education No. 59, pp. 77–88). San Francisco: Jossey-Bass.
Rest, J. R. (1986). *Moral development: Advances in research and theory*. New York: Praeger.
Rest, J. R. (1987). *Guide for the Defining Issues Test*. Minneapolis: Center for the Study of Ethical Development, University of Minnesota.
Richardson, R. C., Fisk, E. C., & Okun, M. A. (1983). *Literacy in the open-access college*. San Francisco: Jossey-Bass.
Rogers, G. P. (1988). *Validating college outcomes with institutionally developed instruments: Issues in maximizing contextual validity*. Milwaukee, WI: Office of Research and Evaluation, Alverno College.
Shapiro, J. Z. (1986). Evaluation research and educational decisionmaking. In J. C. Smart (Ed.), *Higher education: Handbook of theory and research* (Vol. II, pp. 163–206). New York: Agathon.
Sheldon, M. S. (1981). *Statewide longitudinal study: 1978–81 final report*. Los Angeles: Los Angeles Pierce College.

Shulman, L. S. (1987a). Assessment for teaching: An initiative for the profession. *Phi Delta Kappan, 69*(1), 38–44.

Shulman, L. S. (1987b). Assessing content and process: Challenges for the new assessments. In *Three presentations from the Second National Conference on Assessment in Higher Education* (pp. 1–14). Washington, DC: American Association for Higher Education.

Southern Regional Education Board. (1985). *Access to quality undergraduate education: A report to the Southern Regional Education Board by its Commission for Educational Quality*. Atlanta: Southern Regional Education Board.

Stark, J. S., Shaw, K. M., & Lowther, M. A. (1989). *Student goals for college and courses: A missing link in assessing and improving academic achievement* (1989 ASHE-ERIC Report 6). Washington, DC: ERIC Clearinghouse on Higher Education, George Washington University.

Steele, J. M. (1988, May). *Using measures of student outcomes and growth to improve college programs*. Paper presented at the National Forum of the Association for Institutional Research.

Stone, H. L., & Meyer, T. C. (1989). *Developing an ability-based assessment program in the continuum of medical education*. Madison: Medical School, University of Wisconsin.

Terenzini, P. T. (1989). Assessment with open eyes: Pitfalls in studying student outcomes. *Journal of Higher Education, 60*, 644–664.

Thorndike, R. M. (1990). The Washington State assessment experience. *Assessment Update, 2*(2), 7–9.

Thrash, P. A. (1988). Educational "outcomes" in the accrediting process. *Academe, 74*, 16–18.

U.S. Department of Education. (1987). Notice of proposed rulemaking, secretary's procedures and criteria for recognition of accrediting agencies, 34 CFR Parts 602 and 603. *Federal Register, 52*, 33906–33913.

U.S. Department of Education, National Commission on Excellence in Education. (1983). *A nation at risk: The imperative for educational reform* (Report to the nation and the secretary of education). Washington, DC: U.S. Government Printing Office.

University of Virginia, Office of the Provost. (1990). *Undergraduate learning at the University of Virginia: A first report to the UVa community*. Charlottesville: Student Assessment Program, Office of the Provost of the University, University of Virginia.

Vorhees, R. A., & Hart, S. (1989). A tracking scheme for basic skills intake assessment. In T. H. Bers (Ed.), *Using student tracking systems effectively* (New Directions in Community Colleges No. 66, pp. 31–38). San Francisco: Jossey-Bass.

Walleri, R. D., & Japely, S. M. (1986, May). *Student intent, persistence, and outcomes*. Paper presented at the 26th annual forum of the Association for Institutional Research, Orlando, FL.

Warren, J. (1984). The blind alley of value added. *AAHE Bulletin, 37*(1), 10–13.

Warren, J. (1988). Cognitive measures in assessing learning. In T. W. Banta (Ed.), *Implementing outcomes assessment: Promise and perils* (New Directions for Institutional Research No. 59, pp. 29–40). San Francisco: Jossey-Bass.

White, E. M. (1990, June). *Language and reality in writing assessment*. Paper presented at the Fifth National Conference on Assessment in Higher Education, AAHE Assessment Forum, Washington, DC.

Wiggins, G. (1989). A true test: Toward more authentic and equitable assessment. *Phi Delta Kappan, 70*, 703–713.

Winona State University. (1990). *Draft indicators for improving undergraduate instructional quality*. Winona, MN: Office of the President, Winona State University.

Wolff, R. A. (1990, June). *Assessment and accreditation: A shotgun marriage?* Paper presented at the Fifth National Conference on Assessment in Higher Education, AAHE Assessment Forum, Washington, DC.

Zemsky, R. (1989). *Structure and coherence: Measuring the undergraduate curriculum*. Philadelphia: Institute for Research on Higher Education, University of Pennsylvania.

Chapter 4

Sexuality Education and Child Sexual Abuse Prevention Programs in the Schools

N. DICKON REPPUCCI and JANNA HERMAN
University of Virginia

Teenage pregnancy and child sexual abuse are two of the major social problems of our time. The United States leads all other industrialized nations in the percentage of teenage pregnancies (Henshaw, Kenney, Somberg, & Van Vort, 1989), and even the most conservative estimates suggest that 10% of America's female children are subjected to some form of child sexual abuse (Haugaard & Reppucci, 1988). Both statistics provide ample evidence of the need for effective interventions to alleviate these problems.

Although teenage sexual activity is about the same in all industrialized nations, other countries are more tolerant of this behavior than the United States, and are more committed to providing contraceptives and education to prevent pregnancies (C. Donovan, 1990). As syndicated columnist Ellen Goodman (1985) stated:

> In the United States. . . , the public debate hinges on morality as well as practicality. We haven't decided whether our primary mission is to focus on discouraging sex or preventing pregnancy through birth control. We are fighting two half-hearted battles instead of concentrating on the one that we can win: the battle against pregnancy. (p. A4)

In the 1970s, child advocates and feminist groups helped make the general public and professionals aware of the prevalence of child sexual abuse (Finkelhor, 1986). However, the problem was brought to center stage in 1984 by the sensational McMartin Day Care Center case in Los Angeles, in which the center's owner and six teachers were accused of systematically abusing hundreds of children over a 10-year period. The publicity from front-page headlines and evening television newscasts concerning this case and others that followed, as well as from cover stories in *Newsweek* and *Life* and television reports on *Sixty Minutes* and *Nightline*, resulted in "something of a national obsession" ("The Unreliability of Expert Testimony," 1985, p. 429) and in a bandwagon to develop programs to prevent child sexual abuse. Millions of children have now been exposed to these programs.

The purpose of this chapter is to provide a succinct review about sexuality education and child sexual abuse prevention programs. Although we concentrate on research findings, societal context and theoretical perspectives have been included to provide clarity. For example, even though a developmental perspective is clearly important to both sexuality education and abuse prevention programs, we emphasize it regarding abuse prevention because the targets of most of these programs are preschool and younger elementary school children (under the age of 10) whose cognitive capacities tend to be less than those of the targets of most sexuality education programs, who are 11 years or older (Melton, Koocher, & Saks, 1983). Because of such differences, we review each type of program separately, even though our society's ambivalent attitude toward explicit discussion of all matters relating to sexual behavior has had an impact on the nature of programming in both areas. In the first part, we divide our discussion of sexuality education into four sections: (a) an examination of the social and philosophical issues; (b) a description of basic program components; (c) a delineation of value-based programs, secular programs, and school-based clinics, with a special emphasis on evaluative studies; and (d) an update on acquired immune deficiency syndrome (AIDS) education. In the second part, we suggest that child sexual abuse prevention programs must be based on a developmental perspective because the reporting and repelling of sexual abuse are complex acts that require cognitive capabilities and emotional maturity that many children do not possess. We then describe briefly the programs in general, detail a few of the best evaluated ones, suggest that several of the underlying assumptions of these programs are based mainly on clinical anecdote, and argue that caution is warranted regarding their widespread use. We conclude that the major research-action goal of the 1990s for both sexuality education and child sexual abuse prevention should be the development of new and better programs that include systematic evaluation of both positive and negative effects.

SEXUALITY EDUCATION

Social and Philosophical Issues

In the United States, over 1 million adolescent women under 20 years of age become pregnant each year, with about 31,000 being under the age of 16 (Henshaw et al., 1989). Roughly half of these pregnancies end in abortion, resulting in the highest rates of any country that publishes accurate abortion statistics (Henshaw et al., 1989). Billions of dollars are spent annually supporting pregnant teens, teen parents, and their children

(Select Committee, 1985b). Moreover, teen mothers tend to have a reduced level of education, an increased family size, and a lower economic status (Hofferth & Hayes, 1987) that all too often leads to a "vicious cycle of poverty" (Furstenberg, 1976). In order to combat these problems and because parents are regarded as inadequate sex educators (Imber, 1984; Klein, 1983; Trudell, 1985), sexuality education has become a responsibility of our country's school systems.

Educators believe sexuality education programs are necessary for several reasons (Cassell & Wilson, 1989, p. xxiv):

- To help prepare people for upcoming stages of development
- To increase comfort with the topic of sexuality
- To increase the attitude that sexuality is a normal and positive part of human existence
- To provide responsible answers to questions and concerns that arise in an age when the media bombard us with sexual messages
- To increase skills that will enable people to live happy, safe, and responsible lives as sexual beings

These arguments address the need for adolescents to acquire knowledge of and a healthy attitude toward human sexuality (Klein, 1983).

Two basic assumptions underlie these rationales for sexuality education in the schools: (a) Such education can alleviate the social problems that have been blamed on teenage sexual activity (Ravitch, 1984; Trudell, 1985), and (b) accurate information about sexual behavior will yield responsible decisions by adolescents (Kirby, 1980; Trudell, 1985). Therefore, most of these programs have aimed to improve young people's knowledge of sexuality (Richard, 1989), although sparse evidence exists that improved knowledge changes adolescent behavior (Kirby, 1989).

The actual expectation of most sexuality education programs, although not always explicitly stated, is to reduce adolescent pregnancy. Most programs attempt to attain this result by promoting abstinence, delaying onset of coitus, and increasing usage of effective contraception. Some of these goals, and some of the programs, are more controversial than others. With the myriad of parental beliefs regarding appropriate goals, the federal government's stance that localized programs are the best means of satisfying entire communities (Select Committee, 1985a) would apparently be confirmed. However, Hunter (1989) concluded that even if programs are locally developed, at least "one segment of any community . . . will oppose any kind of sex education in the public schools" (p. 113). For the most part, resistance has been successfully contested by parents and community members who favor the development of sexuality programs (Tatum, 1989). Accordingly, educators endorse sexuality education as a cooperative effort between schools and parents so that programs may be designed to be comprehensive while satisfying the majority (Klein, 1983; Trudell, 1985).

Many parents have resisted these programs because they fear that by discussing sexual intercourse and contraceptive techniques, children will believe adults are condoning sexual behavior, and programs will indirectly promote adolescent sexual activity (Klein, 1983). Although several scientific investigations have shown that sexuality program participation does not increase initiation or frequency of sexual activity (Kirby, 1989; Paikoff & Brooks-Gunn, in press) or undermine parental influence (Furstenberg, Moore, & Peterson, 1985), these fears remain widely prevalent. A similar lack of correspondence between sexuality education and decreases in sexual activity has also been found (Kirby, 1989; Paikoff & Brooks-Gunn, in press); however, an association between exposure to sex education and sexual *in*experience substantiates the value of these programs for delaying onset of sexual activity (Furstenberg et al., 1985).

Albeit the ultimate goal of reducing teenage pregnancy is commendable, the following question is seldom asked: "Is it reasonable to ask adolescents to counter their physiological development and their many years of informal sexual education (Kirby, 1980) in order to delay their sexual involvement?" During the 19th century and the first half of the 20th century, adolescent females were frequently experiencing coitus within marital bonds by 16 years of age, because early marriage for women and building of families facilitated the agrarian lifestyle of that time. In dramatic contrast, our present technological culture encourages delay of marriage for both sexes until educations are completed, careers are established, and jobs are secured. To attain these goals before engaging in socially condoned sexual activity would mean that adolescents would be waiting until they were well into adulthood.

Furthermore, a contradictory model of sexual behavior and morality is communicated by the high rates of cohabitation and divorce among adults (C. Donovan, 1990) and a media that glamorizes sexuality outside of marriage (e.g., sexual intercourse occurs 4 to 8 times more frequently among unmarried than among married heterosexual television characters) (Paikoff & Brooks-Gunn, in press). We have created the technology to allow any two consenting adults to engage in coitus without significant fear of procreating (e.g., birth control pills are 95–99% effective) (Francoeur, 1982), yet we instruct adolescents to abstain from sex until they are married because sex is for "making babies." So it appears we are sending our youth mixed messages (Thornburg, 1985).

A vast amount of our children's informal education contradicts the religious values and family morals that many parents endeavor to instill. Our culture highly values beauty and sexuality, and our capitalist economy uses these concepts to maintain its strength by selling products through advertising. The fundamental constitutional right to freedom of speech limits censorship of the media. Thus, it is not realistically possible to shelter adolescents from sexuality in our society. As a result, it may be unreasonable to expect youth, who are physiologically ready to engage in sexual behavior, to remain chaste while society glorifies sexuality. We must, at the very least, provide adolescents with accurate information. Once open communication is established, we can provide the details, nuances, and values that will allow them to behave responsibly.

The Alan Guttmacher Institute (1985) concluded that

> American teen-agers seem to have inherited the worst of all possible worlds regarding their exposure to messages about sex: movies, music, radio and TV tell them that sex is romantic, exciting, titillating . . . yet at the same time, young people get the message good girls should say no. Almost nothing that they see or hear about sex informs them about contraception or the importance of avoiding pregnancy. (cited in Goodman, 1985, p. A4)

C. Donovan (1990) has described how other Western societies have used sexuality education, contraception, and abortion to counteract their liberal sexual cultures and to prevent the high teenage pregnancy rates some believed were inevitable. Instead of denying that adolescents are physiologically prepared for sexual activity, that the majority are engaging in sexual activity while still in high school (Brooks-Gunn & Furstenberg, 1989), and that our culture is encouraging this behavior, it would seem more sensible to equip youth to survive the risks associated with coitus. However, even in this era of high teen pregnancy rates and fear of the AIDS epidemic, many voices are raised against such solutions. The challenge for sexuality education is how to help adolescents negotiate a safe sexual passage to adulthood in a hypocritical society.

Basic Components of Sexuality Education Programs

Once the goals of a sexuality education program are established, issues such as who will teach, what will be taught, and when and how it will be taught come to the fore. Basic components necessary to any successful educational program include qualified teachers, appropriate curriculum, and students with the cognitive and emotional capacity necessary to grasp curriculum topics. National surveys have indicated that consensus exists on these fundamental elements.

Teachers

A recent survey of sex education instructors conducted by Forrest and Silverman (1989) reported that health, physical education, home economics, and biology teachers were most likely to teach sex education because sexuality is most easily incorporated into curricula as a facet of human health, physical well-being, marital relations, or human biology. Because these teachers are generally assigned this responsibility, one would expect training in sex education instruction to be part of their requirements for certification (Forrest & Silverman, 1989; Picker, 1984); however, this is not the case. Only a few of the teachers participating in the Forrest and Silverman (1989) survey were certified sex educators, though a majority reported that they had attended formal seminars, conferences, or workshops on sexuality education during the previous year. Because the success of a sexuality education program depends on its teachers (Klein, 1983; Picker, 1984; Tatum, 1989), having training requirements would seem reasonable. Because frank discussions are crucial to successful sex education, educators must feel comfortable leading and facilitating this type of exchange. Therefore, screening of personal values may also be necessary (Kerr, Allensworth, & Gayle, 1989).

Some school systems have employed a combination of medical, psychological, and education professionals as sexuality education instructors. Many of these professionals have already been well-trained in their specialties to communicate the concepts included in sex education curricula. Regardless of whom is chosen to teach sexuality education, instructors should be informed about current health research, skilled in the principles of decision making and problem solving, sensitive to the variety of values of the families represented in their classes (Picker, 1984; Quinn, Thomas, & Smith, 1990), and able to put their own sexuality into a manageable perspective (Gordon, 1985).

Curriculum

Surveys suggest a surprising concordance in opinions regarding appropriate sex education curriculum. Seventy-seven percent of Americans believe that information about contraception should be provided to 12-year-olds, and approximately two thirds believe that information about homosexuality and abortion should be provided to these children (Kenney, Guardado, & Brown, 1989; Silverstein & Buck, 1986). Although these topics are controversial, growing awareness of the AIDS epidemic has given the public a "life-and-death" reason to teach youth about these issues. In fact, Paikoff and Brooks-Gunn (in press) report that 94% of parents desire AIDS education in the schools.

It is important to note that both males and females can benefit from sexuality education, as peer and media pressure to participate in sexual activity is directed at both sexes, and teenage pregnancy obviously is not the result of the behavior of females alone. Unfortunately, teenage pregnancy has usually been considered the problem of adolescent girls, and boys have often been overlooked by sexuality education (Hofferth &

Hayes, 1987; Select Committee, 1985b). Because gender differences have been found in sexual beliefs and attitudes, like those found in a study of "self-perceived obstacles to safer sex practices" where men chose not to suggest condom usage for fear of offending their dates and women chose not to suggest using a condom for fear they would be perceived as "loose" (G. Melton, personal communication, August 21, 1990), programs must be designed to acknowledge and accommodate these distinctions while being relevant to both sexes.

Developmental Readiness

Cognitive developmental theory holds early adolescence to be an appropriate age for sex education instruction because youths of this age have the capacity to comprehend the abstract concepts necessary for moral reasoning (Kohlberg, 1976). Thornburg (1985) has similarly posited the critical age range for sexuality education to be 11–13 years so that early adolescents' intellectual and emotional development will be synchronized with their physical readiness for engaging in sexual behaviors. Soefer, Scholl, Sobel, Tanfer, and Levy (1985) have demonstrated a strong relationship between onset of menstruation and onset of sexual activity, and resultingly deemed sex education to be requisite at menarche. Marsiglio and Mott (1986) have shown that large proportions of teenagers initiate sexual activity before they have taken a sexuality education course. Because the focus of sex education should be teaching adolescents the consequences of sexual activity before they become sexually active (Baldwin, 1983), 11 years appears to be an appropriate age for imparting sexual knowledge.

Types of Programs

The lack of federal guidelines (Select Committee, 1985a) has led to an array of sexuality education programs, but most can be categorized as either value based or secular. We use the term *secular* to indicate that these programs do not promote the values of any particular religious or moral group; however, they are not value free. Value-based programs emphasize the distinctly human experience of sexual intercourse rather than focusing on physiology. These programs address the motivation to satisfy the need for love, the valuing of this need compared to other adolescent needs, and the ramifications of sexual behavior. Secular or traditional programs (Paikoff & Brooks-Gunn, in press) also teach adolescents to consider the consequences of their behavior; however, because they attempt to do so without including the values of any particular group in the lessons, their curricula center around the reproductive aspects of sexuality, including disease communication and contraceptive technology (Richard, 1989; Strouse & Fabes, 1985). By addressing issues and/or values to help adolescents consider the consequences of sexual activity, both types of programs cultivate decision-making and problem-solving skills. The guiding presumption is that adolescents who discuss and weigh their decisions under the supervision of an instructor will be prepared to act responsibly if they are caught in "the heat of the moment."

Clearly, both value-based and secular education programs teach adolescents decision-making and problem-solving skills, human physiology, and some methods of contraception. However, because value-based programs are promoting the morals of a particular group, that group's favored opinions about teen sexuality will be fostered. For example, a pro-life organization's program may encourage abstinence as the primary method of contraception and adoption as the appropriate solution to the dilemma of unwanted pregnancy, whereas a secular program would additionally discuss birth control pills, diaphragms, and other contraceptive measures, and abortion as another alternative to adoption. By examining all possibilities, secular programs are not ignoring values but attempting to address many values. Therefore, the major distinction between these methods is the context in which sexuality is placed; value-based programs address sex from a moral viewpoint, whereas secular programs attempt to provide a full panorama of perspectives.

Value-Based Sexuality Education

Over 40 years ago recommendations were made that human sexuality should be taught in a positive context (Goffin, 1947; Kirkendall, 1984). Prior to that time, adolescents were taught that sex was bad because it caused the spread of venereal diseases and resulted in unwanted pregnancies. The end result was that adolescents were not becoming healthy sexual beings (Klein, 1983). Research has shown that creating sexual guilt does not hinder sexual activity, but does prevent contraceptive prudence (Gordon, Scales, & Everly, 1979). Thus, a central goal of value-based sexuality education today is to maintain a positive context (Cassell & Wilson, 1989; Klein, 1983) and to communicate the value of human sexual experience (Kirkendall & Libby, 1985; Klein, 1983; Mast, 1989), not to teach adolescents "the evils of sex."

Nevertheless, value-based sexuality education programs are controversial because no moral consensus exists that determines what values should be taught (Mast, 1989). Still, many people believe these programs are necessary and blame the exclusion of specific values for the failure of secular efforts (Cabaniss, 1989; Strouse & Fabes, 1985). Like Dawson's (1986) finding that females who attended church one or more times per week were significantly less likely to engage in premarital sexual activity, some research seems to support incorporating specific values (religious or other) to make programs more effective. Moreover, because American parents agree that public schools should teach values and ethical behavior (Pietig, 1984), and increasing factual knowledge alone appears to have had little effect on behavior (Kirby, 1989), value-based programs seem to have much to offer.

Among the most cited value-based programs are Human Sexuality: Values and Choices (Cabaniss, 1989; Office of Population Affairs, 1989); Me, My World, My Future (Cabaniss, 1989; Office of Population Affairs, 1989); Postponing Sexual Involvement (Howard, 1987); and Sex Respect (Respect Inc., 1988). These programs encourage delay of onset of sexual activity, abstinence from sex, improvement of communication between adolescents and their parents, and values clarification in middle and high school students.[1] Parents and sex educators are united by these programs to teach a combination of values and facts, with the hope of counteracting the onslaught of informal sexuality education that accosts American children (Strouse & Fabes, 1985; Thornburg, 1985). Each program has a unique method for communicating its specific topics and achieving its goals.

For example, the goal of Values and Choices is to teach adolescents seven values: equality, fairness, honesty, promise keeping, respect, responsibility, and self-control. It also teaches parents how to talk with their children about sex. The program is intended to foster definition of values, communication, and abstinence (Office of Population Affairs, 1989).

Commitment, marriage, and the family provide the context for the Me, My World, My Future program. The importance of the family unit is emphasized, as is the full spiritual meaning of coitus. The goals of this program include promoting mutual respect in dating relationships, increasing adolescents' self-worth, developing a respect for the power of procreation, and increasing understanding of the risks of adolescent sexual activity (Office of Population Affairs, 1989). Contemplating the risks of sexual activity simultaneously teaches the negative facets of coitus, so these value-based programs are not completely positively oriented, although they are often described that way.

Postponing Sexual Involvement (PSI) is based on the idea that adolescents' physical development has surpassed their cognitive ability to handle the consequences of that development. Nurses teach the physiological aspects of sexuality, and trained teen leaders conduct discussions with younger adolescents about the peer and social pressures associated with sexuality. PSI's major goal is to help adolescents deal with pressures to become sexually active, and thus delay initiation of coitus until they are ready (Office of Population Affairs, 1989).

Sex Respect teaches adolescents that in the spirit of true sexual freedom, they have the right to say no to premarital sex. The topics covered by this program include decision making, responsibilities of parenthood, and adoption (should pregnancy occur). The alleged aim of this program is to improve the character development and health of young people, although its curriculum topics seem directed toward preventing adolescent sexual activity and abortion (Office of Population Affairs, 1989).

Neither the benefits nor the liabilities of these value-based programs have been fully assessed, as their evaluations tend to thwart accurate appraisals of effectiveness. Evaluation of the Sex Respect program found percentile differences in pre- and postprogram attitude questionnaires to attest to its success (Respect Inc., 1988). However, these attitudinal questionnaires were given immediately after the course, thereby increasing the likelihood of students responding with the "correct" answer regardless of their true attitudes (Kirby, 1989). Although Richard (1989) has asserted that no student participants became pregnant during the 2 years that the Sex Respect program had been implemented in Lamar, Missouri, she neglected to reveal the number of students exposed to the program, whether a comparable control group experienced any pregnancies, or what the pregnancy rate was before the program began.

Similar short-term results were demonstrated in an evaluation of the Me, My World, My Future program. Immediately after the program, statistically significant gains in knowledge were noted, but there was no control group and no longitudinal follow-up (Kirby, 1989). An evaluation of the Values and Choices program has shown that after only a few months, initial increases in knowledge and in communication with parents were no longer significant (Kirby, 1989; Paikoff & Brooks-Gunn, in press).

The Postponing Sexual Involvement program has been evaluated with more sophisticated research designs and has provided more promising results. Because the program was administered in a metropolitan area where reported sexual activity rates were higher than average,[2] improvements in responsible sexual behavior may have been more sensational than if the program had been conducted with a typical sample. Pre-, mid-, and postprogram telephone interviews with the eighth-grade participants indicated a 67% reduction in girls' sexual involvement, although there were no changes for boys (Howard, 1987). Moreover, although no change in contraceptive use was found, those who did use contraceptives said it was a result of what they had learned during the program (Howard, 1987). One year later, when the students were in ninth grade, Howard and McCabe (1990) conducted an additional evaluation with a comparable control group of adolescents who used the same Atlanta hospital facilities and participated in a larger health-habits survey but were not enrolled in schools offering the PSI program. Information from hospital records and the self-report questionnaires was compared. Only 24% of the adolescents who had experienced the PSI program, compared with 36% who had not, had begun participating in sexual intercourse. Both boys and girls benefited from this program: 61% of the boys and 27% of the girls who had not had PSI, compared with 39% of the PSI boys and 17% of the PSI girls, had engaged in sexual intercourse. Of those who had onset of intercourse after PSI, the program students were more likely to have used contraceptives. Although the investigators believed the size of the sample (535) made evaluation of pregnancy prevention tenuous, they calculated that if the program girls had engaged in sex at rates similar to the non-PSI girls, the program would have reduced pregnancy rates by one third. These dramatic behavioral changes are tempered by the program's inability to influence the behavior of those who were sexually active at the start of PSI (Paikoff & Brooks-Gunn, in press) and by the possibility that the changes were not due to program influences at all, but instead were due to a Hawthorne effect or an effect of local history (Cook & Campbell, 1979).

In sum, evaluations have demonstrated some behavioral change with PSI, and unenduring changes in communication, knowledge, and attitudes with other value-based sexuality education programs similar to those reported by Kirby (1989). The importance of such short-term increases is diminished by lack of evidence that these fleeting changes have any influence on adolescents' life courses. Undoubtedly, longer term assessments are a priority for future evaluations.

Secular Sexuality Education

Secular programs attempt to provide information without religious or other specific value judgments. As with value-based programs, evaluations of secular programs have demonstrated general increases in knowledge (Hofferth & Miller, 1989) and shifts in attitudes but inconclusive results regarding behavior change (for a comprehensive review of secular programs, see Kirby, 1984). These programs have also been plagued by methodological problems such as lack of control groups and exclusive use of questionnaire data (Kilmann, Wanlass, Sabalis, & Sullivan, 1981).

Rudimentary descriptions of three programs and their evaluations are furnished below to provide an illustration of secular sexuality education. The Youth and Sexuality Modules program was designed to change knowledge and attitudes about sexuality and is representative of basic secular sex education (Parcel, Luttmann, & Flaherty-Zonis, 1985). Class lessons by trained teachers addressed topics such as decision making, sex roles, contraception, and responsibility for sexual behavior. Parcel et al. (1985) evaluated the program, via questionnaires to 114 ethnically diverse eighth-grade students, and found a significant ($p < .01$) change in knowledge, but not a significant change in attitudes.

Parcel and Luttmann (1981) also evaluated the Sex Education Course for Young Adolescents, which was intended to help eighth graders feel comfortable with their sexuality. The program objectives were to increase knowledge of sexual development, decrease sexual guilt, decrease worry over sexual issues, and increase acceptance of masturbation. Pre- and postcourse questionnaires were given to 100 students who were categorized into three groups: regular attenders, irregular attenders, and nonattenders. The regular attenders demonstrated a significant ($p < .004$) increase in knowledge and an average increase of 21% in approval of masturbation. There were no significant changes in guilt or worry over sexual concerns.

STD: A Guide for Today's Young Adults (Yarber, 1985) is a secondary school curriculum promoted by the Centers for Disease Control (CDC) in Atlanta because it emphasizes attitudes and behavior to prevent the spread of sexually transmitted diseases (STDs). Yarber's (1988) evaluation compared two types of basic secular programs to this STD awareness program. More than 1,000 male and female students in Grades 7–12 from different subcultures participated. Results indicated that the awareness program was effective in changing knowledge and attitudes about STDs in almost all groups.

All of these investigations evaluated only short-term effects; measures were usually taken immediately after the last class. None examined change in behavior, although change in behavioral intention was measured. To assess this variable, adolescents were asked what they believed they would do in a given situation. However, as previously noted with assessments of value-based programs, in these situations teens will probably provide what they believe is the "right" answer rather than what they may truly believe their behavior would be (Kirby, 1989). Proof of actual behavioral intentions, such as hospital records of contraceptive counseling, would provide stronger evidence. Health records of pregnancy or STD infection could also provide confirmatory evidence of program effectiveness and should be used in future evaluations. Given the shortcomings of these programs' assessments, it is difficult to make any judgment regarding their potential value to adolescents' futures.

Paikoff and Brooks-Gunn (in press) attribute traditional sex education programs' failures to demonstrate behavior change to "the sparseness of the offerings" rather than to the inadequacies of the evaluations. Although these investigators report that the majority of high school students have taken a sexuality education course, they also note that less than 10% of the urban school districts surveyed by Sonenstein and Pittman (1984) provided sessions on contraceptives and how to obtain them prior to the ninth grade, and only 20% had such sessions prior to the end of high school. Thus, they believe that the lack of intensive and extensive programs restricts the degree of behavioral change that might be observed. Kirby (1980) similarly contended that high school classes are likely to have limited impact, as they "are typically conservative, cover a limited set of topics and discourage students from becoming sexually active" (p. 560).

School-Based Clinics

Although both standard secular and value-based sexuality programs have demonstrated few solid successes in behavioral change to date, school-based health clinics appear to offer some real hope. Research that revealed that adolescent pregnancy in other developed countries was reduced by the availability of effective contraception influenced the development of school-based clinics in the United States (Trussell, 1988). Other research has indicated that adolescents who receive specific contraceptive information from a trusted source (such as a parent or medical professional) are more likely to use contraceptives (Furstenberg, 1976; Kastner, 1979; Rosoff, 1989), and, equally important for many parents, such teaching does not increase adolescents' sexual activity (Kastner, 1979; Paikoff & Brooks-Gunn, in press; Rosoff, 1989). These findings suggest that clinics may be a viable vehicle for the provision of adolescent contraceptive technology.

As of 1988, there were 138 school-based health clinics in the United States, with 65 more in development (Dryfoos, 1988). Most clinics are individually operated, and about 85% are located within school buildings (Dryfoos, 1988). All school-based clinics provide physical examinations, treatment for illness and accident, and counseling for personal problems, but only some dispense contraceptives (21%), provide gynecological examinations (48%), or offer family planning counseling (31%) (Dryfoos, 1988).

Although few comprehensive evaluations of the effectiveness of these clinics are available (Dryfoos, 1988; Kenney, 1986), positive results have occasionally been presented. Using census data, Ralph and Edgington (1983) evaluated the impact of the West Dallas Youth Clinic (WDYC) on inhibiting teenage fertility. When adjusted for age and race, comparisons of the live birth rate 4 years after the intervention showed the WDYC group to have had significantly fewer births per 1,000 students than a matched nonprogram group (58 births vs. 112, respectively). In Houston, Kansas City, Baltimore, and St. Paul, students who used school-based clinics were significantly more likely to use contraceptives than nonattenders (Dryfoos, 1988). The St. Paul program also achieved a 56% decline in birth rates over a 3-year period (Dryfoos, 1988; Kenney, 1986; Kirby, 1980). These data imply that the dissemination of sexual information and technology in school-related clinics may be an effective means of reducing the number of teenage pregnancies.

The Baltimore Pregnancy Prevention Program for Urban Teenagers, an innovative clinic prototype, provides strong evidence that teenagers will request information about sexuality and contraceptives if it is made available from a trusted source. Zabin, Hirsch, Smith, Streett, and Hardy's (1986) evaluation of this program demonstrates significant changes in knowledge *and* behavior for the 1,033 female and 667 male lower-class, inner-city junior and senior high school participants. This combination school and clinic program used the following procedures. Twice each semester, a social worker (or a nurse) gave a full class presentation to every homeroom in each of the participating schools. These presentations were aimed at raising students' awareness of the consequences of unprotected sexual intercourse and their right to accurate information. Although the classroom provided a setting where over 7,000 students were actively contacted, almost 14,000 voluntary student contacts occurred in group discussions that took place in the school health suites during the 2½ hours that the educators were made available each day (Zabin et al., 1988). After-school health services were available to the students from a nearby storefront clinic. At this clinic, individual counseling, medical visits, and casual discussion took place. Condoms and contraceptive foam were dispensed during individual counseling sessions. Females could receive comprehensive gynecological examinations by medical staff and obtain contraceptive devices (Zabin et al., 1988).

The evaluation of this school-based clinic used control schools, with students of similar socioeconomic status, to establish a baseline for comparison. Self-report questionnaires were administered before, during, and after the 2½-year program to assess changes in knowledge, attitude, and behavior (Zabin et al., 1986). Only students in the program schools significantly increased their knowledge of effectiveness of contraceptive methods, pregnancy risk, and fertile period of the menstrual cycle. The number of female program participants who believed the ideal age for childbearing was lower than the ideal age for marriage declined, as did their overall support for adolescent childbearing.

Changes in sexual behavior appeared substantial. Females in the program postponed onset of sexual activity 7 months longer than a group of students from their own school before the program was implemented. (No data were presented comparing rates to the students in the control schools). Although family planning clinics had been located in the community for some time, program participants were significantly more likely to have used clinic services after the implementation of the program as opposed to 1 year before, whereas no consistent changes occurred in the control groups. A higher percentage of virgins visited the health clinic, and a higher usage of contraceptive techniques was reported for program participants compared with the control group. Most important, after 28 months of the program, pregnancy rates declined over 30% compared to increases in the control schools of over 57%. The comparative increase in the control school rates may reflect a general developmental trend, whereas the interaction of treatment and time implies that the program caused the decline in pregnancy rates. These results are extremely positive and warrant further evaluations of school-based clinics.

Zabin and Hirsch (1988) have suggested that many versions of school-based clinics are possible. For example, clinics may be contained within the school health facility or at adjunct locations such as hospitals. Alternate service organizations, such as abuse prevention centers and athletic leagues, may provide an appropriate location from which to reach adolescents. Whenever clinics are founded, they should provide free, quality services and foster open communication to most effectively encourage preventive behavior (Zabin et al., 1986).

AIDS Education

As of December 1989, almost 2,500 youths (1,643 under 5 years and 813 between 5 and 19 years) had been reported to the CDC as having AIDS (Kerr, 1990), making AIDS the most important impetus for sexuality education today. Public awareness of the epidemic's profound implications has purportedly led to more funding and more attention for sexuality education (Kenney et al., 1989). However, this campaign has also had the paradoxical effect of hindering the development of general sexuality education (Kenney, 1989; Kenney et al., 1989), which is rarely taught independently from AIDS education (Kenney et al., 1989; Quinn et al., 1990). The influx of federal funds to support AIDS education has caused many programs to redirect their goals toward increasing knowledge of AIDS and other STDs (Rosoff, 1989) and changing behaviors linked with acquisition of these diseases (Kasun, 1989), while reducing coverage of sexual decision making and birth control. The Forrest and Silverman (1989) survey indicated that over 90% of sex education teachers covered the topic of AIDS, whereas only an average of 70% said they taught the more general topic of "safe sex."

A recent U.S. Government Accounting Office (GAO) (Nadel, 1990) report showed that although the CDC spends approximately $44 million on AIDS education programs for young people and recommends that all grade levels receive it, only 5% of the sampled school districts actually had such a sequence of programs (Nadel, 1990). The newly designed AIDS curricula may be limited because they provoke community opposition by addressing concepts far more controversial than those ventured by earlier sexuality education efforts. Abstinence is still promoted as a primary means of preventing human immunodeficiency virus (HIV) infection, but curriculum guides also address what AIDS is, how it is transmitted, and how it can be prevented (Kenney, 1989). These topics may appear innocuous, but lessons regarding transmission can easily lead to discussions of oral and anal sex, and prevention lessons will probably include instruction in proper condom use. Most schools provide AIDS education in the 9th and 10th grades, with less coverage in the upper grades. Given the rapid increase in rates of sexual activity as young people become older (Forrest & Silverman, 1989), programs should exist throughout the middle to high school years. Another deficiency is that 66% of AIDS education teachers receive less than the recommended 12 hours of training.

Assessment of AIDS education programs is necessary to ascertain their actual potential for increasing knowledge of AIDS etiology and prevention. Although the CDC recommends that evaluations be conducted by the programs it funds, over 80% of its programs have not even administered questionnaires to students about their knowledge, beliefs, and/or behaviors (Nadel, 1990). Program directors have blamed this lack of evaluation on inadequate staffing and on restrictions to collecting information regarding students' sexual and drug usage activities (Nadel, 1990). These restrictions must be lifted in order to collect the data required for monitoring present programs and for guiding future programs.

A Final Word About Sexuality Education Programs

It is important that every American child have a basic knowledge of the consequences of sexual activity. The Sex Information and Education Council of the United States (SIECUS, 1984) recently stated that "sex education is a basic right of all children in America" (p. 14). Although over 80% of all high school students are reportedly receiving sexuality education (Paikoff & Brooks-Gunn, in press), there is little evidence of effectiveness. The social problems that generated the need for such programs still exist. The serious implications that accompany lack of sexual knowledge make it imperative that we refine our efforts at developing and implementing effective sexuality education programs. P. Donovan (1989) has asserted that sex education curriculum guidelines may provide the necessary direction to attain effective programming. Because there appears to be some consensus, national guidelines to address who is qualified to teach sex education, what concepts should be taught, and when sexuality education should occur are conceivable. Coordination among sex education efforts may be attained by allowing states and localities sufficient latitude to design specific methods of sexuality education to satisfy community differences. We recognize the need to allow communities their choice of approach. However, because open communication about and provision of contraceptives has proven effective in the United

States and abroad, we also recognize the opportunity to resolve the crisis of teen pregnancy and encourage states to choose to win the battle.

CHILD SEXUAL ABUSE PREVENTION PROGRAMS

The widespread documented incidence of child sexual abuse (Finkelhor, 1979; Russell, 1984; Wyatt, 1985), especially the disturbing data that indicate that 25% to 30% of all sexually abused children are under the age of 7 (Finkelhor, 1986; Nibert, Cooper, Ford, Fitch, & Robinson, 1989), and numerous clinical reports of harm to victims (Haugaard & Reppucci, 1988) have highlighted the pressing need for effective prevention programs. To date, the vast majority of programs have focused on empowering children by teaching them concepts and actions for understanding and repelling sexual abuse. The goal is laudatory; however, it may be inappropriate (Melton, in press) in that most children exposed to these programs have been under the age of 10 years. Yet this goal is so prevalent that Leventhal (1987) has called it "the ultimate goal of any program to prevent [child] sexual abuse" (p. 169). In response, Melton (in press) has argued that "the ultimate focus on the behavior of potential victims is unjust, besides being of dubious efficacy."

In this section, we do not mean to be unduly critical regarding efforts to empower young children to become able to recognize and cope with the dangers of sexual abuse. However, we do feel that it is appropriate to question this relatively exclusive focus, which may be placing an inappropriate burden on these children's shoulders; to emphasize that children's developmental capacities must be considered; and to encourage more rigorous evaluations of both positive and negative effects. Moreover, by questioning these efforts, we do not denigrate them. They are important first steps toward the goal of preventing child sexual abuse, and several of them have shown much promise. Nevertheless, our current state of knowledge regarding the best paths toward prevention requires a questioning stance, so that we do not become complacent because we want to believe that we have found an effective solution. Advocates of current approaches must recognize that only by questioning these interventions can we sharpen them and develop new and more effective ones. As children grow to maturity, they experience various ecological contexts (Bronfenbrenner, 1979), including family, school, peer groups, neighborhood, and society as a whole; each influences them and may be the appropriate context for intervention. It is crucial that educators and researchers be open to these contexts as foci for intervention and be supportive of rigorous evaluation.

The Complexity of Sexual Abuse Prevention

Reppucci and Haugaard (1989) emphasized that the process a child must go through either to repel an abusive approach or to report an occurrence of abuse is very complex. In order to repel or report abuse, a child must recognize that he or she is in an abusive situation. Then the child must believe that he or she can and should take some sort of action. Finally, the child must possess and use specific self-protective skills. However, many existing prevention programs seem to be based on the simplistic idea that they can teach children enough information during one or two presentations to enable them both to understand the issues and to protect themselves.

Programs must first inform a child about what sexual abuse is. Most prevention programs have dealt with this definitional issue by trying to teach the concept of good, bad, and confusing touches, even though younger children are very poor at making fine distinctions between such abstract entities (Haugaard & Reppucci, 1988). Moreover, although most adults may agree that certain acts always entail sexual abuse (e.g., a parent having intercourse with a child), considerable disagreement exists about other acts (e.g., whether a 7-year-old girl is experiencing sexual abuse from her father who cleans her genitals each night when he gives her a bath, or whether a 10-year-old is experiencing sexual abuse from his mother when she kisses him on the lips each morning as she leaves for work). Thus, even adults are not clear about what is and is not sexual abuse.

Assuming that a child is able to label a certain experience as sexual abuse, the child must then feel that she or he should report or repel it. Many programs attempt to teach children that they do not have to allow other people to touch them (under most circumstances), and that they have the right to say no to anyone who tries to touch them in an unacceptable fashion. However, children at different cognitive levels often find it difficult to decide when an action should or should not be taken. For example, young children are much better at following broad and general rules, such as "Do not let anyone touch you or your private parts," than they are at following rules that require making distinctions, such as "Doctors or nurses can touch your private parts, and your parents can touch you if they are helping you clean yourself of if you are hurt there, but no one, not even your parents, can touch you there at other times." Such rules may be incomprehensible to many children, who may simplify them so that anyone who is caring for them can touch them in certain places, or no one can touch them or make them do anything they do not want to do.

If a child comprehends that a certain act is sexual abuse and knows that he or she should do something to stop it, then the child must feel empowered to implement a plan of action. Many prevention programs teach that the child should tell a parent or other adult and keep telling adults until someone believes the child. Although this may appear to be a good general approach, it is doubtful whether it gives the child enough information to plan and implement the reporting or repelling. It also does not take into account that a child may be fearful of telling because of threatened or real punishments that might occur. Most adults have been in situations where they know that something should be done, but if they are unprepared or afraid, they prefer to do nothing in order to avoid a wrong or ineffective action. Why then do prevention educators think that children, who usually are not as cognitively or as emotionally competent or as powerful as adults, will be able to engage in these complex behaviors in an emotionally delicate and sometimes frightening situation?

With these developmental issues in mind, we turn to an overview of existing programs.

Programs for School Children

Although a few programs to prevent child sexual abuse have been designed for use with junior and senior high school students, most are for use with preschool and elementary school children. Two very different goals are usually emphasized: (a) *primary prevention* (keeping the abuse from ever occurring) and (b) *detection* (encouraging disclosure of past and ongoing sexual abuse so that children can receive intervention and protection). Programs vary in content, length, format, and instructor.

Content

Programs for children generally address the following topics: educating children about what sexual abuse is; broadening their awareness of possible abusers to include people they know and like; teaching that each child has the right to control access to his or her body; describing a variety of "touches" that a child can experience; stressing actions that the child can take in a potentially abusive situation, such as saying no or leaving or running away; teaching that some secrets should not be kept and that a child is never at fault for sexual abuse; and stressing that the child should tell a trusted adult if touched in an inappropriate manner until something is done to protect the child (Conte, 1988; Conte, Rosen, & Saperstein, 1984; Finkelhor, 1986; Hazzard, Webb, & Kleemeier, 1988).

Finkelhor (1986) reports that there is a general effort to skirt the emotionally charged topic of sexuality in prevention programs. Therefore, child sexual abuse prevention is usually approached from a protective, rather than sexual, standpoint. The concepts of good and bad touching are frequently approached through discussions of bullies or relatives who forcefully try to kiss a child. More intimate or long-term types of sexual abuse and specific discussions of molestation by parents tend to be ignored, as is the information that some "bad" touches can actually feel good. By avoiding these controversial issues, prevention educators claim that they increase the number of schools willing to accept the programs. Unfortunately, by avoiding sexuality, young children may get the message that sexuality is largely secretive and negative.

Length

Some prevention programs involve only one presentation, whereas others involve more than 30 short sessions (Committee for Children, 1983). If primary prevention is the major goal, then more sessions may be required than if the major goal is case identification, because some abused children will identify themselves after even brief prevention efforts (e.g., several children in Seattle identified themselves after viewing a 30-second public service announcement on television).

Format

Prevention educators generally agree that the various formats should be entertaining, of high interest, and nonthreatening (Koblinsky & Behana, 1984). Slide presentations, movies, videotapes, plays, discussions, and role-play situations, as well as printed materials such as pamphlets, coloring books, or comic books, are used. Unfortunately, most of these materials are being widely distributed without any validation. This latter fact is important because a largely unskeptical public, sensitized by the massive publicity, has turned to these commercially available materials in order to protect their children. Questions about the accuracy of the information presented or the demonstrated efficacy of these materials in preventing abuse are rarely asked. In 1987, Shore reviewed nine books to prevent child abuse and found that despite endorsements and expert consultations, all of the materials contained some inaccurate information. Recently, Roberts, Alexander, and Fanurik (1990) surveyed authors and publishers about the development of their commercially available child sexual abuse prevention materials that were being marketed and distributed nationwide. Of the 33 questionnaires returned (36.7%), 12 respondents reported no evaluation of any sort before distribution; 19 reported informal evaluation that entailed having the materials presented to or read by a panel of professional experts or groups of children for their feedback on quality and context; and 2 indicated formal evaluation that used some aspects of accepted research methodology. Even less evaluation was reported following dissemination of the material: 27 reported no evaluation of any sort, 2 reported informal evaluation, and 4 reported some type of formal evaluation. These findings suggest that most of the sexual abuse prevention materials currently being used are of unknown efficacy.

Instructors

The instructors of the programs also vary. Some, such as teachers, are chosen because of their familiarity with the children. Others are specially trained volunteers or mental health professionals who have expertise in the field. Still others, like police officers, are authority figures who have the children's respect. Because most programs take place through the schools, they attempt to make use of teachers because of their ongoing contact with the children, their increased likelihood of being able to deal with a sensitive topic in their classrooms, and their role in identifying and supporting abused children. In addition, teachers are considered potentially ideal discussion leaders even though they are seldom extensively trained for this role (Trudell & Whatley, 1988).

Parent Programs

Although many programs have tried to involve parents, participation rates have been disappointing (Berrick, 1988), and few parent programs have been evaluated (Miller-Perrin & Wurtele, 1988; Reppucci & Haugaard, 1989). One possible reason for low participation is that many parents have a very difficult time talking with children about any sexual topics. Finkelhor (1984) reported survey results indicating that most parents tend to think of their own children as well supervised and able to avoid danger, and they do not want to frighten them unnecessarily. Moreover, those parents who are likely to attend the usual special educational programs tend to be better informed and more likely to discuss these issues with their children anyway (Porch & Petretic-Jackson, 1986). In addition, Berrick (1988) reported that only 39 of 116 parents whose children were participating in prevention programs even attended required parent education meetings, and those who did learned very little.

Reppucci and Haugaard (1989) concluded that in order to reach more parents, educators should try providing programs through places of employment or through community service clubs, such as Kiwanis or the Lions Club. Berrick (1988) not only stressed the potential of in-service training in the workplace, but also suggested the importance of using the mass media to provide information. Such innovations might also reach more men, the major perpetrators and the parent least likely to attend a typical evening session held in schools, churches, or other community centers. One immediate benefit might be to discourage men from becoming abusers, if they believe that children might be more likely to tell someone of an approach (Finkelhor, 1986). Another benefit might be removing the burden from children of being responsible for preventing their own sexual exploitation.

Finally, preventive interventions for school children and their parents have much appeal because of their potential to reach large numbers of children in a relatively cost-efficient fashion and to reduce the number of children affected by sexual abuse. However, as with sexuality education, having positive goals is not enough; effectiveness of intervention is critical. Yet most programs appear to be implemented and continued on the strength of their positive goals rather than on a systematic evaluation of their effectiveness.

Outcome Research for Day-Care and School-Based Prevention Programs

Although several school-based prevention programs have investigated the effectiveness with which children learned the material presented, hundreds have not attempted even this minimal degree of evaluation. We first present a summary of the overall findings of the evaluated programs and then provide a more detailed discussion of a few of the best evaluated studies.

As a whole, the various evaluations provide some limited support for the efficacy of sexual abuse prevention programs (Reppucci & Haugaard, 1989). The most common and consistent finding is a statistically significant, yet often slight (e.g., a 2-point gain on a 20-item questionnaire), increase in knowledge about sexual abuse following a prevention program (Conte, Rosen, Saperstein, & Shermack, 1985; Harvey, Forehand, Brown, & Holmes, 1988; Ray & Dietzel, 1984; Saslawsky & Wurtele, 1986). However, as Leventhal (1987) has pointed out, there is little "evidence that such a change is linked to changes in behavior" (p. 169). In several studies, many children answered a high percentage of the questions accurately even before they participated in the program (Ray & Dietzel, 1984; Swan, Press, & Briggs, 1985), which would suggest that either children know more than prevention educators think they do or that better assessment instruments are needed in order to demonstrate the value of the programs from a cost-benefit perspective. For example, children may have learned more than has been revealed because of possible ceiling effects on limited-item questionnaires that have often been used for evaluation (Conte, 1984; Hazzard & Angert, 1986; Kleemeier & Webb, 1986; Reppucci & Haugaard, 1989).

In the few studies that examined differences between school-aged and preschool children, the younger children learned less (Borkin & Frank, 1986; Conte et al., 1985), which raises the question of whether programs that are useful for school-aged children are appropriate for younger children. Review sessions increased retention of knowledge for all but the youngest age groups (Plummer, 1984; Ray & Dietzel, 1984). Such sessions seem essential because, without them, durability of learning was so weak that any long-term value of the prevention programs was questionable

(Plummer, 1984). Of special concern is Plummer's finding in an 8-month follow-up of 69 fifth-grade students that although the majority of concepts were retained, three crucial concepts in any prevention program (i.e., questions about breaking promises, whether molesters were often people whom the child knew, and who was to blame if the child was touched in a sexual way) were answered incorrectly significantly more often than immediately after the program was completed. Thus, Finkelhor and Strapko's (in press) conclusion that "the overwhelming and irrefutable message of the evaluation studies is that children do indeed learn the concepts they are being taught" must be accepted with caution.

Finally, most of the evaluations had basic design problems. Although a few did use nontreatment control groups (Harvey et al., 1988; Saslawsky & Wurtele, 1986; Wolfe, MacPherson, Blount, & Wolfe, 1986; Wurtele, Kast, Miller-Perrin, & Kondrick, 1989), matched for such variables as age, gender, and socioeconomic status, and a repeated measures design, most did not. Therefore, there is no way to determine whether the programs caused any changes that might have occurred. Other design flaws included small sample sizes, lack of attention to the reliability and validity of the measuring instruments, no pretesting to establish a baseline of knowledge, and short-term follow-up assessments, usually less than 2 months. Clearly, more sophisticated research designs are necessary in order to make any claims regarding the overall positive impact of most currently used interventions.

We now turn to the most extensive study to date of the impact of sexual abuse prevention programs on preschool children, and follow this with a description of a very promising program based on children's active role playing.

The Berkeley Family Welfare Research Group (Daro, 1988; Daro, Duerr, & LeProhn, 1987, Gilbert, Daro, Duerr, LeProhn, & Nyman, 1988) evaluated seven representative curricula for preschool children (Child Assault Prevention; Children's Self-Help; Talking About Touching; Touch Safety; Child Abuse Prevention, Intervention and Education; the Youth Safety Awareness Project; and SAFE—Stop Abuse through Family Education). These programs ranged in duration from a single 15- to 30-minute session to twenty-one 15- to 20-minute sessions over a 3- to 6-week period. Parent meetings lasting 1 to 2 hours were an integral part of each curriculum, and may have contributed to two thirds of the parents discussing some of the concepts with their children following the presentation.

A few findings stand out. Children were more likely to interpret pictures of frequently encountered interactions such as tickling and bathing as evoking a negative affect after participation in prevention training. Furthermore, they appeared unable to comprehend the concept of a mixed-up or confusing touch. Although some children seemed to have a rudimentary grasp of the concept that there is a connection between the physical act of being touched and the emotion that it generates, even at posttest half of the children could not provide an explanation for why they selected a particular affect in response to the pictures they were shown. Given the central importance of this connection as a building block for the prevention programs, it is questionable whether it is expecting too much for children to understand the subtle nuances and emotions described and elicited either during the prevention program or in a case of actual abuse if they cannot explain their own response. Children also found it difficult to distinguish how touches or feelings about touches can change and to differentiate between types of secrets. Even the issue of "stranger danger," one of the least ambiguous ideas presented, was not internalized well enough by many children so that they could apply these teachings. In summary, this investigation clearly raises questions regarding the developmental readiness of preschoolers to comprehend the concepts being taught in prevention programs.

It should be noted that a few studies have found more positive results for preschool children (e.g., Harvey et al., 1988; Nibert et al., 1989), but these interventions have entailed a more active involvement on the part of the child participants than has typically been the case. Although Nibert et al. (1989) specifically contrasted their findings with those of Gilbert et al. (1988), claiming that 3- to 5-year-old children have the ability to recognize and recommend basic prevention strategies in program-specific situations, they tended to disregard or rationalize that they (a) found no statistically significant differences between the intervention group and a control group, (b) had a serious problem with their testing instrument, (c) used a "behavioral" response that consisted of children selecting an illustrated card showing the correct action response (hardly a response that most investigators would claim is behavioral), and (d) collected their postmeasurement within 1 week of the intervention.

Two recent studies by Kraizer and her colleagues (Fryer, Kraizer, & Miyoski, 1987a, 1987b; Kraizer, Witte, & Fryer, 1989) deserve special attention because of their behavioral assessment techniques and their optimistic results. In the first, Fryer et al. (1987a, 1987b) used role-playing techniques to reduce susceptibility to stranger abduction. The program consisted of eight daily 20-minute sessions in which children were taught four concrete rules to follow when approached by a stranger and not accompanied by a caretaking adult. An experimental group of 23 kindergarten, first-grade, and second-grade students participated in the program initially; 21 nonparticipating children from the same grades formed the control group and were given the program later. On the day before the program began and on the day after it ended, each child was sent on an errand by his or her teacher and met one of the reseachers (a stranger), who asked the child to accompany him to his car to help him carry something into the school (an actual *in vivo* abduction situation). The researchers took extraordinary care before, during, and after the program to inform parents and to protect children from any anxiety possibly associated with meeting the stranger.

Before the program, about half of the children in each group agreed to accompany the stranger. Following the program, only 22% of the participating group agreed to go, whereas there was no change in the control group. Six months later, the four participating children who had failed the posttest and the children in the control group were given the training program. Children from all groups were then involved in a similar *in vivo* abduction situation. All of the participating children who had passed the original posttest, all of the control children, and two of the four "retrained" children resisted the abduction situation. This testing demonstrated that almost all of the children had developed and maintained the ability to avoid this type of stranger abduction.

Several lessons are suggested by the success of this program. First, teaching specific concrete rules and steps to follow may be easier for young children to comprehend than the less distinct "good touch/bad touch" idea. Second, using role-playing techniques rather than the typical passive observing or reading techniques may be critical, as other recent research (Harvey et al., 1988; Wurtele, Marrs, & Miller-Perrin, 1987) has also stressed the importance of children's active participation, especially behavioral rehearsal (Melton, in press). Third, the pretesting and posttesting situations may have served to establish and then reinforce the skills taught by the program because none of the control students, each of whom had been susceptible to the stranger's tactics twice before the program, agreed to accompany the stranger after the program. Perhaps when taught these skills, children are able to assimilate their own experiences, thereby increasing their retention of and their ability to transfer them to real life situations. Fourth, a few children were less able to learn the skills, which highlights the need to tailor prevention programs to children's abilities. Fifth, a behavioral assessment such as the *in vivo* abduction situation is the best means of estimating the strength of the behaviors being taught and should be pursued whenever appropriate. Lastly, a word of caution is in order. Although the results of this investigation suggest that stranger avoidance in particular situations may be taught, no evidence exists that the skills taught to children will generalize to other, more complex situations. In fact, Melton (in press) has argued that because "perpetrators commonly used sophisticated techniques of persuasion and social reinforcement (Wolf, Berlinger, Conte & Smith, 1987), little reason exists to believe that training in stranger avoidance would significantly diminish children's vulnerability."

In a second investigation, Kraizer et al. (1989) measured the behavioral skills associated with prevention of victimization before and after children ages 3 through 10 had participated in the Safe Child Personal Safety Training Program. This standardized scripted videotape curriculum provides training for parents and teachers as well as for children in five age-appropriate segments. It teaches basic concepts and role-playing techniques and then develops mastery of skills through role playing and discussion in the classroom. The program teaches assertiveness, decision making, and communication by interweaving these life skills throughout the curriculum, which emphasizes prevention of sexual, physical, and emotional abuse by persons known and unknown to the child.

Program evaluation was completed with 670 children from rural, suburban, and urban schools in three states. Both participants and matched control children were pre- and posttested. Behavioral change attributable to the program was measured by simulation and role play, and these results were correlated with measures of knowledge and self-esteem in order to assess a child's ability to successfully resist victimization.

Kraizer and her colleagues argue that the scripted role play used to measure behavior change is the most critical element. This role play measures the child's ability and willingness to terminate unwanted touch effectively and appropriately in the face of flattery, emotional coercion, rejection, bribery, and secrecy, all behaviors that research has shown to be used by sexual offenders (Conte, Wolf, & Smith, 1989). They explain that each child was asked to help the examiner "learn a little bit more about what you know." The children became rapidly involved and responded as if the role-playing situation was real. For example, children who had been very willing to say no when the examiner had been playing with their hair or pinching their cheek suddenly gave in and agreed to a hug when the examiner acted as if her feelings had been hurt. During the pretests, few children rebuffed the examiner in the role play when the examiner suggested that she might not be the child's friend anymore if the child would not remain close to her. Scoring of this assessment was based on the child's body language and verbal response.

The most important finding was that children who had gone through this program demonstrated skills associated with the reduction of risk for child abuse, and all children, including preschoolers, were able to learn these skills. Moreover, although many of these children had previously participated in more typical child abuse prevention programs, there were no skill differences revealed by the pretesting between these children and the others who had not been in such programs. Upon completion of the postprogram role play, children were asked whether anything in the program had made them feel uncomfortable or afraid. Only 4.5% of the children reported any anxiety or fear, and in only two cases was the anxiety attributable to the program. In both of these cases, the children were put at ease by clarifying a misunderstanding. Kraizer et al. (1989) concluded that prevention training can be effective without introducing specific information about sexual abuse, perpetrators, or physical resistance training, all issues that may have negative side effects. Children do not have to learn distinctions that may be beyond their developmental capacities; rather, they can learn to say no to any touch that makes them uneasy and to tell about any time someone continues to touch them in a way that makes them uncomfortable. In summary, this study suggests that prevention education (a) should be experientially based, (b) can begin in the preschool years, (c) does not work for all children (about 10% of the children did not seem to benefit from the program), and (d) should have an evaluation component.

Untested Assumptions

Most child sexual abuse prevention programs are developed from anecdotal clinical information (Conte, 1984) and are based on several untested assumptions (Reppucci, 1987), including the assumption that we know what types of skills will make a child less susceptible to sexual abuse. However, sexual abuse comes in many different forms (Haugaard & Reppucci, 1988). Skills useful for preventing one type of abuse might not be useful for preventing another very different type, and some skills may be useful for children of one age but not for children of another. Clarity as to the specific skills and behaviors that prevention programs should teach is needed in order to allow researchers to develop means of measuring their acquisition. Kraizer et al.'s (1989) program, which is based on what actually happens in abusive situations as found in recent research with adult abusers who have discussed the techniques that they used to engage their victims, is a step in the right direction. However, *in vivo* assessment situations are very difficult to construct because of various ethical problems, not the least of which is that subjecting children to actual sexual abuse situations in order to assess what prevention behaviors they exhibit is not acceptable.

Another critical assumption is that children will be able to transfer the knowledge gained from prevention programs into effective action when needed; yet, no empirical evidence of such transfer exists. Recently, a psychologist from the Cornell Medical Center informed us of a case in which more than 100 upper-middle-class children, ages 7 to 9 years, all of whom had been exposed to a good touch/bad touch type of prevention program, had been sexually abused by a computer teacher. Yet none of these children ever told anyone because the teacher had threatened to harm them or their parents.

A third assumption is that prevention programs have no negative effects, or that possible negative effects are so minor that they are insignificant when compared to the positive effects. However, no evidence exists about whether programs concerning the incorrectness of some forms of touching will adversely affect children in the long run (e.g., in their comfort with nonsexual physical contact with their parents and others, and/or exploratory sexual play with peers). Although a few investigators (Binder & McNiel, 1987; Hazzard et al., 1988; Miltenberger & Thiesse-Duffy, 1988; Wurtele, 1988; Wurtele & Miller-Perrin, 1987) have found no evidence of increases in fears or other anxieties among children who were participants in prevention programs, others (Daro, 1988; Gilbert et al., 1988; Kleemeier & Webb, 1986; Swan et al., 1985; Wurtele, 1988; Wurtele et al., 1989) have found evidence that at least some small proportion, usually about 5% to 10%, may suffer from nightmares, upset stomachs, or other anxieties after being exposed to these programs. Although Kleemeier and Webb (1986) summarized their results as showing "few negative reactions," the parents of the children studied reported that more than 33% of the children displayed negative emotional reactions such as anxiety and irritability and that 20% exhibited negative behavioral responses. In addition, Garbarino (1987) found that an average of 33% of children who had read the *Spiderman* comic book about sexual abuse prevention without any accompanying training by adults reported that they felt scared or worried. Although this study did not use an appropriate control group of children who read a *Spiderman* comic on another topic and is not representative of prevention programs conducted by professional educators, the high percentage of children reporting being worried or scared cannot be ignored. Moreover, anecdotal evidence suggests temporary negative reactions for some children. For example, some preschool children have been afraid to ride home from school with anyone but their parents (Conte, 1988), whereas others have interpreted the message that a child has the right to say no as being applicable to all realms of their lives (Haugaard & Reppucci, 1988). Finally, neither the evaluation studies nor the anecdotes measured or provided insight into any long-term or subtle effects. Although it is likely that only a few children are adversely affected in any way, the risk of possible negative consequences, such as increased fearfulness or disruption of children's understanding of their world, warrants further investigation.

The crux of the matter is whether any of the programs have actually achieved either of their major goals—primary prevention or detection. Although many well-meaning professionals and parents want to believe that the programs effectively prevent child sexual abuse, no evidence exists, not even a published case example, that primary prevention has ever been achieved. Again, although some professionals suggest that these programs may act as a deterrent to potential abusers, who may be less likely to engage in abusive behaviors because of fear of detection, no evidence exists to support this claim. Finally, if primary prevention is the major goal, then it may be more productive to develop prevention programs that are specifically geared to helping parents and other adults restrain from engaging in abusive sexual behaviors, rather than putting the onus for prevention on young children.

In contrast to primary prevention, some reported instances of successful detection do exist (Finkelhor & Strapko, in press; Hazzard et al., 1988). Individual cases of ongoing or past abuse have been discovered as a result of these interventions, and are often cited as justification for the programs. In fact, Finkelhor and Strapko (in press), without presenting data, claim that the "most important unambiguous finding" is that "prevention education encourages children to report abuse they have already suffered." However, detection is not prevention, and if detection is the main justification, then family privacy may be being unjustly invaded (Goldstein, Freud, & Solnit, 1979). Furthermore, we do not know what the impact of either a valid or false disclosure is on the child or on his or her family. Moreover, the prospect of making the schools *de facto* into law enforcement agencies is troubling (see Melton, in press). Yet, this is exactly what is happening if more arrests or child protection investigations are the major effects of these programs.

On some sort of ethical balancing scale, the judgment that must be made is whether the possible uncovering of a small number of cases of abuse compensates for the seemingly minor negative consequences that have now been documented for some of the participants and for the possible invasion of family privacy: Are these consequences a small price to pay in order to discover and alleviate the possible severe abuse of a few children as documented by case examples?

More definitive information about these untested assumptions and more thorough evaluations of ongoing prevention programs are necessary in order to determine their effectiveness, as well as their potential for injury. As mentioned, the programs may have two types of adverse reactions: (a) They may harm a child's positive relationships with meaningful people in his or her life or cause the child undue worry or fear, at least in the short run; and (b) they may actually place some children at a greater risk for sexual abuse if parents, teachers, and others who work with children abdicate their responsibility as guardians against abuse to these programs. The complexity of the process that a child must go through to repel or report abuse, the variety of abusive situations that a child may encounter, and the short duration of most prevention programs virtually ensure that a child cannot be assumed to be protected simply because of participation in a program. Adults must be encouraged to continue and to increase their protective efforts rather than be reassured that children are learning to be self-protective.

Extensive investigations of the full range of effects of prevention programs must be undertaken. Because the safety of children is the goal of these programs, we need to know much more about which ones work to teach which skills to which children. We must engage in more sophisticated research with the goals of understanding the process that a child must go through to repel or report abuse and determining how this process is experienced by children at various levels of cognitive and emotional development and in varying ecological contexts. We also must engage in more intervention efforts that use behavioral assessments as the major form of evaluation.

Finally, even though prevention programs focusing on environmental change have not yet been developed, attention should be paid to such approaches. The history of public health strongly suggests that prevention programs designed to change individuals' risky behavior are not very successful (Melton, in press). Eliminating or reducing the opportunities for risky behaviors has produced greater increases in safety in other areas than teaching or persuading people to avoid the risky behaviors themselves. For example, child-proof caps and lead-free paints are much more effective at reducing poisoning than programs aimed at increasing parents' vigilance and children's avoidance behaviors, and legal regulation of the marketplace has had more impact on teenagers' smoking and alcohol consumption than health education (Melton, in press). In other words, our relatively exclusive focus on educating the child has conspired to keep us from considering alternative approaches to sex abuse prevention.

FUTURE DIRECTIONS

With the high rates of adolescent pregnancy and child sexual abuse and the increasing rate of AIDS mortality, education has much to accomplish. Its primary goal is to provide accurate information and to decrease misinformation. Our society currently conveys much misinformation via the media and peer networks. It is a known fact that adolescents often engage in risky behaviors (Millstein, 1989; Reppucci, Revenson, Aber, & Reppucci, in press); however, when adolescents believe they are safe from the consequences of risky sexual activities, they are even more likely to participate in these behaviors (Paikoff & Brooks-Gunn, in press). Similarly, if child abusers believe they are immune to negative consequences, they are likely to engage in the abuse, and children can only avoid sexual abuse if they can identify abusive situations before they become enmeshed in them. Clearly, accurate and comprehensible information must be made available to children and adolescents so that they have the opportunity to make informed judgments.

Disseminating Information

At present, the major carriers of informal educational information in our culture—television, radio, and printed publications—often work against sexuality educators. Brown, Childers, and Waszak (1990) report that in 1985, the average American teenager viewed approximately 2,000 sexual references but only a negligible number of references to birth control or STDs. Yet, television has the potential to advance knowledge of adolescent sexuality and child sexual abuse, as demonstrated by the much watched dramas *Daddy* and *Something About Amelia*, which dealt with these topics in a serious and informed fashion. If the media could be used to transmit accurate information about the dangerous consequences of child sexual abuse and the risks of teenage sexual intercourse or, at the very least, to provide positive role models, perhaps educators would have an increased chance of reducing risky behaviors.

As we have noted, peers are also the source of much misinformation about sexuality. If educators are permitted to provide reliable, detailed information to students without fear of adverse consequences, then peer communication networks might actually become an asset to the dissemination of accurate knowledge about sexual behavior (Paikoff & Brooks-Gunn, in press). Investigations about developmental differences in the influence of television and peers on adolescents' perceptions of sexual risk and on their sexual attitudes and behaviors could provide information that might increase the likelihood of them becoming resources instead of obstacles (Paikoff & Brooks-Gunn, in press). We also believe that studies of the influence of media on deterring adults from engaging in child sexual abuse and on children's abilities to resist victimization would be very useful to the development of successful prevention programs.

Developmentally Sensitive Curricula

Educational programs must be sensitive to the developmental status of the students. Melton (in press) has concluded that current sexual abuse prevention programs "generally have failed to consider cognitive-developmental factors" and "look remarkably similar across age groups." The Berkeley Family Welfare Research Group's (Daro, 1988; Daro et al., 1987; Gilbert et al., 1988) finding that young children are often not able to comprehend the meaning of confusing touches or the connection between the physical act of being touched and the emotion that it generates strongly questions the developmental readiness of these children for such programs. In contrast, Howard's (1987) Postponing Sexual Involvement program is a good example of a program's effectiveness when it is tailored to the needs and abilities of its audience. Sexuality and sexual abuse programs that encourage active involvement of the participants seem to provide the best opportunities for assimilation of skills and knowledge. The role-playing activities used by Kraizer and her colleagues (Fryer et al., 1987a, 1987b; Kraizer et al., 1989) in their prevention programs, as opposed to the usual passive reading or observation exercises, resulted in significant behavioral change, while Zabin et al.'s (1988) and Howard and McCabe's (1990) sexuality education programs, which involved active participation in group discussions, had positive effects for delaying onset of sexual activity and decreasing teen pregnancy. It may be that for youth to be able to generalize knowledge and skills learned in the classroom or clinic, opportunity for practice must first be provided. We must engage in more basic research with a goal of understanding how decision-making and action-taking processes are developed and used at various levels of cognitive and emotional development in various situations. Without these evaluations, we risk developing programs that make adults feel better but do not protect children.

Evaluation

In both sexuality education and child sexual abuse prevention programs, evaluation is much discussed but seldom implemented with sophisticated research designs. Short- and long-term evaluations are often considered a drain on resources that could be used for the programs themselves; therefore, long-term evaluations, which are necessary to demonstrate endurance of program outcomes but require the largest investments of time and money, are rare (Cassell & Wilson, 1989). Moreover, most past evaluations have been flawed in that they have failed to use comparable control groups, to make comparisons of programs, or to report findings of ineffectiveness (Strouse & Fabes, 1985). Without the use of experimental designs in evaluation, it is impossible to determine whether changes that have occurred were caused by the program, developmental progress, ecological context, or some combination of these factors (Kirby, 1980; Reppucci, 1987). Poorly designed and executed evaluations have therefore hindered the improvement of programs and the reduction of health and social problems that could accompany effective education.

For efforts at sexuality education to be more effective, appraisals of existing programs are required in order to better select appropriate curricula and teaching methods (Select Committee, 1985b), and more definitive information about the untested assumptions of child sexual abuse prevention programs is necessary in order to be sure of their effectiveness. Zabin and her colleagues (1986) also stressed the importance of scientifically evaluating intervention efforts. Although some of the evaluations we have described used experimental designs, one important area where action has been requested is the evaluation of school-based clinics (Kenney, 1986). Because the safety of youth is the goal, we need to know much more about the aims and procedures of these programs.

Both short- and long-term evaluations using nonequivalent control groups and time series analyses (Linney & Reppucci, 1982) should be part of the design of educational programs. In order to monitor change and effectiveness, they should have clearly stated objectives that can be measured. Intervention efforts that use behavioral assessments as the major form of evaluation must be encouraged. Because most sexuality education programs attempt to decrease adolescent pregnancy rates, program designers could use census data (Gould, Ostrem, & Davey, 1989), which are divisible by school district, or community hospital data (Howard & McCabe, 1990) to determine actual changes in adolescent pregnancy rates. Child sexual abuse prevention programs could similarly use police department or social service statistics of child sexual abuse to compare communities that have programs with those that do not. If changes in knowledge or attitudes are goals of the program, they must be measured as well. When questionnaires are used to assess these changes, it may be better to administer them outside of the schools and clinics where the programs were instituted to assess whether these changes are generalizable to life situations where sexual encounters actually occur. If interviews are used, they should be conducted by raters blind to groupings.

It is ultimately the long-lasting effects of a program, both positive and negative, that are of most interest, as short-term changes in knowledge and attitudes may have little effect on later behavior. Although outcome evaluation is essential, process evaluation (i.e., evaluation of the implementation of the program itself) is equally crucial. Was a comparable version of the program taught in each classroom, or was the program's design so vague that no consistent program could be found between classrooms? When evaluations are conducted on such unmonitored programs and little or no effect is found, one cannot conclude that the program is valueless, because the program, as it was designed, may never have been implemented. In other words, the strength and integrity of a program (Reppucci, 1987) must be evaluated on a regular basis to verify that the program was properly implemented.

Other basic factors of scientific research should be included in education program evaluations. Control groups are needed to monitor the effects of the program as separate from history, growth, regression, or context effects. Validity and reliability of measures should be assessed and reported. In all probability, to ensure adequate evaluation and program implementation, sexuality and prevention educators will need to increase their collaborations with researchers, as researchers have the knowledge of and interest in scientific evaluation and educators have the knowledge of and interest in implementing the programs.

CONCLUSION

Although there is not a large corpus of research that demonstrates extensive effectiveness of either sexuality education or child abuse prevention programs, there are examples of both that have merit. Zabin et al.'s (1988) Baltimore school-based clinic, Howard's (1987) Postponing Sexual Involvement program, and Kraizer and her colleagues' (Fryer et al., 1987a, 1987b; Kraizer et al., 1989) work on the use of role play to prevent child sexual abuse suggest further experimentation on the ability to assimilate program information through active participation. The positive and negative effects of open discussion and provision of contraceptive technology in a variety of ecological settings must also be studied. Given the enormity of the problems and the large number of youth affected, innovative programs must be developed, implemented, and *evaluated.* Our children deserve no less.

NOTES

[1] Most family life education (FLE) is similar to these programs, but FLE concentrates more on issues of the individual in marriage, parenting skills, and budgeting skills and less on sexuality, and therefore is not addressed in this paper.

[2] Inner-city adolescents engage in sexual activity at earlier ages; for example, males in metropolitan locations tend to experience sex by the age of 12 years (Select Committee, 1985a).

REFERENCES

Baldwin, W. (1983). Trends in adolescent contraception, pregnancy and childbearing. In E. R. McAnarney (Ed.), *Premature adolescent pregnancy and parenthood* (pp. 3–19). New York: Grune & Stratton.

Berrick, J. D. (1988). Parental involvement in child abuse prevention training: What do they learn? *Child Abuse and Neglect, 12,* 543–553.

Binder, R. L., & McNiel, D. E. (1987). Evaluation of a school-based sexual abuse prevention program: Cognitive and emotional effects. *Child Abuse and Neglect, 11,* 497–506.

Borkin, J., & Frank, L. (1986). Sexual abuse prevention for preschoolers: A pilot program. *Child Welfare, 6,* 75–83.

Bronfenbrenner, U. (1979). *The ecology of human development.* Cambridge, MA: Harvard University Press.

Brooks-Gunn, J., & Furstenberg, F. (1989). Adolescent sexual behavior. *American Psychologist, 44,* 249–257.

Brown, J., Childers, K., & Waszak, C. (1990). Television and adolescent sexuality. *Journal of Adolescent Health Care, 11,* 62–71.

Cabaniss, N. (1989). A look at the Adolescent Family Life Act. *The World & I: A Chronicle of Our Changing Era, 4,* 605–611.

Cassell, C., & Wilson, P. (1989). *Sexuality education: A resource book.* New York: Garland Publishing.

Committee for Children. (1983). *Talking about touching: A personal safety curriculum.* (Available from the Committee for Children, P.O. Box 15190, Seattle, WA 98115)

Conte, J. R. (1984, August). *Research on the prevention of sexual abuse of children.* Paper presented at the Second National Conference for Family Violence Researchers, Durham, NH.

Conte, J. R. (1988). Research on the prevention of sexual abuse of children. In G. T. Hotaling, D. Finkelhor, J. T. Kirkpatrick, & M. A. Straus (Eds.), *Coping with family violence* (pp. 300–309). Beverly Hills, CA: Sage.

Conte, J. R., Rosen, C., & Saperstein, L. (1984, September). *An analysis of programs to prevent the sexual victimization of children.* Paper presented at the Fifth International Congress on Child Abuse and Neglect, Montreal, Canada.

Conte, J. R., Rosen, C., Saperstein, L., & Shermack, R. (1985). An evaluation of a program to prevent the sexual victimization of young children. *Child Abuse and Neglect, 9,* 319–328.

Conte, J. R., Wolfe, S., & Smith, T. (1989). What sexual offenders tell us about prevention strategies. *Child Abuse and Neglect, 13*(2), 293–301.

Cook, T., & Campbell, D. (1979). *Quasi-experimentation: Design and analysis issues for field settings.* Chicago: Rand McNally College Publishing Company.

Daro, D. (1988). *Prevention programs: What do children learn?* Unpublished manuscript, School of Social Welfare, University of California, Berkeley.

Daro, D., Duerr, J., & LeProhn, N. (1987, July). *Child assault prevention instruction: What works with preschoolers.* Paper presented at the Third National Family Violence Research Conference, University of New Hampshire, Durham.

Dawson, D. (1986). The effects of sex education on adolescent behavior. *Family Planning Perspectives, 18,* 162–170.

Donovan, C. (1990). Adolescent sexuality: Better, more accessible sex education is needed. *British Medical Journal, 300,* 1026–1027.

Donovan, P. (1989). *Risk and responsibility: Teaching sex education in America's schools today.* New York: The Alan Guttmacher Institute.

Dryfoos, J. (1988). School-based health clinics: Three years of experience. *Family Planning Perspectives, 20,* 193–200.

Finkelhor, D. (1979). *Sexually victimized children.* New York: Free Press.

Finkelhor, D. (1984). *Child sexual abuse: New theory and research.* New York: Free Press.

Finkelhor, D. (1986). Prevention: A review of programs and research. In D. Finkelhor with S. Araji, L. Baron, A. Browne, S. D. Peters, & G. E. Wyatt (Eds.), *A sourcebook on child sexual abuse* (pp. 224–254). Beverly Hills, CA: Sage.

Finkelhor, D., & Strapko, N. (in press). Sexual abuse prevention education: A review of evaluation studies. In D. Willis, E. Holden, & M. Rosenberg (Eds.), *Child abuse prevention.* New York: Wiley.

Forrest, J., & Silverman, J. (1989). What public school teachers teach about preventing pregnancy, AIDS and sexually transmitted diseases. *Family Planning Perspectives, 21,* 65–72.

Francoeur, R. (1982). *Becoming a sexual person.* New York: Wiley.

Fryer, G. E., Kraizer, S. K., & Miyoshi, T. (1987a). Measuring actual reduction of risk to child abuse: A new approach. *Child Abuse and Neglect, 11,* 173–179.

Fryer, G. E., Kraizer, S. K., & Miyoshi, T. (1987b). Measuring children's retention of skills to resist stranger abduction: Use of the simulation technique. *Child Abuse and Neglect, 11,* 181–185.

Furstenberg, F. (1976). *Unplanned parenthood: The social consequences of teenage childbearing*. New York: Free Press.

Furstenberg, F., Moore, K., & Peterson, J. (1985). Sex education and sexual experience among adolescents. *American Journal of Public Health, 75,* 1331–1332.

Garbarino, J. (1987). Children's response to a sexual abuse prevention program: A study of the *Spiderman* comic. *Child Abuse and Neglect, 11,* 143–148.

Gilbert, N., Daro, D., Duerr, J., LeProhn, N., & Nyman, N. (1988). *Child sexual abuse prevention: Evaluation of educational materials for pre-school programs*. Unpublished manuscript, Family Welfare Research Group, School of Social Welfare, University of California, Berkeley.

Goffin, J. (1947). What is sex education? *The Journal of School Health, 17,* 151–156.

Goldstein, J., Freud, A., & Solnit, A. J. (1979). *Before the best interests of the child.* New York: Free Press.

Goodman, E. (1985, March 20). Making love, but carefully. *The Daily Progress,* p. A4.

Gordon, S. (1985). Before we educate anyone else about sexuality, let's come to terms with our own. *Journal of Sex Education and Therapy, 11,* 16–21.

Gordon, S., Scales, P., & Everly, K. (1979). *The sexual adolescent: Communicating with teenagers about sex*. North Scituate, MA: Duxbury.

Gould, J., Ostrem, M., & Davey, B. (1989). Analyzing teenage births by school district. *Family Planning Perspectives, 21,* 131–133.

Harvey, P., Forehand, R., Brown, C., & Holmes, T. (1988). The prevention of sexual abuse: Examination of the effectiveness of a program with kindergarten-age children. *Behavior Therapy, 19,* 429–435.

Haugaard, J. J., & Reppucci, N. D. (1988). *The sexual abuse of children: A comprehensive guide to current knowledge and intervention strategies*. San Francisco: Jossey-Bass.

Hazzard, A., & Angert, L. (1986, August). *Child sexual abuse prevention: Previous research and future directions*. Paper presented at the meeting of the American Psychological Association, Washington, DC.

Hazzard, A. P., Webb, C., & Kleemeier, C. (1988). *Child sexual assault prevention programs: Helpful or harmful?* Unpublished manuscript, Emery University School of Medicine.

Henshaw, S., Kenney, A., Somberg, D., & Van Vort, J. (1989). *Teenage pregnancy in the United States: The scope of the problem and state responses*. New York: The Alan Guttmacher Institute.

Hofferth, S., & Hayes, C. (Eds.). (1987). *Risking the future: Adolescent sexuality, pregnancy and childbearing*. Washington, DC: National Academy Press.

Hofferth, S., & Miller, B. (1989). An overview of adolescent pregnancy prevention programs and their evaluations. In J. J. Card (Ed.), *Evaluation program aimed at preventing teenage pregnancies* (pp. 25–40). Palo Alto, CA: Sociometrics Corporation.

Howard, M. (1987, April). *Helping youth postpone sexual involvement*. Paper presented at the Fourth International Symposium on Adolescent Health, Sydney, Australia.

Howard, M., & McCabe, J. (1990). Helping teenagers postpone sexual involvement. *Family Planning Perspectives, 22,* 21–26.

Hunter, L. (1989). Family life education in a public school system. In C. Cassell & P. Wilson (Eds.), *Sexuality education: A resource book* (pp. 95–118). New York: Garland Publishing.

Imber, M. (1984). Toward a theory of educational origins: The genesis of sex education. *Educational Theory, 34,* 275–286.

Kastner, L. (1979). *Adolescent perceptions of personal and ecological factors predicting contraceptive use. A multilevel, multivariable study.* Unpublished doctoral dissertation, University of Virginia.

Kasun, J. (1989). Sex education: The hidden agenda. *The World & I: A Chronicle of Our Changing Era, 4,* 487–503.

Kenney, A. (1986). School-based clinics: A national conference. *Family Planning Perspectives, 18,* 44–46.

Kenney, A. (1989). *Sex education and AIDS education in the schools: A survey of state policies, curricula and program activities.* New York: The Alan Guttmacher Institute.

Kenney, A., Guardado, S., & Brown, L. (1989). Sex education and AIDS in the schools: What states and large school districts are doing. *Family Planning Perspectives, 21,* 56–64.

Kerr, D. (1990). Ryan White's death: A time to reflect on schools' progress in dealing with AIDS. *Journal of School Health, 60,* 237–238.

Kerr, D., Allensworth, D., & Gayle, J. (1989). The ASHA national HIV education needs assessment of health and education professionals. *Journal of School Health, 59,* 301–307.

Kilmann, P., Wanlass, R., Sabalis, R., & Sullivan, B. (1981). Sex education: A review of its effects. *Archives of Sexual Behavior, 10,* 177–205.

Kirby, D. (1980). The effects of school sex education programs: A review of the literature. *The Journal of School Health, 50,* 559–563.

Kirby, D. (1984). *Sexuality education: An evaluation of programs and their effects.* Santa Cruz, CA: Network Publications.

Kirby, D. (1989). Sex education programs and their effects. *The World & I: A Chronicle of Our Changing Era, 4,* 590–603.

Kirkendall, L. (1984). The journey toward SIECUS, a personal odyssey. *SIECUS Report, 12,* 1–4.

Kirkendall, L., & Libby, R. (1985). Sex education in the future. *Journal of Sex Education and Therapy, 11,* 64–67.

Kleemeier, C., & Webb, C. (1986, August). *Evaluation of a school-based prevention program.* Paper presented at the meeting of the American Psychological Association, Washington, DC.

Klein, D. (1983). *Sex education: A historical perspective.* DeKalb, IL: Northern Illinois University. (ERIC Document Reproduction Service No. ED 231 797)

Koblinsky, S., & Behana, N. (1984). Child sexual abuse: The educator's role in prevention, detection, and intervention. *Young Children, 39,* 3–15.

Kohlberg, L. (1976). Moral stages and moralization: The cognitive-developmental approach. In T. Lickona (Ed.), *Moral development and behavior* (pp. 31–53). New York: Holt, Rinehart and Winston.

Kraizer, S., Witte, S. S., & Fryer, Jr., G. E. (1989, September–October). Child sexual abuse prevention programs: What makes them effective in protecting children? *Children Today,* pp. 23–27.

Leventhal, J. M. (1987). Programs to prevent sexual abuse: What outcomes should be measured? *Child Abuse and Neglect, 11,* 169–171.

Linney, J., & Reppucci, N. (1982). Community psychology research methods.

In J. Butcher & P. Kendall (Eds.), *Handbook of research methods in clinical psychology* (pp. 535–566). New York: Wiley.

Marsiglio, W., & Mott, F. (1986). The impact of sex education on sexual activity, contraceptive use and premarital pregnancy among American teenagers. *Family Planning Perspectives, 18,* 151–162.

Mast, C. (1989). Sex and the sanctity of love. *The World & I: A Chronicle of Our Changing Era, 4,* 543–553.

Melton, G. (in press). The improbability of prevention of sexual abuse. In D. Willis, E. Holden, & M. Rosenberg (Eds.), *Child abuse prevention.* New York: Wiley.

Melton, G., Koocher, G., & Saks, M. (Eds.). (1983). *Children's competence to consent.* New York: Plenum.

Miller-Perrin, C., & Wurtele, S. (1988). The child sexual abuse prevention movement: A critical analysis of primary and secondary approaches. *Clinical Psychology Review, 8,* 313–329.

Millstein, S. (1989). Adolescent health: Challenges for behavioral scientists. *American Psychologist, 44,* 837–842.

Miltenberger, R. G., & Thiesse-Duffy, E. (1988). Evaluation of home-based programs for teaching personal safety skills to children. *Journal of Applied Behavior Analysis, 21,* 81–87.

Nadel, M. (1990). *AIDS education: Gaps in coverage still exist* (GAO/T-HRD-90-26, Statement of Associate Director for National and Public Health Issues, Human Resources Division before the Senate Committee on Governmental Affairs). Washington, DC: General Accounting Office.

Nibert, D., Cooper, S., Ford, J., Fitch, L. K., & Robinson, J. (1989). The ability of young children to learn abuse prevention. *Response to the Victimization of Women & Children, 12,* 14–21.

Office of Population Affairs. (1989). *Adolescent Family Life Program: Fact sheet.* Washington, DC: U.S. Department of Health and Human Services.

Paikoff, R., & Brooks-Gunn, J. (in press). Taking fewer chances: Teenage pregnancy prevention programs. *American Psychologist.*

Parcel, G., & Luttmann, D. (1981). Evaluation of a sex education course for young adolescents. *Family Relations, 30,* 55–60.

Parcel, G., Luttmann, D., & Flaherty-Zonis, C. (1985). Development and evaluation of a sexuality education curriculum for young adolescents. *Journal of Sex Education and Therapy, 11,* 38–45.

Picker, L. (1984). Human sexuality education: Implications for biology teaching. *The American Biology Teacher, 46,* 92–98.

Pietig, J. (1984). Values and morality in early 20th century elementary schools: A perspective. In F. Schultz (Ed.), *Education 84/85* (11th ed., pp. 11–14). Guilford, CT: The Dushkin Publishing Group.

Plummer, C. (1984). *Preventing sexual abuse: What in-school programs teach children.* Unpublished manuscript.

Porch, T. L., & Petretic-Jackson, P. A. (1986, August). *Child sexual assault prevention: Evaluation parent education workshops.* Paper presented at the 94th annual convention of the American Psychological Association, Washington, DC.

Quinn, S., Thomas, S., & Smith, B. (1990). Are health educators being prepared to provide HIV/AIDS education? A survey of selected health education professional preparation programs. *Journal of School Health, 60,* 92–95.

Ralph, N., & Edgington, A. (1983). An evaluation of an adolescent family planning program. *Journal of Adolescent Health Care, 4,* 158–162.

Ravitch, D. (1984). The educational pendulum. In F. Schultz (Ed.), *Education 84/85* (11th ed., pp. 11–14). Guilford, CT: The Dushkin Publishing Group.

Ray, J., & Dietzel, M. (1984). *Teaching child sexual abuse prevention.* Unpublished manuscript.

Reppucci, J., Revenson, T., Aber, M., & Reppucci, N. (in press). Unrealistic optimism among adolescent smokers and nonsmokers. *Journal of Primary Prevention.*

Reppucci, N. D. (1987). Prevention and ecology: Teen-age pregnancy, child sexual abuse, and organized youth sports. *American Journal of Community Psychology, 15,* 1–22.

Reppucci, N. D., & Haugaard, J. J. (1989). Prevention of child sexual abuse: Myth or reality. *American Psychologist, 44,* 266–275.

Respect Incorporated. (1988). *The option of true sexual freedom.* Bradley, IL: Author.

Richard, D. (1989). Exemplary abstinence-based sex education programs. *The World & I: A Chronicle of Our Changing Era, 4,* 569–590.

Roberts, M. C., Alexander, K., & Fanurik, D. (1990). Evaluation of commercially available materials to prevent child sexual abuse and abduction. *American Psychologist, 45,* 782–783.

Rosoff, J. (1989). Sex education in the schools: Policies and practice. *Family Planning Perspectives, 21,* 52–64.

Russell, D. E. H. (1984). *Sexual exploitation, rape, child sexual abuse, and work place harassment.* Beverly Hills, CA: Sage.

Sarason, S. (1974). *The psychological sense of community: Prospects for a community psychology.* San Francisco: Jossey-Bass.

Saslawsky, D. A., & Wurtele, S. K. (1986). Educating children about sexual abuse: Implications for pediatric intervention and possible prevention. *Journal of Pediatric Psychology, 11,* 235–245.

Select Committee. (1985a). *Teen pregnancy issues* (Report of the Subcommittee on Public Assistance and Unemployment Compensation of the House Committee on Ways and Means). Washington, DC: U.S. House of Representatives.

Select Committee. (1985b, December). *Teen pregnancy: What is being done? A state-by-state look* (Report of the House Select Committee on Children, Youth, and Families). Washington, DC: U.S. House of Representatives.

Sex Information and Education Council of the United States. (1984). SIECUS position statements 1984. *SIECUS Report, 12*(4), 14–15.

Shore, M. (1987). Review of nine child abuse books. *Children's Health Care, 16,* 60–61.

Silverstein, C., & Buck, G. (1986). Parental preferences regarding sex education topics for sixth graders. *Adolescence, 21,* 971–980.

Soefer, E., Scholl, T., Sobel, E., Tanfer, K., & Levy, D. (1985). Menarche: Target age for reinforcing sex education for adolescents. *Journal of Adolescent Health Care, 6,* 383–386.

Sonenstein, F., & Pittman, K. (1984). The availability of sex education in large city school districts. *Family Planning Perspectives, 16,* 19–25.

Strouse, J., & Fabes, R. (1985). Formal versus informal sources of sex education: Competing forces in the sexual socialization of adolescents. *Adolescence, 20,* 251–263.

Swan, H. L., Press, A. N., & Briggs, S. L. (1985). Child sexual abuse prevention: Does it work? *Child Welfare, 64,* 667–674.

Tatum, M. L. (1989). Overview: A perspective on school programs. In C. Cassell

& P. Wilson (Eds.), *Sexuality education: A resource book* (pp. 95–118). New York: Garland Publishing.

Thornburg, H. (1985). Sex information as primary prevention. *Journal of Sex Education and Therapy, 11,* 22–27.

Trudell, B. (1985). The first organized campaign for school sex education: A source of critical questions about current efforts. *Journal of Sex Education and Therapy, 11,* 10–15.

Trudell, B., & Whatley, M. H. (1988). School sexual abuse prevention: Unintended consequences and dilemmas. *Child Abuse and Neglect, 12,* 103–113.

Trussell, J. (1988). Teenage pregnancy in the United States. *Family Planning Perspectives, 10,* 262–272.

The unreliability of expert testimony on the typical characteristics of sexual abuse victims. (1985). *Georgetown Law Journal, 74,* 429–456.

Wolf, S. C., Berlinger, L. C., Conte, J., & Smith, T. (1987, July). *The victimization process in child sexual abuse.* Paper presented at the Third National Family Violence Research Conference, Durham, NH.

Wolfe, D. A., MacPherson, T., Blount, R., & Wolfe, U. V. (1986). Evaluation of a brief intervention for educating school children in awareness of physical and sexual abuse. *Child Abuse and Neglect, 10,* 85–92.

Wurtele, S. K. (1988, August). *Harmful effects of sexual abuse prevention program? Results and implications.* Paper presented at the meeting of the American Psychological Association, Atlanta.

Wurtele, S., Kast, L., Miller-Perrin, C., & Kondrick, P. (1989). Comparison of programs for teaching personal safety skills to preschoolers. *Journal of Consulting and Clinical Psychology, 57,* 505–511.

Wurtele, S. K., Marrs, S. R., & Miller-Perrin, C. L. (1987). Practice makes perfect? The role of participant modeling in sexual abuse prevention programs. *Journal of Consulting and Clinical Psychology, 55,* 599–602.

Wurtele, S. K., & Miller-Perrin, C. L. (1987). An evaluation of side effects associated with participation in a child sexual abuse prevention program. *Journal of School Health, 57,* 228–231.

Wyatt, G. E. (1985). The sexual abuse of Afro-American and White-American women in childhood. *Child Abuse and Neglect, 9,* 507–519.

Yarber, W. (1985). *STD: A guide for today's young adults.* Waldorf, MD: American Alliance Publications.

Yarber, W. (1988). Evaluation of the health behavior approach to school STD education. *Journal of Sex Education and Therapy, 14,* 33–38.

Zabin, L., & Hirsch, M. (1988). *Evaluation of pregnancy prevention programs in the school context.* Lexington, MA: Lexington Books.

Zabin, L., Hirsch, M., Smith, E., Streett, R., & Hardy, J. (1986). Evaluation of a pregnancy prevention program for urban teenagers. *Family Planning Perspectives, 18,* 119–126.

Zabin, L., Hirsch, M., Streett, R., Emerson, M., Smith, M., Hardy, J., & King, T. (1988). The Baltimore pregnancy prevention program for urban teenagers: How did it work? *Family Planning Perspectives, 20,* 182–186.

II.
POLITICS AND SCHOOL DECISION MAKING

Chapter 5

State Authority and the Politics of Educational Change

THOMAS JAMES
Brown University

The community of scholars has a predilection for converting urgent demands into underlying questions not being asked. If it is true, for example, that most educational reforms since the 1890s have had little impact on classroom practice, and that many proposed changes—no matter how necessary or appealing they may have seemed at the time—tend to recur but are perennially unachievable (Cuban, 1984, 1990), then it is time to change the conversation. Some recent literature points to shifting authority relations within schools and their impact on the instructional process (Hurn, 1985; Powell, Farrar, & Cohen, 1985; Sedlak, Wheeler, Pullin, & Cusick, 1986). Closer study of change within individual institutions draws attention to the combination of that trend with the entry of new groups into mainstream schools where the rules of human association have been altered by public policy (Cusick, 1983; Grant, 1988; Metz, 1978, 1986). Numerous scholars have sought to clarify the assorted forms of control and resistance that collide in school settings as teachers act to protect their autonomy (e.g., McNeil, 1983, 1988; Muir, 1986), and as the schools, despite a plethora of reforms over recent decades, routinely fail to alter their hierarchical and unequal treatment of students from different groups in society (Everhart, 1983; Gamoran, 1987; Oakes, 1985; Willis, 1976).

A further cautionary note is sounded by those who point to change and continuity beyond schooling itself, in the broader streams of social, political, and economic life within which educational practice develops. Such a perspective, variously construed according to the scholar's theoretical point of departure, suggests the need for more encompassing frameworks of interpretation than those that focus on the reform of schooling as such (Apple, 1982; Carnoy & Levin, 1985; Cremin, 1980). But no matter how educational expansion is conceptualized as a process over time (Craig, 1981, reviews the alternatives), and notwithstanding its school versus nonschool facets, education is a contested public good in American society (Levin, 1983, 1987). Agreements forged over the years through social conflict and political consensus become embedded, tacitly or explicitly, in law and policy, in commonsense rules of educational practice, and in public opinion (Tyack, James, & Benavot, 1987). The residue of that process can be discerned most readily in the values and social ideas of dominant groups, professional elites, and political majorities, but also—at times more revealingly—in those of groups and interests whose values are driven to the margins (Jorgenson, 1987; Kaestle, 1983; Reese, 1986; Tyack & Hansot, 1982).

Historical scholarship situates the dilemmas of policy and practice in a longer trajectory of efforts to establish normative structures in the public world. Such work calls attention to the changing social relationships that shape—and are shaped by—those structures as people adapt to new conditions in the world around them. Historically, the process of change has been studied most meticulously in the cities, where ethnic and class conflict tended to be more pronounced, as they are today (Katz, 1968a; Katznelson & Weir, 1985; Labaree, 1988; Perlmann, 1988; Peterson, 1985b; Ravitch, 1974; Tyack, 1974; Wrigley, 1982). By studying the institutionalization of schooling from the broader perspective of educational and societal change, it is possible to gain critical insight into arrangements of power now widely accepted as normal, even necessary, in the public, political world of American education, and to reflect upon alternatives thereby suppressed (D. J. Hogan, 1985; Katz, 1987). A historical perspective suggests that current reform initiatives will continue to be ephemeral if they fail to engage the long-standing social accords that shape the life of schools (D. K. Cohen, 1985; D. K. Cohen & Neufeld, 1981).

Historians are by no means the only party to this conversation. Twenty years ago, Sarason (1971) shed light on the situation by diagnosing the problems encountered by improvers as they ran up against the regularities embedded in schools. His wise counsel, focusing concretely on the question of how people in educational settings relate to one another and how they might learn to work together in new ways, has outlasted myriad policies and programs that failed to heed it. Two decades of implementation research and organizational studies have added to the picture of what happens under the pressure of reform and what can be done to stimulate constructive change (Berman, 1986; Berman & McLaughlin, 1974, 1975, 1977, 1978; Fullan, 1982; Huberman & Miles, 1984a, 1984b; Kirst & Jung, 1980; McLaughlin, 1987). It seems clear from this literature that less prescriptive forms of "mutual adaptation" (McLaughlin, 1976) are most likely to bring genuine change into view.

Does such a view underestimate the structures of continuity that shape educational settings, as identified by critically inclined historians? Perhaps, but the virtue of the implementation research is that it succeeds in distinguishing promising strategies from proven disappointments (Berman

& McLaughlin, 1980; Fuhrman, Clune, & Elmore, 1988). Adopting a pragmatic stance toward the problems of educational change, this literature has contributed to the quest for school improvement by showing that the gulf between policy and practice is not likely to narrow without greater understanding of the actual conditions under which teaching and learning take place. The setting of standards must build upon, rather than seek to coerce, professional capacities and local dispositions (Darling-Hammond & Wise, 1985). If there is a message emblazoned across much of the recent research on planned change in schools, it is to discover kinds of policy that will make it possible to act locally within organizations and cultures and, as Sarason recommended, look at the problem of change in approachable human terms.

The shift toward local knowledge is promising but not without limitations. Despite the intuitive appeal of trying to understand education from the inside out rather than from the outside in, some further concerns immediately come to mind. A distinctive proclivity of the 1980s, cutting across the domains of policy, practice, and research, was the dethroning of authoritative directives from higher levels of government as the perceived prime mover of educational change. Exceptions stand out to prove the rule, such as those very few scholars who called for a redoubled commitment to centralized control and binding state sanctions as a way of achieving crucial changes such as school desegregation (Hochschild, 1984). Nevertheless, a growing trend among those who think seriously about educational practice has been toward more decentralized, voluntary, and locally initiated strategies of change, even in the area of desegregation, where the evidence on magnet schools appears to support further experimentation along these lines (Rossell, 1990). The trend appears to be consistent with a shift in the study of education generally, both in theory-building and empirical studies, away from an insistence upon universal, context-free, hierarchical forms of knowledge, toward more contingent, situational, locally adaptable frames of reference for interpreting the truth of experience.

If one could extrapolate all the various demands for deregulation in policy, practice, and research, what would be the result as far as state authority and educational change are concerned? Pushing these tendencies to see where they might lead, we find that the vision forming in the mind's eye is one of dispersed sovereignties, each empowered to act with a minimum of constraints and a maximum of appropriate incentives within the context of local preferences, resources, and opportunities. At its most extreme—not represented by the literature I have so far discussed—such a vision would sever the school from the state as much as possible, take education out of what Milton Friedman called the "cumbrous political channels" in the public sector, and henceforth let consumer choice shape the market for schooling (Arons, 1983; Chubb & Moe, 1988; Coons & Sugarman, 1978; M. Friedman, 1962, p. 91; Lieberman, 1989). Even the milder versions of disenchantment with centralized authority convey a tacit presupposition that the state and its policy-making capacity are *external* to the life of schools.

As a caution against too readily accepting the argument, frequently mentioned in discussions of public policy during the 1980s, that higher levels of government only fail in their attempts to induce change in social institutions through positive state action (Murray, 1984), some researchers warn that any conclusion along these lines is premature without a more careful look at the evidence across different domains of public policy, because there is much to be seen that turns out to be not only instructive but auspicious (Anton, 1984; Peterson, Rabe, & Wong, 1986). This perspective views intergovernmental relations as a source of something other than red tape, malfeasance, and coercion. It resurrects a legitimate category of social action that historians know to have been of central importance to the rise of common schools in American society: federal-state-local cooperation as the organizing framework for the development of public works and government-sponsored social institutions (Elazar, 1962).

Generally inclined toward skepticism when encountering new waves of reform (Peterson, 1985a), researchers interested in federalism nonetheless seem more optimistic about the uses of authoritative public policy for stimulating educational change. An interest in federalism moves the conversation beyond the misleading question of how educational reforms might be implemented or how to limit their disorienting effects on local organizations. Instead, it refocuses the discussion by asking what kinds of state action are possible and then exploring ways of articulating the relationships among governments and private interests to enable each to do what it does best in the pursuit of educational goals (Elmore, 1986). Acknowledging that political and bureaucratic development is as consequential an issue in our time as deregulation and localization of authority, this view attempts to generate understanding within the most powerfully centralized arenas of decision making in the polity, but a new kind of understanding that will allow productive forms of dispersed control to develop under democratic rule (Yates, 1982).

Much more needs to be done on this score. Although it is crucial that the research community deepen its understanding of the regularities and inner workings of schools, encouraging a variety of historical, local, and critical investigations for that purpose, the value of such knowledge will be lost without a complementary set of inquiries into the possibilities for constructive change within the practical limits of statecraft under American federalism. Paradoxically, only by strengthening the process of governance itself, in ways yet to be imagined, will it be possible to forge the openness and flexibility that can support a more complex vision of educational possibilities.

REDISCOVERING THE STATE

Drawing from scholarship on the history of schooling, public policy analysis, and the politics of education, this chapter explores the relationship between state authority and educational change. For our purposes, the state can be conceptualized in its broader meaning as the totality of public authority that constitutes the political system at all levels, or more concretely as American state governments, which have primary constitutional authority over formal schooling in the United States. Using both perspectives as appropriate, we begin with the observation that researchers find themselves at a particular juncture in the course of reflecting on educational change, marked by contradictory pressures to emphasize, on the one hand, the legitimacy of dispersed and self-initiated processes of change in the smallest units of analysis associated with educational systems—community cases, the school site, classroom practice, even individual students and the strategies of learning they bring to school from their families and social groups. But on the other hand, there is equally strong pressure to recognize, as any observer must, an accelerating tilt toward centralized financing, more commanding policy controls, and generally a more politicized involvement of state governments in school affairs.

These divergent tendencies are difficult to reconcile. The interest in local practice has been more than counterbalanced by the growth of legislation, funding, regulation, and court mandates during the 1980s, all of which tended to increase the states' dominion over schools. Those who have studied the implementation of educational programs are well aware of these contradictory tendencies in research and state action, but they persist in arguing—persuasively—that strategies of change need to be connected as concretely as possible to the local organization of schooling and the practice of teachers (Elmore & McLaughlin, 1988). They suggest, in addition, that a high priority now is to sort out the many changes that have taken place in the highly interactive roles of policy formulation, governance, administration, professional organization, and teaching practice; a clearer understanding is needed of who is in charge, who is doing what, and how the most appropriate channels of communication and action can be strengthened (Elmore, 1986; Kirst, 1988b). At the same time, even though an implicit emphasis on decentralization of authority is much in evidence in recent research, as it is in many current reform discussions, some analysts are casting an increasingly sympathetic eye on the record of state-mandated reforms (Fuhrman, 1987; Fuhrman & Elmore, 1990; Murphy, 1989; Odden & Marsh, 1987).

However one resolves the apparent contradiction between state authority and local self-determination, the fact is that authoritative state systems of governance and legal sanction, which define jurisdictions and delegate powers for local action in the field of education, grew up hand in hand with the schools that exist in American communities. This is not to say that state policy controls local practice, for it does not; nor is this intended to suggest that the federal, state, and local organization of schooling is functionally interdependent to the extent often assumed in centrally promulgated reforms. A wide margin must be allowed in any account for the fragmentation that characterizes governance systems in education (D. K. Cohen, 1982; Scott & Meyer, 1988; Weick, 1976; for an overview of governance systems, see Campbell, Cunningham, Nystrand, & Usdan, 1985). But the state does have an impact on educational institutions, far beyond the control that can be exercised directly through regulatory devices.

The drive for more effective exercise of state authority has accelerated in recent years, despite the countervailing rhetorics of local control, privatization, choice, school-based management, and other labels for dispersed authority. Even taking into account the variety of political cultures and governing structures in the states, the growth of state influence is one of the distinctive changes in American education over the past decade (Kirst, 1988a). Common elements are visible across most states, such as the prominence of legislatures in shaping educational policy (Marshall, Mitchell, & Wirt, 1989, chapter 2; Wirt & Kirst, 1989). The growth of state sanctions has been fueled by court decisions in response to constitutional rights challenges, an upward shift toward the state in the revenue base generated by taxes for public schooling, a growing political interest in education among state leaders, public and media concerns about the disappointing performance of school systems, and increasing staff capacities in state governments for legislative research and bureaucratic oversight related to educational issues.

In view of these developments, it does not seem likely that school-by-school and teacher-by-teacher reform, sporadically developed according to the peculiarities of local organizations, cultures, and practices, will move the overall structure of schooling and its enduring regularities toward a new synthesis without acting as well through the state. Locally initiated reform seems all the more unlikely on any grand scale when it is acknowledged that some of the recent state actions, such as stiffer graduation requirements and intensified use of standardized tests, systematically cut against the dispersal of authority sought by those who favor alternative forms of local, professional, or consumer sovereignty.

Given what they have learned about how improvements occur in local settings, researchers have the potential of helping to envision new ways for the state to act as a source of goals and rules for American schooling. Yet when we set the literatures on implementation, school improvement, and educational change in recent times next to the historical scholarship on past social struggles, and bear in mind the formidable crises beyond schooling itself that rocked the state as it sanctioned the durable structures of school governance and organization we find about us today, it is difficult not to wonder whether the research community is prepared for the rigors that lie ahead if today's school crisis is indeed as severe as many people suspect.

Another segment of the research community has spoken eloquently to this challenge by deliberating upon the theory and practice of the liberal democratic state as related to education (Gutmann, 1987; Strike, 1982; for critical theories of the state, see Carnoy, 1984; Carnoy & Levin, 1985; Shapiro, 1990). Although the appearance of such works is timely, signaling a renewed interest in theoretical and historical studies of the state across several disciplines, the prospect of venturing into such a discussion will be unsettling for many researchers, especially policy researchers, for it suggests that they can no longer rely on specialized, disciplined, technical control of knowledge about educational change. They must strip away the framework of state intentions that implicitly shapes so much of social-scientific inquiry, and they must start back at the beginning with ethical, risky questions about the democratic reasoning that brings states into the morass of education in the first place. To pursue such questions is risky because if that reasoning is not supportable under current institutional arrangements, as some advocates of privatization contend, or if the role of the democratic state cannot possibly be supported with enough strength as it is presently organized in our society, as some of the critical scholarship suggests, or if there are potentially fruitful developments taking place in the democratic reasoning of American statecraft but the researchers studying educational change are failing to connect with them, then it will be time for researchers, too, to change the conversation in which they have been involved through their works.

The disputes joined in these recent books lead back to the essential questions about state authority, the meta-questions of policy analysis: What constitutes democratic political community? What processes must the state embody to earn the consent of a sovereign people? What must the state do to act in accordance with its principles when it confronts the dilemmas of social life that give rise to law, policy, and public institutions? Are current arrangements of statecraft in a liberal democratic polity such as ours capable of meeting such requirements for state action? Can the state as we know it maintain the robust political community needed to foster a democratic way of life in a social order deeply divided along racial and class lines?

These kinds of questions are not new to educators (Bode, 1937; Butts, 1974; Dewey, 1916). Yet they are especially challenging to this generation because there appears to be mounting political will to change the organization of schooling. More new work along these lines is needed, rooted in political philosophy as well as the social sciences and public policy. Going back to the basics of power and political reason, more research is needed to understand the changes taking place in state authority, the impact of state actions on the process of educational change, and the cumulative impact of these changes on the democratic potential and quality of life in American society.

Turning concretely to the American states, we find two types of literature especially relevant to evaluating current understanding of state authority and educational change. The first of the following sections will draw upon studies that interpret the growth of state school systems, reflecting upon embedded structures of educational governance and their implications for changes taking place in the politics of education. Then the next section will examine the relatively limited literature on state-level governance itself. The aim will be to discover ways of bringing together what appear to be promising strategies of educational improvement, based on local initiative and the practice of teaching, and strategies for the renewal of educational governance in the states. The final section will ask whether any generative concepts, ideas capable of improving the policy strategies of the state, can be located in the research on educational change.

THE TRAJECTORY OF STATE AUTHORITY

This section interprets recent scholarship looking at how the American states used their authority to encourage the establishment of common schools, then to support their growth into bureaucratically controlled institutions, and subsequently, prodded by the federal government, to elaborate increasingly detailed, prescriptive, and binding institutional rules within those systems. These three stages—which I shall call constitutive, administrative, and regulatory—reflect momentous changes in intergovernmental relations and legal development over the last two centuries, demonstrating how the particular organization of state expansion in any era influences the ways in which educational issues are settled.

It would be an exaggeration to argue that the state has the last word on the nature of schooling in American society. Cultural configurations, technological and economic development, professionalization, class conflict, social mobility, and crises such as wars and depressions all have strong and interacting effects on the evolution of education. Depending on their presuppositions, historians emphasize the relative value of these and other categories in different ways, but it would hardly be credible now to construe educational change as arising principally from the polity and the public sector. The importance of the state can be defined more precisely, though, not as the cause but as a repository and keeper of changes, once they have been made in social and political history. While all the various other forces are at work in the process of change, the state—public authority as constituted at all levels and in every branch of government—is used over time to enforce the social agreements that people reach about how schooling should be organized. Advocates of privatization cannot achieve their aims in private; sanctions must be created in the public realm through political means to protect nonpublic educational activity. Social upheavals, such as the agrarian and labor unrest around the turn of the century or the civil rights movement after World War II, leave sanctions inscribed in law and institutions—ambiguous, changing, open to interpretation, constantly reshaped through experience, but sanctions nonetheless. The same is true, as will be explored below, for the relationship between the drive for professionalization of schooling after the turn of the century and the structural regularities of schooling today. Recurrent questions in the politics of educational change run up against sanctions that, once established in the public realm, must likewise be changed by the same means as they were established, sometimes rather painfully but democratically through means incorporated for that purpose into the state.

All this can be said of the democratic state in the abstract, but it is especially true of the states as governmental entities in our federalist system. State constitutions embody the provisions authorizing education as a public good in American society. States control the statutory and administrative backbone of public schooling within their borders. They exercise considerable authority over the small minority of private schools as well. The states—not families, not communities, not voluntary associations, not local boards—require and enforce the compulsory school attendance of all young people in this country. Although there is great interstate variation, the states control the tax systems that raise the majority of funds this nation spends to educate its youth in elementary and secondary schools.

Questions of educational value, from wherever they might emerge, cannot help but move into some relationship with social agreements embodied in the state. To say this is not to reify the state as an actor in educational history; it is merely to recognize the prominence that this society has given the state in mediating the many interacting forces of change that shape education as a public good. Schools and states are more inextricably intertwined than any dichotomous conception of public and private can convey. The nature of standards for schools, the rules of association for those who attend, acceptable versus unacceptable inequality in the distribution of resources, the social construction of teachers and administrators as professionals, the use of schools and other agencies for transmitting one culture or excluding another, the channeling of young people toward social futures and occupational roles, the selection of what should be known and who should know it—all these are inscribed in sanctions that remain in force long after the era in which they were produced (van Geel, 1976, 1987).

The interconnected reality of formal education and state authority becomes apparent when we look historically at the ways in which schools acquired their enduring characteristics as state-sponsored institutions.

The Constitutive State and Its Problems

The spread of common schools, which by any yardstick of comparison was one of the most successful reform movements this nation has ever experienced, went hand in hand with the expansion of the national territory, the settling of communities beyond the borders of the original colonies, and the formation of new states. As a social movement in the 19th century, the common school crusade brought together Protestant-style civic religion and a republican fervor carried forward from the American Revolution (Cremin, 1951), along with socially and politically conservative values stressing nativism, work discipline, time control, sobriety, and other traits associated with the maintenance of moral order and civic cohesion in a nascent capitalist economy (Kaestle, 1983; Katz, 1968a; Tyack & Hansot, 1982).

Opening its pupils and their communities to the widening public and cosmopolitan world of 19th-century America, the common school took hold and supplanted most of its nonpublic forebears, which had already succeeded, along with churches and families, in raising literacy rates across the northern states (Kaestle & Vinovskis, 1980). These institutions represented a vision of the common good that applied to most citizens of the day (Katznelson & Weir, 1985; Reese, 1988); however, they also maintained a stance toward many people in the increasingly diverse nation after 1830 that could be characterized as morally reproving (Onuf, in press), religiously intolerant (Glenn, 1988), and pedagogically conformist (Finkelstein, 1989). The legacy of the common school movement was its success in instituting a majoritarian consensus, outside the South at least, that helped to solidify the public culture of the new nation.

State authority was central to the process of expansion (Tyack & James, 1986). Beginning with the Northwest Ordinance of 1787, the federal government provided new states with land grants to support common schools, affirming the proposition that schools were necessary to good government. It did this to stimulate the formation of new states in the Northwest Territories and to suggest some rules, drawn from the political ideals upon which the nation was founded, to guide the process of state building. As the territories formed constitutional conventions to join the Union, levels of expectation rose steadily during the 19th century as to what constituted an adequate school system for statehood. The states copied each other, borrowing what were thought to be the most advanced features of state school systems to incorporate the latest provisions in their constitutions, statutory codes, and other educational requirements.

Hortatory preambles, vague constitutional articles, terse statutes, a feeble administrative apparatus, and grudgingly ceded, poorly implemented tax laws did little more than construct a symbol, yet it was an invitation to which local citizens responded enthusiastically with the raising of common schools. Practically speaking, the ideal was unenforceable; the means of enforcement simply did not exist. Only its attractiveness, the perceived usefulness of literacy, and the indisputable need for unifying elements in so centrifugal a nation sustained the institution powerfully on the social and economic currents of the time.

Without regulating schools directly or belaboring the details of what should happen in classrooms, states constituted schooling as a public good in American society. They did this not by bringing the institution into being—the people and their communities did that—but by framing the activity as a desirable element of the political culture and permanent institutional base of the state. The "system" of schooling, as it was called from the beginning by reformers and lawmakers, was little more than a ritual in which people voluntarily participated. Schools were distant from the reach of the law but not its spirit. Thus, education expanded with the nation, goaded by evangelical school reformers, officiated by callow and impecunious teachers, and proceeding under the watchful eye of locally elected school trustees.

The common schools established in this manner developed unevenly across the states (Richardson, 1984a, 1984b), and they were not without conflict. If it is possible to say that the 19th century produced a consensus, a set of core agreements about schooling that to this day undergirds the institution as a public good, the other side must be acknowledged as well. The common schools were bluntly majoritarian. Often, they simply overrode the conscience of minorities (James, in press), well into the 20th century. For nearly as long, they were closed or harshly insensitive to the needs of those perceived by local majorities as outsiders (J. D. Anderson, 1988; Kaestle, 1983; Tyack & Hansot, 1982).

A further problem that accompanied the spread of common schools was that local partisans occasionally pocketed the proceeds of land grants instead of depositing them in permanent school endowments. Local control had few checks built into it for preventing corruption or remedying poor performance. By necessity, the first and most authoritative acts of state governments often consisted of mandating clearer, more centralized controls over the management of funds. As the nation expanded westward, such provisions became part of the basic package of state controls expected in constitutions for admission to statehood (Tyack & James, 1986).

A third problem for these grass-roots institutions operating under such diffuse central authority was the difficulty of providing a consistent level of funding to sustain qualified instruction, even for the few weeks when children were most likely to attend school. The land endowments furnished an incentive to build schools, but they could not supply adequate funds to continue them. Therefore, "rate bills" or tuition fees were commonplace. The effort to replace those fees with a stable base of public tax revenue was among the most divisive issues in the politics of education before the present century (Kaestle, 1983). When that threshold was crossed, states entered a phase when they began to legislate more comprehensive laws to stipulate the organization, funding, and content of schooling, even going so far as to make attendance compulsory for children of certain ages, though these latter laws were merely symbolic (James, 1986).

In short, the states used constitutional and statutory norms as little more than a suggestive imagery. State authority represented an exhortation more than an injunction to build schools. The financial incentives were weak. More than anything else, widely held beliefs about the need for republican virtue and political community—and, among elites and the respectable class, a fear of the lower classes—made it possible to raise schools under such an aegis. It can truly be said that the early structure of law and policy for state school systems was a source of standards in the process of educational change. Those standards, however, were more like the banners waving at the front of a slowly moving, disorderly pageant, not standards as we generally understand the term today: precise calibrations designed to hold movement within an acceptable range of tolerance in machines. Such imprecise standards worked as well as they did in the past because they were open to, and mostly congruent with, the values of local majorities in a society that believed passionately in direct democracy. Ironically, their very success in creating more universal access to publicly subsidized schooling led to serious problems that such institutions were ill-prepared to address.

State Action and Administrative Hegemony

Between the 1890s and roughly 1930, several changes took place in the organization of schooling that had lasting consequences for educational practice throughout the nation. One must, of course, take into account regional variations, the idiosyncracies of leadership and political cultures, the strength of organized opposition in different localities, and other types of unevenness in the pattern. Nevertheless, over several decades there was a clear trajectory to the national pattern of schooling authority, resulting in major features still in existence today. To the extent that there are recurrent problems with the performance of school systems, whether stemming from academic achievement, students dropping out, or the failure of schools to address social needs, the administrative calculus of schooling systems continues to favor changes consistent with the bureaucratic structures introduced in that earlier era, whereas it tends to reject innovations that are not. A vision of efficiency and economy subdues the spontaneous dynamism of intrinsic educational aims. The embedded sanctions of the institution cause its managers, estranged from the process of instruction, to turn repeatedly to technical and organizational considerations framed at the highest levels of control within the administrative state (Callahan, 1962; James, 1969).

Beginning in urban areas, school systems developed into incipient bureaucracies during the late 19th century (Katz, 1968b; Tyack, 1967). School leaders responded to the unstable social conditions, the ethnic and class conflict, and the vagaries of urban politics by pressing for more formal, hierarchical structures of control and layers of supervisory authority, insulated to a greater degree than in the past from the will of local political authorities and from direct contact with the practice of teaching. During the era of municipal reform around the turn of the century, the centralization of urban school boards paralleled a similar trend in local representative government. Centralization was accompanied by administrative consolidation of school districts from ward and neighborhood units into larger jurisdictions, thus diluting local representation and driving a wedge between school decision making and local politics (Cronin, 1973; Tyack, 1974).

Buttressing these institutional changes were several other reforms that came to the fore in the period. Compulsory schooling laws, backed by stringent means of enforcement such as truant officers and juvenile courts, became increasingly effective during the early decades of the 20th century (Tyack, 1976; Tyack & Berkowitz, 1977). Larger and larger majorities of legally defined schoolchildren came under the regime of formal schooling during their formative years. Alongside these laws and institutional controls were others that excluded children from the labor force during the years of compulsory schooling (S. B. Wood, 1968). As elementary school attendance became more and more universal after the turn of the century and high school attendance began to double every decade from 1890 to World War II, schooling remained a local activity but a national quest, surrounded by a hortatory culture of reform that was marked by wide swings in emphasis between competing views of what schools should accomplish (James & Tyack, 1983).

Professionally initiated reforms during the early decades of this century dealt with the growing diversity of school populations by differentiating school services. They created specialized institutions and tracks for academic, vocational, and commercial interests. They introduced a growing panoply of social services and ancillary activities as part of schooling. The cumulative effect was greater variety, more intensive standardization along with specialization, and administratively controlled correlation of subject matter and school services in the educational program generally (Kliebard, 1987; Krug, 1969, 1972).

One of the salient aspects of educational change in those years was the campaign of university-based experts, federal officials, foundations, and national associations to persuade state and city governments that they should enact laws to consolidate school districts into larger jurisdictions under the centralized control of school administrators. Unlike today's advocates of deregulation and restructuring, the successful reformers in the era of accelerated bureaucratization offered state and local officials a fully elaborated vision of what the modern school should look like under more centralized and consolidated control (Tyack, 1974).

The states were obliging when confronted with the steady persuasion of an authoritative and apparently united professional community. They enacted laws over the years to consolidate jurisdictions and succeeded dramatically in reducing the number of public school districts—from 127,531 in 1932 to 15,577 in 1988 (U.S. Department of Education, 1989, Table 79, p. 90). Especially in the areas of most rapid institutional expansion, notably the high school, state law created a standard set of sanctions to guide the development of local practice toward the professional and bureaucratic norms favored by administrative reformers in the field of education (Troxel, 1928). For their part, parents and students expressed their resistance to those norms—when they chose to do so—by attempting to maintain the integrity and shared universe of meanings they identified with schools as community institutions (D. K. Cohen, 1985; Lynd & Lynd, 1929; Peshkin, 1982).

Strong opposition to bureaucratic centralization came from urban teachers (Urban, 1982; Wrigley, 1982) as well as from local political officials whose educational authority was displaced by the more concentrated power of professionals and newly centralized boards of education. Other reforms, such as vocational education, Americanization, and intelligence testing, created controversies in various places and led to sundry forms of compromise and imposition. On the whole, though, the vision of the administrative reformers became the authoritative structure of schools in the public sector—elementary, junior high, and high schools as well as other specialized institutions. The vision received decisive support from foundations, the federal and state governments, business and professional leaders, the burgeoning cadres of school administrators, and the growing urban professional class.

The administrative reformers of the past succeeded in orchestrating a coordinated set of controls—from constitutional provisions and state school codes to local plans for school reorganization and developed centers for research and professional training. Determined advocates of professionalization, they envisioned a closed system of expert decision making on school matters, working with but also insulated against local democracy and responsive to higher administrative authority in the district and state department of education, to the ideas coming from centralized professional organizations, to the findings of the research community, and to overall direction from more distant, representative organs of government corresponding to higher levels of the governing structure in education. At higher levels of governance the issues of schools and classrooms were typically reframed, translated from instructional or other intraorganizational terms into a language reflecting the operation of administrative systems and overall efficiency—the certification of teachers, allocation of resources, size of schools, levels of attendance, distribution of credits, number of overage and truant students, and so forth. The accountability systems of the day, such as they were, provided formal and administrative information on district operations according to the dictates of this larger institutional structure, which was set up purposefully to control the organization of schools from beyond the sites where instruction occurred.

Such a portrait of how state authority was used during the era of administrative ascendancy should not be taken to mean that states directly controlled the public schools. They did not by any means, and probably never will. Local boards governed directly within the boundaries of the law and sometimes beyond them. Administrators ran the schools as organizations. Teachers taught as they saw fit behind the classroom door. Students invented their own cultures among themselves while learning some of the things they were supposed to along the way. Parents were generally quiescent as long as the symbolic rules of the game were not shifted too abruptly. Taxes remained locally controlled for the most part, though states began to exercise greater control over school finance systems and to create minimum foundation programs to help poor districts (see Mort, 1933). School boards continued to exercise direct oversight of local school operations within the boundaries set by state law. State bureaucracies continued to be minuscule, and even in the most activist states they remained distant from schooling organizations. States did specify the school program to a much greater degree than in the past (Flanders, 1925), in some cases requiring the inculcation of particular values such as temperance and patriotism along with conventional school subject matter (Tyack et al., 1987), but the actions of the states were congruent with the local administrative structures for schooling that they had sanctioned in law and policy.

Not yet could it be said that any branch of the state government was acting in a concerted way to overcome the local consensus about schooling, except to establish the administrative structure and its professional leadership. Thus, school consolidation was a state intervention but not a continuing regulatory act. Once the bureaucratic school was in place, it became the host, not the uninvited guest. Law and policy were framed on the assumption that the school was functioning properly once it had been set up along administrative lines at the local level. In this way, schools were locally controlled, but in educational governance they were treated, once they had been bureaucratized, as if they were within the ambit of the state, which indeed they were in much more than the diffusely symbolic sense that they had been in the past.

Fundamentally, the states sanctioned an administrative system largely under professional control but immersed in local institutional pressures under the limited rule of a school board. School administrators had to deal with the remnants of local democracy in generally unrepresentative school boards (Counts, 1927; Gross, 1958), now sharply confined in their effective powers. They also had to supervise, while seeking working rules of accommodation with, disempowered teachers collectively denied a voice in policy and administration. This politically fragile construction, which was a closed system in some ways but also a volatile human world of suppressed powers, constituted the reality of "the one best system" (Tyack, 1974). Its resilience can be appreciated only by looking at the sustained attacks on that system in later years with the rise of the regulatory state.

The Regulatory State and Its Problems

States constituted school systems in the 19th century; it was enough, then, that schools existed and appeared to serve the interests of the majority who chose to use them. If states had wished to do more, the reality was that they could not, for their governing powers were not elaborated enough to specify local administrative structures or regulate the internal workings of schools. Even the states taken as a whole, the Union, could do no more than symbolize and encourage, unless it raised troops and put an army in the field to break an unacceptable template of local institutions—as in the Civil War.

When states expanded their sanctions over schooling from the 1890s to the 1930s—compelling attendance, placing administrators in charge of local schooling organizations, and regularizing the schools as bureaucratic organizations—still it was enough merely to trace a vague outline for the structure and functioning of the system. The states found it expedient to rely on administrative authority and professional expertise, backed by applied research, but embedded as much as possible (once bureaucratic structures were put in place) in the local consensus about what schooling should be. This was sufficient to maintain and even to continue improving local operations.

To a large degree, despite their expanded sanctions, states still did not enumerate what had to occur within the production process of schooling itself. They did not, and could not, exercise direct control over the decisions that most directly shaped the educational experience of students within local school systems. Professional influence and local consensus tended to determine such decisions. Under this regime of educational control, the key issue for maintaining administrative ascendancy was how to defuse the conflict between professionals, interest groups, local political interests, the shifting boundaries of local public opinion, and disaffected groups. For decades the system proved to be remarkably impermeable to minority dissent in most places. Given the professional dominance of school affairs that came with administrative consolidation, the debates over internal schooling processes and the sorting of students took place most fiercely within the profession, not between levels of government acting to represent different constituencies.

The momentous change that occurred after World War II can be understood most clearly by looking at the transformation of the federal role in education. From the early days of the Republic until the 1950s, the role of the federal government in education had been singularly constitutive, including the gathering of information to demonstrate that school systems in fact existed and were showing progress. As Hyman (1986) has noted, national lawmakers expanded the social rights embodied in American citizenship with landmark enactments that helped to organize whole constellations of social, cultural, and economic activity around them. One such law was the Northwest Ordinance of 1787, which provided land grants for the development of schools. Another was the Morrill Land Grant Act passed during the Civil War, which provided large parcels of land for the founding of state colleges and universities. A third was the G.I. Bill enacted at the end of World War II, channeling millions of Americans—with the help of government funding—into the rapidly expanding systems of higher education. To these laws we might add the government's support of vocational education since World War I (Cuban, 1982) and its creation of adult education and public works programs during the 1930s.

All of these laws channeled dollars from the federal government to individuals, states, institutions, and local jurisdictions, but none of them regulated to any great extent the activity that took place at the local level. Essentially, the laws assumed that states and their dependent jurisdictions would create the administrative structures necessary to carry out the spirit of the law. Alternatively, in the case of the New Deal programs, the federal government set up autonomous structures for providing services that were not connected to state and local governing structures. Not surprisingly, those programs were short-lived (Tyack, Lowe, & Hansot, 1984).

All this began to change in the 1940s. In a series of cases during the interwar years, the U.S. Supreme Court reinterpreted the constitutional standard for applying the Bill of Rights: Federal rights guarantees could be applied directly to the law and policy of state and local jurisdictions. The case of *West Virginia State Board of Education v. Barnette* (1943), in which the court upheld the right of a religious minority not to say the Pledge of Allegiance to the American Flag in school even though state law compelled it, demonstrated that federal authorities could, under some circumstances, regulate the behavioral rules and operational procedures of schools. As the court said emphatically in that case:

> The Fourteenth Amendment, as now applied to the States, protects the citizen against the State itself and all of its creatures—Boards of Education not excepted. (*West Virginia State Board of Education v. Barnette*, 1943)

In 1954, the court's decision in *Brown v. Board of Education* took these powers yet further with the holding that states and school systems engaged in racial segregation were violating the Fourteenth Amendment's guarantee of equal protection under the laws. The decision introduced substantially expanded national authority into educational policy-making. It also reflected the growing influence of organized interest groups outside the traditionally closed system of the administrative state (Kluger, 1975; Tushnet, 1987). The pressure of such coalitions on judicial and legislative policy-making at the national level, then subsequently at the state level as well, has become one of the hallmarks of the regulatory state to our own day (Bailey, 1981; Kirst & Somers, 1981; Mazzoni, 1982; Peterson & Rabe, 1983).

With increased powers of enforcement and compliance on issues stemming from constitutional rights, courts became major players in the politics of educational change (Flicker, 1990; J. C. Hogan, 1974; Horowitz, 1977; Kirp & Jensen, 1986; Nystrand & Staub, 1978; van Geel, 1987; Yudof, Kirp, van Geel, & Levin, 1982). Desegregation became the most salient issue of educational politics in the postwar era (see Wilkinson,

1979), producing a vast literature on the implementation of desegregation and local case studies (e.g., Fine, 1986; Grant, 1988; Kirp, 1982; Peterson, 1976). It is probably no exaggeration to say that the confluence of social movements, a more activist view of judicial interpretation, and the growth of positive state action in the national legislative arena to establish constitutionally grounded entitlements to social benefits have irrevocably altered the terms on which it is possible to negotiate the politics of educational change at the state and local levels.

This is not the whole story, however. Although ostensibly unique to this country, where the historical development of race relations has played a special role in national political development, the use of equality guarantees for enlarging national authority over schooling institutions paralleled a worldwide trend in the industrialized nations toward increased and more centralized governmental authority (Boli-Bennett, 1979). Two world wars and a rapidly integrating world economy tended to push the efficiency of educational systems onto the agenda of public policy in nations everywhere.

In the United States, as elsewhere, federal policy also moved ahead broadly on issues defined as a national interest, beyond specific rights enforcement and entitlements. A salient example was the attempt to spur mathematics and science improvement in schools with the National Defense Education Act after the launching of Sputnik by the Soviet Union. Federal legislation moved ahead on a broad front, including specific equality issues such as race, language, disability, and gender, but also issues of system effectiveness such as curricular improvement, administrative efficiency, and the quality of teachers. Federal intervention through legislation as well as court action became a salient feature in the postwar politics of education (for an overview of the expanding federal role, see Kaestle & Smith, 1982). Studies have looked closely at changes in the politics of education within the federal government itself (Graham, 1984; Sproull, Weiner, & Wolf, 1978) as well as in the effects of federal priorities on the direction of educational systems (Ravitch, 1983; Spring, 1989).

In contrast to earlier forms of statecraft, which provided general goals and formal administrative structures for schools, regulatory action specified activity and demanded precise measures of outcomes. Rights litigation and legislation in support of the handicapped, for example, has seen courts making administrative decisions about the internal operation of schools, far beyond the effective governing capacity of governments in other nations, even those with more centralized states (Kirp & Jung, 1984). Combined with the growing legalization of education to mediate labor disputes with organized teachers, the use of law as an instrument for managing local schools has been a steadily growing trend throughout the country since the 1960s, most evident in leading industrial states (Jensen & Griffin, 1984) but affecting patterns of governance in smaller states as well.

A major reorientation of efforts to change educational practice accompanied this growth in federal policy-making influence. It could still be said that the main features of the administrative state were in place. The sanctions maintaining schools as a formal institution under administrative authority were left intact and even strengthened by the accountability demands of regulation. But the convergence of organized groups upon the state in quest of specific changes for their own particular ends made pressure and conflict a daily fact of life for those who attempted to frame policy, manage schools, or teach there with a chaos of competing demands falling upon them (Tyack & Hansot, 1982).

One visible effect, after a generation of intergovernmental struggle over the control of education, has been a growing rift between the intent of policy directives and the life of schools (Iannaccone, 1982; see also D. K. Cohen, 1982). At its worst, the legalization of school decision making backfires and becomes "regulatory unreasonableness" (Kagan, 1986), paralyzing decision processes within schools. Such interventions are necessary, within the range of activities selected for the enforcement of rights guarantees, to preserve the fundamental interests of the democratic state. But multiple competing controls and fragmentation can in themselves threaten to undermine the effects of such guarantees at the local level—by driving privileged citizens from the public system, for example, and lowering public commitment to maintaining an adequate level of services for the predominantly less privileged citizens who remain (Levin, 1983; Sherman, 1980; see also Hirschman, 1970, 1982). Nevertheless, mandates and funding from higher levels of government have had a substantial impact on services for those who previously had been underserved or systematically excluded (Smith & O'Day, in press-b), though such gains have not been matched by economic gains (Carnoy & Levin, 1985; Levin, 1977; see also Levy, 1987).

Another important lever for creating the regulatory state was the move to overturn locally controlled financing of schools. When viewed against the long trajectory of state involvement in financing schools, this stream of constitutional challenges was tied to accords reached in the constitutive and administrative stages of state building in education. However, no longer would it be appropriate, argued the new wave of court cases in the 1970s and 1980s, to permit such wide latitude for local discretion in generating resources for schools. The inequalities were too great to stand up to the constitutional guarantees for an equal education (Wise, 1968).

Impelled by constitutional interpretation, the school finance issue has gradually been removed from administrative politics within an insulated profession. It has been forced into the more contentious arena of regulatory politics as part of the open strife of the state amidst its embattled constituencies and organized interest groups (Lehne, 1978) as well as its entrenched political cultures (Bennett, 1983). With greater activism by state supreme courts on rights issues generally (Galie, 1982) and growing legislative activism in response to rights demands and concerns about the performance of school systems, state governments joined the federal government in a highly variegated pattern of increased legalization, growing centralized control over funding, and a continuing inability to change the internal processes of schools. Federal and state policy entered the equation of school decision making as ever-present forces to be reckoned with in the politics of educational change.

Some of the early signals that there might be constructive ways to move beyond the policy bind of intervention, compliance, resistance, and fragmentation emphasized the need to dwell less on top-down program priorities and more on how schools mobilize resources from various sources to operate effectively (Porter, 1973). Similarly, the earlier literature contained suggestions that studies should move beyond the conception of schools as merely backwards and refractory if they failed to heed the enlightened dictates of top-down reform. Instead, it is necessary to focus much more precisely on the dynamism of local schools, their sources of adaptation, and their intrinsic dispositions to change (Hawley, 1975; see also Berman & McLaughlin, 1974). To bring about constructive change in schools, according to this perspective, policy authority and funding should be used with greater discretion not merely to regulate but to support crucial processes within schools, such as staff development and organizational leadership.

The possibility on the horizon, indicated by a strong emphasis in the implementation literature on local practice and professional growth, is that the regulatory state might achieve its goals for schooling more readily by transmitting a new generation of enabling rules through the multilayered system of educational governance, conditionally open ended and choice enhancing as long as schools and communities are willing to incorporate basic constitutional guarantees into their responses to the state's invitation to change. Such action would be designed to protect schooling as a public good, but actively invest in local organizations on a basis that will build leadership and self-initiated forms of professional capacity.

A question that will arise with increasing frequency is whether state leaders might be able to learn enough about local practice and the educational process itself to be able to make rules in a form that will lead to willing action and concerted change. As will be shown in the next section, this question forces us to look more closely at the possibilities of state leadership beyond the developed administrative and regulatory capacities that are now in place. Are states capable of entering into a new type of relation with school systems, as they have done at critical junctures in the past when such change was necessary not only for the health of the schools but for the vitality of the state itself?

STATES AND EDUCATIONAL CHANGE

Strategy and Structure

The interest in state governments as a site for educational change quickened after the "New Federalism" of Ronald Reagan began to take effect in the early 1980s. Federal funding and program mandates slackened; civil rights enforcement at the behest of the federal government grew lax. Consolidating program entitlements into block grants and curtailing social spending, the federal government pursued a strategy of devolution (Astuto & Clark, 1988).

In education, this trend reinforced a growing state presence in shaping educational policy. Throughout the 1980s, despite works in the field of educational policy analysis that persisted in emphasizing the need for local and school-site initiative in educational innovation (McLaughlin, 1987), scholars pointed to the emergence of the states as increasingly dominant partners not only in the constitutive and administrative aspects of school governance as in the past, but in a more regulatory and interventionist role (Elmore, 1984; Fuhrman, 1987; Kirst, 1984; McLaughlin & Catterall, 1984). Elmore (1984) noted that, contrary to the rhetoric of devolution, an increasing interdependence of governmental levels, rather than more independent state and local roles, would be necessary for improving education (see also Fuhrman & Elmore, 1990).

Legally and fiscally, the center of gravity for elementary and secondary education in this country resides at the state level. It was for this reason that federal funds from Great Society programs poured through the floodgates of state agencies, attempting to use their administrative leverage for regulatory and interventionist aims. Also for this reason, during the era of maximum federal expansion in the 1960s people like James Conant (1964) and Governor Terry Sanford (1967) called for greater attention to the role of the states in shaping educational policy. They and others pursued this theme despite the poor record of states in achieving regulatory and redistributive goals in public policy. New efforts were made to document the existing state systems of education (Fuller & Pearson, 1969a, 1969b) and outline their major initiatives for extending state control over schooling (Fitzwater, 1968). These studies built upon and extended earlier work done from an administrative perspective (Chase & Morphet, 1949), but they were more closely connected with federal goals and the tacit aim of working through existing policy systems to support local interventions.

Simultaneously, a new generation of political research on the state politics of education began to emerge, conceptualizing educators as but one interest group in a complex arena of policy-making that, with all its limitations, increasingly would hold the purse strings for state school systems (Bailey, Frost, Marsh, & Wood, 1962; Campbell & Mazzoni, 1976; Masters, Salisbury, & Eliot, 1964; Usdan, 1963; Usdan, Minar, & Hurwitz, 1969; Wirt & Kirst, 1972; Zeigler & Johnson, 1972; see also McGivney, 1984). In addition to such studies, comprehensive analyses of legal provisions began to appear (Lawyers' Committee, 1978), along with increasing attention, by economists and by school finance experts drawn from the field of administration, to the specific fiscal processes of state finance systems (e.g., Grubb & Michelson, 1974).

As the study of state governance intensified during the era of federal expansion, more detailed knowledge began to accumulate, but some distortions of perspective began to appear as well. The best new studies viewed the state from the perspective of federal program mandates. Frequently, those studies were funded, in fact, through the federal government's education bureaucracy, which was involved in massive efforts to change state and local education bureaucracies. Researchers interested in state governance became involved in this intergovernmental struggle of policy influence by looking at the state department of education through the lens of federal interventionism. It became fashionable to treat state departments of education as an administrative structure for achieving regulatory aims, and at least implicitly if not explicitly to judge their effectiveness on that basis, rather than viewing state government principally within the social and political contexts out of which state sanctions had been developed for educational systems (Campbell, Sroufe, & Layton, 1967; B. D. Friedman, 1971; B. D. Friedman & Dunbar, 1971; U.S. Department of Health, Education & Welfare, 1970; case studies in Berke & Kirst, 1972; Milstein, 1976; Murphy, 1973, 1974). The tendency to look at state government through the lens of federal programs continues into some of the recent research as well (Darling-Hammond & Marks, 1983; McDonnell & McLaughlin, 1982).

After the rise of federal interventionism in the 1950s and 1960s, the question of how to make the politics of change more susceptible to planned intervention became the obsession of specialized research communities far beyond the scholars who studied state governance. Those communities were becoming, however, much less attached to the controlling professional and administrative elites of school systems than in the past. The channeling of larger subsidies from higher levels of government naturally gave rise to evaluation and policy analysis, tailored to the instrumental aims of federal and philanthropic programs acting to change the delivery of social services through existing structures.

Another trend in educational research appeared in the attempt to provide systemic analyses of the politics of educational change, identifying the political conditions affecting the interventions sought by policymakers. Beyond the literature on state politics and education, a broader literature on the politics of education began to develop, drawing its conceptual forms mostly from political science and systems theory to show analytically how different groups operate in the policy system of school politics (for reviews of the literature, see Iannaccone & Cistone, 1974; Kirst & Mosher, 1969; Peterson, 1974; Wirt, 1972).

Such research offered no brief for administrative supremacy, nor any implicit undercurrent of exhortation for educational expansion. Treating educational institutions as if they were intrinsically no different from other political and institutional phenomena, research of this sort claimed objectivity in its systematic probing of group formations and interests, their interactions in educational policy-making, and rational assessments of the ways in which policy processes allocate power and resources in education. Nevertheless, the study of politics and policy became increasingly intertwined, in large part because elite centers of educational research expanded with the growth of governmental grants and philanthropic initiatives aiming to change education (Clifford & Guthrie, 1988). There was a tacit but widely shared hope that researchers could develop knowledge that would make future innovations more powerful and more easily adopted in American schools.

As state policy influence continued to expand in the 1980s while federal influence declined, a renewed interest in the politics of educational governance began to emerge in the research community. There were calls for greater attention to state governance beyond the state education department and a stronger focus on the dynamics of state-local relations (Murphy, 1980), including that battered ornament of democratic school governance, the local school board (Kirst, 1988b). For larger states, researchers began to look more closely at organizational processes within the state-level education bureaucracy itself (Meltsner & Bellavita, 1983). The approach showed promise in moving the emphasis from the unsuccessful implementation of federal program mandates to state policy formation, intergovernmental relations, and linkages to educational practice. The drawback of the organizational framework at the state level is that it can sometimes lose perspective on the far more powerful and decisive activity of the political process, which in organizational studies is typically viewed as the "environment" of the policy system. Some of the literature, therefore, presses the discussion beyond organizational systems of state policy formation to embrace political communication and the limited influence of the educational bureaucracy on political decisions (Mazzoni,

1985; but see also Masters et al., 1964, for an earlier interpretation of the same phenomenon).

The example of testing reforms in the 1980s shows clearly why an emphasis on agency performance in the educational bureaucracy cannot give a clear reading on the politics of change. Reinforcing the pervasive use of standardized tests in American schools today (see Anderson, 1982, on scope of use), states over the past decade have issued a profusion of legislatively driven policy mandates for more widespread testing at more frequent grade intervals to gauge the performance of school systems (Airasian, 1987; Doyle & Hartle, 1985). Such concerns are not new (Resnick, 1980, 1982), but the sudden visibility and volatility of political will are striking. Along with the demand for better means of assessment have come more complex strategies of technical assistance, dissemination, program development, and scrutiny of plans for school improvement at the local level by state officials (Dougherty, 1983), all showing the concern of elected officials for linking funding to measurable educational outcomes that a discontented public will accept (see Richards, 1988, for an overview of state monitoring systems). The upshot is that agency performance and the organizational realities of professional bureaucracies can offer no privileged view of educational change. Politics—the calculus of consent that puts state leaders face to face with their constituencies without benefit of professional and bureaucratic filters—ultimately drives the agenda for state action in the field of education.

A natural response from those who study classrooms and curricula has been to decry the "external" demands of governing agencies and to lament their damaging impact on instruction (e.g., see Wood, 1988). There is much truth in this claim. Those who study federalism, however, argue that the misalignment has less to do with fundamental aims than with the challenge of working out governing relationships in new ways to strengthen professional capacities and local initiative (Elmore & McLaughlin, 1988; Elmore and Associates, 1990) while at the same time empowering the states to govern in ways that will prove most effective from an educational standpoint (Smith & O'Day, in press-a).

A more fundamental challenge comes from the argument that equates poor agency performance in the federalist system with "politics," declaring that the alternative is to clear away the bureaucratic rubble and reconstitute schools as "markets" (Chubb & Moe, 1988). Of course, this view also must turn to politics in order to change the system in the desired ways. At its root, popular loyalty to schooling is a political act, not strictly an economic term of social life (Tyack, Kirst, & Hansot, 1980).

To refashion the social contract underlying our schooling institutions will mean working against the crystallization of bureaucratic authority and political aggrandizement that endures from the past as an organizing feature of educational governance. If history is any guide, reformers and researchers who truly wish to be part of this change must again enter the realm of politics, as they did many years ago (while pretending not to) when they envisioned the structure of sanctions that buttresses the administrative state. The strategies of reform and research cannot merely forge ahead; they must themselves change, because the era of professional dominance is over in American education. Working in coalitions now, alongside others who see the need for change, including the disaffected, the people most poorly served by existing institutions, reformers and researchers will continue to find themselves irresistibly and ambivalently drawn to each other as they confront the challenge of discovering new ways for state action to stimulate educational improvement.

Here again, the issue of assessment emerges as an important barometer of change. States are attempting to move policy closer to instruction. The aim is to control, but also to understand, and if the latter could become predominant, it would open the former to new possibilities that local practitioners and parents demanding instructional improvement would find immensely rewarding. So far the policy agenda is not well aligned with the efforts of those engaged directly in the educational process at the local level; the overwhelming emphasis is administrative and increasingly regulatory. Scholars familiar with developments taking place within state-level governance detect the possibility of important changes, however, as political will, rough and ready as it may be at certain junctures in educational history, creates demands for better state-local linkages in improving education (Darling-Hammond & Wise, 1985; Fuhrman & Elmore, 1990; Turnbull, 1985). The communication taking place over state assessment embraces not only the development of state policy and the attempt to improve local school performance, but the maintenance of strong public support for schools, including financial support as well as legitimacy (M. Cohen, 1988). Policy mistakes, errors in judgment about what matters most in teaching and learning, will lead to a weakened educational process, worsening schools and generating political crisis for the states. A better understanding of assessment is important for maintaining the momentum of school improvement by continually expanding public awareness of the possibilities for educational excellence beyond narrowly conceived, test-driven schemes of control (Kirst, 1985).

The example of state assessment points to the urgency in discovering more about the inner workings of state governance, including its intergovernmental links to federal and local levels. Testing is tied in with a larger problem of accountability in school systems, a theme that experts in the administrative state thought they had settled, but that has proven to be much more problematic with the rise of regulatory interventionism (Murphy & Cohen, 1974). There have even been recurring doubts about the ability of social science to generate valid knowledge about school productivity, and a sense that new systems, perhaps even new kinds of information, will be necessary (Guthrie, 1976; Odden, 1990). An important task for research on the politics of change will be to discern the implications of various accountability designs proposed or established to influence school practice (Benveniste, 1985; Richards, 1988), making sure that what is measured equals what is sought by states and schools and that the means of measuring it do not prevent teachers and students from seeking it in the best possible ways.

The Allure of Political Culture

The elusive dream of those who studied politics of educational change over the past generation was that if one were able to analyze the policy system, categorize the channels of action that produce its outcomes, and find predictable variables in state political cultures, it might then be possible to influence the policy-making process and thereby achieve beneficial results for the improvement of education. A broader goal among political scientists, who as a group are generally not attached to the administrative structures of education or to school improvement as a professional goal, has been the elucidation of democratic processes with the prospect of strengthening American federalism and improving governmental performance at all levels. These two underlying aims have intertwined to produce an array of comparative studies, taxonomies, and models. Even though the goal has remained elusive, it is useful to consider past literature in formulating new ideas for adapting policy strategies to local initiatives.

A key issue in the literature has been the ways in which interest groups shape educational policy through legislative action and gubernatorial leadership. It has been found that varying political cultures are significant in structuring attention to educational issues at the state level. Those structures, in turn, are tied into statewide policy systems that often differ substantially from one another (Campbell & Mazzoni, 1976; Iannaccone, 1967; Iannaccone & Cistone, 1974).

Traditionally, as we have seen in the rise of the administrative state, professional educators and university-based experts backed by foundations and the federal government had an important strategic influence on the design of governance structures for school systems. In a poignant way, much of the research conducted on the politics of education at the state level over the past generation has been an attempt to recapture lost capacities of authoritative influence, perhaps to impute some remnant of rational structure as the administrative system has become more fragmented. If either systems analysis or political culture could be used predictively for influencing policy, such research would become a player in its own right for shaping educational systems. Methodologically, however, such studies appear to have been more successful in generating case studies and categories than in producing usable knowledge to shape policy formation.

As an example, the degree of state centralization would seem to be a crucial variable in designing reforms for educational systems. Wirt (1977) developed a quantitative model for assessing the degree of centralization in state control over local districts. He took the model another step by using extensive documentation on state law and policy to suggest patterns in the way authority is allocated in the policy systems of states. This effort, like the detailed study of governance models in the work of Campbell and Mazzoni (1976) but more attuned to the processes through which policy outcomes are formed, furnishes good information about variation in state patterns of governance, but it does little to predict, much less to shape, major changes in governmental practice such as the rise of challenges to the school finance systems in a majority of states or the surge of legislation on statewide testing in the 1980s. The same can be said of taxonomies describing the categories of policy through which the state exercises its authority over local districts (Mitchell & Encarnation, 1984). To understand developments over time, one must find conceptualizations not limited to the policy system itself or even to the political culture of the states.

This is not to say that systematic studies of interstate variation and categories of policy authority have no value; they are, in fact, quite useful. Obviously, the shaping of educational policy will proceed differently in New York, Nebraska, or Hawaii. Intriguingly, in a later study Wirt (1980) found that the degree of centralization, at least as represented by level of state funding, did not necessarily correspond to the level of state control over local school funding. Such a finding reaffirms the value of understanding political culture, but it also points to the need for looking more deeply at the social contexts, historical developments, and intergovernmental accords that give rise to state action.

Scholars continue to be fascinated with possibilities of tracking interstate variation in search of policy variables (Coombs, 1980), attitudinal factors (Welch & Peters, 1980), and socioeconomic correlates (Allen & Clark, 1981) toexplain the dynamics of educational change. Such studies have proved valuable in the task of analyzing how things work, but in the end we have the problem of static theory, an equilibrium that cannot explain the primal forces that upset its logic and drive the state to the making of new history. Research along these lines succeeds, principally, in demonstrating the constraints presented by different political cultures, policy systems, and fiscal structures (see Wong, 1989, for the best recent study), thus indicating tactics and a probable scope of action for new initiatives.

With such problems attending the effort to make systematic comparisons among states, the in-depth case study would seem to recommend itself. Although this approach has proved valuable for deepening the context of policy development and giving it a historical dimension (Lovrich, Daynes, & Ginger, 1980), such studies have not proved satisfying in explaining educational change. This deficiency is especially visible when abrupt shifts occur and there are transformations in the way educational issues are framed by lawmakers (Burlingame & Geske, 1979). In a promising development, Marshall et al. (1989) have extended the notion of political culture by including underlying "public values" as well as the "culture" embedded in a state's constitutional and statutory development as active agents capable of precipitating change in educational policy, thus conceptualizing political culture to include normative structures institutionalized in state government, along with the attitudes, values, and behavioral norms of political actors and public officials. To some extent this type of analysis had been done in the past, but in addition to thinking about models and systems, these researchers seek to explain how leaders generate meaning, define the legitimate arena for the exercise of political will, and act on the basis of their shared understandings.

Similarly, but without such impressive development on the conceptual plane, some of the case studies on school finance crises in the states have attempted to locate a more embedded view of the political economy of state action (e.g., Verstegen, Hooker, & Estes, 1986). Such an approach enlarges the focus beyond the identification of governance models in the administrative state. It carries the conversation beyond the heuristic of rational systems producing policy outputs. But still it cannot explain why educational change occurs when it does, and it cannot generate concepts to influence the direction of change.

Further light on the subject comes from recent studies of gubernatorial advocacy in the state policy process. The older research on the politics of education did not pay much attention to this issue. Although governors in the past were generally involved in state planning and the setting of priorities (Beyle & Wright, 1972), they were not as central to the strategic formulation of educational policy as were the key education interests and legislative leaders. Over the last decade, however, many governors have emerged as a dominant force in educational policy-making. Their capacities for educational leadership have been strengthened by organizations such as the National Governors Association and the Education Commission of the States. With better information and more specialized staff, governors are taking the lead in nationwide policy formulation for educational systems, far beyond any expectations that might emerge from a knowledge of interstate variation in governance systems or of distinctive political cultures. The phenomenon of gubernatorial advocacy has become much more than the familiar grandstanding endemic to electoral politics, at times acting as a phalanx in educational reform movements (Achilles, Lansford, & Payne, 1986; Alexander, 1986; Mazzoni, 1989). If the trend continues, researchers will need to revamp their conceptions about educational leadership and policy development at the state level, which are calibrated now to legislative coalitions, interest groups, and the education bureaucracy.

Moreover, it will be necessary to look more broadly at the gubernatorial leadership in relation to other executive agencies besides the state department of education to understand the coordinated development of state policy influence on local affairs (Murphy, 1980). Gubernatorial leadership tends to move on the symbolic level more than on the administrative plane; it seizes upon opportunities to connect with mass movements of thought and value in the electorate. Accordingly, much greater thought will need to be given in the literature on educational change to the symbolic and ideological correlates of school improvement—not just to attitudes and norms in the political culture, but to the ways in which leaders mobilize the aspirations of their constituencies with the language of policy (Burns, 1978).

As governors move aggressively into the domain of educational policymaking, two conditions will become more pronounced than in the past. First, governors are exposed to the vicissitudes of mass opinion, probably more so than other actors in state government and in ways less protected by party organizations. They are more personally and unavoidably caught up in the process of "mutual instruction" through which the populace reluctantly gives its consent to be governed and taxed (see Lutz, 1979). As a result, they are likely to view educational policy development, perhaps more than anyone within or beyond government except for those involved directly in social movements, as a constitutive act, full of exhortation, vague intentions, and a quest for political community. Because they traffick in imagery, not specifics—in this respect they are more like the school crusaders of the 19th century than the educational leaders of more recent times—they are drawn irresistibly to bold and unrefined ideals. They tend to treat policy as something open to political bargaining and elaboration as it reaches the people, not as something rational, predictable, or contingent on mediating structures of administration and professional expertise.

Second, as Alan Rosenthal has argued, one of the most salient political struggles taking place in the states today is between governors and legislatures (Rosenthal, 1990; see also Beyle & Dalton, 1983), and it is over the control of policy formation and oversight. Many of the goals that matter to people who are interested in education hinge on the resolution of that struggle. Both of these issues—the constitutive nature of gubernatorial advocacy and the struggle taking place for policy and budgetary leadership—will enter the consciousness of all educational planners and practitioners with much greater intensity over the next decade as state control continues to grow, indicating a high priority for research.

State legislatures might well be viewed as the supreme policymakers in American education. It is no accident that studies of political culture have focused intensively on their behavior. Studies of legislatures are among the most valuable for understanding the limited range of fundamental adaptation in such things as school funding and institutional redesign (Fuhrman & Rosenthal, 1981; Lehne, 1983; Mazzoni, 1978; Milstein & Jennings, 1973; Rosenthal, 1981; Rosenthal & Fuhrman, 1981). Highly informative studies of the more activist legislatures have appeared (e.g., BeVier, 1979; Bissell, 1979; Kirst, 1981; Mitchell & Iannaccone, 1980; Muir, 1982), as well as comparative studies showing the development of such key policy-making ingredients as legislative staffing (Rosenthal & Fuhrman, 1981), the process of legislative decision making (Mitchell, 1981), and significant capacities for direct oversight of spending programs and state-local relations (Rosenthal, 1983). Over the past decade, a substantial body of knowledge on how legislators work has emerged (Loewenberg, Patterson, & Jewell, 1985; Mitchell, 1981), and there have been seminal studies that explore the interaction between legislatures and state supreme courts (Elmore & McLaughlin, 1982; see also Tarr & Porter, 1988).

As federal legislative and judicial activism has become more attenuated over the past decade, scholars have reconsidered from new perspectives the interacting influence of state and federal legislation (Moore et al., 1983; Smith & Jenkins, 1982) and the capacities of state government for maintaining program priorities established during the era of expanding federal influence. Focusing on the recent waves of reform in the 1980s, researchers have attended closely to the response of legislatures to calls for change, noting, for example, their cautious attitude toward costs of some reforms but their perseverance in maintaining commitments once reforms have been adopted (Firestone, 1990; Kirst, Tyler, Ford, & Rogers, 1986).

In several respects, a new era has dawned in legislative policy-making for education. Interstate variation may not be the issue so much as the acute common problems that outlast economic fluctuations, such as the unavoidable challenge of building a common policy framework for human resource development (Danziger & Witte, 1988). This challenge will necessarily be met on a state-by-state basis, but the legislative leadership, gubernatorial staff, and many governors themselves have caught sight of the larger vision of legislative capacity in the formation of social policy. As Jerome Murphy has pointed out (1982), the states encountering the greatest criticism about the need for reform and school improvement are the very ones that have made the most progress in modernizing and expanding their overall operations. By attempting to bring the reality of school performance into fuller view with better information and refusing to accept the traditional administrative and interest-group filters of an earlier era, legislatures that have developed such capacities for thinking about school improvement are making the first steps toward a different way of dealing with educational issues—through direct political action applied to administrative systems and schooling organizations at much more frequent intervals than in the past. Whether such influence from the state level can help to enlarge, rather than diminish, the educational process in local schooling organizations remains to be seen.

GENERATING NEW CONCEPTS

What does all of this political change in education mean for the research community? There was a high degree of alignment once between the strategy of educational research and the newly emerging structure of schooling institutions. For many serious scholars, the memory of that relationship is an embarrassment, a straw man for critical studies. But it is true: During the first few decades of this century, when the bureaucratization of schooling was successfully implemented, leading administrative reformers assiduously cultivated the support of the research community.

Now the strategy of educational change is different. The situation of researchers as intellectuals within the modern state is far more ambivalent. The prevailing forms of educational governance in American society are undergoing great stress, possibly some lasting change in relation to their origins. New social agreements now affect such things as the distribution of resources (school finance and targeted compensatory assistance) and the rules of human association (desegregation, mainstreaming, sex equity). The much-studied policy system is in disarray. The structures of continuity in educational systems are responding, recalcitrant as they may be in some respects, to more dynamic and politicized relationships among teacher organizations, state agencies, political leadership, professional associations, business leaders, special interest groups, and the media. Some of the central configurations of power are becoming realigned; most notably, as we have seen, political leaders are playing a more direct role in policy formation and in educational change.

Though it is not a new development (Masters et al., 1964), school administrators and their allies are no longer in control of the policy agenda of governing authorities in education. The "zone of tolerance" (Boyd, 1976; McGivney & Moynihan, 1972) in which administrators used to operate with confidence has become a battle zone, frequently—especially in large cities—a disaster area for professional careers. Yet it is probably just as true today as it was in the past that school administrators, along with teachers and researchers, have an irreplaceable role to play in supplying local knowledge of school improvement. Perhaps a better understanding of state governance can help to provide openings for collaboration and shared vision attuned to developing opportunities for political action in support of teaching and learning.

Research on the politics of educational change can contribute to the emerging dialogue in several ways. A salient need, already addressed to some extent in the literature, will be to continue clarifying what states do when they make policy. Further studies are needed, both in-depth and comparative, to analyze the means through which decisions are reached and the ways they address substantive educational goals. It should be possible to use such work to suggest better ways of linking state governance more effectively to the improvement of schools at the local level. Social scientists relying on conventional methodologies will continue to encounter frustration in this quest, for reasons that Mitchell (1984) has identified in a perceptive review of the literature on educational policy analysis. As he points out, the knowledge generated by social scientists employing the methodologies now in use will be meaningful if and only if (a) it can be produced within a theoretically consistent frame of reference specifying the categories of possible state action in educational policy, and (b) the framework is also accepted and used by those involved in the process of formulating policies. This is as much as to say that politics should be rational.

Another approach that holds promise for clarifying state policy is the continuation of implementation studies. The task here will be to refine what is known so that it will be possible to engage local initiative more constructively. A highly refined stream of good advice needs to reach key actors at the state level, particularly in the legislative arena, to alert them to the depth of perspective needed for achieving goals at the levels of local governance, school leadership, and teaching practice (Elmore & McLaughlin, 1988; Kirst et al., 1986). Such research can continue to make lawmakers aware of the need for flexibility in setting policy goals for those who teach and learn in schools. From the standpoint of higher levels of governance, the policy literature suggests that better communication between levels of government can lead to improved performance.

Alongside the need for better policy communication with local schooling organizations looms another goal that might be called the self-education of leaders. The solution to the problem of public-sector performance and implementation failure is not likely to be found only by improving the level of understanding in relation to immediate policies as they are promulgated. After all, legislatures, courts, governors, and the federal government will continue altering priorities and channeling new demands through the structure. It will also be necessary to pursue in greater depth the education of policymakers and political leaders about the nature of teaching and learning as practiced by others and also by themselves (Scheffler, 1984), so that they can use their political will most intelligently to improve school systems and education in general.

That strategy, of course, is what Conant and Sanford were recommending when the Education Commission of the States was launched in the 1960s. It is the guiding light of other associations such as the National Conference of State Legislatures and the National Governors Association. More recently, new research centers on state policy, based in the research community and modeled after the Policy Analysis for California Education (PACE) project, have sprung up (McCarthy & Hall, 1989) to inform elected officials and the public about educational needs. The work of the centers has broken the boundaries of policy analysis by detaching the production of information from agency demands within particular government programs or under the direct auspices of government funding, by removing research production from academic hierarchies and pointing it instead toward the political process with the packaging of ideas and data for that purpose, by networking extensively to overcome institutional boundaries of higher education, and by sharing and receiving timely information to gain more immediate access to policy processes. The result has been the production of information that is authoritative from the perspective of political actors and the state-level education bureaucracy, which often cannot supply such information in the politicized environment of state-level politics. Emerging from this effort, as well, are comprehensive descriptions of educational policy trends and needs in the state (Guthrie et al., 1990) as well as interpretations of the broken front of reform across states and nationally (Guthrie & Koppich, 1990).

These centers are reminiscent of the institutes for educational research set up at places like Teachers College, Stanford, the University of Chicago, and some of the state universities during the interwar years to influence educational policy during the ascendancy of the administrative reformers—who, it will be recalled, succeeded in promoting the bureaucratic regularities that exist in American education today. Yet there was an important difference in the earlier institutes. As they analyzed and documented, they also led the way in introducing generative concepts that helped to organize new policy systems.

Those concepts represented the implicit normative structures to which historians return when studying the impact of social movements, political processes, and economic transformation on the history of education. For the administrative reformers, the generative concepts were such things as *social efficiency* (the power of schools to allocate individuals to probable destinies in the occupational order), *individual differences* (the power of social scientists to scale human traits and measure the student population for sorting individuals into tracked opportunities for instruction), *differentiated curricula* (the power of professional educators to codify knowledge in discrete subject areas and curricular sequences and to develop organized professional interests permanently around the transmission of such knowledge), and *supervision* (the power of administrators, viewed as scientific managers separated from the process of production, to exercise the authority of the state over teachers and measure their performance according to administrative criteria of evaluation).

As promising as today's new policy centers are for extending research efforts beyond the reach of the federal and academic purview, particularly in a state like California where even the tracking of demographic changes is a major undertaking, a historical perspective leads to the following questions: What generative ideas will these centers offer to transform education? Can these centers go beyond gathering information, analyzing needs, and making policy suggestions (Policy Analysis for California Education, 1990) to introduce a more fundamental reorientation into the ways that policymakers and the public understand the relationship between educational policy and practice?

Those who are concerned with studying educational policy seem generally predisposed to search for a basis on which to rationalize the action of the state, even if it means going only so far as to discover the variegated patterns of fragmentation and ambiguity that shape current decision-making processes. This is not enough to understand what impels states toward substantive goals in the long run. A historical perspective suggests that the standing agreements embodied in the state are placed there not by policy deliberation so much as by the changing lives of people in society—their values, the conditions they encounter, the state to which they aspire. When used to propose changes, the languages of research and reform will tend toward stasis, toward unwitting reinforcement of existing configurations of education whatever the social cost, unless they create new vision by mobilizing deeper aspirations and potentials that shape education from beyond the policy system itself.

Are there any themes to be found in the research that might have the potential of becoming generative concepts, provocations in tune with the deepest springs of constitutive state action on the landscape of social and political history? Many, perhaps, but let us pursue just one within the confines of this chapter to see where it might lead. Consider the right to an education under state constitutional law (Hubsch, 1989). Only 20 years ago, several scholars made a connection between constitutional rights and the vast interdistrict disparities in spending on public schools (Coons,

Clune, & Sugarman, 1970; Wise, 1968). It certainly can be said in retrospect that the concept of fiscal neutrality was a generative idea for changing state school systems. The strategy, though based on individual rights, was consistent with the growth of universalistic reasoning as viewed by the reformers and researchers who helped to envision policy strategies for the administrative state in the early years of the 20th century. Once the point of leverage was found in legal argument, the reform began to produce some of the most sweeping changes in educational policy during the last half century—not interventions or innovations merely, but systemic changes from within.

If one goes back to the rationale (Wise, 1968) with fresh eyes, there is not only a federal constitutional justification for the equalization of funding and a careful review of incriminating evidence, but also a challenging interpretation of the legal basis of education in state law. Is education basically a burden on the state, something it must do—but will do minimally—as part of its police powers to maintain order? Or is there a more dynamic and expansive conception to be found, based on rights of citizenship, on the need to activate young minds, to protect their development against unjust treatment, and to prepare them for full membership in the political community? The answer to these questions changes over time. State supreme courts are generally much more active on rights issues today than they were a generation ago (Brennan, 1986; Collins, Galie, & Kincaid, 1986; Thro, 1989).

After the U.S. Supreme Court failed to recognize education as a fundamental interest of the federal government under the Constitution in *San Antonio Independent School District v. Rodriguez* (1973), states began that same year in New Jersey with *Robinson v. Cahill* to develop independent grounds for interpreting individual rights in education to require statewide equalization of school finance. In a stream of new cases across various domains of public policy, those independent grounds are carrying state law and policy beyond the requirements of federal equality guarantees. States are developing conceptions of educational rights grounded not only in equal protection of individuals, but also in universal guarantees to maintain adequate provision of educational services for all citizens under compulsory education laws. As the conception of rights broadens, possibilities arise for interpreting the substantive goals of educational policy (e.g., see Schuman, 1988, on one state's bill of rights provisions). But revealingly, as we saw in reviewing the actions of the regulatory state, the debate on rights within judicial circles has reached the same impasse as the one that has stymied effective implementation, regulation, and control of the educational process in the bureaucratic system of schooling. It is simply not possible to produce the desired results with yet further rationalization and authoritative allocation of resources through existing administrative structures. The result is hyperrationalization (Wise, 1979), whereby systems become merely unresponsive.

How can the state meet its obligation to provide all citizens with an education? This is not only an educational issue, for, as Gutmann (1987) has suggested, nondiscrimination is a principle at the core of the democratic state. Schooling itself, including the irrepressible debate over its value and limits, is part of the democratic process, reproducing over time the civic language of political community as we know it in this nation. If today's administrative systems and regulatory apparatuses cannot perform adequately in seeking that objective, it is no technical or professional matter; nor is it merely a state monopoly waiting to be replaced by a free market. Whatever is done to remedy the situation, states must act, and they must do so before chronic institutional failure threatens their own legitimacy. Government at all levels must speak in the form of law and policy, as before, but the will to improve education must be suffused with a better understanding of how to release the energies and initiative blocked in the system. If state leaders, especially those in the most populous and diverse states, can be persuaded to behave in this manner, it will not be because they miraculously decide to stop being political and finally act in rational ways, but because they perceive that in the long run there will be no choice in the matter. Prodded by citizens who claim that they suffer a degradation unbecoming to a democratic society, the states that educate the majority of schoolchildren in this country will—because they eventually must—dissolve the political and institutional barriers and press hard for a system that delivers the desired results. The dilemma is national in scope, for if the democratic state does not do this, there is danger that it will not be able to maintain a just claim on the consent of the people.

This points to the tremendous significance of black insurgency as the foundation of reform in the 1960s (Lowe & Kantor, 1989). And thus, too, we can sense the potency of the inner city today, the pressure of the urban crisis and its festering inequality on the embedded structures of the state. The inner city places students at risk and requires special programs, interventions, massive intergovernmental subsidy—all the paraphernalia of the regulatory state—but this is the least of it and only the beginning. The persistence of educational failure will put those students beyond the pale of political community. The human condition of the cities will do more than attract governmental assistance for education and social services. Eventually, if it continues to deteriorate, it will move the states to pull apart the embedded structure of assumptions on which all schooling policies are built. Recent legislative actions to decentralize school governance in Chicago show the penchant of states for heroic cures.

As Wise foresaw, the discussion of rights is not static. Formulating the right to an education as an institutional reality must be based on our understanding of education. Court action and public policy cannot proceed far without an ability to detect whether it—whatever "it" is deemed to be—has occurred to a sufficient extent to satisfy any rules that might be made to meet the purposefully vague constitutional standard. The quest for resolution of disputes over the right to an education is much more than legal. To solve the problem of what is adequate and for whom, state officials and educational leaders need to imagine a modus operandi more likely to succeed than the hierarchical frameworks of administrative rationality in which the state has invested its sanctions and resources since the beginning of the century. They must also try to imagine a strategy of change less likely to falter than the later spate of interventions, innovations, and mandates coming from every level and sector of the federalist system, which in effect have attacked the prevailing administrative framework in order to deliver more benefits directly to those whose rights have been abridged.

Even when these incursions succeed, and sometimes they do, they destabilize and fragment the system, weakening the school as an institution. The more fundamental problem is to discover what the state must do to deliver an adequate education (Wise, 1983), not just what can be done administratively to allocate resources or as a regulatory intervention to influence the school program, but what must be produced to help in building institutional capacities (Smith & O'Day, in press-a; Timar & Kirp, 1988) in order to make available the educational outcomes to which people are entitled and upon which the state ultimately depends for its health.

Once the black box of the administratively controlled school can be opened up, once it can be determined more precisely what is to happen there as a constitutionally guaranteed relation between the state and its young citizens, then it will be possible to simplify the policy relationships between the state and the participants in that process. At that point it will also be possible, with the help of local knowledge from participants and researchers, to strengthen the process with more focused and appropriate resources, professionalism, and assessment. What seems most generative about this idea, as far as state authority is concerned, is the dialogue about responsibilities that must begin after one starts down the road of thinking substantively and not just procedurally about educational rights. Only by more concretely, intelligently, and thoroughly meeting its obligations arising from the right to an education will the state be able to untangle the multilayered and fragmented system of controls that now makes schooling so inefficient.

Will this prove to be a false promise, ratcheting up even further the hyperrationalization of the classroom? The answer to this question will depend on whether the state can transform its understanding of the educational process in response to the realities of social crisis and school failure. As a heuristic for suggesting a possible research agenda, let us assume that such change is possible and that the ideas of the research community can make a difference in the transformation. Working on the frontier of legal theory, some scholars are beginning to identify the outlines of a new conceptual framework for regulatory action that will carry the democratic state beyond the "rights revolution" but at the same time will continue to support positive action in public policy (Sunstein, 1990). Taking a cue from Gutmann, we might imagine that this new entity could be called the *democratic state*. If it could be achieved in the compromised world of educational policy and governance, such a state would be distinguished by its capacity to create enabling structures for reflective action and initiative at the levels where services are delivered and social goods are produced. But at the same time, state action would be based on clear, unambiguous standards for issues such as constitutionally protected privacy, fairness, and nondiscrimination.

A further possibility, as Minow (1985) has argued, is that the problem of rights and social services can be reworked without loss of justice as schools become more capable of dealing constructively with differences among their students. Moving beyond the "dilemma of difference" to the provision of a fully adequate education for a wide variety of children, all of whom are different from one another but whose differences are valuable and educationally productive, such a vision challenges the standard of normalcy that was embedded in the administrative state and used by planners to stratify and differentiate the school population. In its early phase, the rights revolution adopted such standards to rectify the differences with an authoritative standard of equality, but in the long run it will be necessary for the state to dissolve the normalcy/difference barrier, along with the administrative and regulatory solutions that serve to perpetuate the difference as well as alleviating its effects. The solution that comes into view with the democratic state is a more fully productive system of sparking education among young people based on their educational needs. Minow suggests that differences are essentially social relations that can be used constructively for the improvement of education. For the state to act on this generative idea, it must discover new ways of releasing the potential of teaching and learning at the local level.

CONCLUSION

To incorporate into state governing capacities a more profound understanding of what it takes to produce an adequate education at the local level will be no simple matter. Some of what is entailed in this task can be accomplished through continuing review and more active use of the implementation literature as it develops over time in relation to state and federal programs. It will also be necessary to look more closely at locally initiated reforms supported by means other than governmental actions (Raywid, 1989, 1990; Timar, 1990; cf. Goodlad, 1975). When governments act to improve education, researchers must be clear-sighted enough to see when the opposite is happening and courageous enough to say so, yet also astute enough to speak as a respected ally of the state in the process of educational change. It will be particularly important to assess the effectiveness and results of the incentives used by the state to encourage local initiatives for improving school performance (Richards & Shujaa, 1990). Continuing review and critique of state education reform is a crucial ingredient of educational improvement (Firestone, Fuhrman, & Kirst, 1989).

The development of local leadership capacity and the testing of alternative conceptions of effective school organization will become an increasingly important stream of information for strategic policy-making at the state level. It seems likely that incentive plans for school performance will continue to shift the focus from district-level administrative offices to the school site in conceptualizing effective schools, and this in turn will create new needs for insight and comparative analysis (Fullan, 1985). The shift toward the smaller units will also require continuing review of the possibilities for greater choice in local schooling (Elmore, 1988; Raywid, 1985), because one way of creating incentives for releasing local initiative is simply to encourage greater variety in organizational forms under public authority.

In general, states will need more information about how local districts, schools, and communities respond to state-level policy initiatives aiming at creating local discretion while establishing standards for performance (Fuhrman & Elmore, 1990; Odden & Marsh, 1990; Timar, 1989). States will also need to develop a more broad-based and participatory mechanism of self-monitoring, closely watching the proliferation of new policy rules at the state level as local schools experiment with new organizational forms and practices, to ensure that state standards and assessments do not squash that discretion with even more binding rules of the game.

The challenge of the future, the democratic challenge par excellence, is to create greater order while exercising less control. This is tricky business, full of pitfalls, sometimes hardly visible when success is close at hand, but a lost cause when people categorically claim to have found the answer. Initiative, discretion, choice—these are indispensable for opening up the process of educational change to new possibilities in schools. Yet they are not sufficient as educational aims in their own right. It is well known that even the most forward-looking programs of change go through surprising metamorphoses at the hands of local service providers (Lipsky, 1980; Weatherley & Lipsky, 1977). A standard of some kind is necessary; it need not be procrustean, educationally unsound, or otherwise inimical to local and professional initiative. States, in any event, must meet their obligation to citizens for the provision of an adequate education. Where is the balance to be found? Research, reform, policy, practice—all are in need of illumination on this point.

Many states are already making greater efforts to understand the local restructuring of schools within their borders (M. Cohen, 1990; David, 1989; David, Cohen, Honetschlager, & Traiman, 1990). Supported by research, this process of deliberation has the potential to press beyond policy analysis to fundamental consideration of the state's aims and needs in defining school improvement more concretely as a social goal. It is much easier for the lens of state-level deliberation to focus on schools as organizations than it is to gain deeper understanding of the elemental processes and professional cultures that produce excellence in teaching and learning, just as it was easier under the administrative state to focus on districts and the rationality of managerial control than it was to look behind the classroom door and see what was happening. There is always a temptation merely to create another black box, not only ignoring but stifling the essence.

The states are capable of shaping without thwarting the vitality present in educational institutions, but this cannot be done without developing new ways of seeing that provide better information at the level of policy about teaching and learning. It should be possible, as part of the commonsense rules of statecraft, to work with greater depth of perspective on schools as learning communities. When states make policy in the future, the main actors in the process should be able to see students as creators of meaning, teachers as professionals, and classrooms as fully activated sites for instructing citizens in the basics of democratic deliberation. What has become invisible must be made visible: the many ways people are disposed to learn, and above all, the means available for activating that process.

REFERENCES

Achilles, C. M., Lansford, Z., & Payne, W. H. (1986). Tennessee educational reform: Gubernatorial advocacy. In V. D. Mueller & M. P. McKeown (Eds.), *The fiscal, legal, and political aspects of state reform of elementary and secondary education: Sixth annual yearbook of the American Education Finance Association 1985* (pp. 223–244). Cambridge, MA: Ballinger.

Airasian, P. W. (1987). State mandated testing and educational reform: Context and consequences. *American Journal of Education, 95*, 393–412.

Alexander, K. (1986). Executive leadership and educational reform in Florida. In V. D. Mueller & M. P. McKeown (Eds.), *The fiscal, legal, and political aspects of state reform of elementary and secondary education: Sixth annual yearbook of the American Education Finance Association 1985* (pp. 145–168). Cambridge, MA: Ballinger.

Allen, R., & Clark, J. (1981). State policy adoption and innovation: Lobbying and education. *State and Local Government Review, 13*, 18–25.

Anderson, B. L. (1982). Test use today in elementary and secondary schools. In A. K. Wigdor & W. R. Garner (Eds.), *Ability testing: Uses, consequences, and controversies. Part II: Documentation section* (pp. 232–285). Washington, DC: National Academy Press.

Anderson, J. D. (1988). *The education of Blacks in the South, 1860–1935*. Chapel Hill: University of North Carolina Press.

Anton, T. J. (1984). Intergovernmental change in the United States: An assessment of the literature. In T. C. Miller (Ed.), *Public sector performance: A conceptual turning point* (pp. 15–64). Baltimore: Johns Hopkins University Press.

Apple, M. W. (1982). *Education and power*. Boston: Routledge & Kegan Paul.

Arons, S. (1983). *Compelling belief: The culture of American schooling*. New York: McGraw-Hill.

Astuto, T. A., & Clark, D. L. (1988). State responses to the new federalism in education. *Educational Policy, 2*, 361–375.

Bailey, S. K. (1981). Political coalitions for public education. *Daedalus, 110*(3), 27–43.

Bailey, S. K., Frost, R. T., Marsh, P. E., & Wood, R. C. (1962). *Schoolmen and politics: A study of state aid to education in the Northeast*. Syracuse, NY: Syracuse University Press.

Bennett, L. L. M. (1983). *Symbolic state politics: Education funding in Ohio 1970–1980*. New York: Peter Lang.

Benveniste, G. (1985). The design of school accountability systems. *Educational Evaluation and Policy Analysis, 7*(3), 261–279.

Berke, J. S, & Kirst, M. W. (1972). *Federal aid to education: Who benefits? Who governs?* Lexington, MA: Lexington Books.

Berman, P. (1986). From compliance to learning: Implementing legally-induced reform. In D. L. Kirp & D. N. Jensen (Eds.), *School days, rule days: The legalization and regulation of education* (pp. 46–62). Philadelphia: Falmer Press.

Berman, P., & McLaughlin, M. W. (1974). *Federal programs supporting educational change, Vol. I: A model of educational change* (Report prepared for the U.S. Office of Education, Department of Health, Education, and Welfare, R-1589/1-HEW). Santa Monica, CA: Rand Corporation.

Berman, P., & McLaughlin, M. W. (1975). *Federal programs supporting educational change, Vol. IV: The findings in review* (Report prepared for the U.S. Office of Education, Department of Health, Education, and Welfare, R-1589/4-HEW). Santa Monica, CA: Rand Corporation.

Berman, P., & McLaughlin, M. W. (1977). *Federal programs supporting educational change, Vol. VII: Factors affecting implementation and continuation* (Report prepared for the U.S. Office of Education, Department of Health, Education, and Welfare, R-1589/7-HEW). Santa Monica, CA: Rand Corporation.

Berman, P., & McLaughlin, M. W. (1978). *Federal programs supporting educational change, Vol. VIII: Implementing and sustaining innovations* (Report prepared for the U.S. Office of Education, Department of Health, Education, and Welfare, R-1589/8-HEW). Santa Monica, CA: Rand Corporation.

Berman, P., & McLaughlin, M. W. (1980). Factors affecting the process of change. In M. M. Milstein (Ed.), *Schools, conflict, and change* (pp. 57–71). New York: Teachers College Press.

BeVier, M. J. (1979). *Politics backstage: Inside the California legislature.* Philadelphia: Temple University Press.
Beyle, T. L., & Dalton, R. (1983). The governor and the state legislature. In T. L. Beyle & L. R. Muchmore (Eds.), *Being governor: The view from the office* (pp. 124–130). Durham, NC: Duke University Press.
Beyle, T. L., & Wright, D. S. (1972). The governor, planning, and governmental activity. In T. L. Beyle & J. O. Williams (Eds.), *The American governor in behavioral perspective* (pp. 193–205). New York: Harper & Row.
Bissell, J. S. (1979). Use of educational evaluation and policy studies by the California legislature. *Educational Evaluation and Policy Analysis, 1*(3), 29–37.
Bode, B. H. (1937). *Democracy as a way of life.* New York: Macmillan.
Boli-Bennett, J. (1979). The ideology of expanding state authority in national constitutions, 1870–1970. In J. W. Meyer & M. T. Hannan (Eds.), *National development and the world system: Educational, economic, and political change, 1950–1970* (pp. 222–237). Chicago: University of Chicago Press.
Boyd, W. L. (1976). The public, the professionals, and educational policy making: Who governs? *Teachers College Record, 77,* 539–577.
Brennan, W. J., Jr. (1986). The Bill of Rights and the states: The revival of state constitutions as guardians of individual rights. *New York University Law Review, 61,* 535–553.
Brown v. Board of Education, 347 U.S. 483 (1954).
Burlingame, M., & Geske, T. G. (1979). State politics and education: An examination of selected multiple state case studies. *Educational Administration Quarterly, 15*(2), 50–75.
Burns, J. M. (1978). *Leadership.* New York: Harper & Row.
Butts, R. F. (1974). Public education and political community. *History of Education Quarterly, 14,* 165–183.
Callahan, R. E. (1962). *Education and the cult of efficiency: A study of the social forces that have shaped the administration of the public schools.* Chicago: University of Chicago Press.
Campbell, R. F., Cunningham, L. L., Nystrand, R. O., & Usdan, M. D. (1985). *The organization and control of American schools* (5th ed.). Columbus, OH: Charles E. Merrill.
Campbell, R. F., & Mazzoni, T. L., Jr. (1976). *State policy making for the public schools: A comparative analysis of policy making for the public schools in twelve states and a treatment of state governance models.* Berkeley, CA: McCutchan.
Campbell, R. F., Sroufe, G. E., & Layton, D. H. (Eds.). (1967). *Strengthening state departments of education.* Chicago: Midwest Administration Center, University of Chicago.
Carnoy, M. (1984). *The state and political theory.* Princeton, NJ: Princeton University Press.
Carnoy, M., & Levin, H. M. (1985). *Schooling and work in the democratic state.* Stanford, CA: Stanford University Press.
Chase, F. S., & Morphet, E. L. (1949). *The forty-eight state school systems.* Chicago: The Council of State Governments.
Chubb, J. E., & Moe, T. M. (1988). Politics, markets, and the organization of schools. *American Political Science Review, 82,* 1065–1087.
Clifford, G. J., & Guthrie, J. W. (1988). *Ed school: A brief for professional education.* Chicago: University of Chicago Press.

Cohen, D. K. (1982). Policy and organization: The impact of state and federal educational policy on school governance. *Harvard Educational Review, 52*, 474–499.

Cohen, D. K. (1985). Origins. In A. G. Powell, E. Farrar, & D. K. Cohen (Eds.), *The shopping mall high school: Winners and losers in the educational marketplace* (pp. 233–308). Boston: Houghton Mifflin.

Cohen, D. K., & Neufeld, B. (1981). The failure of high schools and the progress of education. *Daedalus, 110*(3), 69–89.

Cohen, M. (1988). Designing state assessment systems. *Phi Delta Kappan, 69*, 583–588.

Cohen, M. (1990. Key issues confronting state policymakers. In R. F. Elmore and Associates (Eds.), *Restructuring schools: The next generation of educational reform* (pp. 251–288). San Francisco: Jossey-Bass.

Collins, R. K. L., Galie, P. J., & Kincaid, J. (1986). State high courts, state constitutions, and individual rights litigation since 1980: A judicial survey. *Publius: The Journal of Federalism, 16*, 141–161.

Conant, J. B. (1964). *Shaping educational policy*. New York: McGraw-Hill.

Coombs, F. S. (1980). *Opportunities in the comparison of state education policy systems*. Stanford, CA: Center for Educational Research at Stanford.

Coons, J. E., Clune, W. H., & Sugarman, S. D. (1970). *Private wealth and public education*. Cambridge, MA: Harvard University Press.

Coons, J. E., & Sugarman, S. D. (1978). *Education by choice: The case for family control*. Berkeley: University of California Press.

Counts, G. S. (1927). *The social composition of boards of education*. Chicago: University of Chicago Press.

Craig, J. E. (1981). The expansion of education. In D. C. Berliner (Ed.), *Review of research in education* (Vol. 9, pp. 151–213). Washington, DC: American Educational Research Association.

Cremin, L. A. (1951). *The American common school: An historic conception*. New York: Bureau of Publications, Teachers College, Columbia University.

Cremin, L. A. (1980). *American education: The national experience, 1783–1876*. New York: Harper & Row.

Cremin, L. A. (1988). *American education: The metropolitan experience, 1876–1980*. New York: Harper & Row.

Cronin, J. M. (1973). *The control of urban schools: Perspective on the power of educational reformers*. New York: Free Press.

Cuban, L. (1982). Enduring resiliency: Enacting and implementing federal vocational educational legislation. In H. Kantor & D. B. Tyack (Eds.), *Work, youth, and schooling: Historical perspectives on vocationalism in American education* (pp. 45–78). Stanford: Stanford University Press.

Cuban, L. (1984). School reform by remote control: SB 813 in California. *Phi Delta Kappan, 66*, 213–215.

Cuban, L. (1990). Reforming again, again, and again. *Educational Researcher, 19*(1), 3–13.

Cusick, P. A. (1983). *The egalitarian ideal and the American high school: Studies of three schools*. New York: Longman.

Danziger, S., & Witte, J. F. (Eds.). (1988). *State policy choices: The Wisconsin experience* (La Follette Public Policy Series). Madison: University of Wisconsin Press.

Darling-Hammond, L., & Marks, E. L. (1983). *The new federalism in education: State responses to the 1981 Education Consolidation and Improvement Act*

(Report prepared for the U.S. Department of Education). Santa Monica, CA: Rand Corporation.

Darling-Hammond, L., & Wise, A. E. (1985). Beyond standardization: State standards and school improvement. *The Elementary School Journal, 85*, 315–336.

David, J. L. (1989). *Restructuring in progress: Lessons from pioneering districts*. Washington, DC: National Governors' Association.

David, J. L., Cohen, M., Honetschlager, D., & Traiman, S. (1990). *State actions to restructure schools: First steps*. Washington, DC: National Governors' Association.

Dewey, J. (1916). *Democracy and education*. New York: Macmillan.

Dougherty, V. (1983, October). *State programs of school improvement, 1983: A 50-state survey*. Denver: Education Commission of the States.

Doyle, D. P., & Hartle, T. W. (1985). *Excellence in education: The states take charge*. Washington, DC: American Enterprise Institute for Public Policy Research.

Elazar, D. J. (1962). *The American partnership: Intergovernmental co-operation in the nineteenth-century United States*. Chicago: University of Chicago Press.

Elmore, R. F. (1984). The political economy of state influence. *Education and Urban Society, 16*, 125–144.

Elmore, R. F. (1986). Education and federalism: Doctrinal, functional and strategic views. In D. L. Kirp & D. N. Jensen (Eds.), *School days, rule days: The legalization and regulation of education* (pp. 166–186). Philadelphia: Falmer Press.

Elmore, R. F. (1988). Choice in public education. In W. L. Boyd & C. T. Kerchner (Eds.), *The politics of excellence and choice in education: 1987 Yearbook of the Politics of Education Association* (pp. 79–98). New York: Falmer Press.

Elmore, R. F., and Associates (Eds.). (1990). *Restructuring schools: The next generation of educational reform*. San Francisco: Jossey-Bass.

Elmore, R. F., & McLaughlin, M. W. (1982). *Reform and retrenchment: The politics of California school finance reform*. Cambridge, MA: Ballinger.

Elmore, R. F., & McLaughlin, M. W. (1988). *Steady work: Policy, practice, and the reform of American education* (Report prepared for the National Institute of Education, R-3574-NIE/RC). Santa Monica, CA: Rand Corporation.

Everhart, R. B. (1983). *Reading, writing and resistance: Adolescence and labor in a junior high school*. Boston: Routledge & Kegan Paul.

Fine, D. R. (1986). *When leadership fails: Desegregation and demoralization in the San Francisco schools*. New Brunswick, NJ: Transaction Books.

Finkelstein, B. (1989). *Governing the young: Teacher behavior in popular primary schools in 19th century United States*. New York: Falmer Press.

Firestone, W. A. (1990). Continuity and incrementalism after all: State responses to the excellence movement. In J. Murphy (Ed.), *The educational reform movement of the 1980s: Perspectives and cases* (pp. 143–166). Berkeley, CA: McCutchan Publishing.

Firestone, W. A., Fuhrman, S. H., & Kirst, M. W. (1989, October). *The progress of reform: An appraisal of state education initiatives* (CPRE Research Report Series RP-014). New Brunswick, NJ: Center for Policy Research in Education, Rutgers.

Fitzwater, C. O. (1968). *State school system development: Patterns and trends*. Denver: Education Commission of the States.

Flanders, J. K. (1925). *Legislative control of the elementary curriculum* (Contribution to Education No. 195). New York: Bureau of Publication, Teachers College, Columbia University.

Flicker, B. (Ed.). (1990). *Justice and school systems: The role of the courts in education litigation*. Philadelphia: Temple University Press.
Friedman, B. D. (1971). *State government and education: Management in the state education agency*. Chicago: Public Administration Service.
Friedman, B. D., & Dunbar, L. J. (1971). *Grants management in education: Federal impact on state agencies*. Chicago: Public Administration Service.
Friedman, M. (1962). *Capitalism and freedom*. Chicago: University of Chicago Press.
Fuhrman, S. H. (1987). Educational policy: A new context for governance. *Publius: 1986 Annual Review of Federalism, 17*(3), 131–143.
Fuhrman, S. H., Clune, W. H., & Elmore, R. F. (1988). Research on education reform: Lessons on the implementation of policy. *Teachers College Record, 90*, 237–257.
Fuhrman, S. H., & Elmore, R. F. (1990). Understanding local control in the wake of state education reform. *Educational Evaluation and Policy Analysis, 12*(1), 82–96.
Fuhrman, S. H., & Rosenthal, A. (Eds.). (1981). *Shaping education policy in the states*. Washington, DC: Institute for Educational Leadership.
Fullan, M. (1982). *The meaning of educational change*. New York: Teachers College Press.
Fullan, M. (1985). Change processes and strategies at the local level. *Elementary School Journal, 85*, 391–421.
Fuller, E., & Pearson, J. B. (Eds.). (1969a). *Education in the states, Vol. 1: Historical development and outlook* (A Project of the Council of Chief State School Officers). Washington, DC: National Education Association.
Fuller, E., & Pearson, J. B. (Eds.). (1969b). *Education in the states, Vol. 2: Nationwide development since 1900* (A Project of the Council of Chief State School Officers). Washington, DC: National Education Association.
Galie, P. J. (1982). The other supreme courts: Judicial activism among state supreme courts. *Syracuse Law Review, 33*, 731–793.
Gamoran, A. (1987). The stratification of high school learning opportunities. *Sociology of Education, 60*, 135–155.
Glenn, C. L., Jr. (1988). *The myth of the common school*. Amherst: University of Massachusetts Press.
Goodlad, J. I. (1975). *The dynamics of educational change: Toward responsive schools*. New York: McGraw-Hill.
Graham, H. D. (1984). *The uncertain triumph: Federal education policy in the Kennedy and Johnson years*. Chapel Hill: University of North Carolina Press.
Grant, G. (1988). *The world we created at Hamilton High*. Cambridge, MA: Harvard University Press.
Gross, N. (1958). *Who runs our schools?* New York: Wiley.
Grubb, W. N., & Michelson, S. (1974). *States and schools: The political economy of public school finance*. Lexington, MA: Lexington Books.
Guthrie, J. W. (1976). Social science, accountability, and the political economy of school productivity. In J. E. McDermott (Ed.), *Indeterminancy in education: Social science, educational policy and the search for standards* (pp. 253–308). Berkeley, CA: McCutchan.
Guthrie, J. W., Kirst, M. W., Hayward, G. C., Odden, A. R., Koppich, J. E., Adams, Jr., J. E., & Webb, F. R. (1990). *Conditions of education in California 1989* (Policy paper No. PP90-1-2). Berkeley: Policy Analysis for California Education, University of California, Berkeley.

Guthrie, J. W., & Koppich, J. E. (1990, June). *Politics & educational change: Making sense of port barrels, iron triangles, high politics, and national social reform.* Paper presented at the third annual conference of the U.S. and U.K. Education and Training Policy in Comparative Perspective, Warwick University, Coventry, England.

Gutmann, A. (1987). *Democratic education.* Princeton, NJ: Princeton University Press.

Hawley, W. D. (1975). Dealing with organizational rigidity in public schools: A theoretical perspective. In F. M. Wirt (Ed.), *The polity of the school: New research in educational politics* (pp. 187–210). Lexington, MA: Lexington Books.

Hirschman, A. O. (1970). *Exit, voice, and loyalty: Responses to decline in firms, organizations, and states.* Cambridge, MA: Harvard University Press.

Hirschman, A. O. (1982). *Shifting involvements: Private interest and public action.* Princeton, NJ: Princeton University Press.

Hochschild, J. L. (1984). *The new American dilemma: Liberal democracy and school desegregation.* New Haven, CT: Yale University Press.

Hogan, D. J. (1985). *Class and reform: School and society in Chicago, 1880–1930.* Philadelphia: University of Pennsylvania Press.

Hogan, J. C. (1974). *The schools, the courts, and the public interest.* Lexington, MA: Lexington Books.

Horowitz, D. L. (1977). *The courts and social policy.* Washington, DC: Brookings Institution.

Huberman, A. M., & Miles, M. B. (1984a). *Innovation up close: How school improvement works.* New York: Plenum Press.

Huberman, A. M., & Miles, M. B. (1984b). Rethinking the quest for school improvement: Some findings from the DESSI study. *Teachers College Record, 86*, 34–54.

Hubsch, A. W. (1989). Education and self-government: The right to education under state constitutional law. *Journal of Law and Education, 18*, 93–140.

Hurn, C. (1985). Changes in authority relationships in schools: 1960–1980. *Research in Sociology of Education and Socialization, 5*, 31–57.

Hyman, H. M. (1986). *American singularity: The 1787 Northwest Ordinance, the 1862 Homestead and Morrill Acts, and the 1944 G.I. Bill.* Athens: University of Georgia Press.

Iannaccone, L. (1967). *Politics in education.* New York: Center for Applied Research in Education.

Iannaccone, L. (1982). Changing political patterns and governmental regulations. In R. B. Everhart (Ed.), *The public school monopoly: A critical analysis of education and the state in American society* (pp. 295–324). Cambridge, MA: Ballinger.

Iannaccone, L., & Cistone, P. J. (1974). *The politics of education* (ERIC/CEM State-of-the-Knowledge Series No. 20). Eugene, OR: ERIC Clearinghouse on Educational Management.

James, H. T. (1969). *The new cult of efficiency and education.* Pittsburgh: University of Pittsburgh Press.

James, T. (1986). State politics and educational leadership in California: The ebb and flow of the nineteenth century. *Pacific Historian, 30*(3), 19–33.

James, T. (in press). Rights of conscience and the development of state school systems in nineteenth-century America. In P. Finkleman & S. E. Gottlieb (Eds.), *Toward a usable past: The origins and implications of state protections of liberty.* Athens: University of Georgia Press.

James, T., & Tyack, D. (1983). Learning from past efforts to reform the high school. *Phi Delta Kappan, 64*, 400–406.

Jensen, D. N., & Griffin, T. M. (1984). The legalization of state educational policymaking in California. *Journal of Law and Education, 13*(1), 19–33.

Jorgenson, L. P. (1987). *The state and the non-public school 1825–1925*. Columbia: University of Missouri Press.

Kaestle, C. F. (1983). *Pillars of the republic: Common schools and American society, 1780–1860*. New York: Hill and Wang.

Kaestle, C. F., & Smith, M. S. (1982). The federal role in elementary and secondary education, 1940–1980. *Harvard Educational Review, 52*, 384–408.

Kaestle, C. F., & Vinovskis, M. A. (1980). *Education and social change in nineteenth-century Massachusetts*. Cambridge, MA: Cambridge University Press.

Kagan, R. A. (1986). Regulating business, regulating schools: The problem of regulatory unreasonableness. In D. L. Kirp & D. N. Jensen (Eds.), *School days, rule days: The legalization and regulation of education* (pp. 64–90). Philadelphia: Falmer Press.

Katz, M. B. (1968a). *The irony of early school reform: Educational innovation in mid-nineteenth century Massachusetts*. Cambridge, MA: Harvard University Press.

Katz, M. B. (1968b). The emergence of bureaucracy in urban education: The Boston case, 1850–1884. *History of Education Quarterly, 8*(2 & 3), 155–188, 319–357.

Katz, M. B. (1987). *Reconstructing American education*. Cambridge, MA: Harvard University Press.

Katznelson, I., & Weir, M. (1985). *Schooling for all: Class, race, and the decline of the democratic ideal*. Berkeley: University of California Press.

Kirp, D. L. (1982). *Just schools: The idea of racial equality in American education*. Berkeley: University of California Press.

Kirp, D. L., & Jensen, D. N. (Eds.). (1986). *School days, rule days: The legalization and regulation of education*. Philadelphia: Falmer Press.

Kirp, D. L., & Jung, D. J. (1984). Law as an instrument of educational policymaking. *American Journal of Comparative Law, 32*, 625–678.

Kirst, M. W. (1981). California. In S. H. Fuhrman & A. Rosenthal (Eds.), *Shaping education policy in the states* (pp. 39–55). Washington, DC: Institute for Educational Leadership.

Kirst, M. W. (1984). State policy in an era of transition. *Education and Urban Society, 16*, 225–237.

Kirst, M. W. (1985, July). *Sustaining state education reform momentum: The linkage between assessment and financial support*. Paper presented at the annual meeting of the Education Commission of the States, Philadelphia.

Kirst, M. W. (1988a). Recent state education reform in the United States: Looking backward and forward. *Educational Administration Quarterly, 24*(3), 319–328.

Kirst, M. W. (1988b). *Who should control our schools: Reassessing cuurent policies* (Report 88-CERAS-05). Stanford, CA: Center for Educational Research at Stanford.

Kirst, M. W., & Jung, R. (1980). The utility of a longitudinal approach in assessing implementation. *Educational Evaluation and Policy Analysis, 2*(5), 17–34.

Kirst, M. W., & Mosher, E. K. (1969). Politics of education. *Review of Educational Research, 39*, 623–640.

Kirst, M. W., & Somers, S. A. (1981). California educational interest groups: Collective action as a logical response to Proposition 13. *Education and Urban Society, 13*, 235–256.

Kirst, M. W., Tyler, R. W., Ford, K., & Rogers, J. (1986). *Evaluating state education reforms: A special legislative report*. Washington, DC: National Conference of State Legislatures.

Kliebard, H. M. (1987). *The struggle for the American curriculum 1893–1958*. New York: Routledge & Kegan Paul.

Kluger, R. (1975). *Simple justice: The history of Brown v. Board of Education and Black America's struggle for equality*. New York: Vintage Books.

Krug, E. A. (1969). *The shaping of the American high school: Vol. 1, 1880–1920*. Madison: University of Wisconsin Press.

Krug, E. A. (1972). *The shaping of the American high school: Vol. 2, 1920–1941*. Madison: University of Wisconsin Press.

Labaree, D. F. (1988). *The making of an American high school: The credentials market and the central high school of Philadelphia, 1838–1939*. New Haven, CT: Yale University Press.

Lawyers' Committee for Civil Rights Under Law. (1978). *State legal standards for the provision of public education: An overview*. Washington, DC: National Institute of Education, U.S. Department of Health, Education, and Welfare.

Lehne, R. (1978). *The quest for justice: The politics of school finance reform*. New York: Longman.

Lehne, R. (1983). Research perspectives on state legislatures and education policy. *Educational Evaluation and Policy Analysis, 5*(1), 43–54.

Levin, H. M. (1977). A decade of policy developments in improving education and training for low-income populations. In R. H. Haveman (Ed.), *A decade of federal antipoverty programs: Achievements, failures, and lessons* (pp. 123–188). New York: Academic Press.

Levin, H. M. (1983). Educational choice and the pains of democracy. In T. James & H. M. Levin (Eds.), *Public dollars for private schools: The case of tuition tax credits* (pp. 17–38). Philadelphia: Temple University Press.

Levin, H. M. (1987). Education as a public and private good. *Journal of Policy Analysis and Management, 6*, 628–641.

Levy, F. (1987). *Dollars and dreams: The changing American income distribution*. New York: Russell Sage Foundation.

Lieberman, M. (1989). *Privatization and educational choice*. New York: St. Martin's Press.

Lipsky, M. (1980). *Street-level bureaucracy: Dilemmas of the individual in public services*. New York: Russell Sage Foundation.

Loewenberg, G., Patterson, S., & Jewell, M. (Eds.). (1985). *Handbook of legislative research*. Cambridge, MA: Harvard University Press.

Lovrich, N., Jr., Daynes, B., & Ginger, L. (1980). Public policy and the effects of historical-cultural phenomena: The case of Indiana. *Publius: The Journal of Federalism, 10*(2), 111–125.

Lowe, R., & Kantor, H. (1989). Considerations on writing the history of educational reform in the 1960s. *Educational Theory, 39*, 1–9.

Lutz, D. S. (1979). The theory of consent in the early state constitutions. *Publius: The Journal of Federalism, 9*(2), 11–42.

Lynd, R. S., & Lynd, H. M. (1929). *Middletown, a study in contemporary American culture*. New York: Harcourt, Brace and Company.

Marshall, C., Mitchell, D., & Wirt, F. (1989). *Culture and education policy in the American states*. New York: Falmer Press.

Masters, N. A., Salisbury, R. H., & Eliot, T. H. (1964). *State politics and the public schools: An exploratory analysis*. New York: Alfred A. Knopf.

Mazzoni, T. L. (1978). State legislators and school policy making. *Planning and Changing, 9*, 149–162.
Mazzoni, T. L. (1982). Education interest groups and state school policymaking. *Planning and Changing, 13*, 158–171.
Mazzoni, T. L. (1985). Bureaucratic influence in the formation of state school policy. *Planning and Changing, 16*, 67–81.
Mazzoni, T. L. (1989). Governors as policy leaders for education: A Minnesota comparison. *Educational Policy, 3*, 79–90.
McCarthy, M. M., & Hall, G. C. (1989). The emergence of university-based education policy centers. *Trends and Issues.* Eugene, OR: ERIC Clearinghouse on Educational Management.
McDonnell, L. M., & McLaughlin, M. W. (1982). *Education policy and the role of the states* (Report prepared for the National Institute of Education, R-2755-NIE). Santa Monica, CA: Rand Corporation.
McGivney, J. H. (1984). State educational governance patterns. *Educational Administration Quarterly, 20*(2), 43–63.
McGivney, J. H., & Moynihan, W. (1972). School and community. *Teachers College Record, 74*, 317–356.
McLaughlin, M. (1976). Implementation as mutual adaptation: Change in classroom organization. In W. Williams & R. F. Elmore (Eds.), *Social program implementation* (pp. 167–180). New York: Academic Press.
McLaughlin, M. W. (1987). Learning from experience: Lessons from policy implementation. *Educational Evaluation and Policy Analysis, 9*(2), 171–178.
McLaughlin, M. W., & Catterall, J. S. (1984). Notes on the new politics of education. *Education and Urban Society, 16*, 375–381.
McNeil, L. M. (1983). Defensive teaching and classroom control. In M. W. Apple & L. Weis (Eds.), *Ideology and practice in schooling* (pp. 114–142). Philadelphia: Temple University Press.
McNeil, L. M. (1988). *Contradictions of control: School structure and school knowledge.* New York: Routledge.
Meltsner, A. J., & Bellavita, C. (1983). *The policy organization.* Beverly Hills, CA: Sage Publications.
Metz, M. H. (1978). *Classrooms and corridors: The crisis of authority in desegregated secondary schools.* Berkeley: University of California Press.
Metz, M. H. (1986). *Different by design: The context and character of three magnet schools.* New York: Routledge, Chapman & Hall.
Milstein, M. M. (1976). *Impact and response: Federal aid and state education agencies.* New York: Teachers College Press.
Milstein, M. M., & Jennings, R. E. (1973). *Educational policy-making and the state legislature: The New York experience.* New York: Praeger.
Minow, M. (1985). Learning to live with the dilemma of difference: Bilingual and special education. *Law and Contemporary Problems, 48*, 157–211.
Mitchell, D. E. (1981). *Shaping legislative decisions: Education policy and the social sciences.* Lexington, MA: Lexington Books.
Mitchell, D. E. (1984). Educational policy analysis: The state of the art. *Educational Administration Quarterly, 20*(3), 129–160.
Mitchell, D. E., & Encarnation, D. J. (1984). Alternative state policy mechanisms for influencing school performance. *Educational Researcher, 13*(5), 4–11.
Mitchell, D. E., & Iannaccone, L. (1980). *The impact of California's legislative policy on public school performance* (California policy seminar monograph No. 5). Berkeley: Institute of Government Studies, University of California.

Moore, M. T., Goertz, M. E., Hartle, T. W., Winslow, H. R., David, J. L., Sjogren, J., Turnbull, B. J., Coley, R. J., & Holland, R. P. (1983). *The interaction of federal and related state education programs. Vol. 1* (Report prepared for the School Finance Project, U.S. Department of Education). Princeton, NJ: Educational Testing Service.

Mort, P. R. (1933). *State support for public education.* Washington, DC: American Council on Education.

Muir, W. K., Jr. (1982). *Legislature: California's school for politics.* Chicago: University of Chicago Press.

Muir, W. K., Jr. (1986). Teachers' regulation of the classroom. In D. L. Kirp & D. N. Jensen (Eds.), *School days, rule days: The legalization and regulation of education* (pp. 109–123). Philadelphia: Falmer Press.

Murphy, J. (1989). Educational reform in the 1980s: Explaining some surprising success. *Educational Evaluation and Policy Analysis, 11*(3), 209–221.

Murphy, J. T. (1973, August). Title V of ESEA: The impact of discretionary funds on state education bureaucracies. *Harvard Educational Review, 43*, 362–385.

Murphy, J. T. (1974). *State education agencies and discretionary funds: Grease the squeaky wheel.* Lexington, MA: Lexington Books.

Murphy, J. T. (1980). The state role in education: Past research and future directions. *Educational Evaluation and Policy Analysis, 2*(4), 39–51.

Murphy, J. T. (1982). Progress and problems: The paradox of state reform. In A. Lieberman & M. W. McLaughlin (Eds.), *Policy making in education: Eighty-first yearbook of the National Society for the Study of Education, Part I* (pp. 195–214). Chicago: University of Chicago Press.

Murphy, J. T., & Cohen, D. K. (1974). Accountability in education—The Michigan experience. *Public Interest, 36*, 53–81.

Murray, C. A. (1984). *Losing ground: American social policy, 1950–1980.* New York: Basic Books.

Nystrand, R. O., & Staub, W. F. (1978). The courts as educational policy makers. In C. P. Hooker (Ed.), *The courts and education: 77th yearbook of the National Society for the Study of Education, Part I* (pp. 27–53). Chicago: University of Chicago Press.

Oakes, J. (1985). *Keeping track: How schools structure inequality.* New Haven, CT: Yale University Press.

Odden, A. (1990). Educational indicators in the United States: The need for analysis. *Educational Researcher, 19*(5), 24–29.

Odden, A. R., & Marsh, D. D. (1987, December). *How state education reform can improve secondary schools* (Policy paper No. PC87-12-14-SDE). Berkeley, CA: Policy Analysis for California Education, University of California, Berkeley.

Odden, A., & Marsh, D. (1990). Local response to the 1980s state education reforms: New patterns of local and state interaction. In J. Murphy (Ed.), *The educational reform movement of the 1980s: Perspectives and cases* (pp. 167–186). Berkeley, CA: McCutchan.

Onuf, P. S. (in press). State politics and republican virtue: Religion, education and morality in early American federalism. In P. Finkleman & S. E. Gottlieb (Eds.), *Toward a usable past: The origins and implications of state protections of liberty.* Athens: University of Georgia Press.

Perlmann, J. (1988). *Ethnic differences: Schooling and social structure among the Irish, Italians, Jews, and Blacks in an American city, 1880–1935.* New York: Cambridge University Press.

Peshkin, A. (1982). *The imperfect union: School consolidation & community conflict*. Chicago: University of Chicago Press.

Peterson, P. E. (1974). The politics of American education. In F. N. Kerlinger & J. B. Carroll (Eds.), *Review of research in education, 2* (pp. 348–389). Itasca, IL: F. E. Peacock Publishers.

Peterson, P. E. (1976). *School politics Chicago style*. Chicago: University of Chicago Press.

Peterson, P. E. (1985a). Did the education commissions say anything? In P. G. Altbach, G. P. Kelly, & L. Weis (Eds.), *Excellence in education: Perspectives on policy and practice* (pp. 57–72). Buffalo, NY: Prometheus Books.

Peterson, P. E. (1985b). *The politics of school reform 1870–1940*. Chicago: University of Chicago Press.

Peterson, P. E., & Rabe, B. G. (1983). The role of interest groups in the formation of educational policy: Past practice and future trends. *Teachers College Record, 84*, 708–729.

Peterson, P. E., Rabe, B. G., & Wong, K. K. (1986). *When federalism works*. Washington, DC: Brookings Institution.

Policy Analysis for California Education. (1990). *The new challenge: Rebuilding education in the golden state. A policy plan and action agenda for the 1990's*. Berkeley, CA: PACE, School of Education, University of California.

Porter, D. O., with D. C. Warner & T. W. Porter. (1973). *The politics of budgeting federal aid: Resource mobilization by local school districts*. Beverly Hills, CA: Sage.

Powell, A. G., Farrar, E., & Cohen, D. K. (1985). *The shopping mall high school: Winners and losers in the educational marketplace*. Boston: Houghton Mifflin.

Ravitch, D. (1974). *The great school wars, New York City, 1805–1973: A history of the public schools as battlefield of social change*. New York: Basic Books.

Ravitch, D. (1983). *The troubled crusade: American education, 1945–1980*. New York: Basic Books.

Raywid, M. A. (1985). Family choice arrangements in public schools: A review of the literature. *Review of Educational Research, 55*, 435–467.

Raywid, M. A. (1989, April). *Patterns of constraint and opportunity: The policy environments of three coalition schools*. Paper presented at the Politics Conference, Coalition of Essential Schools, Brown University.

Raywid, M. A. (1990). Rethinking school governance. In R. F. Elmore & Associates (Eds.), *Restructuring schools: The next generation of educational reform* (pp. 152–205). San Francisco: Jossey-Bass.

Reese, W. J. (1986). *Power and the promise of school reform: Grassroots movements during the progressive era*. Boston: Routledge & Kegan Paul.

Reese, W. J. (1988). Public schools and the common good. *Educational Theory, 38*, 431–440.

Resnick, D. (1982). History of educational testing. In A. K. Wigdor & W. R. Garner (Eds.), *Ability testing: Uses, consequences, and controversies, part II: Documentation section* (pp. 173–194). Washington, DC: National Academy Press.

Resnick, D. P. (1980). Minimum competency testing historically considered. In D. C. Berliner (Ed.), *Review of research in education, Vol. 8, 1980* (pp. 3–29). Washington, DC: American Educational Research Association.

Richards, C. E. (1988). A typology of educational monitoring systems. *Educational Evaluation and Policy Analysis, 10*(2), 106–116.

Richards, C. E., & Shujaa, M. (1990). State-sponsored school performance incentive plans: A policy review. *Educational Considerations, 17*, 42–52.

Richardson, J. G. (1984a). Settlement patterns and the governing structures of nineteenth-century school systems. *American Journal of Education, 92*, 178–206.

Richardson, J. G. (1984b). The American states and the age of school systems. *American Journal of Education, 92*, 473–502.

Robinson v. Cahill, 62 NJ 473, 303 A.2d 273 (1973).

Rosenthal, A. (1981). *Legislative life: People, processes, and performances in the states*. New York: Harper & Row.

Rosenthal, A. (1983). Legislative oversight and the balance of power in state government. *State Government, 56*(3), 90–98.

Rosenthal, A. (1990). *Governors and legislatures: Contending powers*. Washington, DC: Congressional Quarterly.

Rosenthal, A., & Fuhrman, S. H. (1981). Legislative education staffing in the states. *Educational Evaluation and Policy Analysis, 3*(4), 5–16.

Rossell, C. H. (1990). *The carrot or the stick for school desegregation policy: Magnet schools or forced busing*. Philadelphia: Temple University Press.

San Antonio Independent School District v. Rodriguez, 411 U.S. 1 (1973).

Sanford, T. (1967). *Storm over the states*. New York: McGraw-Hill.

Sarason, S. B. (1971). *The culture of the school and the problem of change*. Boston: Allyn and Bacon.

Scheffler, I. (1984). On the education of policymakers. *Harvard Educational Review, 54*, 152–165.

Schuman, D. (1988). The right to "equal privileges and immunities": A state's version of "equal protection." *Vermont Law Review, 13*, 221–245.

Scott, W. R., & Meyer, J. W. (1988). Environmental linkages and organizational complexity: Public and private schools. In T. James & H. M. Levin (Eds.), *Comparing public & private schools, Vol. 1: Institutions and organizations* (pp. 128–160). New York: Falmer Press.

Sedlak, M. W., Wheeler, C. W., Pullin, D. C., & Cusick, P. A. (1986). *Selling students short: Classroom bargains and academic reform in the American high school*. New York: Teachers College Press.

Shapiro, S. (1990). *Between capitalism and democracy: Educational policy and the crisis of the welfare state*. New York: Bergin and Garvey.

Sherman, J. D. (1980). Financing local schools: The impact of desegregation. In T. R. Dye & V. Gray (Eds.), *The determinants of public policy* (pp. 75–83). Lexington, MA: Lexington Books.

Smith, M. S., & Jenkins, J. W. (1982). Legislation. In H. E. Mitzel (Ed.), *Encyclopedia of educational research* (5th ed., pp. 1068–1078). New York: Free Press.

Smith, M. S., & O'Day, J. (in press-a). Systemic school reform. In S. H. Fuhrman & B. Malen (Eds.), *The politics of curriculum and testing*. New York: Falmer Press.

Smith, M. S., & O'Day, J. (in press-b). Educational equality: 1966 and now. In D. Verstegen (Ed.), *Spheres of justice in American schools*. New York: Harper and Row.

Spring, J. (1989). *The sorting machine revisited: National educational policy since 1945* (rev. ed.). New York: Longman.

Sproull, L., Weiner, S., & Wolf, D. (1978). *Organizing an anarchy: Belief, bureaucracy, and politics in the National Institute of Education*. Chicago: University of Chicago Press.

Strike, K. A. (1982). *Educational policy and the just society*. Urbana, IL: University of Illinois Press.

Sunstein, C. R. (1990). *After the rights revolution: Reconceiving the regulatory state.* Cambridge, MA: Harvard University Press.

Tarr, G. A., & Porter, M. C. A. (1988). *State supreme courts in state and nation.* New Haven, CT: Yale University Press.

Thro, W. E. (1989). To render them safe: The analysis of state constitutional provisions in public school finance reform litigation. *Virginia Law Review, 75,* 1639–1679.

Timar, T. B. (1989). A theoretical framework for local responses to state policy: Implementing Utah's career ladder program. *Educational Evaluation and Policy Analysis, 11*(4), 329–341.

Timar, T. B. (1990). The politics of school restructuring. In D. E. Mitchell & M. E. Goertz (Eds.), *Education politics for the new century: The twentieth anniversary yearbook of the Politics of Education Association* (pp. 55–74). New York: Falmer Press.

Timar, T. B., & Kirp, D. L. (1988). *Managing educational excellence.* New York: Falmer Press.

Troxel, O. L. (1928). *State control of secondary education.* Baltimore: Warwick and York.

Turnbull, B. J. (1985). Using governance and support systems to advance school improvement. *The Elementary School Journal, 85,* 337–351.

Tushnet, M. V. (1987). *The NAACP's legal strategy against segregated education, 1925–1950.* Chapel Hill: University of North Carolina.

Tyack, D. (1967). Bureaucracy and the common school: The example of Portland, Oregon, 1851–1913. *American Quarterly, 19,* 475–498.

Tyack, D. B. (1974). *The one best system: A history of American urban education.* Cambridge, MA: Harvard University Press.

Tyack, D. (1976). Ways of seeing: An essay on the history of compulsory schooling. *Harvard Educational Review, 46,* 355–389.

Tyack, D., & Berkowitz, M. (1977). The man nobody liked: Towards a social history of the truant officer, 1840–1940. *American Quarterly, 29,* 31–54.

Tyack, D., & Hansot, E. (1982). *Managers of virtue: Public school leadership in America, 1820–1980.* New York: Basic Books.

Tyack, D., & James, T. (1986). State government and American public education: Exploring the "primeval forest." *History of Education Quarterly, 26,* 39–69.

Tyack, D., James, T., & Benavot, A. (1987). *Law and the shaping of public education, 1785–1954.* Madison: University of Wisconsin Press.

Tyack, D. B., Kirst, M. W., & Hansot, E. (1980). Educational reform: Retrospect and prospect. *Teachers College Record, 81,* 253–269.

Tyack, D., Lowe, R., & Hansot, E. (1984). *Public schools in hard times: The Great Depression and recent years.* Cambridge, MA: Harvard University Press.

U.S. Department of Education, National Center for Education Statistics. (1989). *Digest of education statistics 1989* (25th ed.). Washington, DC: U.S. Government Printing Office.

U.S. Department of Health, Education & Welfare, National Center for Educational Research and Development. (1970). *Linking schools to state education departments: Analysis of literature and selected bibliography.* Eugene, OR: ERIC Clearinghouse on Educational Administration, University of Oregon.

Urban, W. J. (1982). *Why teachers organized.* Detroit: Wayne State University Press.

Usdan, M. D. (1963). *The political power of education in New York State.* New York: Institute of Administrative Research, Teachers College, Columbia University.

Usdan, M. D. (1969). The role and future of state educational coalitions. *Educational Administration Quarterly, 5*(2), 26–42.

Usdan, M. D., Minar, D. W., & Hurwitz, E., Jr. (1969). *Education and state politics: The developing relationship between elementary-secondary and higher education*. New York: Teachers College Press.

van Geel, T. (1976). *Authority to control the school program*. Lexington, MA: Lexington Books.

van Geel, T. (1987). *The courts and American education law*. Buffalo, NY: Prometheus Books.

Verstegen, D. A., Hooker, R., & Estes, N. (1986). A comprehensive shift in educational policymaking: Texas educational reform legislation. In V. D. Mueller & M. P. McKeown (Eds.), *The fiscal, legal, and political aspects of state reform of elementary and secondary education: Sixth annual yearbook of the American Education Finance Association 1985* (pp. 277–306). San Francisco: Ballinger.

Weatherley, R., & Lipsky, M. (1977). Street-level bureaucrats and institutional innovation: Implementing special-education reform. *Harvard Educational Review, 47*, 171–197.

Weick, K. E. (1976). Educational organizations as loosely coupled systems. *Administrative Science Quarterly, 21*(1), 1–19.

Welch, S., & Peters, J. G. (1980). State political culture and the attitudes of state senators toward social, economic welfare, and corruption issues. *Publius: The Journal of Federalism, 10*(2), 59–68.

West Virginia State Board of Education v. Barnette, 319 U.S. 624 (1943).

Wilkinson, J. H. (1979). *From Brown to Bakke: The Supreme Court and school integration: 1954–1978*. New York: Oxford University Press.

Willis, P. (1976). The class significance of school counter-culture. In M. Hammersley & P. Woods (Eds.), *The process of schooling* (pp. 188–200). London: Routledge and Kegan Paul.

Wirt, F. M. (1972). American schools as a political system: A bibliographic essay. In M. W. Kirst (Ed.), *State, school and politics: Research directions* (pp. 247–281). Lexington, MA: Lexington Books.

Wirt, F. M. (1977). School policy culture and state decentralization. In J. D. Scribner (Ed.), *The politics of education: The seventy-sixth yearbook of the National Society for the Study of Education, Part II* (pp. 164–187). Chicago: University of Chicago Press.

Wirt, F. M. (1980). Does control follow the dollar? School policy, state-local linkages and political culture. *Publius: The Journal of Federalism, 10*(2), 69–88.

Wirt, F. M., & Kirst, M. W. (1972). *The political web of American schools*. Boston: Little, Brown.

Wirt, F. M., & Kirst, M. W. (1989). *Schools in conflict* (2nd ed.). Berkeley, CA: McCutchan Publishing.

Wise, A. E. (1968). *Rich schools, poor schools: The promise of equal educational opportunity*. Chicago: University of Chicago Press.

Wise, A. E. (1979). *Legislated learning: The bureaucratization of the American classroom*. Berkeley: University of California Press.

Wise, A. E. (1983). Educational adequacy: A concept in search of a meaning. *Journal of Education Finance, 8*, 300–315.

Wong, K. K. (1989). Fiscal support for education in American states: "Parity-to-dominance" view examined. *American Journal of Education, 97*(4), 329–357.

Wood, S. B. (1968). *Constitutional politics in the progressive era: Child labor and the law*. Chicago: University of Chicago Press.

Wood, T. (1988). State-mandated accountability as a constraint on teaching and learning science. *Journal of Research in Science Teaching, 25*, 631–641.

Wrigley, J. (1982). *Class politics and public schools: Chicago, 1900–1950*. New Brunswick, NJ: Rutgers University Press.

Yates, D. (1982). *Bureaucratic democracy: The search for democracy and efficiency in American government*. Cambridge, MA: Harvard University Press.

Yudof, M. G., Kirp, D. L., van Geel, T., & Levin, B. (1982). *Kirp & Yudof's educational policy and the law: Cases and materials* (2nd ed.). Berkeley, CA: McCutchan.

Zeigler, H., & Johnson, K. F. (1972). *The politics of education in the states*. Indianapolis, IN: Bobbs-Merrill Co.

Chapter 6

Review of Research on Teacher Participation in School Decision Making

SHARON CONLEY
University of Arizona

Teacher participation in school decision making remains a persistent theme in this country's educational reform movement. In 1986, the Carnegie Commission called for "giving teachers a greater voice in decisions that affect the school" (p. 57). A second Carnegie Foundation report based on a national survey of public school teachers found that a majority of teachers are not "asked to participate in such crucial matters as teacher evaluation, staff development, [and] budget" (Carnegie Foundation, 1988, p. 1).[1] In 1986, an association of the nation's governors called for teachers to become "involved integrally in making [school] decisions" (National Governor's Association, 1986, p. 6). Finally, the nation's largest teachers' union and administrator organization jointly produced a report calling for teacher participation in "identifying the purposes, priorities and goals of the school" (National Education Association/National Association for Secondary School Principals, 1986, p. 16).

These observations have the common goal of increasing teacher involvement in a wide array of school decisions (e.g., teacher development and evaluation and facilities planning). School governance councils, for example, have been implemented in various forms to achieve this aim. The research literature on teacher participation has been outpaced by these developments, however, because discussion of teacher involvement is often restricted to a narrow range of instructional policy-making areas, such as shaping the curriculum (Conley, Schmidle, & Shedd, 1988). Policymakers who seek to provide teachers with the broader decision-making responsibilities clearly called for in the reform reports might be helped

---

The author thanks consulting editor Larry Cuban (Stanford University), editor Gerald Grant (Syracuse University), colleagues Gary Rhoades and Mike Sacken (University of Arizona), and Richard Wagman (Sunnyside School District) for their helpful comments and suggestions. Yvonne Cano and Joanne Hurley also provided helpful reference and editorial assistance.

by research that examines the potential for and effects of teacher participation in a more extensive selection of school decisions.

Acknowledging the narrow scope of participation assumed in many studies, a reasonably consistent pattern of survey research indicates the importance of teacher participation in efforts to improve individual and organizational performance. Participation has been examined as a key determinant of such individual and organizational school outcomes as teacher job satisfaction (Hoy & Sousa, 1984; Miskel, Fevurly, & Stewart, 1979; Schneider, 1984), stress (Bacharach, Bauer, & Conley, 1986), loyalty (Hoy & Sousa, 1984; Johnston & Germinario, 1985; Miskel et al., 1979), militancy (Alutto & Belasco, 1972), role ambiguity (Mohrman, Cooke, & Mohrman, 1978), role conflict (Alutto & Belasco, 1972), perceived organizational effectiveness (Miskel et al., 1979), collaboration (Rosenholtz, Bassler, & Hoover-Dempsey, 1986), and work alienation (Benson & Malone, 1987). Despite consensus regarding the importance of participation, less agreement exists concerning its meaning. In a variety of organizational settings, participation remains an elusive and polysemous construct; "everyone who employs the term thinks of something different" (Schregle, cited in Hoy & Sousa, 1984). Indeed, work on participation has produced a set of strategic choices rather than a consensus definition. Researchers and policymakers, often unaware of the conceptual framework within which they operate, define participation in varied ways. To give analytic coherence to the material presented in this chapter, a particular framework—the political framework—will be chosen, from which a set of meanings for participation will be derived.

If one focuses on the authority structure of the school, different "shades of participation" exist (Alutto & Belasco, 1972, p. 118); administrators may delegate decisions to teachers or they may consult teachers in making joint decisions (Bridges, 1967). Debates over participation inevitably turn on these concepts (delegation and joint decision making) as well as on their respective sources of power: authority and influence. Focusing on the sources of power underlying decision participation suggests that an explication of the concept may be achieved coherently within a political organizational framework. Political theorists (Bacharach & Lawler, 1980; Ball, 1987; Corwin, 1974, 1981; Hanson, 1979; Hoyle, 1986) traditionally maintain that organizational members constantly negotiate and renegotiate who should have authority and influence on particular decisions. Thus, within a political perspective, a definition of participation would necessarily include two dimensions: (a) who participates in decision making and (b) the types of decisions in which members may participate.

The issue of who participates in decision making turns on the degree of centralization in the organization, that is, the level of the organization at which decisions are approved (Mohrman et al., 1978). Given that a hierarchical structure is emphasized in administrative and bureaucratic bodies of literature, "the dominant image associated with participation in decision making becomes one of decisional influence moving down the hierarchy or a flattening of the organizational structure" (Mohrman et al., 1978, p. 13). For the purposes of this chapter, the first dimension of participation includes administrators delegating specific decisions to teachers as well as teachers and administrators making decisions jointly (casting teachers in an explicitly advisory or consultative role). With regard to the types of decisions, members may participate in work-level decisions (e.g., task execution) or organizational-level decisions (e.g., policy making and resource allocation) (Miskel et al., 1979; Mohrman et al., 1978). The second dimension of participation thus designates involvement in work or policy domains; a teacher making decisions within the confines of a classroom is considered to be participating, albeit in work-level decisions.

This chapter addresses the issue of who participates in decision making by discussing (a) teachers' expectations for participation, (b) forms that participation has taken—and is taking—in schools, and (c) power in decision making. The topic of decision types is addressed by examining the domains of decision making in the organization and the changing conceptualizations of those domains. Finally, because current reform reports focus particularly on teacher participation at the school building level, this review concentrates on teacher participation in decisions at the school rather than at other levels of the educational system (district, state, national). When districts and states are mentioned, it is to frame participation-oriented reform mandates within a broader policy context, for example, teacher participation in the Utah career ladder (e.g., Malen & Ogawa, 1988).

The framework of this review incorporates research examining the decision expectations of teachers regarding participation and the organizational domains in which they may become involved. Then, research delimiting teacher participation to the technical (i.e., work level) domain of organizational decision making is shown to be incomplete in important ways. Traditional and new forms of participation in schools are examined, in turn, as possible mechanisms for enhancing organizational coordination. Finally, dimensions of power represented by participation in decision making (i.e., teacher authority and influence) are discussed, and issues for further research are suggested. Because teacher participation takes place in professional bureaucracies, it is important to emphasize the manner in which schools represent bureaucratic organizations. Therefore, the next few paragraphs briefly outline some of the assumptions of teacher participation research in this context, a literature that normally assumes the importance of participation, although in the pursuit of divergent aims.

THE AIMS OF PARTICIPATION

What are the aims, or purposes, of participation? Researchers' perspectives regarding participation purposes vary according to their explicit or implicit assumptions regarding schools as organizations. Although multiple theoretical frameworks, such as political and human relations models (Bolman & Deal, 1985; Morgan, 1986), exist for analyzing schools, participation researchers often fail to identify their framework explicitly or acknowledge that multiple models for analyzing schools exist. Most participation research implicitly adopts either a bureaucratic model of schools or an unclear hybrid of bureaucratic and human relations models. The blending of bureaucratic and human relations approaches is due to a tendency in many studies to examine job satisfaction and morale as criterion variables and also to stress the formal properties of schools as bureaucratic organizations (e.g., the hierarchical setting and authority structure). Thus, participation research is traditionally dominated by bureaucratic or administrative bodies of thought seeking humanistic ends. However, recent debates on participation have drifted toward an image of schools that is congruent with a professional model of school organizations, carrying with it a different set of aims for participation. Thus, the appropriate frameworks or models to adopt in understanding or evaluating participation research appear to be the bureaucratic (accepting a human relations overlay) and the professional. Thus, these models receive primary consideration in this section.

Current debates concerning the conceptualization and design of participation are driven, implicitly, by the differences between the aforementioned ideal models or types (Corcoran, 1987). The bureaucratic or administrative model emphasizes the formal authority of administrators to delegate responsibilities to subordinates, formulate rules to govern subordinate behavior, and implement centralized control, planning, and decision making. The professional model emphasizes the professional discretion and expertise of teachers in diagnosing and addressing student learning needs (Bacharach & Conley, 1986). The bureaucratic model suggests that participation serves to gain teacher compliance with administrative decisions. The professional model suggests that an aim of participation is to accord teachers the rights they expect, as professionals, in the school workplace.

Both of these perspectives coexist with a human relations model of school organizations in that employee job satisfaction and morale are viewed as primary aims of participation. However, researchers adhering to one or the other perspective differ in their emphasis on the needs of the administrative bureaucracy versus the needs of professionals. On one hand, researchers following administrative bodies of thought (Johnston

& Germinario, 1985; Miskel et al., 1979) emphasize the importance of participation for the administrative supervision of teachers and the building of teacher loyalty to superiors: "The most effective teacher-administrator relationship, in terms of both morale and productivity, is a participative one" (Johnston & Germinario, 1985, p. 91). For example, Miskel et al. (1979) related teacher involvement in policy decisions (through decentralization) with increased satisfaction, organizational effectiveness, and teacher loyalty—employee attributes that translate to fewer problems for administrators. Studies aligned more with a professional orientation tend to emphasize the significance of participation for enhancing teachers' organizational roles as professional decision makers. Lack of participation is then viewed as depriving teachers of the decisional power they expect and deserve in the workplace, leading to dissatisfaction, stress, or work alienation. Such a perspective on participation has been taken in studies in other professional settings, such as nursing: "A critical set of activities for professional employees [nurses] is the maintenance of autonomy through participation in decision making in the face of organizationally defined constraints" (Alutto & Vredenburgh, 1977, p. 344). In education, Bacharach et al. (1986), working within a professional conceptual framework, hypothesized that teachers who were denied opportunities to participate would feel a sense of powerlessness based on their professional expectations for discretion and involvement. They related increased teacher powerlessness (operationalized in terms of low decision influence) with increased teacher stress. (See also Corcoran's [1987, p. 4] discussion of participation as an ethical imperative and a cornerstone of workplace democracy.)

Thus, researchers following administrative or managerial bodies of thought tend to identify teacher loyalty to administrators and teacher acceptance and compliance with administrative decisions as critical goals and rationales of participation. Typical of the human relations model in business, the overriding strategy is to promote employee compliance with administrative decisions. The professional model views employee satisfaction, morale, and workplace democracy as ends in themselves rather than as means to compliance.

A contribution of studies following administrative bodies of thought has been to demonstrate that teacher-principal relationships are strengthened—and teachers are more accepting of administrators' directives—when administrators adopt a participative or human relations management style (Hoy & Brown, 1988; Kunz & Hoy, 1976). However, because this literature tends to focus on the "blind" acceptance of management directives by teachers, it seems out of pace with current calls for genuine teacher participation in decision making. On the other hand, a professional orientation, while sensitizing researchers and practitioners to teacher expectations, generally fails to deal with the issue of organizational constraints on decision making, acknowledge much need for the exercise of managerial authority, or speak to the implications for relations between teachers and principals. Taken to its extreme, it suggests that empowerment alone will solve educational problems.

It is important to note that neither perspective (bureaucratic or professional) addresses educational outcomes directly. For example, do students actually learn more or drop out less in a more participatory school environment? Both models exclude direct consideration of students and their parents, yet both assume that participation is good for the school. Thus, both exclude direct organizational benefits and focus instead on indirect organizational benefits accrued by teachers (i.e., job satisfaction and morale). However, the indirect benefits of participation received by employees (e.g., satisfaction) provide an unpersuasive rationale for participation in many organizations, because the benefits of participation are likely to be viewed by managers as one-sided (Shedd, 1987).

Even when the aim of participation is framed as a "transaction cost" for administrators—that is, they receive teachers' cooperation in management decisions in exchange for giving teachers the opportunity to participate—the acceptance of management-initiated change is still only an indirect organizational benefit and thus is likely to engender minimal administrator and teacher commitment to participation. Thus, a need exists to identify a middle ground that relates the aims of participation to a recognition of the professional needs of teachers as well as the coordinative needs of managers.

In sum, the bureaucratic model, taken to its extreme, suggests that employees should either not participate or should participate only to gain acceptance for decisions made by administrators. The professional model metaphorically suggests that teacher empowerment and morale alone represent an appropriate solution to managerial problems in schools. In trying to break out of the metaphorical extremes promoted by both models, the next section addresses two critical issues: What are the expectations of professional teachers with regard to participation, and in what decision domains may they participate?

TEACHER EXPECTATIONS AND ORGANIZATIONAL DECISION DOMAINS: IN WHICH DECISIONS MAY TEACHERS PARTICIPATE?

This section examines teachers' desires for participation and, more particularly, the types of decisions in which they may become involved. As suggested earlier, a primary assumption in the professional model is that teachers expect to be afforded opportunities to participate in organizational decision making based on their possession of a body of knowledge and expertise. In this context, it is critical to examine the nature and extent of decision making desired by teachers. In addition, one must examine two issues: (a) the nature of decision making in the school organization and (b) the specific decision areas in which professional teachers may become involved. Literature examining the first issue focuses on uncovering possible discrepancies between teachers' expectations for decision making and the decisional opportunities afforded them. Recognizing that schools are complex professional bureaucracies, literature examining the second issue focuses on various sets of decisions characterizing these work organizations. Obviously, the two issues are related, and recent research tends to examine both simultaneously (e.g., Bacharach, Bamberger, & Conley, 1990; Mohrman et al., 1978). An additional task in this section is to identify points where research remains unclear, for example, the specific nature and content of decision domains in the organization. The studies cited in this section use survey methods to examine these issues, reflecting research in the field of educational administration in general (see Miskel & Sandlin, 1981).

Professional Expectations of Teachers

A critical issue in examining teachers' expectations for participation is whether teachers assess their decision participation in relative or absolute terms (Alutto & Belasco, 1972). Relative participation means that teachers assess their need for participation based on how much influence they currently have (on organizational decision making) compared to how much they desire. This issue may be viewed as critical in professional organizations, where members may expect a high level of autonomy and decision participation. Absolute participation means that teachers assess their need for participation without reference to the amount of participation they would like to have but only how much they currently receive.

This distinction is important, because research prior to the 1970s often conceptualized and operationalized participation in absolute terms; that is, teachers were asked to report their opportunities to participate but not the amount of participation they desired (Alutto & Belasco, 1972). This approach was criticized on two grounds. First, it seemed important in a professional occupation such as teaching to assess teachers' expectations. Second, an "absolute measure" assumes that organizational members are "homogeneous in attitudes, sentiments and expectations" concerning decision making (Alutto & Belasco, 1972, p. 118). In any particular school, teachers may be far from uniform in their desires for participation.

A "relative" conceptualization and measure of participation addresses both of these concerns by placing an emphasis on the discrepancy between teachers' current and preferred levels of participation across several decision areas. This method, initially advocated by Alutto and Belasco

(1972) in their study of teachers in two districts, measured participation according to three decisional states: deprived, saturated, and in equilibrium. Alutto and Belasco found that teachers were more likely to report being decisionally deprived than in equilibrium or saturated; furthermore, male and secondary school teachers were more decisionally deprived than their female and elementary school teacher counterparts. Expectations for participation also exceeded actual participation among younger teachers working in a rural as opposed to urban setting. Consistent with the predictions of Alutto and Belasco, decisionally deprived teachers reported greater militancy and role conflict than teachers who were saturated or in equilibrium.

Subsequently, investigations over nearly a 20-year period confirm that (a) the decisional state of deprivation characterizes a majority of teachers (Bacharach et al., 1990; Benson & Malone, 1987; Conway, 1976; Johnston & Germinario, 1985; Mohrman et al., 1979; Schneider, 1984)[2] and (b) decisional deprivation is related to important outcomes, such as teacher satisfaction (Bacharach et al., 1990; Schneider, 1984), stress (Bacharach et al., 1986), and loyalty (Johnston & Germinario, 1985). That is, when the professional expectations of teachers for participation exceed current opportunities in the school, teachers report more dissatisfaction, more stress, and less loyalty to principals.

It should be noted that over this 20-year period, there has been an increasing amount of debate over the utility of the saturation and equilibrium decisional states that originally engendered much interest. In the 1970s, the use of these decisional states in research was advocated on the grounds that increasing participation for segments of the organization that are saturated or in equilibrium is of doubtful value (Alutto & Belasco, 1972; Conway, 1976). In addition, it was argued that the concepts of saturation and equilibrium allow the researcher to posit a curvilinear relationship between decisional conditions and attitudinal work outcomes: Organizational members who are closer to equilibrium are at the peak of the curve and have the most positive perceptions of the school organization, whereas decisionally deprived and saturated members make up the extreme ends of the curve and hold negative perceptions of the organization (Conway, 1976). Recent research (Schneider, 1986), however, tends to disagree with this conceptualization and posits a linear association between decisional deprivation and work outcomes. These studies have focused on decisional deprivation as a critical participation variable predicting outcomes (e.g., Bacharach et al., 1990; Schneider, 1984). The virtue of this approach (focusing on decisional deprivation) is that it places an emphasis on discovering the consequences of the decisional state experienced by the majority of teachers. Finally, it should be noted that the use of deprivation scores has generated debate in the literature due to possible social desirability effects (Alutto & Vredenburgh, 1977).[3]

In sum, Alutto and Belasco (1972) raised the issue of the relative nature of the decision construct. Such a conceptualization of participation carries with it the dual assumptions that (a) participation should be assessed in reference to a teacher's expectations and (b) desires for participation are not uniform within an organization. However, Alutto and Belasco did not examine teachers' decisional states in relation to particular decision domains in the school, though they did speculate that the effect of decision deprivation on work outcomes may depend on the type of decision issue being assessed. In the context of educational policy, examination of teachers' current and desired levels of participation—in relation to specific decision areas—emphasizes increasing participation in those areas in which teachers' desires for participation are not being met.

Bacharach et al. (1990) provide a useful summary of 14 studies, catalogued according to whether the research assumed participation to be relative or absolute in nature and according to whether participation was assumed to be a unidimensional or multidimensional construct. The reader is referred to Bacharach et al. for a more detailed treatment of these conceptual and methodological assumptions; however, the study is helpful for the purposes of this review in suggesting that the most feasible—and least used—research method is one that assumes that participation is (a) based on teacher's expectations (relative) and (b) multidimensional in nature. The remainder of this section examines the latter assumption—the domain-specific nature of the participation construct.

Decision Domains in School Organizations

The previous section discussed research examining teachers' expectations for participation. However, this is only one half of the equation. Other studies have examined the organizational subsystems or domains of decision making that characterize school organizations. Only by examining specific decisions in the school organization can we begin to identify the decision areas in which teachers may increase their involvement. This section addresses research examining two aspects of this problem: multidimensional aspects of participation and the content specificity of domains.

Multidimensional Aspects

Is participation in school organizations characterized by different domains of decision making, or is it a single, global construct? On one hand, teachers may form an overall or summary judgment of their decision participation across different decision areas (Alutto & Belasco, 1972). On the other hand, it is perhaps more plausible to maintain that teachers may distinguish among participation in different decision domains owing to the complex decisional nature of school organizations (Benson & Malone, 1987; Mohrman et al., 1978). If the latter possibility (termed the multidimensional approach) is correct, then the use of aggregate (or global) conceptualizations and operationalizations of participation has weaknesses for both research and practice. For research, global approaches would fail to capture the actual domain-specific nature of decision participation. For practice, such methods may encourage reformers to increase participation across the board rather than to evaluate strategically (and set priorities about) whether participation is needed in some areas more than others. That is, studies may be less than helpful in their lack of specificity concerning decision areas that could become the focus for increasing teacher involvement.

The multidimensional approach places a premium on discovering the content-specific nature of decision domains. In this sense, it emphasizes the horizontal characteristics of decision participation rather than the more typically examined vertical distribution of decision-making involvement (Mohrman et al., 1978). Studies examining vertical participation focus on the issue of decision-making power and seek to discover the degree of authority or influence exercised by members at different hierarchical levels of the organization. For example, Hage and Aiken (1967) conceptualized hierarchy of authority in terms of whether the job incumbent or the incumbent's superior has the authority to make work-level decisions. In a sense, studies addressing vertical and horizontal participation both consider individual-organization fit; however, whereas the former explores the "fit between the individual and the amount of participation, [the latter explores the] fit between the individual and the domain of participation" (Mohrman et al., 1978, p. 15). Only a handful of studies have empirically dealt with the content specificity of decision domains since Mohrman et al.'s writing in 1978 (e.g., Bacharach et al., 1990; Johnston & Germinario, 1985; Miskel et al., 1979; Schneider, 1986).

This paucity of literature is curious given educational scholars who have hinted at the multidimensional nature of the participation construct. Bridges (1967) distinguished between organizational decisions falling outside and within teachers' "zone of indifference" (p. 51). (For the originator of the concept of "zone of indifference," see Barnard [1938].) Decisions falling outside the zone essentially tap classroom decisions (e.g., teaching methods); decisions falling inside the zone relate to organizational issues (e.g., attendance procedures). More recent scholarly work has progressed beyond this delineation by clarifying specific decisions within these broad zones (Mohrman et al., 1978), by examining domains empirically (Bacharach et al., 1990), and—through more exploratory, field-based investigations—by proposing intermediate or contested zones of decision making (discussed later) (Hanson, 1979).

The Content of Decision Domains

Mohrman et al. (1978) exemplify a content-oriented approach to studying decision participation. Drawing on Parsons (1960), they distinguish between two broad decision domains or organizational subsystems, each associated with a unique set of decision areas: technical and managerial (see Parsons, 1960, for a discussion of institutional, managerial, and technical subsystems). The "technical domain" consists of decisions related to task execution (e.g., selecting texts, resolving learning problems). The "managerial domain" consists of decisions related to what Mohrman et al. term "managerial support functions" (e.g., hiring personnel, planning budgets) (p. 19). Mohrman et al. sought to demonstrate empirically the utility of a multidimensional approach by demonstrating (a) strong interrelationships among items measuring decision participation in each hypothesized domain and (b) differential relationships of the two domains to attitudinal work outcomes. The study examined patterns of actual and desired levels of participation—and decision deprivation—in each domain. A factor analysis of decision deprivation in 12 decisional areas supported the proposed technical-managerial distinction.[4] In addition, the two domains were differentially associated with affective work outcomes; for example, intrinsic and extrinsic satisfaction and role ambiguity were associated with teacher participation (controlling for participation in other domains) only in technical decisions. The results supported the multidimensional conceptualization of participation: Teachers distinguished between participation in decisions that are more central versus those more marginal to their professional task (Mohrman et al., 1978). Furthermore, the results indicated that although teachers both desire and actually have more participation in the technical domain than in the managerial domain, they feel most deprived of decision-making influence in the managerial domain (see also Johnston & Germinario, 1985, who found that correlations between actual and desired levels of decision making were greater for technical decisions than for managerial decisions). However, the researchers did not examine the possibility of differential results for teachers working in elementary and secondary school organizations.

Recently, Bacharach et al. (1990) modified the domains proposed by Mohrman et al. (1978) in two respects. First, because the technical domain deals with carrying out immediate work activities, it was viewed as operational in nature; because the managerial domain deals with broad organizational resource allocation decisions and overarching policies, it appeared strategic in nature. Second, the authors drew a distinction between whether operational or strategic decisions primarily affected individuals or the organization as a whole. Four distinct decision areas or domains were proposed: (a) strategic-organizational, (b) strategic-individual, (c) operational-organizational, and (d) operational-individual. Using a nationwide sample of 1,531 teachers, the researchers conducted a factor analysis of decision deprivation scores in 19 decision areas. Examples of decisions receiving high factor loadings (for both elementary and secondary schools) on the strategic domain are budget development and expenditure priorities (organizational) and school and classroom assignments (personal); examples of decisions loading on the operational domain are student rights and reporting procedures (organizational) and books used and books available for use (personal) (see Table 7 [p. 152] in Bacharach et al., 1990). Consistent with earlier findings (Mohrman et al., 1978), Bacharach et al. found that participation in the operational domain (measured in terms of decision deprivation) showed a stronger pattern of relationships with outcomes than participation in the strategic domain.[5]

Thus, consistent with previous empirical (Mohrman et al., 1978) and conceptual (Bridges, 1967) work, teachers appear to desire more influence on operational decisions pertaining to direct student instruction than to strategic school administration. However, decidedly different operational decision domains must be considered in this context; teachers report being more decisionally deprived in the organizational (e.g., student rights) domain than in the personal (e.g., books used) domain. Thus, teachers appear to feel most deprived in decisions, such as those involving student rights, reporting procedures, and grading policies, that regulate the boundary between the classroom and organization.[6]

Comment

The relative and multidimensional nature of participation indicates the complexity of the subject of decision participation. The contribution of the multidimensional perspective is that it is rooted in the types of decision issues that teachers encounter and their perspectives regarding their influence on those decisions. If the work is to become more valid, research must address itself to several deficiencies in this line of inquiry. First, a lack of consensus exists regarding the exact typology of decision-making domains (Bacharach et al., 1990; Mohrman et al., 1978). More field-based, exploratory approaches will probably be useful in accomplishing greater clarification in this area. Second, research has not generally examined the issue of multiple domains separately for elementary and secondary school organizations. The dimensionality of the vertical distribution of decision-making involvement has been examined in this context (see Bacharach et al., 1986; Bishop & George, 1973); however, more work is needed on the content specificity of horizontal domains in these distinct types of organizations. Finally (as suggested in the next section), research on the multidimensionality of participation is not well integrated into other (teacher) participation literature; this latter body of literature tends to confine its discussion to participation in the classroom domain. The literature cited in this section noted that although teachers desire the most participation in these areas, they also feel most deprived of decision making in "managerial" domains (e.g., budget; Schneider, 1984), as well as in making decisions close to the boundary of the classroom (e.g., grading policies and student placement).

BEYOND DECISION DOMAINS: CHANGING RATIONALES AND CONCEPTUALIZATIONS OF TEACHER PARTICIPATION IN SCHOOLS

Thus far, teacher participation has not been considered in the context of the daily managerial realities of schools. Schools are marked by a "traditional influence pattern" (Malen & Ogawa, 1988) in which decisions are differentiated by locale and position; strategic decisions typically are made outside of classrooms by administrators, and operational decisions are those made within classrooms by teachers. This pattern exists at the same time that research on the work of teachers and the insular structure of schooling is providing powerful rationales for involving teachers more fully in schools' decision-making processes.

Recently, scholars (Shedd, 1987) have suggested that we may need to progress beyond decision domains and "zones of acceptance"—which carve out separate areas of influence for teachers and administrators—to some new framework that emphasizes the coordination of teachers' and adminstrators' decisions and the ability of each party to achieve influence over decisions previously left to the other. Such arguments draw explicitly, if not exclusively, from a political model of organizations that views schools as a contested terrain where individuals and groups negotiate the decisions in which various parties will become involved. It is argued in this section that within the context of a negotiated order of schooling, the precise line delineating managerial and technical domains of decision making—and the separate "work" of teachers and administrators—may soften, blur, or disappear.

Beyond the Narrow Scope of Teacher Participation

Although the private-sector effective-organizations research literature has long stressed the importance of employee participation in strategic organizational decisions (concerning overall policies and goals), as well as in operational work decisions (concerning specific tasks or means) (e.g., Bailyn, 1985), this advice has not been widely adopted in schools (Bacharach & Conley, 1986). In education, administrators make strategic decisions outside of classrooms and teachers make operational decisions inside of classrooms.

The teacher participation literature tends to support this influence pattern by favoring a limited role for teacher involvement in school decision making in terms of both scope and intensity. Arguments (Bridges, 1967) for restricting scope turn on the relevance of decisions to classroom work and teacher expertise; "managerial" decisions may lack direct relevance to teachers' classroom responsibilities and access matters in which teachers may possess few qualifications. To invoke participation in such decisions may thus span teachers' "zone of indifference" and elicit participation in decisions in which teachers do not have a high personal stake. Arguments (Lortie, 1977) favoring a restricted intensity of teacher involvement in management turn on teachers' concentrated involvement in classroom work. Lortie maintains that the intense classroom environment acts as an "organizationally 'centrifugal' effect" pressing teachers further into the classroom and away from involvement in general school affairs (p. 359). Observations regarding scope and intensity thus promote a sharp distinction between the decision making of teachers and administrators and constrain teacher participation to the classroom domain. Unfortunately, it is unclear how approaches that construe a narrow scope of teacher involvement—limited to such issues as student discipline codes and grading policies—will be reflected in current calls for teacher involvement in a wide array of management decisions.

The precise line dividing the two domains—classroom and organization—may represent an "institutional myth" (Meyer & Rowan, 1977) serving teachers' and administrators' interests, for different reasons. Teachers may view the division between classroom and organization as safeguarding their discretion: "Teachers purchase discretion within classrooms by relinquishing their opportunity to influence school policy" (Corwin, 1981, p. 267). Administrators may view such a division as clearly preserving their authority over decisions made outside of the classroom. In reality, however, many decisions span the border between school and classroom (discussed earlier); thus, positing a sharp division between the two domains is misleading.

If this is the case, how, then, do we view new participation experiments, such as school-based management, that are clearly under way in many schools (Lieberman, 1988; McDonnell & Pascal, 1988)? Traditionally, administrators have employed distant forms of control such as technology and standardization, more so than close supervision, to integrate teachers' and administrators' decision making (Corwin, 1974, 1981). These controls often reflect administrators' dependence on teachers for the information they need to make strategic decisions; for example, school managers frequently employ uniform reporting requirements to acquire student and teaching data (e.g., student attendance). New forms of participation appear to represent a more organic approach to integrating decision making between administrators and teachers (Conley et al., 1988).

In a political conceptualization of participation, Shedd (1988) views new participation mechanisms as making more sophisticated uses of power, coupled with a growing awareness of how participation may capitalize on the dependency relationships among organizational participants. This viewpoint addresses participation from a power and dependence perspective, examining what different parties have to gain from employee input in management decisions (Shedd, 1988). Hence, in many organizational settings, managers recognize that they benefit from the perspectives of those who have closest contact with the organization's products or clients (Shedd, 1987). In some settings more than others, managers view employee participation as something they need to ensure quality management decisions. In education, one of the strongest benefits of participation to managers would thus lie in the organizational roles of teachers.

Teachers are the organization's "line professionals" in the sense that they are "on the line" with clients (students), handling uncertainty for the organization (Bacharach & Conley, 1989). Indeed, teachers are already heavily involved in operational decision making concerning the means for carrying out their classroom work activities. Teachers make decisions in an uncertain and unpredictable work context stemming from (a) the variable and changing needs of clients; (b) expectations that teachers pursue multiple, and often conflicting, goals in relation to clients; and (c) the need to work with individual clients in a highly interactive group setting (Doyle, 1986; Lampert, 1985). Integration of separate responsibilities occurs in the context of ongoing modifications; teachers in one study noted that they repeatedly "shift gears" and change plans during the course of instruction based on their evaluation of classroom events (Shedd & Malanowski, 1985). Thus, teachers are individually responsible for making their own immediate work decisions, and they deal with large amounts of information to be gathered, analyzed, and evaluated.

Teachers, as line professionals, are the only individuals who have direct and ongoing contact with the school system's primary clients (the students). As just stated, they are the primary reservoir of organizational knowledge, the ones most knowledgeable about clients' instructional, counseling, and classroom managerial problems and needs. In this context, administrators need the knowledge teachers have to make effective managerial decisions (Bridges, 1967). The fact that, to date, these professionals have not been sufficiently integrated into the formal decision-making process of schools (Duke, Showers, & Imbers, 1981; Glasman & Hajnik, in press) provides an important rationale for increasing teacher participation; formal mechanisms for teacher participation have not facilitated greater integration in decision making (Corcoran, 1987).

Conley et al. (1988) contend that the literature that does address the teacher's role in school management tends to restrict its discussion to the teacher's role in basic policy decisions to the exclusion of other management functions. In this context, four components of school management are proposed as possible focuses for increasing teacher participation:

- Direction: the specification of collective or individual responsibilities in terms of purpose, activity, or both (e.g., assigning a teacher a particular subject).
- Organization: the structuring of relationships between and among individuals and groups (e.g., setting schedules for teachers and students).
- Support: the provision of human, material, and other resources needed to execute responsibilities (e.g., providing a teacher with a mentor).
- Monitoring: the ongoing collection and evaluation of information related to performance (e.g., evaluating a teacher's classroom performance). (p. 267)

Although setting basic policy direction is arguably one element in directing the organization, it is equally important to recognize that policy directives must become integrated with other management functions. For example, once a course of policy action is set, systems must exist for collecting information and securing the resources necessary to execute plans.

Significantly, teachers are already responsible for these management functions—setting goals, planning activities, providing support, and monitoring progress—albeit at the classroom level (Doyle, 1986). Thus, although Mohrman et al. (1978) imply that teachers' operational decisions are not managerial in nature, in some respects they are. Teachers, as line professionals, are responsible for inferring a great deal of their own responsibilities in the context of multiple school goals and unpredictable and changing student needs. Hanson (1979) notes that teachers are, in Lipsky's (1980) terms, "street-level bureaucrats" whose discretion results in "their actually making policy for their organizations" (p. 101). Teachers "decide which of the organization's policies to carry out and how they will do so" (Hanson, 1979, p. 102). Thus, those at higher administrative levels rely on street-level bureaucrats (teachers) to determine which strategic board and administrative policies will actually be implemented. (See also Cuban's [1988] discussion of the political image of teaching where teachers stand between policy-making and what occurs in classrooms. "By their decisions and actions, teachers determine [whether] policy is implemented . . . transformed . . . or ignored" [p. 33].)

In this context, research describing a weak integration of teachers' and administrators' decision making appears particularly debilitating. Glasman and Hajnik (in press), for example, conducted 2-day visits with 13 principals for the purpose of observing principal-teacher interactions. They found that, on average, principals were in contact with teachers for less than one fourth of the total work day (22%). In addition, a majority of contacts centered on decision issues primarily affecting individual teachers (e.g., an isolated student problem) rather than matters affecting teachers as a whole. Of the 9% of total interactions dealing with schoolwide issues, curriculum planning accounted for about one third (34%). In descending order of frequency, student affairs (25%), personnel planning (19%), personnel administration (17%), and materials and supplies (13%) accounted for the remaining discussions. However, interactions concerning personnel planning and administration tended to occur in formal staff meetings dominated by the principal. The research also found that a majority of interactions (64%) occurred with a select group of teachers labeled "repeaters" (e.g., specialists). Thus, principals appeared to involve teachers only intermittently in schoolwide issues (see also Duke et al., 1981).

Studies of principals' general conceptions of leadership complement field studies documenting principals' unwillingness to have teachers participate in schoolwide decision making. Drawing on socialization perspectives (Lortie, 1975), Conley and Rhoades (1990) interviewed prospective principals concerning their conceptions of leadership and teachers. They found that prospective principals viewed the principal, rather than the teachers, as the linchpin of change in schools. In addition, principals (rather than teachers) were thought to possess a moral imperative to act in the best interests of the school and children, underlying their claim to decision-making authority in the school (see also Rhoades & Slaughter, in press). More research is needed to connect teacher participation literature with studies on how principals form their conceptions of leadership, teachers, and power.

Research generating additional conclusions about the importance of how principals and teachers conceive of power in schools has examined the bureaucratic-professional interface. The notion dovetails nicely with some of the research cited in the previous section, addressing different domains of organizational decision making from a political-organizational perspective. Using a field-based approach and drawing from research in other professional settings (e.g., hospitals; Strauss, Schatzman, Ehrlich, Bucher, & Sabshin, 1963), Hanson (1979) maintains that a "contested zone" of decision making in schools intercedes between decisions belonging primarily to administrators and teachers. Five decision areas are proposed: (a) allocation decisions, including teacher scheduling and teacher assignments; (b) security decisions, including attendance policies and student rights; (c) boundary decisions, including parental problems and the parent-teacher interface; (d) evaluation decisions, including teacher promotion and evaluation; and (e) instructional decisions, including school curricular policies.

Appendix A provides illustrations of decisions within the contested zone and decisions falling largely within the classroom and school realm. A distinction may be drawn between allocation decisions, which appear strategic in nature, and the other four, which appear operational. In addition, allocation and boundary decisions appear to affect primarily individuals (e.g., teacher scheduling and the parent-teacher interface), whereas security, evaluation, and instructional decisions appear to have more of an organizationwide impact (e.g., student rights, teacher promotion, and school curricular policies). Using this model as a conceptual framework, Hanson's (1979) case study of one district suggests that administrators and teachers frequently disagree about the degree of influence each party should exercise on each of the "contested" decisions. In addition, Isherwood and Taylor's (1978) survey study of the implementation of teacher councils in Quebec found that teachers advocated—and principals opposed—council involvement in teacher evaluation decisions.

Although more research is needed regarding contested decisions, the model tentatively identifies decisions that address the interface between school and classroom. Whereas the bureaucratic and professional models (discussed earlier) focus either on the needs of administrators or teachers, respectively, a political model encompasses both sets of actor interests. Contested decisions may require greater coordination between teachers and administrators than those falling clearly within either the school or classroom domain. With regard to current reform mandates, Hanson's (1979) study reveals a double-edged sword: Increasing teacher participation in the intermediate, contested zone may engender conflict between teachers and administrators, but it may also allow reform efforts to place a primary emphasis on decisions that border each party's traditional decision-making realm (i.e., those areas where each party has a significant stake).

Reconceptualizing Teacher Participation: Vertical and Horizontal Coordination in Decision Making

Thus far, discussion has focused on expanding the vertical participation of teachers (i.e., teacher participation in decisions made at higher organizational levels). However, participation may also be lateral in nature (i.e., teachers may participate with peers in decisions made at the same organizational level). Indeed, an important rationale for increasing lateral participation in schools stems from the cellular, insular structure of schooling. The human relations perspective that has dominated research on teacher participation tends to evaluate participation benefits in terms of those gained by individual teachers (e.g., individual job satisfaction). With some exceptions (e.g., Duke et al., 1980; Little, 1982), teacher collegiality is infrequently viewed as a primary benefit of participation. However, given the infrequent opportunities teachers have to engage in substantive dialogue and information exchanges (Lortie, 1975), collegiality may be one of the more important outcomes. The solitary nature of instruction, the physical layout of school facilities, and restrictive time schedules usually preclude much peer interaction (Lortie, 1975). Hence, research suggests that the need for greater collegial interaction and information exchange constitutes another benefit of enhanced teacher participation. In this sense, participation includes not only vertical influence (from subordinate to superordinate) but lateral (peer) influence as well. (For an opposing definition, see Corcoran [1987], who maintains that participation "excludes those activities described as collegial or cooperative" [p. 7].)

Recognizing the importance of coordination among peers reframes the issue of participation from merely assessing downward methods of supervision and control to addressing multidirectional organizational coordination (Hinckley, 1985; Smith & Peterson, 1988). With regard to vertical coordination, Firestone (1977) distinguishes upward influence from downward social control aspects of participation. Observers thus appear to be abandoning the notion that organizational "effectiveness" hinges on the willingness of subordinates to accept the formal directives of managers in favor of an approach that also emphasizes the capacity of subordinates, individually and collectively, to assume responsibility for coordinating their own work activities (Smith & Peterson, 1988). However, because the participation literature is marked by a vertical emphasis, the research should be expanded to connect it to lateral (peer) influence patterns as well.

Comment

Because teachers make their decisions on the "line," teacher participation literature tends to restrict its discussion to the teacher's role in what Mohrman et al. (1978) term the "technical" domain (e.g., decisions about textbooks, instructional policy) rather than the "managerial" domain (e.g., decisions about hiring, determining work assignments). This sharp division in the locus of influence (i.e., teachers make operational decisions inside classrooms and administrators make strategic decisions outside classrooms) is reflected in studies of principals as well as sociological studies of teaching. That such a division reflects typical practice in schools (Glasman & Hajnik, in press) means that the perspectives of line professionals are characteristically not well integrated into managerial decision making, a troublesome fact for a professional organization. In this context, recent participation literature (derived from a political perspective) suggests rethinking the conventional wisdom that the components of school management belong necessarily and exclusively to administrators. It also requires recasting the rationales and benefits of participation from benefiting only teachers to benefiting managers as well.

The human relations perspective that has dominated research on participation infrequently considers the benefits that participation may offer managers. It instead focuses (as suggested at the beginning of this chapter) on indirect organizational benefits accrued by teachers that offer a weak rationale for participation to managers. The acceptance of management-initiated change by teachers also provides a less than satisfactory rationale, as it may be perceived by administrators and teachers as an irrelevant exercise. Recently, scholars (Shedd, 1987) suggested a different aim for teacher participation: the coordination of teachers' and administrators' decisions in school management. In this political perspective, the benefits of participation increasingly would lie in the ability of teachers and administrators to influence decisions previously left to the other.

FORMS OF PARTICIPATION

Thus far, this review has not addressed the forms that participation has taken (or may take) in schools. Previous researchers (e.g., Duke et al., 1981) have suggested that forms of participation in schools have certain benefits, but these benefits have not been framed in terms of coordination. Similarly, participation problems or costs have not been addressed in terms of obstacles that preclude such integration. Framing the issue of participation as chiefly a problem of organizational coordination provides a conceptual tool for examining research on forms of participation.

Traditional Forms of Participation

It is important to note that researchers examining educational systems from a variety of perspectives have historically called, implicitly or explicitly, for more collegial, organic, and participative forms of school management. For example, writing from a democratic theory viewpoint, Gutman (1988) suggests that Dewey's (1956) prominent Chicago lab school ascribed clearly to such an approach: "Dewey treated teachers . . . as colleagues; they met with him weekly to discuss curriculum and other educational matters" (p. 195). With others (Boyer, 1983; Lightfoot, 1983),

Gutman suggests that recent attempts to organize large schools into several smaller "schools-within-a-school" illustrate this democratic, participatory practice: "Schools-within-a-school can prevent educational bureaucracies from destroying professional autonomy while creating the potential for more local [teacher and citizen] participation" (p. 193).

Although observers (Boyer, 1983; Lightfoot, 1983) tend to deal with teacher participation as a subsidiary effect (or by-product) of school change, others describe and analyze participation efforts as a primary focus. Research has, for example, addressed itself to traditional (Bridges, 1967; Corcoran, 1987; Duke et al., 1981; Johnson, 1988) and current (Kerchner & Koppich, in press; Malen & Ogawa, 1988) forms of participation. Appendix B provides examples of both forms of participation. A critical issue is the degree to which these forms provide teachers with an advisory or consultative role (influence) or with final decision-making power (authority). Research is not clear on this question; however, it appears that many traditional forms appear to be advisory or consultative in nature, thereby representing mechanisms for increasing teachers' influence on decisions. New forms may allocate authority to teachers; for example, shared governance and career ladder systems may provide teachers with authority over program or personnel decisions previously made by administrators. In practice, however, only minimal teacher or parent influence on decisions may result. In a school governance experiment in Utah that attempted to allocate authority to a team of teachers, principals, and parents, principals continued to retain the majority of authority in (and influence on) school decisions.

The importance of distinguishing between traditional and new forms lies in emphasizing that forms for participation have always existed in schools providing mechanisms for teacher influence on administrators' decisions. For example, departmental structures, teacher teams, and grade-level meetings are typical in secondary, middle, and elementary schools, respectively; teacher committees and school councils are common across school levels.[7] Thus, rather than simply assuming that established forms of participation are not working, the question becomes, What are the specific advantages and disadvantages of these forms? That is, to what degree have more conventional participation forms offered teachers opportunities for involvement in school decisions? Research on traditional forms provides, in some cases, an explanation of barriers that limit teachers' exercise of influence on school decisions.

Corcoran's (1987) case studies of a midwestern and West Coast high school suggest that department chairs may give scant attention to teacher involvement, provide little time for quality interaction, and limit the options that teachers may consider in group decision making. "Dominance by the chair and quick acceptance of his/her views to gain favor is . . .

likely to be a problem'' (p. 32) (see also Wood, 1984). In addition, Corcoran (1987) suggests that although teacher committees do produce ''policy and program changes'' they are often dominated in meeting agendas, scheduling, and conduct by principals and thus afford teachers little influence (p. 33). ''Face-saving'' behavior (Malen & Ogawa, 1988) also diminishes teachers' involvement; teachers are ''reluctant to speak up for fear of unfavorable reactions from colleagues'' (Corcoran, 1987, p. 14). In addition, time constraints frequently hamper the scheduling of committee and council meetings and diminish involvement.

Johnson's (1988) field study of 25 teachers nominated as exemplary by their principals affirms some of the weaknesses of traditional participation approaches. Teachers noted that they lacked opportunities for input generally—and in committees and faculty meetings particularly. Reports and recommendations produced in such forums are infrequently entertained seriously or (even less often) approved at higher organizational levels. A limited scope of discussion and administrator domination of the agenda characterize most faculty meetings; additionally, faculty senates and principals' cabinets perform an explicitly—if not intentionally—advisory role. Johnson (1988) suggests that time constraints, the insular structure of schooling, and the lack of administrative expectations for teacher involvement additionally limit (or preclude) collegial and teacher-administrator interactions.

Duke et al. (1980, 1981) examined teachers' attitudinal reactions to several traditional forms of ''shared decision making'' implemented in five schools. These forms included school-site councils, advisory boards, a decision-making board, and a constitutionally based shared governance system (Duke et al., 1981). The researchers posited a number of teacher benefits (e.g., self-efficacy) and costs of participation (e.g., loss of autonomy). Survey and interview data suggested that teachers perceived a number of benefits, including higher quality joint decisions, a sense of workplace democracy, teacher compliance with decisions, closer relationships among teachers, and opportunities for teacher career progression. The data also revealed several costs, including lack of time, loss of autonomy, teacher skepticism, and jeopardizing collective bargaining agreements (Duke et al., 1980). An implication of these data is consistent with Alutto and Belasco (1972): Teachers may differ markedly in their attitudes toward participation. However, Duke et al. (1981) maintain that, in general, teachers believe that the benefits outweigh the costs.

Recently, researchers have contemplated the aforementioned costs of participation in broader discussions of school management. Observers suggest that the fundamental structure of schools is time prohibitive (Lieberman, Saxl, & Miles, 1988); teaching loads, inflexible schedules, and reporting requirements virtually guarantee that every hour (or minute) of a teacher's day is prearranged (Goodlad, 1984). Time problems are exacerbated by the insular structure of schools and "egalitarian norms" that prohibit information seeking (and giving). Teachers thus spend excessive amounts of time acquiring information (e.g., about students and teaching practices) that their colleagues in other classrooms could have easily provided (Conley et al., 1988). Participation, in facilitating exchange of information with supervisors and colleagues, may thus alleviate rather than amplify teachers' time pressures.

Concerning teacher cynicism, observers maintain that teacher suspicion of administrators' motives in initiating participation may be well founded (Shedd, 1987). Teachers notice that the advice of committees supposedly designed to gain teacher input often goes unheeded (Johnson, 1988). In other cases, teachers suspect that participation is a method to induce them to contribute additional (unpaid) labor (Bacharach & Conley, 1989), "share the blame for unpopular or risky actions" (Corcoran, 1987, p. 12), or carry out "decisions which someone higher in the authority structure has already made" (Wood, 1984, p. 58). Recent research thus characterizes teacher cynicism as a contextual or moderating factor affecting the success of participation efforts (Corcoran, 1987).

Finally, Duke et al. (1980) express the concern that school-based participation mechanisms may be in conflict with district collective bargaining agreements. Recent observers suggest that, on the contrary, the two structures may complement each other, one as a vehicle for teacher participation in broad strategic issues (e.g., teacher salaries and class size) and the other a mechanism for gaining input into daily school management (Conley & Bacharach, 1990). Indeed, although contractual negotiations regarding such issues as working hours have been viewed as potential obstacles to teacher participation, recent research suggests that districts are accommodating participation initiatives through flexible arrangements developed by collective bargaining. For example, McDonnell and Pascal (1988) describe the establishment of collectively bargained "shared decision making" school teams in one Florida district; teacher teams addressed such issues as the number and length of class periods, curricular changes, and peer assistance. Administrator-union collaboration and the incorporation of plans into collective bargaining agreements assisted the implementation of these teams. Local and national union leaders, who have historically been uneasy about administrator-led participation efforts,[8] now appear eager to take the lead in such efforts when opportunities for teacher involvement appear genuine (Futrell, 1988; Shanker, 1986).

Thus, costs of traditional participation efforts often implicitly address basic difficulties in coordinating individual efforts (e.g., among administrators, teachers, and students) in schools generally. Restrictive time schedules, teacher suspicion, and insular school structures, for example, present barriers to such integration. Benefits of participation frequently address successful coordination and information exchange (e.g., closer relationships among teachers and higher quality management decisions respecting the individual and collective judgments of teachers). Observers suggest that the success of new forms of participation may hinge on the degree to which the forms are able to extend the strengths and amend the weaknesses of previous approaches.

New Forms of Participation

Recent research has addressed itself to examining critically whether and how new forms of participation in schools provide opportunities for increased teacher involvement. A promising vehicle for increasing teacher participation may be school-based management, a form of shared governance and one of the most active areas of policy experimentation. Although new models of participation may emerge in these efforts, research on school site management is highly descriptive and tentative (see David, 1990). Malen and Ogawa (1988) and Kerchner and Koppich (in press) examined two types of shared governance arrangements: school councils and educational policy trust agreements, respectively. Malen and Ogawa's (1988) study investigated eight schools employing school councils in a district in Salt Lake City, Utah. The research examined whether school site-based governance structures actually enabled teachers—and parents—to influence school and district issues. At the onset of the study, the researchers viewed the district's "shared governance" model as having significant advantages over previous approaches. Under the new model, councils purportedly had the authority to make decisions and were not simply advisory bodies. Furthermore, power was to be equally distributed to principals, teachers, and parents for decision making (i.e., no single member, including the principal, could veto council decisions). Contrary to expectations, however, analysis of in-depth interviews, observations, council agendas, minutes, and surveys failed to confirm these changes in school and district decision making. For example, Malen and Ogawa (1988) found council agendas and meetings to be restricted in scope and limited to such routine organizational matters as parent conference schedules and facility safety improvements (notably, Hanson, 1979, suggests that parent conference schedules are part of the "contested zone" of decision making). Discussions concerning significant (strategic) issues related to budgets, programs, and personnel (e.g., staff hiring) were rare or nonexistent. Thus, the councils upheld a conventional pattern of school influence where "principals control building policies and procedures, teachers control the instructional component, and parents provide support" (p. 258). Principal control over stages of group decision making apparently perpetuated this pattern (e.g., principals determined the agenda, set the meeting times, and dominated council discussions). Both teachers and parents performed an explicitly advisory role, and parents had less input than teachers. More field-based studies of this type that capture in detail the dynamics of school decision making (e.g., issues of the domain, extent, and stage of decision making) are needed.

Kerchner and Koppich (in press) describe the implementation of educational policy trust agreements designed to expand teacher participation in decision making beyond making formal policies to a broader array of management decisions (e.g., peer assistance and supervision). Trust agreements are negotiated compacts that specify a problem and allocate resources for addressing it. Although agreements are formulated at the district level, they are also intended to expand teacher influence at the school site. Case studies of three districts highlight the political and organizational factors that emerge from teacher involvement in new decision areas. For example, one district's choice of staff development as the issue to be worked on generated tension between teachers and administration over the extent of teacher involvement in the teacher evaluation system and dismissal policies. Principals were especially concerned that trust agreements would erode their authority to make teacher evaluation decisions.

Enhanced by political and organizational perspectives, field studies ground their analysis in local contexts and the perceptions of school actors. In addition, they complement recent examinations of new participation forms in which participation may be an inadvertent effect. Although it may not have been an initial or primary goal of such plans, the current middle-school movement, career ladders, and peer assistance may potentially increase teacher involvement as well as the coordination of decisions between teachers and administrators and among teachers. Although it is too early to tell whether these structures involve providing teachers with more influence over decisions or delegating decision-making power to them, like the shared governance models discussed above, research is tentatively uncovering strengths as well as potential shortcomings of these various forms.

Observers (e.g., Clark & Clark, 1987) suggest that interdisciplinary teacher teaming in the current middle-school movement enhances closer coordination of teachers' efforts through scheduling and subject-matter integration. Teachers in the team are often assigned the same planning period and assume responsibility for grouping students (Clark & Clark, 1987; Maeroff, 1990). Subject-matter specialists are often additionally responsible for integrating content and instruction (Clark & Clark, 1987). Thus, such teams may develop closer working relationships among teachers, as well as (collective) teacher influence on student scheduling and discipline policies; indeed, in some teams teachers appear to have the final decision-making power to schedule students. More research is needed to clarify the advantages these new structures offer over more traditional teacher teams. Although current observers are optimistic (Maeroff, 1990), given the recency of middle-school approaches and the transitory history of teacher teams in middle schools (Corcoran, 1987), it is possible that innovation may decline over time (Binko & Lawlor, 1986). In addition, experimentation tends to be viewed as appropriate for the sixth, seventh, and eighth grades rather than as an approach that may be applicable to school management generally.

Career ladders and mentor or master teacher plans constitute another recent innovation that at least partially increases the prospect of teacher participation in decision making (Devaney, 1987; Griffin, 1985; Holmes Group, 1986). Specifically, observers (Devaney, 1987) suggest that master or mentor teachers would serve a representation function, injecting teachers' views into school decision making. It appears that these mentors would be afforded greater influence than other teachers in making school decisions but that they would still operate within the formal authority structures (e.g., with principals having final decision-making power). In the context of lateral coordination (discussed earlier), peer assistance roles assumed by mentor or master teachers may additionally increase collegial interaction and information exchange (Griffin, 1985).

Career ladders are among the most popular of recent reform efforts; 25 states have implemented some form of a career ladder or teacher incentive plan (Career Ladder Clearinghouse, 1987). Career ladders are difficult to separate from mentor teacher plans because teachers at the top levels of the system often have mentoring responsibilities; these teachers are afforded more decision-making power than other teachers and perhaps take responsibility for making or influencing evaluation decisions. However, case studies (Malen & Hart, 1987; Schlechty, 1989) suggest that significant components of state mandates may not be implemented. Malen and Hart's (1987) study of the Utah career ladder suggests that the original intent of the program was compromised at each level of implementation (i.e., state, district, and school site).[9] Drawing from literature documenting the "vanishing effects" of job redesign experiments (Hackman & Oldham, 1980), Malen and Hart show that the state legislature reduced the original $40 million proposed funding level to $15 million in 1984, with only a $5 million increase in 1986. In addition, attempts to require 25% of career ladder funding for teacher salary redistribution were subsequently cut to 10%. Pressures on local districts and school sites to implement career ladder plans brought additional compromises within 6 months. For instance, districts and schools funded previously planned short-term activities rather than new long-term career assignments. Malen and Hart suggested that state mandates may be successful if provided sufficient state monies to fund egalitarian distribution of benefits, a reasonable schedule to ensure sound strategic planning, and adequate monetary and information resources to support comprehensive district career ladder committee work. Unfortunately, because of current state funding priorities, brief legislative timetables, and the need to accommodate diverse state political interests, the aforementioned resource requirements are rarely met.[10] Finally, Malen and Hart found that teachers' reactions to newly expanded roles were mixed. Some teachers reported greater collaboration with peers and supervisors, but others perceived that status differences engendered resentment and isolation.

These patterns are consistent with related research. Because participation includes lateral as well as vertical influence (discussed earlier), it is important to note the barriers to closer working relationships among peers. Status differentials may violate long-standing teacher egalitarian norms and confer a superior status on the advice giver (Glidewell, Tucker, Todt, & Cox, 1983). A negative evaluation of the competence of the teacher requesting assistance may additionally deter interaction (Smylie, 1989). Furthermore, teacher inequities may generate excessively dominant or deferent behavior from members of different status (Smylie, 1989). Finally, scarce local and state monies may produce stringent quotas for top positions (Malen & Hart, 1987), augmenting the aforementioned difficulties and causing additional teacher competition, suspicion, and hostility (Schlechty, 1989). Perhaps most debilitating is the possible withholding of teacher support when schools actually need closer, more facilitative relationships among teachers (Glidewell et al., 1983).

With regard to representation, promoted teachers may lose credibility with the majority of teachers in the school if a promotion removes them from the classroom and places them in quasi-administrative roles (Smylie & Denny, 1990). Master teachers report that a majority of their time is spent working with administrators and not with fellow teachers (Smylie & Denny, 1990). In addition, quotas limiting the number of teachers who may apply and be promoted to representational roles may limit teachers' voices in decision making. Finally, teacher representation appears to be conditioned by whether the system specifies schoolwide responsibilities as a prerequisite or an obligation of teachers occupying the top levels of the system. Assigning schoolwide responsibilities only to teachers who secure a promotion will probably restrict such participation to a small minority; specifying such responsibilities as something that must be demonstrated prior to receiving a promotion (e.g., see Arizona Education Association, 1986) will probably involve a larger number.

Finally, experiments with peer assistance are another vehicle for increasing the likelihood that teacher participation in decision making will facilitate lateral coordination of teachers' efforts. Peer assistance is, by implication, one element of mentor teacher plans; it is typically a component of career ladder and master teacher plans as well. Of course, peer assistance may also be conducted among participants of equal status (Smylie, 1989). Observers (e.g., Showers, 1985) suggest that peer assistance systems primarily designed to enhance lateral coordination may have vertical effects as well. For example, peer assistance originally intended to inculcate a common language regarding teaching practices may facilitate development of schoolwide curricular and disciplinary policies (Showers, 1985).

Smylie (1989) suggests that assistance conducted among teachers of the same status offers advantages over career ladder and master teacher plans. Because such systems (e.g., "peer coaching" and "peer support groups") do not involve differences in rank, they promote "greater equality in participant status and reciprocity in interaction" (Smylie, 1989, p. 3). Although they operate under formal rules and expectations, the absence of status distinctions encourages a more informal tone of interaction (Smylie, 1989). However, they may share with career ladders the violation of teacher autonomy and privacy norms (Lortie, 1975); teachers may believe that receiving help threatens autonomy by creating "indebtedness" or exhibits inadequacies through public exposure of problems (Smylie, 1989, p. 21).

In sum, traditional and new forms may be promising vehicles. The research is not clear about the type of power being afforded teachers in many of the new forms, whether authority or influence; however, some tentative speculations are possible. Most new forms of participation appear to be extending decision-making influence rather than authority to teachers. In addition, whereas some forms are oriented toward vertical coordination between teachers and administrators (e.g., school governance teams), others are directed at lateral coordination (e.g., peer assistance), and some plans have elements of both (e.g., career ladders).

Finally, it should be noted that although the above literature focuses on teacher participation in school buildings, mechanisms also exist for increasing teacher participation at other educational levels. One illustration is the recently established National Board for Professional Teaching Standards, which has a majority of teacher members. In addition, McDonnell and Pascal's (1988) study of teacher unions found that these unions shape decision making and policy-making in local districts, state legislatures, and national reform movements. Malen and Hart (1987) also reported influence by teachers and their representatives at higher levels of education (district and state) in their analysis of career ladders in Utah. The teacher participation literature should be expanded to connect it to the exercise of influence at other levels of public education.

Comment

In some cases, new forms of participation appear to offer advantages over traditional systems; in other cases, the advantages they offer are unclear. The benefits of participation (e.g., collegiality) may be framed in terms of successful organizational coordination generally; the costs (e.g., time) have been cited in other literatures as general problems in organizational coordination (for a discussion of time and participation, see Duke et al., 1981, and Firestone & Herriott, 1981; for time and career ladders, see Richardson-Koehler & Fenstermacher, 1987). The next section provides a framework for addressing the questions of whether and how new participation mechanisms may be increasing teachers' decision-making power vis-à-vis administrators.

DELIMITING PARTICIPATION: THE ISSUE OF TEACHER POWER IN SCHOOL DECISION MAKING

New forms of participation, such as school governance structures (Malen & Ogawa, 1988), appear to be generating uneasiness among teachers and administrators as both parties reassess their respective roles (Lieberman, 1988). Apprehension may be partially due to a failure to distinguish between two critical dimensions of power: authority and influence (introduced earlier). Unfortunately, research on forms of participation often fails to adopt an explicitly political, analytical framework; thus, with the exception of Malen and Ogawa (1988), it is difficult to ascertain the type(s) of power being tapped by these forms. Authority deals with final decision-making power, referring to the ability of an organizational member to say yes or no to a particular decision. Authority stems from the legal right to make decisions governing others; for example, principals have the authority to assign students and teachers to classes, and teachers have the (de facto) authority to implement instruction (Bacharach & Mitchell, 1987). Influence, by contrast, stems from the capacity to shape decisions through informal or nonauthoritative means, including personal characteristics (e.g., charisma), expertise, informal opportunity, and resources (Bacharach & Lawler, 1980). In theory, increases in either teachers' decision-making authority or influence may serve to expand teachers' participatory role. Indeed, the delegation of formal authority to teachers for making specific decisions has been examined as one way to increase teacher involvement (Bridges, 1967; Hoy & Sousa, 1984). However, teachers may also gain participation through increasing their influence on decisions without necessarily possessing final implementation authority. One consideration in implementing this latter option is that it could increase participation without fundamentally altering the formal authority structure of the school. For example, Malanowski, Kennedy, and Kachris

(1986) describe the implementation of teacher teams designed to expand teacher involvement in the selection of problems and design of solutions; administrators retained final decision-making control. The teams were thus intentionally formulated to increase teacher participation without altering the location of final authority or lessening managerial control (Malanowski et al., 1986). Few studies address the question of how to broaden the scope of teacher involvement without also appropriating managerial authority.

Research from a variety of perspectives implicitly suggests that influence, not authority, may be the underlying issue in current reform efforts. Observers (Lieberman, 1988; Mertons & Yarger, 1988) encourage teachers to assume greater responsibility for school leadership; in doing so, they frequently focus on increasing teacher influence capacities apart from their formal positions. Similarly, writers examining collegial systems in education (Smylie, 1989) suggest, often implicitly, that teachers may expand their lateral influence through expertise. With regard to administrators, the emphasis being placed on symbolic (Bolman & Deal, 1985) and instructional (Sergiovanni, 1989) aspects of leadership encourages principals to draw on influence sources (e.g., charisma and expertise) outside of the formal authority of their positions. Similarly, research (Hallinger & Murphy, 1985) suggesting that effective principals display a visible presence in classrooms encourages the expansion of influence, at least in part, through informal access to information.

Writers advocating an increase in teacher and administrator influence in school systems need not represent opposing viewpoints, however. In this context, two theoretical properties of influence may be considered (Bacharach & Lawler, 1980). First, influence is multidirectional: It may be initiated at any organizational level, flowing from lower (e.g., teacher) to higher (e.g., administrator) positions or vice versa (or laterally). Second, influence is non-zero sum in nature: Although only one organizational position may wield final decision-making power, conceivably all organizational members may exercise influence on decisions. Together, these properties suggest that decisions influenced by teachers do not necessarily cause a decrease in administrator influence on or authority in those same decisions.

Research has recently addressed itself to examining upward teacher influence in school (Ginsburg & Berry, 1988; Wilson, 1988). One strand of research examines teacher influence as a criterion variable in studies of school change. For example, Wilson (1988) found that organizational process variables (e.g., goal consensus and communication) predicted teacher consensus concerning perceived influence on school decisions (e.g., resource allocation) vis-à-vis their principals. Others focus more generally on the tactics teachers use to gain power in relation to principals

(Blase, 1989; Tewel, 1988). Still others (Ginsberg & Berry, 1988) look at teachers' use of informal influence to circumvent bureaucratic reform mandates. Although these studies suggest that influence patterns may be changing because of such reform mandates as school-based management, others disagree; notably, Malen and Ogawa (1988) found no evidence that influence patterns were altered following the implementation of a school-site management initiative. Consequently, the effect of reform measures on influence patterns is a point of debate in the literature and a focus of growing inquitry.

Indeed, the study of influence continues to be problematic and imprecise (Malen & Ogawa, 1988). Malen and Ogawa found that extensive interviews, follow-up probes, and survey items were unsuccessful in uncovering possible teacher and parent influence through informal contacts and conversations outside the participation (i.e., school council) arena (p. 258). In addition, studies of teacher influence seldom explicitly address—or analyze the trade-offs between—decision-making influence and authority. One study (Bacharach et al., 1986) posited that both absence of authority and deprivation of desired influence would be predictive of stress among elementary and secondary teachers. The study found that only lack of influence (not authority) predicted stress among elementary teachers; neither dimension of power predicted stress among secondary teachers. The differential results suggest that teachers may not expect to exercise final decision-making power. In addition, secondary teachers may be more sensitive to influence on a departmental, rather than school-wide, basis. Finally, teachers' expectations may depend on the nature of the teacher-client relationship. Elementary teachers may feel more strongly about their participatory role than secondary teachers because of their more all-encompassing responsibility for students and concomitant belief that they know pupils best.

Unless research addresses the distinction between authority and influence in decision making, it will offer minimal practical guidance in current participation debates about whether teachers should wield final decision-making power or whether their involvement should be limited to influence (and on what decisions). That is, studies that use these terms interchangeably will continue to be unclear about the dimension of power possessed by teachers. Only allocating final decision-making power to teachers would require a change in the formal authority structure of the school.

Researchers (Benson & Malone, 1987; Bridges, 1967) have examined alternative models for distributing decision-making authority and influence in schools. Bridges (1967) proposes three decision-making models: participant-determining, parliamentarian, and democratic-centralist. In participant-determining groups, members (e.g., teachers and administrators) have equal influence over the decision, with consensus required for final decisions. In parliamentarian groups, members exert equal influence but make final decisions according to majority vote. In the democratic-centralist group, the principal retains final decision-making authority. All three encompass teacher influence, and only the last clearly allocates authority to one party or the other. However, as Malen and Ogawa (1988) suggest, in any participatory group, members' actual influence may be constrained by a variety of contextual and mediating factors (e.g., principal control of the agenda and scheduling). In addition, with the exception of Malanowski et al. (1986), research has not tended to address itself to developing analytical models of groups in which teachers are the sole members. In the context of new interdisciplinary teams and peer groups, for example, this would appear to constitute an important area of investigation.

Research (Bridges, 1967; Duke et al., 1981) has also addressed itself to phases of the participation process. Duke et al. (1981) suggest five participation stages: (a) setting the agenda, (b) determining guidelines, (c) gathering information in relation to problems, (d) designing (solution) choices, and (e) expressing (solution) preferences. At each stage, implementors need to consider strategically whether teachers will exercise influence or authority in decision making. For example, Wood (1984) suggests that a primary source of teacher skepticism over participation is the failure to include teachers in the setting of an agenda. Also, Firestone (1977) suggests that a lack of teacher influence on final decisions may negate the effects of involvement in all previous stages. Indeed, in groups such as interdisciplinary teams, teachers may have the authority to set the agenda. In addition, teachers may or may not influence the determination of group guidelines, or they may have the authority to do so. Finally, administrators or teachers may possess final implementation authority. If the administrator exercises this authority, teachers may still wield influence on this decision. In other cases, as in teacher-run schools, teachers might have final implementation authority.

Debates concerning the design of authority and influence are likely to turn on the differences between the two ideal models (professional and bureaucratic) examined at the beginning of this chapter. The bureaucratic model metaphorically suggests that teachers should have little influence in school-level decision making or that participation can be used manipulatively to buy teacher acceptance of decisions that have already been made. The professional model metaphorically maintains that empowering teachers to make both classroom and school decisions is the sole key to educational improvement; hence, the administrator's role in school management is limited. Current participation debates should, therefore, strive to define a realistic middle ground based on management's recognition of teachers as professionals and teachers' recognition that they work in an organizational setting requiring coordination with supervisors and peers. In this context, schools are complex organizational settings, requiring both vertical and horizontal coordination and subject to important, constraining forms of external authority (e.g., school boards, departments of education, accreditation agencies). A critical remaining question then becomes how to design systems of participation that incorporate the organizational concerns embedded in professional and bureaucratic frameworks, that is, how to design participation systems that allow teachers to broaden their decision making beyond the scope of their immediate classrooms (the professional model) without necessarily threatening the legitimate authority structure of schools and school districts (the bureaucratic model).

CONCLUSION

A major challenge in school improvement efforts has been the involvement of teachers in the broad array of school decisions called for in recent reform reports. It was suggested early in this chapter that researchers examining this broader participatory role should acknowledge that multiple frameworks exist for analyzing schools and, moreover, should clearly state the organizational model they use. This chapter introduced some ideas regarding how bureaucratic, professional, human relations, and political models may be used to evaluate participation research and attempted to integrate research related to four major topics: (a) teacher expectations and organizational decision domains, (b) changing rationales for teacher participation, (c) forms of participation, and (d) issues of teacher power (authority and influence) in decision making.

The section on teacher expectations reviewed education literature grounded in two primary organizational concepts. Specifically, the first literature dealt with teachers' expectations for decision participation, that is, whether they judge their participation in absolute terms or weigh their perceptions against expectations. Teachers experience three decisional "states"—deprivation, saturation, and equilibrium. Over a 20-year period, interest in examining the states of saturation and equilibrium has waned, and interest in studying deprivation has increased. A second body of literature dealt with the dimensionality and content of decision domains. This literature underscores that schools are organizations marked by an array of decision-making responsibilities. It was suggested that although teachers desire the most participation in decisions clearly within the classroom, they feel the most deprived in managerial decisions. However, a drawback of the literature reviewed in this section is that it is not grounded in the daily internal workings of schools.

In an attempt to frame the issue of participation in terms of schools' daily realities, the next section reviewed literature that captures the organizational roles, structures, and working relationships that are unique in schools. For example, research emphasizes that teachers already are heavily involved in decision making but that decision making occurs in isolation from supervisors and peers. In this context, participation may help ensure greater (vertical and lateral) coordination of decisions between teachers and supervisors and among individual teachers. Another area of research investigates those decision-making areas over which teachers and administrators make claims in the school organization. Negotiation of a contested zone of decisions appears to be central in the political, internal machinations in schools. However, in general, a managerial perspective marks this literature. Participation continues to be thought of as a problem of downward supervision rather than a problem of multidirectional organizational coordination.

The third section attempted to frame different forms of participation in terms of coordination. It was argued that the literature on costs of participation (e.g., time and teacher cynicism) addresses general difficulties in coordinating individual efforts in schools. This literature highlights the wide array of (traditional and new) participation forms that show potential for increasing teacher involvement in school decision making. However, the literature is not clear regarding the advantages new approaches to participation offer over more traditional approaches. In addition, research is needed to clarify why some participation experiments are not increasing teacher participation in decision making as anticipated.

The closing section addressed the dimensions of power represented by participation in decision making: authority and influence. Although these dimensions originate from the general organizational behavior literature, they offer insights into the teacher participation literature. To give a simple illustration, a teacher team might call for teachers to have the authority to select an agenda, determine guidelines, and design solutions, with the administrator possessing final implementation power. Such an arrangement would preserve traditional managerial authority while giving teachers authority over several stages of the decision-making process. However, teachers may feel that they will not actually influence final implementation decisions or that in time their influence will erode.[11] In addition, administrators may feel that they should have authority over these stages of the decision-making process (determining an agenda, guidelines, or preferred solutions).

In closing, the literature suggests some directions for future research. First, researchers analyzing current participation forms should become specific about dimensions of decision-making power, domains of decisions, and actors' interests being served by different methods. Few studies include all three of these variables in their investigations, and very few address the distinction between authority and influence in decision making. Unless we become clear about these dimensions, research will continue to be vague as to which domain of power is being tapped by various forms of participation. In addition, the work that has been done by scholars such as Duke et al. (1980) and Bridges (1967) on different participation structures (parliamentarian, advisory, and decision-making groups; e.g., Bridges, 1967) and different phases of decision making (identifying problems, determining solutions; Duke et al., 1980) is rarely examined in research on specific forms of participation. Research should address itself to applying these conceptual frameworks to examining particular decision-making structures and altered roles for teachers and administrators in group decision making.

Second, although research has addressed itself to identifying decision domains, we know little about how teachers and administrators interpret, protect, and negotiate these decisions in daily school management. More field-based, exploratory research should assist in these efforts. Finally, the focus of this review has been on teacher participation in school-site decision making (individual or collective) in school buildings. However, teachers play significant participatory roles at other levels of our educational system, evidenced recently, for example, by teacher involvement in the National Board for Teaching Standards. Thus, an underresearched area is the nature of teacher participation at other levels of public education: in districts, state departments of education, national networks, and teacher unions. Because teachers shape district and state decision making and policy-making as well as state and national reform movements (National Educational Association, 1988), these roles should provide a fruitful avenue for further research. Meanwhile, in school buildings, we wait to evaluate the success of the many different forms of participation being tested nationwide.

NOTES

[1] The percentages of teachers reporting that they were "not very involved" in decision making were as follows: choosing textbooks, 21%; shaping the curriculum, 37%; setting standards for student behavior, 53%; deciding whether students are tracked into special classes, 55%; designing staff development and in-service programs, 57%; setting promotion and retention policies, 68%; deciding school budgets, 80%; evaluating teacher performance, 90%; selecting new teachers, 93%; and selecting new administrators, 93%.

[2] For example, Schneider reported only a small fraction of respondents in her study—less than 5%—to be either saturated or in equilibrium; others found no instances of decision saturation in their samples either in total (Mohrman, Cooke, & Mohrman, 1978) or on average (Bacharach, Bamberger, & Conley, 1990).

[3] The operationalization of decision deprivation has also been a point of debate in the literature (see Conway, 1976). Following Conway, recent research (e.g., Bacharach, Bamberger, & Conley, 1990; Mohrman, Cooke, & Mohrman, 1978;

Schneider, 1984) substitutes a Likert-type scale for the original (Alutto & Belasco, 1972) "yes-no" response format. Under this method, the researcher subtracts the desired participation from the actual participation score on each item; a negative number indicates deprivation, zero indicates equilibrium, and a positive number indicates saturation. These values are then summed to yield a single score.

[4] It should be noted that when actual participation was factor analyzed, a third factor—labeled negotiation—incorporated two items from the managerial domain (salaries and grievances).

[5] The four outcomes examined were job satisfaction, role ambiguity, role conflict, and goal commitment. Of eight correlation coefficients within the two operational domains, six and seven were significant for elementary and secondary teachers, respectively. With regard to the strategic domains, only three were significant for elementary teachers and two for secondary teachers.

[6] For both strategic and operational decisions, teachers report more decisional deprivation in the organizational domains (e.g., budget development [strategic] and student rights [operational]) than in the personal domains (e.g., school assignments [strategic] and books used [operational]) (Bacharach et al., 1990).

[7] For a historical perspective on teacher curriculum committees, see Cuban (1988). For example, Cuban notes that in the 1920s in Denver under the leadership of Superintendent Jesse Newlon about one fourth (376) of Denver teachers served on curriculum committees. Almost half of the secondary teachers and 10% of elementary teachers worked on these committees (see footnote 43 on page 257). However, subsequent experimentation seldom had "the intensity that Newlon and his successors brought to it" and thus did not become as powerful or pervasive a vehicle for participation as the originator intended (p. 23).

[8] For a historical examination lending considerable insight into union uneasiness regarding participation, see Urban (1982). For example, teacher councils were used by superintendents (such as McAndrew in Chicago) to circumvent union growth in the early part of this century.

[9] Malen and Hart (1987) suggest that the original intent provided for "staff differentiation and work redesign" (p. 13).

[10] Malen and Hart's (1987) larger point is that the need to accommodate different state political interest groups leads to a diffusion of monies across multiple components of the legislative bill.

[11] A counterpoint to this argument is that teacher authority over stages of the problem-solving process could legitimize teachers' upward influence on final decisions and may transform the traditional authority relationship (see Conley, 1989).

REFERENCES

Alutto, J. A., & Belasco, J. A. (1972). A typology for participation in organizational decision-making. *Administrative Science Quarterly, 9*(1), 27–41.

Alutto, J. A., & Vredenburgh, D. (1977). Characteristics of decisional participation by nurses. *Academy of Management Journal, 20,* 341–347.

Arizona Education Association/National Education Association Research. (1986). *Career development system.* Phoenix, AZ: Arizona Education Association.

Bacharach, S. B., Bamberger, P., & Conley, S. (1990). The dimensionality of decision participation in educational organizations: The value of a multi-domain evaluative approach. *Educational Administration Quarterly, 26*(2), 126–167.

Bacharach, S. B., Bauer, S., & Conley, S. (1986). Organizational analysis of stress: The case of elementary and secondary schools. *Work and Occupations, 13*(1), 7–32.

Bacharach, S. B., & Conley, S. C. (1986). Education reform: A managerial agenda. *Phi Delta Kappan, 67*(9), 641–645.

Bacharach, S. B., & Conley, S. (1989). Uncertainty and decision-making in teaching: Implications for managing line professionals. In T. J. Sergiovanni & J. H. Moore (Eds.), *Schooling for tomorrow: Directing reforms to issues that count* (pp. 311–329). Boston: Allyn and Bacon.

Bacharach, S. B., & Lawler, E. E. (1980). *Power and politics in organizations: The social psychology of conflict, coalitions and bargaining*. San Francisco: Jossey-Bass.

Bacharach, S. B., & Mitchell, S. (1987). The generation of practical theory: Schools as political organizations. In J. W. Lorsch (Ed.), *Handbook of organizational behavior*. Englewood Cliffs, NJ: Prentice-Hall.

Bailyn, L. (1985). Autonomy in the industrial R&D lab. *Human Resource Management, 24*(2), 129–146.

Barnard, C. (1938). *The functions of the executive*. Cambridge, MA: Harvard University Press.

Ball, S. J. (1978). *The micro-politics of school organization*. New York: Methuen.

Benson, N., & Malone, P. (1987). Teachers' beliefs about shared decision making and work alienation. *Education, 107,* 244–251.

Binko, J., & Lawlor, J. (1986). Middle schools: A review of current practices—How effective are they? *NASSP Bulletin, 70,* 81–87.

Bishop, L., & George, J. (1973). Organizational structure: A factor analysis of structural characteristics of public elementary and secondary schools. *Educational Administration Quarterly, 9*(3), 66–80.

Blase, J. J. (1989). The micropolitics of the school: The everyday political orientation of teachers toward open school principals. *Educational Administration Quarterly, 25*(4), 377–407.

Bolman, L., & Deal, T. (1985). *Modern approaches to understanding and managing organizations*. San Francisco: Jossey-Bass.

Boyer, E. L. (1983). *High school: A report on secondary education in America*. New York: Harper and Row.

Bridges, E. M. (1967). A model for shared decision making in the school principalship. *Educational Administration Quarterly, 20*(3), 11–40.

Career Ladder Clearinghouse. (1987). *More pay for teachers and administrators who do more: Incentive pay programs*. Atlanta, GA: Southern Regional Education Board.

Carnegie Commission on Teaching as a Profession. (1986). *A nation prepared: Teachers for the 21st century*. Hyattsville, MD: Carnegie Forum on Education and the Economy.

Carnegie Foundation for the Advancement of Teaching. (1988). *Teacher involvement in decisionmaking: A state-by-state profile*. Washington, DC: Author.

Clark, S. N., & Clark, D. C. (1987). Interdisciplinary teaming programs, organization, rationale and implementation. In National Association for Secondary School Principals, *Schools in the middle: A report on trends and practices* (pp. 1–6). Reston, VA: NASSP.

Conley, S. (1988). Reforming paper pushers avoiding free agents: The teacher as a constrained decision-maker. *Educational Administration Quarterly, 24*(4), 393–404.

Conley, S. (1989). Who's on first: School reform, teacher participation and the decision-making process. *Education and Urban Society, 21*(4), 366–379.

Conley, S., & Bacharach, S. (1990). From school site management to participatory school site management. *Phi Delta Kappan, 71*(7), 539–544.

Conley, S. C., & Rhoades, G. (1990, April). *Prospective principals and school leadership*. Paper presented at the annual meeting of the American Educational Research Association, Boston.

Conley, S. C., Schmidle, T., & Shedd, J. B. (1988). Teacher participation in the management of school systems. *Teachers College Record, 90*(2), 259–280.

Conway, J. (1976). Test of linearity between teachers' participation in decision-making and their perceptions of their schools as organizations. *Administrative Science Quarterly, 21*(1), 130–139.

Corcoran, T. B. (1987). *Teacher participation in public school decision-making: A discussion paper*. Paper prepared for the Work in America Institute.

Corwin, R. G. (1974). Models of educational organizations. In F. N. Kerlinger (Ed.), *Review of research in education* (Vol. 2, pp. 247–295). Washington, DC: American Educational Research Association.

Corwin, R. (1981). Patterns of organizational control and teacher militancy: Theoretical continuities in the idea of "loose coupling." In A. C. Kerckhoff (Ed.), *Research in the sociology of education and socialization* (Vol. 2, pp. 261–291). Greenwich, CT: JAI Press.

Cuban, L. (1988). *The managerial imperative and the practice of leadership in schools*. Albany: State University of New York Press.

David, J. W. (1989). *Restructuring in progress: Lessons from pioneering districts*. Washington, DC: National Governors' Association.

Devaney, K. (1987). *The lead teacher: Ways to begin*. Washington, DC: Task Force on Teaching as Profession, Carnegie Forum on Education and the Economy.

Dewey, J. (1956). The school and society. In *The child and the curriculum and the school and society*. Chicago: University of Chicago Press.

Doyle, W. (1986). Classroom organization and management. In M. C. Wittrock (Ed.), *Handbook of research on teaching* (pp. 392–431). New York: Macmillan.

Duke, D. L., Showers, B. K., & Imber, M. (1980). Teachers and shared decision making: The costs and benefits of involvement. *Educational Administration Quarterly, 16*(1), 93–106.

Duke, D. L., Showers, B. K., & Imber, M. (1981). Studying shared decision making in schools. In S. B. Bacharach (Ed.), *Organizational behavior in schools and school districts* (pp. 245–276). New York: Praeger.

Firestone, W. A. (1977). Participation and influence in the planning of educational change. *Journal of Applied Behavioral Science, 13*, 167–187.

Firestone, W. A., & Herriott, R. E. (1981). Images of organization and the promotion of educational change. In A. C. Kerckhoff (Ed.), *Research in the sociology of education and socialization* (Vol. 2, pp. 221–260). Greenwich, CT: JAI Press.

Futrell, M. H. (1988). Teachers in reform: The opportunity for schools. *Educational Administration Quarterly, 24*(4), 374–380.

Ginsberg, R., & Berry, B. (1988, April). *Influencing superiors' perceptions: The fudge factor in teacher and principal evaluation*. Paper presented at the annual meeting of the American Educational Research Association, New Orleans.

Glasman, N. S., & Hajnik, S. R. (in press). Participative decision making in schools: Do principals facilitate teacher participation? In S. C. Conley & B. Cooper (Eds.), *Exploring the teacher work environment: New perspectives*. Boston: Allyn & Bacon.

Glidewell, J. C., Tucker, S., Todt, M., & Cox, S. (1983). Professional support systems: The teaching profession. In A. Nadler, J. Fisher, & B. Depaulo (Eds.), *New directions in helping, 3* (pp. 189–212). New York: Academic Press.

Goodlad, J. I. (1984). *A place called school: Prospects for the future*. New York: McGraw-Hill.

Griffin, G. (1985). The school as a workplace and the master teacher concept. *The Elementary School Journal, 86,* 1–15.

Gutman, A. (1988). Democratic theory and the role of teachers in democratic education. In J. Hannaway & R. Crowson (Eds.), *Politics of Education Association yearbook* (pp. 183–199). New York: Falmer Press.

Hackman, J. P., & Oldham, G. R. (1980). *Work redesign*. Reading, MA: Addison Wesley.

Hage, J., & Aiken, M. (1967). Relationship of centralization to other structural properties. *Administrative Science Quarterly, 12*(1), 72–92.

Hallinger, P., & Murphy, J. (1985). Assessing the instructional management behavior of principals. *Elementary School Journal, 86,* 217–247.

Hanson, E. M. (1979). *Educational administration and organizational behavior*. Boston: Allyn & Bacon.

Hinckley, S. R. (1985). A closer look at participation. *Organizational Dynamics, 13*(3), 57–67.

Holmes Group. (1986). *Tomorrow's teachers: A report of the Holmes Group*. East Lansing, MI: Author.

Hoy, W. K., & Brown, B. L. (1988). Leadership behavior and the zone of acceptance of elementary teachers. *Journal of Educational Administration, 26*(1), 23–38.

Hoy, W., & Sousa, D. (1984). Delegation: The neglected aspect of participation in decision making. *The Alberta Journal of Educational Research, 30,* 320–331.

Hoyle, E. (1986). *The politics of school management*. London: Hodder & Stoughton.

Isherwood, G. B., & Taylor, R. M. (1978). Participatory decision making via school councils. *The High School Journal,* 255–270.

Johnson, S. M. (1988). Schoolwork and its reform. In J. Hannaway & R. Crowson (Eds.), *Politics of Education Association yearbook* (pp. 95–102). New York: Falmer Press.

Johnston, G. S., & Germinario, V. (1985). Relationship between teacher decisional status and loyalty to the principal. *Journal of Educational Administration, 23*(1), 91–105.

Kerchner, C. T., & Koppich, J. E. (in press). Redesigning teacher work roles through the educational policy trust agreement. In S. Conley & B. Cooper (Eds.), *The school as a work environment: Implications for reform*. Boston: Allyn & Bacon.

Kunz, D. W., & Hoy, W. K. (1976). Leadership style of principals and the professional zone of acceptance of teachers. *Educational Administration Quarterly, 12*(3), 49–64.

Lampert, M. (1985). How do teachers manage to teach: Perspectives on problems in practice. *Harvard Education Review, 55,* 178–194.

Lieberman, A. (1988). Teachers and principals: Turf, tension, and new tasks. *Phi Delta Kappan, 69*(9), 648–653.

Lieberman, A., Saxl, E. R., & Miles, M. B. (1988). Teacher leadership: Ideology and practice. In A. Lieberman (Ed.), *Building a professional culture in schools* (pp. 148–166). New York: Teachers College Press.

Lightfoot, S. L. (1983). *The good high school*. New York: Basic Books.

Lipsky, M. (1980). *Street-level bureaucracy: Dilemmas of the individual in public services*. New York: Russell Sage Foundation.

Little, J. W. (1982). Norms of collegiality and experimentation: Workplace conditions of school success. *American Educational Research Journal, 19*, 325–340.

Lortie, D. (1975). *School teacher: A sociological study*. Chicago: University of Chicago Press.

Lortie, D. (1977). The balance of control and autonomy in elementary school teaching. In D. A. Erickson (Ed.), *Educational organization and administration* (pp. 335–371). Berkeley, CA: McCutchan.

Maeroff, G. A. (1990). Getting to know a good middle school: Shoreham-Wading River. *Phi Delta Kappan, 71*(7), 505–511.

Malanowski, R. M., Kachris, P., & Kennedy, V. (1986, April). *Professional analysis teams in schools: A case study*. Paper presented at the annual meeting of the American Educational Research Association, San Francisco.

Malen, B., & Hart, A. W. (1987). Career ladder reform: A multi-level analysis of initial efforts. *Educational Evaluation and Policy Analysis, 9*(1), 9–23.

Malen, B., & Ogawa, R. T. (1988). Professional-patron influence on site-based governance councils: A confounding case study. *Educational Evaluation and Policy Analysis, 10*(4), 251–270.

McDonnell, L. M., & Pascal, A. (1988). *Teacher unions and educational reform*. Santa Monica, CA: The Rand Corporation.

Mertens, S., & Yarger, S. J. (1988). Teaching as a profession: Leadership, empowerment and involvement. *Journal of Teacher Education, 39*(1), 32–37.

Meyer, J., & Rowan, B. (1977). Institutionalized organizations: Formal structure as myth and ceremony. *American Journal of Sociology, 82*(7), 440–463.

Miskel, C. G., Fevurly, R., & Stewart, J. (1979). Organizational structures and processes, perceived school effectiveness, loyalty and job satisfaction. *Educational Administration Quarterly, 15*(3), 97–118.

Miskel, C., & Sandlin, T. (1981). Survey research in educational administration: A critical analysis. *Educational Administration Quarterly, 17*(4), 40–56.

Mohrman, A. M., Cooke, R. A., & Mohrman, S. A. (1978). Participation in decision making: A multidimensional perspective. *Educational Administration Quarterly, 14*(1), 13–29.

Morgan, G. (1986). *Images of organization*. Beverly Hills, CA: Sage.

National Association of Secondary School Principals/National Education Association. (1989). *Ventures in good schooling: A cooperative model for a successful secondary school*. Reston, VA: Author.

National Education Association. (1988). *Employee participation programs: Considerations for the school site*. Washington, DC: Author.

National Governor's Association. (1986). *Time for results: The governor's 1991 report on education*. Washington, DC: Author.

Parsons, T. (1960). *Structure and process in modern societies*. Glencoe, IL: Free Press.

Rhoades, G., & Slaughter, S. (in press). The public interest and professional labor: Research universities. In W. Tierney (Ed.), *Culture and ideology in higher education: Advancing a critical agenda*. New York: Praeger.

Richardson-Koehler, V., & Fenstermacher, G. (1987, May). *Graduate programs of teacher education and the professionalization of teaching*. Paper presented at the Rutgers Invitational Symposium on Education, New Brunswick, NJ.

Rosenholtz, S. J., Bassler, O., & Hoover-Dempsey, K. (1986). Organizational conditions of teacher learning. *Teaching and Teacher Education, 2*(2), 91–104.

Schlechty, P. C. (1989). Career ladders: A good idea going awry. In T. J. Sergiovanni & J. H. Moore (Eds.), *Schooling for tomorrow: Directing reforms to issues that count* (pp. 356–376). Boston: Allyn & Bacon.

Schneider, G. T. (1984). Teacher involvement in decision making: Zones of acceptance, decision conditions, and job satisfaction. *Journal of Research and Development in Education, 18*(1), 25–32.

Schneider, G. T. (1986). The myth of curvilinearity: An analysis of decision-making involvement and job satisfaction. *Planning and Changing, 17*(3), 146–158.

Sergiovanni, T. (1989). The leadership needed for quality schooling. In T. Sergiovanni & J. H. Moore (Eds.), *Schooling for tomorrow: Directing reforms to issues that count.* Boston: Allyn & Bacon.

Shanker, A. (1986). Teachers must take charge. *Educational Leadership, 44*(1), 12–13.

Shedd, J. B. (1987). *Involving teachers in school and district decision-making.* Manuscript prepared for the State Education Department, the University of the State of New York, Organizational Analysis and Practice.

Shedd, J. B. (1988). Collective bargaining, school reform and the management of school systems. *Educational Administration Quarterly, 24*(4), 405–415.

Shedd, J. B., & Malanowski, R. (1985). *From the front of the classroom: A study of the work of teachers.* Ithaca, NY: Organizational Analysis and Practice, Inc.

Showers, B. (1985). Teachers coaching teachers. *Educational Leadership, 42*(7), 43–48.

Smith, P. B., & Peterson, M. F. (1988). *Leadership, organizations and culture: An event management model.* London: Sage.

Smylie, M. A. (1989, March). *Teachers' collegial learning: Social and psychological dimensions of helping relationships.* Paper presented at the annual meeting of the American Educational Research Association, San Francisco.

Smylie, M. A., & Denny, J. W. (1990). Teacher leadership: Tensions and ambiguities in organizational perspective. *Educational Administration Quarterly, 26*(3), 235–259.

Strauss, A., Schatzman, L., Ehrlich, D., Bucher, R., & Sabshin, M. (1963). The hospital and its negotiated order. In E. Friedson (Ed.), *The hospital in modern society* (pp. 147–169). New York: The Free Press.

Tewel, K. J. (1988). The best child I ever had: Teacher influence on the decision making of three urban high school principals. *Urban Education, 23*(1), 24–41.

Urban, W. (1982). *Why teachers organized.* Detroit: Wayne State University Press.

Wilson, B. L. (1988, April). *The effect of organizational factors on variation of influence in schools.* Paper presented at the annual meeting of the American Educational Research Association, New Orleans.

Wood, C. J. (1984). Participatory decision making: Why doesn't it seem to work? *The Educational Forum, 49*(1), 55–64.

APPENDIX A
Examples of Classroom, Contested, and School Organizational Decisions

Classroom decisions

1. Books used

Note. Examples of classroom and school organizational decisions are adapted from Mohrman, Cooke, and Mohrman (1978) and Bacharach, Bamberger, and Conley (1990). Illustrations of decisions in the contested zone are adapted from Hanson (1979) and Bacharach et al. (1990).

2. Books available for use
3. How to teach
4. What to teach

Contested decisions

1. Teacher scheduling (allocation)
2. Student rights (security)
3. Parent-teacher interface (boundary)
4. Teacher promotion (evaluation)
5. School curricular policies (instructional)

School organization decisions

1. Budget development
2. Expenditure priorities
3. Facilities planning

APPENDIX B
Illustrations of Traditional and Current Forms of Participation

Traditional illustrations

1. Departmental structures
2. Teacher teams
3. Grade-level meetings
4. School councils and committees
5. Faculty senates
6. Advisory boards

Current illustrations

1. Shared governance models
2. Educational policy trust agreements
3. Middle-school movement (interdisciplinary teams)
4. Career ladders
5. Peer assistance

III.
GENDER AND RACE

Chapter 7

The Issue of Gender in Elementary and Secondary Education

MYRA SADKER AND DAVID SADKER
American University

SUSAN KLEIN
U.S. Department of Education

During colonial times in New England, schools were for male students only; yet 50 years after the American Revolution coeducation had become the norm in public elementary education. This change emerged gradually and with little public discussion. In rural communities most parents did not think it worth the prohibitive cost to educate boys and girls separately, and the one-room, coeducational school district was typical, viewed as a natural extension of male and female participation in the family and church (Hansot & Tyack, 1988).

In contrast to the rural one-room school, the high schools of the nation's urban areas were larger, more bureaucratic, and structurally further removed from the model of the family. In these schools, coeducation generated more controversy; parents and educators worried not only about the sexual involvement from such close contact during adolescence, but also about the need to prepare boys and girls for their different roles in the largely segregated world of work. In response to such concerns, the curriculum was consciously designed to meet the "different needs" of female and male students. For example, girls were required to take courses in homemaking to prepare them for their designated roles as wives

Myra Sadker and David Sadker thank Elise Lindemuth and Jackie Sadker for their research assistance. Susan Klein, author of the administration section, thanks the following colleagues for supplying information: Carol Dwyer, Norman Brandt, Patrick Forsyth, Dolores Grayson, Paul Hersey, Gwendolen Ingraham, Claradine Johnson, Effie Jones, Jeannie Lathroum, Martha McCarthy, Barbara Pavan, Myra Sadker, Mary Scherr, Patricia Schmuck, Charol Shakeshaft, Lynn Spencer, and Judy Stark.

Although Susan Klein is employed by the U.S. Department of Education, she contributed to this article in her private capacity; her views are her own, and no official support by the U.S. Department of Education is intended or should be inferred.

and mothers, whereas boys were required to take vocational training to ready them for work in the salaried labor force.

Throughout the 20th century gender distinctions were more blurred in school than in the workplace. Nonetheless, as recently as the 1960s, school policies including dress code regulations and curricular separation made it clear that, on the whole, schools expected boys and girls to fulfill distinctly different roles. The following description of a 1960s experiment in sex segregation in Fairfax County, Virginia, makes clear the differential expectations of the times; it also offers a startling contrast to the rationale provided by proponents of single-sex education today (Lyles, 1966).

> In working with boys, we employ more science materials and experiments. There is more emphasis on building things and on studies of transportation. As a result, we can create and maintain a high level of interest. We have found it well to let the interests of the classes guide the teacher in areas such as science and social studies. Depending on the sex of the group, this sometimes results in quite different activities. From studying the atom, for example, a boy's class moved easily into a study of nuclear fission. It is unlikely that girls would respond in this way. Or, another example, mold can be studied from a medical standpoint by boys and in terms of cooking by girls. (p. 41)

When the issue of gender did reach public debate, it was usually because of concern for the education of male students. Typically, educators worried about the emasculation of boys in the "feminine" elementary school (Sexton, 1965, 1969).

> Boys and the schools seem locked in a deadly and ancient conflict that may eventually inflict mortal wounds on both. . . . The problem is not just that teachers are too often women. It is that the school is too much a woman's world, governed by women's rules and standards. The school code is that of propriety, obedience, decorum, cleanliness, physical and, too often, mental passivity. (Sexton, 1965, p. 57)

Even as educators were designing various forms of sex separation to best meet the needs of boys in school, the 1960s witnessed ideas and events that would set the stage for a new field of study. Betty Friedan (1964) published her landmark book, *The Feminine Mystique*, and gave voice to the dissatisfaction of a generation of women who were beginning to view automatic channeling into the role of housewife and mother as an unjust limitation to diverse interests and talents. President Kennedy established the Commission on the Status of Women, and the 1964 Civil Rights Act was passed with its inclusion, almost by accident, of provisions against sex discrimination. These set the stage for the efforts to expose and eradicate sexism in education that took place throughout the 1970s.

During the 1970s, concerns given voice in *The Feminine Mystique* were clearly articulated as arguments for equality and justice in the treatment of women and men in many social institutions, including schools. Economic pressure gave weight to arguments of principle as increasing numbers of women entered the salaried labor force, most often because of economic necessity. Several developments indicated that the field of education was becoming aware of these changes in the role and lifestyle of American women. The 1970s saw the passage of Title IX of the 1972 Education Amendments, which prohibited sex discrimination in schools receiving federal financial assistance, and the Women's Educational Equity Act whereby educators received grants to develop nonsexist curricular material and programs. The mission of desegregation assistance centers, funded by the 1964 Civil Rights Act to confront race desegregation, was expanded to include gender. Women's studies became a legitimate area of scholarship and teaching on the nation's campuses. There was a dramatic increase in athletic opportunities as well as professional graduate education as increasing numbers of women entered the traditionally male areas of medicine, law, and business. Funding cutbacks and psychological backlash slowed but did not halt progress toward educational gender equity during the 1980s.

Focusing on the remarkable developments in gender equity in education occurring during a quarter of a century, this chapter will review four major areas in which gender equity research has been active: curriculum, administration, instruction, and educational outcomes. It will discuss the research on sex-role stereotyping in the curriculum, with emphasis on the roles of females and males in textbooks. Studies on gender inequity in classroom interaction will be discussed, particularly as these relate to research on effective teaching. Sexism in the leadership and management of educational institutions, a third strand of research emerging during these years, will be reviewed. Also, developments and controversy over gender differences in intellectual ability will be assessed. Finally, the issue of gender equity within the contexts of teacher preparation and educational reform will be discussed.

In the 1960s, one could search the library for articles or books on gender equity or sexism in education and find almost no entries. During the past 25 years, gender-related research and publication has become voluminous; consequently, it is not possible to review all areas of scholarship under these four themes, and certain limitations are necessary. Gender equity in athletics will not be discussed, nor will computers and other selected aspects of technology. So many developments have occurred in postsecondary education that this level of education deserves a review of its own. Research in this area will be noted only when it has been especially pertinent to developments in elementary and secondary education. Similarly, although the intersection of race and gender will be alluded to, it is not a key focus of this chapter. Particularly relevant studies on race will be noted, but it would do a disservice to the complexity and importance of this issue, as well as the focus of the chapter, to attempt more extensive analysis. As Grant and Sleeter (1986) note, there has been inadequate attention to how race and sex intersect, and an exploration of this nature deserves its own research review.

THE PORTRAYAL OF GENDER IN TEXTBOOKS AND CHILDREN'S LITERATURE

Instructional materials create the foundation of most classroom activities, and the majority of classroom teaching is driven by commercially produced textbooks such as basal readers. Given the importance, widespread use, and highly visible nature of instructional materials, it is not surprising that studies of sex roles in texts and children's books first called attention to the issue of sexism and education. Several studies were conducted during the early 1970s, and their findings, jolting at the time, gained the attention of education professionals and the public alike. This section will review two decades of content analysis research of both textbooks and children's literature, including a discussion of methodological problems in these studies and a consideration of the impact of instructional materials on attitudes and comprehension of studies.

Textbooks

During the first half of the 1970s, a number of studies analyzed basal readers in widespread use in elementary schools and found that women and girls were underrepresented; when included, females were sex-role stereotyped in terms of character traits and career roles (Britton, 1975; Chase, 1972; Frasher & Walker, 1972; Gersoni-Stavn, 1975; Graebner, 1972; Key, 1972; O'Donnell, 1973; Oliver, 1974; Saario, Jacklin, & Tittle, 1973; Schnell & Sweeney, 1975; Schulwitz, 1976; Staven, 1971; Stefflre, 1969; Stewig & Knipfel, 1975; U'Ren, 1971; Weitzman & Rizzo, 1974; Women on Words and Images, 1972, 1975). In *Dick and Jane as Victims* (1972, 1975), the Women on Words and Images gained national attention as their analysis of 134 readers from 16 different publishers disclosed omission of females. They found a 5 to 2 ratio of boy-centered stories to girl-centered stories, a 3 to 1 ratio of adult male main characters to adult female main characters, a 6 to 1 ratio of male biographies to female biographies, a 4 to 1 ratio of male folk or fantasy stories to female folk or fantasy stories, and a 2 to 1 ratio of male animal stories to female animal stories.

Their findings also indicated sex-stereotyped portrayals. They tabulated 147 different occupations for males and only 25 for females; they found male characters portrayed as creative, brave, persevering, achieving, and capable of solving problems. In contrast, they found female characters drawn as dependent, passive, incompetent, fearful, and concerned about physical appearance. Women on Words and Images (1975) noted denigrating comments about women such as the following:

Women's advice is never worth two pennies. Yours isn't worth even a penny. (p. 53)

Look at her, Mother, just look at her. She is just like a girl. She gives up. (p. 51)

We are willing to share our great thoughts with mankind. However, you happen to be a girl. (p. 55)

Weitzman and Rizzo (1974) broadened content analysis from basal readers to those elementary texts most widely used between 1967 and 1972 not only in reading, but also in the content fields of science, mathematics, spelling, and social studies. In terms of illustrations, they found that (a) females represented only 31% of the textbook total; (b) their representation decreased as the grade level increased; and (c) whereas men were represented in 150 roles, almost all women were portrayed as housewives. Moreover, minority women suffered particular exclusion, for they were pictured only half as many times as minority males. In an analysis of elementary science texts (1972), Scardina also found females underrepresented and less frequently portrayed as grade level increased. DeCrow (1972) analyzed social studies series produced by 10 publishing houses and found no women working outside the home except as teachers and nurses.

Fewer studies of secondary texts were undertaken, but those available also showed patterns of omission and stereotyping. Arnold (1975) found females omitted from illustrations in earth science texts and ignored in discussions of science as a career. In a widely publicized study, Trecker (1971) analyzed 12 of the most widely used secondary history texts, documented the invisibility of female characters, and concluded that students reading these texts would be limited to the following description of the experiences and contributions of women in the history of the United States:

Women arrived in 1619 (a curious choice if meant to be their first acquaintance with the new world). They held the Seneca Falls Convention on Women's Rights in 1848. During the rest of the 19th century, they participated in reform movements, chiefly temperance, and were exploited in factories. In 1923 they were given the vote. They joined the armed forces for the first time during the Second World War and thereafter have enjoyed the good life in America. (Trecker, p. 252)

Trecker found that one text, in its discussion of the frontier period, allocated five pages to the six-shooter and scarcely five lines to the frontier woman. In another two-volume text, there were only two sentences allocated to the women's suffrage movement, one sentence in each volume.

Another text spent more space on women's fashions than on their struggle to win the vote.

As a result of public concern about such distortions, publishers developed and disseminated guidelines to achieve production of more equitable texts. Scott, Foresman (1972) was the first company to issue guidelines to improve the image of women in textbooks. Other companies followed suit: Ginn (1973), McGraw-Hill (1974), Macmillan (1975), Houghton Mifflin (1975), and Holt, Rinehart, and Winston (1975). Typically, these guidelines indicated that texts teach subliminal messages as well as explicit academic content. For example, the Macmillan guidelines stated: "These children are not simply being taught mathematics and reading; they are also learning—sometimes subliminally—how society regards certain groups of people." Ginn's guidelines noted:

> Educational materials teach far more than information and a way of learning. In subtle—often unconscious—ways, the tone and development of the content and illustrations foster in a learner positive or negative attitudes about self, race, religion, regions, sex, ethnic and social class groups, occupations, life expectations, and life chances. Inadvertent bias, as often the result of omission as commission, can influence the impact of educational programs.

Researchers attempted to determine whether these guidelines, once published, resulted in the publication of more equitable texts. Britton and Lumpkin (1977) compared reading, literature, and social studies texts for Grades 1–12 published between 1958 and 1970 with texts published between 1974 and 1976. They found that between 1958 and 1970, 60% of main characters were male, 14% were female, and 26% were "other" (an inanimate object or of indeterminate gender). Nine percent of main characters were minority males and 2% were minority females. In texts published during 1974–1976, they found improvement negligible. Sixty-one percent of main characters were male, 16% were female, and 23% were other. They concluded that the publishers had not lived up to their guidelines. Marten and Matlin (1976), replicating Graebner's earlier study of elementary texts (1972), found that slight progress had been made in terms of representation, but that texts remained highly stereotyped. Other studies published during the late 1970s documented ongoing bias. For example, Heikkinen (1978), analyzing 17 secondary science texts, found that males were included with far greater frequency and in a much wider variety of roles. Taylor (1979) analyzed secondary physics texts and found little female involvement. Gallagher (1980) carried out an extensive study of elementary science texts adopted in California; books adopted in 1980–1981 were compared with those adopted in 1970–1971. Findings indicated that although females in illustrations had increased, they were still drawn less frequently than males.

Many of these studies claimed that the publishers had not fulfilled their guidelines. But such criticism could be seen as somewhat premature; from a practical standpoint, one could claim that more than 5 or 6 years are necessary for the successful development and publication of nonsexist texts. Therefore, later context analysis research, carried out during the 1980s, could be considered more indicative of publishers' willingness to change.

Between 1980 and 1990 content analysis studies were mixed in their findings. Hitchcock and Tompkins (1987) found equal numbers of males and females in textbooks published in 1985–1986. Rupley, Garcia, and Longnion (1981) analyzed 25,709 stories included in four basal reading series published in 1976 and four published in 1978. Whereas an imbalance remained in the 1976 texts, the books published in 1978 showed almost equal numbers of male and female characters. Replicating the research design used by the Women on Words and Images (1972, 1975), Purcell and Stewart (1990) analyzed 62 elementary readers disseminated by four publishers included on the 1987 Texas Approved Textbook List. In contrast to the ratio of seven male characters for every female character reported by the Women on Words and Images in 1972, Purcell and Stewart found girls and boys included in equal numbers, and girls were shown in a wide range of activities. However, they were still portrayed as more helpless than male characters. Nibbelink, Stockdale, and Mangru (1986), comparing elementary arithmetic texts published from the 1930s through the 1980s, found the 1980s portrayals more equitable in terms of representation and less stereotyped in terms of roles. Powell and Garcia (1985) analyzed seven elementary science series published between 1981 and 1984. Coding 6,000 illustrations of humans, they found that approximately half represented females. Women were involved in a wide variety of science career roles; however, they were shown in these roles less often than men. Gains in history texts were less impressive; a recent review of 31 U.S. history textbooks found that the contributions of women continue to be minimized (Davis, Ponder, Burlbaw, Garza-Lubeck, & Moss, 1986).

Children's Literature

Given the current movement toward whole language, the trend away from heavy reliance on the basal reader, and the increasing use of children's literature, it is important to review studies analyzing the portrayal of gender roles in children's books. One of the earliest content analysis studies was conducted by the Feminists on Children's Literature (1971), who examined 49 Newbery Medal winners, those books receiving the American Library Association's award for the best book published for older children each year. In their analysis of these 49 books, the researchers found that books about boys outnumbered books about girls by

3 to 1. They also found that the books contained sex stereotypes as well as derogatory comments about females.

Weitzman, Eifler, Hodaka, and Ross (1972) analyzed the depiction of sex roles in picture books that won the Caldecott Medal, awarded by the American Library Association for the best picture book of the year. The books analyzed were the Caldecott winners and runners-up between 1953 and 1971. In this sample, the ratio of males to females in illustrations was 11 to 1, and the ratio of male to female animals was a staggering 95 to 1. In close to one third of the books, there were no women at all. Moreover, the researchers found pervasive sex-role stereotyping of characters, with male characters portrayed as independent and active and female characters as passive observers. Women left housemaking activities to assume only three other roles—fairy, fairy godmother, and underwater maiden. Nilsen (1971) analyzed 80 of the Caldecott winners and Honor books from 1950 to 1970 and found a consistent decline in books about girls during that time period. Of the 80 books in her sample, only 10 had female main characters, and 9 of these 10 were written during the 1950s. From 1951 to 1955, the percentage of girls pictured in the Caldecott sample was 46%, whereas from 1966 to 1970 only 26% of characters pictured were female. It is important to note similar problems of omission and invisibility characterizing the portrayal of minority characters. For example, more than 90% of children's books published during the first half of the 1960s did not include a single black character (Larrick, 1969).

Following public and professional awareness of sexism in children's literature, the development of nonsexist guidelines by publishing companies, and the emergence of nonsexist publishers such as the Feminist Press and Lollipop Power, researchers attempted to determine whether more recent Newbery and Caldecott winners and Honor books had become more gender fair in terms of language, representation, and nonstereotyped character portrayals. Kinman and Henderson (1985) analyzed Newbery Medal winners and Honor books published between 1977 and 1984. These books included 18 female main characters and 12 male main characters; positive images of females were portrayed in 18 of the books, whereas 6 presented negative images. Dougherty and Engel (1987) analyzed the Caldecott winners and Honor books of the 1980s and, comparing their findings with earlier studies, found a significant shift toward greater equality in representation, with 57% of characters male and 43% female.

It appears that award-winning books, selected by committees sensitive to issues of cultural pluralism and nonsexist portrayals, are improving. However, studies of children's literature other than the few books that win awards are not as promising. White (1986) analyzed children's book summaries included in the 1983–1984 issues of *Publisher's Weekly* and found nearly equal numbers of female and male main characters. However, supporting characters were far more likely to be male, and characters were sex-role stereotyped, with the majority of female main characters needing help and the majority of male main characters giving help. Tetenbaum and Pearson (1989) analyzed contemporary fiction selected from children's favorite books as listed between 1974 and 1984 in *The Reading Teacher*. Drawing on criteria established by Lyons (1983), they found males demonstrating a morality of justice, whereas female characters were more likely to demonstrate a morality of care. Christian-Smith (1989) analyzed 34 contemporary best-selling teen romance novels, highly popular with female reluctant readers, and found that they transmitted a clear message that in contrast to men, women have little sense of purpose or identity until they fall in love; in these books, the woman's place was in the home, with salaried career a distant second in priority if mentioned at all.

New books appear to be more fair and inclusive than those of the past. However, because most teachers themselves grew up with older books representing highly traditional gender roles, the influence of these more sexist books remains pervasive. For example, Smith, Greenlaw, and Scott (1987) interviewed 254 elementary teachers concerning their favorite books to read aloud in the classroom. Of these teachers' top 10 favorites, 8 books had male main characters, 1 had a female protagonist, and 1 had both male and female main characters. The adult women were mothers and homemakers exclusively. In contrast to self-sufficient males, the women were pictured as neurotic, selfish, and needing assistance. There were no female protagonists of elementary school age, and the only admirable female characters were animals. Although newer books evidence a trend toward greater equity, popular favorites from earlier times, less likely to be gender fair, evidently remain in widespread use in classrooms.

Many of the earlier studies on gender in instructional materials lacked well-structured research designs; consequently, systematic replication has been difficult (Tibbets, 1979). Moreover, several different content analysis instruments have been developed, and definitions of categories have varied across studies. For example, some studies include personified animals (e.g., Sylvester the donkey) in their analysis of male and female characters, whereas others categorized personified animals and objects in a different category, often termed "other." Because children's reading material includes large numbers of personified animals, this difference in categorization had a significant impact on findings. Also, nonverbal cues such as clothes and body position, used to establish gender, varied from study to study. Therefore, it is not always possible to determine whether it is the books that have changed, or the instruments researchers use to assess the books.

Another area of concern is that content analysis research assessing portrayals of males and females in instructional material decreased precipitously during the 1980s. At this point, there is not a sufficiently comprehensive and systematic body of research to offer a clear picture of the current state of gender equity in school texts and children's literature. If such research is not conducted and current publications are not monitored, the gains that appear to have been made could be lost.

The Impact of Traditional and Nontraditional Instructional Materials

One reason males have been overrepresented in school texts and children's literature has been the widespread notion that whereas boys would not read books about girls, girls would be willing to read about characters of either gender. In fact, through teacher preparation texts, new teachers have been encouraged to adopt an uncritical stance toward this notion and to emphasize male-oriented books in classroom reading and libraries. M. Sadker and Sadker (1980), in their content analysis of best-selling teacher education texts, reported comments such as the following taken from Rubin's *Teaching Elementary Language Arts* (1975):

> However, what we know about children's attitudes toward choosing books should also be taken into account. For example, it has been found that boys will not read "girl books" whereas girls will read "boys books." Therefore, the ratio of "boy books" should be about two to one in the classroom library collection. Examples for "girl-type" books are *Little Women* by Louisa May Alcott and many of the Laura Ingalls Wilder books such as *Little House in the Big Woods*. (p. 191)

Such pronouncements have had anticipated results—the production of a disproportionate number of books about male protagonists. When Scott O'Dell sought a publisher for *Island of the Blue Dolphins*, eventually a Newbery Award winner, he was informed by several publishers that a "minor" change would be needed in his superb book: He should change his intrepid female protagonist to a male because boys will not read books about a girl. Fortunately, O'Dell refused, and his book offers one of the best portrayals of a courageous girl struggling to survive in a solitary natural environment.

There are studies indicating that boys do prefer stories about male main characters, but much of the research is dated (Droney, Cucchiara, & Scipione, 1953; Jennings, 1975; Norvell, 1958). More recent studies also support this finding but question girls' satisfaction with reading male-oriented books (Bleakley, Westerberg, & Hopkins, 1988; D. Johnson, Peer, & Baldwin, 1984). Bleakley et al. (1988) found that when male and female fifth-grade students were exposed to adventure, mystery, and humorous stories, boys rated stories more interesting when the main characters were male; girls were more interested in reading about female protagonists, although their preference was less pronounced. Schau and Scott (1984) point to sex stereotyping as the reason why some boys prefer reading about male characters; plots about males are more likely to be filled with action and interesting details. Other studies indicate that both girls and boys rate stories with main characters who are female and nontraditional as high or higher than stories about traditional male main characters (Scott, 1980; Scott & Feldman-Summers, 1979).

Most educators agree on the value of literature in helping children become more understanding of others, especially those who may be somewhat different from themselves. If it is accepted practice that boys should not be expected to read about girls, an opportunity to create understanding is lost. Several studies show fewer biased responses by readers after exposure to nonsexist materials (Barclay, 1974; Berg-Cross & Berg-Cross, 1978; Flerx, Fidler, & Rodgers, 1976; Greene, Sullivan, & Beyard-Tyler, 1982; Hurwitz & White, 1977; Lutes-Duckley, 1978; Schau, 1978; Scott & Feldman-Summers, 1979). For example, Scott and Feldman-Summers (1979) found that after reading about female characters engaged in nontraditional activities, 3rd- and 4th-grade students were more likely to think that girls could participate in the nontraditional behavior represented in the story; however, perceptions regarding other nontraditional activities were not affected. Scott (1986) gave students from the 4th, 7th, and 11th grades a set of four narrative stories to read with main characters drawn as traditional female, traditional male, nontraditional female, and nontraditional male. When students read about a female involved in an activity traditionally regarded as male (e.g., skydiving), both girls and boys were more likely to think that females could and should participate in that activity. When they read about a male main character involved in an activity such as child care, typically regarded as female, they were more likely to think that males could and should take care of babies. Scott and Schau summarize the research on the impact of instructional materials on readers' attitudes as follows:

> (1) Exposure to sexist materials may increase sex-typed attitudes, especially among young children; (2) exposure to sex equitable materials and to same-sex characters results in decreased sex-typed attitudes in students from 3 to at least 22 years of age; (3) the effects of sex equitable materials do not usually generalize to areas not specifically covered in the materials, especially for pre-school and elementary age students, although there may be some generalization for older students, especially those who are initially more sex-typed; and (4) attitude change toward equity increased with increased exposure. (1985, p. 221)

Some studies show that students are more likely to recall traditional gender role content (Koblinsky, Cruse, & Sugawara, 1978; McArthur & Eisen, 1976); other studies indicate that students are more likely to recall nontraditional material (Frasher & Frasher, 1978; Jennings, 1975). Kropp and Halverson (1983), Scott (1986), and Bleakley, Westerberg, and Hopkins (1988) report no difference in reading comprehension for traditional or stereotypical content. According to Schau and Scott (1984), more investigation in this area is needed.

EQUITY THROUGH EDUCATIONAL ADMINISTRATION

Most of the gender equity research during the past 20 years dealing with educational administration has focused on the underrepresentation of women in high-level administrative positions such as principal or superintendent. Relatively little attention has been paid to the role of male or female administrators in advancing gender equity in their schools or districts. Although there have been some analyses of governmental policies intended to promote equity, most have focused on descriptions of federal and state legislation and regulations rather than on the implementation of these policies at the district and school level or the incorporation of gender equity into local policies such as codes for student conduct. In addressing each of these aspects of achieving equity through educational administration, we will contrast the concerns in the late 1960s and early 1970s with those of today.

Women in Educational Administration: The Numbers

Despite the fact that most administrators come from the ranks of teachers and the majority of teachers are women, the vast majority of educational administrators are men. Contrary to popular belief, this situation has not always been so inequitable. In 1928 over half of all principals were women. But, by 1988, whereas women continued to hold over half of the private school principalships, they held only 24.5% of the generally better-paid public school K–12 principalships (Hammer & Gerald, 1990). In 1972, 19.6% of elementary principals, 1.4% of secondary principals, and 1% of superintendents were female (Shakeshaft, 1987, p. 20). The parallel figures for 1988 showed some improvement: 28.8%, 11.6%, and 3.7% (E. Jones & Montenegro, 1988).

The current underrepresentation of women in key administrative positions cannot be tied to their lack of academic degrees, administrator certification, or assessment center performance. In 1969–1970 women earned 3 times as many bachelor's degrees in education as men and 1.2 times as many master's degrees; men, however, earned almost 4 times as many education doctorates. By 1986–1987 women increased their representation in the doctoral ranks, earning 1.2 times as many doctorates in education as men, and they earned slightly more than 3 times as many bachelor's degrees and 2.8 times as many master's degrees (National Center for Education Statistics, 1989, p. 256). In 1970 women earned 20% of master's degrees in general educational administration and 8.6% of the doctorates (National Center for Education Statistics, 1972). By 1988 women earned 57% of the master's degrees in general educational administration and 48% of the doctoral degrees (National Center for Education Statistics, 1990). Although there are no national data on recipients of administrator certifications by sex, Pavan (1985) noted that in Pennsylvania, the percentage of women certified each year was much greater than the percentage employed in administrative positions. Also, an estimated 50% of the graduates of administrator assessment centers are female, as are 50% of the assessors and 65% of the participants in the assessment center development programs (P. Hersey, personal communication, May 15, 1990). In some states administrator certification is tied to successful participation in assessment centers (P. Hersey, personal communication, May 15, 1990). Thus, there are plenty of qualified women for educational administration positions, but they are not being hired in equitable numbers.

When women administrators are hired, inequities continue. There are sex inequities in qualifications and earnings of public and private school administrators, but the patterns are not parallel. In 1988, 56% of male public school principals had a master's as their highest degree, compared to 46% of female principals; 34% of the males' highest degree was education specialist, compared to 31% for females, and 8% of the males had doctorates as their highest degree, compared to 11% for female principals. The highest degree for more than 25% of private school principals or heads was the bachelor's (compared to under 3% of public school principals). But the gender distribution of private school principals with master's and specialist degrees slightly favored women, whereas men had more of the doctorates. Despite this fairly equal distribution of degrees, female private school principals earned about $7,000 less than their male peers per year, and female public school administrators earned about $1,000 less than their male colleagues (Hammer & Gerald, 1990). Minority women are the most underemployed and underpaid in school administration (Shakeshaft, 1985, p. 130; Valverde & Brown, 1988; Yeakey, Johnston, & Adkison, 1986).

Although more women have become education administration professors over the past 15 years, like the administrators in their classes, they have not attained equity in numbers of paychecks. In 1975 2% of the professors of educational administration were women; the percentages had increased to 8% by 1983 (Ortiz & Marshall, 1988, p. 130) and 12% by 1986 (McCarthy, Kuh, Newell, & Iacona, 1988). Female professors of educational administration received about $5,000 less in annual salary than their male peers, even when rank and experience were controlled for (McCarthy et al., 1988). In 1990, Charol Shakeshaft was the first woman elected to head the division of the American Educational Research Association (AERA) concerned with educational administration.

In summary, these numbers suggest that in 1991, women entering educational administration should be hired and paid equally to their male peers because they have the same amount of experience and the same qualifications. The same equity standard would suggest that women should be employed as professors of educational administration at the 48% rather than the 12% level of representation.

Women's Roles in Managing Education

The research on women in educational administration has reflected sex bias in some of its focus and methodology. For example, relatively little attention has been given to the large proportion of women in central administration who are not principals, and little attention has been given to the school leadership roles of teachers. Also, early research often tended to compare male and female administrators using "male" standards and neglected many of the more subtle issues that were important to women. In contrast, some recent studies illustrate how many of women administrators' practices should be used by all administrators to improve education.

Limited Emphasis on the Wide Range of Women's Administrative Roles

In 1973 most of the research on women administrators focused on the few female principals or superintendents, not on the more numerous central office administrators, who were over 35% female (E. Jones & Montenegro, 1988; Ortiz, 1982; Ortiz & Marshall, 1988). The percentage of female central office administrators declined to under 20% during the rest of the 1970s and was 30% by 1988 (E. Jones & Montenegro, 1988). Schmuck (1987b) points out that most administrative staff positions held by women are likely to deal directly with students. Yeakey et al. (1986) and Valverde and Brown (1988) describe how minority administrators are frequently assigned to schools and special projects concerned with minorities rather than overall policy responsibilities.

With the current restructuring movement, there has been increased examination of the role of an educational leader, and the rhetoric suggests somewhat less demarcation between teachers and administrators. This shift reflects a broader acknowledgment of diverse leadership roles. For example, there is now greater attention to the important leadership nature of assistant superintendents and other supervisory central office staff (positions that are increasingly likely to be held by women) and to more dispersed leadership though efforts to restructure schools to facilitate participation and collaboration of all staff.

Shifts in Research on Gender Differences of Educational Administrators

Early research on women in educational administration documented the dearth of women in key administrative positions and sex differences in their characteristics and career paths. These studies found that female administrators were older, had more instructional experience, and were more diverse in respect to race, religion, and ethnicity than their male peers and that male administrators came from the ranks of coaching and band directing (M. Sadker, 1985; Shakeshaft, 1987, p. 73).

The next research emphasized internal (psychological) and external (institutional) barriers to female and minority advancement in educational administration. For example, these researchers tried to learn "why women—who are the majority of teachers—are the minority of managers and administrators" (Schmuck, 1987a, p. 9). Reviews of research from the 1960s and early 1970s indicated that (a) more women than men lacked self-confidence; (b) fewer women than men aspired to administrative positions; (c) home and family responsibilities, particularly lack of child care, created barriers for women; (d) women were less likely than men to receive encouragement and have sponsors and networks; (e) there was a pervasive bias against female administrators in patriarchal educational systems; (f) administrator preparation programs were sex-biased; and (g) few women had formal administrator preparation and certification (Biklen, 1980, p. 15; Ortiz, 1982, p. 59; Ortiz & Marshall, 1988, pp. 126, 131; Schmuck, 1986, pp. 178–179; Shakeshaft, 1985).

By the mid-1980s there were no longer major sex differences in academic credentials and certification; Pavan (1989) found that previous stereotypes about men trying harder than women to obtain administrative positions were not true. Women made greater job search efforts than men by four criteria: more applications, more formal and informal job-seeking techniques, and more months spent looking for their first administrative job. Men, however, received more district encouragement and more interviews and had a higher likelihood of being hired per each application than women. Pavan (1989) also found that men applied for more out-of-district jobs and that women were still asked illegal questions about their family situations during the hiring process. Calabrese and Wallich (1989) found that many male administrators made administration hiring decisions based on ingrained, socially reinforced personal biases such as beliefs that women are too sexual or emotional.

Shakeshaft (1987, p. 13) and Schmuck (1987a, p. 12) describe the next stage of research as studying women "on their own terms" instead of against typical behaviors and standards used for male administrators. This stage is exemplified by Edson's (1988) study of women administrator aspirants from 1979 to 1985, which indicated that assumptions about women's lack of motivation for these positions were often inaccurate. Edson found that female educational administrator aspirants were highly motivated, knew that they must have superior determination and credentials, and wanted to push to their personal limits to improve schools (p. 241). In 1990 the Office of Educational Research and Improvement of the U.S. Department of Education supported the final stages of a somewhat similar in-depth study conducted by Colleen Bell and Susan Chase at the University of Tulsa (1990): "Women's Educational Leadership: A Study of Superintendents and Gate Keepers."

Increased Focus on Structural Issues Related to Educational Leadership

Recent research has identified more subtle structural issues relating to assumptions about male leadership and new visions of leadership based on female and humanist principles. These issues include double standards for female and male administrators (giving women less support for their actions than men and viewing women in power as exceptional), women in a token status, sexuality-related constraints (such as when a man avoids hiring an attractive female administrator to work with him), and the identification and sharing of effective female administrative practices that should be used by all administrators (M. Sadker, 1985; M. Sadker, Sadker, & Shakeshaft, 1989; Shakeshaft, 1988, p. 405).

Research reporting the superior performance of female administrators is particularly important because as these administrators' attributes and behaviors are identified, they may be taught to male administrators as well. The 1964 research by Gross and Trask (1976) was the first large-scale study to show that female principals were more effective than their male colleagues. Subsequent research also indicated the superior performance of female principals compared to male principals (Ortiz & Marshall, 1988, p. 133; Shakeshaft, 1985, 1987, p. 166) and the special attributes that women often bring to the work. Such valued female administrator attributes include concern for others; a greater focus on teaching and learning; a more democratic, participative style; greater effectiveness in representing the school and working with the community; more emphasis on using outside resources to apply new ideas to improve instruction; and increased attention to monitoring student participation and evaluating student learning (M. Sadker, 1985; Shakeshaft, 1988, pp. 404–405). By 1990, over 13,000 people had participated in the National Association of Secondary Schools administrator assessment centers for elementary and secondary education. Women performed better than men in all 12 skill areas, and spectacularly better in written communication (P. Hersey, personal communication, May 15, 1990; M. Johnson & Douglas, 1985; Schmitt & Cohen, 1989).

Strategies to Increase the Participation and Effectiveness of Women in Educational Administration

The following strategies address both internal and external barriers to women in educational administration. Although there is no evidence on the relative effectiveness of each type of strategy, logic suggests that many of these approaches need to be used together to increase the participation and effectiveness of women in educational administration.

Research Justifications for Fairness and Excellence

Research is often used to identify or support changes in education. The results of the study by Gross and Trask (1976) indicating that "the professional performance of teachers and pupils' learning were higher on the average in schools administered by women than by men" (p. 219) were used to attack three commonly used arguments to justify giving preference to hiring male administrators: (a) Male principals would outperform female principals; (b) male teachers needed the occupational advancement provided by principalships to stay in education; and (c) female and male teachers prefer to work with male administrators. Gross and Trask suggested that the women's schools were better because many of the male principals lacked instructional leadership skills as a result of their limited teaching experience. In addition to abandoning male preference policies (that were fairly overt prior to Title IX in 1972), they recommended that women receive equal opportunities to become elementary principals and that the current male principals be given in-service training to upgrade their instructional leadership skills.

By 1990, research was used to show how women's ways of managing are congruent with the findings from research on effective schools and to suggest that schools and conceptions of educational administration should be restructured to take advantage of these female strengths, ranging from frequent evaluations of student progress to support for teachers and their efforts to attain common goals (Shakeshaft, 1987, pp. 199–200, 1988).

Recruitment, Preparation, and Selection

Starting in the early 1970s, special programs were created to recruit and prepare women for educational administration, and federally sponsored training materials were developed for men and women to decrease sex stereotyping about women in educational administration. Resource manuals, financial aid for participation in preparation programs, job banks, candidate pool projects, hiring guidelines, internships, networks, and support systems such as mentor programs were also developed to help women enter and succeed in administrative positions (Coursen, Massarella, Jeffress, & Hadderman, 1989; Edson, 1988; Leadership in Educational Administration Development, 1990; Shakeshaft, 1985, 1987). Some of the programs were designed specifically for women and focused on teaching them skills (such as assertiveness training, balancing home and work, catching a sponsor, or male rules of the game) to survive in a sexist world (Shakeshaft, 1987, p. 127). Shakeshaft (1987, p. 135) reports that little is known about the effectiveness or continued use of these materials.

One example of a university-level response was a University Council for Educational Administration project funded by the Women's Educational Equity Act Program in the U.S. Department of Education to develop a self-assessment instrument for departments of educational administration. This instrument is designed to identify and eliminate a wide range of university-imposed barriers to sex equity for education administration graduate students and faculty (L. Webb, Stout, & Metha, 1986).

More recently, administrator assessment centers have established systematic and equitable procedures to help potential administrators understand their strengths and prepare for advancement. Because districts that agree to use these assessment centers are required to interview the qualified center participants, more women are now being considered for higher level administrative positions. In some instances, the assessment center results provided "the only evidence of administrative skills in their credentials" (M. Johnson & Douglas, 1985, p. 109). However, only one third of the assessment center participants have been promoted since 1978 and, despite the assessment of superior skills, only one half of those promoted have been women (Hersey, 1990).

On-the-Job Support and Advancement

Because many able women who participated in programs to prepare for educational administration are exiting education (Ortiz & Marshall, 1988, p. 137), some recent attention has been given to providing entry-level support to women leaders through Leadership in Educational Administration Development (LEAD) mentoring and entry-year support programs. Early on-the-job support programs had emphasized obtaining family support and sponsors and participating in networks. Additionally, some recent attention has been given to promoting the advancement of women and minorities in educational administration.

Policies to Increase Equitable Participation in Educational Administration

Federal, state, and local policies and structures for implementing and enforcing laws such as Title IX of the 1972 Education Amendments (which prohibits discrimination on the basis of sex in programs or activities that receive federal financial assistance) and Title VII of the Civil Rights Act of 1964 (which prohibits employment discrimination on the basis of sex, race, or national origin) have had some success, yet a wide gap remains between policy and practice (Schmuck, 1986, p. 179). Edson (1988, p. 218) notes that it is difficult for women who are discriminated against to use the legal process, but that women who do so have a strong commitment to the principle of equal treatment.

In addition to enforcing these federal laws, Congress has provided the U.S. Department of Education with program mandates and funds to support sex equity in education. Since 1974, these funds have supported many of the sex equity materials for in-service administrator training and recruitment through the Women's Educational Equity Act. When the Congressionally mandated LEAD program was established in 1988 to support training and technical assistance centers in each of the states, it included "particular emphasis upon improving access for women and minorities to administrative positions" (LEAD, 1990, p. 2). Organizations such as the National School Boards Association and the American Association of School Administrators also have policies and programs to appoint and advance women and minorities in educational administration. In April 1990, the National Policy Board for Educational Administration (representing 10 national organizations concerned with educational administration) issued a new statement of purpose that advocates a professional certification process for school administrators as well as concern for improved recruitment and selection of women and minorities.

Change the Structure of the Organization

Perhaps the most promising approach is to change the structure of the organization to make it more congruent with feminist values and leadership attributes. Shakeshaft (1988, pp. 406–407) describes this as helping women value and implement leadership by relying on female administrator strengths such as "clear educational goals, supported by a value system that stresses service, caring and relationships" rather than trying to copy male administrators. Scherr (1986) reported that women suppressed their own views and perceptions in order to fit into organizations instead of speaking out to help humanize organizations. The attributes of effective women administrators are congruent with principles found in effective schools and with the current ideas about restructuring schools.

The Role of Administrators in Advancing Gender Equity

Many assume that women administrators who may have faced discrimination themselves will work hard to advance gender equity in their districts and schools. There is little research to support or refute this assumption. Many believe that women administrators serve as valuable role models, but the evidence of their positive effects on career aspirations of their female staff and students is anecdotal. Gross and Trask (1976, p. 223) reported "that male administrators of low SES schools displayed on the average less concern for individual differences among children and for their social and emotional development than women principals." However, in a study of 19 female principals, Schmuck and Schubert (1986) found that they made only modest gestures toward initiating equity activities in their schools and concluded that they had *not* been trained to be sensitive observers of inequities. A related study of women on school boards points out that although women had more positive attitudes about sex equity than men, "there is little evidence that a board's activity in this area reflects the presence of women as board members" because women are rarely board leaders, and if they push their views in the women's equity area, they may be considered uncooperative and a threat to board harmony (M. Johnson & Crowley, 1978, pp. 16–17). D. A. Grayson (personal communication, May 16, 1990) reports that some women administrators have even counseled other women not to "stick their necks out on behalf of sex equity because they may become identified as interested in only this one issue." Schmuck and Schubert (1986) note that the "advocacy organizations for women administrators have been too narrow in their support. They have promoted self-interest in career mobility but not promoted a sense of responsibility for providing equality for students and other employees" (p. 15). To partially counteract this, the theme of a recent summer institute for women administrators was how to create change without losing your job (C. Shakeshaft, personal communication, May 15, 1990).

The Role of Administrator Training in Developing Equity Knowledge and Skills

Educational administrators can do many things to implement sex equity from the management of knowledge such as collecting statistics by sex/race/ethnicity or ensuring that textbooks are sex fair (Baptiste, Waxman, Walker de Felix, & Anderson, 1990; Ortiz & Marshall, 1988, p. 126; Scott & Schau, 1985). They also have the responsibility for developing and implementing administrative and curriculum policies both to ensure equity and to assess classroom interactions and curricula. To do these things well, administrators need to know about equity laws and research on what works to promote equity in education. For example, Shakeshaft (1988, p. 409) points out that if administrators know about common sex biases such as the likelihood that men will be rated as more competent for identical performance or that they are more likely to be given corrective feedback, they can guard against this in their own supervisory actions. They can also make sure that these sex biases are counteracted in all recruitment, hiring, and management policies and procedures used in their district. Additionally, Shakeshaft (1988, p. 412) notes that women are more likely than men to empower others and work collaboratively to achieve group goals.

The research review in this section has attempted to assess what administrators were taught about equity in their university administration programs and whether organizations concerned with these programs had any equity goals beyond the entry and advancement of women and minorities into educational administration. The executive director of the University Council for Educational Administration, which represents administration professors, noted that his constituents have been dealing with structural issues relating to recruitment, selection, and assessment and are now starting to focus on curriculum issues. Thus, the time is ripe to ask about including equity in preservice and in-service administrator training programs (P. Forsyth, personal communication, May 16, 1990).

A 1981 analysis of best-selling educational administration textbooks found little information on women in educational administration or guidance about eliminating sexism (Tietze & Davis, 1981). Similar analyses of journals for school administrators found little emphasis on attaining sex equity (Ortiz & Marshall, 1988, p. 136). Schmuck and Schubert (1986) stated that social science theories of objective, value-free inquiry in organizational settings have been dominant in training school administrators and that equity concerns are not included within the curriculum. Like other female students, McCarthy and Webb (1990) observed that female administration students are still likely to receive inappropriate treatment by male faculty and peers such as sexist comments and devaluations of their class contributions. A 1989 study of 28 graduate students in educational administration in three colleges revealed that "there has been very little systematically and formally taught in the areas of race, gender, ethnicity, social class and other areas of difference" but that the students acquired some informal insights from their peers who were urban administrators (Parker & Shapiro, 1990, p. 14). Thus, it is no wonder that administrators tend not to address equity very systematically in their schools. A recent informal survey of professors concerned with equity suggests that any inclusion of equity content in administration courses is dependent upon the individual professor's interests. So equity issues may be well covered in one professor's education law course but barely mentioned in another's, even in the same university. To our knowledge there are no laws for administrators similar to an Oregon law that states that teachers need to demonstrate knowledge of antidiscrimination laws (Shakeshaft, 1985, 1987, p. 143).

Given this confirmation of limited attention to equity in formal administrative training programs, Shakeshaft (1990) recommends that these programs incorporate equity into the central core of what an administrator should know. In doing so, university programs would model equity in their behavior toward their own administration students and staff; teach administration students to understand the role of race, ethnicity, and gender in their own administrative styles; and help aspiring administrators learn how to achieve equity as they influence the teaching and learning processes in their own schools. In addition to incorporating information on equity in all administration classes, a separate course on equity should be required for all.

Although piecemeal and inconsistent, efforts to involve administrators in in-service equity workshops and training have been more extensive than most preservice efforts. The Women's Educational Equity Act and some foundations and associations have supported the development of training materials for sex equity in education. Whereas some programs, such as Sex Equity in Educational Leadership, have focused on increasing the numbers of women in educational administration, others, such as Expanding Options, Becoming Sex Fair, and Organizing for Change: PEER's Guide to Campaigning for Equal Education, have provided training on a wide variety of sex equity topics—usually to combined groups of administrators and teachers. Two of the most recent programs use the trainer of trainers approach. Myra and David Sadker's Principal Effectiveness–Pupil Achievement (PEPA) program was developed for administrators to promote equity in their role as instructional leaders and to train their teachers to increase equity in classroom interactions. PEPA is widely used in U.S. in-service training, and anecdotal reports suggest positive reactions. Dolores Grayson's program, The Equity Principal: Infusing an Equity Agenda into School Districts, is designed to "equip a cadre of practitioners to model the concepts at their own sites and to conduct workshops with current and aspiring administrators" (Grayson, 1990, abstract). Both approaches help participants understand equity and effective schools research and become more aware of inequities in how they treat their teachers and in how teachers treat students. For example, the principals often found that "they tended to avoid their perceived low achieving staff members and did not initiate as many opportunities for positive interaction with them," and that gender and race often influenced their perceptions of perceived ability (Grayson, 1990, p. 75). More research is needed to fully assess whether training administrators in gender equity results in long-term change in teacher behavior.

Administrative Policies to Promote Equity

Administrators, in theory, do have an accountability role in implementing educational equity policies developed at the federal, state, or district level. They also should have a leadership role in developing formal and informal policies in their own districts and schools. However, there is little indication that administrators are being assessed on their on-the-job success in attending to and attaining equity. This lack of attention to equity is particularly disturbing when we consider the increasingly multicultural nature of our public school population and our nation's economic needs for the full participation of women, minorities, and persons with disabilities in all aspects of our lives.

National attention to equity policies in education was given a significant boost in 1964 with the federal Civil Rights Act and again in 1972 with Title IX. Materials to identify and interpret federal equity policies were prepared by the U.S. Office of Education (McCune & Matthews, 1975); the National Organization for Women (NOW) Legal Defense and Education Fund, Project on Equal Education Rights (Peer) (Verheyden-Hilliard & Steele, 1978); and many others at the state and local levels. In 1982 the Council of Chief State School Officers (Bailey & Smith) published an excellent compilation of state sex equity policies, but Schmuck et al. (1985) report little documentation on the extent to which local school districts may have developed their own equity policies or how they responded to federal or state equity policies. Although the national education reform reports starting with *A Nation at Risk* (National Commission on Excellence in Education, 1983) suggested that education can be improved by establishing and enforcing standards, they failed to mention equity policies or standards. However, with the exception of the 1984 Supreme Court Grove City College ruling that limited the scope of coverage of Title IX until the Civil Rights Restoration Act of 1988 (National Coalition for Women and Girls in Education, 1988), equity policies at the federal, state, and local levels designed to eliminate discrimination and reduce stereotyping remained in place. And some states continued to develop their own stronger versions of Title IX that went beyond the federal Title IX and prohibited discrimination in textbooks (Klein, 1986). Some of the local district educational equity policies or standards included equity—in competencies required of beginning teachers, in school appraisal criteria or performance indicators, in criteria for textbook selection, and in student codes of conduct (Klein, 1986).

Ironically, policies or goals may have differential effects on females and males, even though this was not their intent. For example, some policies designed to raise standards, such as the "no-pass, no play" and the "C" average policies, may limit boys' participation in extracurricular activities more than girls', because girls generally receive higher grades. It is also possible that policies specifically intended to promote equity may not have an equitable impact. Thus, trying to promote equity by eliminating all sex segregation may result in outlawing some valuable all-female special focus programs that would help women achieve equitable outcomes in areas where there are different needs or where interactions in a male-dominated group would be detrimental (Klein, 1987, 1988). In summary, formal public equity policies and administrator leadership to articulate, implement, and analyze the effects of policies by gender, race, ethnicity, and handicapping condition should become salient aspects of excellence in educational administration during the 1990s.

Issues of the 1990s That May Influence Achieving Equity Through Administration

Three issues may significantly affect achieving equity through administration in the 1990s. They are career paths, particularly for teachers; projected administrator vacancies; and school restructuring.

Career Paths

The need to attract and maintain quality teachers may lead to the development of more career paths for females and minorities in education. In the late 1960s one of the arguments for hiring male rather than female administrators was that men needed to see some possibilities for career advancement as incentives to enter teaching (Gross & Trask, 1976). Recently, Yeakey, Johnston, and Adkison (1986, p. 133) noted the sex stereotyping inherent in teachers' "careerless orientations" that is also associated with a "relatively flat salary scale and the absence of vertical differentiation and mobility." However, despite recent attention to the development of teacher mentors and board certification procedures for advanced teachers and the fact that most excellent educational administrators have extensive teaching experience, C. Dwyer (personal communication, May 15, 1990) observes that many teachers may resist career ladders and merit pay systems because they perceive in them an unwelcome element of competition with other teachers. However, others such as M. Sadker (1985) note that "Women's aspirations increase when they perceive genuine opportunities in educational administration. In 1958, only 9 percent of women surveyed were interested in educational administration. In 1977, 50 percent of women surveyed said they were interested in this career."

Projected Extensive Administrator Vacancies

Because it is likely that there will be an increased need for educational administrators due to projected retirements of half of the U.S. principals in the next decade (Coursen et al., 1989), some have suggested that it would be appropriate to hire noneducators with management experience from business or the military. The research reviewed here suggests that such a strategy would be unwise for the following reasons:

1. There are many women in the administrator pipeline with a great deal of important instructional experience, and research suggests that they will be more effective than many of their male predecessors.
2. It would discriminate against advancing the large numbers of women and minorities already in education because most transfers from business and military would be white males.
3. Validity studies of administrator assessment centers suggest that they are an effective way to identify talented administrators and to also make sure that women and minorities obtain equal opportunities for success. They are expanding, and some states are already using their results for administrator certification decisions.

Restructuring the Schools

School restructuring should help break down the excessive dichotomy between administrators and teachers, and in some cases school-based management may be led by a school team rather than a principal (Council of Chief State School Officers, 1990). This decentralized decision making is congruent with a female-defined organizational structure that would have less differentiation of administrators and teachers and less extreme hierarchies (Shakeshaft, 1988, p. 412). Shakeshaft (1987, p. 139) also reports that "organizations that allowed decisional flexibility for teachers were also the ones in which the teachers had more interest in administration." Valverde and Brown (1988, p. 155) urge the "restructuring of educational institutions to eliminate inequity and social injustice" and suggest that administrators can help with this by establishing "goals broad enough to foster and encompass cultural pluralism as well as the common wealth."

Recommendations to Achieve Equity Through Educational Administration

Those interested in achieving educational equity through administration should make every effort to ensure that the following recommendations are heeded:

1. An equitable proportion of women and minorities should be selected

to fill the projected administrative vacancies. In connection with this goal, well-qualified women and minorities should continue to be prepared and certified in educational administration; be trained and selected without experiencing either overt or subtle discrimination based on sex, race, ethnicity, or sexual orientation; and receive pay and prestige at least equivalent to their male, nonminority peers. Federal, state, and local affirmative action and equal employment opportunity policies such as Title VII of the Civil Rights Act of 1964 and the Civil Rights Act of 1990 (if enacted) should be used to supplement the *educational* equity safeguards in Title IX and the Civil Rights Restoration Act of 1988.

2. All administrator preparation, support, and evaluation activities should take advantage of school restructuring opportunities and increased societal needs for achieving educational equity. This can be accomplished by continuing research on the identification and support of effective democratic values such as decreasing educational hierarchies and increasing participative decision making associated with school restructuring. Relatedly, because it is unrealistic to believe that all education professions will be seen as equivalently desirable in prestige and pay, the most stereotyped differentiations, such as paying teachers and administrators in schools with the youngest (or poorest) children least, should be ameliorated.

3. Educational administration should be used as a primary mechanism to actively ensure equity for traditional and restructured schools. In addition to establishing and using policies intended to eliminate discrimination and decrease stereotyping, administrators—and those who hire them—should be accountable for assessing success in achieving the desired equity outcomes. Richards (1988, p. 160) reminds us that educational institutions should serve as models of democratic ideals and that they will do so "when they practice what they teach."

GENDER EQUITY IN TEACHER-STUDENT INTERACTION

The research and analysis of classroom interaction has taken several dramatic turns during the 20th century. Research well into the 1970s focused on the travails and tribulations suffered by boys. Reflecting the tenor of the times, male achievement was of paramount concern as educators focused on lower male performance on report card grades and lower reading proficiency scores. The higher rate of grade repeaters among males was yet another area of concern. For most of this century, gender-related criticism of schools, especially elementary schools, focused on boys as victims of a hostile feminine school environment (Austin, Clark, & Fitchett, 1971; Ayres, 1909; Sexton, 1969). Brophy and Good (1974) reviewed numerous studies characterizing a culture conflict between the passive, docile, and conforming students desired by teachers and the active, independent, assertive behaviors associated with boys. Compounding this culture clash was the overwhelming proportion of female teachers, especially in the preschool and elementary school environment. Some educators attributed poor male performance in schools to a "self-fulfilling prophecy," in which the cadre of female teachers, expecting boys to do poorly, became educational accomplices to male underachievement. The higher incidence of behavior and discipline problems associated with boys represented yet another example of the ill-fitting male student in a female school environment. Studies into the early 1970s (and beyond) indicated that even the minority of teachers who were male defined "good" students as docile and conforming, criticizing males more frequently for misbehavior and awarding higher report card grades to females (Goffman, 1977; Good, Sikes, & Brophy, 1973). In terms of gender differences, research priorities and poor school performance of males was the major priority of educational concern.

The 1970s marked a profound turnabout in the perception of classroom interaction and in the body of gender-related research. Frazier and Sadker (1973) identified the female as the primary at-risk student whose academic failure was marked not by overt signs such as poor report cards and school discipline problems, but by a far more extensive, subtle, and enduring bias. Frazier and Sadker described a detrimental "trade-off" between teachers and docile students; whereas females received higher grades for conforming to classroom norms, males received more active instruction and developed stronger self-esteem and higher career goals because of their more assertive and central classroom role. As feminists decried the lack of political, legal, and economic power of women in society at large, many educators saw schools in a new light, and female students now assumed a more central role.

Paralleling the heightened concern about female performance in the classroom was a growing body of research underscoring the importance of the nature and frequency of classroom interaction in the educational achievement of students (Fennema & Peterson, 1978; Otto & Schuck, 1983; Redfield & Rousseau, 1981). Research investigations during the 1970s and 1980s emphasized the importance of direct instruction (Good, 1979), and male-female classroom interactions were analyzed through this new viewing glass. No longer limited to overt and gross classroom artifacts (grade repeaters, disciplinary actions, and the "female" nature of classroom life), researchers became more concerned with the specific dynamics of teacher-student interaction. A more precise and focused investigation of teacher-student interaction along with a concern for faltering female performance on measures such as standardized tests has the direction of a major avenue of research during the past two decades.

The Distribution of Interaction

Studies at the preelementary school level indicate that gender-different teacher behaviors can be documented from the earliest years. One of the first investigations in this area, conducted by Serbin, O'Leary, Kent, and Tonick (1973), studied 15 preschool classes and found that boys received more instructional time, more nurturant instructional attention, and more hugs, whereas girls were more likely to be ignored, except when they were physically beside the teacher. Cherry (1975) also found more teacher contacts with preschool male students, but indicated that many of these contacts reflected needs to supervise and control boys. Although Honig and Wittmer (1982) found no significant difference in the number of male and female preschool interactions, they did find that girls were asked significantly more personal-social questions than boys, reflecting a stereotyped line of teacher inquiry. Choices made by girls in preschool activities also reflected gender bias, according to Ebbeck (1984). In this study of 30 early childhood classes, girls were found less likely to participate in block play, climbing, sand play, and construction play; in addition, teachers spent nearly two thirds of their time with male students. Serbin and O'Leary (1975) reported that teachers gave preschool boys over 1.5 times more attention than girls and were 2.5 times as likely to engage in extended conversation with boys.

Although much of the early work on the frequency of interaction was performed at the preschool level, research rapidly expanded to the higher grades. At all levels of schooling, studies continue to reflect a greater number of teacher interactions with male students (Brophy & Good, 1974; Etaugh & Hughes, 1975; G. Jones, 1989; M. Jones, 1987; Leinhardt, Seewald, & Engel, 1979; M. Lockheed, 1982, 1985; Lockheed & Harris, 1984, 1989; Mahoney, 1983; M. Sadker & Sadker, 1985b; Spaulding, 1963). Sikes (1971) reported a higher level of academic contacts at the junior high school level with boys, as well as more complex and abstract questions being directed at male students. A study of 105 gifted students revealed that teachers initiated more talk with boys and were more restrictive toward girls (Cosper, 1970). A major study of over 100 classrooms in five states at Grades 4, 6, and 8 in language arts, math, and social studies revealed a higher number of teacher–male student interactions than teacher–female student interactions (M. Sadker & Sadker, 1984).

Other studies in science and math classrooms (Bean, 1976; Morse & Handley, 1982; Parsons, 1979; Stage, Kreinberg, Eccles-Parsons, & Becker, 1985) also reflect more interactions between teachers and male students. In fact, Morse and Handley (1985) found that the discrepancy in teacher interactions with male and female students became greater as the students moved from seventh to eighth grade. In the seventh grade, girls initiated 41% of the student-to-teacher interactions, a figure that dropped to 30% by the eighth grade. In contrast, male initiation of class comments rose from 57% to 70% over the same 2-year period, suggesting that girls were becoming less assertive over time. Studies at the secondary and postsecondary levels generally substantiate this trend.

At the postsecondary level, M. Sadker and Sadker (1986), in a study of 46 college classrooms, found that males were twice as likely as females to dominate classroom interaction, whereas females were twice as likely as males to be nonparticipants and to silently sit and observe classroom interaction. Krupnick (1985) reported similar findings in 24 classrooms at Harvard. Hall and Sandler (1982) reported that students at six different eastern colleges believed that male students received more recognition and encouragement than female students. Students reported their perceptions that males were called on more frequently and given more praise. To investigate these perceptions, Wingate (1986) recorded observations in 11 college classrooms, determining that a greater percentage of male students participated in these classrooms.

A number of postsecondary investigations have examined the effect of instructor gender on interaction. Boersma, Gay, Jones, and Morrison (1981) studied interactions in 50 college classrooms, finding that males received more interactions only in female-taught classes. However, most studies have found no interaction differences in male- or female-taught classes (M. Sadker & Sadker, 1985b) or that female instructors were more equitable. Sternglanz and Lyberger-Ficek (1977) examined 60 college classrooms, finding that male students received more interactions in classrooms with male instructors but equal interactions in female-taught classrooms. Karp and Yoels (1976) found males receiving more attention in all 10 classrooms they observed, but recorded a greater inequity in male-taught classes. Evaluating 24 videotapes of classes at Harvard, Krupnick (1985) found that female students spoke three times longer in classes with female instructors. Postsecondary interaction studies differ significantly in this regard from elementary and secondary studies, suggesting that the gender of the instructor may influence the nature of student-teacher interaction in college classes. Yet the lack of consensus in the research suggests a possible confounding effect by other variables. For instance, might a female instructor role model have a greater impact in historically all-male institutions or programs of study? Might some female professors exhibit more effective teaching behaviors in promoting equitable interaction? Clearly, more studies are needed to determine if and how the gender of the instructor affects interaction.

Several explanations have been offered for the higher frequency of male interactions at all levels. D. Sadker, Sadker, and Thomas (1981) reported that boys were eight times more likely than girls to call out in elementary and middle school classrooms. When boys called out, the teacher's most frequent response was to accept the call out and continue with the class. When girls called out, a much rarer phenomenon, the teacher's most typical response was to remediate or correct the inappropriate behavior with comments such as "in this class, we raise our hands." Becker (1981) studied geometry classes and found that females were generally given fewer opportunities to participate. M. Jones and Wheatley (1989) observed 60 science classes using the Brophy-Good Teacher-Child Dyadic Observation Instrument and found that males not only called out more frequently, but even when they did not call out, teachers more frequently called on them directly (see also M. Sadker & Sadker, 1985a). Jones and Wheatley reported that when science teachers in their study called for volunteers, males were more likely to be the volunteers. When science teachers organized demonstrations, 79% were carried out by males and only 21% by females. In examining science classrooms in Australia, Tobin and Garnett (1987) observed similar classroom behaviors, including more frequent hand raising by males to volunteer answers and a greater likelihood that males would be involved in manipulating science equipment.

The preponderance of study findings at all educational levels indicates that males are both given, and through their behaviors attract, a higher number of teacher interactions. Whereas males generally are the beneficiaries of this higher level of teacher attention, not all males are recipients. There is not only inequity between genders; there is also inequity within gender. M. Sadker and Sadker (1985b) reported that a few "salient" or "star" students tend to receive much more attention and interactions than one would normally predict. They reported that one or two students receive about 20% of teacher interactions. Tobin (1988) also reported the dominance of classroom interaction by a few "target" students, as did Karp and Yoels (1976). M. Sadker and Sadker (1984, 1985b) reported a decreasing level of interaction through the higher grades, with postsecondary classes being the least interactive and the most likely to be dominated by a few salient students who were twice as likely to be male than female.

Research offers us insights into which males are most likely to become target or salient students (Tobin & Gallagher, 1987). Teachers are more likely to interact with high-achieving boys than high-achieving girls (Good et al., 1973). Reyes and Fennema (1982) report that teachers interacted more with boys who indicated a high degree of confidence in their math ability than with girls who indicated similar levels of confidence. Moreover, teachers interacted with these males at a higher cognitive level. Brophy and Good (1974) reported that in addition to gender, student achievement and behavior must be considered as variables in the unequal distribution of teacher attention. High-achieving boys and boys exhibiting behavior problems capture much of the teacher's attention, whereas other boys and girls are less likely to be the target of teacher interaction (Bank, Biddle, & Good, 1980).

Finally, the research suggests that the ethnicity and racial background of the student also serve as predictors of the level of classroom interaction. Minority group students, both male and female, receive less teacher attention than majority group students. Majority males are more likely to interact with the teacher than minority males, and majority females are more likely to interact than minority females (Brophy & Good, 1974; Rubovits & Maehr, 1973; M. Sadker & Sadker, 1984). In analyzing the imbalance in teacher-student interaction, it is useful to keep in mind that many males are not the recipients of significant teacher interaction and that there is significant inequity within gender groups as well as between them.

There is a tendency, when considering the frequency of interactions, of losing one's way in the numbers. In the end, we must attempt to sort out the impact of the differential number of interactions, especially when these numerical differences may not appear to be great. Kelly (1986) estimated, in her meta-analysis of gender differences in teacher-student interactions, that teachers are involved in 56% of their interactions with males and 44% with females. Although an 8% discrepancy may not, at first, appear great, over the length of a 15,000-hour school career males would average 1,800 more instructional hours than females. Assuming a class size of 30, the average girl would end up with 60 fewer hours of individual attention than the average boy. When we consider the disparities within gender that are masked by most studies, the differences are even more pronounced. Or we may consider these differences in nonstatistical terms. Kahle (1983) points out the impact of these gender differences on a single field, in this case science:

> The most critical difference in the science education of boys and girls occurs in the science classroom. Research shows that girls have fewer experiences with the instruments, materials or techniques of science. This difference must be addressed by every science teacher in every science classroom to eliminate the inequalities in science education. As long as the majority of our citizens have fewer opportunities to observe natural phenomena, to use scientific experiments, or to go on science-related field trips, they are disadvantaged in terms of their science education. (p. 1)

Evaluation and Attribution

In *A Place Called School* (1984), John Goodlad noted that "learning is enhanced when students understand what is expected of them, get recognition for their work, learn about their errors and receive guidance in improving their performance" (p. 111). Other researchers also have emphasized the pivotal role of corrective teacher comments in shaping and directing student behavior (Berliner, 1984; Brophy, 1981, 1985; Brophy & Good, 1969, 1970; Gardner, Mason, & Matyas, 1989). Brophy (1981) reported that effective praise delivered by the teacher can improve the academic achievement of students. Effective praise, as defined by Brophy, includes specific comments delivered with sincerity, comments directly related to student performance and using past performance as a context, and remarks that inform students about the importance of their accomplishments and attribute their success to ability or effort. Similarly, corrective teacher comments can also be influential in developing student achievement and maintaining positive student attitudes. Criteria for effective critical comments by teachers include focusing on specific student performance rather than on the student as a person, providing an environment in which mistakes are permitted, offering a specific plan for improvement, and encouraging students to make efforts that will lead to success. In short, it is not only the number of questions and frequency of teacher-student interactions that create classroom learning opportunities and contribute to student success, but also the specificity and skill demonstrated by the teacher in responding to student comments. Research studies suggest that sex differences exist in the influential area of teacher evaluation and attribution.

Spaulding (1963), investigating 24 elementary classrooms, found that boys received more comments of both disapproval and approval. Other researchers have also identified a pattern of males receiving more praise and/or more criticism (Baker, 1986; Berk & Lewis, 1977; Brophy & Good, 1970; Felsenthal, 1970; M. Jones, 1987, 1989; V. Jones, 1971; Morse & Handley, 1985; M. Sadker & Sadker, 1984; Sikes, 1971). With few exceptions (Dweck, Davidson, Nelson, & Enna, 1978), most researchers have found that males receive more frequent and more precise teacher evaluation of their classroom comments. Boys are more likely than girls to be rewarded for a correct answer or remediated or criticized for an incorrect answer (Becker, 1981; Evertson, Emmer, Clements, Sanford, & Worsham, 1984; M. Sadker & Sadker, 1985a).

In a large, 3-year study of more than 100 fourth-, sixth-, and eighth-grade classrooms in four states and the District of Columbia, Sadker and Sadker tabulated four types of teacher evaluation: praise-positive remarks (good, excellent), acceptance-neutral remarks (OK, I see, uh huh), remedial-corrective comments (check your addition), and critical-negative comments (no, that's wrong). They found that male students were more likely to receive all four types of teacher reaction. The most frequent teacher reaction given in class was a neutral and diffuse acceptance; teachers used acceptance comments on an average of one per minute, more than all other reactions combined. Remediation, which constituted approximately one third of all teacher reactions, was the second most frequent teacher response. Praise accounted for 11% and criticism only 5% of teacher comments. For all four areas, males consistently received more teacher reactions than females. However, as the teacher reactions became more specific (praise, criticism, remediation), the imbalance became greater. In short, the more precise, the more valuable, and the more evaluative the teacher comments, the more likely they were to be directed at male students. The Sadker and Sadker findings are congruent with other studies that indicate that for both academic and conduct-related behaviors, male students receive more precise praise, criticism, and assistance than do females, teacher reactions that provide clarity and instruct, encourage, and sustain student performance (Becker, 1981).

Although this review focuses primarily on gender issues, it is both useful and appropriate to include some reference to the roles of race, ethnicity, and socioeconomic status in classroom interaction. A review of the literature reveals that most studies investigate single student variables, such as race or gender, rather than the impact of multiple student characteristics on classroom interaction. Because students in fact represent multiple characteristics, the current body of research offers a fragmented and limited view of classroom interaction. The few studies investigating multiple characteristics (Daminco & Scott, 1988; M. Sadker & Sadker, 1985b) suggest that white, majority culture males are more likely to be the target of frequent and productive interaction, whereas minorities and females receive less frequent and less precise interaction. Studies on ethnic and racial minorities as well as research involving students from lower socioeconomic class backgrounds indicate that they also are the less valued members of the class and less likely to receive positive or productive teacher behaviors. In a highly influential study, Rosenthal and Jacobson (1968) indicated that teacher expectations both predict and create the level of student achievement. Although the methodology of their research on the concept of "self-fulfilling prophecy" has received significant criticism, the influence of teacher expectations generally has been validated in numerous other studies that indicate that racial and ethnic minorities are not "expected" to do as well as white children by most teachers (Forehand, Ragosta, & Rock, 1976; Weinberg, 1977; Williams & Muehl, 1978; Woodworth & Salzer, 1971). Lower teacher expectations for minority student performance have been attributed to a variety of factors, including less effective use of standard English (Bikson, 1974; Choy & Dodd, 1976; R. Smith & Denton, 1980; F. Williams, Whitehead, & Miller, 1972), perceived less physical attractiveness (Adams & Cohen, 1974; Clifford & Walster, 1973; DeMeis & Turner, 1978; Dusek & Joseph, 1983), perceived lower achievement of the minority group as a whole being ascribed to each member (Crowl, 1971; J. Williams & Muehl, 1978), and miscommunication of both verbal and nonverbal messages due to cultural differences (Byers & Byers, 1972; Feldman, 1985; LaFrance & Mayo, 1976). Research studies have identified a number of ways that teachers behave differently toward students perceived as low achievers. Teachers interact less with these students and interrupt them more, demand less from them, pay them less attention, and smile and praise them less while disciplining them more (Emihouvich, 1983; Gollub & Sloan, 1978; Good, 1981). Clearly, the intricate but powerful relationship between gender, race, ethnicity, and social class of students and the quantity and quality of teacher interaction represents a critical research priority for educators in the years ahead.

Although some research documents shorter wait-time (associated with lower expectations) being awarded to minority children (Good, 1981), studies on the amount of wait-time distributed to males as compared to females have been less definitive. Wait-time, the silent waiting period after a teacher question and after a student response, has been associated with a number of positive classroom conditions. Longer wait-time has been found to increase the frequency and enhance the quality of student responses (Row, 1974, 1986; M. Sadker & Sadker, 1990). Whereas some studies suggest that males are given longer wait-time to respond to teacher questions (Gore & Roumagoux, 1983), others have found no sex differences (Morse & Handley, 1982). A review of the literature does not reveal any studies reporting longer wait-time being awarded to females.

One of the more fascinating areas of gender interaction research explores the concept of learned helplessness and the role of attributions in teacher-student feedback. The concept of learned helplessness was first investigated by Seligman and Maier (1967), whose experiments with animals revealed that some animals had learned to give up—to passively accept pain rather than to explore behaviors that would free them from pain. Those animals exhibiting learned helplessness had been put in situations where, regardless of their actions, they were subjected to electric shock; they "learned" that all future actions on their part would be futile. As a result, they no longer tried to avoid shock in other situations, even those in which their actions would have been fruitful: They had learned to be helpless.

Applying this concept to children, educators have attempted to explain why some children, usually male, actively and continuously pursue solutions to problems and other children, usually female, abandon fruitful action and are more likely to give up (Dweck & Goetz, 1978; Dweck & Repucci, 1973). Females have been reported as entering learning situations with lower expectations of success and with a lack of self-confidence in their ability to accomplish a task, even when such beliefs may be unsupported by objective measures (Crandall, 1969; Dweck, Goetz, & Strauss, 1980; Feather & Simon, 1973; Goetz, 1981; Lenney, 1977; Maccoby & Jacklin, 1974; Parsons & Ruble, 1977). These attitudes have a negative impact on subsequent efforts and performance, as females are less likely to pursue tasks (Dweck & Elliot, 1983; Felson, 1984; Shephard & Hess, 1975; Stein & Smithells, 1969; Stewart & Corbin, 1988).

Along with the concept of learned helplessness, gender differences in causal attribution have been investigated. Boys are more likely to attribute success to ability and failure to lack of effort. Girls are more likely to attribute success to luck or effort and failure to lack of ability. As a result, boys are more likely to feel a sense of mastery and control over their fate, to experience a higher level of self-confidence, to demonstrate greater persistence in academic tasks, and, therefore, to gain greater opportunity for academic achievement (Armstrong, 1981; Bar-Tal, 1978; Bar-Tal & Frieze, 1977; Deaux, 1976; Dowling, 1978; Dweck & Bush, 1976; Dweck et al., 1980; Fennema, 1984; Fennema, Peterson, Carpenter, & Lubinski, 1990; Fennema & Sherman, 1978; Frey & Ruble, 1987; Hrdy, 1981; Nicholls, 1979; Phillips, 1984; Reyes, 1980, 1984a, 1984b; Wolleat, Pedro, Becker, & Fennema, 1980).

To explore the reasons for sex differences in learned helplessness and attribution, Dweck and Goetz (1978) analyzed sex differences emerging in teacher criticism of children. They reported that teacher criticism of boys was concerned with nonintellectual behavior such as conduct and neatness. Boys were led to believe that although they made mistakes, these were not reflective of intellectual failings. Dweck and Goetz reported that teachers were eight times more likely to make statements attributing male errors to effort, suggesting that if boys tried harder, they would succeed. In contrast, they found that when teachers criticized girls, the negative feedback waas usually directed at intellectual inadequacy (88%). Girls were less likely to be told that their achievement would increase if they would try harder. Dweck and Goetz indicated that the nature of the feedback they receive may cause girls to see their failure as a result of intellectual inadequacy, beyond their control for alteration or improvement.

A number of studies have failed to replicate the findings by Dweck and Goetz that females receive more intellectual criticism. D. Sadker et al. (1981), Meyer and Thompson (1956), and Simpson and Erickson (1983) found that male students received more interactions and more teacher attention of all kinds, including intellectual criticism. Rather than attributing the lower self-esteem and confidence of females to a higher level of intellectual criticism, these researchers see the greater number of interactions and the more precise evaluation being given to boys as serving to boost their confidence and self-esteem. As males become more central in classroom interaction, their status, attitudes, and achievement are enhanced. These researchers suggest that teachers may be communicating a continuous if subtle set of signals indicating that males are the more valued students (Oren, 1983; M. Sadker & Sadker, 1984).

Teacher evaluation behaviors may also be shaped in part by the subject being taught. Licht, Stader, and Swenson (1989) found that sex differences in attribution were more likely to be found in social studies and science classes, where students reported infrequent and ambiguous feedback, than in math and reading classes, where feedback was more frequent and more precise. Graham (1984), examining the affective dimension of teacher feedback, indicated that when teachers exhibited sympathy concerning student performance, students felt that failure was unavoidable. When teachers expressed anger, students believed that failure could and should be avoided. More research on the affective component of teacher feedback would be useful.

Although studies continue to document attribution and attitudinal gender differences, not all studies connect the teacher with the cause or the potential remediation of these differences. Some investigators explain these differences in terms of pervasive social forces, positing that culturally sex-stereotyped messages as to appropriate and inappropriate career paths and the lower value ascribed to females in our society could, in fact, be the cause of the lower self-confidence expressed by girls in the classroom (Bottomley & Ormerod, 1981; Eccles-Parsons, 1983; Eder, 1985; Eder & Hallinan, 1978; Kahle & Lakes, 1983; Pattison & Grieve, 1984; Reyes & Padilla, 1985; Ridley & Novak, 1983). Female modesty, as contrasted with male boastfulness (Corbin, Landers, Feltz, & Senior, 1983), has been advanced to explain this gender gap in confidence and task persistence. Finally, peer pressure, classroom climate, and subjective personal perceptions (Eccles & Blumenfeld, 1985; Peterson & Fennema, 1985) have been used to explain this difference as well. Whether the reasons for lower academic confidence and persistence experienced by females are to be found within the classroom or beyond the school walls, research and remediation will continue to be educational objectives in the decade ahead.

Cooperative Learning

Cooperative learning, a relatively recent organizational strategy, is seen by some educators as a potential weapon in reducing sex segregation. This approach is designed to eliminate the negative impact of classroom competition while increasing heterogeneous student relationships. Heterogeneous student groups work and are evaluated on a group as well as individual basis (Aronson, 1978; DeVries & Edwards, 1974; Okebukola, 1986; Slavin, 1977; Weigel, Wiser, & Cook, 1975), an approach that equalizes status while increasing interdependence and group cohesion (Sharan, Hare, Webb, & Hertz-Lazarowitz, 1980). Cooperative learning attempts to develop strong interpersonal relationships and put these relationships to work to achieve academic objectives (Bossert, 1979; D. Johnson & Johnson, 1974; Shrum & Cheek, 1988). Positive effects of cooperative learning have been focused for increasing cross-race friendships, academic achievement, mainstreaming handicapped students, and developing mutual student concern (Blaney, Stephan, Rosenfield, Aronson, & Sikes, 1977; DeVries & Edwards, 1973; Sharan et al., 1980; Slavin, 1980, 1981; Weigel et al., 1975).

However, perhaps because race desegregation and mainstreaming are viewed as more critical educational objectives, there has been less assessment of cooperative learning on promoting cross-sex interaction. Yet, the body of research suggests a clear need to investigate cross-gender learning situations (Lee & Bryk, 1986; Thorne, 1985; Thorne & Luria, 1983, 1986; Weisfeld, Weisfeld, Warren, & Freedman, 1983; Wilkinson, Lindow, & Chiang, 1985).

Peterson and Fennema (1985) found that competitive classroom climates may be more helpful to male academic achievement than female academic achievement. Cognitive gain for girls was negatively related to the frequency of competitive interactions and positively related to the frequency of opportunities for individualized or cooperative learning. However, not all studies show that cooperative learning is a positive instructional strategy for girls. Positive cross-ethnic and handicap-non-handicap relationships may be easier to promote than positive relationships between males and females (Cooper, Johnson, Johnson, & Wilderson, 1980). Differing friendships and communication patterns between males and females emerge as challenges to the effectiveness of cooperative learning. Hallinan (1977), Best (1983), Eccles-Parsons (1984), and Hallinan and Tuma (1978) report on the high degree of sex segregation and same-sex friendships in the elementary and middle school years. M. Lockheed, Finkelstein, and Harris (1979) found that over 65% of elementary students surveyed preferred single-sex work groups. From nursery school through adolescence, studies report on the strong and pervasive disposition of students to form sex-segregated work groups, play groups, and friendships. Moreover, females are more likely to use indirect communication patterns, such as questioning and speech tentativeness, whereas males are more likely to dominate conversations, make declarative statements, and even interrupt (Eakins & Eakins, 1978; Henley & Thorne, 1977; Lakoff, 1976; Savin-Williams, 1976). The preference for same-sex friendships and dominant-submissive language styles creates unique barriers to effective cooperative learning groups.

In one study, M. Lockheed and Harris (1984) found that the infrequent use of small, unstructured work groups was not effective in reducing gender stereotypes, and, in fact, could increase sex stereotyping. In their analysis of 29 classrooms, Lockheed and Harris concluded that cooperative groups provided boys with leadership experiences that strengthened their self-perceptions. Male students viewed themselves as problem solvers and leaders and viewed females as followers. Girls involved in these groups were actually less likely to want to work in mixed-sex groups in the future. However, other studies by the same researchers (M. Lockheed & Harris, 1982) had reported previously that students in mixed-sex science groups expressed more positive attitudes toward cross-sex collaboration, showed a reduced level of sex stereotyping, and were less sex-biased in their perceptions of student competence than students with less cross-sex collaborative experiences. Other studies indicate a decrease in female achievement, academic and physical, when females are placed in mixed-sex groups (Weisfeld et al., 1983), or indicate that pupils actually develop negative attitudes about mixed-sex groups (M. Lockheed, 1984; Serbin, Tonick, & Sternglanz, 1977) or the need to devise special strategies to overcome these barriers (Fennema & Peterson, 1985; Fennema, Reyes, Perl, Konsin, & Drakenberg, 1980; Fennema, Wolleat, Pedro, & Becker, 1981).

Several studies have suggested explanations for the different performance of males and females in cooperative learning groups, and they shed some light on the reasons for different gender-related findings concerned with the efficacy of such groups on female performance and attitudes. For instance, subject matter mastery may affect the educational impact of cooperative learning; M. Lockheed and Hall (1976) found that intragroup dominance was likely when high school students had no previous experience with the material discussed. However, when students had previous experience with the material, male dominance was less likely.

Another explanation for male and female cooperative learning performance differences concerns communication differences. In small groups males were more successful than females in obtaining help when requested. Females were responsive to male requests for help. When females asked males for help and explanations, they were frequently ignored. These patterns were particularly characteristic of high achievement groups (Wilkinson et al., 1985).

Some researchers suggest that within cooperative learning, as well as other settings, gender may operate as a status characteristic (Berger, Cohen, & Zelditch, 1972; Berger, Conner, & Fisek, 1974). Therefore, males might hold positions of power and prestige within the group (M. Lockheed & Hall, 1976; M. Lockhead & Harris, 1984) and exhibit their social dominance by being selective in choosing to whom they talk. This hypothesis is particularly pertinent to high achieving males and content areas stereotyped as masculine, such as mathematics (Fennema & Sherman, 1978; Fox, 1977; Peterson, Wilkinson, Spinelli, & Swing, 1984;

Reyes & Fennema, 1981). Others have looked to the culturally encouraged female inhibition and deference in mixed-sex groups (Lever, 1976; Maltz & Borker, 1983; Weisfeld et al., 1983), the negative relationships between cooperative female behaviors and achievement (Engelhard & Monsaas, 1989), or the degree of competition that is productive rather than destructive to group cohesion and performance (Warring, Johnson, Maruyama, & Johnson, 1985). Unlike the research on cross-race relations, the success of cooperative learning on cross-gender relationships and performance is less consistent.

The different and contradictory findings of the relatively few studies analyzing cross-gender performance in cooperative learning organizations suggest that, by itself, the implementation of cooperative learning groups does not necessarily lead to a more equitable and effective learning environment for females. In fact, the data suggest that educators need to attend to the impact of extensive sex segregation and culturally inspired differences between male and female students in researching relevant cooperative learning variables and organizing effective cooperative learning groups. Recommendations for attaining gender equity within cooperative learning range from teacher structuring and monitoring student interactions to teaching females to be more precise and direct in their communication patterns (N. Webb & Kenderski, 1985). Scott (1985) suggests that teachers use small, mixed-sex groups more frequently, monitor and remediate problems, demonstrate a strong commitment to mixed gender work groups, and teach directly about the restrictions of sex stereotyping and different gender communication patterns. Scott and others believe that without intentional teacher behaviors such as these, equitable relationships and interactions may not be fostered in cooperative learning environments.

GENDER DIFFERENCES IN INTELLECTUAL ABILITIES

By the mid-1800s, most students were attending coeducational schools but were entering a largely gender segregated world of work. Throughout the next century, gender differences in intellectual abilities and personality characteristics were assumed to be biologically determined, and these assumptions resulted in career and lifestyle destiny, with women "naturally" suited to a limited range of roles. As late as the mid–20th century, elementary school boys, in general, envisioned a wide range of future careers, but girls aspired to only four occupational paths—teacher, nurse, secretary, or mother. Moreover, their commitment to professional careers declined during high school and college (Bruemmer, 1969; Hawley, 1971; O'Hara, 1962; Slocum & Bowles, 1968).

During the second half of the 20th century, the idea of naturally determined roles for women and men was shaken as the nation, more technologically oriented and facing new challenges in a global arena, was increasingly willing to draw its labor force from diverse talent pools, including women. In 1974 Maccoby and Jacklin published their landmark book, *The Psychology of Sex Differences;* after a comprehensive literature review, these researchers concluded that most assumptions about psychological sex differences were myths or that there was insufficient research evidence to support them. However, Maccoby and Jacklin did determine that there were fairly well-established differences in quantitative, spatial, and verbal abilities, with males favored in the first two and females in the latter. They and other researchers also established that these differences were relatively modest, with greater range within gender than between genders. From the perspective of the 1990s, *The Psychology of Sex Differences* may seem unremarkable, even serving to support arguments for stereotypic gender roles and a gender-divided world of work. However, within the context of the 1970s, the book sounded an early challenge to entrenched stereotypes.

The work of Maccoby and Jacklin and subsequent researchers sparked a classic nature-nurture debate over the reasons for gender differences. Those turning to biological mechanisms noted that exposure to adrenal/gonadal hormones might result in biological gender differences (Geary, 1989; Resnick, Berenbaum, Gottesman, & Bouchard, 1986). The cerebral cortex, they argued, is divided into two hemispheres specialized for different mental processes, with the left side controlling language and other sequential skills and the right side controlling spatial relations. Males have greater right-hemisphere specialization, and this dominance of the right cerebral hemisphere may explain their superior performance in spatial visualization (Dimond & Beaumont, 1974; Seward & Seward, 1980; Springer & Deutsch, 1981; Wheatley, Mitchell, Frankland, & Kraft, 1978). According to Restak (1979), measurement of brain activity showed that boys activate only the right hemisphere of the brain, but female test takers activate both hemispheres, demonstrating that "spatial ability is more widely dispersed in the female brain" (p. 234). Geschwind and Behan (1979) concluded that males are exposed to increasing amounts of in utero testosterone, which inhibits the development of the left hemisphere and causes the right hemisphere to become dominant, thereby encouraging male superiority in spatial abilities. Many researchers have suggested that spatial visualization is related to achievement in math and science, an assertion that remains highly controversial.

Other researchers noted variation in socialization, child rearing, and schooling to explain differences in verbal, quantitative, and spatial skills. In general, their position was as follows. Boys are more likely to play with erector sets, blocks, models, and other construction toys that may yield spatial abilities. They are allowed more independence in negotiating space further from their homes and participate more in sports such as football, which may develop spatial ability. Moreover, differential achievement in math and science could be explained by textbooks, children's literature, television, and other media demonstrating sex-stereotyped roles, with men typically portrayed using science and mathematics. Differential course enrollment, teacher interactions, and counselor and parental expectations encourage stereotypic behavior and a gender gap in academic achievement (Klein, 1985; M. Sadker & Sadker, 1982, 1985b, 1986; see also the previous sections of this chapter).

Recently meta-analytic reviews have shed new light on gender-difference research; these reviews indicate that differences in math, verbal, and spatial skills have been declining over recent years. These changes in sex differences over a small period of time speak against a heavy reliance on biological arguments (Halpern, 1989). In the words of Rosenthal and Rubin, such changes are happening "faster than the gene can travel" (1982, p. 711). The remainder of this section will review findings on the current state of the gender gap in math, science, spatial visualization, and verbal skills.

Quantitative Abilities

In no area has there been more controversy than that concerning the gender gap in quantitative skills. Typically, researchers have found no differences until the age of 10 (Callahan & Clements, 1984; Dossey, Mullis, Lindquist, & Chambers, 1988; McKay, 1979; Siegal, 1968). Those differences that do occur in the early years are found to favor females (Brandon, Newton, & Hammond, 1987; Hawn, Ellet, & Des Jardines, 1981; Potter & Levy, 1968; Shipman, 1972). A mixed pattern emerges in the middle school years, with slight differences in favor of girls (Tsai & Walberg, 1979), slight differences in favor of boys (Hilton & Berglund, 1974), or no differences (Connor & Serbin, 1985). Studies of highly gifted youth are exceptions, with results favoring males (Benbow & Stanley, 1980, 1982; Weiner, 1984). Differences favoring males generally occur during the high school years (Carpenter, Lindquist, Mathews, & Silver, 1983; L. Jones, Burton, & Davenport, 1984; Ramist & Arbeiter, 1986; Swafford, 1980).

Pallas and Alexander (1983) and Wise, Steel, and MacDonald (1979) have suggested that differential course enrollment in mathematics explains these variations. However, other research indicates that differential course participation does not completely account for the gender gap in mathematics achievement (Armstrong, 1981; Benbow & Stanley, 1982; Friedman, 1989; Ramist & Arbeiter, 1986). Female students indicate less interest in mathematics and less understanding of its usefulness (Fennema & Sherman, 1977; Hilton & Berglund, 1974). Some speculate that spatial visualization affects mathematics achievement, but this is an area of great controversy (Armstrong, 1981; Connor & Serbin, 1985; Fennema & Sherman, 1977; Fennema & Tartre, 1985; Pattison & Grieve, 1984; Weiner, 1984).

Since Maccoby and Jacklin's research indicating that sex differences in quantitative abilities were fairly well established, especially by adolescence, new studies suggest that these differences are diminishing. In her meta-analyses, Hyde (1981) also found sex differences in quantitative abilities, but she determined that these differences were not large. Feingold (1988) examined normative data obtained from technical reports and test manuals to analyze current and past sex differences on the eight scales of the Differential Aptitude Test (DAT) and the Preliminary Scholastic Aptitude Test (PSAT). When the DAT and PSAT were normed in 1947 and then again in 1960, gender differences were found on all tests. Currently, however, girls no longer lag in the DAT's numerical ability scale, and they have cut in half the gap on the PSAT-Math. Marsh (1989), in his recent analysis of the High School and Beyond data, found a "relative lack of strong sex differences" (p. 217), with male performance only slightly stronger than female performance in mathematics. In her analysis of seventh- and eighth-grade data from eight countries in the recent International Mathematics Study (IMS), Ethington (1990) concluded that there were "no substantial gender effects . . . and the slight effects shown favored girls more often than boys" (p. 79). Hyde, Fennema, and Lamon (1990) indicate that since 1974, the magnitude of sex differences in quantitative ability has declined. Linn and Hyde (1989) conclude that (p. 19) "average quantitative gender differences have declined to essentially zero" and that "age trends indicate that females are superior at computation at all ages and that differences favoring males on problem-solving emerge in high school." They emphasize that the Scholastic Aptitude Test–Math is idiosyncratic in its indication of larger sex differences favoring males than occur in nationally representative samples.

Friedman (1989) performed a meta-analytic review of 98 studies, contrasting more recent research with the older studies reviewed by Maccoby and Jacklin (1974). She found a "striking" difference between the earlier and the more recent research, with sex differences in quantitative skills favoring males decreasing over time. According to Friedman, SAT-M data, which she considered separately, also support the conclusion that gender differences favoring males in quantitative performance are decreasing over time. Friedman concludes (pp. 205–206):

> The sex difference in favor of males is decreasing over short periods of time. This is evidence for environmental explanation of sex differences, for surely it is not biology but environmental influence that has been changing at the same time that sex differences have been

decreasing. . . . A substantial amount of concrete evidence has been brought to bear against the tenet that women are irreversibly inferior in mathematical capabilities. The second conclusion that can be drawn from the statistical analyses reported here is that the average sex difference is now very small. Whatever the contributions of heredity and environment to the explanation of sex differences in mathematical tasks, the finding that they are now very small should have considerable practical import. Changes in guidance, hiring, and general admission practices, already well under way, should be accelerated in the years to come.

Science

Frequently associated with sex differences in mathematics is a gender gap in science achievement. As Howe and Doody comment (1989):

It is no longer news that boys score higher than girls on large scale science tests. This sex related difference has now been documented so often and so well that it is not an artifact of testing or testing procedures. (p. 703)

According to Benbow and Minor (1986), gender differences in science and achievement are found in highly able populations and may be related to mathematical reasoning; the greatest gender difference is in the area of physics.

Some researchers suggest that, as with mathematics, the gender gap in science achievement is related to sex differences in spatial functioning, a factor that may have a biological component. Those who take a primarily sociocultural perspective note that (a) males take more advanced science courses; (b) science, like math, is considered a male domain; (c) textbooks omit females from narrative and pictures and show few women in careers as scientists; (d) boys evidence more positive attitudes toward science and are more likely to interact with the teacher and participate in experiments in science class; and (e) males rate the environment in science classes more positively than do females (see prior sections of this chapter).

According to Linn and Hyde (1989), meta-analytic reviews show that the gender gap in science is also decreasing. They note that sex differences for science processes are not as great as for science knowledge and appear related to learning opportunities both inside and outside of school. In the general population, when science knowledge is distinguished from science processes, sex differences occur only on science knowledge (Hueftle, Rakow, & Welch, 1983; Zimmerer & Bennett, 1987).

Spatial Abilities

After a thorough review of the literature, Maccoby and Jacklin (1974) concluded that spatial ability was an area of reliable sex difference favoring males. Other researchers have supported this conclusion (Harris, 1981; Liben, 1981; Sherman, 1980). Although it has been frequently asserted that differences in spatial abilities contribute to gender differences in math and science, recent meta-analyses provide no support for this hypothesis. Instead, they reveal:

> (a) Gender differences occur on spatial processes not obviously related to science or mathematics, (b) gender differences in spatial ability are declining, and (c) processes revealing gender differences in spatial ability respond to training. (Linn & Hyde, 1989, p. 18)

Spatial ability is a broad category consisting of a variety of diverse tasks. In their meta-analysis of gender differences in spatial abilities, Linn and Peterson (1985) concluded that in the area of spatial visualization, the process of reasoning about spatially presented information, gender differences have been declining to the extent that they no longer exist. This finding is supported by Feingold (1988) and, in earlier work, by Rosenthal and Rubin (1982). However, gender differences continue to appear in abilities of mental rotation, the process of rapidly rotating a figure through space.

Several studies indicate that spatial abilities respond to training (Baenninger & Newcombe, 1989; Ben-Chaim, Lappen, & Houang, 1988). Baenninger and Newcombe (1989) performed two series of meta-analyses indicating that spatial experience is related to good performance on spatial tests. For both sexes, participation in spatial activities was related, at least weakly, to spatial ability. Baenninger and Newcombe (1989) stress the need to strengthen measures designed to assess spatial activity participation with preschool and school-aged populations to better determine whether early spatial activity promotes better spatial performance in later life (Connor & Serbin, 1977).

In a second meta-analysis, Baenninger and Newcombe (1989) found that direct, test-specific spatial training appears to offer fairly strong but perhaps narrow improvement for both genders on spatial test scores. Both males and females profit from spatial training. It is important to note that whereas schools offer education in verbal, quantitative, and science skills, training for spatial abilities is rarely an integral part of the school curriculum; such omission continues the disadvantage of female students in this area.

Verbal Abilities

Gender differences in verbal skills, claiming superiority for females throughout the life cycle, have been established as psychological fact and transmitted through highly regarded texts such as Anastasi's *Differential Psychology* (1958) and Tyler's *The Psychology of Human Differences* (1965). Maccoby and Jacklin (1974) differed from these prior assertions in their conclusion of no gender difference in the early years; however, they noted divergence in verbal ability at approximately age 11, with female verbal superiority increasing throughout high school and perhaps beyond. In general, more recent reviews (Denno, 1982; Halpern, 1986) support these conclusions, which continue to be reported in widely read psychology texts (Mussen, Conger, Kagan, & Huston, 1984).

To extend knowledge about gender differences in verbal ability, Hyde and Linn (1988) performed a meta-analysis comparing the Maccoby and Jacklin studies (1974) to those reported more recently. They omitted a large single study providing data for Scholastic Aptitude Test (SAT) takers in 1985 (Ramist & Arbeiter, 1986) because the enormous number of subjects overshadowed other studies considered in the meta-analysis. Hyde and Linn found that the sex difference was significantly smaller in more recent studies and concluded (1988, p. 62):

> We are prepared to assert that there are not gender differences in verbal ability at least at this time, in American culture, in the standard ways that verbal ability has been measured. . . . A gender difference of one tenth of a standard deviation is scarcely one that deserves continued attention in theory, research, or textbooks.

Other investigations support the Linn and Hyde conclusions (Feingold, 1988; Rosenthal & Rubin, 1982). Hyde and Linn (1988) also note that the reversal on the verbal section of the Scholastic Aptitude Test (SAT-V), with boys outscoring girls since 1972, may reflect the inclusion in recent years of more technical items, on which boys usually do better. They also cite the larger numbers of disadvantaged females, as judged by parental income and education, taking the SAT in the years being studied.

The College Board Report, Sex Differences in Test Performance: A Survey of the Literature summarizes the research on intellectual gender differences as follows:

> Insofar as there is convergence among the studies (and there continues to be controversy about many of the major findings), it is that the disparities between the sexes are slowly (perhaps too slowly for some) diminishing. Males appear to have caught up with females on tests of verbal ability and achievement to the point where the absolute differences can be considered insignificant. And females have gained on but not equalled males in performance of mathematics ability and achievement, accompanied by increases in their participation in mathematics and their interest and self-confidence in that domain. With the exception of some limited domains of spatial ability and performance at the top levels of mathematics achievement, women are improving their position relative to men. In nationally representative samples, against a backdrop of declining performance through the early 1980s, the tendency for the disparities to have diminished is quite evident. (Wilder & Powell, 1989, pp. 30–31)

Although most assessments indicate that the gender gap is diminishing, legal and scholarly controversy over tests and their findings continues; even small differences can yield significant disparity in financial aid and access to college, graduate schools, and professional schools, as well as careers. It is important to question the impact of testing on the shortages of women in math and science fields. It is also worth noting the emphasis on remediating verbal deficits in public schools and the lack of attention to remediating problem areas for female students, such as spatial skills. In fact, academically disabled female students typically exhibit greater deficit than males before they are identified for special services, and less is known about their characteristics and needs (Vogel, 1990).

GENDER EQUITY, TEACHER EDUCATION, AND REFORM

As this chapter indicates, a significant body of research on gender equity in education has mounted over the past two decades; although much of this research has generated interest from the press and lay public, its influence on teacher preparation and education reform remains marginal. For example, M. Sadker and Sadker (1980) analyzed the best-selling teacher education texts published between 1973 and 1978 in the areas of foundations, psychology of education, and teaching methods in reading, language arts, social studies, mathematics, and science. As a result of a line-by-line content analysis, they found that 95% of the 24 most widely used teacher education textbooks devoted less than 1% of book space to the issue of sexism. Texts in methods for teaching science and math allocated almost no content to sexism, sex differences, or the experiences and contributions of women. As a result of their analysis, Sadker and Sadker concluded that the nation's future teachers "are being prepared with textbooks more likely to promote and reinforce sex bias than to reduce and eliminate such prejudice" (1980, p. 550).

More recent content analysis of teacher education books is not available, but it is hoped that, as with elementary and secondary texts, trends toward improvement emerged during the 1980s. However, content analysis of influential reports on education reform issued during the 1980s show continued invisibility of gender equity as an issue of educational concern. Tetreault and Schmuck (1985) analyzed *A Nation at Risk*, *Making the Grade*, *Action for Excellence*, *A Place Called School*, *The Good High School*, and *Horace's Compromise* and found little mention of the new scholarship on gender equity in education. M. Sadker, Sadker, and Steindam (1989) conducted a line-by-line content analysis of 138 articles appearing on reform between 1983 and 1987 in nine prominent educational journals. Similar to the teacher education texts published in the 1970s, the articles written about education reform in the 1980s allocated less than 1% of space to gender equity. Not a single article made reference to gender difference in academic performance, and only one discussed sex-differential treatment in curriculum and instruction.

Studies on gender and education, such as those discussed in this chapter, must move into the educational mainstream and inform both policy and practice, and increased attention should stimulate new research to respond to provocative questions and persistent problems. For example, more research is needed on intellectual gender differences and potential bias in assessment instruments. We need to identify factors that lower achievement and self-esteem for girls, especially during early adolescence; this information must be sufficiently broad to address circumstances in various racial and ethnic groups. Although some information on effective interventions is available (Guttentag & Bray, 1976; D. Sadker, Sadker, & Garies, 1980; Scott, 1984), we need greater clarity on characteristics of schools and programs at different levels of education that promote achievement for both male and female students. Questions related to this issue abound. Do females and males exhibit different learning styles, and what are the differences, if any, in moral development? What is the impact of coeducation and single-sex education on male and female students at different stages of development?

Invisibility is one of the most pernicious forms of bias, and gender equity must not remain a blind spot in the process of educational restructuring and reform. If we are to prepare a work force built upon the talent of all of our students, gender equity will need to become a mainstream issue in education research and efforts to reform and restructure schools.

REFERENCES

Adams, G. R., & Cohen, A. S. (1974). Children's physical and interpersonal characteristics that affect student-teacher interactions. *Journal of Experimental Education, 43*, 1–5.

Anastasi, A. (1958). *Differential psychology* (3rd ed.). New York: Macmillan.

Armstrong, J. M. (1981). Achievement and participation of women in mathematics: Results of two national surveys. *Journal for Research in Mathematics Education, 12*, 356–372.

Arnold, L. (1975). Florence Bascom and the exclusion of women from the earth science curriculum materials. *Journal of Geological Education, 23*, 110–113.

Aronson, E. (1978). *The jigsaw classroom*. Beverly Hills, CA: Sage.

Austin, D., Clark, B., & Fitchett, G. (1971). *Reading rights for boys*. New York: Appleton-Century-Crofts.

Ayres, L. (1909). *Laggards in our schools*. New York: Russell Sage Foundation.

Baenninger, M., & Newcombe, N. (1989). The role of experience in spatial test performance: A meta-analysis. *Sex Roles, 20*, 327–344.

Bailey, S., & Smith, R. (1982). *Policies for the future: State policies, regulations, and resources related to the achievement of educational equity for females and males*. Washington, DC: Chief State School Offices.

Baker, D. (1986). Sex differences in classroom interactions in secondary science. *Journal of Classroom Interaction, 22*, 212–218.

Bank, B., Biddle, B., & Good, T. (1980). Sex roles, classroom instruction, and reading achievement. *Journal of Educational Psychology, 72*, 119–132.

Baptiste, H. P., Waxman, H. C., Walker de Felix, J., & Anderson, J. E. (Eds.). (1990). *Leadership, equity, and school effectiveness*. Newbury Park, CA: Sage.

Barclay, K. L. (1974). The emergence of vocational expectations in preschool children. *The Journal of Vocational Behavior, 4*, 174.

Bar-Tal, D. (1978). Attributional analysis of achievement-related behavior. *Review of Educational Research, 48*, 259–271.

Bar-Tal, D., & Frieze, I. (1977). Achievement motivation for males and females as a determinant of attributions for success and failure. *Journal of Sex Roles, 3*, 301–313.

Bean, J. P. (1976, April). *What is happening in mathematics and science classrooms: Student-teacher interaction.* Paper presented at the annual meeting of the American Educational Research Association, San Francisco.

Becker, J. (1979). *A study of differential treatment of females and males in mathematics classes.* Unpublished doctoral dissertation, University of Maryland.

Becker, J. R. (1981). Differential treatment of females and males in mathematics classes. *Journal for Research in Mathematics Education, 12*, 40–53.

Bell, C. S., & Chase, S. S. (1990). *Women's educational leadership: A study of superintendents and gatekeepers.* (A proposal submitted to the U.S. Department of Education Field Initiated Studies Program)

Benbow, C. P., & Minor, L. (1986). Mathematically talented males and females and achievement in the high school sciences. *American Educational Research Journal, 23*, 425–436.

Benbow, C. P., & Stanley, J. C. (1980). Sex differences in mathematical ability: Fact or artifact? *Science, 210*, 1262–1264.

Benbow, C. P., & Stanley, J. C. (1982). Consequences in high school of sex differences in mathematical reasoning ability: A longitudinal perspective. *American Educational Research Journal, 19*, 598–622.

Ben-Chaim, D., Lappen, G., & Houang, R. (1988). The effect of instruction on spatial visualization skills of middle school boys and girls. *American Educational Research Journal, 25*, 51–71.

Berg-Cross, L., & Berg-Cross, G. (1978). Listening to stories may change children's attitudes. *Reading Teacher, 31*, 659–663.

Berger, J., Cohen, B. P., & Zelditch, M., Jr. (1972). Status conceptions and social interaction. *American Sociological Review, 37*, 241–255.

Berger, J., Conner, T. L., & Fisek, M. H. (Eds.). (1974). *Expectation states theory: A theoretical research program.* Cambridge, MA: Winthrop.

Berk, L. E., & Lewis, N. C. (1977). Sex role and social behavior in four school environments. *Elementary School Journal, 3*, 205–217.

Berliner, D. (1984). The half-full glass: A review of research on teaching. In P. Hosferd (Ed.), *Using what we know about teaching.* Alexandria, VA: Association for Supervision and Curriculum Development.

Best, R. (1983). *We've all got scars.* Bloomington: Indiana University Press.

Biklen, S. K. (1980). Introduction: Barriers to equity—Women, educational leadership, and social change. In S. K. Biklen & M. B. Brannigan (Eds.), *Women and educational leadership.* Lexington, MA: Lexington Books, D. C. Heath and Co.

Bikson, T. K. (1974). *Minority speech as objectively measured and subjectively evaluated.* Bethesda, MD: ERIC Document Reproduction Service, ED 131 135.

Blaney, N. T., Stephan, C., Rosenfield, D., Aronson, E., & Sikes, J. (1977). Interdependence in the classroom: A field study. *Journal of Educational Psychology, 69*, 121–128.

Bleakley, M., Westerberg, V., & Hopkins, K. (1988). The effect of character of sex on story interest and comprehension in children. *American Educational Research Journal, 25*, 145–155.

Boersma, P., Gay, D., Jones, R., & Morrison, L. (1981). Sex differences in college student-teacher interactions: Fact or fantasy? *Sex Roles, 7*, 775–784.

Bossert, S. (1979). *Task structures and social relationships*. Cambridge, MA: Cambridge University Press.

Bottomley, J., & Ormerod, M. B. (1981). Stability and lability in science interest from middle schools to the age of science choices (14+). *European Journal of Science Education, 3*, 329–338.

Brandon, P., Newton, B., & Hammond, O. (1987). Children's mathematics achievement in Hawaii: Sex differences favoring girls. *American Educational Research Journal, 24*, 437–461.

Britton, G. (1975). Danger: State adopted texts may be hazardous to our future. *The Reading Teacher, 29*, 52–58.

Britton, G., & Lumpkin, M. (1977). For sale: Subliminal bias in textbooks. *Reading Teacher, 31*, 40–45.

Brophy, J. E. (1981). Teacher praise: A functional analysis. *Review of Educational Research, 51*, 5–32.

Brophy, J. (1985). Interactions of male and female students with male and female teachers. In L. Wilkinson & C. Marrett (Eds.), *Gender influences in classroom interactions*. Orlando, FL: Academic Press.

Brophy, J., & Good, T. (1969). *Teacher-child dyadic interaction: A manual for coding classroom behavior* (Report Series No. 27). Austin: The University of Texas, Research and Development Center for Teacher Education.

Brophy, J. E., & Good, T. L. (1970). Teachers' communication of differential expectations for children's classroom performance: Some behavioral data. *Journal of Educational Psychology, 61*, 365–374.

Brophy, J., & Good, T. (1974). *Teacher-student relationships: Causes and consequences*. New York: Holt, Rinehart & Winston.

Bruemmer, L. (1969). The condition of women in society today: A review—Part I. *Journal of the National Association of Women, Deans and Counselors, 33*(1), 18–22.

Byers, P., & Byers, H. (1972). Nonverbal communication and the education of children. In C. B. Cazden, V. P. John, & D. Hymes (Eds.), *Functions of language in the classroom*. New York: Academic Press.

Calabrase, R. L., & Wallich, L. (1989). Attribution: The male rationale for denying women access into school administration. *High School Journal, 72*(3), 105–110.

Callahan, L. G., & Clements, D. H. (1984). Sex differences in rote-counting ability on entry to first grade: Some observations. *Journal for Research in Mathematics Education, 15*, 378–382.

Carpenter, T. P., Lindquist, M. M., Mathews, W., & Silver, E. A. (1983). Results of the third NAEP mathematics assessment: Secondary school. *Mathematics Teacher, 76*, 652–659.

Chase, D. J. (1972). Sexism in textbooks? *Nations Schools, 90*, 31–35.

Cherry, L. (1975). The preschool teacher-child dyad: Sex differences in verbal interaction. *Child Development, 46*, 532–535.

Choy, S. J., & Dodd, D. H. (1976). Standard-English-speaking and nonstandard Hawaiian-English-speaking children: Comprehension of both dialects and teachers' evaluations. *Journal of Educational Psychology, 68*, 184–193.

Christian-Smith, L. (1989). New directions for curriculum content. *Contemporary Education, 61*, 11–14.

Clifford, M. M., & Walster, E. (1973). Research note: The effect of physical attractiveness on teacher expectations. *Sociology of Education, 46*, 248–258.

Connor, J. M., & Serbin, L. A. (1977). Behaviorally based masculine and feminine activity preference scales for preschoolers: Correlates with other classroom behaviors and cognitive tests. *Child Development, 48*, 1411–1416.

Connor, J. M., & Serbin, L. A. (1985). Visual-spatial skill: Is it important for mathematics? Can it be taught? In S. F. Chipman, L. R. Brush, & D. M. Wilson (Eds.), *Women and mathematics: Balancing the equation* (pp. 151–174). Hillsdale, NJ: Erlbaum.

Cooper, L., Johnson, D. W., Johnson, R., & Wilderson, F. (1980). The effects of cooperation, competition, and individualization on cross-ethnic, cross-sex, and cross-ability friendships. *Journal of Social Psychology, 111*, 243–252.

Corbin, C. B., Landers, D. M., Feltz, D. L., & Senior, K. (1983). Sex differences in performance estimates: Female lack of confidence vs. male boastfulness. *Research Quarterly for Exercise and Sport, 54*, 407–410.

Cosper, W. (1970). *An analysis of sex differences in teacher-student interaction as manifest in verbal and nonverbal cues*. Unpublished doctoral dissertation, University of Tennessee.

Council of Chief State School Officers Resource Center on Educational Equity. (1990, January). A concern about school restructuring for improved learning by all students, particularly those at risk of school failure. *Concerns, 29*.

Coursen, D., Massarella, J. A., Jeffress, L., & Hadderman, M. (1989). Two special cases: Women and blacks. In S. C. Smith & P. K. Piele (Eds.), *School leadership: Handbook for excellence* (2nd ed., pp. 85–106). ERIC Clearinghouse on Educational Management, ED 309 506.

Crandall, V. C. (1969). Sex differences in expectancy of intellectual and academic reinforcement. In C. P. Smith (Ed.), *Achievement-related behaviors in children*. New York: Russell Sage Foundation.

Crowl, T. K. (1971). White teachers' evaluations of oral responses given by white and Negro ninth grade males. *Dissertation Abstracts International, 31*, 4540-A.

Daminco, S. B., & Scott, E. (1988). Behavior differences between black and white females in desegregated schools. *Equity and Excellence, 23*, 63–66.

Davis, O. L., Ponder, G., Burlbaw, L., Garza-Lubeck, M., & Moss, A. (1986). A review of U.S. history textbooks. *The Education Digest, 52*, 50–53.

Deaux, K. (1976). Sex: A perspective on the attribution process. In J. Harvey, W. Ickes, & R. Kidd (Eds.), *New directions in attributional research, 1*. Hillsdale, NJ: Erlbaum.

DeCrow, K. (1972). Look Jane look! See Dick run and jump! Admire him! In S. Anderson (Ed.), *Sex differences and discrimination in education*. Worthington, OH: Charles A. Jones.

DeMeis, D. K., & Turner, R. R. (1978). Effects of students race, physical attractiveness, and dialect on teachers' evaluations. *Contemporary Educational Psychology, 3*, 77–86.

Denno, D. (1982). Sex differences in cognition: A review and critique of the longitudinal evidence. *Adolescence, 17*, 779–788.

DeVries, D. L., & Edwards, K. J. (1973). Learning games and student teams: Their effect on classroom process. *American Educational Research Journal, 10*, 234–242.

DeVries, D. L., & Edwards, K. J. (1974). Student teams and learning games: Their effects on cross-race and cross-sex interaction. *Journal of Educational Psychology, 66*, 741–749.

Dimond, S. J., & Beaumont, J. G. (Eds.). (1974). *Hemisphere function in the human brain*. New York: Wiley.

Dossey, J. A., Mullis, I. V. S., Lindquist, M. M., & Chambers, D. L. (1988). *The mathematics report card: Are we measuring up? Trends and achievement based on the 1986 National Assessment.* Princeton, NJ: Educational Testing Service.

Dougherty, W., & Engel, R. (1987). An 80s look for sex equality in Caldecott winners and Honor Books. *Reading Teacher, 40*, 394–398.

Dowling, D. M. (1978). The development of a mathematics confidence scale and its applications in the study of confidence in women college students (Doctoral dissertation, Ohio State University, 1978). *Dissertation Abstracts International, 39*, 4790A. (University Microfilms No. 79-02,111)

Droney, M. L., Cucchiara, S. M., & Scipione, A. M. (1953). Pupil preferences for titles and stories in basal readers for the intermediate grades. *Journal of Educational Research, 47*, 271–277.

Dusek, J. B., & Joseph, G. (1983). The bases of teacher expectancies: A meta-analysis. *Journal of Educational Psychology, 75*, 327–346.

Dweck, C. S., & Bush, E. S. (1976). Sex differences in learned helplessness: I. Differential debilitation with peer and adult evaluators. *Developmental Psychology, 12*, 147–156.

Dweck, C., Davidson, W., Nelson, S., & Enna, B. (1978). Sex differences in learned helplessness: II. The contingencies of evaluative feedback in the classroom; III. An experimental analysis. *Developmental Psychology, 14*, 268–276.

Dweck, C. S., & Elliot, E. S. (1983). Achievement motivation. In P. Mussen & E. M. Hetherington (Eds.), *Handbook of child psychology* (Vol. 4). New York: Wiley.

Dweck, C., & Goetz, T. (1978). Attributions and learned helplessness. In J. Harvey, W. Ickes, & R. Kidd (Eds.), *New directions in attribution research, 2*. Hillsdale, NJ: Erlbaum.

Dweck, C. S., Goetz, T. E., & Strauss, N. L. (1980). Sex differences in learned helplessness: IV. An experimental and naturalistic study of failure generalization and its mediators. *Journal of Personality and Social Psychology, 38*, 441–452.

Dweck, C.S., & Repucci, N. D. (1973). Learned helplessness and reinforcement responsibility in children. *Journal of Personality and Social Psychology, 25*, 109–116.

Eakins, B. W., & Eakins, R. G. (1978). Sex roles, interruptions, and silences in conversation. In B. Thorne & N. Henley (Eds.), *Sex differences in human communication*. Boston: Houghton Mifflin.

Ebbeck, M. (1984). Equity for boys and girls: Some important issues. *Early Child Development and Care, 18*, 119–131.

Eccles, J., & Blumenfeld, P. (1985). Classroom experiences and student gender: Are there differences and do they matter? In L. C. Wilkinson & C. B. Marrett (Eds.), *Gender influences in classroom interaction* (pp. 79–114). Orlando, FL: Academic Press.

Eccles-Parsons, J. S. (1983). Expectancies, values, and academic choice: Origins and change. In J. Spence (Ed.), *Achievement and achievement motivation*. San Francisco: W. H. Freeman.

Eccles-Parsons, J. (1984). Sex differences in mathematics participation. In M. Steinkamp & M. Maehr (Eds.), *Women in science*. Greenwich, CT: JAI Press.

Eder, D. (1985). The cycle of popularity: Interpersonal relations among female adolescents. *Sociology of Education, 58*, 154–165.

Eder, D., & Hallinan, M. T. (1978). Sex differences in children's friendships. *American Sociological Review, 43*, 237–250.

Edson, S. K. (1988). *Pushing the limits: The female administrative aspirant.* Albany: State University of New York Press.

Emihouvich, C. A. (1983). The color of misbehaving: Two case studies of deviant boys. *Journal of Black Studies, 13*, 259–274.

Engelhard, G., & Monsaas, J. A. (1989). Academic performance, gender, and the cooperative attitudes of third, fifth and seventh graders. *Journal of Research and Development in Education, 22*, 13–17.

Etaugh, C., & Hughes, V. (1975). Teachers' evaluations of sex-typed behaviors in children: The role of teacher sex and school setting. *Developmental Psychology, 11*, 394–395.

Ethington, C. (1990). Gender differences in mathematics: An international perspective. *Journal for Research in Mathematics, 21*, 74–80.

Evertson, C. M., Emmer, E. T., Clements, P. S., Sanford, J. P., & Worsham, M. I. (1984). *Classroom management for elementary teachers.* Englewood Cliffs, NJ: Prentice-Hall.

Feather, N. T., & Simon, J. G. (1973). Fear of success and causal attributions for outcome. *Journal of Personality, 41*, 525–542.

Feingold, A. (1988). Cognitive gender differences are disappearing. *American Psychologist, 43*, 95–103.

Feldman, R. S. (1985). Nonverbal behavior, race, and the classroom teacher. *Theory into Practice, 24*, 45–49.

Felsenthal, H. (1970). *Sex differences in expressive thought of gifted children in the classroom.* Washington, DC: American Educational Research Association.

Felson, R. B. (1984). The effect of self-appraisals of ability on academic performance. *Journal of Personality and Social Psychology, 47*, 944–952.

Feminists on Children's Literature. (1971). A feminist look at children's books. *School Library Journal, 17*, 19–24.

Fennema, E. (1984). Girls, women, and mathematics. In E. Fennema & M. J. Ayer (Eds.), *Women and education: Equity or equality?* (pp. 137–164). Berkeley, CA: McCutchan.

Fennema, E., Peterson, P., Carpenter, T. P., & Lubinski, C. A. (1990). Teachers' attributions and belief about girls, boys, and mathematics. *Educational Studies in Mathematics, 21*, 55–69.

Fennema, E., & Peterson, P. L. (1978). Effective teaching for girls and boys: The same or different? In D. C. Berliner & B. V. Rosenshine (Eds.), *Talks to teachers* (pp. 111–125). New York: Random House.

Fennema, E., & Peterson, P. L. (1985). Autonomous learning behavior: A possible explanation of gender-related differences in mathematics. In L. C. Wilkinson & C. B. Marett (Eds.), *Gender-related differences in classroom interaction.* Orlando, FL: Academic Press.

Fennema, E., Reyes, L. H., Perl, T. H., Konsin, M. A., & Drakenberg, M. (1980, April). *Cognitive and affective influences on the development of sex-related differences in mathematics.* Symposium presented at the annual meeting of the American Educational Research Association, Boston.

Fennema, E., & Sherman, J. (1976). Fennema-Sherman Mathematics Attitude Scales. JSAS: *Catalogue of Selected Documents in Psychology, 6*, 31. (Ms. No. 1225)

Fennema, E., & Sherman, J. (1977). Sex-related differences in mathematics achievement, spatial visualization, and affective factors. *American Educational Research Journal, 14*, 51–57.

Fennema, E., & Sherman, J. (1978). Sex-related differences in mathematics achievement and related factors: A further study. *Journal for Research in Mathematics Education, 9*, 189–203.

Fennema, E., & Tartre, L. A. (1985). The use of spatial visualization in mathematics by girls and boys. *Journal for Research in Mathematics Education, 16*, 184–206.

Fennema, E., Wolleat, P., Pedro, J., & Becker, A. (1981). Increasing women's participation in mathematics: An intervention study. *Journal for Research in Mathematics Education, 12*, 3–14.

Flerx, V., Fidler, D., & Rodgers, R. (1976). Sex-role stereotypes: Developmental aspects and early intervention. *Child Development, 47*, 998–1007.

Forehand, G. Z., Ragosta, M., & Rock, D. A. (1976). *Conditions and processes of effective school desegregation. Final report.* Princeton, NJ: Educational Testing Service.

Fox, L. H. (1977). The effects of sex role socialization on mathematics participation and achievement. In L. H. Fox, E. Fennema, & J. Sherman (Eds.), *Women and mathematics research perspectives for change*. Washington, DC: National Institute of Education.

Frasher, R. S., & Frasher, J. M. (1978). Influence of story character's roles on comprehension. *Reading Teacher, 32*, 160–164.

Frasher, R. S., & Walker, A. (1972). Sex roles in early reading textbooks. *Reading Teacher, 25*, 741–749.

Frazier, N., & Sadker, M. (1973). *Sexism in school and society*. New York: Harper and Row.

Frey, K. S., & Ruble, D. N. (1987). What children say about classroom performance: Sex and grade differences in perceived competence. *Child Development, 58*, 1066–1078.

Friedan, B. (1964). The feminine mystique. New York: Dell.

Friedman, L. (1989). Mathematics and the gender gap: A meta-analysis of recent studies on sex differences in mathematical tasks. *Review of Educational Research, 59*, 185–213.

Gallagher, V. G. (1980). *A comparative study of the female image in selected elementary school science textbooks*. Unpublished doctoral dissertation, University of the Pacific.

Gardner, A. L., Mason, C. L., & Matyas, M. L. (1989). Equity, excellence & just plain good teaching! *The American Biology Teacher, 51*, 72–77.

Geary, D. (1989). Comment: A model for representing gender differences in the pattern of cognitive-abilities. *American Psychologist, 44*, 1155–1156.

Gersoni-Stavn, D. (1975). Feminist criticism: An overview. *School Library Journal, 20*, 22.

Geschwind, N., & Behan, P. (1979). Left-handedness: Association with immune disease, migraine, and developmental learning disorder. *Proceedings of the National Academy of Science of the USA, 79*(13), 5097–5100.

Ginn. (1973). *Treatment of minority groups and women*. New York: Author.

Goetz, J. P. (1981). Children's sex role knowledge and behavior: An ethnographic study of first graders in the rural south. *Theory and Research in Social Education, 8*, 31–54.

Goffman, E. (1977). The arrangement between the sexes. *Theory and Society, 4*, 301–336.

Gollub, W. L., & Sloan, E. (1978). Teacher expectations and race and socioeconomic status. *Urban Education, 13*, 95–106.

Good, T. (1979). Teacher effectiveness in the elementary school. *Journal of Teacher Education, 33*, 55–61.

Good, T. (1981). Teacher expectations and student perceptions: A decade of research. *Educational Leadership, 38*, 415–422.

Good, T., Sikes, J., & Brophy, J. (1973). Effects of teacher sex and student sex on classroom interaction. *Journal of Educational Psychology, 65*, 74–87.

Goodlad, J. (1984). *A place called school: Prospects for the future*. New York: McGraw-Hill.

Gore, D. A., & Roumagoux, D. V. (1983). Wait-time as a variable in sex-related differences during fourth-grade mathematics instruction. *Journal of Educational Research, 76*, 273–275.

Graebner, D. (1972). A decade of sexism in readers. *Reading Teacher, 26*, 52–58.

Graham, S. (1984). Teacher feeling and student thoughts: An attributional approach to affect in the classroom. *The Elementary School Journal, 85*, 91–104.

Grant, C., & Sleeter, C. (1986). Race, class, and gender in education research: An argument for integrative analysis. *Review of Educational Research, 56*, 195–211.

Grayson, D. A. (1990). *Designing and implementing a research-based intervention program to transform education for the 21st century: An inclusive approach to excellence*. Unpublished dissertation.

Greene, A. L., Sullivan, H. J., & Beyard-Tyler, K. (1982). Attitudinal effects of the use of role models in information about sex-typed careers. *Journal of Educational Psychology, 74*, 393–398.

Gross, N., & Trask, A. E. (1976). *The sex factor and the management of schools*. New York: Wiley.

Guttentag, M., & Bray, H. (1976). *Undoing sex stereotypes: Research and resources for educators*. New York: McGraw-Hill.

Hall, R. M., & Sandler, B. R. (1982). *The classroom climate: A chilly one for women?* Washington, DC: Association of American Colleges.

Hallinan, M. T. (1977). *The evolution of children's friendship cliques*. (ERIC Document Reproduction Service No. ED 161 556)

Hallinan, M. T., & Tuma, N. B. (1978). Classroom effects on change in children's friendship. *Sociology of Education, 51*, 170–282.

Halpern, D. F. (1986). *Sex differences in cognitive abilities*. Hillsdale, NJ: Erlbaum.

Halpern, D. (1989). The disappearance of cognitive gender differences: What you see depends on where you live. *American Psychologist, 44*, 1156–1157.

Hammer, C., & Gerald, E. (1990). *Selected characteristics of public and private school administrators (principals): 1987–88*. Washington, DC: National Center for Education Statistics, Office of Educational Research and Improvement, U.S. Department of Education.

Hansot, E., & Tyack, D. (1988). Gender in American public schools. *Signs: Journal of Women in Culture and Society, 13*, 741–760.

Harris, L. J. (1981). Sex-related variations in spatial skill. In L. S. Liben, A. H. Patterson, & N. Newcombe (Eds.), *Spatial representation and behavior across the life span: Theory and application*. New York: Academic Press.

Hawley, P. (1971). What women think men think. *Journal of Counseling Psychology, 18*, 193–194.

Hawn, H. C., Ellet, C. D., & Des Jardines, L. (1981, April). *Differences in mathematics achievement between males and females in grades 1–3*. Paper presented at the annual meeting of the Eastern Educational Research Association, Philadelphia.

Heikkinen, H. (1978). Sex bias in chemistry texts: Where is a woman's place. *The Science Teacher, 45*, 16–21.

Henley, N., & Thorne, B. (1977). Woman speak and man speak: Sex differences and sexism in communications, verbal and nonverbal. In A. Sargent (Ed.), *Beyond sex roles*. St. Paul, MN: West Publishing Company.

Hilton, T. L., & Berglund, G. W. (1974). Sex differences in mathematics achievement—A longitudinal study. *Journal of Educational Research, 67*, 232–237.

Hitchcock, M. E., & Tompkins, G. E. (1987). Basal readers: Are they still sexist? *Reading Teacher, 29*, 764–767.

Holt, Rinehart, & Winston. (1975). *Guidelines for the development of elementary and secondary instructional materials: The treatment of sex roles*. New York: Author.

Honig, A. S., & Wittmer, D. S. (1982). Teacher questions to male and female toddlers. *Early Child Development and Care, 9*, 19–32.

Houghton Mifflin. (1975). *Avoiding stereotypes*. Boston: Author.

Howe, A., & Doody, W. (1989). Spatial visualization and sex-related differences in science achievement. *Science Education, 73*, 703–709.

Hrdy, S. (1981). *The woman that never evolved*. Cambridge, MA: Harvard University Press.

Hueftle, S. J., Rakow, S. J., & Welch, W. W. (1983). *Images of science*. Minneapolis: University of Minnesota, Science Assessment and Research Project.

Hurwitz, R. E., & White, M. A. (1977). Effect of sex-linked vocational information on the reported occupational choices of high school juniors. *Psychology of Women Quarterly, 2*, 149–156.

Hyde, J. S. (1981). How large are cognitive gender differences? A meta-analysis using w^2 and d. *American Psychologist, 36*, 892–901.

Hyde, J. S., Fennema, E., & Lamon, S. J. (1990). Gender difference in mathematics performance: A meta-analysis. *Psychological Bulletin, 107*, 139–155.

Hyde, J. S., & Linn, M. C. (1988). Gender differences in verbal activity: A meta-analysis. *Psychological Bulletin, 104*, 53–69.

Jennings, S. A. (1975). Effects on sex typing in children's stories on preference and recall. *Child Development, 46*, 220–223.

Johnson, D. M., Peer, G. G., & Baldwin, R. S. (1984). Protagonist preferences among juvenile and adolescent readers. *Journal of Educational Research, 77*, 147–150.

Johnson, D. W., & Johnson, R. T. (1974). Instructional goal structure: Cooperative, competitive, or individualistic. *Review of Educational Research, 44*, 213–240.

Johnson, M., & Crowley, J. (1978). *Women and men on school boards: A summary report to participants in a study of thirty-seven New Jersey boards*. New Brunswick, NJ: Center for the American Woman and Politics, The Eagleton Institute of Politics, Rutgers, The State University.

Johnson, M. C., & Douglas, J. R. (1985). Assessment centers: What impact have they had on career opportunities for women? *NAASP Bulletin, 69*, 105–111.

Jones, E. H., & Montenegro, X. P. (1988). *Women and minorities in school administration facts & figures 1987–88*. Arlington, VA: American Association of School Administrators.

Jones, G. (1989). Gender bias in classroom interactions. *Contemporary Education, 60*, 216–222.

Jones, L. V., Burton, N. W., & Davenport, E. C., Jr. (1984). Monitoring the mathematics achievement of black students. *Journal for Research in Mathematics Education, 15*, 154–164.

Jones, M. G. (1987). *Gender differences in student-teacher interactions in physical science and chemistry classes.* Doctoral dissertation, North Carolina State University.

Jones, M. G. (1989). Gender issues in teacher education. *Journal of Teacher Education, 49,* 33–38.

Jones, M. G., & Wheatley, J. (1989). *Gender differences in teacher-student interactions.* Manuscript submitted for publication.

Jones, V. (1971). *The influence of teacher-student introversion, achievement, and similarity on teacher student dyadic classroom interaction.* Unpublished dissertation, University of Texas.

Kahle, J. B. (1983). *The disadvantaged majority: Science education for women* (AETS outstanding paper). Burlington, NC: Carolina Biological Society.

Kahle, J. B., & Lakes, M. K. (1983). The myth of equality in science classrooms. *Journal of Research in Science Teaching, 20,* 131–140.

Karp, D., & Yoels, W. (1976). The college classroom: Some observations on the meanings of student participation. *Sociology and Social Research, 60,* 421–439.

Kelly, A. (1986). *Gender differences in teacher-pupil interactions: A meta analytic review.* Manuscript submitted for publication.

Key, M. R. (1972). Male and female in children's books—Dispelling all doubts. *Wilson Library Bulletin, 46,* 167–176.

Kinman, J., & Henderson, D. (1985). An analysis of sexism in Newbury Medal Award Books from 1977–1984. *Reading Teacher, 38,* 885–889.

Klein, S. S. (Ed.). (1985). *Handbook for achieving sex equity through education.* Baltimore: Johns Hopkins University Press.

Klein, S. S. (1986). Identifying elements of equity in federal, state and local educational standards. *Equity and Excellence: The University of Massachusetts School of Education Quarterly, 22,* 132–138.

Klein, S. S. (1987). The role of public policy in the education of girls and women. *Educational Evaluation and Policy Analysis, 9,* 219–230.

Klein, S. S. (1988). Using sex equity research to improve education policies. *Theory into Practice, 27,* 152–160.

Koblinsky, S., Cruse, D., & Sugawara, A. (1978). Sex role stereotypes and children's memory for story content. *Children Development, 49,* 452–458.

Kropp, J. J., & Halversen, C. (1983). Preschool children's preference and recall for sex-appropriate and sex-inappropriate stories. *Sex Roles, 9,* 261–272.

Krupnick, C. (1985). Women and men in the classroom. *On Teaching and Learning, 12,* 18–25.

LaFrance, M., & Mayo, C. (1976). Racial differences in gaze behavior during conversation. *Journal of Personality and Social Psychology, 33,* 547–552.

Lakoff, R. (1976). *Languages and women's place.* New York: Harper Colophon Books.

Larrick, N. (1969). The all white world of children's books. *Saturday Review, 48,* 84–85.

Leadership in Educational Administration Development Study Group on Women and Minorities. (1990). *Strengthening support and recruitment of women and minorities to administrative positions: A resource manual.* Washington, DC: National Leadership Network.

Lee, V., & Bryk, A. (1986). Effects of single-sex secondary schools on student achievement and attitudes. *Journal of Educational Psychology, 78,* 381–395.

Leinhardt, G., Seewald, A., & Engel, M. (1979). Learning what's taught: Sex differences in instruction. *Journal of Educational Psychology, 71,* 432–439.

Lenney, E. (1977). Women's self-confidence in achievement settings. *Psychological Bulletin, 84*, 1–13.

Lever, J. (1976). Sex differences in the games children play. *Social Problems, 23*, 478–487.

Liben, L. S. (1981). Spatial visualization and behavior between multiple perspective. In L. S. Liben, A. H. Patterson, & N. Neucombe (Eds.), *Spatial representation and behavior across the life span: Theory and application* (pp. 3–36). New York: Academic Press.

Licht, B. G., Stader, S. R., & Swenson, C. C. (1989). Children's achievement-related beliefs: Effects of academic area, sex, and achievement level. *Journal of Educational Research, 82*, 253–260.

Linn, M. C., & Hyde, J. S. (1989). Gender, mathematics, and science. *Educational Researcher, 18*, 17–19, 22–27.

Linn, M. C., & Peterson, A. C. (1985). Emergence and characterization of sex differences in spatial ability: A meta-analysis. *Child Development, 56*, 1479–1998.

Lockheed, M. (1982, March). *Sex equity in classroom interaction research: An analysis of behavior chains*. Paper presented at the annual meeting of the American Educational Research Association, New York.

Lockheed, M. (1984). *Final report: A study of sex equity in classroom interaction*. Washington, DC: National Institute of Education.

Lockheed, M. (1985). Some detriments and consequences of sex segregation in the classroom. In L. C. Wilkinson & C. B. Marret (Eds.), *Gender influences in classroom interaction*. Orlando, FL: Academic Press.

Lockheed, M. E., Finkelstein, K. J., & Harris, A. M. (1979). *Curriculum and research for equity: Model data package*. Princeton, NJ: Educational Testing Service.

Lockheed, M., & Harris, A. (1989, April). *Classroom interaction and opportunities for cross-sex peer learning in science*. Paper presented at the annual meeting of the American Educational Research Association, New York.

Lockheed, M. E., & Hall, K. P. (1976). Conceptualizing sex as a status characteristic: Applications to leadership training strategies. *Journal of Social Issues, 32*, 111–124.

Lockheed, M. E., & Harris, A. M. (1984). Cross-sex collaborative learning in elementary classrooms. *American Educational Research Journal, 21*, 275–294.

Lockheed, M. F., & Harris, A. M. (1982). Classroom interaction and opportunities for cross-sex peer learning in science. *Journal of Early Adolescence, 2*, 135–143.

Lutes-Duckley, C. J. (1978). Sex-role preferences as a function of sex of story teller and story content. *Journal of Psychology, 100*, 151–158.

Lyles, T. (1966). Grouping by sex. *National Elementary Principal, 46*, 38–41.

Lyons, N. (1983). Two perspectives: On self, relationships, and morality. *Harvard Educational Review, 55*, 125–145.

Maccoby, E. E., & Jacklin, C. N. (1974). *The psychology of sex differences*. Stanford, CA: Stanford University Press.

Macmillan. (1975). *Guidelines for creating positive sexual and racial images in educational materials*. New York: Author.

Mahoney, P. (1983). How Alice's chair really came to be pressed against her foot: Sexist processes of interaction in mixed-sex classrooms. *Women's Studies International Forum, 6*, 107–115.

Maltz, D. N., & Borker, R. A. (1983). A cultural approach to male-female miscommunication. In J. J. Gumperz (Ed.), *Language and social identity*. New York: Cambridge University Press.

Marsh, H. (1989). Sex differences in the development of verbal and mathematics constructs: The High School and Beyond study. *American Educational Research Journal, 26*, 191–225.

Marten, L., & Matlin, M. (1976). Does sexism in elementary readers still exist? *The Reading Teacher, 29*, 764–767.

McArthur, L. A., & Eisen, S.V. (1976). Achievements of male and female storybook characters as determinants of achievement behavior by boys and girls. *Journal of Personality and Social Psychology, 33*, 467–479.

McCarthy, M. M., Kuh, G. D., Newell, L. J., & Iacona, C. M. (1988). *Under scrutiny: The educational administration professorate*. Tempe, AZ: University Council of Educational Administrators.

McCarthy, M. M., & Webb, L. D. (1990). Equity and excellence in educational leadership: A necessary nexus. In H. P. Baptiste, H. C. Waxman, J. Walker de Felix, & J. E. Anderson (Eds.), *Leadership, equity, and school effectiveness* (pp. 9–13). Newbury Park, CA: Sage.

McCune, S., & Matthews, M. (1975). *Programs for educational equity: Schools and affirmative action*. Washington, DC: Office of Education, U.S. Department of Health, Education and Welfare.

McGraw-Hill. (1974). *Guidelines for equal treatment of the sexes in McGraw-Hill Book Company publications*. New York: Author.

McKay, L. R. (1979). Sex differences in cognitive styles and mathematics achievement in fourth and eighth graders (Doctoral dissertation, University of Texas at Austin, 1978). *Dissertation Abstracts International, 39*, 4103A.

Meyer, W. J., & Thompson, G. G. (1956). Sex difference in the distribution of approval and disapproval among sixth-grade children. *Journal of Educational Psychology, 47*, 385–396.

Morse, L. W., & Handley, H. M. (1982). *Relationship of significant others, parental and teacher influences to the development of self-concept, science attitudes and achievement among adolescent girls* (Final Report, NIE-G-79-0159). Mississippi State, MS: Bureau of Educational Research.

Morse, L. W., & Handley, H. M. (1985). Listening to adolescents: Gender differences in science classroom interaction. In L. C. Wilkerson & C. B. Marrett (Eds.), *Gender influences in classroom interaction* (pp. 37–56). Orlando, FL: Academic Press.

Mussen, P. H., Conger, J. J., Kagan, J., & Huston, A. C. (1984). *Child development and personality* (6th ed.). New York: Harper and Row.

National Center for Education Statistics. (1972). *Digest of education statistics*. Washington, DC: U.S. Department of Education.

National Center for Education Statistics. (1989). *Digest of education statistics 1989* (25th ed). Washington, DC: U.S. Department of Education.

National Center for Education Statistics. (1990). *Digest of education statistics 1990* (26th ed). Washington, DC: U.S. Department of Education.

National Coalition for Women and Girls in Education. (1988). *Title IX: A practical guide to achieving sex equity in education*. Washington, DC: National Women's Law Center.

National Commission on Excellence in Education. (1983). *A nation at risk*. Washington, DC: U.S. Government Printing Office.

Nibbelink, W., Stockdale, S., & Mangru, M. (1986). Sex role assignments in elementary school mathematics textbooks. *Arithmetic Teacher, 34*, 19–21.

Nicholls, J. G. (1979). Development of perception of own attainment and causal attribution for success and failure in reading. *Journal of Educational Psychology, 71*, 94–99.

Nilsen, A. P. (1971). Women in children's literature. *College English, 32*, 918–926.

Norvell, G. W. (1958). *What boys and girls like to read.* Morristown, NJ: Silver Burdett.

O'Donnell, R. W. (1973). Sex bias in primary social studies textbooks. *Educational Leadership, 31*, 137–141.

O'Hara, L. (1962). The roots of careers. *Elementary School Journal, 62*, 277–280.

Okebukola, P. A. (1986). Cooperative learning and students' attitude to laboratory work. *Social Science and Mathematics, 86*, 582–590.

Oliver, L. (1974). Women in aprons: The female stereotype in children's readers. *Elementary School Journal, 74*, 253–259.

Oren, D. L. (1983). Evaluation systems and attributional tendencies in the classroom: A sociological approach. *Journal of Educational Research, 76*, 307–312.

Ortiz, F. I. (1982). *Career patterns in education: Women, men and minorities in public school administration.* New York: Praeger.

Ortiz, F. I., & Marshall, C. (1988). Women in educational administration. In N. J. Boyan (Ed.), *Handbook of research on educationl administration: A project of the American Educational Research Association* (pp. 123–141). New York: Longman.

Otto, P. B., & Schuck, R. F. (1983). The effect of a teacher questioning strategy training program on teaching behavior, student achievement, and retention. *Journal of Research in Science Teaching, 20*, 521–528.

Pallas, S. M., & Alexander, K. L. (1983). Sex differences in quantitative SAT performance. New evidence on the differential coursework hypothesis. *American Educational Research Journal, 20*, 165–182.

Parker, L. J., & Shapiro, J. P. (1990, April). *Graduate students' voices on exposure to diversity in educational administration: An analysis for program of change.* Paper presented at the annual meeting of the American Educational Research Association, Boston.

Parsons, J. (1979, April). *The effects of teachers' expectancies and attributions on students' expectancies for success in mathematics.* Paper presented at the annual meeting of the American Educational Research Association, San Francisco.

Parsons, J. E., & Ruble, D. N. (1977). The development of achievement-related expectancies. *Child Development, 48*, 1075–1079.

Pattison, P., & Grieve, N. (1984). Do spatial skills contribute to sex differences in American types of mathematical problems? *Journal of Educational Psychology, 76*, 678–689.

Pavan, B. N. (1985, October). *Certified but not hired: Women administrators in Pennsylvania.* Paper presented at the Annual Research on Women in Education Conference, Boston.

Pavan, B. N. (1989, October). *Searching for female leaders for America's schools. Are the women to blame?* Paper presented at the University Council for Educational Administration convention, Scottsdale, AZ.

Peterson, P. L., & Fennema, E. (1985). Effective teaching, student engagement in classroom activities, and sex-related differences in learning mathematics. *American Educational Research Journal, 22*, 267–288.

Peterson, P. L., Wilkinson, L. C., Spinelli, F., & Swing, S. (1984). Merging the process-product and sociolinguistic paradigms: Research on small-group processes. In P. L. Peterson, L. C. Wilkinson, & M. Hallinan (Eds.), *The social context of instruction: Group organization and group processes*. New York: Academic Press.

Phillips, D. (1984). The illusion of incompetence among academically competent children. *Child Development, 55*, 2000–2016.

Potter, M. C., & Levy, E. (1968). Spatial enumeration without counting. *Child Development, 39*, 265–272.

Powell, R., & Garcia, J. (1985). The portrayal of minorities and women in selected elementary science series. *Journal of Research in Science Teaching, 22*, 519–533.

Purcell, P., & Stewart, L. (1990). Dick and Jane in 1989. *Sex Roles, 22*, 177–185.

Ramist, L., & Arbeiter, S. (1986). *Profiles of college-bound seniors; 1985*. New York: College Entrance Examination Board.

Redfield, D., & Rousseau, E. (1981). A meta-analysis of experimental research on teacher questioning behavior. *Review of Educational Research, 51*, 237–247.

Resnick, S. M., Berenbaum, S. A., Gottesman, I. I., & Bouchard, T. J. (1986). Early hormonal influences on cognitive functioning in congenital adrenal hyperplasia. *Developmental Psychology, 22*, 191–198.

Restak, R. (1979). The other difference between boys and girls. *Educational Leadership, 37*, 232–235.

Reyes, L. H. (1980). Attitudes and mathematics. In M. M. Lindquist (Ed.), *Selected issues in mathematics education* (pp. 161–184). Berkeley, CA: McCutchan.

Reyes, L. H. (1984a). Affective variables and mathematics educations. *Elementary School Journal, 84*, 558–581.

Reyes, L. H. (1984b, August). *Mathematics classroom processes*. Paper presented at the Fifth International Congress on Mathematical Education, Adelaide, Australia.

Reyes, L. H., & Fennema, E. (1981). *Classroom processes: Observer manual*. Madison: Wisconsin Center for Education Research.

Reyes, L. H., & Fennema, E. (1982, April). *Sex and confidence level differences in participation in mathematics classroom processes*. Paper presented at the annual meeting of the American Educational Research Association, New York.

Reyes, L., & Padilla, M. (1985). Science, math and gender. *The Science Teacher, 53*, 46–48.

Richards, C. (1988). The search for equity in educational administration: A commentary. In N. J. Boyan (Ed.), *Handbook of research on educational administration: A project of the American Educational Research Association* (pp. 159–168). New York: Longman.

Ridley, D., & Novak, J. (1983). Sex-related differences in high school and mathematics enrollments: Do they give males a critical headstart toward science- and math-related careers? *Alberta Journal of Educational Research, XXIX*, 308–318.

Rosenthal, R., & Jacobson, L. (1968). *Pygmalian in the classroom: Teacher expectations and pupils' intellectual development*. New York: Holt, Rinehart, and Winston.

Rosenthal, R., & Rubin, D. (1982). Further meta-analytic procedures for assessing cognitive gender differences. *Journal of Educational Psychology, 74*, 708–712.

Rowe, M. B. (1974). Wait-time and rewards as instructional variables: Their influence on language, logic, and fate control (Part 1). *Journal of Research in Science Teaching, 11*, 81–94.

Rowe, M. B. (1986). Wait-time: Slowing down may be a way of speeding up! *Journal of Teacher Education, 37*, 43–50.

Rubin, D. (1975). *Teaching elementary language arts*. New York: Holt, Rinehart, and Winston.

Rubovits, P., & Maehr, M. (1973). Pygmalion black and white. *Journal of Personality and Social Psychology, 25*, 210–218.

Rupley, W. H., Garcia, J., & Longnion, D. (1981). Sex role portrayal in reading materials: Implications for the 1980s. *Reading Teacher, 24*, 786–791.

Saario, T., Jacklin, C., & Tittle, C. (1973). Sex role stereotyping in the public schools. *Harvard Educational Review, 43*, 151–155.

Sadker, D., Sadker, M., & Garies, R. (1980, April). *Development of field testing of nonsexist teacher educational materials*. Paper presented at the annual meeting of the American Educational Research Association, Boston.

Sadker, D., Sadker, M., & Thomas, D. (1981). Sex equity and special education. *The Pointer, 26*, 33–38.

Sadker, M. (1985). *Women in educational administration: The report card #4*. Washington, DC: Mid-Atlantic Center for Sex Equity, The Network, Inc.

Sadker, M., & Sadker, D. (1980). Sexism in teacher education texts. *Harvard Educational Review, 50*, 36–46.

Sadker, M. P., & Sadker, D. M. (1982). *Sex equity handbook for schools*. New York: Longman.

Sadker, M., & Sadker, D. (1984). *Year 3: Final report, promoting effectiveness in classroom instruction*. Washington, DC: National Institute of Education.

Sadker, M., & Sadker, D. (1985a). Is the O.K. classroom O.K.? *Phi Delta Kappan, 66*, 358–361.

Sadker, M., & Sadker, D. (1985b, March). Sexism in the schoolroom of the 80s. *Psychology Today*, pp. 54–57.

Sadker, M., & Sadker, D. (1986). Sexism in the classroom: From grade school to graduate school. *Phi Delta Kappan, 68*, 512.

Sadker, M., & Sadker, D. (1990). Questioning skills. In J. Cooper (Ed.), *Classroom teaching skills*. Lexington, MA: D. C. Heath.

Sadker, M., Sadker, D., & Shakeshaft, C. (1989). Sex, sexism and the preparation of educators. *Peabody Journal of Education, 64*, 213–224.

Sadker, M., Sadker, D., & Steindam, S. (1989). Gender equity and education reform. *Educational Leadership, 46*, 44–47.

Savin-Williams, C. (1976). An ethnological study of dominance formation and maintenance in a group of human adolescents. *Child Development, 47*, 972–979.

Scardina, F. (1972). *Sexism in textbooks in Pittsburgh public schools*. (ERIC Document Reproduction Service No. ED 096224)

Schau, C. (1978, April). *Evaluating the use of sex role-reversed stories for changing children's stereotypes*. Paper presented at the annual meeting of the American Educational Research Association, Toronto, Ontario, Canada.

Schau, C. G., & Scott, K. P. (1984). The impact of gender characteristics on instructional materials: An integration of the research literature. *Journal of Educational Psychology, 76*, 173–183.

Scherr, M. (1986, April). *Women as outsiders within organizations*. Paper presented at the annual meeting of the American Educational Research Association, San Francisco.

Schmitt, N., & Cohen, S. A. (1989). *Criterion-related validity of the National Association of Secondary School Principals' Assessment Center. A report.* East Lansing: Michigan State University.
Schmuck, P. A. (1986). School management and administration: An analysis by gender. In E. Hoyle & A. McMahon (Eds.), *The management of schools: World-yearbook of education 1986* (pp. 173–183). New York: Nichols Publishing Company.
Schmuck, P. A. (1987a). *Women educators: Employees of schools in western countries* (pp. 1–17). Albany: State University of New York Press.
Schmuck, P. A. (1987b). Women school employees in the United States. In P. A. Schmuck (Ed.), *Women educators: Employees of schools in western countries* (pp. 1–17). Albany: State University of New York Press.
Schmuck, P. A., Adkison, J. A., Peterson, B., Bailey, S., Glick, G. S., Klein, S. S., McDonald, S., Schubert, J., & Tarason, S. (1985). Administrative strategies for institutionalizing sex equity in education and the role of government. In S. S. Klein (Ed.), *Handbook for achieving sex equity through education* (pp. 95–123). Baltimore: Johns Hopkins University Press.
Schmuck, P. A., & Schubert, J. (1986, November). *Women administrators' views on sex equity: Exploring issues of information, identity and integration.* Paper presented at the annual meeting of the American Educational Research Association, Washington, DC.
Schnell, T., & Sweeney, T. (1975). Sex role bias in basal readers. *Elementary English, 52*, 735–742.
Schulwitz, B. S. (1976). Coping with sexism in reading materials. *Reading Teacher, 29*, 768–791.
Scott, Foresman. (1972). *Guidelines for improving the image of women in textbooks.* Glenview, IL: Author.
Scott, K. (1980). Sexist and nonsexist materials: What impact do they have? *The Elementary School Journal, 81*, 47–51.
Scott, K. (1984). Effects of an intervention on middle school pupils in decision making, achievement, and sex role flexibility. *Journal of Educational Research, 77*, 369–375.
Scott, K. P. (1985). Social interaction skills: Perspectives on teaching cross-sex communication. *Social Education, 47*, 610–615.
Scott, K. (1986). Effects of sex-fair reading materials on pupils' attitudes, comprehension, and interests. *American Educational Research Journal, 23*, 105–116.
Scott, K. P., & Feldman-Summers, S. (1979). Children's reactions to textbook stories in which females are portrayed in traditionally male roles. *Journal of Educational Psychology, 71*, 396–402.
Scott, K. P., & Schau, C. G. (1985). Sex equity and sex bias instructional materials. In S. S. Klein (Ed.), *Handbook for achieving sex equity through education* (pp. 218–232). Baltimore: Johns Hopkins University Press.
Seligman, M. E. P., & Maier, S. F. (1967). Failure to escape traumatic shock. *Journal of Experimental Psychology, 74*, 1–9.
Serbin, L., & O'Leary, D. (1975, July). How nursery schools teach girls to shut up. *Psychology Today*, pp. 56–58, 102–103.
Serbin, L., O'Leary, K., Kent, R., & Tonick, I. (1973). A comparison of teacher response to the pre-academic and problem behavior of boys and girls. *Child Development, 44*, 796–804.
Serbin, L. A., Tonick, I. J., & Sternglanz, S. H. (1977). Shaping cooperative cross-sex play. *Child Development, 48*, 924–929.

Seward, J. P., & Seward, G. H. (1980). *Sex differences: Mental and temperamental.* Lexington, MA: D. C. Heath.

Sexton, P. (1965, June 19). Are schools emasculating our boys? *Saturday Review,* p. 57.

Sexton, P. (1969). *The feminized male: Classrooms, white collars and the decline of manliness.* New York: Random House.

Shakeshaft, C. (1985). Strategies for overcoming the barriers to women in educational administration. In S. S. Klein (Ed.), *Handbook fo achieving sex equity through education* (pp. 124–144). Baltimore: Johns Hopkins University Press.

Shakeshaft, C. (1987). *Women in educational administration.* Newbury Park, CA: Sage.

Shakeshaft, C. (1988). Women in educational administration: Implications for training. In D. Griffiths, R. T. Stout, & P. B. Forsythe (Eds.), *Leaders for America's schools: The report and papers of the National Commission on Excellence in Educational Administration* (pp. 403–416). Berkeley, CA: McCutchan.

Shakeshaft, C. (1990). Administrative preparation for equity. In H. P. Baptiste, H. C. Waxman, J. Walker de Felix, & J. E. Anderson (Eds.), *Leadership, equity, and school effectiveness* (pp. 213–223). Newbury Park, CA: Sage.

Sharan, S., Hare, P., Webb, C. D., & Hertz-Lazarowitz, R. (Eds.). (1980). *Cooperation in education.* Provo, UT: Brigham Young University Press.

Shephard, W., & Hess, D. (1975). Attitudes in four age groups toward sex role division in adult occupations and activities. *Journal of Vocational Behavior, 6,* 27–39.

Sherman, J. A. (1980). Mathematics, spatial visualization, and related factors: Changes in girls and boys, grades 8–11. *Journal of Educational Psychology, 72,* 476–482.

Shipman, V. C. (1972). *Disadvantaged children and their first school experiences* (Head Start Longitudinal Study Report PR-72-18). Princeton, NJ: Educational Testing Service.

Shrum, W., & Cheek, N., Jr. (1988). Friendship in school: Gender and racial homophilid. *Sociology of Education, 61,* 227–239.

Siegal, L. S. (1968). The development of the ability to process information. *Journal of Experimental Child Psychology, 6,* 368–383.

Sikes, J. N. (1971). Differential behavior of male and female teachers with male and female students. *Dissertation Abstracts International,* 33, Sec 1A. (University Microfilms No. 72-1967)

Simpson, A. W., & Erickson, M. T. (1983). Teachers' verbal and nonverbal communication patterns as a function of teacher race, student gender, and student race. *American Educational Research Journal, 20,* 183–198.

Slavin, R. E. (1977). How student learning teams can integrate the desegregated classroom. *Integrated Education, 15,* 56–58.

Slavin, R. E. (1980). Cooperative learning. *Review of Educational Research, 50,* 315–342.

Slavin, R. E. (1981). Cooperative learning and desegregation. In W. Hawley (Ed.), *Effective school desegregation.* Berkeley, CA: Sage.

Slocum, W., & Boles, R. (1968). Attractiveness of occupations to high school students. *Personnel and Guidance Journal, 46,* 754–761.

Smith, N., Greenlaw, M., & Scott, C. (1987, January). Making the literate environment equitable. *Reading Teacher,* pp. 400–407.

Smith, R. P., & Denton, J. J. (1980). The effects of dialect, ethnicity and orientation to sociolinguistics on the perceptions of teaching candidates. *Education Research Quarterly, 5*, 70–79.

Spaulding, R. (1963). *Achievement, creativity, and self-concept correlates of teacher-pupil transactions in elementary school* (Cooperative Research Project No. 1352). Washington, DC: U.S. Department of Health, Education and Welfare.

Springer, S. P., & Deutsch, G. (1981). *Left brain, right brain.* San Francisco: W. H. Freeman.

Stage, E. K., Kreinberg, N., Eccles-Parsons, J., & Becker, J. R. (1985). Women in mathematics, science and engineering. In S. S. Klein (Ed.), *Achieving equity through education.* Baltimore: Johns Hopkins University Press.

Staven, D. (1971). The skirts in fiction about boys: A maxi-mess. *School Library Journal Book Review, 5*, 66–70.

Stefflre, B. (1969). Run mama run: Women workers in elementary readers. *Vocational Guidance Quarterly, 18*, 99–102.

Stein, A. H., & Smithells, V. (1969). Age and sex differences in children's sex role standards about achievement. *Developmental Psychology, 1*, 252–259.

Sternglanz, S., & Lyberger-Ficek, S. (1977). Sex differences in student-teacher interactions in the college classroom. *Sex Roles, 3*, 345–352.

Stewart, M. J., & Corbin, C. B. (1988). Feedback dependence among low confidence preadolescent boys and girls. *Research Quarterly for Exercise and Sport, 59*, 160–164.

Stewig, J., & Knipfel, M. (1975). Sexism in picture books: What progress? *Elementary School Journal, 76*, 151–165.

Swafford, J. O. (1980). Sex differences in first-year algebra. *Journal for Research in Mathematics Education, 11*, 335–346.

Taylor, J. (1979). Sexist bias in physics textbooks. *Physics Education, 14*, 277–280.

Tetenbaum, T., & Pearson, J. (1989). The voices in children's literature, the impact of gender on the moral decisions of storybook characters. *Sex Roles, 20*, 382–395.

Tetreault, M. K., & Schmuck, P. (1985). Equity, education reform, and gender. *Issues in Education, 3*, 45–67.

Thorne, B. (1985). Girls and boys together . . . but mostly apart: Gender arrangement in elementary schools. In W. W. Hartup & Z. Rubin (Eds.), *Relationships and developments.* Hillsdale, NJ: Erlbaum.

Thorne, B., & Luria, Z. (1983, August). *Sexuality and gender in children's daily worlds.* Paper presented at the annual meeting of the American Sociological Association, Stanford, CA.

Thorne, B., & Luria, Z. (1986). Sexuality and gender in children's daily worlds. *Social Problems, 33*, 176–190.

Tibbets, S. L. (1979). Research in sexism: Some studies of children's reading material revisited. *Educational Research Quarterly, 4*, 34, 39.

Tietze, I. N., & Davis, B. H. (1981, April). *Sexism in texts in educational administration.* Paper presented at the annual meeting of the American Educational Research Association, Los Angeles.

Tobin, K. (1988). Target student involvement in high school science. *International Journal of Science Education, 10*, 317–330.

Tobin, K., & Gallagher, J. J. (1987). The role of target students in the science classroom. *Journal of Research in Science Teaching, 24*, 61–75.

Tobin, K., & Garnett, P. (1987). Gender related differences in science activities. *Science Education, 71*, 91–103.

Trecker, J. (1971). Women in U.S. history textbooks. *Social Education, 35*, 248–260.

Tsai, S. L., & Walberg, H. J. (1979). Mathematics achievement and attitude productivity in junior high school. *Journal of Educational Research, 76*, 267–272.

Tyler, L. E. (1965). *The psychology of human differences* (3rd ed.). New York: Appleton-Century-Crofts.

U'Ren, M. (1971). The image of women in textbooks. In V. Gornick & B. Moran (Eds.), *Woman in sexist society* (pp. 318–328). New York: Basic Books.

Valverde, L. A., & Brown, F. (1988). Influences on leadership development among racial and ethnic minorities. In N. J. Boyan (Ed.), *Handbook of research on educational administration: A project of the American Educational Research Association* (pp. 143–158). New York: Longman.

Verheyden-Hilliard, M. E., & Steele, C. (1978). *Cracking the glass slipper: Peers guide to ending sex bias in your schools*. Washington, DC: Project on Equal Educational Rights, NOW Legal Defense and Education Fund.

Vogel, S. (1990). Gender difference in intelligence, language, visual-motor abilities, and academic achievement in students with learning disabilities: A review of the literature. *Journal of Learning Disabilities, 23*, 44–52.

Warring, D., Johnson, D. W., Maruyama, G., & Johnson, R. (1985). Impact of different types of cooperative learning on cross-ethnic and cross-sex relationships. *Journal of Educational Psychology, 77*, 53–59.

Webb, L. D., Stout, R. T., & Metha, A. (1986). *Overcoming sex disequity in educational administration*. Tempe, AZ: University Council for Educational Administration.

Webb, N. W., & Kenderski, C. M. (1985). Gender differences in small group interaction and achievement in high- and low-achieving classes. In L. C. Wilkinson & C. B. Marrett (Eds.), *Gender influences in classroom interaction*. Orlando, FL: Academic Press.

Weigel, R. H., Wiser, P. L., & Cook, S. W. (1975). The impact of cooperative learning experiences on cross-ethnic relations and attitudes. *Journal of Social Issues, 3*, 219–244.

Weinberg, M. (1977). *Minority students: A research appraisal*. Washington, DC: National Institute of Education.

Weiner, N. C. (1984). Cognitive aptitudes, personality variables, and gender difference effects on mathematical achievement for mathematically gifted students (Doctoral dissertation, Arizona State University, 1983). *Dissertation Abstracts International, 44*, 361A.

Weisfeld, C. C., Weisfeld, G. E., Warren, M. A., & Freedman, D. G. (1983). The spelling bee: A naturalistic study of female inhibitions in mixed-sex competitions. *Adolescence, 18*, 695–708.

Weitzman, L., Eifler, D., Hodaka, K., & Ross, C. (1972). Sex role socialization in picture books for preschool children. *American Journal of Sociology, 77*, 1125–1150.

Weitzman, L., & Rizzo, D. (1974). *Biased textbooks: Images of males and females in elementary school textbooks*. Washington, DC: National Foundation for the Improvement of Education.

Wheatley, G. H., Mitchell, R., Frankland, R. L., & Kraft, R. (1978). Hemisphere specialization and cognitive development: Implications for mathematics education. *Journal for Research in Mathematics Education, 9*, 20–32.

White, H. (1986). Damsels in distress: Dependency themes in fiction for children and adolescents. *Adolescence, 21*, 251–256.

Wilder, G., & Powell, K. (1989). *Sex differences in test performance: A survey of the literature* (College Board Report No. 89-3). New York: College Entrance Examination Board.

Wilkinson, L. C., Lindow, J., & Chiang, C. P. (1985). Sex differences and sex segregation in students' small-group communication. In L. C. Wilkinson & C. B. Marret (Eds.), *Gender influences in classroom interaction.* Orlando, FL: Academic Press.

Williams, F., Whitehead, J. L., & Miller, L. (1972). Relations between language attitudes and teacher expectancy. *American Educational Research Journal, 9*, 263–277.

Williams, J. H., & Muehl, S. (1978). Relations among student and teacher perceptions of behavior. *Journal of Negro Education, 47*, 328–336.

Wingate, N. (1986). Sexism in the classroom. *Equity and Excellence, 22*, 105–110.

Wise, L., Steel, L., & MacDonald, C. (1979). *Origins and career consequences of sex differences in high school mathematics achievement.* Palo Alto, CA: American Institutes for Research. (ERIC Document Reproduction Service No. ED 180 846)

Wolleat, P., Pedro, J., Becker, A., & Fennema, E. (1980). Sex differences in high school students' causal attributions of performance in mathematics. *Journal for Research in Mathematics Education, 11*, 356–366.

Women on Words and Images. (1972). *Dick and Jane as victims: Sex stereotyping in children's readers.* Princeton, NJ: Carolingian Press.

Women on Words and Images. (1975). *Dick and Jane as victims: Sex stereotyping in children's readers* (expanded ed.). Princeton, NJ: Author.

Woodworth, W. P., & Salzer, R. T. (1971). Black children's speech and teacher evaluations. *Urban Education, 6*, 167–173.

Yeakey, C. C., Johnston, G. S., & Adkison, J. A. (1986). In pursuit of equity: A review of research on minorities and women in educational administration. *Educational Administration Quarterly, 22*, 110–149.

Zimmerer, L. K., & Bennett, S. M. (1987, April). *Gender differences on the California statewide assessment of attitudes and achievement in science.* Paper presented at the annual meeting of the American Educational Research Association, Washington, DC.

Chapter 8

School Desegregation and Intergroup Relations: A Review of the Literature

JANET WARD SCHOFIELD
University of Pittsburgh

The history of black-white contact in the United States is long and complex. However, the last 35 years have seen changes in relations between blacks and whites of a magnitude virtually unparalleled before, except for the period immediately after the Civil War. One of the most controversial of these changes was the decision handed down in the *Brown v. Board of Education* (1954) case in 1954, in which the Supreme Court overturned the earlier doctrine that "separate but equal" public facilities for blacks and whites could be mandated by state law. Instead, it argued that such separation in the schools "generates a feeling of inferiority (in black children) that may affect their hearts and minds in a way unlikely ever to be undone." Thus, enforced segregation of the schools by race was held to violate the equal protection clause of the U.S. Constitution (Read, 1975; Wisdom, 1975) and to provide an inherently unequal education for black and white children.

The *Brown* decision and later attempts to implement it raised a storm of controversy (Edelman, 1973; Hochschild, 1984; Kluger, 1976; Lukas, 1985). White resistance to the policy was expressed in an extraordinary number of ways, ranging from physical attacks on black students attempting to enroll in previously all-white schools, to legal stratagems aimed at delaying desegregation, to the founding of over 3,000 private academies set up to serve as alternatives to desegregated schools. Prince Edward County in Virginia literally closed down its public school system for several years rather than desegregate until the Supreme Court ruled that unacceptable (Bell, 1980; Kluger, 1976; Smith, 1965).

Thus, efforts to achieve school desegregation were stymied for over 10 years. In fact, in 1964, a full 10 years after the *Brown* decision, about

---

The author wishes to express her thanks to Beatriz Arias, John Levine, Richard Moreland, and John Ogbu for their constructive comments on an earlier draft of this chapter.

98% of the black children in the South were still enrolled in all-black schools (Holsendolph, 1976; Jaynes & Williams, 1989). However, the passage of the Civil Rights Act of 1964 and the Elementary and Secondary Education Act of 1965 finally created effective pressures toward change. Thus, a substantial amount of desegregation occurred between 1965 and 1973 in the South, the region of the country characterized by de jure segregation, that is, by state-supported dual systems of the kind specifically dealt with in the *Brown* decision. In sharp contrast, little change occurred in those years in the North. For example, the proportion of black students in predominately white schools in the North and West shifted almost imperceptibly (from 28% to 29%) between 1968 and 1972 (Feagin, 1980).

Overall national statistics show the current amount of desegregation to be remarkably similar to that achieved by 1972. Specifically, Orfield, Monfort, and Aaron (1989) report national statistics demonstrating that whereas the percentage of black students in predominately minority schools (less than 50% white) fell from 76.6% to 63.6% between 1968 and 1972, it remained virtually unchanged in the following decade and a half, standing at 63.3% in 1986. Similarly, between 1968 and 1972 the percentage of black students in intensely segregated schools (90% or more minority enrollment) in the United States dropped sharply from 64.3% to 38.7%, but this figure declined only marginally thereafter to 32.5% in 1986. Of course, these national statistics do not tell the full story. There have been and continue to be marked variations in the amount of desegregation occurring in various regions of the country, with trends toward increased desegregation in some areas counterbalanced by trends in the other direction elsewhere (Orfield, 1983; Orfield et al., 1989). However, discussion of the national figures will serve for the purposes of this review as long as the three trends noted below are taken into consideration.

Three striking changes are obscured by the figures showing an overall stability in the percentage of black students in desegregated schools since 1972. First, there has been major growth in the number of Hispanic, Asian, and other minority students in the public school systems in the United States. Although Mexican-American parents went to court as far back as 1947 in *Westminister v. Mendez* seeking to prevent the segregation of their children, Hispanics in all regions have experienced a high and increasing degree of segregation over the years (Arias, 1986). National figures show that whereas roughly 55% of all Hispanic students were enrolled in predominantly minority schools in 1968, over 71% are now found in such schools (Orfield et al., 1989). The Supreme Court's 1973 *Keyes* decision extended the *Brown* decision to cover Mexican-Americans, although the position of the courts with regard to other Hispanic groups is unclear (Orfield, 1978). No matter what the official legal status of Hispanics in various desegregation plans, their presence in many areas in which blacks and other minority group members are also concentrated affects desegregation plans in important ways. For example, for many Hispanics concern over bilingual-bicultural education far outweighs concern about desegregation (Orfield, 1978). Historically, the impetus for desegregation has usually come from minority parents concerned about their children's education. Thus, the presence of a large Hispanic population that may fear that dispersion of Hispanic students throughout the school system could weaken special language programs can create competing interests between different minority groups.

A second major change obscured by the stability of the overall national figures on black segregation since 1972 is the increasing difficulty of creating and maintaining desegregated schools in numerous large urban centers, especially those outside the South. Differential minority and majority group immigration and birth rates, differential usage of private schools, and the differential flow of white and minority families to the suburbs have led to increasing racial isolation in the schools in many cities. Although "white flight" from desegregated school systems accounts for some of this change (Armor, 1988; Rossell, 1990a), the increasing concentration and isolation of minority groups in large urban centers is also a pronounced and common pattern in cities with no mandatory desegregation plans such as New York and Chicago. In the southern and border states, the impact of these demographic changes on the city schools has been mitigated in a number of areas by mandatory metropolitan area desegregation plans that have merged and integrated previously separate city and suburban school districts and by the long-standing existence of county-wide school districts that include both the center city and many suburban areas. However, even the South experienced some increase in the segregation of black students in the 1980s (Orfield et al., 1989).

The third major change that has occurred since the early 1970s and is not reflected in the overall statistics about the amount of existing desegregation is the shift in the public's attitude toward this policy. The shift among whites has been dramatic (Taylor, Sheatsley, & Greeley, 1978). For example, Schuman, Steeh, and Bobo (1985) report that between 1942 and 1982, the percentage of whites giving a response that supported the principle of school desegregation rose 58 points. Although there is strong evidence of a major change in such attitudes, it is also important to point out that attitudes concerning the implementation of these principles have not shown a comparable shift. In addition, the absolute level of endorsement of implementation policies is lower than one might expect from the level of support for the related principles. For example, although the overwhelming majority of whites state they favor desegregation in principle, three quarters of the whites surveyed in 1986 opposed cross-district busing for the purpose of school desegregation, a figure only somewhat lower than the 87% who opposed it in 1972 (Davis & Smith, 1987, cited in Jaynes & Williams, 1989).

Not surprisingly, both actual attitudes toward desegregation and patterns of change are somewhat different for Hispanics and blacks than for whites. The attitudes of Hispanics toward desegregation have not received much study. However, it appears that, generally speaking, Hispanics are somewhat more in favor of desegregation than whites, although concern about desegregation's impact on special language programs is strong (Orfield, 1986). Overall, black support for the principle of school desegregation has been strong and consistent, showing relatively little change over time (Jaynes & Williams, 1989). However, like whites, blacks are more likely to endorse principles supporting equality and integration than they are to endorse actual implementation efforts. In fact, Schuman et al. (1985) demonstrated that blacks became more negative toward implementation efforts in many realms, including certain policies relating to school desegregation, from the early 1970s to the mid-1980s at the same time that support for the principle of school desegregation remained very high. This increasing skepticism is evidenced in essays written by a number of eminent blacks, including some who played an important role in the early push for desegregation, who argue that focusing on the quality of the education black children receive, rather than on desegregation per se, would be the wisest course for the black community (Bell, 1980; Blakey, 1989; Edmonds, 1980; Hamilton, 1968; Sampson & Williams, 1978; Sizemore, 1978). This shift in emphasis appears to have resulted partly from the demographic shifts discussed above that make it increasingly evident that exceedingly large numbers of black children are likely to remain in racially isolated schools. Another important contributing factor is awareness on the part of blacks that, generally speaking, they have borne the greater burden in the desegregation process (Arnez, 1978; Sizemore, 1978). For example, many desegregation plans have disproportionately fired black staff, bused black children, and closed black schools (Butler, 1974; Hamilton, 1968; Haney, 1978; Orfield, 1975; Spruill, 1966).

Widespread active political support for new mandatory desegregation efforts is not very likely at this point in time given the attitudes of both whites and minority group members toward the implementation efforts discussed above. However, the fact remains that very large numbers of students, from majority and minority groups alike, are now enrolled in racially and ethnically mixed schools. Demographic trends that lead experts to expect that an increasingly large proportion of the school-aged children in the United States will be minority group members (Henry, 1990) and the overall stability in the degree of desegregation nationally since 1972 combine to make it reasonable to expect that racially and ethnically mixed schools will continue to be a fact of life in many American communities. Thus, in spite of the present lull in new desegregation activity, it remains vitally important to understand how attending such schools affects students' development.

THE IMPORTANCE OF EXPLORING THE IMPACT OF SCHOOL DESEGREGATION ON INTERGROUP RELATIONS

The lion's share of the research on the effect of school desegregation has focused on its impact on academic achievement (for reviews of this literature see Armor, 1984; Bradley & Bradley, 1977; T. Cook, 1984; Crain, 1984; Krol, 1978; Mahard & Crain, 1983; Miller & Carlson, 1984; Stephan, 1978, 1984; St. John, 1975; Walberg, 1984; Weinberg, 1977; and Wortman, 1984). However, a fairly large body of research has also addressed the issue of desegregation's impact on intergroup relations, the topic of this review. Although many of the parties concerned with desegregated schools tend to be relatively uninterested in how interracial schooling affects intergroup relations, there are some compelling arguments in favor of giving serious attention to the matter. Much social learning occurs in schools, whether or not it is planned. Hence, racially or ethnically mixed schools cannot choose to have no effect on intergroup relations, only whether the effect will be planned or unplanned. Even a laissez-faire policy concerning intergroup relations conveys a message—that either school authorities see no serious problem with relations as they have developed or they do not feel that the nature of intergroup relations is a legitimate concern for an educational institution. So those who argue that schools should not attempt to influence intergroup relations miss the fundamental fact that whether or not they consciously try to influence such relations, schools are extremely likely to do so in one way or another (Schofield, 1989).

Because of the pervasive residential segregation in our society, students frequently have their first relatively intimate and extended intergroup experiences in schools. Hence, whether racial and ethnic hostility and stereotyping grow or diminish may be critically influenced by the particular experiences students have there. Although there may still be considerable argument about whether the development of close ties between students from different racial or ethnic backgrounds should be a high priority in this country, there is a growing awareness of the very real societal costs of intergroup hostility and stereotyping. It is clear that, under many conditions, intergroup contact can lead to increased hostility. Hence, unless racially or ethnically mixed schools are carefully planned, there is the real possibility that they will exacerbate the very social tensions and hostilities that many initially hoped they would diminish. In addition, Jencks et al. (1972) have suggested that more attention should be paid to structuring schools so that they are reasonably pleasurable environments for students. This viewpoint emphasizes that in addition to being institutions that prepare students for future roles, schools are also the environments in which many people spend nearly one third of their waking hours for a significant portion of their lives. This line of argument suggests that even if positive or negative interracial experiences do not cause change in intergroup behaviors and attitudes outside the school situation, positive relationships within the school setting may be of some value.

Yet another reason for concern about the impact of desegregation on intergroup relations is the evidence that social relations between students in interracial schools may affect minority students' academic achievement or their later occupational success (Braddock & McPartland, 1987; Crain, 1970; Katz, 1964; McPartland & Crain, 1980; Pettigrew, 1967; Rosenberg & Simmons, 1971; U.S. Commission on Civil Rights, 1967). For example, Katz's early (1964) work suggests that the academic performance of blacks may be markedly impaired in biracial situations that pose a social threat. The potentially constructive effect of positive intergroup relations on minority group outcomes is highlighted by Braddock and McPartland's (1987) finding that black high school graduates who use desegregated social networks in their job search are likely to attain positions with a substantially higher salary than are those who use segregated social networks. They also work in environments that have, on the average, a higher percentage of white workers.

Finally, the ability to work effectively with out-group members is an important skill for both majority and minority group members in a pluralistic society striving to overcome a long history of discrimination in education and employment. Many individuals lack this ability (Pettigrew & Martin, 1987), but population trends that suggest that an increasingly large proportion of the population will be composed of minority group members make this an increasingly important aspect of children's education. Such skills are unlikely to develop in desegregated schools characterized by intergroup tension, separation, and high levels of anxiety, providing yet another reason for paying attention to the quality of intergroup relations in desegregated schools.

RESEARCH ON DESEGREGATION AND INTERGROUP RELATIONS

School desegregation itself occurred in definite historical periods, as discussed earlier: 1954–1968, during which desegregation was the law but was rarely implemented; 1968–1973, which saw the fastest and most far-reaching change; and the post-1973 period in which increases in desegregation at certain times and in certain regions were offset by countervailing tendencies at other times and places. Not surprisingly, research on school desegregation also progressed through various periods. My primary concern in this chapter is to assess the current state of the literature on school desegregation, rather than to try to write a detailed history of the field. However, using historical periods is a convenient way to provide context for this endeavor, to indicate the connections between the political and legal situation at various periods and the research that emerged from those periods, and to lay out the deficiencies and scholarly controversies in the field and their origins. Thus, for heuristic purposes, I have used time periods as an organizing device. It should, of course, be understood that these periods overlap somewhat and that the precise years proposed as break points between them are necessarily somewhat arbitrary.

The Pre-Brown Years: 1954 and Before

As one might expect, in the years before the 1954 *Brown* decision there was very little research on the impact of school desegregation on intergroup relations. Schools in the South were very heavily segregated, making such research there essentially impossible. There was also a substantial amount of racial isolation in other parts of the country, making racially mixed schools the exception rather than the rule. However, there was a body of research pertinent to issues relating to the probable impact of school segregation and desegregation (for more extended discussions of this research see S. Cook, 1979; Gerard, 1983; Klineberg, 1986; and Stephan, 1978). Some of this research came from the study of adults in other milieus, such as job situations (Harding & Hogrefe, 1952; Saenger & Gilbert, 1950; Stouffer et al., 1949), public housing complexes (Deutsch & Collins, 1951; Jahoda & West, 1951; Wilner, Walkley, & Cook, 1955), and coal mines (Minard, 1952). Some of the research compared students in existing, racially mixed northern schools to those in segregated schools in southern or border states (Clark, 1939a; Clark & Clark, 1947, 1950), thus confounding region and desegregation. Others compared the racial awareness, racial self-identification, and racial attitudes of black and white children or of different groups of black children (Clark, 1939b; Clark & Clark, 1940, 1947; Goodman, 1952; Horowitz, 1939; Landreth & Johnson, 1953; Stevenson & Steward, 1958; Trager & Yarrow, 1952). Although these latter studies did not bear directly on the impact of school desegregation, the fact that many of them demonstrated that black children were less likely to identify with a "black" doll than white children were with a "white" doll and that they were more likely to attribute negative characteristics to same-race dolls than were white children was taken as evidence of the damage that blacks' position in our society inflicted upon black children.

In spite of the relative paucity of strong, direct scientific evidence on the impact of segregated education on blacks or the consequences of school desegregation, there was very broad agreement among social scientists that state-mandated segregation had "detrimental psychological effects on both members of racial and religious groups which are segregated and on those who do the segregating, even when equal facilities were made available to both groups" (Deutscher & Chein, 1948, p. 268). In fact, a survey of social scientists that demonstrated this broad consensus was presented by a psychologist who served as an expert witness in one of the five cases that were dealt with in the *Brown* ruling. The active participation by a number of psychologists who testified on behalf of the plaintiffs in the *Brown* case laid the basis for a scholarly controversy that emerged three decades later about whether social scientists had misled the Supreme Court. However, in the postwar years immediately preceding *Brown,* when awareness of the atrocities that Hitler's theories of racial inferiority had led to was still very fresh and the odious Jim Crow laws were still in place in the South, support for desegregation was widespread and generally noncontroversial among scholars studying race relations and related issues.

The Immediate Post-Brown Years (1955–1967)

Research on school desegregation and intergroup relations remained sparse until around 1968, partly because so little desegregation actually occurred. This situation was also partly due to researchers' tendency to focus on academic achievement (D. Cohen & Weiss, 1977). Studies such as those of S. Aronson and Nobel (1966), E. Campbell (1956), Dwyer (1958), Fox (1966), Jansen and Gallegher (1966), Lombardi (1962), Mann (1959), McWhirt (1967), Singer (1966), Webster (1961), and Yarrow, Campbell, and Yarrow (1958) that explored student relations in racially mixed environments or compared the attitudes of students in desegregated and segregated environments began to appear. They were not very numerous, however, especially in the period before 1965.

The most detailed and influential study of this time period bearing directly on the issue of how racially mixed schooling might affect intergroup relations was *Racial Isolation in the Public Schools,* published by the U.S. Commission on Civil Rights in 1967. This lengthy report documented the extent of the racial isolation existing in the nation's schools, explored the factors perpetuating it, examined the connection between racially isolated schooling and various academic and social outcomes, and discussed numerous programs that had been proposed to narrow the black-white achievement gap and diminish racial isolation. The conclusions of the report most relevant for this review were quite consistent with the ethos of the late 1960s, as well as with the positive attitudes toward desegregation expressed by social scientists in their testimony in the *Brown* case and in the earlier Deutscher and Chein (1948) survey. This report used large-scale survey data to argue that racial isolation in the schools led to a continuing preference for racial isolation on the part of both black and white students. Specifically, the report concluded that attendance at desegregated schools led to a more positive attitude toward out-group members as expressed in an increased willingness to reside in an interracial neighborhood, to have one's children attend desegregated schools, and the like.

The Active Empirical Years (1968–1975)

The implementation of numerous desegregation plans in the late 1960s and early 1970s provided the first widespread opportunities to examine the effect of desegregation on intergroup relations. A large number of researchers seized this opportunity (e.g., Armor, 1972; Barber, 1968; Carrigan, 1969; Crooks, 1970; Evans, 1969; Gardner, Wright, & Dee, 1970; Garth, 1969; Green & Gerard, 1974; Justman, 1968; Koslin, Pargament, & Waxman, 1972; Kurokawa, 1971; Lewis, 1971; Orost, 1971; Patchen & Davidson, 1973; Porter, 1971; St. John, 1969; St. John & Lewis, 1973; Schmuck & Luszki, 1969; Shaw, 1973; Silverman & Shaw, 1973; Smith, 1969; Stephan, 1977; Useem, 1971; Walker, 1969; Williams, Best, & Boswell, 1975).

Unfortunately, most of this research tended to ask what, in hindsight, was an overly simplistic question. In most cases it was simply "What is the effect of desegregation on intergroup relations?" Thus, children in desegregated settings, from preschool on up, were compared to peers in segregated settings. Common dependent measures were racial attitude questionnaires, social distance scales, and sociometric measures, often those asking children to list a small number of classmates who were their closest friends. Many of these studies were marred by conceptual and methodological flaws. By and large, these flaws also characterize more recent quantitative work on school desegregation. Thus, they are worth serious attention, not only for the historical record but out of concern for improvement in future work as well.

Design Flaws

Focus on a narrow range of outcomes rather than on process.[1] Typically, in the pre-1975 period, researchers studying desegregated schools tried to assess the effects of desegregation without simultaneously exploring the social processes that accounted for these effects (National Institute of Education, 1974; St. John, 1975). The lack of attention to social process is striking. There are some clear exceptions, such as a study by Gerard and Miller (1975) that set out not only to attempt to determine the impact of school desegregation on various academic and social outcomes, but also to measure the variables thought to mediate many of these outcomes. Similarly, a study of the desegregation of Indianapolis high schools conducted in the 1970s and reported most fully in Patchen (1982) also made a sophisticated attempt to understand and document the causes of change. However, with the exception of a few such studies and a group of qualitative studies that began to appear in the late 1970s (which will be discussed later), the focus of research on desegregation and intergroup relations has clearly been on outcomes rather than on the processes that might account for these outcomes.

The focus on desegregation's effects undoubtedly stemmed at least partially from the fact that researchers and funding agencies often hoped to use the results of the research in political ways to support or, less frequently, to undermine it as a national policy. Obviously, for political purposes, it is much more useful to be able to say that desegregation improves or harms intergroup relations than it is to delineate the processes that may lead to these results. The heavy emphasis on effects to the exclusion of process is an especially severe problem because desegregation research tends to be nonexperimental and does not lend itself well, from a statistical point of view, to unambiguous causal statements. Given this state of affairs, the causal conclusions drawn would be much more convincing if one could demonstrate both processes that occur and plausible links between the processes and the outcomes that are found (Suchman, 1967).

Frequent use of cross-sectional designs. It is far from easy to assess the impact of an ongoing and highly controversial social policy. As Crain (1976) points out, there are strong pressures on researchers involved with studies on desegregation to complete their work rapidly. Often, school boards give permission for studies in their districts in the hope that they will supply useful information for decision making. Similarly, funding agencies or the governing bodies of which the funding agencies are a part have often sponsored desegregation research in order to generate data to guide policy decisions. These decisions are frequently pressing, so the idea of waiting for research results for any large number of years is highly unattractive (cf. Weiss, 1977). These pressures for rapid results are, of course, compounded by the academic reward structure, which also strongly encourages rapid publication. Hence, for a variety of reasons, including the fact that cross-sectional studies are generally less expensive than longitudinal studies, the majority of the research dealing with desegregation and intergroup relations is cross-sectional rather than longitudinal. Rather ironically, cross-sectional studies, which are attractive to policymakers because of their relatively low cost and quick payoff, do not allow one to make the causal inferences with which policymakers are frequently concerned. For example, it seems about as reasonable to interpret the positive relation McPartland (1968) found in survey data between intergroup contact and racial attitudes as suggesting that positive attitudes lead to contact as it does to interpret it as suggesting that contact leads to positive attitudes.

Control group and attrition problems in longitudinal designs. Although longitudinal studies have a distinct advantage over cross-sectional studies, they, too, frequently have serious problems. First, one must have the financial resources and long-term cooperation from a school system that longitudinal studies require. The pressures and difficulties of doing long-term longitudinal work are so great that very few desegregation studies span more than 1 year. Although occasional studies do span 2 to 5 or more years (e.g., Gerard & Miller, 1975; Schofield & Sagar, 1977), they almost inevitably tend to encounter potentially serious problems. For example, in the 3 years between 1966 and 1969, Gerard and Miller (1975) lost approximately one third of their original sample. The tendency of longitudinal studies to cover short periods at the beginning of students' desegregated schooling severely limits the extent to which it is appropriate to generalize from their findings.

In addition to covering short periods of time, many longitudinal studies of desegregation use no control group. Rather, they simply measure a group of students before and after desegregation. Writing about this kind of design, D. Campbell and Stanley (1963) state that "while this design . . . is judged as . . . worth doing where nothing better can be done . . . it is introduced . . . as a 'bad example' " (p. 7) of a research strategy. Campbell and Stanley go on to point out the serious threats to internal validity in designs such as this. Because there is no control group, the researcher has little idea of whether the effect found, if any, stems from factors such as historical change or maturation of the subjects or from the treatment being investigated.

The importance of having control groups in longitudinal studies of school desegregation and intergroup relations is heightened by the fact that research suggests there are indeed both age trends and clear historical trends in interracial attitudes and behavior. For example, Criswell's (1939) early work on age trends suggests that black and white children interact fairly readily until third grade, when students increasingly begin to interact with others of their own race. Other research supports Criswell's early finding of increasing hostility and racial cleavage in the upper elementary and later grades (S. Aronson & Nobel, 1966; Dwyer, 1958; Schofield, 1979; Trager & Yarrow, 1952). Hence, changes in interracial attitudes owing to age may confound changes resulting from desegregation unless a control group is available to which the desegregated group can be compared. Similarly, as mentioned earlier, survey research suggests that there have been major shifts in the racial attitudes of both whites and blacks during the last 35 years (A. Campbell, 1971; Jaynes & Williams, 1989; Schuman & Hatchett, 1974; Schuman et al., 1985). Thus, there is the possibility that in research without a control group, changes resulting from desegregation will be confounded with changes owing to larger societal trends. The desirability of having control groups in longitudinal studies of desegregation is illustrated by a study performed by Williams and Venditti (1969). These researchers found that, over the course of a year, black students in both segregated and desegregated schools became more negative in their attitudes toward certain aspects of their schools and the students in these schools. If measures had been taken only in the desegregated schools, the changes in attitudes might well have been incorrectly attributed to the desegregation experience.

Desegregation researchers recognize the importance of control groups but often are unable to locate or gain access to such groups in spite of serious thought and effort. Finding appropriate control groups is much more difficult than it might appear, as many of the desegregation programs that are most easily accessible to researchers are voluntary programs. Inasmuch as volunteers in these programs are self-selected for their interest in attending a desegregated school, a control group of students who have not volunteered for such a program is of questionable value. Students interested in the desegregation program who were not admitted would make a good control group only if a random selection process were used in deciding which of the applicants would be admitted to the program.

Studies attempting to judge the impact of desegregation on interracial behavior, whether they use observational measures or sociometric techniques, face a special control-group problem. As St. John (1975) points out, "Interracial behavior cannot be compared in segregated and integrated settings or before and after desegregation; it can be examined only if the races are in contact" (p. 65). One can compare responses of segregated and desegregated students to attitude measures such as social-distance questions, but one can hardly make meaningful comparisons between the in-school interracial behavior of segregated and desegregated students because segregated students have no out-group members with whom they can interact. In essence, this means that studies of behavior are hard pressed to find reasonable control groups. There are a number of partial solutions to this problem, although none are completely satisfactory. First, if longitudinal studies with no control group find trends that are clearly counter to the trends one might expect due to maturation or historical trends, one can at least make a reasonably strong argument that desegregation is responsible for that effect. This argument would be greatly strengthened if hypotheses about the effects of desegregation based on our theoretical understanding of the process had been formulated in advance.

There is another way to handle the control-group problem in studies of intergroup behavior methodologically more satisfying than the one just discussed. One could present students actually enrolled in segregated and desegregated schools with an interracial situation outside of their schools in which their behavior could be observed. Assuming that segregated students who constitute a reasonable control group could be found (this is the same problem found in attitude studies), the behavior of the segregated and desegregated students could be compared. For example, students from segregated and desegregated schools could be observed during a summer camp experience. Using this strategy, one could assess quite well whether interracial schooling influences students' behaviors in quite different interracial situations. However, it is important to recognize that this is a very stringent test of desegregation's impact, because it is really a test of whether change presumed to occur within the school will generalize to other individuals in a quite different situation. Failure to find change would not indicate that behavior changes owing to desegregation were failing to occur in the desegregated school itself.

Finally, there are problems even with a design that has longitudinal data on reasonably well-matched students at one desegregated and one segregated school. The principal problem is that the impact of the schools as institutions may be confounded with the impact of desegregated classrooms, which is only one aspect of those schools. Obviously, schools that are similar in most objective respects on which "experimental" and "control" schools are usually matched can differ significantly in other respects that may have implications for the students' development. For example, a number of studies have suggested that the principal of a desegregated school has a major impact on how intergroup relations develop (Collins, 1979; St. John, 1975; Wax, 1979). Hence, the conclusions drawn from research comparing racial attitudes in one desegregated and one segregated school might be affected greatly by the principals who happened to be at the schools in question. To avoid such problems, one could study a whole array of segregated and desegregated schools, but this strategy requires vast amounts of time, money, and effort. In addition, the error variance due to differences between the various desegregated schools might well mask whatever effects desegregation might have.

In addition to facing several control-group problems, desegregation studies are often plagued by self-selection problems, both at the institutional and the individual level, that limit their external validity. As Pettigrew (1969) points out, schools that agree to make themselves available to researchers interested in desegregation are clearly not a random sample of all desegregated schools. For example, school systems such as those in New Haven, Connecticut, White Plains, New York, and Berkeley, California, have allowed significant studies of desegregation. Many less well-regarded systems, including those in Cleveland, Chicago, and Los Angeles, have been less open, refusing even to participate in a major federal survey of desegregated schools in spite of the fact that such participation was ordered by Congress in the Civil Rights Act of 1964 (Pettigrew, 1969). Similarly, it is reasonable to hypothesize that children whose parents refuse to let them participate in research on desegregation may not be a random sample of all children in such schools.

Measurement Problems

Measuring intergroup attitudes. Researchers who want to investigate the impact of desegregation on interracial attitudes face a very difficult task. First, they must face the numerous thorny issues routinely encountered in attempts to measure attitudes (Dawes & Smith, 1985). Second, they are likely to have to deal with the complex technical issues often involved in the measurement of change (Cronbach & Furby, 1970; Feldt & Brennan, 1989; Harris, 1963). As each of these topics has a large literature of its own, I will not review these problems here. Rather, I turn now to a brief consideration of the special problems faced by researchers trying to measure attitudes in an area as controversial and emotionally involving as race relations.

Rosenberg (1969) has argued convincingly that participants in the research process are often quite concerned with presenting themselves in a way that will earn the researcher's approval. Although this "evaluation apprehension" is operative in a wide variety of research situations, it seems especially likely to influence subjects' responses when the research is dealing with a controversial topic such as race relations. Subjects concerned about making a good impression may be particularly careful to present their racial attitudes in a way they believe will win favor because these attitudes are so closely linked to cultural norms and values. A recent study suggests that there is reason for real concern about this issue. Specifically, Miller (1990b) reports that college students indicated on pen-and-paper measures that they were more positive about a hypothetical black individual with whom they expected to interact than about a similar hypothetical white peer. However, physiological measures of facial muscle movements suggested precisely the opposite conclusion.

Gaertner and his colleagues (Gaertner, 1976; Gaertner & Dovidio, 1986) point out that, when responding to questions about their social attitudes, individuals are presenting themselves not only to the researcher but also to themselves. Following a train of thought similar to D. Katz's (1960) description of the value-expressive function that attitudes can serve, Gaertner argues that many whites desire to see themselves as unprejudiced even though their basic feelings about blacks may be negative or ambivalent. Hence, they may well make unprejudiced statements in order to convince themselves as well as others that they are not prejudiced. This line of reasoning gains empirical support from the finding that, among white liberals, those whose affective responses to blacks are the least positive sometimes act in the most positive manner toward blacks (Weitz, 1972), as if they are anxious about denying their negative or ambivalent feelings. Although less attention has been devoted to the issue, concerns about evaluation apprehension and self-image may also impede the accurate measurement of minority group members' attitudes toward whites and each other.

Another serious and often unrecognized problem that has impeded research on the impact of desegregation on intergroup relations is the fact that intergroup attitudes have generally been conceived rather simplistically in desegregation research. In practice, researchers have generally assumed that the racial attitudes of majority and minority group members are quite similar in meaning and structure. It is common to present minority and majority group students with the same attitude scales (differing only in whether the out-group referred to is labeled black, white, Hispanic, etc.) and to use some kind of simply constructed composite scale score as the dependent variable. The problem with this approach is that it does not adequately recognize the possibility of real asymmetry in the content, structure, and determinants of intergroup attitudes. Yet, there are data that suggest these asymmetries do exist. For example, one study found that whereas black children rated black and white peers whom they considered close friends very similarly on a variety of personality dimensions, white children, in contrast, rated their close friends who were white more positively than close friends who were black (Damico, Bell-Nathaniel, & Green, 1981). One implication of this study is that the statement that one has a close friend of the other race may mean something rather different to white and black children—a potentially serious problem given the widespread use of sociometric measures as indicators of intergroup relations in desegregated schools.

In addition to this kind of problem, there is reason to believe that the structure of intergroup attitudes may be much more complex than desegregation researchers have assumed. A study conducted as early as 1967 by Woodmansee and Cook and replicated by Brigham, Woodmansee, and Cook (1976) suggested that white college students' racial attitudes are multidimensional and that attitudes relating to certain aspects of intergroup relations, such as acceptance of out-group members in close personal relationships, may not predict attitudes toward other aspects of intergroup relations. This conclusion is supported by Kawwa's (1968) finding that British adolescents' level of prejudice toward an out-group was not related to whether or not they had friends belonging to that group. A study by Bank, Biddle, Keats, and Keats (1977) demonstrated a different kind of complexity when it showed that both black and white adolescents respond quite differently to questions about school desegregation depending on whether one assesses norms, preferences, or beliefs. Yet the distinctions suggested by such studies have not generally been recognized in desegregation research, which has tended to treat measures of friendship, prejudice, and the like as virtually interchangeable indicators of the generalized construct of intergroup relations.

In addition, the structure of racial attitudes may be different for students belonging to different racial or ethnic groups. For example, Patchen and his colleagues have demonstrated (Patchen, 1982; Patchen, Davidson, Hofmann, & Brown, 1977) that whereas white students tend to see blacks in terms of two general clusters of traits, black students tend to see their white classmates in terms of six more specific underlying dimensions such as unfriendliness and the tendency to violate school norms. Also, the factors that influence black and white students' attitudes may be different. For example, Patchen (1982) reports that when black students expressed negative attitudes towards whites, their criticisms centered on what they perceived as a lack of friendliness and a sense of superiority. On the other hand, whites' complaints about blacks centered on their perceptions of blacks as dangerous and disruptive. In an almost surprising convergence between two studies that differed dramatically in methodology, locale, age group, and kind of desegregation, Schofield (1989) reported identical findings. Thus, it appears that more attention needs to be given to the issue of how to measure intergroup attitudes in a way that takes account of their complexity and of the potential difference in the structure of such attitudes in students from different backgrounds.

Another set of problems that may sometimes impede the fruitful study of interracial attitudes in a desegregated school stems from the ethical and practical dilemmas of assessing actively hostile feelings or negative stereotypes. In a great many desegregated schools, there is at least the potential for outbursts of negative feeling or behavior between students from different backgrounds. Hence, administrators and teachers in such schools are often, with good reason, leery of letting a researcher employ a balanced attitude-assessment instrument that may contain negative as well as positive statements. There is always the possibility that the presentation of such negative statements will help legitimize stereotyped negative points of view or serve as a trigger to set off undesirable conflict. Also, sometimes university-based committees set up for the protection of human subjects are hesitant to allow the use of such measures for similar reasons. Thus, study after study has focused on friendship and interracial acceptance. Two exceptions to this generalization are Patchen's (1982) analysis of intergroup relations in the Indianapolis high schools, which explicitly looked at avoidance, unfriendly contact, and the like, and a group of qualitative studies that included consideration of negative as well as positive relations (cf. Clement & Livesay, 1979; Eddy, 1975; G. Grant, 1988; Rist, 1979; Schofield, 1989). However, there is still a tendency for researchers to use measures of friendship and social choice rather than measures explicitly designed to capture strong negative feelings and behaviors.

One major factor contributing to the reluctance to use measures of negative relations, above and beyond the considerations mentioned above, is an implicit assumption that positive and negative attitudes are merely opposite ends of a continuum so that by studying "more positive" and "less positive" attitudes one is really tapping both positive and negative affect. Yet, empirical work on racial attitudes challenges this assumption. Patchen, Hofmann, and Davidson (1976) report, for example, a factor-analytic study of the racial attitudes of desegregated high school students that concludes that whites' attitudes are best described as grouping into two independent factors, including both a general negative evaluation of blacks and a general positive evaluation of blacks.

Given the difficulties that plague relatively straightforward attempts to measure racial attitudes, measures that are unlikely to arouse subjects' awareness that their racial attitudes are being studied seem desirable on methodological grounds. Recently, Greenwald (1990) has also argued, on theoretical grounds, that measures of unconscious prejudice may be more fruitful than those of conscious opinions or beliefs. A number of relatively nonreactive measures of attitudes have been developed (cf. Crosby, Bromley, & Saxe, 1980; Gaertner, 1976), including judgment of voice tone (Weitz, 1972) and Gaertner and Bickman's (1971) wrong-number technique. Sears and his colleagues (Kinder & Sears, 1981; McConahay & Hough, 1976; McConahay, Hardee, & Batts, 1981; Sears & Allen, 1984; Sears, Hensler, & Speer, 1979) have also attempted to develop, validate, and measure symbolic racism, which has been defined as "the expression in terms of abstract, ideological symbols and symbolic behaviors of the feeling that blacks are violating cherished values or making illegitimate demands for changes in the racial status" (McConahay & Hough, 1976, p. 38). Taking a rather different approach, Cooper and Pollack (1959) and Martinez-Monfort and Dreger (1972) have attempted to assess racial attitudes using physiological measures. Although such measures are hardly unobtrusive, physiological responses may not be under the subject's conscious control to the extent that written attitude measures are.

Measures such as those discussed above, however, have rarely been used in the study of the effects of school desegregation on interracial attitudes. One exception to this general pattern is the work of Koslin and her colleagues (Koslin et al., 1968, 1969, 1972), who developed some "quasi-disguised measures" of young children's racial attitudes. One of these measures has children indicate their preference for one of several classrooms that vary in racial composition as well as in activity (to disguise the intent of the measure). Another is very similar to a procedure developed by Schofield (1968) that was designed to capture racial attitudes by measurement of the physical distance between the placement of a figure representing the self and other figures representing black, white, or racially mixed groups of peers.

Measuring intergroup behavior. The majority of the studies designed to investigate the relation between desegregation and interracial behavior use sociometric techniques. In fact, to my knowledge, only three studies on desegregation and intergroup behavior published before the end of the active period in 1975 used actual observation of behavior (Shaw, 1973; Silverman & Shaw, 1973; Yarrow et al., 1958). The most commonly used sociometric measure is a peer nomination technique in which students are asked to list three or four friends or preferred partners for various kinds of activities. Somewhat less widely used is a roster and rating technique that has students rate on a 5- or 7-point scale a list of peers, usually including all of their classmates. Unfortunately, there are several potentially serious problems with the use of such techniques, especially with the peer nomination technique.

First, there are some technical problems with the peer nomination approach that are not specific to its use as a measure of interracial behavior. For example, there is a substantial amount of evidence that this procedure distorts the data by both overstating the number of relationships that isolated individuals have and understating the number of relations that very popular individuals have. Furthermore, to my knowledge there is really no good way to correct these distortions (Holland & Leinhardt, 1973).

Second, sociometric measures may well be as open to distortion by evaluation apprehension as attitude measures. This concern can be allayed somewhat by a study conducted in a desegregated middle school by Sagar, Schofield, and Snyder (1983), which collected observational data and sociometric ratings by sixth graders of all their classmates as potential work and play partners. Both methods of data collection led to similar conclusions, even to the extent of showing a similar three-way interaction. However, the possibility remains that sociometric measures may be responsive to evaluation apprehension, especially if the researchers administering them do not consciously consider how to minimize the potential for this.

Third, even if sociometric measures are strongly associated with actual behavioral patterns in desegregated classrooms, there is still some question of how appropriate traditional peer nomination sociometric techniques are for assessing the impact of desegregation on intergroup behavior. Peer nomination measures typically allow assessment of the child's closest friends or most preferred partners. They are generally very insensitive to changes in patterns of social interaction that do not involve the development of especially strong relationships. Yet it is only logical to expect that one might find more change in weak ties between students in desegregated schools than in the strong tie of friendship, as Granovetter (1986) and Schofield and Francis (1982) have pointed out. In fact, Clement and Livesay's (1979) analysis of social relations in five desegregated schools concludes that the development of really close social relationships between black and white students is quite unusual, although students often interact in relatively harmonious and cooperative ways. Obviously, the preceding is not a criticism of the peer nomination technique per se. Rather, it is a suggestion that sociometric techniques often tap a specific kind of intergroup behavior that may be less likely to change than other behaviors.

In addition, it should be noted that the peer nomination technique, which typically asks about close friendships, tends to assess a relationship that is relatively unlikely to develop in a short period of time. In light of this fact, it is especially unfortunate that studies of school desegregation often span just the first year of the desegregation process. In addition, the majority of desegregation studies have been conducted in schools where desegregation stems from the transfer of children from one school to another rather than from residential desegregation. There is evidence suggesting that new children in a school, regardless of their race, do not immediately become fully integrated into the peer network (St. John & Lewis, 1975; Willie, 1973). In such situations, at a minimum, researchers who want to use sociometric peer nomination techniques might consider asking about *new* friends rather than just friends. In spite of the logical obviousness of this suggestion, I am aware of only one published sociometric study asking about new friends (Roberts, 1989).

The inhibiting effect of ethical and practical constraints on investigation of negative intergroup relations (mentioned briefly in the previous section) can be seen in an examination of the sociometric measures used to explore intergroup relations in desegregated schools. Although there are notable exceptions (Shaw, 1973), studies using sociometric peer nomination techniques generally ask children to name those they want to interact with most but avoid asking for the names of those with whom they least want to interact. The same tendency to avoid strong negative categories is also clear in sociometric rating studies in which children are asked to rate others on a continuum. For example, Schofield's (1978) five rating categories range from "I'd like to work with this person very much" to "I'd rather not work with this person." There is no strong negative statement such as "I'd dislike working with this person very much" to parallel the rather strong positive statement. Not infrequently, attempts to avoid negative statements while keeping a continuum with 5 or more points lead to psychometric problems. For example, St. John and Lewis (1975) instructed students to designate "best friends" by a 1, "good friends" by a 2, "kids who are not your friends but OK" by a 3, and "kids you don't know very well" by a 4. The researcher then assigned a 5 to children who were not rated on a given paper on the assumption that these were the respondents' "least liked or most ignored classmates" (p. 350). As can be seen, the first three ratings on the scale seem to refer to the degree of positive affect. The fourth, however, refers to degree of acquaintance, which may be quite different, for it seems quite possible that a student might want to be friends with another student whom he or she does not happen to know well. The fifth catchall rating could, in actuality, indicate anything from a careless failure to rate a classmate to strong negative feelings. Hence, the 5-point linear scale shifts the entity it measures in midstream. The St. John and Lewis (1975) scale is not unique in this respect.

This tendency to avoid the measurement of negative behavior and to focus on more positive behaviors may have serious consequences. The work of Patchen et al. (1977) suggests that the best predictors of positive interracial behavior are not the same factors that best predict negative behavior, so work that focuses primarily on factors influencing positive behavior may be of little help to theorists or practitioners who are trying to understand the origins of negative behaviors and mechanisms for reducing such behaviors.

Given the many problems associated with using sociometric techniques, especially the peer nomination technique, direct measurement of intergroup behavior itself seems preferable. Of course, it is possible that behavior may be influenced by evaluation apprehension, but investigators have found ways to record behavior that appear to be quite nonreactive. For example, Silverman and Shaw (1973) had graduate assistants with counters concealed in their pockets loiter where they could see students leaving school at the end of the day. Schofield and Sagar (1977) had observers stationed on a ramp overlooking the school cafeteria code the race and sex of students seated next to each other at the lunch tables.

Another advantage of behavioral measures is that they can be used to measure things, like casual classroom interaction, that may well be influenced by relatively small amounts of change in the state of intergroup relations. The more intense relationships that peer nomination techniques are designed to tap are most likely much slower to change. In addition, behavioral measures can be used, when desired, to tap the same sort of choice behavior that peer nomination sociometric techniques are usually used to measure. For example, Schofield (1976) developed a game run by teachers as part of ordinary classroom activity that allowed direct observation of student friendship choices.

Given the numerous advantages of behavioral measures for assessing change in intergroup behavior, the question arises of why sociometric techniques have been so much more widely used than direct observation. Practical considerations most probably account for this situation. Specifically, sociometric questionnaires can be administered relatively quickly and easily to large numbers of students. In addition, they pose relatively little threat to teachers or administrators, although they may pose more of a threat to students than relatively unobtrusive behavioral measures. On the other hand, behavioral observations in the classroom generally require the presence of the researcher while the teacher is actually teaching, thus posing more of a threat to the teacher whose permission is necessary before research can be conducted. Also, although there are numerous widely known and used observational systems that focus on teacher-student interaction, there are fewer that focus on student-student interaction, especially the kind of social interactions most appropriate for assessing intergroup relations. Thus, researchers primarily interested in desegregation and interracial interaction are compelled to use sociometric techniques or relatively simple coding systems unless they want to work on a quite different and extremely time-consuming task—the development of measures of peer interaction. Finally, there is the fact that intergroup behaviors may be very strongly influenced by the particular milieu that is chosen for observation. For example, Schofield and Sagar's (1977) observation of cafeteria seating patterns in a desegregated middle school suggested extremely low levels of cross-race interaction. Yet observation of classroom settings in the same school demonstrated a substantial amount of cross-racial interaction, virtually all of which was positive or neutral in tone (Sagar et al., 1983; Schofield & Francis, 1982). Rogers, Hennigan, Bowman, and Miller (1984) report a parallel finding. Thus, one's conclusions about the state of intergroup relations in a particular institution are likely to be influenced to a great extent by the places one chooses to observe.

Review, Disillusionment, and Redirection: 1975–1983

Reviews of Desegregation and Intergroup Relations

The spate of research on school desegregation and intergroup relations made possible by the actual implementation of many desegregation plans in the late 1960s and early 1970s quite naturally led to attempts to synthesize the overall conclusions that emerged from the literature. Thus, a substantial number of reviews of the literature appeared, most of them published in the 1975–1979 period (Carithers, 1970; E. Cohen, 1975; McConahay, 1978, 1979; St. John, 1975; Schofield, 1978, 1983; Slavin & Madden, 1979; Stephan, 1978). These reviews share three common themes. First, most conclude that the literature is quite inconclusive. Second, most descry methodological problems in the literature. Third, they discuss the sorry state of theory in desegregation research. These three themes will be dealt with in turn.

Inconclusiveness of the literature. In general, the reviews of desegregation and intergroup relations were unable to come to any conclusion about what the probable effects of desegregation were. In fact, St. John (1975) even concluded that the most striking feature of the literature was its inconclusiveness. Numerous studies found generally positive effects (Gardner et al., 1970; Koslin et al., 1968; Orost, 1971; Patchen & Davidson, 1973; Schofield, 1979; Silverman & Shaw, 1973; Singer, 1966; U.S. Commission on Civil Rights, 1967). At least as many found generally negative effects (e.g., Armor, 1972; Barber, 1968; Dentler & Elkins, 1967; Gerard, Jackson, & Conolley, 1975; Green & Gerard, 1974; Lachat, 1972; Stephan, 1977). A substantial number found mixed results, that is, positive for one group and neutral or negative for other groups (e.g., Criswell, 1939; Fox, 1966; Porter, 1971; Schofield & Sagar, 1977; Webster, 1961; Yarrow et al., 1958). Finally, some found no effects (e.g., Horowitz, 1936; Lombardi, 1962; Seidner, 1971; Williams et al., 1975). Thus, virtually all of the reviewers determined that few, if any, firm conclusions about the impact of desegregation on intergroup relations could be drawn.

Although some reviewers attributed much of the inconclusiveness to methodological or theoretical problems, as will be discussed below, it is clear that one other very simple factor also contributed substantially—the probably inevitable failure of researchers in the field to agree on an operational definition of the concept of desegregation.

Laboratory researchers working on a topic at very different institutions will frequently use the same or extremely similar methods of operationalizing a concept. Although the exclusive use of a single specific operationalization of a concept leaves unanswered serious questions about the generality of the phenomenon under study, as both Cartwright (1973) and D. Campbell and Fiske (1959) have noted, it is, of course, conducive to consistency of results. However, researchers studying the impact of desegregation have not been in a position to create instances of desegregation that embody precisely the characteristics they see as crucial to the concept or to control for or eliminate unwanted aspects of the situation they are studying. In fact, with the exception of Pettigrew (1973), who has made a basic distinction between *desegregation,* which refers to the physical presence of members of previously segregated groups in given social situations or institutions, and *integration,* which involves racial mixing under certain conditions seen as conducive to positive outcomes, it is not clear that most researchers have any operational definition of desegregation independent of the legal or popular definition of that term (Rose, 1983). Typically, researchers hear about instances of racially or ethnically mixed schools somewhere in their general locale and then try to gain access to these schools for study. There is often little motivation to go through the conscious step of deciding how one can best operationalize the concept of desegregation, for the practical problems involved in finding and gaining access to sites that embody those characteristics are often overwhelming.

Yet the social situations that our society labels as "desegregated schools" vary to an extraordinary extent. For example, a suburban school that receives bused inner-city blacks, like the school Useem (1976) studied, is called "desegregated" even though it is less than 5% black. In sharp contrast, in some urban settings a school would not be considered desegregated unless it were at least 40% or 50% minority (Schofield, 1989). Research has quite clearly shown that the proportion of students from different groups in a desegregated situation influences intergroup relations (Dentler & Elkins, 1967; Hallinan, 1982; Hallinan & Smith, 1985; Hallinan & Teixeira, 1987; McPartland, 1968; Patchen, 1982; St. John & Lewis, 1975; U.S. Commission on Civil Rights, 1967). Hence, in practice, researchers have studied very different situations without always recognizing that the fact that a situation is legally or popularly dubbed as desegregated does not guarantee that it has a great deal in common with other similarly labeled situations.

Evaluation researchers stress the importance of recognizing that programs vary tremendously in the degree to which and in the way in which they are implemented (T. Cook & Campbell, 1976; T. Cook, Levitan, & Shadish, 1985; Cronbach, 1982; Guttentag & Struening, 1975). Thus, even if one program looks superficially like another, one cannot safely assume that they actually take similar shape. Even if the instances of desegregation studied were similar in the racial or ethnic composition of their student bodies and surrounding communities, there would probably still be such substantial differences between the situations that they might be expected to produce widely varying results. For example, some schools distribute minority and majority group students throughout their classes in proportions roughly similar to their proportion in the school (Schofield, 1976). Others resegregate black and white students within the school building (National Institute of Education, 1977). Thus, two schools with different policies in this regard could have entirely different effects on the intergroup attitudes of their students.

The fact that instances of desegregation that appear similar on the surface may differ markedly in critical aspects of implementation has important implications for the interpretation of large-scale studies that analyze outcome variables in a number of segregated and desegregated schools and conclude that desegregation has no impact. Indeed, it could be that desegregation has an impact that is masked because of the tremendous variance caused by other uncontrolled variables. Alternatively, the positive impact of desegregation in some schools' classrooms might be counterbalanced by the negative impact in others. Sometimes investigators recognize these kinds of problems (Biener & Gerard, 1975). More often, however, they do not.

Methodological problems. Most of the reviews also discuss serious methodological problems, such as those described earlier, that may, at least in part, account for the inconclusiveness of the literature. Because these methodological shortcomings have already been discussed, I will not enumerate them here. However, it is important to indicate the magnitude of the problem. The nine reviews cited above, taken together, mention over 100 studies dealing with some aspect of desegregation and intergroup relations. Yet the literature available dealing specifically with the question of how desegregation influences intergroup relations is much more sparse than one might infer from this. For example, McConahay (1979) wrote, "In my . . . review of over 50 published and unpublished studies done between 1960 and 1978, I did not find even one true experiment and only four of the quasi-experimental studies had enough methodological rigor to make them worth reporting in any detail" (p. 1). The four studies mentioned were Gerard and Miller (1975), Schofield and Sagar (1977), Shaw (1973), and Silverman and Shaw (1973). Stephan's (1978) review defined the literature on the impact of desegregation on prejudice as consisting of 10 published and 8 unpublished studies. The most recent review, Schofield and Sagar (1983), is based on only 17 studies (11 published, 6 unpublished), 3 of which were published subsequent to the earlier reviews. These two later reviews make explicit their decision to use even fairly seriously flawed studies because so few methodologically exemplary studies are available.

It is impossible to say definitely how the flaws commonly found in studies of desegregation influenced their finding. It is, however, worth noting that a number of these flaws may have tended to lead to underestimates of positive effects. First, as discussed earlier, a great many studies were conducted in the first year or two of desegregation, which are commonly marked by more turmoil than later years when the school, students, and community have adjusted to the new situation. Second, studies often span no more than a year or two. Many cover even shorter periods of time. It may be unrealistic to expect substantial improvement in intergroup relations over such short periods of time. On the other hand, fairly dramatic negative shifts can occur quite rapidly when particular incidents crystallize underlying tensions. Third, the general developmental trend toward greater racial cleavage over time means that studies with no control groups may conclude that no change has occurred or even that negative change has occurred over time when, in fact, relations are more positive at the later point in time than they would be if the students had no prior classroom contact with each other. Fourth, as discussed at length earlier, the tendency to look for change in close friendships is conducive to findings of no effect, even when less intense relationships have changed. Although certain flaws, like poor attitude measurement, could lead to underestimates of both positive and negative change, in general it seems reasonable to argue that the particular kinds of problems found in this literature are more likely to lead to underestimating desegregation's positive effects than to overestimating them.

Dissatisfaction with theory and its use in research. A third theme common to virtually all of these reviews is a dissatisfaction with the state of theory in the area of desegregation and intergroup relations. E. Cohen (1975), St. John (1975), and Schofield (1978) all argue that the lack of theoretical perspective has been a major contributing factor to the inconclusiveness of the literature taken as a whole. Typically, researchers study a particular example of desegregation and look for changes in students' attitudes or behaviors that can be attributed to their desegregated experience. Because they bring no theoretical framework that would suggest what characteristics of the desegregated setting might relate to those changes, most researchers have paid little attention to what the desegregated setting was actually like. Because desegregated schools differ so dramatically, contradictory outcomes are found. Without a theoretical perspective, one has little idea of what patterns to look for in the data, and confusion abounds.

For many years the most widely shared theoretical perspective among researchers on desegregation and intergroup relations was that suggested by Allport's (1954) contact theory. Allport argued that intergroup contact may reinforce previously held stereotypes and increase intergroup hostility unless the contact situation is structured in a way that provides equal status for minority and majority group members and provides strong institutional support for positive relations. Allport also stressed the necessity of cooperative interaction aimed toward the achievement of shared goals. According to Allport, unless these conditions are met, improvement in intergroup relations is unlikely.

Although for many years contact theory was routinely invoked in reports on desegregation research, it had a remarkably small impact on the actual design and reporting of that research. For example, researchers often tip their hats to contact theory in the introductory passages of a research report and then fail entirely to give information on topics that it suggests should be vital to predicting the probable outcomes of the contact experience.

The number of studies that omit basic descriptive data on the desegregated situation, as well as the sort of data that contact theory suggests, is extraordinary. Studies frequently neglect to indicate whether the school studied was experiencing mandatory, voluntary, or neighborhood desegregation, and even whether classrooms within the school were desegregated. Many studies fail to mention the proportion of the student body from different racial and ethnic backgrounds, and the majority neglect to give such information about the school's staff. E. Cohen (1975) found that only 3 of the 24 studies she reviewed included detailed information on the intergroup attitudes of teachers and administrators.

Unfortunately, although contact theory has often been used to explain the results of studies that found that interracial contact led to increased friction or to no change, it has infrequently been used to structure studies of desegregation's effects. The studies that have taken contact theory seriously have had generally promising results (e.g., S. Cook, 1978; Lachat, 1972; Schofield, 1979; Schofield & Sagar, 1977). Consistent with the prediction that flows from contact theory, there is strong support for the idea that carefully structured cooperative learning activities can improve intergroup relations (see E. Aronson, Blaney, Sikes, Stephan, & Snapp, 1978; Bossert, 1988–1989; Johnson & Johnson, 1982; Sharan, 1980; Slavin, 1983a). However, in summary, it seems fair to say that with the exception of playing a role in stimulating this important work on cooperative learning teams, contact theory did not fundamentally influence the conduct of much empirical work on school desegregation.

There was one other theoretical stance that had enough impact on desegregation research preceding 1984 to deserve mention—a theory of status characteristics and expectation states developed by Berger, Cohen, and Zelditch (1966, 1972). In brief, this theory argues that the status order in society engenders expectations about competence that become widely held by members of both the higher ranked and the lower ranked groups. When members of these groups come in contact, these mutually held expectations about competence may lead to dominance and actually superior performance by the higher ranked group. The theory also holds that expectations need not be conscious to influence behavior.

E. Cohen (1972) argues that, in American society, race is one of the status characteristics that lead to the self-fulfilling prophecy predicted by the theory. This argument gains strong support from Cohen's demonstration that white junior high school students working in biracial groups dominate interactions even when the experimental situation is carefully constructed to eliminate all factors, aside from the students' expectations, that might promote dominance by either race. I. Katz (1964) and his colleagues had previously found similar dominance by white college students in biracial work groups.

E. Cohen and Roper (1972) reasoned that if expectation states help to account for white domination of interaction in biracial situations, then changes in expectations should lead to changes in such patterns. Hence, they used a specially designed training experience to influence children's expectations about their own competence. They concluded, as a result of their research on changing such expectations, that unequal interaction patterns will persist unless the expectations of both groups are treated. Although this theoretical position has important implications for structuring desegregated schools, empirical research on it remained confined mainly to a small group of researchers consisting mainly, though not exclusively, of Cohen and her students and colleagues (E. Cohen, 1980, 1982, 1984; E. Cohen, Lockheed, & Lohman, 1976; Riordan & Ruggiero, 1980; Rosenholtz & Cohen, 1985). Given the generally modest impact of both contact theory and the theory of status characteristics and expectation states on desegregation research in the active period, it is hardly surprising that reviewers generally called for more attention to theory in future work.

Disillusionment

In light of social scientists' historic support for and belief in the policy of school desegregation, it should come as little surprise that the inconclusive results of the reviews of the literature led to considerable disappointment, even disillusionment. This disillusionment had two conceptually separable but closely intertwined components. First, as discussed above, there was dissatisfaction with the research itself, which led to a deemphasis on continued quantitative research asking "Does desegregation improve intergroup relations?" This aspect of the discouragement and disillusion formed the basis for two quite new and different kinds of efforts—qualitative research on social processes in desegregated schools and efforts to discover "what works"—as will be discussed shortly. However, the other aspect of the disillusionment was a sense of profound disappointment in the results of desegregation and a questioning of whether social scientists had been naive in expecting desegregation to improve intergroup relations. Although contact theory had clearly specified that contact would improve intergroup relations only under certain circumstances that are not readily attainable without effort and planning, many social scientists had acted as if they expected desegregation itself to improve intergroup relations. What else could explain the large number of studies of desegregated schools chosen with so little attention to the contact conditions that information on fundamental aspects of these conditions was never even mentioned in research reports, let alone incorporated into the research design? When the reviews suggested that desegregation in and of itself had no clear predictable effect on intergroup relations, the question arose of whether the social scientific community's long-held expectations had any defensible empirical or theoretical basis.

The sense of disillusionment that characterized the late 1970s and the early 1980s was reflected in and heightened by a special issue of the *Journal of Negro Education* published in 1978, as well as by a paper published in 1983 by Harold Gerard. The special issue (Martin, 1978) presented numerous papers written by black scholars very critical of aspects of desegregation ranging from its basic premises to implementation strategies. Gerard's paper lambastes the social science statement submitted to the Supreme Court in 1954 by social psychologists in support of the plaintiffs in the *Brown v. Board of Education* case. Writing of the "heartache and disappointment" resulting from his work in the area, Gerard (1983, p. 875) concludes:

> Social scientists were wrong in the belief that change would come easily. . . . Simply mixing children in the classroom and trusting to benign human nature could never have done the trick. . . . What I am questioning here are the assumptions underlying the belief that school desegregation, as implemented in the typical school district, will be an instrument to achieve [equal opportunity for all].

Gerard concludes that social scientists lost credibility by entering the political arena before they had much to offer that was based on hard data rather than on well-meaning but basically empty rhetoric. He calls for serious and intensive research and development efforts, while simultaneously recognizing that the current academic reward structure and government funding priorities make it unlikely that this call will be heeded. His critique of the field was lent weight by his involvement as one of the principal investigators of a massive and sophisticated study of school desegregation (Gerard & Miller, 1975).

S. Cook (1979), one of the signers of the social science statement, provided a spirited reply to Gerard's charges. First, he argues that Gerard misread the social science statement, attributing to it predictions it never made. In addition, he points out that the statement was focused on the harmful effects of de jure segregation, which was the issue before the court, and that it was therefore unfair to judge its accuracy by studies conducted decades later in situations very different from those with which the case dealt.

My goal in mentioning this controversy here is not to examine all of the issues it raised; rather, it is to indicate the degree to which the aura of optimism and consensus that had characterized social scientists in earlier years had dissipated by the early 1980s. The more conservative zeitgeist of the Reagan era compounded by the disappointing results of studies of the impact of desegregation led to an atmosphere of discouragement and uncertainty. Thus, many voices in the social science community were raised to assert or acknowledge that desegregation accomplished less than many had hoped it would (Blalock, 1986; Miller, 1980; Rist, 1980). One frequently published scholar captured the situation poignantly when he explained to me why he had never completed a book on desegregation he had contemplated writing in the early 1980s—"Nobody seemed interested in it any longer."

New Directions in the 1975–1983 Period

Although the sense of disappointed expectations and disillusionment described above was quite widespread, it did not bring a complete halt to work in the area of desegregation and intergroup relations. In fact, two quite vigorous new lines of work characterized the 1975–1983 era. First, there was a sudden spurt of qualitative studies of desegregated schools (Aspira of America, 1979; Carew & Lightfoot, 1979; Clement, Eisenhart, & Harding, 1979; Collins, 1979; Collins & Noblit, 1981; Eddy, 1975; G. Grant, 1988; L. Grant, 1984; Hanna, 1982; Heath, 1982; Kochman, 1981; Lukas, 1985; Metz, 1978, 1986; Noblit & Collins, 1980; Noblit & Johnson, 1982; Ogbu, 1974; Ortiz, 1988; Rist, 1978; Scherer & Slawski, 1979; Schofield, 1989; Schofield & Sagar, 1979; Solomon, 1988; Stanlaw & Peshkin, 1988; Sullivan, 1979; Warren, 1982; Willie, 1973). Second, there was a marked increase in research and writing on how to make desegregation successful. Although some researchers continued with studies that, like those of the active period, asked, "What is the effect of school desegregation?" (Schweitzer & Griffore, 1981; Sheehan, 1980; Stephan & Rosenfield, 1978a, 1978b), a new interest in the question "What works?" began to be apparent.

The growth of qualitative research. Concern about sometimes seemingly insurmountable methodological problems, weak theory, and a growing awareness of the extremely varied nature of desegregated situations, which makes cumulating results difficult, led to a situation ripe for a new approach. Thus, the latter part of the 1970s and the early 1980s were characterized by greatly heightened interest in qualitative studies of desegregation. The hope was that such studies could illuminate the social processes occurring in desegregated schools and thus provide a richer understanding of the factors accounting for the varied outcomes documented by the preceding quantitative work.

There is no simple way to summarize the results of these qualitative studies because the schools and situations studied were extremely varied, as were the backgrounds and theoretical predilections of the researchers involved. Two efforts at synthesis of a number of these studies were commissioned back in 1979 by the National Institute of Education (NIE), which had earlier funded a group of five ethnographic studies of desegregated schools (Clement, Eisenhart, Harding, & Livesay, 1978; Collins & Noblit, 1978; Ianni, Sullivan, Orr, Henry, & Mavros, 1978; Scherer & Slawski, 1978; Schofield & Sagar, 1978). The first of these synthesis efforts was the commissioning of a number of cross-site essays—papers intended to illuminate certain important issues based on a comparison or synthesis of relevant information from all five NIE-funded research sites (Clement & Livesay, 1979; Noblit & Collins, 1979; Schofield & Sagar, 1979; Scherer & Slawski, 1979; Sullivan, 1979). The other synthesis effort was a more general attempt to summarize and integrate the five studies (Wax, 1979). Although LeCompte (1979) has made a number of trenchant criticisms of the latter synthesis effort, I think it is fair to say that, as a group, these papers and the other ethnographic studies appearing in the same general time period added a much needed dimension to desegregation research in at least two important ways. First, they made clear in a vivid way the remarkable, even daunting, complexity of the desegregation process and the extent to which school outcomes are influenced by larger social forces. Second, they suggested that in spite of this complexity and the ultimate uniqueness of each situation, there are some recurring problems and processes of which scholars and educators concerned about desegregated schools need to be aware. Each of these contributions is discussed below in turn.

The complexity of the desegregation process. As previously discussed, most of the research on school desegregation in the active period asked simply, "What is the effect of desegregation?" The fact that these studies did not cumulate led to a greater realization of the necessity of looking at the process of desegregation in order to have any hope of predicting its outcomes. The results of the qualitative studies underlined this conclusion by laying out in vivid detail descriptions of how differently this process operated in different settings. More than that, they expanded the kind of variables seen by many researchers as having important consequences for intergroup relations in desegregated schools.

Quantitative research on school desegregation and intergroup relations has historically had a rather psychological orientation. To the extent that it has looked at all at factors likely to influence intergroup relations, it has examined immediate features of the contact situation such as the proportion of minority and majority group students (Hallinan, 1982; Patchen, 1982; St. John & Lewis, 1975; Shaw, 1973), the extent to which the contact situation encourages cooperation (Slavin & Madden, 1979), and the relative status of minority and majority group students (Amir, Sharan, Rivner, Ben-Ari, & Bizman, 1979). Similarly, research on "what works" has also tended to take a "micro" rather than a "macro" perspective because much of it was funded specifically to evaluate how various school-level programs or policies have worked. Although examination of these kinds of variables is undoubtedly very important, it does not tell the whole story.

For example, Ogbu (1979) points out that the ethnographic studies of school desegregation demonstrate that the failure of schools to engage in certain efforts that might well have improved intergroup relations was frequently due to pressure exerted by white parents, who often had the kind of personal characteristics or political clout that made school-level personnel more responsive to them than to black parents. Thus, this approach demonstrates how the unequal status of blacks and whites in the larger setting may impede efforts to achieve equal status within the contact situation. This knowledge does not negate or nullify the importance of work on classroom social processes, but expands the area of inquiry by exploring further back along what can be thought of as a causal chain. One of the cross-site essays, written by Sullivan (1979), explicitly calls for the use of conceptual frameworks that include culture and community, concepts generally ignored or given short shrift in the majority of the literature on school desegregation and intergroup relations. This expansion of focus is hardly surprising, given that the disciplinary background of most of those producing desegregation ethnographies was sociology or anthropology. However, it is very useful in a field that has tended to ignore the importance of such factors.

Recurring processes, problems, and issues. The desegregated schools studied by qualitative researchers vary markedly. In spite of this great variation in size, region, student composition, and desegregation history, a number of common themes recur. For example, Rosenbaum's (1979) summary of the five NIE-funded studies points out that all of these studies found some significant degree of resegregation within the desegregated schools. In addition, virtually all of the studies indicated that desegregation led to heightened attention to maintaining order and avoiding conflict. All of the ethnographers reported some racial tensions, although none found any serious racially motivated violence during the course of their studies. Rather, students generally appeared to handle tensions by avoiding each other or taking care to try to "make it work," "get along," and "not make trouble" (Scherer & Slawski, 1979). In one case these efforts led to the development of a norm of "polite cooperation" (Clement et al., 1979); in another they led to a virtual taboo against explicitly mentioning race (Schofield, 1989). In most cases the tensions were fundamentally linked to white students' generally greater success in meeting the academic and behavioral norms of their schools. Although social class disparities, which were common, contributed greatly to this situation, students tended to interpret the differences as racial ones (Noblit & Collins, 1979; Schofield, 1989).

Increased emphasis on research on making desegregation work. The very mixed results of work asking "Does desegregation improve intergroup relations?" led not only to a considerable amount of qualitative research but also to an increased interest in the somewhat more complex question "What works?"—that is, "What particular conditions or practices are conducive to leading to positive outcomes?" Work asking this sort of question certainly began to appear before 1975 (E. Cohen & Roper, 1972; National Opinion Research Center, 1973; Resource Management Corporation, 1971; Stern & MacLennan, 1974). However, much of this literature consisted of conference papers or research reports that were never published. Furthermore, many of these papers were not widely cited in other scholarly work on school desegregation.

In the post-1975 period this situation changed. A large number of papers on "what works," many written by well-known researchers in the area of desegregation, began to appear. The majority of this work fell into three general categories. First, there was a set of integrative essays on what theory and research suggest about constructive ways of structuring intergroup contact in desegregated environments. These papers and books typically did not report new empirical work, but sought to pull together what was known, or suspected, on the basis of other work (examples of this genre, which I will call prescriptive essays, include Chesler, Bryant, & Crowfoot, 1981; E. Cohen, 1980; Crowfoot & Chesler, 1981; Forehand & Ragosta, 1976; Hawley et al., 1983; McConahay, 1981; Mercer, Iadicola, & Moore, 1980; Miller, 1980; and Sagar & Schofield, 1984). Second, there was a series of correlational studies that examined the relationship between various school characteristics and practices and intergroup outcomes (typical of this approach are Carriere et al., 1978; Coulson et al., 1977; Damico et al., 1981; Epstein, 1985; Forehand, Ragosta, & Rock, 1976; Hallinan, 1982; Hallinan & Smith, 1985; Hallinan & Teixeira, 1987; Patchen, 1982; Slavin & Madden, 1979; Wellisch, Carriere, MacQueen, & Duck, 1977; and Wellisch, Marcus, MacQueen, & Duck, 1976). Third, there was a set of studies, generally experimental in nature, designed to assess the impact of one or a few specific techniques designed to improve race relations (E. Aronson et al., 1978; E. Aronson & Osherow, 1980; Best, Smith, Graves, & Williams, 1975; Blanchard, Adelman, & Cook, 1975; Blanchard & Cook, 1976; Blanchard, Weigel, & Cook, 1975; Blaney, Stephan, Rosenfield, Aronson, & Sikes, 1977; E. Cohen, 1984; DeVries, Edwards, & Slavin, 1978; Johnson & Johnson, 1981; Johnson, Johnson, & Maruyama, 1984; Katz & Zalk, 1978; Landis, Day, McGrew, Thomas, & Miller, 1976; Landis, Hope, & Day, 1984; Lee, 1980; Miller, Brewer, & Edwards, 1985; Mumpower & Cook, 1978; Riordan & Ruggiero, 1980; Slavin, 1978, 1979, 1980, 1983a, 1983b; Weigel, Wiser, & Cook, 1975a; Yawkey, 1973; Yawkey & Blackwell, 1974). It is clearly beyond the scope of this review to try to summarize the results of all three lines of work. However, a brief discussion of each follows.

The prescriptive essays. Many of these essays focus on ways to avoid or minimize what came to be called "second generation" desegregation problems, that is, problems often arising in racially or ethnically mixed schools rather than during the initial desegregation of a school system. Examples of such problems include resegregation within desegregated schools, the disproportionate suspension or expulsion of minority students, and issues relating to ensuring that a school's staffing patterns, curriculum, and reward structures do not discourage or discriminate against minority group members. The goal of these papers was to provide information on how to construct environments likely to produce positive intergroup relations.

Consideration of just one of these second generation problems, resegregation, will show how complex and multifaceted such problems can be. Resegregation can and does occur in many desegregated school systems through an extraordinary variety of routes. First, of course, is the possibility of resegregation that may follow desegregation if whites choose to leave the desegregating school or system, either by moving elsewhere or transferring to a private school. Research on just how rapid and how major such white flight is has produced a longstanding major controversy (Armor, 1980, 1988; Rossell, 1983, 1985, 1990a; Smylie, 1983). However, for the purposes of this paper, it seems sufficient to say that there is substantial evidence that, especially in nonmetropolitan desegregation plans, some white flight due to school desegregation is likely to occur. This tendency is compounded by societal trends such as differential fertility and immigration rates for minority and majority group members, different age structures in the minority and majority group populations, and whites' tendency to migrate from urban to suburban areas even in the absence of urban school desegregation plans. All of these factors mean that desegregated systems with a large minority population may find it increasingly difficult to enroll enough white students to create meaningful chances for contact between white and minority students within their schools. In addition, extreme racial segregation in housing patterns, fiscal constraints, and a tendency for many minority and majority group parents to object to busing to achieve desegregation also create forces at the system level conducive to resegregation.

Even when such forces do not lead to resegregation at the building level, many school-level factors can create resegregation within schools (Epstein, 1985; National Institute of Education, 1977b; Patchen, 1982; Schofield, 1989). Sometimes this can be extreme, as in the case of a southern high school studied by Collins and Noblit (1978) in which one student aptly remarked, "They put all the segregation in the city in this school" (p. 195).

A number of common educational practices lead, often inadvertently, to partial or complete resegregation within desegregated schools. The most obvious and widespread are practices designed to reduce academic heterogeneity within classrooms (Epstein, 1985). A host of social and economic factors contribute to the fact that black and Hispanic students in desegregated schools tend to perform less well academically than their white peers. Thus, schools that categorize students on the basis of standardized tests, grades, or related criteria tend to have resegregated classrooms.

The degree to which practices designed to minimize academic heterogeneity can resegregate students is clearly illustrated by a study conducted by Schofield (1989) in a racially mixed middle school. Over 80% of those assigned to the academically accelerated track in the eighth grade were white, just as over 80% of those in the regular track were black. In the sixth and seventh grades, which did not have formal tracks, some teachers nonetheless grouped their students so that they had a "fast" class, some "average" classes, and a "slow" class. This practice led to considerable resegregation. For example, one black math teacher had a fast class that was entirely white and a slow group that was entirely black except for one white boy. Teachers who taught more academically heterogeneous classes frequently divided children *within* each class into three or more groups. Again, it was not uncommon for the top group to be all white, or virtually so, and for the bottom group to be entirely or almost entirely black. Most teachers were aware that such grouping practices undercut the potential of their school to foster positive contact between black and white children but saw this as a relatively unimportant sacrifice to be made in order to pursue the more important goal of teaching their subject matter as effectively as possible (Schofield & Sagar, 1979).

Although much resegregation stems from policies such as tracking or ability grouping, it is undeniable that students do often voluntarily resegregate themselves. Significant amounts of classroom resegregation can occur even in schools that do not track students when black and white students choose to enroll in different kinds of courses (Collins & Noblit, 1978; G. Grant, 1988). Students may also resegregate themselves in a variety of situations, from lunch to extracurricular activities. For example, Collins (1979) studied a southern school in which whites dominated activities such as the student government, the yearbook, and golf, whereas blacks populated the chorus and the basketball and football teams. The extent of such voluntary resegregation is sometimes surprising. For example, in one set of studies the seating patterns in the cafeteria of a school whose student body was almost precisely half black and half white were mapped for 2 years. On a typical day, when the seating positions of approximately 250 students during any particular lunch period were recorded, fewer than 15 of them sat next to someone of the other race (Schofield, 1979; Schofield & Sagar, 1979). This was so in spite of the fact that there was little overt racial friction. Other studies have reported similarly marked cleavage by race (Cusick & Ayling, 1973; Gerard et al., 1975; G. Grant, 1988; Rogers et al., 1984).

The essays and books written in this period attempt to go beyond isolating problems such as resegregation to suggesting ways to handle or avoid them. In fact, a number of them develop fairly specific prescriptive guidelines for use by educators (Chesler et al., 1981; Crowfoot & Chesler, 1981; Hawley et al., 1983; McConahay, 1981; Mercer et al., 1980; Miller, 1980). For example, many suggest the use of multiethnic texts, endorse strong efforts to ensure a racially and ethnically mixed faculty at desegregated schools, and suggest avoiding or minimizing tracking and ability grouping to the extent possible. Although most of the prescriptions contained in these papers seem sensible and useful, the research base supporting them varies markedly. For example, Stephan and Stephan's (1984) review of the research on multiethnic programs concludes that a substantial, if methodologically flawed, set of studies generally suggest a positive effect, at least when the programs are of some reasonable complexity and duration. On the other hand, there is little, if any, literature on how the racial composition of the faculty affects peer relations, although both contact theory (Allport, 1954; S. Cook, 1969) and status expectation state theory (Berger et al., 1966, 1972) provide a clear rationale for the prediction that a racially and ethnically diverse faculty would promote positive interaction among the students in schools with heterogeneous student bodies. The prescriptive essays are generally appropriately cautious, stating explicitly that their research base is often weak. Some of them use not only the empirical literature but interviews with practitioners involved with desegregated schools to help fill out their knowledge base (Hawley et al., 1983). Although these essays may be of use to practitioners, in general they were not intended to, and did not, move theory or research in the field forward, except perhaps by helping to make even more salient the complexity of the desegregation process and the multitude of factors that can affect its outcomes.

Large-scale correlational studies of school practices and intergroup relations. In the early 1970s the U.S. Office of Education began funding over 900 desegregating school districts under a program known as the Emergency School Assistance Program (ESAP). Evaluations of the impact of this program provide a rich source of information about "what works" based on over 9,000 interviews as well as observations at a large number of schools (Carriere et al., 1978; Coulson et al., 1977; National Opinion Research Center, 1973; Resource Management Corporation, 1971; Wellisch et al., 1976, 1977). Federal funding was also made available for other large-scale correlational studies of the links between school policies and characteristics and student outcomes, both academic and social (Forehand et al., 1976). I will not attempt to summarize the results of these studies here because many of them are weighty tomes, often more than 200 pages in length. However, as a group they reinforce the conclusion emerging from the reviews of the literature—that desegregation is implemented very differently in different places and that these differences do influence intergroup relations. For example, Wellisch et al. (1977) concluded that schools using ethnically diverse reading materials and having assemblies with multicultural or intergroup relations themes were more likely to be characterized by high levels of intergroup interaction at recess and lunchtime than were schools that did not emphasize respect for minority group members and positive intergroup relations in these ways. Forehand et al. (1976) came to a similar conclusion.

Somewhat surprisingly, many of these studies have not become well integrated into the scholarly literature on desegregation. Perhaps this is partially due to many scholars' preference for experimental rather than correlational studies of what works, because the direction of causality is often quite unclear in the correlational studies. However, other factors, such as the fact that they are reports from contract research companies rather than papers prepared in an academic context, may also contribute to their relative neglect. This speculation is supported by the fact that Slavin and Madden's (1979) paper, which was published in a respected journal, is quite commonly cited although it is based on correlational data.

Experimental studies of specific practices designed to improve race relations. Although there have been experimental studies of a number of approaches to improving intergroup relations in desegregated schools, there is one general approach that has received much more attention than others. This is the creation of cooperative work groups within racially or ethnically diverse classrooms. Most of this research has focused on one of five rather similar models and on groups of black and white children, although there are some studies that include Mexican-American children (E. Aronson & Gonzales, 1988; E. Cohen, Lotan, & Catanzarite, 1986; Geffner, 1978; Gonzalez, 1979; Slavin, Sharon, Katan, & Hertz-Lazarowitz, 1985; Weigel, Wiser, & Cook, 1975b). All five techniques have been researched in classroom settings, and most have books or manuals that explain their implementation.

In some of these techniques cooperation between students on racially or ethnically mixed teams is induced through task interdependence; that is, no individual child can fulfill his or her assignment without the assistance of others. In other cases cooperative behavior is induced through reward interdependence; that is, each child's grade is partially dependent on the success of other group members. Although they differ in many ways, most of these techniques have mechanisms that allow lower achievers to contribute substantially to the attainment of the group goals. In spite of the rather important conceptual differences in the way in which cooperation is induced in the different team learning programs, there is a noticeable similarity in their outcomes. The large majority of studies suggest that use of these techniques leads to improvement in intergroup relations, even if the student teams are used for a small part of the school day for no more than 2 or 3 months (for reviews of this literature, see E. Aronson et al., 1978; E. Aronson & Gonzales, 1988; Bossert, 1988–1989; S. Cook, 1985; Johnson & Johnson, 1982; Johnson et al., 1984; Sharan, 1980; and Slavin, 1983a, 1983b, 1985). It is also noteworthy that quite a bit of research has been done on the academic impact of these strategies. Typically, these studies suggest that the impact is positive, especially for originally low achieving students (Slavin, 1980, 1983b). Another added benefit is that such strategies may be more consistent with the cultural backgrounds of some black and Hispanic children than present practices that emphasize competition. For example, there is a body of research that suggests that Mexican-American children, especially first generation children, may be more cooperatively oriented than their Anglo peers (Diaz-Guerrero, 1987; Kagan, 1980; Kagan & Knight, 1981). The same may be true of blacks to a lesser extent (Kagan, 1980).

There is some evidence that cooperation in other spheres at school also encourages the development of positive intergroup relations. The potential for cooperative involvement in extracurricular activities to improve intergroup relations is suggested by Patchen's (1982) work, which found that participation in such activities had a stronger impact on interracial friendships than almost any of the other numerous variables in his study. Similarly, Hallinan and Teixeira (1987) report that both black and white students who participate in such activities make more cross-race best friend choices than do students who do not participate. In addition, Slavin and Madden (1979) found that participation on integrated athletic teams was related to a variety of positive intergroup attitudes and behaviors. The correlational nature of these studies leaves the direction of causality unspecified. Yet, given the clearly demonstrated positive effects of cooperative learning activities on intergroup relations, it seems reasonable to assume that at least some of the relation stems from the positive impact of joint activity on students' feelings about each other.

Recent Years: 1984 to the Present

The disenchantment with desegregation as a social policy described earlier and the concern about the probable usefulness of further studies asking simply about "the effect" of desegregation on intergroup relations continue to affect the field. The demographic realities in many large urban school districts and a much more sophisticated understanding of the complexities of creating environments likely to yield significant positive change in intergroup relations have led many researchers concerned with equality, equity, and the education of minority students to focus on areas such as "effective schools" and the education of "at-risk" students rather than school desegregation, as they might have 20 years ago. Even those who continue to believe that desegregation, if properly implemented, is a sufficiently promising and important tool for the education of this nation's children to merit substantial continued research have had to face the fact that funding for this sort of work is currently very difficult to obtain. This is a major problem because sophisticated studies of this topic, whether quantitative or qualitative, are inevitably too expensive to conduct without substantial external funding. A telling although perhaps rather ad hoc indication of the low level of activity in the field is that only one session at the 1990 annual meeting of the American Educational Research Association was devoted to desegregation issues compared to a full 10 sessions a decade earlier at the 1980 meeting.

Lest I paint too gloomy a picture, let me hasten to point out one very promising characteristic of recent years. Specifically, this has been a time of considerable theoretical ferment. Roughly speaking, it is possible to categorize this work into three areas of discussion and theory building. The first area concerns the purpose of desegregation. The second is an attempt to critique, refine, and go beyond contact theory. The third, arising independently of traditional work on desegregation and intergroup relations, can be characterized as theory and research on intergroup relations as a generic issue. Next, I will discuss each of these three types of work.

Desegregation and Intergroup Relations: What Should We Strive For?

The question posed above is one of values that I do not intend to try to answer here, although I have written about it elsewhere (Sagar & Schofield, 1984). However, consideration of this question is vital not only for educators but also for researchers. As indicated earlier in this chapter, too often researchers have selected outcome measures on the basis of convenience or custom without giving sufficiently serious thought to what the probable or desirable outcomes of desegregated schooling might be. Awareness that the potential intergroup goals of desegregation can range from the cultural and/or structural assimilation (Gordon, 1964) of minority group members to greater appreciation for diversity on the part of majority group members raises important questions about the outcome measures that are appropriate in desegregation research.

One might expect that both educators and researchers would long ago have given a substantial amount of very serious attention to the issue of what the precise intergroup goals of desegregation are or should be. Yet much less has been written on this issue than one might expect. Perhaps because desegregation mandated by the courts is a legal requirement and voluntary efforts at desegregation are often seen by their supporters as a moral imperative, the question of what precisely the intergroup goals are has received less attention than it deserves. Also contributing importantly to this situation is the fact that the original impetus for desegregation in the minority community came primarily from a desire for a better education for minority group students rather than from a desire for improved intergroup relations (Bell, 1980; Blakey, 1989; Martin, 1978). Studies of desegregation in both the United States and Israel have found that school authorities themselves often ignore or gloss over the issues of whether and how their schools should try to influence intergroup relations (Klein & Eshel, 1980; Sagar & Schofield, 1984; Schofield, 1989). One major factor contributing to this is the primacy of the emphasis naturally given to the academic mission of schools. However, undoubtedly contributing to this situation is the fact that explicit discussion of what kind of intergroup goals a school should have is likely to be controversial and politically dangerous because opinions on this matter are often both diverse and highly charged.

Historically, researchers too have not paid a great deal of attention to the issue of what desegregated schools should or actually do try to accomplish. On the one hand, this is hardly surprising, because social scientists' claim to certain conceptual and methodological skills does not translate in any direct way into a claim to have special expertise relating to questions of values. On the other hand, social scientists do have both theory and data relevant to the probable consequences of pursuing different goals. This seems to me to give them reason to enter the fray about what goals should be. For example, back in 1969 Pettigrew wrote a paper in which he employed a great deal of social psychological theory and research to assess the probable consequences of separatist and integrationist policies.

It is certainly true that some social scientists addressed themselves explicitly to the issue of what desegregated schools could or should strive to accomplish well before the mid-1980s. However, discussion of this issue took a more prominent role in this period than it had before, perhaps partly because of the decline in the amount of new empirical work being produced. In the 1970s it was common for edited books or special issues of journals dealing with topics such as racism or school desegregation to omit extended discussions of what precisely school desegregation should achieve in the intergroup realm (Ashmore, 1976; Katz, 1976; St. John, 1975). In fact, this question received so little attention that Yinger (1986), in an essay entitled "The Research Agenda: New Directions for Desegregation Studies," wrote:

> We need, in my judgment, much more research on the goals of desegregation for various groups and study of the extent to which they are shared. . . . We are confronted not simply with technical problems (how to do it), but also with social, moral, and political problems (whether to do it, to what degree, as well as how—for methods affect outcomes). (p. 234)

Although there has not been much research on such topics, in the 1980s discussion of such issues became a common feature of books dealing with desegregation, racism, and the like (Ben-Ari & Amir, 1986; Berry, 1984; Pettigrew, 1988; Ramirez, 1988; Sagar & Schofield, 1984; Triandis, 1988; Yinger, 1986).

The papers dealing with the issue of desegregation's goals are hard to summarize briefly in any way that does them justice. However, as Yinger (1986, p. 234) noted, there is one core issue with which any current consideration of this question must deal—"the degree to which school desegregation should permit, perhaps even encourage, distinctive group identities or, on the other hand, should be color-blind and culture-blind." As our society has become more diverse and issues of ethnic pride and identity have become more salient in the last few decades, more and more voices have been raised urging multiethnic schools explicitly to take account of, and even foster, cultural diversity. Yet there are also those who are concerned about how such goals can be accomplished without creating tension and exacerbating existing racial and ethnic isolation. At least three research issues are raised by this debate. First, what cultural differences actually exist? Second, which of these are relevant to the school situation? Third, what should the schools' stance be toward these differences? Let me briefly discuss each of these issues in turn.

Early research on school desegregation and intergroup relations essentially ignored the question of cultural differences. This was no accident. First, the earliest research was conducted before the late 1960s, when issues of ethnic pride began to gain such salience in our society. Second, in the early years desegregation was generally seen as a phenomenon that involved only two groups, blacks and whites. Blacks were not generally perceived by majority group members as having much in the way of a separate culture that was relevant to schooling. Differences that were perceived to exist were often seen as a result of cultural deprivation and disadvantage in an era that operated through the lens of a deficit model in looking at black/white differences (Valentine, 1971). Thus, they were not perceived as cultural differences to which schools should accommodate.

However, more recently there has been much more emphasis in theory and research on aspects of black culture (Hale-Benson, 1986; J. Jones, 1986, 1988; R. Jones, 1980; Kochman, 1981; Ogbu, 1986, 1988; White, 1984). In addition, the rapid growth of immigrant populations, which bring with them their own cultures, has made the issue of cultural differences in multiethnic schools inescapable. In some cases, such as that in which children's native language is not English, cultural differences are obvious. However, in other cases research can help illuminate substantial but less immediately apparent group differences in values, behavioral style, or the like. For example, Heath's (1982, 1983) work suggests different patterns of questioning in black and white homes. Phinney and Rotheram (1987) found Mexican-American children to be somewhat more passive than black children, as well as more attentive to social stimuli and more deferential to authority. Work by Kagan and his colleagues, as well as others (De la Serna, 1982; Diaz-Guerrero, 1987; Kagan, 1980; Kagan & Knight, 1981; Kagan & Madsen, 1971), suggests a more cooperative orientation on the part of some Mexican-American children than Anglo children.

Once research has established that certain cultural differences exist, a second question that arises is which of these are relevant to the school situation. In some cases the relevance is obvious (Boateng, 1990; Hale-Benson, 1986, 1990). Take again, for example, the issue of language. Schools with linguistically diverse populations must grapple with the issue of what to do. Similarly, the research suggesting a cooperative rather than competitive orientation in some groups of Hispanic[2] children has clear relevance to schools' practices. Also of obvious relevance is the work of Ogbu (1988), which suggests that one reaction that some black students have to the caste-like racially based social stratification in this country is to develop an oppositional identity in which compliance with the normative demands of the school is seen as "acting white" and is thus rejected. Matute-Bianchi (1986) discusses a similar phenomenon in certain subgroups of Mexican-American students. However, in other cases, the relevance is less clear. For example, J. Jones (1988) argues that the Afro-American perspective on spirituality is somewhat different from the Euro-American perspective. Is such a difference irrelevant for schooling, or does a perspective that deemphasizes personal control and earthly accomplishment have implications in the school setting? Both theory and research on learning and classroom social processes may help to clarify questions about the relevance of particular aspects of culture to schooling.

As indicated earlier, once cultural differences have been established and their relevance to schooling made apparent, the next question one must face is what the schools' stance toward these differences should be. This issue stands out in clearest relief in the increasing number of racially or ethnically mixed schools that enroll students for whom English is not a first language. Controversy over the kind and amount of instruction that should be offered in languages other than English has been sharp (Crawford, 1989; National Institute of Education, 1977a; Orfield, 1986; Rossell, 1990b), with some scholars arguing for programs that move students as fast as possible toward English and others arguing for a policy that supports and encourages learning in both the students' home language and English. However, in this case the decision does not rest with the schools. As a result of the Supreme Court's finding in *Lau v. Nichols* (1974), students with limited English proficiency must receive educational services that facilitate access to English. In many other cases, though, the school must decide on its reaction to cultural differences without the guidance of legal requirements. For example, should schools adjust in situations in which Hispanic students are more cooperatively oriented than Anglo children, or do the minority group students need to adjust as part of their preparation to function in the broader society? One's answer to this question depends heavily on one's attitudes toward the desirability and feasibility of achieving cultural and/or structural assimilation, one's views about the degree to which a cultural "mismatch" between student and school is likely to impede learning, whether one believes that children can be bicultural (in the sense of switching back and forth between two sets of cultural patterns depending on which is appropriate given the context in which they are functioning) without considerable stress, and the like.

As should be apparent from the preceding brief discussion, questions of fact and value are highly intermingled in this area. However, social scientists can make a substantial contribution to thinking out some of the complex issues involved. It is unfortunate for the state of research as well as public policy that more attention was not devoted to these questions earlier. Further, this work will have much less impact than it might if researchers see it as relevant only to social policy but not to the research community. One's goals for desegregation have immediate implications for design and measurement issues. Let me give just one brief example. Triandis (1988) argues that the goal of intergroup contact "should be to create in the shortest possible time the largest number of . . . 'successful interpersonal relationships' " (p. 47). Braddock (1985), on the other hand, is more concerned with the degree to which desegregation fosters structural assimilation, which he defines as "entry into the social cliques, organizations, institutional activities, and general civic life of the majority society" (p. 10). The implications of this difference in focus are profound. Researchers accepting Triandis's view would do well to focus on the quantity and quality of the personal relationships developing in desegregated schools. Roster and rating sociometric techniques or classroom observations would be very appropriate. Those more influenced by Braddock's view would want to follow his footsteps in exploring the long-term impact of desegregation on college choice, residential choice, occupational desegregation, and the like (Braddock, 1980, 1985; Braddock & McPartland, 1982; Braddock, McPartland, & Trent, 1984; McPartland & Braddock, 1981).

Contact Theory and Beyond

In the mid-1970s reviewers complained accurately that theoretical issues had received too little attention in the desegregation literature. Several scholars devoted careful attention to assessing the evidence relating to the contact theory (Amir, 1969, 1976; McClendon, 1974; Riordan, 1978). However, as indicated earlier, with the exception of S. Cook (1969, 1978, 1984, 1985; S. Cook & Selltiz, 1955) few researchers engaged in sustained efforts to test and develop this theoretical approach.

One encouraging feature of work in the last several years is the serious attempt to move theory in this area forward. Efforts have been made both to critique and improve contact theory and to go beyond it. One line of work, exemplified in a book edited by Hewstone and Brown (1986), has tried to expand our understanding of the impact of intergroup contact by exploring contact in a more diverse array of national settings than was typical in earlier work. This volume contains papers on contact between Arab and Israeli youth in Israel, Germans and immigrant populations in Germany, Catholics and Protestants in Northern Ireland, and blacks and whites in South Africa. Thus, it highlights the fundamental ways in which political, historical, and economic factors shape intergroup contact and makes some of the limitations of the traditional contact theory approach apparent.

In contrast to this kind of work, which has tended to focus attention on "macro" level variables, recently there has also been work aimed at elucidating the role of more "micro" level variables that might clarify how and why contact might or might not have an effect on intergroup relations. For example, Rothbart and John (1985) discuss how several features of the way in which people process information impede the reduction of stereotyping in contact situations. Focusing on affective rather than cognitive processes, Stephan and Stephan (1985) explore the relation between intergroup anxiety and intergroup contact.

In addition to this kind of work, which provides many insights relevant to contact theory but is not primarily focused on assessing the current status of the theory itself, a number of mainly or exclusively theoretical papers have appeared that go beyond most earlier theoretical efforts in an important way. Earlier work tended either to delineate specific situational factors that might influence contact or to assess the evidence relevant to their effectiveness (Amir, 1969, 1976; S. Cook, 1979; McClendon, 1974; Riordan, 1978). However, the 1980s witnessed a number of papers that stepped back a bit further in an effort to trace contact theory's historical roots, to delineate and assess the validity of the assumptions on which it is based, and the like (Brewer & Miller, 1984; Hewstone & Brown, 1986; Miller et al., 1985; Pettigrew, 1986). Because a number of the criticisms that have been aimed at contact theory have important implications for future research, I will discuss below those that are the most important.

Brown and Turner (1981) argue that a major flaw with contact theory is that it takes an interpersonal approach to what is basically an intergroup issue. Because in their view intergroup behavior is not simply an extension of interpersonal behavior, this is a fundamental problem. More recently, Pettigrew (1986) has made a similar point in a somewhat different way. He criticizes contact theory for focusing so heavily on the problem of individual prejudice. He writes (1986, p. 172): "Prejudice is an important, but not the fundamental, component in intergroup relations. Institutionalized discrimination is the core of the problem; prejudice both supports and is derived from these institutionally-restrictive arrangements." These critiques have very serious implications for theory and research. For example, if Pettigrew is correct, as he may well be, the utility of focusing on racial attitudes as outcome measures in desegregation research is open to serious question. Instead, one might want to look at behavioral indices of discrimination at both the personal and the institutional level.

Pettigrew (1986) also points out that underlying contact theory is the belief that individuals from different groups are fundamentally rather similar and that similarity creates attraction. According to this view, putting individuals from different groups together in the right kind of situation clears barriers to their recognition of their mutual humanity and ultimate similarity. Thus, bringing individuals together is seen as a basis for reducing group stereotypes. Yet, in an era in which large numbers of children from Hispanic, Asian, and other cultures somewhat different from the majority culture are attending school, it is not clear that contact will enable individuals to perceive their basic similarity rather than to become more aware of differences. Even in the case of black-white contact, where cultural differences are not as profound, social class differences can create real barriers to the disconfirmation of racial stereotypes and the discovery of mutual interests (Schofield, 1989). Thus, theories concerned with improving intergroup relations need to pay more attention to how to manage actual diversity and difference than contact theory does.

Yet another important criticism of contact theory, as well as of desegregation research more broadly, is that it has not focused sufficient attention on the generalizability of any change that does occur (Hewstone & Brown, 1986; Miller et al., 1985). Specifically, one can ask about at least two kinds of generalizability. First, does change within a situation carry over and affect the behavior of the same individuals outside of that situation? Second, does change occurring in response to contact with certain members of an out-group generalize to other members of that group or to one's thinking about and behavior toward that out-group as a group? This issue is hardly a new one. Studies of intergroup contact in the late 1940s and early 1950s sometimes made such distinctions (e.g., Deutsch & Collins, 1951). S. Cook (1978) explicitly addressed this issue in his research as well. However, typically such distinctions have been ignored in desegregation research, even though they have crucial implications for the choice of outcome variables to be measured.

Research on Intergroup Relations

Rather ironically, the very years that have seen stagnation and disillusionment in empirical work on desegregation and intergroup relations have seen a virtual flood of basic theoretical and empirical work on intergroup relations as a generic field. Reviews of this work are available elsewhere (Brewer, 1979; Messick & Mackie, 1989; Stephan, 1985; Wilder, 1986), so I will not duplicate them here. However, this work deserves some mention because of the possibilities it presents for providing new approaches to work on desegregation and intergroup relations.

Two lines of work have together created a tremendous amount of interest in research and theory on intergroup relations. The first of these grows out of the pioneering work of Tajfel (1969, 1970, 1978, 1982) and his colleagues (Billig, 1976; Tajfel & Turner, 1979; Turner, 1975, 1978, 1982; Turner & Giles, 1981), who developed an approach to understanding intergroup relations known as social identity theory. Basically, this approach argues that individuals' identities are strongly influenced by their membership in social categories or groups. When group membership is salient in a particular situation, a need for a positive self-identity leads individuals to perceive their own group more favorably than the out-group, to behave in a way that favors the in-group, and the like. It is important to note that work growing out of this tradition has demonstrated such tendencies in situations where the basis for assignment to groups is trivial. In fact, in the early experiments (Tajfel, 1970; Tajfel, Billig, Bundy, & Flament, 1971), as well as subsequent ones, efforts were made to create "minimal groups," that is, groups in which there was no face-to-face contact between members, no financial or other tangible gain from in-group favoritism, no real social significance to the basis for group assignment (overestimating or underestimating dots), and so forth.

The second recent and very active line of research concerned with intergroup relations has been characterized by Stephan (1985) in his review of this field as a cognitive information processing approach. Stimulated by the rapid burgeoning of the field of cognitive psychology, this approach has brought a new perspective to the study of topics such as prejudice and stereotyping. Turning earlier views on their heads, this approach sees stereotyping not as the product of "sick" or "faulty" reasoning, but as an almost inevitable outgrowth of the fact that the human mind simplifies the complex input it receives by grouping similar things into categories as part of its normal functioning. A good example of this kind of approach is Rothbart and John's (1985) paper subtitled "A cognitive analysis of the effects of intergroup contact." The authors (p. 82) "consider the process of stereotype change produced through contact with individual group members as an example of the general cognitive process by which attributes of category members modify category attributes." According to this perspective, there is much to be learned about intergroup relations by thinking of stereotypes as social categories much like the other categories that the human mind normally uses in processing information.

Given the historical tendency of the literature on desegregation and intergroup relations to neglect theoretical development, the intense activity in what can be thought of as the "social identity" and the "social categorization" approaches to intergroup relations poses a real opportunity. Perhaps because of the low level of empirical activity currently exploring intergroup relations in desegregated schools, this opportunity has, to date, not been fully exploited. In fact, to my knowledge, Brewer, Miller, and their colleagues (Brewer & Miller, 1984, 1988; Miller, 1990a, 1990b; Miller, Brewer, & Edwards, 1985) are virtually unique in attempting to draw out the implications of this work for desegregated schools and then to test their ideas. However, even they use a laboratory analogue to the desegregated school involving "minimal groups" (dot overestimators and underestimators) rather than actual social categories such as African-American, Mexican-American, Anglo, and the like.

WHERE DO WE GO FROM HERE?

Shifting the Underlying Research Question

The prototypical study of desegregation and intergroup relations attempted to assess "the effect" of desegregation on some indicator of relations between blacks and whites, such as racial attitudes or the formation of close friendships. This paradigm is not very useful for future work for several reasons. First, as can be seen with the benefit of hindsight, this formulation of the question, which implicitly or explicitly formed the basis of so much of the research in the "active years," was never really satisfactory. It violates the basic contention of contact theory, which is that the consequences of intergroup experiences are very dependent on the structure of the contact situation. Future work needs to keep this elementary but often ignored caveat in mind. Second, desegregation is not what it used to be. In the prototypical study of the effects of desegregation, students or school systems that had been segregated at some point in the very recent past were studied as they had their early experiences with legally mandated desegregation. Much more common today are situations in which schools have had a heterogeneous student body for some time, frequently but not exclusively as the result of earlier desegregation orders. Thus, it is not so much the process of "de-segregation" of the schools one can now study. Rather, it is the processes of biracial or multiethnic schooling. Perhaps the biggest change in the nature of the situation is the need to recognize that desegregation is no longer simply or primarily a phenomenon involving blacks and whites, as it has historically been conceptualized. The marked growth in the Hispanic population in this country along with the increased numbers of immigrants from Asia and elsewhere means that a tremendous number of the nation's largest school systems must grapple with how to educate students from extremely diverse cultural and linguistic backgrounds. Black/white relations remain a problem of vital concern that still needs great attention. However, it is also increasingly important to look at relations between whites and members of various minority groups, as well as between members of different minority groups themselves.

If research should no longer be guided by the question "What is the effect of desegregation on intergroup relations?" what orienting questions should replace the earlier one? I propose two. The first can be stated most generally as "What is going on here?" The second is "What works?" Let me discuss each of these questions briefly.

In suggesting that research should focus on "What is going on here?" I mean that we need to pay much more attention to the social processes that lead to various kinds of intergroup outcomes. I am not suggesting that we try to describe the "typical" biracial or multiethnic school. Circumstances are too varied for that. In fact, the "here" in "What is going on here?" calls attention to the fact that just as there is no one dependable effect of desegregation, there may be no one dependable set of processes that always occur. However, I am suggesting that there may be issues that occur predictably in different kinds of biracial or multiethnic schools and that attention to the question of what is going on will help to isolate them. To give just one example, a study I conducted of a "model" desegregated school in which the white students typically came from more educated and affluent backgrounds than the black students demonstrated numerous ways in which whites' generally privileged status in our society made it difficult to create a truly equitable institution (Schofield, 1989). This same theme comes up frequently in discussions of magnet schools (Metz, 1986) and of how black students' academic performance can be undermined by the structural constraints blacks have faced for so long in the U.S. labor market (Ogbu, 1986). It has also been a concern underlying the critiques of desegregation by many minority scholars (Bell, 1980). Thus, questions connected to how and why majority group privilege in the broader society impedes the creation of equitable school environments and whether such tendencies are malleable would, in my view, be one example of valuable kinds of process questions that could be stimulated by asking "What is going on here?" Whether probed through open-ended qualitative methods or through quantitative methods that specify antecedent conditions, moderating and/or mediating variables, and predicted outcomes, there is much to be learned from asking "What is going on here?"

I would also argue that we need to focus much more attention on "What works?" In spite of the low prestige often accorded to applied research in academic circles, the fact remains that there is an urgent need to know how to make schools with diverse student bodies function more effectively in the social as well as the academic domain. Research on cooperative learning teams, discussed earlier, has provided a real success story in this realm. Such methods are currently used by many thousands of educators in this country and elsewhere (S. Cook, 1985). However, much remains to be done in suggesting and developing other procedures that also work. One barrier to this kind of research (which has not been a problem for the study of cooperative work groups, which are also designed to improve academic achievement) is the low priority schools often put on intergroup relations. However, it is my admittedly very subjective impression that some of the horrific incidents of recent years, such as the racially motivated attacks and murders in places like Howard Beach and Bensonhurst, and the publicity given to the continuing harassment of minority group students on college campuses across the country have made the importance of intergroup relations more salient to school personnel and other "gatekeepers" of the research process than it has been for some time. So it may be possible to overcome this barrier with careful selection of sites.

In focusing on both "What is going on here" and "What works," it is important to go beyond simple description to analysis of why certain things happen or why given practices work. Otherwise, it is likely that this research will be plagued by a problem analogous to the one that is so apparent when one examines research on "the effect" of desegregation—the problem of inconsistent and even contradictory results that cannot be cumulated in a way that is very useful from either a scholarly or a practical standpoint. Different processes may well occur in different milieus. So, too, practices shown to work in one racially or ethnically heterogeneous milieu cannot be assumed to work in all other ethnically heterogeneous milieus. Numerous factors, including the specific groups involved, the community context, and the grade level studied, might be reasonably expected to influence "What is going on here" or "What works." However, attention to why certain processes are set in motion or why certain practices are effective should add greatly both to our theoretical understanding and to our ability to make wise decisions about which practices might be useful in specific situations.

Taking Theory More Seriously

In the pursuit of knowledge relating both to "What is going on here" and to "What works," it is important that we take theory more seriously than it has been taken in the past. This same exhortation was characteristic of the reviews emerging in the 1970s. Unfortunately, the most that can be said is that this call has had a very modest effect on empirical work. This failure to take theory as seriously as desirable may have stemmed partly from the fact that many researchers in this area are urgently motivated by personal values and social concerns. Thus, doing the research, which many believed would demonstrate the value of desegregation, may have seemed more important than stopping to work out theoretical formulations. Second, theory is not easy to develop. It is one thing to call for the use or development of theory and another to do it, especially in an era when the academic job market is very tight and outlets for empirical publications are, in most relevant fields, more numerous than those for exclusively theoretical efforts. There is always the possibility that my plea for greater attention to theory will go virtually unheeded for similar reasons. However, there is one aspect of the current situation that increases the chance that this call will have some impact—the existence of current vigorous theoretical and empirical activity in the "social identity" and "social categorization" traditions described earlier.

The existence of these two bodies of literature provides both a rich opportunity and a potential trap for researchers interested in exploring either "What is going on here" or "What works." Let me explain. On the one hand, these two lines of research are full of ideas that seem to have direct implications for understanding intergroup relations in racially or ethnically mixed schools. For example, Doise and his colleagues have conducted numerous experiments to test the idea, derived from work within the social identity tradition, that the existence of cross-cutting social categories should reduce the discrimination faced by out-group members. Thus, in one study, Deschamps and Doise (1978) found that crossing the preexisting social categories of boy and girl with an experimentally introduced category of "red group" and "blue group" led to a diminution of the favoritism that boys and girls showed toward their own gender group in the absence of this cross-cutting category. This kind of finding has obvious implications for researchers interested in "What works." Although it would be unforgivably naive to expect that placing students from different racial or ethnic groups in artificially created "red" or "blue" groups would suddenly eliminate in-group favoritism, there is some evidence that creating important cross-cutting ties can, in fact, improve peer relations in desegregated schools (McGivern & Schofield, 1979). (It is even possible to speculate that the creation of cross-cutting categories might be one reason why cooperative learning teams have the positive impact on intergroup relations that they do.) Thus, close examination of these bodies of work for insights useful in illuminating social processes in desegregated schools is a very real and exciting possibility.

On the other hand, there are two traps of which researchers must be wary. The first is the danger of too ready a leap from the world of the "minimal group" into the world of real groups with long histories, varied cultures, and very different positions in the larger social structure. The second, which is especially dangerous for those drawing on work coming out of the social categorization approach, is the danger of focusing too exclusively on individual mental processes. Any approach that does this neglects the kinds of variables that qualitative studies of desegregation have demonstrated are so important—culture, social power, stratification systems, and the like. I would like to discuss these two potential problems in turn.

One extended example will be used to make clear the danger of too quick and direct a translation from work growing out of the minimal group paradigm to the actual functioning of racially or ethnically diverse schools. An obvious implication of such work is that increasing the salience of group boundaries is likely to increase intergroup bias and discrimination, whereas decreasing their salience reduces such tendencies (Brewer, 1979; Gaertner & Dovidio, 1986; Wilder, 1978, 1986; Worchel, 1979, 1986). The research evidence on this point is multifaceted and quite consistent. Thus, it might be tempting to jump to the conclusion that, based on this literature, one should advocate a "color-blind" perspective for school policy and practices.

Yet, the research on which this generalization is based has generally not been conducted in situations directly parallel to racially or ethnically mixed schools. For example, in the laboratory it is possible to create situations in which one can compare the behavior of people for whom group membership is made salient by an experimental manipulation and individuals for whom the issue of group membership does not arise. However, in many real-life situations, including a great many schools with racially and ethnically mixed student bodies, this is hardly a realistic possibility. Group membership is the "ground" against which everyday interaction plays itself out (Ianni et al., 1978; Lukas, 1985; Peshkin, in press; Schofield, 1986, 1989). Ethnicity may be more or less salient at certain times or places in such schools, but the control group condition of absolute "no category salience" is often just not a realistic option.

Furthermore, rather ironically, an attempt to adopt the "no salience" color-blind perspective in too thoroughgoing a way may actually lead to increased category salience. How might this occur? First, there is some evidence that consciously trying not to think about something is often ineffective and may actually increase the frequency with which one thinks about it (Wegner, 1989). Second, and more important, white students in a diverse school frequently come from wealthier and more educated backgrounds than their minority group peers. In such cases a color-blind policy that treats each child as an individual and considers notice of group membership inappropriate tends to lead to a school in which whites constantly "win"—filling up the advanced classes, receiving the honors, running many extracurricular activities, and so forth. Such a situation may well increase group salience because of conflicts that arise as minority group members react in terms of their group identity to what they are likely to perceive as institutional racism. This situation is also conducive, in and of itself, to out-group stereotyping and hostility irrespective of any impact it might have on group salience.

The foregoing example is not meant to downplay the potential contributions of work stemming from the minimal group paradigm to our understanding of "What is going on here" or "What works." Rather, it is presented as a cautionary case to show how careful analysis of the intergroup situation is necessary before applying theoretical insights from this tradition in too facile a manner.

The second caution that I believe is necessary is the warning not to let the vigor of the work on the cognitive aspects of intergroup relations lead researchers to concentrate on such factors to the exclusion of other important factors about which we currently have less knowledge or theory. There is no doubt that analyses in this cognitive vein, such as Wilder's (1986) work on the factors that are likely to affect in-group bias, hold considerable promise for helping us understand the consequences of attending schools with a racially or ethnically diverse student body. But just as contact theory has been criticized for being too "cold" (Pettigrew, 1986), that is, for tending to ignore affect, so too the cognitive information processing approach tends to downplay the role of intense affect to an unfortunate extent.

I think it is important to recognize the fundamental role that preexisting affect plays in intergroup situations and to find acceptable, effective, and constructive ways to study conflicted intergroup situations in which there is a great deal of negative affect. Numerous factors, including ethical concerns about exacerbating problems, personal concerns about stress and safety, and practical concerns about access, have kept most researchers from focusing on the difficult cases in which affect is strong and negative. Yet positive and negative intergroup relations are really not just two ends of the same continuum. Practices designed to facilitate positive intergroup relations, such as cooperative learning teams, may well not have much impact on extremely negative aspects of intergroup relations such as intergroup violence. Strong negative affect and its expression is likely to be more influenced by factors such as the school and community climate with regard to violence and more generally by the way in which the school handles disciplinary matters (G. Grant, 1988; Schofield, 1989). Studies undertaken to illuminate why such conflict occurs and how it can best be handled would be especially important in this area because there is the real chance that the mere descriptive highlighting of cases in which intergroup relations are very negative is more likely to fuel intergroup animosities than to help solve such problems. Because negative intergroup relations within schools are often a direct consequence of the political and social forces surrounding the schools (Dentler & Scott, 1981; G. Grant, 1988; Lukas, 1985), studies on this topic would most likely also have to be especially tuned to such connections.

In fact, even more fundamental than the issue of whether one studies primarily cognition or affect is the level of analysis to which theory directs one. The cognitive approach typically directs one to processes in the individual's mind as the focus for study. As crucial as such processes are, study of them may not be the most efficient or effective way to gain insight into "What is going on here" or "What works." These issues are so vitally influenced by cultural norms and patterns, social power, social and racial stratification patterns, and other social rather than individual level variables that an information processing approach is incomplete at best. The challenge presented in 1983 by Prager, Longshore, and Seeman and their colleagues to researchers to advance the art of inquiry in desegregation research by developing theory that better reflects the components of situational variables and situational variability has not really been met in the ensuing years. Thus, taking theory more seriously includes developing theory that can handle these social variables as well as exploring their links to microsocial and psychological processes. This will not be an easy task, but new work within sociology on linking social structure at the "macro" level to both social structure at the "micro" level and psychological processes may provide some help (House & Mortimer, 1990; Morgan & Schwalbe, 1990). Other important work coming out of anthropology also suggests ways of linking "macro" variables like racial stratification systems with cultural attitudes and behaviors that manifest themselves at the "micro" level (Ogbu, 1986, 1988). Finally, it is encouraging to see researchers within the social identity tradition beginning to explore issues related to the impact of power and status on intergroup relations (Ng, 1982; Ng & Gram, 1988; Sachdev & Bourhis, 1990). Theoretical approaches that ignore or deny the importance of such "macro" variables will surely fail to capture the impact of forces crucial to the shaping of intergroup relations.

Improving Measurement

As pointed out earlier in this review, research on desegregation and intergroup relations has suffered from serious design and measurement flaws. Attention to recognizing and rectifying these flaws is definitely needed. In this closing section, I would like to highlight a few of the methodological problems that are in especially urgent need of attention.

As argued earlier, researchers concerned with desegregation and intergroup relations need to pay much closer attention than they generally have to selection and measurement of their outcome variables. Friendship patterns, fear, prejudice, and long-term social integration are all aspects of intergroup relations. Such outcomes are conceptually distinct and may be uncorrelated or only weakly correlated with each other. Thus, choosing which aspects of intergroup relations to study is an important decision that should not be determined by custom or by the ready availability of convenient instruments. Multiple measures of various aspects of intergroup relations are desirable. Choices about which areas to study should ideally be based on a careful theoretical analysis of what outcomes are likely to be influenced by the situation in question as well as by consideration of the social importance of these outcomes.

A second area in which improvement would be especially beneficial is in the extent to which researchers recognize the complexity, situational dependence, and subjectivity of intergroup relations. As discussed previously, different groups of individuals involved in biracial or multiethnic schools may have very different concerns and perceptions. Thus, different aspects of intergroup relations might change for different groups. The particular milieu in which intergroup relations are studied also can have a major impact on one's conclusions, even when the same individuals are involved, as discussed earlier. Finally, as Patchen's (1982) previously cited work suggests, the structure of the intergroup attitudes of minority and majority group members may not be parallel.

These facts need to be considered not only in selecting particular outcomes for study, but also in thinking about the measurement process itself. Specifically, it is vital to do everything possible to be sure that measures of racial attitudes or the like developed using only white students or focusing on the aspects of intergroup relations most salient to majority group members are not inappropriately used as generic measures of intergroup relations. There are numerous ways to accomplish this goal, including the use of qualitative studies, because one of the hallmarks of this approach is an attempt to delineate the perspectives of those being studied. Other possible approaches include the building of multiethnic research teams and open-ended interviewing with study participants as a means of eliciting the concerns or perspectives of all groups involved before more structured data collection instruments are used.

A CONCLUDING NOTE

In many ways this review has been pessimistic. It has taken a critical stance toward the existing literature on desegregation and intergroup relations, highlighting its deficiencies in the belief that problems must be faced before they can be overcome. Yet looking at the literature from a different vantage point, one could be much more optimistic. For example, although many methodological and theoretical problems still remain to be faced, one has only to compare studies like those of Patchen (1982) or Gerard and Miller (1975) to studies published in the late 1960s or early 1970s to see the vast methodological and conceptual strides the field has made. Our understanding of the nature and texture of intergroup relations has also been enriched greatly by the "inside look" at biracial and multiethnic schools that qualitative researchers have provided. The theoretical ferment in recent years, both inside the field and in more generic social identity and social categorization approaches to intergroup relations, provides a rich source of ideas for future work.

D. Cohen and Weiss (1977) contend that improving research on social issues leads not to greater clarity about what to do but to a greater sense of complexity and to a reformulation of the issues. If this is true, then the disillusionment stemming from the inconclusiveness of the earlier reviews may be at least partially a consequence of inappropriate expectations. Conceptions of the issues that school desegregation raises have changed dramatically over the past 35 years. To some extent, these changes are an immediate reflection of the shifting social and political context in which our schools function and of the changing educational challenges they face. However, there is no doubt that the body of research reviewed here has also contributed substantially to enhancing our understanding of the phenomenon and of the things we need to know in order to create schools that help to prepare students to function effectively in our increasingly heterogeneous society.

NOTES

[1] Portions of pages 339–356 are taken from "School Desegregation and Intergroup Attitudes" by J. W. Schofield, 1978, in D. Bar-Tal & L. Saxe (Eds.), *Social Psychology of Education: Theory and Research,* Washington, DC: Halsted Press. Copyright 1978 by Halsted Press. Reprinted by permission.

[2] The term *Hispanic,* of course, refers to a large number of groups including but far from limited to individuals of Mexican, Puerto Rican, and Cuban descent (Arias, 1986). There are enough elements of shared culture so that it makes sense to speak of "Hispanic cultural patterns" in a review of this sort. However, it is important to point out that this practice glosses over distinctive aspects of the culture of each group as well as each group's social position in the United States. These would need to be considered in a more detailed analysis of the issues discussed here.

REFERENCES

Allport, G. W. (1954). *The nature of prejudice*. Cambridge, MA: Addison-Wesley.

Amir, Y. (1969). Contact hypothesis in ethnic relations. *Psychological Bulletin, 71,* 319–342.

Amir, Y. (1976). The role of intergroup contact in change of prejudice and ethnic relations. In P. A. Katz (Ed.), *Towards the elimination of racism* (pp. 245–308). Elmsford, NY: Pergamon Press.

Amir, Y., Sharan, S., Rivner, M., Ben-Ari, R., & Bizman, A. (1979). Group status and attitude change in desegregated classrooms. *International Journal of Intercultural Relations, 3,* 137–152.

Arias, M. B. (1986). The context of education for Hispanic students: An overview. *American Journal of Education, 95,* 26–57.

Armor, D. J. (1972). The evidence on busing. *The Public Interest, 28,* 90–126.

Armor, D. J. (1980). White flight and the future of school desegregation. In W. G. Stephan & J. R. Feagin (Eds.), *Desegregation: Past, present, and future* (pp. 187–226). New York: Plenum Press.

Armor, D. J. (1984). The evidence on desegregation and black achievement. In T. Cook, D. Armor, R. Crain, N. Miller, W. Stephan, H. Walberg, & P. Wortman (Eds.), *School desegregation and black achievement* (pp. 43–67). Washington, DC: U.S. Department of Education, Office of Educational Research and Improvement, National Institute of Education.

Armor, D. J. (1988). School busing: A time for change. In P. A. Katz & D. A.

Taylor (Eds.), *Eliminating racism: Profiles in controversy* (pp. 259–280). New York: Plenum Press.

Arnez, N. L. (1978). Implementation of desegregation as a discriminatory process. *Journal of Negro Education, 47,* 28–45.

Aronson, E., Blaney, N., Sikes, J., Stephan, G., & Snapp, M. (1978). *The jigsaw classroom.* Beverly Hills, CA: Sage.

Aronson, E., & Gonzalez, A. (1988). Desegregation, jigsaw, and the Mexican-American experience. In P. A. Katz & D. A. Taylor (Eds.), *Eliminating racism: Profiles in controversy* (pp. 301–314). New York: Plenum Press.

Aronson, E., & Osherow, N. (1980). Cooperation, prosocial behavior, and academic performance: Experiments in the desegregated classroom. In L. Bickman (Ed.), *Applied social psychology annual* (Vol. 1, pp. 163–196). Beverly Hills, CA: Sage.

Aronson, S., & Noble, J. (1966). *Urban-suburban school mixing: A feasibility study.* Unpublished manuscript, West Hartford Board of Education.

Ashmore, R. D. (1976). The today and likely tomorrow of American race relations. *Journal of Social Issues, 32*(2), 1–7.

Aspira of America, Inc. (1979). *Trends in segregation of Hispanic students in major school districts having large Hispanic enrollment: Ethnographic case studies* (Final Report, Vol. 2). New York: Author. (ERIC Document Reproduction Service No. ED 190 271)

Bank, B. J., Biddle, B. J., Keats, D. M., & Keats, J. A. (1977). Normative, preferential, and belief modes in adolescent prejudice. *The Sociological Quarterly, 18,* 574–588.

Barber, R. W. (1968). *The effects of open enrollment on anti-negro and anti-white prejudices among junior high students in Rochester, New York.* Unpublished doctoral dissertation, University of Rochester.

Bell, D. (1980). *Brown* and the interest-convergence dilemma. In D. Bell (Ed.), *Shades of Brown: New perspectives on school desegregation* (pp. 91–106). New York: Teachers College Press.

Ben-Ari, R., & Amir, Y. (1986). Contact between Arab and Jewish youth in Israel: Reality and potential. In M. Hewstone & R. Brown (Eds.), *Contact and conflict in intergroup encounters* (pp. 45–58). Oxford, England: Basil Blackwell.

Berger, J., Cohen, B. P., & Zelditch, M. (1966). Status characteristics and expectation states. In J. Berger, M. Zelditch, & B. Anderson (Eds.), *Sociological theories in progress* (Vol. 7, pp. 29–46). Boston: Houghton Mifflin.

Berger, J., Cohen, E., & Zelditch, M. (1972). Status conceptions and social interaction. *American Sociological Review, 37,* 241–255.

Berry, J. W. (1984). Cultural relations in plural societies: Alternatives to segregation and their socio-psychological implications. In N. Miller & M. B. Brewer (Eds.), *Groups in contact: The psychology of desegregation* (pp. 11–27). Orlando, FL: Academic Press.

Best, D. L., Smith, S. C., Graves, D. J., & Williams, J. E. (1975). The modification of racial bias in preschool children. *Journal of Experimental Child Psychology, 20,* 193–205.

Biener, L., & Gerard, H. (1975). Effects of desegregation on achievement-relevant motivation. In H. B. Gerard & N. Miller (Eds.), *School desegregation* (pp. 121–150). New York: Plenum Press.

Billig, M. (1976). *Social psychology and intergroup relations.* New York: Academic Press.

Blakey, W. A. (1989). *Public school desegregation: Education, equal protection and equality of opportunity.* University of Oklahoma, Center for Research on Minority Education.

Blalock, H. (1986). A model for racial contact in schools. In J. Prager, D. Longshore, & M. Seeman (Eds.), *School desegregation research* (pp. 111–141). New York: Plenum Press.

Blanchard, F. A., Adelman, L., & Cook, S. W. (1975). Effect of group success and failure upon interpersonal attraction in cooperating interracial groups. *Journal of Personality and Social Psychology, 31,* 1020–1030.

Blanchard, F. A., & Cook, S. W. (1976). Effects of helping a less competent member of a cooperating interracial group on the development of interpersonal attraction. *Journal of Personality and Social Psychology, 34,* 1245–1255.

Blanchard, F. A., Weigel, R. H., & Cook, S. W. (1975). The effect of relative competence of group members upon interpersonal attraction in cooperating interracial groups. *Journal of Personality and Social Psychology, 32,* 519–530.

Blaney, N. T., Stephan, S., Rosenfield, D., Aronson, E., & Sikes, J. (1977). Interdependence in the classroom: A field study. *Journal of Educational Psychology, 69,* 121–128.

Boateng, F. (1990). Combatting deculturalization of the African-American child in the public school system: A multi-cultural approach. In K. Lomotey (Ed.), *Going to school* (pp. 73–84). Albany: State University of New York Press.

Bossert, S. T. (1988–1989). *Cooperative activities in the classroom.* In E. Z. Rothkopf (Ed.), *Review of research in education* (Vol. 15, pp. 225–250). Washington, DC: American Educational Research Association.

Braddock, J. H. II. (1980). The perpetuation of segregation across levels of education: A behavioral assessment of the contact hypothesis. *Sociology of Education, 53,* 178–186.

Braddock, J. H. II. (1985). School desegregation and black assimilation. *Journal of Social Issues, 41*(3), 9–22.

Braddock, J. H. II., & McPartland, J. (1982). Assessing school desegregation effects: New directions in research. In R. Corwin (Ed.), *Research in sociology of education and socialization* (Vol. 3, pp. 209–282). Greenwich, CT: JAI Press.

Braddock, J. H. II., & McPartland, J. (1987). How minorities continue to be excluded from equal employment opportunities: Research on labor market and institutional barriers. *Journal of Social Issues, 43*(1), 5–39.

Braddock, J. H. II., McPartland, J., & Trent, W. (1984, April). *Desegregated schools and desegregated work environments.* Paper presented at the meeting of the American Educational Research Association, New Orleans.

Bradley, L. A., & Bradley, G. W. (1977). The academic achievement of black students in desegregated schools: A critical review. *Review of Educational Research, 47,* 399–449.

Brewer, M. B. (1979). In-group bias in the minimal intergroup situation: A cognitive-motivational analysis. *Psychological Bulletin, 86,* 307–334.

Brewer, M. B., & Miller, N. (1984). Beyond the contact hypothesis: Theoretical perspectives on desegregation. In N. Miller & M. B. Brewer (Eds.), *Groups in contact: The psychology of desegregation* (pp. 281–302). Orlando, FL: Academic Press.

Brewer, M. B., & Miller, N. (1988). Contact and cooperation: When do they work? In P. A. Katz & D. A. Taylor (Eds.), *Eliminating racism: Profiles in controversy* (pp. 315–326). New York: Plenum Press.

Brigham, J. C., Woodmansee, J. J., & Cook, S. W. (1976). Dimensions of verbal racial attitudes: Interracial marriage and approaches to racial equality. *Journal of Social Issues, 32*(2), 9–21.

Brown, R. J., & Turner, J. C. (1981). Interpersonal and intergroup behaviour. In J. C. Turner & H. Giles (Eds.), *Intergroup behaviour* (pp. 33–65). Chicago: University of Chicago Press.

Brown v. Board of Education of Topeka, 347 U.S. 483 (1954).

Butler, J. S. (1974). Black educators in Louisiana—A question of survival. *Journal of Negro Education, 43,* 22–24.

Campbell, A. (1971). *White attitudes toward black people.* Ann Arbor, MI: Institute for Social Research.

Campbell, D. T., & Fiske, D. W. (1959). Convergent and discriminant validation by the multitrait-multimethod matrix. *Psychological Bulletin, 56,* 81–105.

Campbell, D. T., & Stanley, J. (1963). *Experimental and quasi-experimental designs for research.* Chicago: Rand-McNally.

Campbell, E. Q. (1956). *The attitude effects of educational desegregation in a southern community.* Unpublished doctoral dissertation, Vanderbilt University.

Carew, J. V., & Lightfoot, S. L. (1979). *Beyond bias: Perspectives on classrooms.* Cambridge, MA: Harvard University Press.

Carithers, M. W. (1970). School desegregation and racial cleavage, 1954–1970: A review of the literature. *Journal of Social Issues, 26*(4), 25–47.

Carriere, R. A., Coulson, J. E., Cromer, F. E., Doherty, W. J., Hanes, S. D., & MacQueen, A. H. (1978). *Emergency School Aid Act (ESAA) evaluation: Results of supplemental analyses in the contract extension period.* Santa Monica, CA: System Development Corporation.

Carrigan, P. M. (1969). *School desegregation via compulsory pupil transfer: Early effects on elementary school children.* Unpublished manuscript, Michigan Public Schools, Ann Arbor.

Cartwright, D. (1973). Determinants of scientific progress: The case of research on the risky shift. *American Psychologist, 28,* 222–231.

Chesler, M., Bryant, B., & Crowfoot, J. (1981). *Making desegregation work: A professional guide to effecting change.* Beverly Hills, CA: Sage.

Clark, K. B. (1939a). Segregation as a factor in the racial identification of negro pre-school children. *Journal of Experimental Education, 8,* 161–164.

Clark, K. B. (1939b). The development of consciousness of self and the emergence of racial identification in negro pre-school children. *Journal of Social Psychology, 10,* 591–599.

Clark, K. B., & Clark, M. (1940). Skin color as a factor in racial identification of negro pre-school children. *Journal of Social Psychology, 11,* 159–169.

Clark, K. B., & Clark, M. (1947). Racial identification and preference in negro children. In T. M. Newcomb & E. L. Hartley (Eds.), *Readings in social psychology* (pp. 169–178). New York: Holt, Rinehart, & Winston.

Clark, K. B., & Clark, M. (1950). Emotional factors in racial identification and preference in negro children. *Journal of Negro Education, 19,* 341–350.

Clement, D. C., Eisenhart, M., & Harding, J. R. (1979). The veneer of harmony: Social-race relations in a southern desegregated school. In R. C. Rist (Ed.), *Desegregated schools: Appraisals of an American experiment* (pp. 15–64). New York: Academic Press.

Clement, D. C., Eisenhart, M., Harding, J. R., & Livesay, M. (1978). *The emerging order: An ethnography of a southern desegregated school* (Final Report). Washington, DC: National Institute of Education.

Clement, D. C., & Livesay, J. M. (1979). The organization and representation of social race relations in six desegregated schools. In M. L. Wax (Ed.), *When schools are desegregated: Problems and possibilities for students, educators, parents and the community* (pp. 39–57). Washington, DC: National Institute of Education.

Cohen, D. K., & Weiss, J. A. (1977). Social science and social policy: Schools and race. *Education Forum, 41,* 393–413.

Cohen, E. (1972). Interracial interaction disability. *Human Relations, 25,* 9–24.

Cohen, E. (1975). The effects of desegregation on race relations. *Law and Contemporary Problems, 39,* 271–299.

Cohen, E. (1980). Design and redesign of the desegregated school: Problems of status, power, and conflict. In W. G. Stephan & J. R. Feagin (Eds.), *School desegregation: Past, present, and future* (pp. 251–278). New York: Plenum Press.

Cohen, E. (1982). Expectation states and interracial interaction in school settings. *Annual Review of Sociology, 8,* 209–235.

Cohen, E. (1984). The desegregated school: Problems in status power and interethnic climate. In N. Miller & M. B. Brewer (Eds.), *Groups in contact: The psychology of desegregation* (pp. 77–96). Orlando, FL: Academic Press.

Cohen, E., Lockheed, M., & Lohman, M. (1976). The center for interracial cooperation: A field experiment. *Sociology of Education, 49,* 47–58.

Cohen, E., Lotan, R., & Catanzarite, L. (1986, April). *Treating status problems in the cooperative classroom.* Paper presented at the meeting of the American Educational Research Association, San Francisco.

Cohen, E., & Roper, S. (1972). Modification of interracial interaction disability: An application of status characteristics theory. *American Sociological Review, 36,* 643–657.

Collins, T. W. (1979). From courtrooms to classrooms: Managing school desegregation in a deep south school. In R. C. Rist (Ed.), *Desegregated schools: Appraisals of an American experiment* (pp. 89–113). New York: Academic Press.

Collins, T. W., & Noblit, G. W. (1978). *Stratification and resegregation: The case of Crossover High School, Memphis, Tennessee* (Final Report). Washington, DC: National Institute of Education.

Collins, T. W., & Noblit, G. W. (1981). Qui bono?: White students in a desegregated high school. *Urban Review, 13,* 217–225.

Cook, S. W. (1969). Motives in a conceptual analysis of attitude-related behavior. In W. J. Arnold & D. Levine (Eds.), *Nebraska Symposium on Motivation* (Vol. 17, pp. 179–235). Lincoln: University of Nebraska Press.

Cook, S. W. (1978). Interpersonal and attitudinal outcomes in cooperating interracial groups. *Journal of Research and Development in Education, 12,* 97–113.

Cook, S. W. (1979). Social science and school desegregation: Did we mislead the Supreme Court? *Personality and Social Psychology Bulletin, 5,* 420–437.

Cook, S. W. (1984). Cooperative interaction in multiethnic contexts. In N. Miller & M. B. Brewer (Eds.), *Groups in contact* (pp. 156–186). New York: Academic Press.

Cook, S. W. (1985). Experimenting on social issues: The case of school desegregation. *American Psychologist, 40,* 452–460.

Cook, S. W., & Selltiz, C. (1955). Some factors which influence the attitudinal outcomes of personal contacts. *International Sociological Bulletin, 7,* 51–58.

Cook, T. D. (1984). What have black children gained academically from school integration?: Examination of the meta-analytic evidence. In T. Cook, D. Armor, R. Crain, N. Miller, W. Stephan, H. Walberg, & P. Wortman (Eds.), *School desegregation and black achievement* (pp. 6–42). Washington, DC: U.S. Department of Education, Office of Educational Research and Improvement, National Institute of Education.

Cook, T. D., & Campbell, D. T. (1976). The design and conduct of quasi-experiments and true experiments in field settings. In M. D. Dunnette (Ed.), *Handbook of industrial and organizational psychology* (pp. 223–326). Chicago: Rand-McNally.

Cook, T. D., Levitan, L. C., & Shadish, W. R., Jr. (1985). Program evaluation. In G. Lindzey & E. Aronson (Eds.), *Handbook of social psychology* (Vol. 1, pp. 699–777). New York: Random House.

Cooper, J. B., & Pollack, D. (1959). The identification of prejudicial attitudes by the galvanic skin response. *Journal of Social Psychology, 50,* 241–245.

Coulson, J. E., Ozenne, D. G., Hanes, S. D., Bradford, C., Doherty, W. J., Duck, G. A., & Hemenway, J. A. (1977). *The third year of Emergency School Aid Act (ESAA) implementation.* Santa Monica, CA: System Development Corporation.

Crain, R. L. (1970). School integration and occupational achievement of negroes. *American Journal of Sociology, 75,* 593–606.

Crain, R. (1976). Why academic research fails to be useful. *School Review, 84,* 337–351.

Crain, R. (1984). *Is nineteen really better than ninety-three?* Washington, DC: U.S. Department of Education, National Institute of Education.

Crawford, J. (1989). *Bilingual education: History, politics, theory and practice.* Trenton, NJ: Crane Publishers.

Criswell, J. H. (1939). A sociometric study of racial cleavage in classrooms. *Archives of Psychology, 33*(Whole No. 235).

Cronbach, L. J. (1982). *Designing evaluations of educational and social programs.* San Francisco: Jossey-Bass.

Cronbach, L. J., & Furby, L. (1970). How we should measure "change"—or should we? *Psychological Bulletin, 74,* 68–80.

Crooks, R. C. (1970). The effects of an interracial pre-school program upon racial preferences, knowledge of racial differences and racial identification. *Journal of Social Issues, 26*(4), 137–144.

Crosby, F., Bromley, S., & Saxe, L. (1980). Recent unobtrusive studies of black and white discrimination and prejudice: A literature review. *Psychological Bulletin, 87,* 546–563.

Crowfoot, J. E., & Chesler, M. A. (1981). Implementing "attractive ideas": Problems and prospects. In W. D. Hawley (Ed.), *Effective school desegregation* (pp. 265–295). Beverly Hills, CA: Sage.

Cusick, P., & Ayling, R. (1973, February). *Racial interaction in an urban secondary school.* Paper presented at the meeting of the American Educational Research Association, New Orleans.

Damico, S. B., Bell-Nathaniel, A., & Green, C. (1981). Effects of school organizational structures on interracial friendships in middle school. *Journal of Educational Research, 74*(6), 388–393.

Davis, J. A., & Smith, T. W. (1987). *General social surveys, 1972–1987* [Machine-readable datafile]. Chicago: National Opinion Research Center.

Dawes, R. M., & Smith, T. L. (1985). Attitude and opinion measurement. In G. Lindzey & E. Aronson (Eds.), *Handbook of social psychology* (Vol. 1, pp. 509–566). New York: Random House.

De la Serna, M. (1982). Competitive behaviors among urban Mexican-Americans and Anglo-American children. *Revista Interamericana de Psicologia, 16,* 70–76.

Dentler, R. A., & Elkins, C. (1967). Intergroup attitudes, academic performance, and racial composition. In R. A. Dentler, B. Mackler, & M. E. Warshauer (Eds.), *The urban R's* (pp. 61–77). New York: Praeger.

Dentler, R. A., & Scott, M. B. (1981). *Schools on trial: An inside account of the Boston desegregation case.* Cambridge, MA: Abt Books.

Deschamps, J. C., & Doise, W. (1978). Crossed category memberships in intergroup relations. In H. Tajfel (Ed.), *Differentiation between social groups* (pp. 141–168). London: Academic Press.

Deutsch, M., & Collins, M. E. (1951). *Interracial housing: A psychological evaluation of a social experiment.* Minneapolis: University of Minnesota Press.

Deutscher, M., & Chein, I. (1948). The psychological effects of enforced segregation: A survey of social science opinion. *Journal of Psychology, 26,* 259–287.

DeVries, D. L., Edwards, K. J., & Slavin, R. E. (1978). Biracial learning teams and race relations in the classroom: Four field experiments on Teams-Games-Tournament. *Journal of Educational Psychology, 70,* 356–362.

Diaz-Guerrero, R. (1987). Historical sociocultural premises and ethnic socialization. In J. S. Phinney & M. J. Rotheram (Eds.), *Children's ethnic socialization: Pluralism and development* (pp. 239–250). Newbury Park, CA: Sage.

Dwyer, R. J. (1958). A report on patterns of interaction in desegregated schools. *Journal of Educational Sociology, 31,* 253–256.

Eddy, E. M. (1975). Educational innovation and desegregation: A case study of symbolic realignment. *Human Organization, 34,* 163–172.

Edelman, M. W. (1973, May). Southern school desegregation. 1954–1973: A judicial-political overview. *Annals of the American Academy of Political and Social Science, 407,* 32–42.

Edmonds, R. R. (1980). Effective education for minority pupils. *Brown* confounded or confirmed. In D. Bell (Ed.), *Shades of Brown: New perspectives on school desegregation* (pp. 109–123). New York: Teachers College Press.

Epstein, J. L. (1985). After the bus arrives: Resegregation in desegregated schools. *Journal of Social Issues, 41*(3), 23–43.

Evans, C. L. (1969). *The immediate effects of classroom integration on the academic progress, self-concept and racial attitudes of negro elementary children.* Unpublished doctoral dissertation, North Texas State University.

Feagin, J. R. (1980). School desegregation: A political-economic perspective. In W. G. Stephan & J. R. Feagin (Eds.), *School desegregation: Past, present, and future* (pp. 25–50). New York: Plenum Press.

Feldt, L. S., & Brennan, R. L. (1989). Reliability. In R. L. Linn (Ed.), *Educational measurement* (pp. 105–146). New York: American Council on Education and Macmillan Publishing Co.

Forehand, G. A., & Ragosta, M. (1976). *A handbook for integrated schooling.* Washington, DC: U.S. Department of Health, Education, and Welfare.

Forehand, G. A., Ragosta, M., & Rock, D. (1976). *Conditions and processes of effective school desegregation* (Final Report). Princeton, NJ: Educational Testing Service.

Fox, D. J. (1966). *Free choice open enrollment—Elementary schools.* Unpublished manuscript, Center for Urban Education, New York.

Gaertner, S. (1976). Nonreactive measures in racial attitude research: A focus on liberals. In P. A. Katz (Ed.), *Towards the elimination of racism* (pp. 183–211). New York: Pergamon.

Gaertner, S., & Bickman, L. (1971). Effects of race on elicitation of helping behavior: The wrong number technique. *Journal of Personality and Social Psychology, 20,* 218–222.

Gaertner, S. L., & Dovidio, J. F. (1986). The aversive form of racism. In J. F. Dovidio & S. L. Gaertner (Eds.), *Prejudice, discrimination, and racism* (pp. 61–89). Orlando, FL: Academic Press.

Gardner, B. B., Wright, B. D., & Dee, R. (1970). *The effect of busing black ghetto children into white suburban schools.* (ERIC Document Reproduction Service No. ED 048 389)

Garth, C. E. (1969). *Self-concept of negro students who transferred and did not transfer to formerly all-white schools.* Unpublished doctoral dissertation, University of Kentucky.

Geffner, R. A. (1978). *The effects of interdependent learning on self-esteem, inter-ethnic relations, and intra-ethnic attitudes of elementary school children: A field experiment.* Unpublished doctoral dissertation, University of California, Santa Cruz.

Gerard, H. B. (1983). School desegregation: The social science role. *American Psychologist, 38,* 869–877.

Gerard, H., Jackson, D., & Conolley, E. (1975). Social context in the desegregated classroom. In H. Gerard & N. Miller (Eds.), *School desegregation: A long-range study* (pp. 211–241). New York: Plenum Press.

Gerard, H. B., & Miller, N. (1975). *School desegregation.* New York: Plenum.

Gonzalez, J. M. (1979). *Bilingual education in the integrated school.* Arlington, VA: National Clearinghouse for Bilingual Education.

Goodman, M. E. (1952). *Race awareness in young children.* Cambridge, MA: Addison-Wesley.

Gordon, M. (1964). *Assimilation in American life.* New York: Oxford University Press.

Granovetter, M. (1986). The micro-structure of school desegregation. In J. Prager, D. Longshore, & M. Seeman (Eds.), *School desegregation research* (pp. 81–110). New York: Plenum Press.

Grant, G. (1988). *The world we created at Hamilton High.* Cambridge, MA: Harvard University Press.

Grant, L. (1984). Black females' "place" in desegregated classrooms. *Sociology of Education, 57,* 98–111.

Green, J. A., & Gerard, H. B. (1974). School desegregation and ethnic attitudes. In H. Fromkin & J. J. Sherwood (Eds.), *Integrating the organization: A social psychological analysis* (pp. 291–311). New York: Free Press.

Greenwald, A. G. (1990). What cognitive representations underlie social attitudes? *Bulletin of the Psychonomic Society, 28,* 254–260.

Guttentag, M., & Struening, E. (1975). The handbook: Its purpose and organization. In M. Guttentag & E. Struening (Eds.), *Handbook of evaluation research* (Vol. 2, pp. 3–7). Beverly Hills, CA: Sage.

Hale-Benson, J. (1986). *Black children: Their roots, culture and learning styles.* Baltimore: The Johns Hopkins University.

Hale-Benson, J. (1990). Visions for children: Educating black children in the context of their culture. In K. Lomotey (Ed.), *Going to school* (pp. 209–222). Albany: State University of New York Press.

Hallinan, M. T. (1982). Classroom racial composition and children's friendships. *Social Forces, 61*(1), 56–72.

Hallinan, M. T., & Smith, S. S. (1985). The effects of classroom racial composition on students' interracial friendliness. *Social Psychology Quarterly, 48*(1), 3–16.

Hallinan, M. T., & Teixeira, R. A. (1987). Students' interracial friendships: Individual characteristics, structural effects and racial differences. *American Journal of Education, 95,* 563–583.
Hamilton, C. V. (1968). Race and education: A search for legitimacy. *Harvard Educational Review, 38,* 669–684.
Haney, J. E. (1978). The effects of the Brown decision on black educators. *Journal of Negro Education, 47,* 88–95.
Hanna, J. L. (1982). Public social policy and the children's world: Implications of ethnographic research for desegregated schooling. In G. Spindler (Ed.), *Doing the ethnography of schooling: Educational anthropology in action* (pp. 317–355). New York: Holt, Rinehart, and Winston.
Harding, J., & Hogrefe, R. (1952). Attitudes of white department store employees towards negro co-workers. *Journal of Social Issues, 8*(1), 18–28.
Harris, C. W. (1963). *Problems in measuring change.* Madison: University of Wisconsin Press.
Hawley, W., Crain, R. L., Rossell, C. H., Schofield, J. W., Fernandez, R., & Trent, W. P. (1983). *Strategies for effective desegregation: Lessons from research.* Lexington, MA: Lexington Books, D. C. Heath.
Heath, S. B. (1982). Questioning at home and at school: A comparative study. In G. Spindler (Ed.), *Doing the ethnography of schooling: Educational anthropology in action* (pp. 103–131). New York: Holt, Rinehart, and Winston.
Heath, S. B. (1983). *Ways with words: Language, life, and work in communities and classrooms.* Cambridge, MA: Cambridge University Press.
Henry, W. A. III. (1990, April 9). Beyond the melting pot. *Time,* pp. 28–31.
Hewstone, M., & Brown, R. (1986). Contact is not enough: An intergroup perspective on the "contact hypothesis." In M. Hewstone & R. Brown (Eds.), *Contact and conflict in intergroup encounters* (pp. 1–44). Oxford, England: Basil Blackwell.
Hochschild, J. L. (1984). *The new American dilemma.* New Haven, CT: Yale University Press.
Holland, P., & Leinhardt, S. (1973). The structural implications of measurement error in sociometry. *Journal of Mathematical Sociology, 8,* 85–111.
Holsendolph, E. (1976, June 20). Figures show integration. *New York Times,* p. 24.
Horowitz, E. L. (1936, January). The development of attitude toward the negro. *Archives of Psychology,* p. 194.
Horowitz, R. E. (1939). Racial aspects of self-identity in nursery school children. *Journal of Psychology, 7,* 91–99.
House, J. S., & Mortimer, J. T. (1990). Social structure and the individual: Emerging themes and new directions. *Social Psychology Quarterly, 53*(2), 71–80.
Ianni, F. A. J., Sullivan, M. L., Orr, M., Henry, S., & Mavros, J. (1978). *A field study of culture contact and desegregation in an urban high school* (Final Report). Washington, DC: National Institute of Education.
Jahoda, M., & West, P. (1951). Race relations in public housing. *Journal of Social Issues, 7*(1, 2), 132–139.
Jansen, V. G., & Gallagher, J. J. (1966). The social choices of students in racially integrated classes for the culturally disadvantaged talented. *Exceptional Children, 33,* 222–226.
Jaynes, G. D., & Williams, R. M., Jr. (Eds.). (1989). *Common destiny: Blacks and American society.* Washington, DC: National Academy Press.
Jencks, C., Smith, M., Acland, H., Bane, M. J., Cohen, D., Gintis, H., Heyns, B., & Michelson, S. (1972). *Inequality.* New York: Basic Books.

Johnson, D. W., & Johnson, R. T. (1981). Effects of cooperative and individualistic learning experiences on interethnic interaction. *Journal of Educational Psychology, 73,* 444–449.

Johnson, D. W., & Johnson, R. T. (1982). The study of cooperative, competitive, and individualistic situations: State of the area and two recent contributions. *Contemporary Education, 1*(1), 7–13.

Johnson, D. W., Johnson, R. T., & Maruyama, G. (1984). Goal interdependence and interpersonal attraction in heterogeneous classrooms: A meta analysis. In N. Miller & M. B. Brewer (Eds.), *Groups in contact: The psychology of desegregation* (pp. 187–212). Orlando, FL: Academic Press.

Jones, J. M. (1986). Cultural differences in temporal perspectives: Instrumental and expressive behaviors in time. In J. McGrath (Ed.), *The social psychology of time* (pp. 21–38). Beverly Hills, CA: Sage.

Jones, J. M. (1988). Racism in black and white: A bicultural model of reaction and evolution. In P. A. Katz & D. A. Taylor (Eds.), *Eliminating racism: Profiles in controversy* (pp. 117–157). New York: Plenum Press.

Jones, R. L. (1980). *Black psychology.* New York: Harper & Row.

Justman, J. (1968). Children's reactions to open enrollment. *The Urban Review, 3,* 181–184.

Kagan, S. (1980). Cooperation-competition, culture, and structural bias in classrooms. In S. Sharan, P. Hare, C. D. Webb, & R. Hertz-Lazarowitz (Eds.), *Cooperation in education* (pp. 197–211). Provo, UT: Brigham Young University Press.

Kagan, S., & Knight, G. (1981). Social motives among Anglo-American and Mexican-American children: Experimental and projective measures. *Journal of Research in Personality, 15,* 93–106.

Kagan, S., & Madsen, M. C. (1971). Cooperation and competition of Mexican, Mexican-American and Anglo-American children of two ages under four instructional sets. *Developmental Psychology, 5,* 32–39.

Katz, D. (1960). The functional approach to the study of attitudes. *Public Opinion Quarterly, 24,* 163–204.

Katz, I. (1964). Review of evidence relating to effects of desegregation on the performance of negroes. *American Psychologist, 19,* 381–399.

Katz, P. A. (1976). The acquisition of racial attitudes in children. In P. A. Katz (Ed.), *Towards the elimination of racism* (pp. 125–154). New York: Pergamon.

Katz, P. A., & Zalk, S. R. (1978). Modification of children's racial attitudes. *Developmental Psychology, 14,* 447–461.

Kawwa, T. (1968). A survey of ethnic attitudes of some British secondary school pupils. *British Journal of Social and Clinical Psychology, 7,* 161–168.

Keyes v. School District No. 1. Denver, Colorado, 413 U.S. 189 (1973).

Kinder, D. R., & Sears, D. O. (1981). Prejudice and politics: Symbolic racism versus racial threats to the good life. *Journal of Personality and Social Psychology, 40,* 414–431.

Klein, Z., & Eshel, Y. (1980). *Integrating Jerusalem schools.* New York: Academic Press.

Klineberg, O. (1986). SPSSI and race relations, in the 1950s and after. *Journal of Social Issues, 42*(4), 53–59.

Kluger, R. (1976). *Simple justice: The history of Brown v. Board of Education and Black America's struggle for equality.* New York: Alfred A. Knopf.

Kochman, T. (1981). *Black and white styles in conflict.* Chicago: University of Chicago Press.

Koslin, S., Amarel, M., & Ames, N. (1969, October). A distance measure of racial attitudes in primary grade children: An exploratory study. *Psychology in the Schools,* pp. 382–385.

Koslin, S., Koslin, B. L., Cardwell, J., & Pargament, R. (1969). Quasi-disguised and structured measure of school children's racial preferences. *Proceedings of the 77th Annual Convention of the American Psychological Association.*

Koslin, S., Koslin, B. L., Pargament, R., & Waxman, H. (1972). Classroom racial balance and students' interracial attitudes. *Sociology of Education, 45*(4), 386–407.

Krol, R. A. (1978). *A meta-analysis of comparative research on the effects of desegregation on academic achievement.* Unpublished doctoral dissertation, Western Michigan University. (University Microfilms No. 79-07962)

Kurokawa, M. (1971). Mutual perceptions of racial images; White, black, and Japanese Americans. *Journal of Social Issues, 27*(4), 213–235.

Lachat, M. (1972). *A description and comparison of the attitudes of white high school seniors towards black Americans in three suburban high schools: An all white, a desegregated and an integrated school.* Unpublished doctoral dissertation, Columbia University.

Landis, D., Day, H. R., McGrew, P. L., Thomas, J. A., & Miller, A. B. (1976). Can a black "culture assimilator" increase racial understanding? *Journal of Social Issues, 32*(2), 169–183.

Landis, D., Hope, R. O., & Day, H. R. (1984). Training for desegregation in the military. In N. Miller & M. B. Brewer (Eds.), *Groups in contact: The psychology of desegregation* (pp. 257–278). Orlando, FL: Academic Press.

Landreth, C., & Johnson, B. C. (1953). Young children's responses to a picture and inset test designed to reveal reactions to persons of different skin color. *Child Development, 24,* 63–80.

Lau v. Nichols, 414 U.S. 563 (1974).

LeCompte, M. D. (1979). Less than meets the eye. In M. Wax (Ed.), *Desegregated schools: An intimate portrait based on five ethnographic studies* (pp. 118–131). Washington, DC: National Institute of Education.

Lee, M. K. (1980). *Attitudinal changes in a cultural heritage course about Black Americans.* Washington, DC: National Institute of Education. (ERIC Document Reproduction Service No. ED 195 622)

Lewis, R. G. (1971). *The relationship of classroom racial composition to student academic achievement and the conditioning effects of interracial social acceptance.* Unpublished doctoral dissertation, Harvard Graduate School of Education, Harvard University.

Lombardi, D. N. (1962). *Factors affecting changes in attitudes toward negroes among high school students.* Unpublished doctoral dissertation, Fordham University.

Lukas, J. A. (1985). *Common ground.* New York: Alfred A. Knopf.

Mahard, R. E., & Crain, R. L. (1983). Research on minority achievement in desegregated schools. In C. H. Rossell & W. D. Hawley (Eds.), *The consequences of school desegregation* (pp. 103–125). Philadelphia: Temple University Press.

Mann, J. H. (1959). The effects of inter-racial contact on sociometric choices and perceptions. *Journal of Social Psychology, 50,* 143–152.

Martin, C. A. (Ed.). (1978). Desegregation in the 1970's: A candid discussion [Special issue]. *Journal of Negro Education, 47.*

Martinez-Monfort, A., & Dreger, R. M. (1972). Reactions of high school students to school desegregation in a southern metropolitan area. *Psychological Reports, 30,* 543–550.

Matute-Bianchi, M. E. (1986). Ethnic identities and patterns of school success and failure among Mexican-descent and Japanese-American students in a California high school: An ethnographic analysis. *American Journal of Education, 95,* 233–255.

McClendon, M. J. (1974). Interracial contact and the reduction of prejudice. *Sociological Focus, 7,* 47–65.

McConahay, J. (1978). The effects of school desegregation upon students' racial attitudes and behavior: A critical review of the literature and a prolegomenon to future research. *Law and Contemporary Problems, 42*(3), 77–107.

McConahay, J. (1979, October). *Reducing prejudice in desegregated schools.* Paper presented at the meeting of the National Panel on School Desegregation Research, Key West.

McConahay, J. (1981). Reducing racial prejudice in desegregated schools. In W. D. Hawley (Ed.), *Effective school desegregation* (pp. 35–53). Beverly Hills, CA: Sage.

McConahay, J. B., Hardee, B. B., & Batts, V. (1981). Has racism declined in America? It depends on who is asking and what is asked. *Journal of Conflict Resolution, 25,* 563–579.

McConahay, J. B., & Hough, J. C., Jr. (1976). Symbolic racism. *Journal of Social Issues, 32*(2), 23–45.

McGivern, E. & Schofield, J. W. (1979). The development of interracial bonds in a desegrated school. In R. Blumberg & J. Roye (Eds.), *Interracial bonds* (pp. 106–119). New York: General Hall.

McPartland, J. M. (1968). *The segregated student in desegregated schools: Sources of influence on Negro secondary students* (Report No. 21). Baltimore: Center for the Study of Social Organization of Schools, Johns Hopkins University.

McPartland, J. M., & Braddock, J. (1981). Going to college and getting a good job: The impact of desegregation. In W. Hawley (Ed.), *Effective school desegregation* (pp. 141–154). New York: Sage.

McPartland, J. M., & Crain, R. L. (1980). Racial discrimination, segregation, and processes of social mobility. In V. T. Covello (Ed.), *Poverty and public policy* (pp. 97–125). Cambridge, MA: Schenkman.

McWhirt, R. A. (1967). *The effects of desegregation on prejudice, academic aspiration and the self-concept of tenth grade students.* Unpublished doctoral dissertation, University of South Carolina.

Mercer, J. R., Iadicola, P., & Moore, H. (1980). Building effective multiethnic schools: Evolving models and paradigms. In W. G. Stephan & J. R. Feagin (Eds.), *School desegregation: Past, present, and future* (pp. 281–307). New York: Plenum Press.

Messick, D. M., & Mackie, D. M. (1989). Intergroup relations. In M. R. Rosenzweig & L. W. Porter (Eds.), *Annual review of psychology* (Vol. 40, pp. 45–83). Palo Alto, CA: Annual Reviews, Inc.

Metz, M. H. (1978). *Classrooms and corridors: The crisis of authority in desegregated secondary schools.* Berkeley, CA: University of California Press.

Metz, M. H. (1986). *Different by design.* New York: Routledge & Kegan Paul.

Miller, N. (1990a, October). Parameters of successful intergroup contact. In S. Hinkle (chair), *Intergroup behavior.* Symposium conducted at the annual meeting of the Society for Experimental Social Psychology, Buffalo, NY.

Miller, N. (1990b, October). Negative features of cooperative dependence. In M. Zanna (chair), *Prejudice and stereotypes*. Symposium conducted at the annual meeting of the Society for Experimental Social Psychology, Buffalo, NY.

Miller, N. (1980). Making school desegregation work. In W. G. Stephan & J. R. Feagin (Eds.), *School desegregation: Past, present, and future* (pp. 309–348). New York: Plenum Press.

Miller, N., Brewer, M. B., & Edwards, K.(1985). Cooperative interaction in desegregated settings: A laboratory analogue. *Journal of Social Issues, 41*(3), 63–79.

Miller, N., & Carlson, M. (1984). School desegregation as a social reform: A meta-analysis of its effects on black academic achievement. In T. Cook, D. Armor, R. Crain, N. Miller, W. Stephan, H. Walberg, & P. Wortman (Eds.), *School desegregation and black achievement* (pp. 89–130). Washington, DC: U.S. Department of Education, Office of Educational Research and Improvement, National Institute of Education.

Minard, R. D. (1952). Race relationships in the Pocohantos coal field. *Journal of Social Issues, 8*(1), 29–44.

Morgan, D. L., & Schwalbe, M. L. (1990). Mind and self in society: Linking social structure and social cognition. *Social Psychology Quarterly, 53,* 148–164.

Mumpower, J. L., & Cook, S. W. (1978). The development of interpersonal attraction in cooperating interracial groups: The effects of success-failure, race and competence of groupmates, and helping a less competent groupmate. *International Journal of Group Tensions, 8*(3, 4), 18–50.

National Institute of Education. (1974). *Field studies in urban desegregated schools*. Washington, DC: U.S. Government Printing Office.

National Institute of Education. (1977a). *Desegregation and education concerns of the Hispanic community*. Washington, DC: U.S. Government Printing Office.

National Institute of Education. (1977b). *Resegregation: A second generation school desegregation issue*. Unpublished manuscript.

National Opinion Research Center. (1973). *Southern schools: An evaluation of the effects of the Emergency School Assistance Program and of school desegregation*. Chicago: Author.

Ng, S. H. (1982). Power and intergroup discrimination. In H. Tajfel (Ed.), *Social identity and intergroup relations* (pp. 179–209). Cambridge, England: Cambridge University Press.

Ng, S. H., & Cram, F. (1988). Intergroup bias by defensive and offensive groups in majority and minority conditions. *Journal of Personality and Social Psychology, 55,* 749–757.

Noblit, G. W., & Collins, T. W. (1979). The social context of alienation: New policy research on lower-class black students in desegregated schools. In M. Wax (Ed.), *When schools are desegregated: Problems and possibilities for students, educators, parents and the community* (pp. 59–70). Washington, DC: National Institute of Education.

Noblit, G. W., & Collins, T. W. (1980). Cultural degradation and minority student adaptations: The school experience and minority adjustment contingencies. In M. Sugar (Ed.) *Responding to adolescent needs* (pp. 73–87). New York: Spectrum Press.

Noblit, G. W., & Johnson, B. (Eds.). (1982). *The school principal and school desegregation*. Springfield, IL: Charles C Thomas.

Ogbu, J. (1974). *The next generation: An ethnography of education in an urban neighborhood*. New York: Academic Press.

Ogbu, J. (1979). Desegregation, integration, and interaction theory: An appraisal. In M. L. Wax (Ed.), *Desegregated schools: An intimate portrait based on five ethnographic studies* (pp. 84–103). Washington, DC: National Institute of Education.

Ogbu, J. (1986). Structural constraints in school desegregation. In J. Prager, D. Longshore, & M. Seeman (Eds.), *School desegregation research* (pp. 21–45). New York: Plenum Press.

Ogbu, J. (1988). Class stratification, racial stratification, and schooling. In L. Weis (Ed.), *Class, race, and gender in American education* (pp. 163–182). Albany: State University of New York Press.

Orfield, G. (1975). How to make desegregation work: The adaptation of schools to their newly-integrated student bodies. *Law and Contemporary Problems, 39,* 314–340.

Orfield, G. (1978). *Must we bus? Segregated schools and national policy*. Washington, DC: The Brookings Institute.

Orfield, G. (1983). *Public school desegregation in the United States, 1968–1980*. Washington, DC: Joint Center for Political Studies.

Orfield, G. (1986). Hispanic education: Challenges, research, and policies. *American Journal of Education, 95,* 1–25.

Orfield, G., Monfort, F., & Aaron, M. (1989). *Status of school desegregation: 1968–1986*. Alexandria, VA: National School Boards Association.

Orost, J. H. (1971, February). *Racial attitudes among white kindergarten children from three different environments*. Paper presented at the meeting of the American Educational Research Association, New York.

Ortiz, F. I. (1988). Hispanic-American children's experiences in classrooms: A comparison between Hispanic and non-Hispanic children. In L. Weis (Ed.), *Class, race, and gender in American education* (pp. 63–86). Albany: State University of New York Press.

Patchen, M. (1982). *Black-white contact in schools: Its social and academic effects*. West Lafayette, IN: Purdue University Press.

Patchen, M., & Davidson, J. D. (1973). *Patterns and determinants of interracial interaction in the Indianapolis public high schools*. Unpublished manuscript.

Patchen, M., Davidson, J., Hofmann, G., & Brown, W. (1977). Determinants of students' interracial behavior and opinion change. *Sociology of Education, 50,* 55–75.

Patchen, M., Hofmann, G., & Davidson, D. (1976). Interracial perceptions among high school students. *Sociometry, 39,* 341–354.

Peshkin, A. (in press). *The color of strangers, the color of friends: The play of ethnicity in school and community*. Chicago: University of Chicago Press.

Pettigrew, T. (1967). Social evaluation theory: Convergences and applications. In D. Levine (Ed.), *Nebraska Symposium on Motivation* (Vol. 15, pp. 241–311). Lincoln: University of Nebraska Press.

Pettigrew, T. (1969). The Negro and education: Problems and proposals. In I. Katz & P. Gurin (Eds.), *Race and the social sciences* (pp. 49–112). New York: Basic Books.

Pettigrew, T. (1973). The case for the racial integration of the schools. In O. Duff (Ed.), *Report on the future of school desegregation in the United States* (pp. 52–93). Pittsburgh: University of Pittsburgh, Consultative Resource Center on School Desegregation and Conflict.

Pettigrew, T. F. (1986). The intergroup contact hypothesis reconsidered. In M. Hewstone & R. Brown (Eds.), *Contact and conflict in intergroup encounters* (pp. 169–195). New York: Basil Blackwell.

Pettigrew, T. F. (1988). Integration and pluralism. In P. A. Katz & D. A. Taylor (Eds.), *Eliminating racism: Profiles in controversy* (pp. 19–30). New York: Plenum Press.

Pettigrew, T. F., & Martin, J. (1987). Shaping the organizational context for black American inclusion. *Journal of Social Issues, 43*(1), 41–78.

Phinney, J. S., & Rotheram, M. J. (Eds.). (1987). *Children's ethnic socialization: Pluralism and development*. Newbury Park, CA: Sage.

Porter, J. D. R. (1971). *Black child—white child.* Cambridge, MA: Harvard University Press.

Prager, J., Longshore, D., & Seeman, M. (1983). *The desegregation situation* (Report No. TM-7081/001/01). Santa Monica, CA: System Development Corporation.

Prager, J., Longshore, D., & Seeman, M. (Eds.). (1986). *School desegregation research: New directions in situational analysis*. New York: Plenum Press.

Ramirez, A. (1988). Racism toward Hispanics: The culturally monolithic society. In P. A. Katz & D. A. Taylor (Eds.), *Eliminating racism: Profiles in controversy* (pp. 137–157). New York: Plenum Press.

Read, F. (1975). Judicial evolution of the law of school integration since *Brown v. Board of Education. Law and Contemporary Problems, 39,* 7–49.

Resource Management Corporation. (1971). *Evaluation of the emergency school assistance program* (Final Report UR-163). Washington, DC: U.S. Department of Health, Education, and Welfare.

Riordan, C. (1978). Equal status interracial contact: A review and revision of the concept. *International Journal of Intercultural Relations, 2,* 161–185.

Riordan, C., & Ruggiero, J. (1980). Producing equal status interracial interaction: A replication. *Social Psychology Quarterly, 43,* 131–136.

Rist, R. C. (1978). *The invisible children: School integration in American society.* Cambridge, MA: Harvard University Press.

Rist, R. C. (1979). *Desegregated schools: Appraisals of an American experiment.* New York: Academic Press.

Rist, R. C. (1980). On the future of school desegregation: A new American dilemma? In W. G. Stephan & J. R. Feagin (Eds.), *School desegregation: Past, present, and future* (pp. 117–131). New York: Plenum Press.

Roberts, G. J. (1989). The effect of achievement on student friendships in desegregated schools. *Equity and Choice, 5,* 31–36.

Rogers, M., Hennigan, K., Bowman, C., & Miller, N. (1984). Intergroup acceptance in classrooms and playground settings. In N. Miller & M. B. Brewer (Eds.), *Groups in contact: The psychology of desegregation* (pp. 213–227). New York: Academic Press.

Rose, H. M. (1983). Demography and school desegregation research. In *Advancing the art of inquiry in school desegregation research* (Report No. TM-7081/001/01, pp. 271–323). Santa Monica, CA: System Development Corporation.

Rosenbaum, P. (1979). Five perspectives on desegregation in schools: A summary. In M. L. Wax (Ed.), *When schools are desegregated: Problems and possibilities for students, educators, parents and the community* (pp. 95–103). Washington, DC: National Institute of Education.

Rosenberg, M. J. (1969). The conditions and consequences of evaluation apprehension. In R. Rosenthal & R. L. Rosnow (Eds.), *Artifact in behavioral research* (pp. 279–349). New York: Academic Press.

Rosenberg, M., & Simmons, R. (1971). *Black and white self-esteem: The urban school child.* Washington, DC: American Sociological Association.

Rosenholtz, S. J., & Cohen, E. G. (1985). Status in the eye of the beholder. In J. Berger & M. Zelditch, Jr. (Eds.), *Status, rewards, and influence* (pp. 430–444). San Francisco: Jossey-Bass.

Rossell, C. H. (1983). Applied social science research: What does it say about the effectiveness of school desegregation plans? *Journal of Legal Studies, 12,* 69–107.

Rossell, C. H. (1985). Estimating the net benefit of school desegregation reassignments. *Educational Evaluation and Policy Analysis, 7,* 217–227.

Rossell, C. H. (1990a). *The carrot or the stick for school desegregation policy.* Philadelphia: Temple University Press.

Rossell, C. H. (1990b). The research on bilingual education. *Equity and Choice, 6,* 29–36.

Rothbart, M., & John, O. P. (1985). Social categorization and behavioral episodes: A cognitive analysis of the effects of intergroup contact. *Journal of Social Issues, 41*(3), 81–104.

Sachdev, I., & Bourhis, R. Y. (1990, October). Power and status differentials in minority and majority group relations. In S. Hinkle (chair), *Intergroup behavior.* Symposium conducted at the annual meeting of the Society for Experimental Social Psychology, Buffalo, NY.

Saenger, G., & Gilbert, E. (1950). Customer reactions to the integration of negro sales personnel. *International Journal of Opinion and Attitude Research, 4,* 57–76.

Sagar, H. A., & Schofield, J. W. (1984). Integrating the desegregated school: Problems and possibilities. In M. Maehr & D. Bartz (Eds.), *Advances in motivation and achievement: A research manual* (pp. 203–242). Greenwich, CT: JAI Press.

Sagar, H. A., Schofield, J. W., & Snyder, H. N. (1983). Race and gender barriers: Preadolescent peer behavior in academic classrooms. *Child Development, 54,* 1032–1040.

St. John, N. H. (1969). *School integration research: The Pittsburgh study.* Unpublished manuscript.

St. John, N. H. (1975). *School desegregation: Outcomes for children.* New York: Wiley.

St. John, N. H., & Lewis, R. (1973). *Children's interracial friendships: An exploration of the contact hypothesis.* Unpublished manuscript.

St. John, N. H., & Lewis, R. (1975). Race and the social structure of the elementary classroom. *Sociology of Education, 48,* 346–368.

Sampson, W. A., & Williams, B. (1978). School desegregation: The non-traditional sociological perspective. *Journal of Negro Education, 47,* 58–69.

Scherer, J., & Slawski, E. J., Jr. (1978). *Hard walls—soft walls: The social ecology of an urban desegregated high school* (Final Report). Washington, DC: National Institute of Education.

Scherer, J., & Slawski, E. (1979). Color, class, and social control in an urban desegregated school. In R. C. Rist (Ed.), *Desegregated schools: Appraisals of an American experiment* (pp. 117–153). New York: Academic Press.

Schmuck, R. A., & Luzki, M. B. (1969). Black and white students in several small communities. *Applied Behavioral Review, 30,* 203–220.

Schofield, J. W. (1968). *Integration and racial identification: A study of Negro children's drawings.* Unpublished honor's thesis, Harvard University.
Schofield, J. W. (1976). *Ethnographic study of a "nearly integrated" middle school.* Unpublished manuscript, University of Pittsburgh.
Schofield, J. W. (1978). School desegregation and intergroup attitudes. In D. Bar-Tal & L. Saxe (Eds.), *Social psychology of education: Theory and research* (pp. 330–363). Washington, DC: Halsted Press.
Schofield, J. W. (1979). The impact of positively structured contact on intergroup behavior: Does it last under adverse conditions? *Social Psychology Quarterly, 42,* 280–284.
Schofield, J. W. (1983). Black-white conflict in the schools: Its social and academic effects. *American Journal of Education, 92,* 104–107.
Schofield, J. W. (1986). Causes and consequences of the colorblind perspective. In S. Gaertner & J. Davidio (Eds.), *Prejudice, discrimination and racism: Theory and practice.* New York: Academic Press.
Schofield, J. W. (1989). *Black and white in school: Trust, tension, or tolerance?* New York: Teachers College Press.
Schofield, J. W., & Francis, W. D. (1982). An observational study of peer interaction in racially-mixed "accelerated" classrooms. *The Journal of Educational Psychology, 74,* 722–732.
Schofield, J. W., & Sagar, H. A. (1977). Peer interaction patterns in an integrated middle school. *Sociometry, 40,* 130–138.
Schofield, J. W., & Sagar, H. A. (1978). *Social process and peer relations in a "nearly integrated" middle school* (Final Report). Washington, DC: National Institute of Education.
Schofield, J. W., & Sagar, H. A. (1979). The social context of learning in an interracial school. In R. C. Rist (Ed.), *Desegregated schools: Appraisals of an American experiment* (pp. 155–199). New York: Academic Press.
Schofield, J. W., & Sagar, H. A. (1983). Desegregation, school practices and student race relations. In C. Rossell & W. Hawley (Eds.), *The consequences of school desegregation* (pp. 58–102). Philadelphia: Temple University Press.
Schuman, H., & Hatchett, S. (1974). *Black racial attitudes: Trends and complexities.* Ann Arbor, MI: Institute for Social Research.
Schuman, H., Steeh, C., & Bobo, L. (1985). *Racial attitudes in America: Trends and interpretations.* Cambridge, MA: Harvard University Press.
Schweitzer, J. H., & Griffore, R. J. (1981). A longitudinal study of attitudes of students and parents coincident with court-ordered school desegregation. *Urban Review, 13,* 111–119.
Sears, D. O., & Allen, H. M., Jr. (1984). The trajectory of local desegregation controversies and whites' opposition to busing. In N. Miller & M. B. Brewer (Eds.), *Groups in contact: The psychology of desegregation* (pp. 124–151). Orlando, FL: Academic Press.
Sears, D. O., Hensler, C. P., & Speer, L. K. (1979). Whites' opposition to "busing": Self-interest or symbolic politics? *American Political Science Review, 73,* 369–384.
Seidner, J. (1971). *Effects of integrated school experience on interaction in small bi-racial groups.* Unpublished doctoral dissertation, University of Southern California.
Sharan, S. (1980). Cooperative learning in teams: Recent methods and effects on achievement, attitudes, and ethnic relations. *Review of Educational Research, 50,* 241–272.

Shaw, M. E. (1973). Changes in sociometric choices following forced integration of an elementary school. *Journal of Social Issues, 29*(4), 143–157.
Sheehan, D. S. (1980). A study of attitude change in desegregated intermediate schools. *Sociology of Education, 53,* 143–157.
Silverman, T., & Shaw, M. (1973). Effects of sudden mass school desegregation on interracial interaction and attitudes in one southern city. *Journal of Social Issues, 19*(4), 133–142.
Singer, D. (1966). *Interracial attitudes of negro and white fifth grade children in segregated and unsegregated schools.* Unpublished doctoral dissertation, Teachers College, Columbia University.
Sizemore, B. A. (1978). Educational research and desegregation: Significance for the black community. *Journal of Negro Education, 47,* 58–68.
Slavin, R. E. (1978). Student teams and achievement divisions. *Journal of Research and Development in Education, 12,* 39–49.
Slavin, R. E. (1979). Effects of biracial learning teams on cross-racial friendships. *Journal of Educational Psychology, 71,* 381–387.
Slavin, R. E. (1980). Student team learning: A manual for teachers. In S. Sharan, P. Hare, C. D. Webb, & R. Hertz-Lazarowitz (Eds.), *Cooperation in education* (pp. 82–135). Provo, UT: Brigham Young University Press.
Slavin, R. E. (1983a). *Cooperative learning.* New York: Longman.
Slavin, R. E. (1983b). When does cooperative learning increase student achievement? *Psychological Bulletin, 94,* 429–445.
Slavin, R. E. (1985). Cooperative learning: Applying contact theory in desegregated schools. *Journal of Social Issues, 41*(3), 45–62.
Slavin, R. E., & Madden, N. A. (1979). School practices that improve race relations. *American Educational Research Journal, 16,* 169–180.
Slavin, R. E., Sharon, S., Katan, S., & Hertz-Lazarowitz, R. (Eds.). (1985). *Learning to cooperate: Cooperating to learn.* New York: Plenum Press.
Smith, B. (1965). *They closed their schools: Prince Edward County, Va. 1951–1964.* Chapel Hill: University of North Carolina Press.
Smith, M. B. (1969). The schools and prejudice: Findings. In C. Y. Glock & E. Siegelman (Eds.), *Prejudice U.S.A.* (pp. 112–135). New York: Praeger.
Smylie, J. A. (1983). Reducing racial isolation in large school districts. *Urban Education, 17,* 477–502.
Solomon, R. P. (1988). Black cultural forms in schools: A cross national comparison. In L. Weis (Ed.), *Class, race, and gender in American education* (pp. 249–265). Albany: State University of New York Press.
Spruill, A. W. (1966). The negro teacher in the process of desegregation of schools. *Journal of Negro Education, 29,* 80–84.
Stanlaw, J., & Peshkin, A. (1988). Black visibility in a multi-ethnic high school. In L. Weis (Ed.), *Class, race, and gender in American education* (pp. 209–229). Albany: State University of New York Press.
Stephan, W. G. (1977). Cognitive differentiation and intergroup perception. *Sociometry, 40,* 50–58.
Stephan, W. G. (1978). School desegregation: An evaluation of predictions made in *Brown v. Board of Education. Psychological Bulletin, 85,* 217–238.
Stephan, W. G. (1984). Blacks and Brown: The effects of school desegregation on black students. In T. Cook, D. Armor, R. Crain, N. Miller, W. Stephan, H. Walberg, & P. Wortman (Eds.), *School desegregation and black achievement* (pp. 131–159). Washington, DC: U.S. Department of Education, Office of Educational Research and Improvement, National Institute of Education.

Stephan, W. G. (1985). Intergroup relations. In G. Lindzey & E. Aronson (Eds.), *The handbook of social psychology* (Vol. 2, pp. 599–658). New York: Random House.

Stephan, W. G., & Rosenfield, D. (1978a). Effects of desegregation on race relations and self-esteem. *Journal of Educational Psychology, 70,* 670–679.

Stephan, W. G., & Rosenfield, D. (1978b). Effects of desegregation on racial attitudes. *Journal of Personality and Social Psychology, 36,* 795–804.

Stephan, W. G., & Stephan, C. W. (1984). The role of ignorance in intergroup relations. In N. Miller & M. B. Brewer (Eds.), *Groups in contact: The psychology of desegregation* (pp. 229–255). Orlando, FL: Academic Press.

Stephan, W. G., & Stephan, C. W. (1985). Intergroup anxiety. *Journal of Social Issues, 41*(3), 157–175.

Stern, E., & MacLennan, B. W. (1974). Integrating minority and majority youth: A socio-drama group as a human relations model. *Journal of Non-White Concerns in Personnel and Guidance, 2,* 146–155.

Stevenson, H. W., & Steward, E. C. (1958). A developmental study of racial awareness in young children. *Child Development, 29,* 399–409.

Stouffer, S. A., Lumsdaine, A. A., Lumsdaine, M. H., Williams, R. M., Smith, M. B., Janis, I. L., Starr, S. A., & Cottrell, L. S. (1949). *The American solider* (Vol. 2). Princeton, NJ: Princeton University Press.

Suchman, E. A. (1967). *Evaluative research: Principles and practice in public service and social action programs*. New York: Sage.

Sullivan, M. L. (1979). Contacts among cultures: School desegregation in a polyethnic New York City high school. In R. C. Rist (Ed.), *Desegregated schools: Appraisals of an American experiment* (pp. 201–240). New York: Academic Press.

Tajfel, H. (1969). Cognitive aspects of prejudice. *Journal of Social Issues, 25*(4), 79–97.

Tajfel, H. (1970). Experiments in intergroup discrimination. *Scientific American, 223,* 96–102.

Tajfel, H. (Ed.). (1978). *Differentiation between social groups*. London: Academic Press.

Tajfel, H. (1982). Social psychology of intergroup relations. *Annual Review of Psychology, 33,* 1–39.

Tajfel, H., Billig, M., Bundy, R. P., & Flament, C. (1971). Social categorization and intergroup behavior. *European Journal of Social Psychology, 1*(2), 149–178.

Tajfel, H., & Turner, J. C. (1979). An integrative theory of intergroup conflict. In W. Austin & S. Worchel (Eds.), *The social psychology of intergroup relations* (pp. 33–47). Monterey, CA: Brooks/Cole.

Taylor, D. G., Sheatsley, P. B., & Greeley, A. M. (1978). Attitudes toward racial integration. *Scientific American, 238*(6), 42–50.

Trager, H. G., & Yarrow, M. R. (1952). *They learn what they live*. New York: Harper.

Triandis, H. C. (1988). The future of pluralism revisited. In P. A. Katz & D. A. Taylor (Eds.), *Eliminating racism: Profiles in controversy* (pp. 31–50). New York: Plenum Press.

Turner, J. C. (1975). Social comparison and social identity: Some prospects for intergroup behaviour. *European Journal of Social Psychology, 5,* 5–34.

Turner, J. C. (1978). Social categorization and social discrimination in the minimal group paradigm. In H. Tajfel (Ed.), *Differentiation between social groups* (pp. 101–140). New York: Academic Press.

Turner, J. C. (1982). Towards a cognitive redefinition of the social group. In H. Tajfel (Ed.), *Social identity and intergroup relations* (pp. 15–40). Cambridge: Cambridge University Press.

Turner, J. C., & Giles, H. (Eds.). (1981). *Intergroup behavior.* Chicago: University of Chicago Press.

U.S. Commission on Civil Rights. (1967). *Racial isolation in the public schools.* Washington: U.S. Government Printing Office.

Useem, E. L. (1971). *White suburban secondary students in schools with token desegregation: Correlates of racial attitudes.* Unpublished doctoral dissertation, Harvard University.

Useem, E. L. (1976). Correlates of white students' attitudes towards a voluntary busing program. *Education and Urban Society, 8,* 441–476.

Valentine, C. A. (1971). Deficit, difference and bicultural models of Afro-American behavior: Challenging the myths, the schools, the blacks, and the poor. *Harvard Educational Review, 41,* 137–157.

Walberg, H. J. (1984). Desegregation and education productivity. In T. Cook, D. Armor, R. Crain, N. Miller, W. Stephan, H. Walberg, & P. Wortman (Eds.), *School desegregation and black achievement* (pp. 160–193). Washington, DC: U.S. Department of Education, Office of Educational Research and Improvement, National Institute of Education.

Walker, D. K. (1968). *Effects of social and cultural isolation upon the self-concepts of negro children.* Unpublished doctoral dissertation, University of Miami, Miami, FL.

Warren, R. L. (1982). Schooling, biculturalism, and ethnic identity: A case study. In G. Spindler (Ed.), *Doing the ethnography of schooling: Educational anthropology in action* (pp. 382–409). New York: Holt, Rinehart and Winston.

Wax, M. (Ed.). (1979). *Within these schools.* Washington, DC: National Institute of Education.

Webster, S. W. (1961). The influence of interracial contact on social acceptance in a newly integrated school. *Journal of Educational Psychology, 32,* 292–296.

Wegner, D. M. (1989). *White bears and other unwanted thoughts: Suppression, obsession, and the psychology of mental control.* New York: Viking Press.

Weigel, R. H., Wiser, P. I., & Cook, S. W. (1975a). Participation in decision-making: A determinant of interpersonal attraction in cooperating interracial groups. *International Journal of Group Tensions, 8*(3, 4), 18–50.

Weigel, R. H., Wiser, P. I., & Cook, S. W. (1975b). Impact of cooperative learning experiences on cross-ethnic relations and attitudes. *Journal of Social Issues, 31*(1), 219–245.

Weinberg, M. (1977). *Minority students: A research appraisal.* Washington, DC: U.S. Department of Health, Education & Welfare, National Institute of Education.

Weiss, C. (1977). *Using social research in public policy making.* Lexington, MA: Lexington Books.

Weitz, S. (1972). Attitude, voice and behavior: A repressed affect model of interracial interaction. *Journal of Personality and Social Psychology, 24,* 14–21.

Wellisch, J. B., Carriere, R. A., MacQueen, A. H., & Duck, G. A. (1977). *An in-depth study of Emergency School Aid Act (ESAA) schools: 1975–1976.* Santa Monica, CA: System Development Corporation.

Wellisch, J. B., Marcus, A. C., MacQueen, A. H., & Duck, G. A. (1976). *An in-depth study of Emergency School Aid Act (ESAA) schools: 1974–1975.* Santa Monica, CA: System Development Corporation.

Westminister v. Mendez, 161 F.2d 774 (9th Cir. 1947).

White, J. L. (1984). *The psychology of blacks: An Afro-American perspective.* Englewood Cliffs, NJ: Prentice-Hall.

Wilder, D. A. (1978). Reduction of intergroup discrimination through individuation of the out-group. *Journal of Personality and Social Psychology, 36,* 1361–1374.

Wilder, D. A. (1986). Cognitive factors affecting the success of intergroup contact. In S. Worchel & W. G. Austin (Eds.), *Psychology of intergroup relations* (2nd ed., pp. 49–66). Chicago: Nelson-Hall.

Williams, J. E., Best, D. L., & Boswell, D. A. (1975). The measurement of children's racial attitudes in the early school years. *Child Development, 46,* 494–500.

Williams, R., & Vendetti, F. (1969). Effect of academic integration on southern negro students' expressed satisfaction with school. *Journal of Social Psychology, 20,* 203–209.

Willie, C. (1973). *Race mixing in the public schools.* New York: Praeger.

Wilner, D. M., Walkley, R., & Cook, S. W. (1955). *Human relations in interracial housing: A study of the contact hypothesis.* Minneapolis: University of Minnesota Press.

Wisdom, J. (1975). Random remarks on the role of social sciences in the judicial decision-making process in school desegregation cases. *Law and Contemporary Problems, 39*(1), 135–149.

Woodmansee, J. J., & Cook, S. W. (1967). Dimensions of verbal racial attitudes: Their identification and measurement. *Journal of Personality and Social Psychology, 7,* 240–250.

Worchel, S. (1979). Cooperation and the reduction of intergroup conflict: Some determining factors. In W. G. Austin & S. Worchel (Eds.), *The social psychology of intergroup relations* (pp. 262–273). Monterey, CA: Brooks/Cole.

Worchel, S. (1986). The role of cooperation in reducing intergroup conflict. In S. Worchel & W. G. Austin (Eds.), *Psychology of intergroup relations* (pp. 288–309). Chicago: Nelson-Hall.

Wortman, P. M. (1984). School desegregation and black achievement: An integrative view. In T. Cook, D. Armor, R. Crain, N. Miller, W. Stephan, H. Walberg, & P. Wortman (Eds.), *School desegregation and black achievement* (pp. 194–224). Washington, DC: U.S. Department of Education, Office of Educational Research and Improvement, National Institute of Education.

Yarrow, M. R., Campbell, J. D., & Yarrow, L. J. (1958). Acquisition of new norms: A study of racial desegregation. *Journal of Social Issues, 14*(1), 8–28.

Yawkey, T. D. (1973). Attitudes toward black Americans held by rural and urban white early childhood subjects based upon multi-ethnic social studies materials. *Journal of Negro Education, 42,* 164–169.

Yawkey, T. D., & Blackwell, J. (1974). Attitudes of four-year-old urban black children toward themselves and whites based upon multi-ethnic social materials and experiences. *Journal of Educational Research, 67,* 373–377.

Yinger, J. M. (1986). The research agenda: New directions for desegregated studies. In J. Prager, D. Longshore, & M. Seeman (Eds.), *School desegregation research* (pp. 229–254). New York: Plenum Press.

IV.
MORAL EDUCATION

Chapter 9

The Moral Role of Schooling in a Liberal Democratic Society

KENNETH A. STRIKE
Cornell University

For man, when perfected, is the best of animals, but, when separated from law and justice, he is the worst of all. (Aristotle, *Politics*, p. 1130)

Ours is a liberal democratic society. This assertion, as much aspiration as description, is central in understanding and appraising the American educational system. It does not fully fix the aims of education. There are issues that one might raise about moral education or the ends of schooling that are independent of it. Yet few would deny that schools are supposed to serve the political aspirations of our society. They must educate liberal democratic citizens, and they must do so in a liberal democratic way. Thus, the political character of our society would seem to require some ends and instructional strategies and, perhaps, to forbid others.

Today, discourse about the democratic purposes of schooling seems hortatory, mere ritual to be gotten by so that real business can be attended to. Even when manifestly sincere, such discourse may not do useful work. Exhibit A may be *A Nation at Risk* (National Commission on Excellence in Education, 1983). The ritual is satisfied by references to the importance of a shared education to a free democratic society (p. 7) and a quote from Thomas Jefferson. But the concern of the tract is for America's economic competitiveness and the development of human capital. It is not obvious that the expressions of democratic sentiment affect the recommendations.

What seems lacking in the discourse about the connection of liberal democratic aspirations with schooling is an attempt to come to terms with what these aspirations mean and what they require. Those who do engage

Several people provided valuable assistance with this chapter. Tom Green and Gerald Grant provided useful comments on the text. Pamela Moss helped with the bibliography, did some editing, and contributed several paragraphs to the text. Berni Oltz helped with editing and typing. To each my sincere thanks.

in such attempts, principally philosophers, generally lack entree to real policy dialogue. Their work is thought (not always without justification) to be arcane, esoteric, and impractical. That the professionalization of academic philosophy has produced a literature addressed largely to other philosophers, not to the public, has done little to alter such perceptions. *Real* policy research is done by people who approach policy problems "scientifically." They collect data and analyze it. For those trained in such research traditions, *philosophical research* may be an oxymoron. Because philosophy deals with *values* that are inherently subjective, discourse about political values is inevitably merely hortatory. Those who seek to treat such matters as scholarly topics do little more than present personal opinion dressed in emperor's clothes of academic jargon.

Thus, one who sets out to review research on the moral purposes of schooling must confront both the spirit of the age and a dearth of suitable recent literature. The professionalization of philosophy and the prevalence of positivist sentiment about research is not conducive to the generation of quality public philosophy of the sort done by Dewey or Jefferson. It is conducive to a literature that steps quickly from punditry to esoteric debates. It is unclear whether either genre of literature will be counted as research given a conception of research that treats evidence and argument as synonymous with empirical data and statistical analysis.

Thus, the moral purposes of schooling in a liberal democratic society is not a topic on which there is an obvious literature to be reviewed. We lack much genuine "public philosophy," philosophy that is publicly accessible and directed toward serious issues of public life but is, at the same time, grounded in the best of our intellectual life. Such philosophy seeks to understand, criticize, and redirect our society from a moral perspective. It is the kind done by Plato (1962) and Aristotle (1941), Locke (1960), Mill (1956) and Rousseau (1968), and Jefferson (Lee, 1961) and Dewey (1916). Such a literature is required if a society is to be conscious and reflective about its public life. Yet this genre of literature has much abated in our society. The debates of philosophers and economists about public affairs are conducted in locations and in a manner that makes them inaccessible to the public. What the public receives seems to come more from Madison Avenue.

Without public philosophy a society cannot be both democratic and intelligent.[1] Intelligent democratic decision making requires that the citizenry have entree to the intellectual life of its culture and that the culture's intellectual life have relevance for public decisions. A society that conducts its policy debates in academic journals and its politics on Madison Avenue is unlikely to be both intelligent and democratic at the same time. This problem is not merely one of the absence of public philosophy. It is also one of the inability of the public to consume sophisticated discussions about public life. A public philosophy requires a public with the interest, will, and capacity to consume public philosophy. If the public should believe that values are largely matters of personal preference instead of objects of social reflection and if the educational system should behave as though employment is central and citizenship peripheral to meaningful lives, the interest, will, and capacity to consume public philosophy will fail. Policy issues will be formulated as technical questions about how people's preferences can be aggregated and maximized. No amount of suitable literature will suffice to make the workings of society transparent or to make its collective conception of good lives or a good society a matter of serious public discussion. The ability to consume public philosophy, civic literacy (Matthews, 1984), is part of a democratic character and is a requirement of a society that can be intelligent and democratic about its civic life. Similarly, it is a requirement of a society that can be intelligent and democratic about its schools.

LIBERAL DEMOCRACY: FIRST THOUGHTS

"Liberal" and "democratic" do not mean the same thing (see Beyer, 1988). The center of liberalism is a commitment to human freedom. Often, this is expressed by the idea that people have rights against the state (Locke, 1960) or that there are limits to the authority of the state over individuals (Mill, 1956). Thus, one central problem of liberalism is to find a principled way of separating life into a public sphere where the state may exercise authority and a private sphere where it may not.

A liberal society need not be democratic. One might imagine, for example, a monarchy in which there was a commitment that the authority of the state was limited, but where public decisions were the province of a titled aristocracy.

Democracy refers to procedures for making decisions that respect the equal sovereignty of the people (Benn & Peters, 1959; Wringe, 1984). Whatever respecting equal sovereignty might require, no democratic society could be ruled by a monarch. However, a society might democratically determine an official religion and impose it on religious minorities. Such a society would be democratic, but not liberal.

Both liberalism and democracy can be given differing and conflicting interpretations. Versions of liberalism have been developed within a natural rights tradition (Hobbes, 1968; Locke, 1960), within utilitarianism (Bentham & Mill, 1961), and within American pragmatism (Dewey, 1963). Recent incarnations have emphasized a reformulation of the classical doctrine of a social contract (Rawls, 1971).

Some critics see liberalism as nothing more than the political ideology of capitalism (Bowles & Gintis, 1976). Others see its central commitments as independent of capitalism (for discussion see Bowles & Gintis, 1986;

Strike, 1989). It has adherents whose economic theories run from *laissez faire* to socialist. Interpretations of democracy are equally diverse. Some interpretations see it as a means for resolving conflicting interests (Dahl, 1972). Others see it as a community process of deliberation wherein the common good is sought (see Mansbridge, 1990) and community is created (Barber, 1984). Attempts to use schools to promote liberal democratic values must not uncritically assume that we are in agreement as to what these values are.

Liberalism and democracy may be in tension. When we ascribe rights to people, we remove decisions from the public arena. Insofar as people have a right to religious liberty, religion is not a matter of public authority. Insofar as people have a right to private property, the public may not take an interest in the disposition of that property. When people's exercise of their rights has public consequences, individuals are able to impose costs on others that cannot be redressed by democratic means. Where people have many rights against public authority, individuals may be able to impose many costs on others. However, when the state expands its authority over formerly private conduct, rights may be eroded. Thus, any liberal democratic society must solve a problem of balancing the scope of rights against democratic decision making.

The attempt to define the public sphere is at once an attempt to define the scope of democratic authority, the scope and character of democratic community, and the nature of citizenship in a democratic society. Suppose one held that all communities should be voluntary associations and that the state should be only a means to regulate the cooperation and competition between individuals or between such communities as they had associated themselves with. Cooperation and competition between individuals would be regulated by a theory of justice. Such a theory of justice would also define what members of a given polity ought to have in common and would define the meaning of citizenship. It would have a minimal view of the meaning of both.

In contrast, one might hold that a democratic polity ought to be a robust community in its own right. To use Dewey's (1916) phrase, democracy should be a way of life. Whatever exactly this means, it seems at least to mean that democracy is more than a way that people whose lives are lived in private communities adjudicate the requirements of cooperation and competition. It envisions a democratic community as a place in which people find much of the meaning and good that is to permeate their lives. Suppose that one held that a democratic society cannot adequately function unless it has a common culture. Some (Bellah, Madsen, Sullivan, Swidler, & Tipton, 1985) have claimed that American democracy was grounded in civic republicanism and the biblical tradition and that its continued viability depends on the maintenance of such traditions. If so, the content of the democratic community and the meaning of citizenship will have expanded. Liberals may regard this expansion as illiberal. Such a conception of a democratic community may marginalize or oppress those who choose not to find the meaning of their lives within the democratic community or whose culture is not mainstream. Here, too, democracy and liberalism are in tension.

This is not to say that the same society cannot be both democratic and liberal. Nor does it mean that there are not less antagonist connections. Liberalism and democracy can be seen as sharing common conceptual roots. If we believe that human beings are both free and equal, we might believe as a consequence that they are entitled both to the right to be free of unreasonable state interference and to the right to participate in such public decisions as are necessary. Thus, both liberalism and democracy can be rooted in a common view of human nature and of moral obligation.

Furthermore, liberal freedoms may be required for democratic purposes. Such liberties as freedom of speech, freedom of the press, and freedom of assembly may be required in order to conduct the public deliberations on which democratic decision making depends.

Conversely, the defense of various liberties may depend on democracy. Democratic decision making may inhibit the consolidation of political power required to restrict liberty. Liberalism may be logically consistent with monarchism, but liberal institutions are likely to be less threatened by democracy.

Thus, the connections and tensions between the liberal and the democratic strains in our political heritage are numerous and complex. Understanding the aims of schooling in a liberal democratic society requires some sophistication about these matters.

I shall consider three different problems. The first of these is the problem of democratic character. It has been noted from antiquity (Plato's [1962] *Republic*, Aristotle's [1941] *Politics*) that a stable society requires coherence between the society's "constitution" and the character of its citizens. Different societies require different characteristics of their citizens. Thus, we need to inquire about the virtues, values, beliefs, and skills appropriate to citizens of democratic societies.

Second, we need to understand how democratic character is formed. Part of this inquiry must be a consideration of what students in a democratic society should be taught and how they should be taught it. However, we should not lose sight of the "dialectical" connection between character and institutions. Not only is it the case that a given set of institutions requires people with a certain character, it is also true that institutions form character. A society's laws are its schoolmasters. The character of students may be more influenced by the structure and practices of a society's educational institutions than by its curriculum and instructional methods. Thus, we need to look at the kinds of institutions that are required for the development of democratic character.

Finally, there is the problem of *e pluribus unum*. It is not possible to get a purchase on what can be meant by democratic character until we understand both what should unite the citizens of a democratic society and the ways in which they permissibly differ. This problem is central.

Consider two issues: First, liberalism has been accused of being excessively individualistic. It is thought by some to dissolve communities into competing individuals, rootless, spiritually isolated, and uncaring about the welfare of the community (see Tocqueville, 1969). What is the cure for individualism? Perhaps it is a common culture. What then of pluralism? The "civic republicanism" that some hope will unite us (Nash & Griffen, 1987; Pratte, 1988) will seem to others to involve male, Eurocentric domination or perhaps the rule of unitarians. How, then, are we to balance the call for democratic community and the imperative for diversity?

The second issue concerns the extent to which liberalism is seen as connected to capitalism. Does liberalism entail a right of private property? If so, is this a good thing? Many will argue that private property or limited government is prerequisite for liberty (Friedman, 1962; Hayek, 1960; Nozick, 1974). Others note that capitalism allows some to gain economic power over others unfettered by democratic authority and that it creates a sector of society that operates nondemocratically (Bowles & Gintis, 1986; Carnoy & Levin, 1985). They may see these factors as unjust, miseducative, and inconsistent with democratic community.

These comments set out the agenda I shall seek to address in this chapter. I shall emphasize the problem of *e pluribus unum*. In many ways a grasp of the issues raised by this problem is central to the others. After an initial characterization of some educational issues that have been raised about education and community, I will focus my efforts on several models of community and education that will allow us to get some purchase on the options and issues.

E PLURIBUS UNUM: ISSUES OF SCHOOLING AND COMMUNITY

A number of authors have worried about the erosion of community in American schools. Some writers have expressed this concern in a way that sees the problem as one of an excess of individualism (for representative discussions of individualism and community in education, see Benne, 1985; Green, 1984; Greene, 1984, 1988; Lukes, 1973; Prakash, 1984; Raywid, 1988; Sichel, 1988; Stoutland, 1990; and Worsfold, 1987). Many have laid some of the blame for this decline of community at the feet of liberalism (see Beyer, 1988; Schwandt, 1989). Gerald Grant, in *The World We Created at Hamilton High* (1988), expresses one version of this communitarian concern. Grant suggests that the past two and a half decades have seen a steady erosion in the sense of community formerly characterizing schools. For Grant, "the sharing of attitudes, values, and beliefs . . . bond[s] disparate individuals into a community" in the school (Grant, 1988, p. 117). In schools with a strong community ethos, expectations are high and students learn avidly. Conversely, the lack of a positive ethos has adverse effects on learning: "Teachers may waste a quarter of the hour before getting down to business, homework will not be collected regularly, and many pupils will be absent" (p. 117).

Other writers agree on the need to create and nurture a sense of community in schools. Sarah Lawrence Lightfoot (1983) ethnographically portrays several schools with a strong community ethos in *The Good High School: Portraits of Character and Culture*, and Michael Rutter and others (1979) examine the sense of community characterizing "effective" schools in *Fifteen Thousand Hours: Secondary Schools and Their Effects on Children*. Concern about schools as communities also pervades Eliot Wigginton's (1985) *Sometimes a Shining Moment*. However, none of these works analyzes the causes of the decline of community, as Grant does.

In *The World We Created at Hamilton High*, Grant describes the transformation of authority relations in the modern high school and argues that teachers have come to feel themselves as functionaries laboring in a world created by others in places distant from their control. In part, Grant traces these changes in the lives of teachers and the decline of community in schools generally to excessive concern about student rights, which delegitimized teacher authority. The liberalism of the late 1960s and 1970s destroyed the value consensus that he assumes existed prior to this turbulent period, and opened all authority to question. Grant's cure for ailing school communities thus calls for more power for teachers, because they have the responsibility and expertise to shape a school ethos conducive to learning. Simultaneously, he would limit students' rights against teachers and administrators, because individualistic rights undermine the authority and value cohesiveness necessary to a strong school community. In addition, Grant (like Bloom, 1987, in *The Closing of the American Mind*; Boyer, 1983, in *High School*; and Goodlad, 1984, in *A Place Called School*) favors a core curriculum for all students as a means to foster the common values underlying a well-knit school (or national) community.

Consider a second perspective on community. James Coleman and Thomas Hoffer (1987) begin their book, *Public and Private High Schools*, with the claim that throughout American history there have been two different orientations to schooling. In their words:

> The first orientation sees schools as society's instrument for releasing a child from the blinders imposed by accident of birth into this family or that family. (p. 3)

However, there is a second orientation.

> This second orientation to schooling sees a school as an extension of the family, reinforcing the family's values. . . . The school is in this orientation, an efficient means for transmitting the culture of the community from the older generation to the younger. It helps create the next generation in the image of the preceding one. (pp. 3, 4)

Coleman and Hoffer (1987) note that because of changes in communities and families, it can no longer be taken for granted that children are raised in coherent communities where the values of home, community, and school are mutually reinforcing. They suggest (p. 19) that if the function of schools is to help parents raise their children well, then policy must address the question of the resources that are required to assist families whose capacity for child rearing has been much eroded.

Is it the function of schools to help parents raise their children well? Would it be a good thing if children were raised and schooled in more coherent communities? These are not merely empirical questions about the effects of community on growth, as though such questions could be addressed by looking at the effects of different types of school communities on achievement scores. We must also have a view of the kinds of goods to which initiation into valuationally coherent communities can contribute and those they might inhibit.

Valuationally coherent communities might offend against two types of moral ideals. One is pluralism. The second is autonomy. Pluralism is threatened in that, when the values of one group are dominant, other groups may experience schools as oppressive. Autonomy may be threatened by an environment that prevents students from developing as independent selves. Calls for community in education thus must be appraised by noting their educational consequences, but also by noting their cost in decreased cultural pluralism and individual autonomy.

Although both Grant and Coleman are concerned with the erosion of community in schools, the character of their concern differs. Coleman sees communities as particularistic things. They are constituted by the sharing of values that unite their members but also separate them from other communities. The universalizing function of schooling weakens community. In becoming acquainted with a wider range of values, the student's ties with his or her own community may be diminished.

Grant, however, opposes community with individualism. To be an individual is to be disconnected from others and unconcerned for their welfare. Schools consisting of disconnected individuals are miseducative. But Grant does not see communities as inherently local or parochial. He appears to believe that public schools can be communities in a way that does not require their members to adhere to particularistic or parochial values.

Are these views of schooling and community inconsistent, or do they merely represent different emphases? Coleman's view and Grant's view have a certain unity in that Grant's concern with individualism and Coleman's anxieties about the universalizing role of schooling express an underlying theme. Both express concern about a political liberalism that regards human associations not freely chosen by the individual as suspicious and that therefore tends to understand autonomy as linked with overcoming the parochialism of such communities. This process of "liberalization" may be part of the process that produces disconnected individuals and miseducative schools. If so, Grant's worries about individualism and Coleman's distrust of the universalizing function of schooling may represent conceptually linked concerns about liberalism. However, Coleman's vision of a desirable community seems different from Grant's. Coleman's communities seem to be local communities, the kinds of things that divide Americans into subgroups. They are the *pluribus* in *e pluribus unum*. Grant's communities, however, bind individuals into unities of common regard and purpose. He does not associate communities with parochialism. Instead, his communities seem organized around what he sees as shared public values and common learnings that make possible desirable forms of unity for public schools.

Public school communities may not exhibit much parochialism, or else school communities would represent the conquest of some cultures by others. Coleman's communities are, paradigmatically, religious groups and small towns united by a common culture. Although it may be desirable to try to reproduce some of the structural characteristics of the schools of such communities in public contexts, the difficulties involved in seeking to build public school communities around such shared values are obvious. To advocate that such communities be made more important to schooling in our society must also lead to a significant privatization of schooling (see Coleman, 1981).

Thus, it may be that Coleman and Grant have a common foil. Both may be concerned with the corrosive consequences of liberalism on community. However, their conceptions of desirable communities differ. Grant's discussion points toward an attempt to find the basis for an inclusive democratic community. Coleman's discussion suggests that we should seek more particularistic communities and move toward the privatization of schooling. Advocates of community for the schools of a liberal democratic society owe us an account of community that is decently consistent with the maintenance of some form of pluralism. They need to be clear about the nature of the "glue" that binds diverse people together and the nature of the diversity that is to be permitted. In what follows, I will try to sketch some alternative responses to these questions.

E pluribus unum: Competing Views

Community as Polis

> Every state is a community of some kind, and every community is established with a view to some good; for mankind always act in order to obtain that which they think good. But, if all communities aim at some good, the state or political community, which is the highest of all, and which embraces all the rest, aims at good in a greater degree than any other, and at the highest good. (p. 1127)

These are the opening words of Aristotle's *Politics* (1941). Aristotle held, in his *Politics*, that human beings are by nature political creatures who depend, for their development and for the realization of a good life, on associations with others in a *polis*. According to Aristotle, outside of the *polis* there are no human beings. There are only gods or beasts (p. 1130). Individuals, according to Aristotle, cannot become fully human apart from their associations with others. Further, for Aristotle, it is the chief business of the state to pursue the highest good for human beings.

Here Aristotle suggests a view of a community in which citizens are bound together in a state for the sake of their development and for the achievement of common goods in which all share. It is a view that is likely both to attract and frighten people raised in modern liberal societies. It offers far deeper bonds between individuals than are likely to be found in modern societies. It promises "the goods of community" in abundance. But it threatens to submerge individuality in community and to deny to individuals the chance to be the authors of their own conception of their own good. It is not a vision of society that can be transported easily into the modern, liberal, democratic Western world. Yet it does provide a vision of what a "deep" community might be like.

Below I note several ideas that seem to me to be important to such a view of community. Not all of these ideas are held by Aristotle, and it is not my intent to exegete Aristotle's texts. Rather, my intent is to construct a model of a deep community that reflects the deliberations of philosophers on Aristotle or on the Greek *polis*. This "Aristotelian" view thus characterizes a tradition that runs from Aristotle to Hegel (see C. Taylor, 1984) and contributes to the thought of writers as diverse as Marx, Dewey, Tocqueville, and MacIntyre. We might refer to it as "Aristotelian communitarianism."

This tradition sees human beings as inherently social and political. Human societies are not mere instruments employed by individuals to serve independently conceived goals. The connection between human beings and their communities is more intimate. What might this mean?

It might mean that human beings are formed by their human associations. The community is not merely an association that serves wants or desires formed independently of society. Neither is human nature somehow prior to society. Instead, human beings become real persons through their communities. They are social beings in that their community is essential to their development, to their nature, and to the construction of their selves. Perhaps the strongest version of the claim that people are socially formed is that their community is part of who they are, part of their selves. Michael Sandel (1982) has expressed this idea by means of a distinction between what a person owns and what a person is, a distinction between what is mine and what is me. The deepest connection between an individual and a community is that community membership is more than something the individual has chosen to appropriate, but is part of what the person is (see also MacIntyre 1981; Sandel, 1988; C. Taylor, 1989). The following comments by MacIntyre (1981) suggest the flavor of this notion:

> We all approach our own circumstances as bearers of a particular social identity. I am someone's son or daughter, someone else's cousin or uncle; I am a citizen of this or that city, a member of this or that guild or profession; I belong to this clan, this nation. Hence what is good for me has to be the good for one who inhabits these roles. As such, I inherit from the past of my family, my city, my tribe, my nation, a variety of debts, inheritances, rightful expectations and obligations. These constitute the given of my life, my moral starting point. This is in part what gives my life its moral particularity. (pp. 204, 205)

The suggestion that people are formed by their community is often linked to the rejection of ethical theories that pretend to high levels of abstraction and universality and that, as a consequence, attempt to distance themselves from particular settings and contexts. One philosopher has characterized such theories as "the view from Nowhere" (Nagel, 1986) (for related discussion, see Pincoffs, 1986; Walzer, 1983; Williams, 1985). Ethical conceptions are not universal principles that pertain to all human beings independently of time and place. They are the principles of particular peoples situated in particular historical locations. Hegel (1967, 1977), for example, distinguished between *sittlitkeit* and *moralitat*. The latter was identified with Kant's (1956) ethics. It proposes a morality of universal principles and of respect for persons as moral agents. It is the morality of what ought to be (C. Taylor, 1984). *Sittlitkeit*, however, is an ethic of custom and local practices. It is the ethic that flows from the real life of a real people.

Other philosophers have held that ethical reflection always occurs within a particular conceptual tradition (MacIntyre, 1988). MacIntyre (1981) and others (for examples, see Hauerwas, 1977; Mitscerlich & Mitscerlich, 1975) have noted the importance of history, of narrative (an individual's or a group's story) in ethical reflection. Perhaps the point of this way of thinking can best be seen by asking what kinds of reasons are viewed as appropriate in making ethical decisions. For some ethical theories, ethical reasons must meet tests of generality or universalizability. Appeals to the maximization of the average utility or to the categorical imperative may be seen (by different theories) to be standards to be applied to all choices for all people in any time or place. However, for Aristotelian communitarians, ethical reasons need not meet such a standard. Instead, ethical reasons appropriately reflect particular histories or particular situations. Thus, claims such as "I am a member of this group, and this is what we do" or "My (our) history (story, narrative) is such that this seems the proper course of action" will count as ethical reasons.

It is the purpose of the community and its political organization to achieve the good. Here this most emphatically does not mean that the best political organization is that which permits individuals to successfully pursue such goods as they may have chosen for themselves. Instead, it means that the *polis* will be devoted to the realization of a collectively held conception of human flourishing, one to which a form of human association and the virtues that support it are central. Thus, one cannot know what the ideal state is like or what virtues should be cultivated until it is known what the best life is like. If, as Aristotle held, we consider the best life to consist of a life of wisdom and virtue, then the best state is that which is conducive to wisdom and virtue and, consequently, is ruled by those who possess these virtues. For Aristotle, and to use a title from George Will (1983), statecraft is soulcraft.

Those goods that constitute human flourishing are inherently social and cannot be achieved apart from the *polis*. Friendship is impossible outside of human society. But the life of virtue requires not only other people with whom one is associated, but a state. Here virtue is more than the individual's disposition to do what is right. The virtues are both the chief ends at which the *polis* aims and the means for the happiness of the individual and the *polis*. The chief purpose of the state is to make people virtuous. Moreover, the state is the context in which the virtues have meaning and can be expressed. The virtues enable not only individual flourishing, but a harmonious life together. The exercise of wisdom and virtue are best expressed in the life of the citizen, in the practical activities of living together, and in ruling and being ruled. Thus, the good life is social and political in its character. The life of the citizen is not merely an instrument to accomplish goods chosen by individuals. It is the good life that is not to be realized apart from life in the *polis*.

Can people who live in such a *polis* be free? If we understand freedom as it is understood in liberal societies, there are reasons to view such a state as oppressive. It recognizes no private sphere beyond the authority of the state. It has a collective conception of a good life that is assumed as the basis of community life. It recognizes no right of individuals to choose their own goods or to create themselves through their choices. If our concept of freedom treats autonomy as central or if it emphasizes what some (Berlin, 1969) have called negative freedom, the absence of social or political constraints on our choices and actions, the *polis* will provide reasons in abundance for people to seem unfree.

Consider another conception of freedom, one that derives more from Rousseau (1968) and Hegel than from Anglo-American liberalism. Suppose that we see freedom as the capacity to act in accordance with our basic nature, and that we see institutions as free when they are viewed as the expression of our rational will (see C. Taylor, 1984). When people can do that which nature inclines them to do and when they live together under the ministrations of political and social institutions that they affirm, they experience themselves as free. They may do so even though there is no recognized private sphere of conduct where the state or society may not reach and even though there is much that they may not do.

If people are to experience themselves as free in this way, there must be cultural homogeneity. People must value the same kind of lives and affirm the same institutions. To the degree that they differ, some will experience their actions as constrained and their institutions as imposed by others (C. Taylor, 1984). There must also be an education in which people's natures and wills are formed in line with the requirements of the community's culture and institutions. Such an education must form the wants and desires of individuals in a way that is consistent with what can be pursued in the shared culture, and it must promote the affirmation of social and political institutions. If such an education does not exist, then people will form wants and desires that cannot be achieved in the culture and will experience its social and political institutions as alien.

This view sees the task of creating free people as a matter of creating a harmony between individual aspirations and social institutions. It is a task that requires both collective reflection on the character of the society's shared conception of a good life and an education that successfully initiates children into the society's shared life. Although, in our century, this view of freedom has been most closely associated with fascist and Marxist tyrannies and has consequently become an object of some suspicion, we need to avoid too quick and superficial a condemnation of it. Features of this view of freedom are assumed by people who fall within a democratic tradition. For example, Irving Kristol (1976) distinguishes among legitimate authority, authoritarianism, and permissiveness. His vision of permissiveness is an education in which adults have no moral ideals, but see their role largely as legitimating institutions by accommodating them to what students currently want and by broad participation in decision making. Authoritarianism is the unrestrained use of the power to coerce. Authority, however, is characterized in a way that incorporates a variation of the above conception of freedom.

> I am talking about authority, in which power is not experienced as coercive because it is infused, however dimly, with a moral intention which *corresponds to the moral sentiments and moral ideals of those who are subject to this power*. [italics added] Education, in its only significant sense, is such an exercise in legitimate authority. And when educators say that they don't *know* what their moral intention is, that they don't *know* what kinds of human beings they are trying to create, they have surrendered all claim to legitimate authority. (Kristol, 1976, pp. 381, 382)

In the article from which this quote is taken, Kristol claims to be writing about moral and ethical development in a democratic society. There is nothing in the article that suggests that he is not. Yet the view of freedom expressed in this passage assumes, if not a shared culture, at least a shared morality. Authority is consistent with freedom because of the correspondence of moral sentiments. This is not an implausible view. If members of a society share no common morality, especially if they share no common views about what legitimates civil authority, then the practices and institutions of that society must be experienced as oppressive by those who do not share the moral convictions on which they are based.

Practical reasoning in this tradition is conceived as a social matter and as internal to a conceptual tradition (MacIntyre, 1988, p. 12) that, to a degree, defines and constitutes the group. Moreover, practical rationality is connected to character. Skill in practical reasoning will not be merely a cognitive skill (e.g., applying rules rigorously to cases; see Piaget, 1932). Rather, it will require such virtues as wisdom and justice that are as much character traits and virtues as cognitive skills. Thus, for Aristotle, as MacIntyre (1988, p. 128) notes, "One cannot be practically rational without being virtuous, any more than one can be virtuous without being practically rational."

A conception of education associated with Aristotelian communitarianism has the following features:

1. Education will first and foremost be seen as a matter of initiating children into the culture of the group, of developing the character traits and the virtues that are required for successful living in the community, and of forging a self-concept to which group identity and group affirmation are central. Education is thus a matter of initiation and identification. Conversely, it is not a matter of self-definition or of choosing those goods that one will pursue in one's life. Education will assume a shared conception of a good life as the basis of community, and it will seek to equip children with those character traits and sense of identity that are required by this shared vision.

2. The central goal of education is the development of character. Those character traits that are desired are usually referred to as virtues. The virtues are constitutive of, and instrumentally related to, both an individual good life and the good of the community. To think of the moral life in this way is to see it centrally as a matter of developing certain

dispositions that are central to group living and to the group's shared concept of a good life. Although being a virtuous person involves reasoning, it is primarily a matter of being a person of a certain character and has its beginnings in proper training. Such a view of character development is sharply opposed to views of moral education (such as those of Kohlberg, 1971b) that see correct conduct as a product of cognitive development.

3. Education begins in habituation. Moreover, the development of the capacity for practical reasoning assumes that early training has been properly accomplished. Those who are damaged in their early education cannot develop such virtues as wisdom or judgment (see Williams, 1985). Paul Taylor (1964–1965) provides a modern statement of this Aristotelian view. His view is summarized by Bricker (1989):

> Education in non-obligatory virtues like amiability and generosity involves (1) habituating persons to actions that are consistent with the virtues, (2) placing persons in situations where moral feelings and attitudes are appropriate, (3) challenging persons to imagine what it would be like to be the one affected by their actions, and (4) helping persons become as clear and consistent as possible about the principles behind the virtues. (Bricker, 1989, p. 72)

It is unclear why this process should be limited to nonobligatory virtues. It seems a plausible account about how any virtue might be acquired. Note especially how appropriate feelings and appropriate reasons are built on a substratum of habit. Note also that the suggestion that education begins in habituation involves more than a view about effective moral education. It also involves some degree of confidence as to the features of a worthwhile and ethical life. It assumes that virtues established first by habit will commend themselves to students as they acquire a capacity for rationality, and not merely because they have been indoctrinated into them.

Aristotelian communitarianism, as I have described it, is not an option for our society and cannot be the basis of our society's educational system. It assumes the existence of a degree of cultural homogeneity that does not characterize modern societies and, short of substantial oppression, cannot be made to characterize them. I have sketched it because it represents a view in which the community is central, because it has been and continues to be influential, and because it has many admirable features. Although it is not possible in our society, it may nevertheless contain features that we would do well to incorporate. At this point, however, it is most important to understand the difficulties involved in trying to see this view of community as a view of the moral life and the educational system of a modern nation state. These are:

1. This view of community (and its associated view of freedom) requires a high degree of moral consensus, and mechanisms for achieving

such consensus, that are not coercive or manipulative. Absent such consensus, some portion of society will find that its view of a good life is rejected by the state and that its children are subjected to indoctrination by the educational apparatus of the state. In the modern nation state, where wide disagreement about the nature of a good life is a given, thinking of the nation as a *polis* writ large must inevitably result in subjecting a significant portion of the population to the cultural and educational dominance of some cultural elite or dominant group. Such dominance is not constrained by any notion that some areas of life are inherently private and thus beyond political control.

2. In the *polis*, the state and the community are not differentiated. The *polis* is both state and community at once. The state is not merely the government or an administrative agency with limited powers and a limited role. The state is the dominant form of social life. Similarly, the role of citizen is not differentiated from the notion of full membership in the community. To be a citizen is not merely to possess a set of political rights. In the *polis*, those roles that are seen as most central to the living of a good and worthwhile human life are absorbed into the role of citizen. The costs of this are that those who are deemed unworthy to be citizens are excluded from the central roles of the community as well and those who are alienated from the community's vision of the good life may find that they cannot be regarded as good citizens. In the *polis*, heresy is treason.

3. This view lacks generalizable moral standards. Its concept of the ethical life (*sittlitkeit*) is local. It is the expression of the mores and customs of the group. Reflection occurs within a tradition. Consequently, it is unclear how critical distance on the group's practices is achieved or how one local group can engage in reasoned discussion with others. In a world where moral consensus cannot be assumed, some such "rules of engagement" are required or the relations between diverse groups will be characterized by manipulation and coercion.

4. Finally, the collective life envisioned in this view is difficult on a large scale. Aristotle was convinced that there was an optimal size for a *polis*. It needed to be big enough to provide the various necessities for life but small enough to provide personal, face-to-face interaction between the citizens.

These comments suggest that Aristotelian communitarianism is inherently illiberal, but not that it is inherently undemocratic. Although Aristotle was not overly complimentary about democracies as he understood them and was especially hostile to "extreme democracy," in which offices are open to all regardless of their character and where majority rule substitutes for law, the governance of Aristotle's ideal state involves a high level of participation and office holding by citizens. Thus, its spirit is not radically hostile to a form of democracy. Nevertheless, because public activity is dominated by a shared and public conception of a good life, its spirit is manifestly illiberal. We shall soon look at a set of views that attempt to adapt the idea of a *polis* to the requirements of a modern, democratic nation state. The difficulties sketched above are the problems such views must solve.

Liberalism

Locke (1960) begins the argument of the *Second Treatise* with the following words:

> To understand political power right, and derive it from its Original, we must consider what State all Men are naturally in, and that is, a State of perfect Freedom to order their Actions, and dispose of their Possessions, and Persons as they think fit, within the bounds of the Law of Nature, without asking leave, or depending upon the will of any other Man. . . . A State also of Equality, wherein all the Power and Jurisdiction is reciprocal, no one having more than another. (p. 309)

If men are by nature free, then how do they come to live in civil society, and how is any political authority over them justified? The following is Locke's response to these questions:

> The Natural Liberty of Man is to be free from any Superior Power on Earth, and not to be under the Will or Legislative Authority of Man, but to have only the Law of Nature for his Rule. The Liberty of Man in Society, is to be under no other Legislative Power, but that established, by consent, in the Common-wealth, nor under the Dominion of any will, or Restraint of any Law, but what the Legislature shall enact, according to the Trust put in it. (p. 324)

These are familiar doctrines. Human beings are naturally free and equal. Consequently, they cannot be subjected to any authority except by their own consent. In society, their freedom thus consists in living by institutions to which they consent and in living according to laws that are promulgated by a legislative authority that has the consent of the governed. Civil authority thus rests on a social contract. Such authority as the legislature has is limited. It may not subject individuals to arbitrary power. It must provide them the equal protection of the laws. It may not violate their natural rights.

Such ideas are crucial to the American political tradition and to American conceptions of liberty and of rights. Jefferson's Declaration of Independence is an indictment of George III for breach of the social contract. Its affirmation of inalienable rights echoes Locke's view that rights are natural and may not be violated by civil authorities. Americans have historically seen the state both as necessary for the protection of their liberties and as a potential threat to these same liberties, and, thus, as something to be limited in its scope and power and checked by a balance of power.

The idea that people have natural rights that they possess prior to their entry into civil society needs to be understood in context. Locke is often accused of the historical absurdity of treating the state of nature and the social contract as historical events, and he is often seen as holding that human nature somehow exists apart from any social influence. (This view is disavowed in Locke's educational writings; see Locke [1964].) Whether or not Locke held such doctrines is unclear. However, Locke's appeals to nature are best seen as appeals to what is rational (Gough, 1950). Although they suggest an asocial view of rationality, they are not principally claims about human development.

The import of Locke's claims is that authority requires justification. He is refuting the claim that monarchy is a form of authority that is both natural and God given. Also, Locke is insisting that people own themselves. No one is, by nature, a slave. Self-ownership is understood to give individuals at least a prima facie right to self-determination with respect to their lives and their labor. Thus, for Locke, the claims that people are naturally free and have natural rights need to be understood in opposition to monarchy and slavery.

Locke's doctrines lead to an individualism inconsistent with the state as *polis*. Locke's state exists to protect rights and property. It is not a moral community intended to pursue a common conception of a good life or to make people virtuous. It is a voluntary association of individuals described as having rights and a conception of their lives prior to and independently of the ministrations of the state.

The struggle for religious liberty has been important to the development of liberalism (Rawls, 1985). If the state is to be a *polis* and if, in the Christian West, the *polis* is to be dominated by a religiously based ethic and conception of a good life, then we will find it hard to avoid the conclusion that the nature of the true religion is a matter of civic importance. We cannot determine the character of virtue and the common good apart from religious knowledge. Suppose we cannot agree? Then dissenters will find themselves alienated from the state. Conversely, the orthodox of the moment must regard dissenters as both heretical and treasonous.

In a state where people are not agreed about religion, what are the alternatives? There are at least two. One is coercion and violence. The heretical and the treasonous must be suppressed. The second is to achieve a conception of the state where its legitimacy does not depend on a particular religion. Such a conception of the state requires that religion be regarded as a private matter and that the state remain neutral concerning religion. It also requires a moral basis (or moral bases) for the state that can be accepted by individuals regardless of their religious convictions. Such a justification of the state must be "thin." That is, it cannot appeal to moral claims that are likely to be rejected by significant groups in the population. It must seek a moral common denominator or an "overlapping consensus" (Rawls, 1985; see also Ackerman, 1980, pp. 359–369, on paths to the liberal state). Its political language must be a kind of "moral pidgin" (Stout, 1988; Strike, 1990, in press).

Modern versions of liberalism take the fact that societies consist of people and groups that disagree, not only about religion but about the nature of a good life, as central in their view of the state. They broaden religious neutrality to require neutrality between all competing conceptions of the good. Thus, modern liberal views are committed to the idea that people are free to choose their own conception of their own good within limits imposed by a liberal theory of justice. For this reason, modern liberal theories of justice are often called "deontological" as opposed to "teleological." This means that in such views a theory of right (justice) is achieved by arguments that do not depend on a particular conception of a good life, whereas, for teleological theories, conceptions of justice are argued by showing that they contribute to the realization of a particular conception of a good life (three central instances of deontological liberalism can be found in Ackerman, 1980; Dworkin, 1984; and Rawls, 1971). Thus, a central commitment of deontological liberalism is the claim that the state must be neutral to conflicting conceptions of a good life. Ackerman (1980) provides a quotable formulation of this conception of neutrality.

> A power structure is illegitimate if it can be justified only through a conversation in which some person (or group) must assert that he is (or they are) the privileged moral authority:
>
> Neutrality. No reason is a good reason if it requires the power holder to assert: (a) that his conception of the good is better than that asserted by any of his fellow citizens, *or* (b) that, regardless of his conception of the good, he is intrinsically superior to one or more of his fellow citizens. (pp. 10, 11)

Ackerman's conception of neutrality has two parts. Part (b) asserts the fundamental equality of all human beings. It is widely held by those who are not liberals. Thus, it is not what is distinctive of deontological liberalism. What is distinctive is part (a). State power must be justified by arguments that are neutral to differing concepts of the good.

It is important not to misunderstand neutrality. Liberals do not argue for "value neutrality." That is, although liberals insist that the state be neutral between differing conceptions of good lives, they are equally insistent that the state's responsibility is to promote and secure justice. Because claims about justice are moral claims and, presumably, a subset of value claims, liberalism is not neutral about all values. Liberal discourse on this topic assumes a distinction between notions about right conduct (including justice) and notions about the nature of good lives and insists on governmental neutrality about only the latter. Moreover, the chief reason for liberal neutrality about the good is not moral skepticism. Liberal tolerance need not be justified by denying the objectivity of knowledge about the character of good lives or by holding that the goods people choose are merely matters of taste or personal preference. Likewise, religious tolerance need not be justified by any denial of the possibility of religious truth. Instead, and this has been the historical liberal position, religious tolerance is supported primarily by reasons that show why those who accept some set of religious claims should, nevertheless, tolerate the errors of those who deny them (see Locke, 1946). Reasons for religious tolerance or liberal neutrality include the moral centrality of freedom of conscience and a pragmatic assessment of the social costs of attempting to have an official public commitment on matters on which individuals are deeply divided. Ackerman (1980, p. 369) suggests that there are four main highways to the liberal state: "realism about the corrosiveness of power; recognition of doubt as a necessary step to moral knowledge; respect for the autonomy of persons; and skepticism concerning the reality of transcendent meaning" (p. 369). Although Ackerman includes religious skepticism as a path to liberalism, it should be noted that it is only one path, not a necessary one, and that Ackerman does not claim that skepticism about the possibility of knowledge concerning the nature of good lives is such a justification.

These points indicate that the education of individuals in a liberal state would not be value neutral in any broad way. Indeed, it cannot be value neutral because liberalism entails an affirmative duty to secure and promote justice. Thus, the educational system of a liberal state would have as a central concern the promotion of citizens who are concerned for justice and who have such dispositions as are required to act justly. A liberal education should thus be distinguished from educational viewpoints such as "values clarification" (Raths, Harmin, & Simon, 1966) insofar as they assert a much more generalized form of value neutrality and regard ethical relativism as a requirement of a free society (for discussion, see Baer, 1980; Lockwood, 1976; Strike, 1982). Similar observations might be made of the educational views of individuals such as Carl Rogers (1983) or A. S. Neill (1960). Although these theories often appeal to a concern for freedom and thus seem to share common commitments with liberalism, the value neutrality they require is different and far broader than that of liberalism. Also, they sometimes violate liberal neutrality by advancing conceptions of a good life in which such values as authenticity, pleasure maximization, or an absence of repression are central. Thus, their value neutrality is not liberal neutrality. Moreover, it is often most unclear what forms of public or civic morality they will tolerate or support.

One version of deontological liberalism seeks to justify its conception of justice by reformulating the notion of a social contract. John Rawls (1971), in his *Theory of Justice* (possibly the most important work in political philosophy in English in this century), argues that the principles of justice are those principles that rational self-interested agents would choose in a fair bargaining situation (for discussion, see Wolff, 1975). For Rawls, this bargaining situation is constructed by means of a thought experiment in which agents are said to be in the "original position" and behind a "veil of ignorance." These agents must choose principles of justice without knowing who they are, what their view of a good life is, or facts about their life situation such as their religion, affluence, natural capacities, or social class. They must choose as though they might come out from behind the veil of ignorance to find that they are among the least favored members of society. Rawls assumes that under such conditions, they will choose principles that seek to advance the position of the least advantaged members of society.

The following are the principles Rawls (1971, p. 302) claims would be the result of a fair bargaining situation:

First principle: Each person is to have an equal right to the most extensive total system of equal basic liberties compatible with a similar system of liberty for all.

Second principle: Social and economic inequalities are to be arranged so that they are both (a) to the greatest benefit of the least advantaged, consistent with the just savings principle, and (b) attached to offices and positions open to all under conditions of fair equality of opportunity.

Rawls (1971) claims that these principles serve to regulate the basic structure of society and that they distribute certain universal instrumentalities that he terms primary goods. These are goods that rational persons want whatever else they want. Rawls lists them as rights and liberties, opportunities and powers, income and wealth, and self-respect (p. 92).

Rawls provides two interpretations of his theory. The first, advanced in *Theory of Justice*, is a Kantian interpretation that sees justice as rooted in such notions as autonomy and respect for persons (see Dworkin, 1977, chap. 6). The second, expressing his current view (Rawls, 1985), is the pragmatic interpretation. It sees liberal justice as an accommodation achieved between members of civil society who have differing, and even incommensurable, views of a good life. Its enables them to live together cooperatively without coercion or domination.

Ackerman (1980) takes a different approach. He argues that a liberal state is one in which claims to power over resources are justified by neutral dialogue. Although both Rawls and Ackerman insist that neutrality is central to the liberal state, Ackerman's concern for liberal dialogue replaces the original position and the veil of ignorance as a means of securing neutrality. It has some educational implications that differ from those of Rawls.

For my purpose, the import of this discussion of deontological liberalism can be expressed in four ideas:

1. The concept that people are entitled to their own conception of their own good is central to deontological liberalism. It is the source of liberalism's insistence on government neutrality. In some interpretations this view is rooted in a belief in the moral centrality of autonomy and respect for persons. People are seen as autonomous choosers of ends. In others it expresses the meaning of disagreement for the politics of a modern state. In Lockean terms, it appears as a consequence of self-ownership. But it is the principal reason why the liberal state cannot be the kind of moral community required by the *polis*.

2. Liberalism need not see people as selfish or egoistic. Nor need it reject cooperation in favor of competition. But it does see people as in competition for the resources required for the realization of their conceptions of a good life. Thus, liberal states must have a theory of justice as the basis of cooperation and competition. A theory of justice is a theory of fair competition.

3. Communities in the liberal state are voluntary associations. Liberalism should not be seen as individualistic in the sense that it resists people's organization of themselves into communities. Indeed, one may conceive liberalism as providing considerable protection for communities from state interference (see Buchanan, 1989). But it will resist linking community with civil authority except when the basis of community is justice.

4. The "glue" that creates the civil community is a shared conception of justice. Rawls speaks of liberal societies as a union of social unions. This union consists of free associations of individuals joined to pursue commonly agreed upon goods who are further united into a political and civil union solidified by a shared conception of justice.

Given this, the educational system of a liberal society might be said to have two principal goals. The first is to provide the opportunity for children to explore and freely choose among as wide a range of cultural goods and patterns of life as is practical and to develop such capacities and acquire such resources as are required to realize their choices. I shall call this kind of education "neutral education." The second is to develop such characteristics as are required for citizenship in liberal society. Thus, liberalism's view of education can be developed by addressing two questions: What is the character of a neutral education? and What are the educational requirements of a liberal view of citizenship?

Neutral education cannot aim to promote some particular conception of a good human life. Instead, it will emphasize autonomy (for an excellent and generally liberal discussion of autonomy and its educational implications, see Callan, 1988). Pursuantly, liberal education cannot have a preferred conception of an educated person insofar as such a conception presupposes a conception of a good life. Neutral education might include the following components:

1. It would promote such personal characteristics as are prerequisite of autonomous choice.
2. It would provide as wide a range of educational options to choose from as is practical.
3. It would provide such educational resources as function to support a wide range of differing types of lives.
4. It would make educational resources available in a just or equitable fashion.
5. It would avoid the twin evils of transcultural and transgenerational dominance.

Liberalism provides considerable support for curricular diversity. At the higher levels of education, liberalism might support a curriculum that would be largely elective.[2] The diversity of offerings involved in liberalism's conception of education is subject to two kinds of constraints in addition to those of practicality. The first is that the goods that are made available must be consistent with the requirements of liberal justice (Rawls, 1988). Second, the foundation of a liberal education should involve instruction or experiences intended to realize three goals: (a) to develop the capacity for autonomous choice, (b) to provide instruction in those kinds of learning that are foundational to the diverse kinds of lives that are likely to be available in liberal society, and (c) to develop the requirements of citizenship in liberal society.

Many philosophers have held that autonomy is an achievement (see Strike, 1989). There is sharp disagreement about what exactly is required. Callan (1988), for example, holds that an education for autonomy requires significant attention to the child's current interests. If so, then education for autonomy must be significantly child centered. Others, J. P. White (1973, 1982), for example, have emphasized that autonomy depends on a well-developed breadth of understanding and a curriculum designed by adults to produce it. Most liberals (see Rawls, 1971) have followed Mill in holding that the doctrine of liberty "is meant to apply only to human beings in the maturity of their faculties" (Mill, 1956, p. 13). Liberals have typically not viewed children as possessing the capacities of autonomy and have seen educational paternalism toward children as consistent with and even required by the goal of autonomy. They have also seen the development of autonomy as inconsistent with certain pedagogical practices, especially indoctrination (see Snook, 1972), and as requiring a form of teaching emphasizing the giving of reasons along with the development of what Green (1971) calls enabling beliefs such as respect for truth.

For liberals, the harder problem has been to decide who is entitled to exercise paternalism over children. Mill (1955) was opposed to publicly operated education, regarding it as likely to produce indoctrination in some official viewpoint. Many current advocates of voucher plans echo his views (see Coons & Sugarman, 1978; Friedman, 1962). Others (Crittenden, 1988), although recognizing the legitimacy of public education, nevertheless still locate the primary right to educate with parents. As will be shown below, liberals are also likely to be anxious about any special role of parents in forming the values and beliefs of their children (for additional discussion, see Aiken & La Follette, 1980; Bull, 1989; Gutmann, 1980; Schrag, 1978; P. White, 1983; and Wringe, 1981).

In addition to promoting autonomy, the curriculum of schools in a liberal state might have as a central task the promotion of such knowledge and skills as are instrumental to a variety of good lives. One might approach the identification of such "universal instrumentalities" by asking what educational resources and experiences are required for the attainment of Rawls's primary goods. Although here, too, disagreement about the nature of these educational instrumentalities is possible, it seems likely that they would include both the skills of political participation and of economic sufficiency.

This view of a basic liberal curriculum has an instrumental character to it. This is not because liberalism has any special preference for instrumental educational goods. (Any sane educational philosophy will recognize that an adequate education involves transmission of educational goods that are of intrinsic worth as well as goods that are of instrumental value.) However, liberals are also likely to see those educational goods that are pursued because they are of intrinsic worth as private in the sense that their pursuit should be a matter of choice by the individual. In public schools, those purposes that can be agreed to and treated as appropriate for the entire school population, without violating neutrality, are likely to be the more instrumental ends of schooling.

Liberals will see the activities of public schools as constrained by neutrality. I have suggested that neutrality vis-à-vis education can be construed as having two features. First, it prohibits transcultural dominance. Neutrality is violated when one individual or members of one group attempt to enforce their conception of a good life on another culture or group. The imperative to avoid transcultural domination is paradigmatically expressed in religious tolerance, but it is also the basis of cultural pluralism. Second, neutrality prohibits transgenerational dominance. For liberals, parents may not treat their children as though they were their property. Liberals characteristically recognize that the initial socialization of children cannot be the responsibility of everyone (Ackerman, 1980), and they often argue that parents are the most suitable and convenient primary educators, that they are responsible for the initial education of their children, and, therefore, that they are entitled to such authority as is required by this responsibility (Crittenden, 1988). However, parents must respect the status of their children as future citizens of the liberal state and must rear them in a way that respects their ultimate freedom to choose their own lives (for discussion, see Bilow, 1990). They may not attempt to train them in such a way as to seek the uncritical acceptance of the parents' views of a good life.

These two requirements of neutrality are in tension. The most obvious way to avoid transcultural dominance in education is to give parents or their basic cultural group full responsibility for education. This might be best institutionalized by some sort of voucher system where parents, if they wished, could send their children to schools that were distinctively attentive to advancing the parents' particular conception of a good life. At the same time, such an arrangement might be inconsistent with the child's development of autonomy and with transgenerational neutrality.

Liberals are not so foolish as to imagine that it is possible or desirable for children to be brought up in a way that is entirely neutral. Children brought up in a given society will learn a particular language and much else. Any suggestion that children be socialized so as to preserve neutrality between such things as languages or other basic cultural orientations is impossible to realize and inconsistent with the child's development. Here Ackerman (1980) speaks of the need for the child to develop "cultural coherence" and suggests that this need is the basis of a liberal theory of the role of the family (p. 141) (see Gutmann, 1987, pp. 35, 36, for discussion). Although Ackerman recognizes that "the degree of cultural coherence required is a matter of great dispute" (p. 141), he also talks about it as though it were largely a requirement for infants and that it could be largely accomplished in the early years of a child's life.

One challenge to a liberal view of education concerns the nature of prerequisites for choice in the liberal educator's "cafeteria" of educational goods. Presumably, what liberals desire is that the free choices of individuals be autonomous and rational. Expressing this requirement as a demand for cultural coherence suggests that what children need to make choices is an adequate orientation to their own culture so as to know how to communicate their desires, understand what options are available, and engage in dialogue with others concerning these choices. Given this, the child may then make such choices as seem appropriate given current wants and desires. Ackerman does suggest that liberal parents may exercise guidance over their children once control is no longer warranted (1980, pp. 149, 150). However, guidance is conceived instrumentally in relation to the child's desires.

Two questions must be raised: Is "cultural coherence" sufficient for reasonable choice between cultural goods? and Is it reasonable for a child's current desires to play this role in choice? Communitarians have given three kinds of arguments that suggest a negative response to these questions. First, they have argued that reasonable choice must be made in the context of an adequately formed sense of self-identity. Sandel (1982) suggests that "on the deontological view deliberation about ends can only be an exercise in arbitrariness" (p. 180). Second, MacIntyre (1981) has argued that many goods are internal to practices. One characteristic of practices is that the standards for their appraisal are acquired in the process of their mastery. People who have not made some progress in internalizing the skills and understandings associated with a practice are not in a position to fully understand the ends of the practice or to appraise the excellence of the activities done in pursuit of these ends. Finally, MacIntyre (1981, 1988) has argued (echoing in ethics a theme argued by Kuhn, 1970) that rationality is internal to particular traditions.

These claims suggest that reflective choice is not possible for people unless they have traveled fairly far along a particular path. They must have become particular people, acquired particular commitments, begun to master particular activities, and internalized a particular ethical or moral tradition. Such people can reflect on their ends. They can do so in terms of their own sense of self, in terms of the standards of excellence of various practices that they have mastered, and in terms of the standards of some moral tradition. This is not to say that their desires are unimportant in their reflections, but it recognizes the extent to which desires are socially formed and modified. It also suggests that people who are given choices to make that they must make with only "cultural coherence" and relatively unformed desires will not be in a position to appreciate much that human beings have found value in. In short, people with the rather minimal socialization suggested by Ackerman's analysis are not in a position to make reasonable choices. To organize education on the assumption that they are is an invitation to shallowness on their part and to giving unformed desire free reign in their lives. People who are in a position to make such choices have been committed to a particular line of development to a much greater extent than transgenerational neutrality would seem to permit. Thus, these communitarian arguments concerning the conditions of reflective choice pose a significant dilemma for the coherence of the liberal requirement of transgenerational neutrality.

Much of what liberals have to say about education has to do with citizenship and its educational requirements. Two basic strains can be identified. One sees the essential element of becoming a citizen in the liberal state as the acquisition of a sense of justice. The second sees it as the development of the capacity for liberal dialogue. I will develop the first view primarily through an examination of Rawls and the second through Ackerman.

Rawls (1971, p. 505) characterizes moral persons as beings who are capable of having a conception of their own good and a sense of justice that is described as "a normally effective desire to apply and to act upon the principles of justice." Thus, the development of a moral personality requires both the development of a sense of one's own good and the development of a sense of justice. To account for the latter, we must discuss how people come to understand the requirements of justice and how they acquire the desire to act on it.

A further concept required to grasp Rawls's view is his notion of the union of social unions. Rawls develops the notion of a social union by contrast with private society. Private society is understood as a social state of affairs in which individuals have competing or noncomplementary ends and where social institutions have no intrinsic value. Social unions ("community" is a reasonable synonym for "social union") express the social nature of human beings and consist of social situations in which people have shared ends and value their common institutions and activities as good in themselves. Rawls regards social unions as means whereby "each person can participate in the sum total of the realized natural assets of the others" (1971, p. 523) and as essential to the development of sophisticated and complex ends. Art, science, religion, and culture require such unions.

According to Rawls (1971), a well-ordered society is a union of social unions. It has both characteristics of a social union. It has shared ends and its institutional forms and activities are viewed as good in themselves. Its central feature is described as follows:

> In a well-ordered society each person understands the first principles that govern the whole scheme as it is to be carried out over many generations: and all have a settled intention to adhere to these principles in their plan of life. (p. 528)

This notion of a well-ordered society does not establish any "dominant end" such as religious unity, cultural excellence, or a national culture as the basis of unity. Rather, it is the acquisition of a sense of justice that binds individuals together into a civil society, and it is the acquisition of a sense of justice that is central to citizenship in liberal society.

How then do people acquire a sense of justice, and what is its content? The sense of justice is not acquired by being explicitly taught. No doubt

Rawls would hold that the content of justice can be taught by, for example, teaching the content of a just constitution, but the sense of justice is acquired largely as a consequence of participating in institutions and relationships that have certain features. What is crucial is that individuals come to see that just institutions affirm their dignity and worth and permit them to pursue their conception of a good life. The essence of moral education is that people live under transparently just institutions that they perceive as affirming themselves and their ends. Rawls regards a just society as stable because people who live under just institutions tend to acquire a sense of justice as a matter of course.

The sense of justice emerges in three stages. First, there is the morality of authority; second, the morality of association; and third, the morality of principles. Here the influence of Piaget (1932) and Kohlberg (1963, 1969) is evident and acknowledged (Rawls, 1971, pp. 460, 461). Progression through these stages is mediated by what Rawls (1971, pp. 490, 491) calls the three laws of psychological development: (a) In a just and loving family, children come to love their parents; (b) in just social arrangements people develop trust and friendly feelings toward others; and (c) in a just society people acquire the corresponding sense of justice as they recognize that they and those for whom they care are the beneficiaries of these arrangements. As people progress through these stages, emotional attachments and the cognitive content of morality develop. At the highest level, people have a principled understanding of the content of justice and are able to attach it to persons as such.

Although these ideas have some connection to the views of Kohlberg, it is also important to note how they differ. Kohlberg provides an account of movement between stages that is largely cognitive. Stage movement is governed by the inability of individuals to assimilate some morally problematic dilemma to current moral conceptions and the consequent need for a transformation of one's basic moral understanding. For Rawls, however, moral development is a consequence of an expanding set of human relationships and attachments. Cognitive transformations are consequent on the need to conceptualize this widening of attachment from parents to friends to human beings generally.

This difference has three noteworthy implications. First, Rawls has a plausible account of the development of both the content of moral concepts and the content of moral motivation. Such an account seems largely missing from Kohlberg, who has generally held (1971a) that "knowledge is virtue." Second, several authors (Gilligan, 1982; Noddings, 1984) have criticized an ethic of principle as representing a male view of morality. This male view is distinguished from a feminine ethic emphasizing caring and relationships. The foil of these arguments is often Kohlberg. However, it is less clear how or whether these arguments apply to Rawls. His moral psychology makes the emotional bonds formed in the family and in broader associations crucial to moral development. Moreover, although moral growth ends in the acquisition of a sense of justice wherein people are governed by duties that are owed to moral agents per se, there is no reason to believe that Rawls would hold that such bonds as are formed in families and other associations are either unimportant or rejected in the acquisition of a sense of justice. Third, Rawls's view implies a different picture of what is required for moral development than does Kohlberg's. For Kohlberg, moral development is spurred primarily by cognitive conflict. Moral growth occurs when people are unable to resolve moral dilemmas without altering their basic moral conceptions. Thus, the centerpiece of Kohlberg's pedagogy is providing students with moral dilemmas (this seems true even of Kohlberg's, 1980, more recent work on just schools). For Rawls, it would seem that what is crucial to moral development is establishing a broadening network of relationships and associations in which individuals find that they are loved, cared for, treated justly, and affirmed.

This last point suggests that treating students justly is important for their development of a sense of justice. But it also suggests that the highly individualistic character of student work in schools is part of a miseducative hidden curriculum and that a sense of justice as well as other liberal values might be better promoted by forms of cooperative learning (see Bricker, 1989).

Although Rawls (1971) does claim that the principle of equal liberty includes the principle that people have an equal right to take part in the constitutional process by which laws are made and Rawls affirms majority rule, properly circumscribed by a just constitution that protects basic rights, he also explicitly denies (p. 227) that the principle of participation defines an ideal of citizenship or that there is any duty to take an active part in politics. For liberals, the purpose of democratic institutions is to facilitate justice. Democracy is likely to be viewed as a set of procedures for allocating scarce resources to individuals and judged according to the fairness of its procedures. Democratic participation is not quintessentially the basis of community. Thus, one would suppose that liberals would find it necessary to school students in the skills of political participation in order to ensure the fair value of their equal liberty and the effectiveness of democratic processes. They would agree with Jefferson that an educated citizenry is required for a democratic society. At the same time, the acquisition of such skills is not seen as the basis of citizenship, moral personality, or community.

For liberals, the purpose of justice is primarily to secure individual rights so that individuals may cooperate and compete with one another on a fair basis. Although justice is at the root of the liberal political community, the purpose of this community is to establish the conditions under which people can pursue their own lives as they conceive them. It is rooted in the presumption that people are fundamentally equal (see Dworkin, 1977). It thus is strong on liberty and equality. However, it does not encourage strong bonds to others in a civic community. As Rawls (1971, p. 105) notes, fraternity has a lesser place in liberal theory. Although Rawls suggests that liberals may value benevolence, he also claims that benevolence, unlike justice, is voluntary. Indeed, generally liberals see most personal relationships in this way. Such relations as caring or friendship may be part of the individual's conception of a good life, but they are not required by justice and not owed to everyone. Thus, liberal justice does not state an ideal of human relationships. Rather, it functions as a kind of moral safety net specifying such duties as we may owe to those about whom we may not care and to whom we are bound by no special feelings. Thus, the civic community is a thin community for liberals. People need not live their lives in the civic sphere. Civic friendship is permissible but not required. The curricular implications of such a view are that instructional emphasis is likely to be placed on developing an understanding of such notions as religious and racial tolerance, free speech and a free press, and the documents and governmental structures that give meaning to these ideas. Democracy will be seen as a means to secure equal rights in public decision making. However, there will be less emphasis on democracy as a form of community and on realizing such relational values as solidarity or fraternity. The public square will be the place where the requirements of a just society are debated, where conflicting interests are adjudicated, and where public goods (such as investment in commodities where there are significant neighborhood effects) are pursued. But it will not be the principal form of community in people's lives.

Here Ackerman (1980) provides a different picture than Rawls. For Ackerman, a liberal state is essentially a political community in which power must be legitimated by reasons. Such reasons are expressed through dialogue that, if it is to be liberal dialogue, must provide neutral reasons. Thus, it is liberal dialogue that characterizes liberal community, and it is the capacity for such dialogue and willingness to settle disputes by it that characterizes citizenship in the liberal state. Ackerman comments:

> We can make sense of citizenship only by rooting it in more fundamental ideas of political community. In liberal theory, the polity achieves its distinctiveness by a commitment to a process by which questions are, in principle, achieved by rational answers. Nor can answers take any form the power wielders find convenient. Instead when faced with the question of legitimacy, the challenged party cannot respond by asserting the moral inferiority of the questioner. It is this basic idea that is particularized by Neutrality's guarantee to all "cit-

izens'' of the liberal state. Yet this basic idea also applies to the conversation that determines the citizenship status of persons capable of participating in a liberal polity. The liberal state is . . . a public dialogue by which each person can gain social recognition of his standing as a free and rational being. (p. 93)

In Ackerman's (1980) version of liberalism, the willingness and capacity for neutral dialogue substitute for a sense of justice in his definition of citizenship and political community. This gives his view of citizenship education a somewhat different content, and citizens are created by a different process. Ackerman suggests that the essence of this process is participation.

Instead, they [liberal citizens] achieve this form of self-consciousness by participating in a distinctively *social* process. Day after day, each citizen finds himself exercising power over scarce resources; at any time, he may be called upon by his fellows to justify his power; and when the question is raised, he must be prepared to answer: ''Because I'm just as good as you are.'' . . . In a liberal state, the individual does not ''precede'' society; nor the society the individual. Instead, citizens create a *society of individuals* by talking to one another. (p. 100)

Note, however, that although liberal dialogue constitutes political community and the capacity for and willingness to engage in it defines citizenship, Ackerman is not claiming that people in a liberal society must or should (although presumably they may) achieve their good in political participation. Participation in political community does not represent the fullest expression of human nature. Politics is largely instrumental. It is concerned with the just distribution of those resources that people require to achieve their own conceptions of their own good.

Here liberalism differs sharply from Aristotelian communitarianism. For the latter, politics constitutes part of the good life. However, for liberals politics is an instrumental activity. Liberals see politics as part of a distributive process by means of which resources are allocated. Fairness requires that such processes be just. And presumably people who wished to do so might find their good in politics. But political participation is not a requirement of a good life. Life may be fully lived in private associations.

This discussion of liberalism suggests that those critics of liberalism who accuse it of having an asocial view of human nature or of asserting individualism in a way that erodes community may have overstated their case. Contemporary liberals are quite attentive to the various ways that human beings depend on society for their development and are likewise attentive to the ways in which the development and pursuit of a satisfactory conception of a good life depends on community life. What liberals must reject is the merging of the social and communal with the political and with civil life. If communities are to be voluntary associations, they cannot be the state. Liberals need not deny that people are social animals, and they need not deny that participation in robust communities is crucial for the development of a satisfactory conception of a good life. However, they must deny that people are political animals, and they must insist on a plurality of communities.

As I noted earlier in this chapter, some authors have suggested that liberalism has contributed to the erosion of community in society generally or at least in schools. Have we found any reason to agree? Several comments are required.

First, liberals might well wish to take credit for the erosion of certain forms of community. We should recall, as Grant (1988) is careful to point out, that some forms of community in schools were based on notions of racial supremacy, cultural superiority, or the dominance of elites. Many who attended public schools in the 1950s or 1960s or earlier will recall the kinds of schools described by Grant (1988), which were dominated by the values of a white Protestant middle class to which those who were not white, Protestant, or reasonably affluent were expected to conform. Liberals might wish to take credit for the erosion of these forms of dominance and the unequal communities that they spawned.

Second, liberals might wish to reject the charge that liberalism is inherently opposed to community. Rawls insists that social unions are essential for the realization of various types of goods in people's lives. His view of moral development gives significant place to deep emotional bonds. Liberals need not, and modern liberals generally do not, reject the importance of society and community for individual welfare and development. What they reject is the linking of these aspirations with the power of the state in a way that gives some particular vision of society and community the power to dominate over others.

However, it can be argued that liberalism, as a philosophy of public schooling, can have miseducative consequences. Grant (1988) argues that the miscarriage of liberal reforms has made schools into rule-governed and litigious institutions. Surely it is true that it is not a good thing if the first question administrators ask is "Is it legal?" instead of "Is it educational?" or "Is it right?" And it is not healthy to have too much educational policy made by judges and lawyers. However, as an argument that liberalism is inherently miseducative, this complaint would be more impressive if the abuses that lead to it were less real. We should recall, as Grant does, that the army of lawyers and judges now swarming around the schoolhouse door was invited by such factors as segregated schools, unjust fiscal arrangements, and significant denials of free speech and due process. The restoration of a less litigious environment for schools might best be preceded by the establishment of an atmosphere in which rights are secured by common conviction.

More interestingly, public schools run on liberal assumptions may erode community in a way that many liberals will find undesirable. Many liberals recognize that various forms of community are important for moral development and for the conception and realization of a good life. They merely insist that the forms of community in which these things happen be private. Schools, however, are public institutions. As such, this means that they cannot be organized around a robust and agreed upon conception of a worthwhile life. Although they may promote common instrumental goods and a sense of justice, beyond this they will, at best, be a kind of cafeteria of competing educational wares in which the adults who operate them cannot be expected to share a common view of a worthwhile life or a good education. Yet children are institutionalized into these instrumentally oriented and valuationally contentious institutions at a very young age. Schools dominate the education of children. They take them out of other available communities and locate them in institutions whose structure minimizes the influence of adults on value formation (Coleman, 1974). Liberals who recognize the importance of robust communities for development and possess aspirations for growth in community that exceed the requirements of cultural coherence, but who also insist that robust communities not be creatures of the state, must then place a high value on the educational functioning of private associations. Unhappily, many factors in our society mitigate against private associations playing this kind of role in the lives of children. One such factor may be the dominance of schools operated on liberal assumptions (see Strike, 1982). If so, liberalism, as a philosophy of schooling, may contribute to the erosion of community in children's lives.

The ambiguous status of rationality in liberalism generates a final concern about liberal education. This comment may seem surprising, given liberalism's roots in the Enlightenment and its general commitment to the rule of reason in human affairs. However, one should also note that rationality can conflict with freedom of conscience. The principle of equal liberty precludes the state from regulating the affairs of citizens because it finds their beliefs absurd or their convictions untenable. Courts in our society have, for example, generally held that a religious conviction has constitutional standing when it is sincerely held (see *Mozart v. Hawkins County Public Schools*, 1986). It is not the business of a court to inquire as to its reasonableness or truth. In such cases liberty trumps rationality. In liberal society, even "nuts" have equal rights.

As an educational philosophy, the view that liberty trumps rationality has some drawbacks. It may, for example, constrain public schools in their efforts to teach disciplines to children when those disciplines are at odds with sincerely held religious (or secular) convictions. Similarly, liberalism may require the state to tolerate parents or communities inculcating ideas that may make their adherents quite parochial in their outlook and alienated and withdrawn from the larger society. That these convictions are believed to be false and untenable by secular scholars does not, in itself, justify state interference. The state must also find some public interest, some matter of justice, in the matter. Thus, liberalism may constrain the extent to which the intellectual traditions represented in various secular forms of thought can be treated as decisive in the curriculum of public education.

Are there alternatives to the kind of comprehensive civic community represented in Aristotelian communitarianism and the rather astringent view of the civic community required by liberal neutrality? If so, do these alternatives provide a vision of education for a liberal democratic society that gives more voice to the need for community without the risk of cultural dominance found in Aristotelian communitarianism? I want to consider three such views. One sees the basis of civic community as participation in democratic decision making. This form of civic community has most notably been represented in the works of Dewey (Dewey, 1916, 1927, 1930, 1963) but has more recently been argued by Amy Gutmann (1987, 1989) and others (see Preskill, 1990; for a rejoinder, see Pepperell, 1990). Following a suggestive title by Barber (1984), I shall label this view *strong democracy*. Its essential thrust is to resist what it sees as the excessive individualism and emphasis on individual liberty in liberalism and to attempt to realize more of the values associated with community by attempting to make democratic participation itself the basis of community.

A second perspective is one that seeks to ground a civic community in a core of common learning while legitimating a range of diversity around this core. It often emphasizes the importance to a democratic society of a common liberal curriculum stressing the humanities. It is represented in the works of such individuals as Butts (1980), Adler (1982, 1983a, 1983b), Hutchins (1953), Bloom (1987), and Bennett (1984). Advocates of this position often argue that a pluralistic and democratic society must be rooted in a common cultural tradition that is inclusive enough to respect pluralism and diversity but substantive enough to create the common understandings and civic virtues that make a democratic society possible. I shall call this view *democratic traditionalism*. These two traditions can be merged in a view that sees what is sometimes called *civic republicanism* as the moral basis of a civic and democratic culture (see Bellah et al., 1985; Pratte, 1988; Sullivan, 1982).

These various strains have in common the desire to root democratic institutions in a cultural or intellectual tradition that is "thicker" than the thin civic culture that deontological liberalism permits. They seek a kind of democratic *polis* but one consistent with the diversity of a modern nation state. As will become clear, these three strains can weave together. Thus, in some cases, my classification scheme may be cleaner than justified by the views of those authors whom I discuss. Although this is regrettable, I also believe that it is warranted by the utility of the classificatory scheme in focusing issues.

Strong Democracy

This view of community is characterized by the conviction that liberalism corrodes community. It aspires to build community around democratic processes and considers a range of freedoms justified as requirements of democracy. It emphasizes development of democratic character as a central goal of democracy. I shall look at this vision in three incarnations: Dewey's version, the version presented by Amy Gutmann in *Democratic Education* (1987), and the version that has emerged from the neo-Marxist critique of education.

Although Dewey is often regarded as the quintessential American liberal, much of his work devolves from a criticism of the liberalism of his day (see Dewey, 1922, 1930, 1963) and represents an attempt to reformulate the liberal tradition. Dewey's criticism is focused on the atomistic psychology often associated with liberalism and on the notion of natural law. Dewey emphasizes that the individualism appropriate for a society consisting largely of independent farmers is not appropriate for a society in which most people work in large industrial facilities. He is especially concerned that an "inalienable" right to private property tends to remove issues of significant public concern from the arena of public discussion and action. Moreover, he sees the class structure of a capitalist society as inconsistent with the deliberative requirements and the social forms of life required in a democratic society.

However, Dewey does not seek to restore community by looking for some basis of community in any cultural or religious tradition or in any canon of central texts. Nor does he attempt to specify a particular conception of a good life as central to community. Dewey insists that there are no fixed ends of human conduct, no final unchanging goods, and, consequently, no fixed ends at which education must aim. The most Dewey is willing to say is that the overall aim of education is growth. Growth, in Dewey's view, entails no fixed aims (Dewey, 1916). Instead, the aims of life and of education should be subject to constant scientific scrutiny, reappraised in the light of new experience, and revised as reflection indicates. This process of deliberation is a social enterprise requiring the formation of groups that Dewey calls publics (Dewey, 1927). For Dewey (1927), a public arises when private actions have public consequences. Ecological issues provide a good example. When private manufacturing decisions have consequences for the welfare of those who are not party to them, then a public is created. The public consists of those who are left out of the action but are affected by its consequences. However, Dewey calls such publics inchoate. For a genuine public to exist, people must also form institutions and practices that create an enduring dialogue about such matters. Such a public must be conscious of itself and its nature, must act in concert for the sake of its provisionally identified interests, and must sustain those institutions that enable public dialogue. The "dialogical" process that characterizes publics is the center of Dewey's conception of democracy, which he characterizes as a way of life. The formation of publics precludes any fixed boundaries between what is public and what is private. Thus, traditional liberal formulations often preclude the formation of such publics. Moreover, one of the central tasks of schools is the formation of a public (see Feinberg, 1990).

Crucial to this idea of democracy is the notion of collective problem solving through informed discussion. For Dewey, a central role of education is to create such dialogue and persons capable of participating in it. Conversely, institutions and practices that close off dialogue, restrict it to some particular group or interest, or make it dogmatic and uninformed are the chief obstacles to a democratic society.

Thus, a primary goal of schooling is to create people who can engage in informed dialogue. (This is why the spirit of Dewey's philosophy is antithetical to the social reconstructionists who often saw themselves as Dewey's allies, but who sought to build a new socialist order even through indoctrination [see Counts, 1932].) Dewey's vision of education emphasizes the "method of intelligence,' which he identifies with the scientific method (Dewey, 1939).

The process of schooling (and society) must enable democratic dialogue. This means that schooling must not reflect the class structure of a capitalist society. Such an education merely seeks to train, not educate, some people, thus denying them the cognitive resources for democratic participation. Moreover, by restricting leadership roles to those with a particular form of education, it narrows the range of those who can participate in democratic dialogue to an elite and restricts the range of experiences that can enter into the dialogue (in many ways Dewey anticipates the concern for undominated dialogue found in Habermas, 1979, 1984; see Burbules, 1988).

Dewey's view contains many of the "rights" envisioned by liberal political philosophers but reconceptualizes them as requirements of growth and of a democratic community. Because the idea of dialogue is central to democratic community, a democratic society must, above all, protect freedom of information. Also, it must not generate inequalities or other social structures that exclude some from the democratic dialogue. Thus, forms of freedom are not justified in terms of natural law, a social contract, or as required by fairness in a society that seeks to allow people the maximum freedom to pursue their own concept of a good life. They are justified as requirements of a form of community.

A similar point of view has recently been argued by Amy Gutmann (1987) in *Democratic Education*. Gutmann begins with the assumption that substantial disagreement about the nature of good lives precludes any philosophy of education that assumes a normative vision about what the best life is like. At the same time, she finds that the liberal solution to disagreement, centered in liberal neutrality, uncritically assumes that freedom should be the central social value. Nevertheless, it is important that social reproduction be conscious. This requires that education be dominated by goals that are democratically chosen.

This emphasis on democratic social reproduction leads to the following goals for democratic education: (a) the development of democratic character, and (b) the pursuit of such other goals as may be democratically chosen provided that they are consistent with the principles of nondiscrimination and nonrepression.

The development of democratic character is not subject to democratic decision. A society committed to democratic and conscious social reproduction must also commit itself to the production of individuals capable of participating in democratic processes. Gutmann (1987) claims that democratic character is closely linked to a capacity for deliberation and that it consists in developing character and teaching moral reasoning. Although she provides some discussion of views that are to be distinguished from this notion, she is surprisingly sparing with details of what is to count either as character development or moral reasoning. The flavor of her view can be gleaned from the following:

> In practice, the development of democratic character is essential to realizing the ideal of a democratically sovereign society. Democracy depends on a mutual commitment and trust among its citizens that the laws resulting from the democratic process are to be obeyed except when they violate the basic principles on which democratic sovereignty rests. Deliberative citizens are committed, at least partly through the inculcation of habit, to living up to the routine demands of democratic life, at the same time they are committed to questioning those demands whenever they appear to threaten the foundational ideas of democratic sovereignty, such as respect for persons. The willingness and ability to deliberate set morally serious people apart from both sophists, who use clever argument to elevate their own interests into self-righteous causes, and traditionalists, who invoke established authority to subordinate their own reason to unjust causes. (p. 52)

Other educational goals may be pursued as they are democratically chosen. However, choices must conform to the principles of nondiscrimination and nonrepression. Nonrepression precludes the provision of an education in such a way as to "restrict rational deliberation of competing conceptions of the good life and the good society'' (Gutmann, 1987, p. 44). It generally provides for such liberties as freedom of speech and press and the rejection of censorship. However, Gutmann notes that it is compatible with forms of education that inculcate ''character traits such as honesty, religious toleration and mutual respect for persons, that serve as foundations for rational deliberation of differing ways of life'' (p. 44).

Nondiscrimination requires that all educable children be educated. Its point is to bring everyone into the process of democratic deliberation and to prevent educational processes that tend to exclude people or to retard the development of the prerequisite competencies for democratic participation. Its main application is an equity standard that Gutmann calls the *democratic threshold* principle. Roughly, this principle permits the allocation of educational resources to be democratically determined (and thus rejects any requirement that the allocation of resources conform to some principle of distributive justice) so long as all educable children have the resources needed to raise them above the minimal level required for democratic participation.

Thus, Gutmann, like Dewey, develops democratic versions of intellectual liberty and equity. Their conceptions differ from liberal formulations of rights in that they are seen as means to the creation and preservation of democratic communities and democratic processes instead of means to allow individuals to freely and fairly pursue their own conception of their own good with a fair share of social resources and without unreasonable state interference. One example may help to illuminate the consequence of this difference.

In a discussion of religious tolerance, Gutmann (1987) holds that we must examine the separation of church and state in light of the requirements of democratic education. She argues that a religious rejection of the standards of scientific reasoning is problematic because secular and scientific standards are important for democratic dialogue. This is a reason for rejecting the teaching of scientific creationism. She claims:

> The case for teaching secular but not religious standards of reasoning does not rest on the claim that secular standards are neutral among religious beliefs. The case rests instead on the claim that secular standards constitute a better basis upon which to build a common education for citizenship. (p. 103)

This perspective leads Gutmann (1987) to reject the prevailing three-part test for religious neutrality asserted by the Supreme Court in *Lemon v. Kurtzman* (1971) and to claim that democratic governments need not recognize the right of groups such as the Amish (see *Wisconsin v. Yoder*, 1972) to exemption from compulsory education requirements ''if this right would result in a significant shortening of the time that Amish adolescents were exposed to knowledge and ways of thinking essential to democratic deliberation'' (p. 123). Generally, the civic purposes that govern the separation of church and state as they have been expressed by the federal court emphasize two values. The first is freedom of conscience, and the second is the avoidance of civil strife. These seem reasonably consistent with liberal neutrality. Although *Yoder* does indicate that a state interest in citizenship exists that might override religious liberty, it construes this interest narrowly to emphasize economic competence and obedience to the law. Thus, the view that religious liberty is superseded by the requirements of democratic deliberation involves a significant shift in standards for religious tolerance, the meaning of which should be fully explored.

Indeed, a political theory that is dominated by a concern for strong democracy may generate a broadly different set of standards for the liberty of its citizens than will liberal neutrality. Under democratic theory, rights are contingent in a way they are not under liberal neutrality. The rights one has depend on what is believed about the empirical conditions of achieving democratic community. In many cases, liberal neutrality is likely to provide more extensive rights. Although liberals formulate the standard differently themselves, they generally refrain from interfering in someone else's conduct unless that conduct violates others' liberty. Rawls, for example, insists that we should have the greatest possible liberty consistent with an equal liberty for others. The question that liberals would pose to creationists or the Amish is whether their beliefs and practices are inconsistent with the liberty of others. Thus, creationists might be prevented from having creationism taught in schools if that was seen as an attempt to impose religious belief on others, and the Amish[3] might be compelled to comply with compulsory education statutes if their noncompliance somehow damaged the rights of others. But interference would not be justified on the grounds that it furthers the development of democratic character. Such interference for the sake of democratic community is not limited to the practices of public schools. Gutmann is clear that private schools are not exempt from the requirement to promote democratic character. (Indeed, it is not clear why the argument that Gutmann uses to exclude teaching creationism in schools would not preclude it being taught anywhere, including home and church.) Finally, rationality connects to democratic theory differently than it does to liberal theory. For Gutmann and Dewey, secular forms of rationality are important because they are the lingua franca of democracy. Liberals value rationality principally for its connections to autonomy. They are likely to interfere with the educational decisions of parents when those decisions violate transgenerational neutrality. Transgenerational neutrality might be thought to preclude indoctrination and to require those forms of learning that promote rational decision making. However, for democratic theory, the capacity to practice secular rationality is part of democratic character.

What is at stake here is not so much the tolerance of error as the toleration of irrationality. Liberalism was, in part, born in religious confrontation. Thus, freedom of conscience is central. The state is entitled neither to a judgment on the truth of religious convictions nor to one on the reasonableness with which they are held. There is no public interest that conflicts with unreasoning faith so long as it does not yield unjust behavior. But, for democratic theory, the interest in promoting secular forms of rationality is stronger. It is perhaps strong enough to bring the state into conflict with groups whose religious visions seem to reject secular forms of thought.

Thus, democratic theory can generate a different picture of liberty than liberalism in two ways. First, democratic decision making is not bound by liberal neutrality. Democratically made educational decisions can aim at goals that would violate liberal neutrality so long as they do not violate nonrepression and nondiscrimination. Second, the imperative to produce democratic character and its connection with secular rationality provide reasons to interfere with the transmission of religious conviction that liberal neutrality would probably preclude.

Those whose view of education is dominated by a concern for the creation of democratic citizens may also provide equity standards that differ from the meritocratic conception of equal opportunity sometimes associated with liberal views. I have noted that Gutmann's understanding of the principle of nondiscrimination leads her to conclude that democratic education must, first and foremost, see to it that everyone is raised above a minimum standard she terms the democratic threshold. Michael Walzer (1983), whose larger views should not be identified with those of the advocates of strong democracy but who does see the principal end of education as the development of citizens, suggests an even stronger standard. He suggests that democratic schools must be inclusive and must emphasize *simple equality*. Simple equality seems to mean that the political equality of each citizen provides a reason why the schools should "try to establish a shared education among their students and to raise them to something like the same level" (p. 203). Walzer applies this standard to the basic education that is prerequisite for citizenship. He concludes:

> Teaching children to read is, after all, an egalitarian business, even if teaching literary criticism (say) is not. The goal of the reading teacher is not to provide equal chances but to achieve equal results. Like the democratic theorist, he assumes that all his students have an interest and are able to learn. He doesn't try to make it possible for students to read; he tries to engage them in reading and *teach them to read*. (pp. 203, 204)

This task is seen as requiring democratic specification and as properly occurring in a public context.

The community has an interest in the education of its children, and so do the children, which neither parents or children adequately represent. But that interest must be publicly debated and given specific form. That is the work of democratic assemblies, parties, movements, clubs, and so on. And it is the pattern of association necessary for this work that basic education must anticipate. Private schools don't do that. The communal provision of educational goods, then, has to take a more public form—else it won't contribute to the training of citizens. (p. 219)

Two things should be noted: First, the preparation of citizens to participate in a democratic society seems to provide reasons for a view of the distribution of educational resources that emphasizes need and equal outcomes and deemphasizes a more meritocratic distribution in which educational resources go disproportionately to those with the ability to profit. Second, it provides a reason why education should take place in "public space." We should not uncritically assume that public educational functions can only be accomplished in publicly operated schools. Nevertheless, as the public functions of schooling expand, it becomes increasingly attractive to conduct schooling in public institutions. Thus, views that focus on educating for citizenship and have extensive or exacting requirements for citizenship are likely to be suspicious of entrusting the performance of these public functions to private schools.[4]

An interesting test case for a comparison of liberalism and strong democracy might be to ask about the status of private fundamentalist schools. Alan Peskin (1986), for example, describes a school he calls Bethany Christian School in a book entitled *God's Choice*. This school is not long on promotion of dialogical competence. A particular religious conception is taught as THE TRUTH. Engagement with outsiders is devalued as worldly and corrupting. Faith triumphs over secular rationality. Censorship is widespread. Intolerance of various sorts seems rife. (There is also a marvelously coherent community.) The Supreme Court (*Pierce v. Society of Sisters*, 1925) has upheld the right to send one's children to a private school as part of religious liberty. For liberals, tolerance of such schools turns on whether they are just, and the central concern will be whether transgenerational neutrality is violated. For strong democracy, the central concern is the failure to promote democratic character. There is thus a case against Bethany on either view. But the democratic case seems far stronger. Liberals must balance transgenerational neutrality against transcultural neutrality. (In *Yoder*, transcultural neutrality won as it has generally done in liberal societies.) It is less clear that strong democracy provides sufficient reason to tolerate Bethany.

One characteristic that liberal theory and democratic theory seem to share is a healthy respect for the importance of disagreement about the nature of good lives. Thus, although democratic theory allows the democratic selection of goals in a way that is inconsistent with liberal neutrality, it need not be grounded in a substantive vision of the nature of a good life. Dewey insists that ends are always provisional. Gutmann presents her view of democratic education as a response to disagreement about the nature of good lives and interprets the principle of nonrepression so as to permit those who have been defeated in the democratic arena to continue to make the case for their preferred views. However, an alternative construction of strong democracy is available. One might also (or instead) value democracy because it served a particular conception of a good life, one, for example, in which fraternity or "civic friendship" was highly valued. Such a view of democracy would have taken a significant step further toward a kind of democratic version of Aristotelian communitarianism. Although neither Dewey nor Gutmann seem predisposed to travel very far down this path, it should be noted that many advocates of strong democracy value democracy because of the intrinsic worth of the forms of human association to which it leads. Here lies the road to the democratic *polis*.

A final perspective on democratic education can be obtained from those who are heirs to the neo-Marxist critique of education. This critique of schooling in capitalist societies is best represented in the work of Samuel Bowles and Herbert Gintis, *Schooling in Capitalist America* (1976). Bowles and Gintis argued that, despite the rhetoric of public education, schools in capitalist societies do not provide equality of opportunity. Nor do they promote personal development or produce citizens for a democratic society. In fact, they serve principally to reproduce the inequalities of a capitalist class system. They do this by a correspondence between the structure of schooling and the structure of the workplace that serves to create the values, habits, and expectations of a hierarchically organized undemocratic workplace. At the same time, schools differentially socialize students, depending on their anticipated niche in the class structure, and legitimate these inequalities by creating the illusion of equal opportunity. In capitalist schools, liberalism functions as an ideology to legitimate capitalist oppression to its victims.

The capitalist class system is itself objectionable in that it undercuts the requirements for human growth and development and frustrates participation in democratic institutions. Capitalist institutions on Marxist theory are inherently undemocratic in their organization. Decisions are made on the basis of an unfair contract where workers sell their labor to the capitalist in exchange for a wage. Having purchased workers' labor, capitalists are free to dispose of it as they desire. Moreover, because capitalist organizations are undemocratic, they undermine the conditions for individual growth. Growth requires the opportunity to engage in activities that elicit reasoning, creativity, and cooperation in the pursuit of shared goals. This is precisely what is elicited by democratic participation and what the organization of capitalist work precludes. When schooling is structured along the lines of the capitalist workplace, opportunity to develop such capacities is similarly denied.

Much of this critique has been abandoned. Although the reasons are complex, a central one is that the critique came to be seen as too firmly embedded in a kind of Marxist determinism (see Apple, 1982a, 1982b; Aronowitz & Giroux, 1985; Bowles & Gintis, 1986; Willis, 1977; for discussion, see Strike, 1989) that left the revolution to the laws of history and that provided little space for human agency and comprehending resistance. Studies that viewed social reproduction in education apart from the lens of Marxist orthodoxy soon came to find the process more complex than Bowles and Gintis had assumed.

Nevertheless, some facets of a Marxist view remain. Many recent philosophers (Buchanan, 1982; Miller, 1984; Wood, 1981) have noted Marx's opposition to liberal justice. Marx (Tucker, 1978) regarded liberalism as the ideology of capitalism and saw liberal rights as expressing the alienation of human beings from their community. He substituted an ethic that emphasized such communal values as fraternity and solidarity and the growth that he saw as requiring rich communities. And he insisted that capitalism was inconsistent with such communities. Democratic communities require forms of cooperation and association that are inconsistent with capitalist work.

Although Marx's economic determinism has been substantially abandoned by individuals such as Apple and Bowles and Gintis, much of his sense that liberal justice is alienating and that capitalism precludes the expansion of democratic social organization and its potential for growth remains. They are thus inclined to see modern liberal democracies as contradictory in that they have a civic order in which democratic institutions prevail and an economic order in which capitalism dominates. But democracy and capitalism are inconsistent types of social organization. This conflict will be especially acute in education. Thus, Carnoy and Levin (1985) observe:

> The relationship between education and work is dialectical—composed of a perpetual tension between two dynamics, the imperatives of capitalism and those of democracy in all its forms. . . . This tension illustrates a basic principle, the centrality of contradiction, that we believe characterizes the democratic capitalist state and all of its institutions. . . . For example, we have indicated that schools must respond to the needs of unequal hierarchies associated with the capitalist workplace as well as to the democratic values and expectations associated with equality of access to citizens rights and opportunities. (p. 4)

These authors suggest that arguments for strong democracy provide reasons for a commitment to some form of democratic socialism. Liberalism sees democratic decision making as part of a theory of distributive justice. Its purpose is to provide a fair procedure for distributing social resources. Strong democracy, however, sees democracy as a form of community that expresses such values as fraternity, friendship, and solidarity and provides the conditions for growth. Strong democracy thus provides a set of reasons for wishing to democratize a wide range of social institutions, especially economic ones, because it sees these both as central in human life and, under capitalism, as significantly miseducative.

I conclude this discussion of strong democracy by noting some of its implications for pluralism. There is much in strong democracy that is supportive of pluralism. Advocates of strong democracy are insistent on intellectual liberty and on the democratic virtues of sharing diverse perspectives and experiences. Toleration of diversity is part of dialogical competence. Democracy requires undominated dialogue. Thus, advocates of strong democracy are likely to insist that different groups, especially those who have been oppressed, be given a voice in public dialogue. They are thus likely to be strong advocates for the democratic participation of women, minorities, or workers in public affairs. Finally, they are resistant to any conception of education that is dominated by fixed ends or *a priori* visions of an educated person. Thus, all visions of the good will be given a democratic hearing.

At the same time, there are reasons to suppose that strong democracy is not fully a friend to pluralism. Strong democracy is not committed to liberal neutrality. This means (at least in Gutmann's, 1987, version) that the goals of education may be collectively chosen and that the preferences of some may be democratically rejected so long as nonrepression and nondiscrimination are respected. It is important to note that nonrepression and nondiscrimination are dialogical rights. They guarantee a right to democratic participation to all. They do not guarantee a right to pursue one's own conception of one's own good in free association with others. Individual preferences can be overridden by collective choice or by the imperative to promote democratic character. Liberalism may provide stronger protection to cultural pluralism.

Also, advocates of strong democracy have generally held views of rationality that do not see rationality as conducted within the parameters of a particular tradition. Some recent communitarians (MacIntyre, 1988) hold that coherent moral reasoning can take place only within a tradition. Dewey, however, provides a conception of scientific reasoning in which tradition is not especially important. Indeed, Dewey (1920) often insists that many moral and religious traditions are obstacles to scientific problem solving. Insofar as a capacity for secular reasoning is part of dialogical competence and part of democratic character, strong democracy is brought into opposition with the outlook of groups that function within a particular moral tradition, especially if that tradition is religious. We should carefully note the potential of such educational ideas to bring educational institutions dominated by the ideals of strong democracy into conflict with some religious groups. In our society, where a significant form of diversity is religious and where ethnic diversity is strongly associated with religious diversity, schools devoted to strong democracy may easily become the means whereby the secular values of academic elites come to dominate religious conviction.

These claims may be put generally by noting that strong democracy has a different view of the relationship between primary and secondary associations than does liberalism. Here primary associations (see Cooley, 1909; Pratte, 1988) are those groups in which people may live their immediate lives. Secondary associations tend to be more formal, instrumental, and impersonal. One's family, religious group, and ethnic group are primary associations. Schools and governments are secondary. Liberalism is inclined to provide a high level of independence to primary associations so long as their members treat outsiders justly. But strong democracy wishes to create a strong civic culture. Although it might be excessive to suggest that strong democracy wishes to see a civic culture become the dominant primary association, the civic culture is imbued with many of the features of a primary culture and other associations must give way when they conflict. Although liberalism need not value the insularity of various primary associations, it tolerates it so long as justice is served. It is less clear that such forebearance is consistent with strong democracy. "Mind your own business" is not a slogan that immediately comes to mind as capturing its *geist*.

Finally, although strong democracy can be seen as a form of communitarian ethic, we should be clear that it is not necessarily supported by or consistent with the forms of communitarianism that have recently become popular in philosophy. The kinds of community advocated by those such as MacIntyre and Sandel take local communities and moral traditions in all their particularity as the models of community. Although they generally treat liberalism as their foil, liberalism may well be more compatible with a society in which such communities are educationally central, indeed dominant, than is strong democracy. Strong democracy has a yen for a national *polis* organized around the values of democratic participation. Local community, diverse moral traditions, and other forms of moral particularity may not live comfortably in this national democratic *polis*.

Democratic Traditionalism

A Nation at Risk contains the following rather paradoxical passage:

> Our concern, however, goes well beyond matters such as industry and commerce. It also includes the intellectual, moral and spiritual strengths of our people which knit together the

very fabric of our society. The people of the United States need to know that individuals in our society who do not possess the levels of skill, literacy, and training essential to this new era will be effectively disenfranchised, not simply from the material rewards that accompany competent performance, but also from the chance to participate fully in our national life. A high level of shared education is essential to a free democratic society and to the fostering of a common culture, especially in a country that prides itself on pluralism and individual freedom. (p. 7)

I do not know whether these comments significantly affected the recommendations of *A Nation at Risk* or whether they are simply rhetorical flourishes in a document dominated by a concern for human capital development. *A Nation at Risk* does recommend a substantial increase in academic subject matter at the secondary level. It is not obvious that this demand for a common academic curriculum is fully warranted by the nation's economic needs. Perhaps it might be understood as a step toward a common curriculum for a common culture. But how is this concern for a common culture linked to pluralism, and how does it serve democratic institutions?

William Bennett (1984) provides some illumination for these questions in a report oriented to higher education:

We are a part and a product of Western civilization. That our society was founded upon such principles as justice, liberty, government with the consent of the governed, and equality under the law is the result of ideas descended directly from great epochs of Western civilization—Enlightenment England and France, Renaissance Florence, and Periclean Athens. These ideas, so revolutionary in their times yet so taken for granted now, are the glue that binds together our pluralistic nation. . . . The core of the American college curriculum—its heart and soul—should be the civilization of the West, source of the most powerful and pervasive influences on America and all of its people. (Bennett, 1984, p. 30)

How might the creation of a common culture, a common intellectual culture, contribute to democracy? Consider an argument against the position of strong democracy. Strong democracy is deficient in that it does not understand that democratic processes require a supporting democratic culture, or else it does not fully appreciate what the nature of that culture must be. Strong democracy sees democracy as consisting in certain processes, institutions, and values. Dialogue is important. Thus, the development of democratic character requires dialogical competence. Democratic participation requires freedom of expression. Thus, it is important to protect free speech and a free press. Moreover, democracy involves certain values. It assumes tolerance of divergent views. It assumes a right of equal participation. Perhaps it promotes such goods as civic friendship, fraternity, or solidarity. However, the advocates of strong democracy fail to grasp the cultural grounding of democratic institutions. They do not understand, for example, that democratic ideas are the product of a certain intellectual history apart from which they are unintelligible. They do not understand that democratic participation requires an identification among the participants that is rooted in a shared culture. They do not see that democracy rests upon a rationality that can only be produced by initiating at least some people into a common intellectual culture. Or they do not see that democratic character is, in part, a product of an immersion into a body of ideas that form the character in a certain way. In short, democracy is not just a process of participation connected to certain institutions and values. It is the expression of a definite inherited culture, grounded in a particular body of written texts, and its health requires the maintenance of that culture. Thus, although the advocates of strong democracy are correct to see the civic functions of schooling as central to education, they fail to see the extent to which these functions require intellectual substance as well as democratic process.

The implication of this argument for education is that the curriculum of the public schools of a liberal democratic society ought to emphasize the transmission of some core ideas and familiarity with a canonical body of text. The details of what, when, and for whom vary. We should also note that an emphasis on the claim that democracy requires a shared culture represents a further step toward a conception of a liberal democracy as a kind of democratic *polis*. Like any *polis*, it may be given to elitism in that the rule of the virtuous may be emphasized. Moreover, like any *polis*, the status of pluralism requires attention.

The connection between intellectual culture and democracy can be given the following subthemes:

1. A shared culture is a condition of "democratic bonding." It is what allows us to identify with one another sufficiently so as to care for the welfare of the civic community and for the welfare of its members. It allows us to know who "us" is.

2. A shared culture is a condition of "democratic comprehension." It is what allows us to understand one another sufficiently that we can communicate effectively. Initiation into this culture is prerequisite for the mastery of dialogical competence.

3. A shared culture is a condition of "democratic consciousness." It is a precondition of an outlook, of moral sensibilities that allow individuals to experience democratic institutions as expressing their freedom and as nonalienating and nonrepressive.

4. A shared culture is a condition of "democratic rationality." It provides the intellectual resources on which a rational democratic citizenry depends.

5. A shared culture is a condition of "democratic virtue." It provides the cognitive resources needed for the development of the virtuous individuals required by a democratic polity.

The view that a democratic society is grounded at least partly in the transmission of a common liberal arts curriculum has been associated, for some years, with the writings of Robert Hutchins (1953) and Mortimer J. Adler. In recent years, it has been especially triumphed by Adler, who seems the guiding light of the Paideia proposal (1982, 1983a, 1983b). The Paideia proposal claims that there are three kinds of learning:

1. The acquisition of organized knowledge in subject matter. The subject matters noted are language, literature, the fine arts, mathematics, natural science, history, geography, and the study of social institutions.
2. The development of intellectual skills.
3. The enlarged understanding of ideas and values.

Each of these is associated with its own form of teaching, didactic instruction, coaching and practice, and socratic questioning. For purposes of citizenship education, it is especially important that students study certain central texts. Adler (1983a) writes:

> What is required here is the reading and discussion of the basic documents that throw light on the political principles of our democratic republic. I have in mind such documents as the *Declaration of Independence*, the Constitution of the United States, the *Federalist Papers*, Tocqueville's *Democracy in America*, Lincoln's *Gettysburg Address*, Theodore Roosevelt's Progressive Party Platform of 1912, and Franklin Delano Roosevelt's Message to Congress in 1944, and so on. (p. 37)

This common education is connected with citizenship by means of three key assumptions. First, Adler usually juxtaposes the idea of a common curriculum with vocational tracking. Tracking is seen as a violation of equal opportunity and as inconsistent with the values of a society that is politically classless. Second, such a curriculum is viewed as providing the cognitive basis of citizenship in a democratic society. Third, Adler (1983b) claims that "the objectives of basic schooling should be the same for all because what is common to all is more fundamental than the ways in which human beings differ from one another as individuals" (p. 5). Here one should note the strong Aristotelian flavor that has generally characterized the work of Hutchins and Adler. Once we have expunged Aristotle of his unfortunate conviction that some were deficient in human nature, it becomes possible to imagine a democratic *polis* in which the potential in the nature of all people is realized through the development of their intellect and their association together as citizens in a democratic society.

Analogous sentiments have been expressed by R. F. Butts (1980, 1982, 1983). Butts (1983) argues:

> The fundamental ideas and values upon which our constitutional order is built should be the core of sustained and explicit study, based upon realistic and scholarly knowledge and searching criticism, carried on throughout the school years from kindergarten through high school. (p. 48)

To identify these fundamental ideas and values that are the foundation of a renewed civic culture and of a liberal education that promotes it, Butts proposes what he calls a "decalogue of democratic civic values." These are provided (1982, p. 392) along with a list of their perversions. This list is divided into those values that appropriately unify us and those where we are appropriately many. The unifying values are justice, equality, authority, participation, and personal obligation for the public good. Their perversions are law and order, enforced sameness, authoritarianism, majoritarianism, and chauvinism. The "true forms of pluribus" are freedom, diversity, privacy, due process, and international human rights. Their perversions are anarchy, unstable pluralism, privatism, being soft on criminals, and cultural imperialism. This decalogue is to be the basis of education for a civic culture and a renewed liberal education that will promote stable pluralism with cosmopolitan civism.

It is difficult to reject this decalogue. Who among us wishes to be against justice, freedom, or the public good? And who wishes to promote permissiveness or authoritarianism? At the same time, there is more than a hint here of unity through ambiguity. Butts (1982) is lavish in his praise of Rawls and his conception of justice. He likewise takes his conception of freedom from Rawls. At the same time, he argues with some passion for the need to promote a civic culture, a notion about which Rawls would have grave reservations. A view of American democracy that can invoke Rawls and civic republicanism in the same few pages is not likely to be noteworthy for its consistency. Likewise, as Pratte (1988) notes, Butts provides little clear idea as to the specific virtues and forms of human flourishing required by his decalogue. At the same time, Butts is commendably sensitive to the need to attend to pluralism in his characterization of common learning.

Alan Bloom, in *The Closing of the American Mind* (1987), argues that universities (in his conception of them) are crucial for liberal democratic society. Liberal democracies, according to Bloom, represent the realization of the Enlightenment project of institutionalizing the rule of reason in society. The university is the principal organ of this rule of institutionalized reason.

Bloom's vision of the university's role comes in two versions, one more elitist than the other. Sometimes one gets the picture of the university as a haven for rational thought that purchases the toleration of society for its general impracticality and its constant questioning by buying off the *hoi polloi* with applied technology and the political science required for competent government. A second and less elitist image is one where the role of the university is to shine the light of reason into Plato's cave. "Enlightenment meant to shine the light of being in the cave and dim forever the images on the wall. Then there would be unity between the people and the philosopher" (Bloom, 1987, p. 265). Only in a society where the populace at large is enlightened can the rule of reason be consistent with democracy.

Historically, according to Bloom, the chief enemies of the rule of reason have been the gods and the priests. Until the Enlightenment it was taken for granted that the prevailing dogmas would rule in the state. Thus, the creation of liberal democracy required deposing the priests. But the modern enemies of the liberal democratic state are not the priests but the German barbarians—philosophers such as Nietzche and Heidegger—who have unleashed an attack on reason itself and whose thought is at the bottom of the 1960s culture that Bloom believes to have undermined the university and its role in liberal democratic society.

Bloom (1987) provides the following account of the academy:

> Knowledge is the goal; competence and reason are required of those who pursue it. The disciplines are philosophy, mathematics, physics, chemistry, biology and the science of man, meaning a political science that discerns the nature of man and the ends of government. This is the academy. Dependent on it are a number of applied sciences—particularly engineering, medicine and law—that are lower in dignity and derivative in knowledge, but produce the fruits of science and benefit the unscientific and make them respectful of science. (p. 261)

Moreover, it is crucial that the study of the liberal arts be integrated and whole. Such an education is not promoted by distribution requirements or by cross-disciplinary studies. It requires a central emphasis on philosophy. Although Bloom stops short of a recommendation of the great books approach to higher education, he claims that it is the only approach to a curriculum that seriously addresses the problem. The value of this curriculum is not only that it is the source of democratic wisdom. Also, because it acquaints students with the great questions and the great ideas, it is the source of the great souls, the virtuous people, that a democratic society requires for its leaders.

What of pluralism? Those who see the intellectual tradition of the West as the glue that binds our culture together seem collectively to have little to say about pluralism. Bloom is largely crabby about most of its manifestations in the university. But at least we might note that the Western intellectual tradition reflects a rather large degree of diversity of both opinion and theme. If it is the basis of some form of unity, it will be a unity of questions, not of answers, of common concerns, not common belief. There is some pluralism here. At the same time, if this tradition is to be valued not only as an intellectual resource, but because it is *our* tradition, then it should be noted that the *us* that this tradition selects is somewhat less than the entire population of the nation. And we should not be too surprised if those who are left out of this *us* wonder whether the preference for the Western tradition is not Eurocentric. Here pluralism seems to have more to do with free inquiry than cultural diversity.

A rather different version of the claim that a common culture is required for a democratic society has been provided by Hirsch (1987). Hirsch is concerned by what he sees as the decline of cultural literacy and its implications for democracy. He understands cultural literacy in terms of the possession of a store of shared, literate, background knowledge. This shared knowledge need not be sophisticated or deeply grasped. Indeed, it seems amenable to description in a list of terms and dates. But it plays an orienting role. It allows people within a given nation to communicate meaningfully with one another because they share a common group of terms, a mutually grasped frame of reference. Moreover, cultural literacy is important to basic literacy, to the ability to read, and, thereby, to democracy. Hirsch (1987) describes the connection among cultural literacy, literacy, and democracy as follows:

> Both of these leaders [Martin Luther King and Thomas Jefferson] understood that just having the right to vote is meaningless if a citizen is disenfranchised by illiteracy or semiliteracy. Illiterate and semiliterate Americans are condemned not only to poverty, but also to the powerlessness of incomprehension. Knowing that they do not understand the issues, and feeling prey to manipulative oversimplifications, they do not trust the system of which they are supposed to be masters. They do not feel themselves to be active participants in our republic, and they often do not turn out to vote. The civic importance of cultural literacy lies in the fact that the true enfranchisement depends upon knowledge, knowledge upon literacy, and literacy upon cultural literacy. (p. 12)

Hirsch's (1987) views might be given a narrow and a broad interpretation. In the narrow interpretation, Hirsch is making a point about how people learn to read. Learning to read is misunderstood if it is seen as merely learning to decode symbols. Research suggests that learning to read requires a context for the interpreting of the text. "What counts," Hirsch (1987) says, "is our ability to grasp the general shape of what we are reading and to tie it to what we already know" (pp. 14, 15). However, Hirsch's comments might also be treated as a broader theory of communication. The intelligibility of any sort of message depends on more than a mere grasp of the individual words. Communication requires a background of shared assumptions, a common context. Otherwise, meaning cannot be shared. This understood, cultural literacy would be a requirement not only of the ability to read, but also of the ability to participate intelligibly and intelligently in the conversations of one's society. It would be a requirement of dialogical competence. Thus, there is a public democratic interest in developing and maintaining a shared national culture.

Hirsch (1987) is aware that this view is in tension with American pluralism. His solution is worth noting. He (1987) suggests that we think of American public culture as existing in three parts:

> At one end is our civil religion, which is laden with definite value traditions. Here we have absolute commitments to freedom, patriotism, equality, self-government, and so on. At the other end of the spectrum is the *vocabulary* of our national discourse, by no means empty of content but nonetheless value-neutral in the sense that it is used to support all the conflicting values that arise in public discourse. . . . Between these two extremes lies the vast middle domain of culture proper. Here are the concrete politics, customs, technologies, and legends that define our current attitudes and actions and our institutions. (pp. 102, 103)

Hirsch regards the American civil religion as the source of our national unity. It is a curious form of unity. It seems more a unity of symbols than ideas. It is "capacious and vague," "big-tented and tolerant." Those secularists who reject the American civil religion as expressed in our national symbols and rituals forget that it is "a central source of coherence in American public culture, holding together various and even contradictory elements of its tradition" (p. 99). This sense that the civil religion creates a unity of symbol rather than ideas is enhanced by the fact that its language turns out not to be the real language of public debate. That, it seems, is Hirsch's vocabulary of national discourse, which is seen as value neutral and capable of serving as a vehicle in which numerous conflicting claims can be pressed.

Although I have put Hirsch together with other advocates of the notion that a democratic society requires a common culture, some significant differences need to be noted. In the vision shared by Bennett, Adler, and Bloom, the Western intellectual tradition is supposed to do real cognitive work. It is the source of great ideas, rationality, and virtue. Its role as a storehouse of symbols, objects of loyalty, means of mutual intelligibility, or vehicle of bonding is minimized. No doubt, this is reasonable. One may imagine being edified by a reading of, say, Kant's *Critique of Practical Reason* (1956) or Hegel's *Phenomenology of Spirit* (1977), but their appeal as sacred texts is limited. At the same time, those who advocate the Western tradition as the center of a democratic culture seem inattentive to the role symbols and sacred texts play in achieving cultural unity. Hirsch cannot be faulted here. However, we should also note the extent to which the vision of a democratic society governed by the rule of reason and of education as involving the democratic distribution of rationality has been lost. Hirsch's unity is one of symbols, not ideas. His national vocabulary and cultural literacy involves learning a little about a long list. An education dedicated to these chunks of curriculum is apt to be long on patriotism and rote learning and short on rationality and deliberative competence.

Moreover, we should be suspicious of its claims to permit pluralism. The national vocabulary may be classless, but the civil religion, for all its vacuity, is suspect. Hirsch notes that "secularists" are alienated by its frequent uses of religious images and terms. One supposes that the seriously religious may be equally offended by a use of the divine that they might well see as somewhere between blasphemy and idolatry. The suggestion that the vacuity of the civil religion ensures its neutrality is suspect.

Thus, these visions of a democratic culture seem deficient. They offer an unhappy choice. On one hand, we are offered a high culture that contains intellectual resources for understanding our polity, producing dialogical competence, and perhaps creating a virtuous citizenry. At the same time, the suggestion that this tradition is Eurocentric and inaccessible to many is surely not bizarre. Moreover, its potential as a source of symbols and civic bonding is not great. On the other hand, we are offered a civil religion and a national vocabulary that is long on symbols, sacred texts, and bonding, but where the cultivation of civic intelligence and dialogical competence seems in doubt.

None of the works discussed has a genuine view of citizenship, of civic virtues, or of the nature of civic participation. Pursuantly, they lack a view of education that goes much beyond the cognitive. There is little sense of how citizens are to be initiated into democratic practices because there is little sense of what democratic practices are. Although the advocates of strong democracy might be accused of emphasizing democratic practices apart from any substantive content for a democratic culture, here the difficulty is reversed. There is content aplenty, but little sense of institutions and practices. Pursuantly, there is little sense of what democratic education might be that goes beyond curricular specification and examines institutional forms as vehicles for democratic education.

Civic Republicanism

Civic republicanism might be viewed as incorporating elements of both strong democracy and democratic traditionalism. It has a view of the cognitive traditions that underlie democratic polity. These are identified as the biblical tradition and the republicanism of ancient Greece and Rome. But there is often also a vision of civic practices, citizenship, and the virtues. Moreover, the content of civic republicanism seems to be understood in a way that does not retreat into high culture. One can imagine it serving to illuminate discourse at a high school or a community college, not just at the faculty club at the University of Chicago. Civic republicanism thus has much in common with Dewey's vision of a democratic polity, but it has a greater respect for substantive traditions. Moreover, in some of its formulations, it is more self-consciously Aristotelian in its character than is strong democracy. The aspiration for a democratic *polis* is clear. Finally, civic republicanism is self-consciously antagonistic to liberalism. The works of its advocates seem characterized by lavish praise of Tocqueville's (1969) insights into the destructive role of individualism in American society and are dedicated to the proposition that the bearer of the evil of individualism is liberalism (see Bellah et al., 1985; Pratte, 1988; Sullivan, 1982).

Recent interest in civic republicanism has been stimulated by Bellah's book, *Habits of the Heart* (Bellah et al., 1985), where Bellah traces the erosion of community and the dominance of individualism through the lives of several individuals whom he interviews in depth. He opposes this individualism to the biblical and republican strands in American culture. The biblical strand is represented by the Puritans and John Winthrop, who wished to create "a community in which a genuinely ethical and spiritual life could be lived" (p. 29). The republican tradition is represented by Jefferson, who is said to have been guided throughout his life by "the ideal of a self-governing society of relative equals in which all participate" (p. 30). Both Winthrop and Jefferson are held to have rejected a "formal freedom" that would allow people to do what they pleased and to have favored a form of freedom that takes "on its real meaning in a certain kind of society with a certain form of life" (p. 31).

For civic republicanism, civil participation is more than a form of benevolence or of concern for the welfare of others. Civic republicanism is strongly imbued with the Aristotelian vision that the nature of the good is a public concern and is to be found in public life. Sullivan (1982) writes:

> What is ultimately at issue is the radical question of what is a worthwhile life. A republican public philosophy begins with the realization that this is necessarily a public concern, precisely because human life is interdependent, requiring mutual trust even for individual survival. However, while this is true for any human society, a public life develops only when a society realizes that reciprocity and mutual aid are worthy of cultivation both as good in themselves and as providing the basis of the individual self. (p. 10)

Pratte (1988), in *The Civic Imperative*, a book devoted to exploring the educational implications of civic republicanism, characterizes civic republicanism as concerned with civic virtue and with the public good:

> Civic virtue (*arete*, or the good traits of moral and intellectual character) suggests the ideal of civic excellence—certain skills and character traits the possession and exercise of which tend to enable us to achieve a kind of integrity and unity of self. The possessor of civic

virtue is guided by moral and intellectual considerations in an attempt to balance private interest with the *public good.* This is an ideal state whereby solidarity, friendship, trust, and tolerance are collective, communal relationships guided by moral principles and reasoning. The recognition of this role makes public life something to be celebrated and valued, something that reflects credit upon the individual, rather than something to be ridiculed or grudgingly engaged in. (p. 40)

Here, too, the center of a worthwhile human life consists in civic participation, which is supported by civic virtue. An education for participation in such a community would, presumably, attempt to describe the civic virtues and to devise a pedagogy for their achievement. Such would be the education of a citizen.

What, then, are the virtues of civic republicanism? Pratte (1988) suggests that civic republicanism rests on an ethic of obligation that consists in character traits of concern, caring, and tolerance and an ethic of civil service that is a "practical means for achieving the bond of loyalty, empathy and fidelity, and solidarity so fundamental to the well-being of a community" (p. 74). This ethic requires "*social habits of willing action beneficial to others*" (p. 74). Pratte also mentions certain civic competencies, civic literacy, civic conscience, practical reasoning skills, and reflective thinking. One would suppose that these are virtues as well.

A pedagogy for producing such citizens might have several components. The explicit curriculum might emphasize a grasp of some of the basic texts of the American polity. Pratte suggests the Declaration of Independence, the Constitution, the *Federalist Papers, Democracy in America*, and Lincoln's Gettysburg Address. (There seems much agreement on the sacred texts of the civil religion.)

A view of education that seeks to establish a form of community and to cultivate civic virtues must also attend to its own institutional forms and not only those of the school. The laws are educators. Thus, Pratte notes that civic education is influenced by the total school environment and expresses concern about the hidden curriculum. Sullivan worries about the uneasy tension between commerce and the democratic republic. One would suppose that in a participatory democracy where civic friendship is a central good of life, significant inequalities of wealth or class or bureaucratic hierarchies will be frowned upon. Insofar as virtues are best formed by participation in such institutions rather than by bad example, such inequalities would be particular liabilities in the education of the young. Thus, the schools of civic republicans would be noteworthy for their classlessness, for their participatory character, and for their deemphasis of professional expertise. As Giroux (1986) notes, "Professionalism as it is presently defined has little to do with democracy as a social movement" (p. 37).

Finally, the pedagogy that is most suitable for the development of democratic virtues is likely to emphasize habituation and identification. Presumably, these are features of a participatory environment. Thus, Pratte commends Green's (1984) notion of "the voice of conscience as membership." Green, in turn, explicates this notion with an appeal to Durkheim (see Durkheim, 1961). Green claims:

> Durkheim says that the first step in moral education is discipline, that is, the setting of boundaries, the bringing of order to the child's behavior. The second step, however, is "attachment to a social group." (p. 9)

Green notes that such attachment involves strong normation:

> The point is that norm acquisition is not displayed merely in the fact that the behavior of persons conforms to a certain pattern. Rather, the existence or failure of norm acquisition is displayed in the presence or absence of certain feelings associated with departure from what the norm requires. (p. 10)

Green (1984) concludes his discussion by describing what he calls a curriculum of moral competence. This curriculum emphasizes problems of collective decision making and requires that the following questions be addressed: "(1) Whose interests are you expressing? (2) Whose interests are you not expressing? and (3) How does your proposal balance the goods being sought?" (p. 13). Addressing such questions provides a vehicle for acquiring empathy and the kinds of practical wisdom "that are needed for moral conduct or moral thinking within the context of some public." Because Green does not suggest that the object of this membership must be the *polis*, one should not uncritically view his intent as a description of the kind of moral education uniquely suited to civic republicanism. Nevertheless, it is adaptable to that purpose.

Because civic republicanism involves elements of a substantive cultural tradition as well as a distinctive set of virtues and institutional practices, we need to look carefully at its conception of pluralism. Pratte (1988) suggests that although pluralism and civic republicanism are in some tension, it is a mistake not to recognize their common ground. This involves a recognition of the value of human dignity and mutual respect and of the democratic principles of social justice, community, and fairness. Moreover, Pratte expresses some affection for Dewey's claim that the national community cannot possess all of those desirable qualities that characterize local community and that it must be seen as a means of ordering and enriching the experience that is had in local associations. Nevertheless, he also insists that in areas of conflict, the larger association of the nation state must take precedence. These, of course, are soothing words. Much depends on what precisely they mean.

Because I have suggested the Amish as a kind of barometer for liberal tolerance and because I have expressed concern for how the desire for the democratic *polis* is related to freedom of conscience, we might test Pratt's sentiments by asking how religion fares. His (1988) response to this problem involves a contrast between civic conscience, which is always general, common, communal, and secular, and religious conscience, which

> involves a sectarian, sacerdotal, nonsecular, or worshipful set of moral principles informing conduct that is private, privileged, particular, intimate, personal, confidential, and devotional. . . . It is precisely because religious conscience connects the self to God that it sustains itself by informing the personal, the private, by specifying what is best for one to do in one's understanding and covenant with God, that is, with the meaning of one's life, not all others' lives. (p. 166)

Although Pratte stops well short of claiming that religion should be inhibited for the sake of the democratic community, it is clear that he views religion as undermining the civic conscience that is the basis of democratic community. Civic republicanism is grounded in a biblical tradition, but it seems antithetical to a biblical faith. In such a vision, "I must obey God rather than man" has little standing, and much is rendered unto Caesar. In appreciating the conflict between liberalism and these several varieties of democratic communitarianism, it seems generally to be the case that freedom of conscience is subordinate to establishing the conditions of democratic community. Whether this is a good thing is properly a matter of debate, but we do not understand what is at stake if we are inattentive to the conflict. In the democratic *polis*, rights are contingent. The good is prior.

I wish to suggest three lines of criticism of civic republicanism. First, civic republicanism, like the other versions of the democratic *polis*, places rights, especially freedom of conscience, at risk, because it makes them subordinate to the social conditions required for the maintenance of the democratic polity. Deontological liberals will find this a concern whenever the right is contingent on a vision of the good life. Second, the arguments of civic republicanism may overstate the individualist character of liberalism. Liberals need not deny that human beings are social animals whose development is dependent on the quality and character of the forms of community available to them. What they must deny is the assimilation of community or society into the state or the polity. Often, democratic communitarians attack liberals by asserting that people are social animals but draw conclusions that require the premise that people are political animals. The latter claim is far stronger than the former and requires stronger arguments than are often given. Finally, civic republicanism, especially in Pratte's version, involves an assimilation of Dewey and the tradition of strong democracy into that of civic republicanism. A question of the consistency of these strains of the democratic *polis* should be raised. One can grant that they have much in common. Yet Dewey, at least, might be troubled by the emphasis on the special status of biblical principles and republican traditions in civic republicanism. One must recall the extent to which Dewey sees religion and classical civilization as antithetical to the scientific spirit that animates his vision of the democratic community. Moreover, the dominance of the goods of association, and of civic friendship, might represent more of a determinate set of fixed ends than Dewey's growth ethic, with its constant reappraisal of ends, is consistent with.

A NOTE ON RESEARCH ON STRUCTURAL CHARACTERIZATIONS OF COMMUNITY

There has been a vast interest in recent years in the characteristics of effective schools (see Good & Brophy, 1986). Some of this work deals with the structural or organizational characteristics of such schools (see Rowan, 1990). Thus, the work of Coleman and Hoffer (1987) discussed at the beginning of this chapter seems primarily interested in discovering the structural characteristics of effective school communities and whether these characteristics can be replicated. Likewise, Chubb (1988) and Chubb and Moe (1990) argue that what they see as ''democratic'' governance of schools tends to produce organizational structures that are less effective.

A common measure of school effectiveness in these studies is scores on various standardized tests. Such tests most frequently measure some form of literacy. I have no wish here to dispute the value or appropriateness of this work. It is quite clear that a democratic society has a compelling interest in the wide distribution of literacy among its citizens. Nor do I wish to be numbered among those philosophers who believe that the use of test scores to measure school achievement is itself some form of evil. I do, however, wish to note three cautions that apply to the particular context of this paper.

1. This emphasis on effectiveness tends to ignore those values that constitute the social glue that maintains the community. For example, Catholic schools are studied in a way that ignores anything that is uniquely Catholic. This has at least two liabilities. First, it may be inadequately sensitive to the extent to which the structural characteristics of such effective schools are internal to those values that organize the community in a way that makes it unlikely that such characteristics can be attached to communities organized around different values. Different religions have different views of authority and different community structures. These views are internal to the faith. It is unclear as to the extent that the structural characteristics of parochial schools are what they are be-

cause of the theological convictions that motivate the school community. Second, an emphasis on effectiveness as measured by test scores can displace notions of effectiveness that are more internal to the values that maintain the community. One supposes that those who operate most parochial schools are interested in the academic progress of the children they teach. One might also suppose that few of them would trade a modest increase in the test scores of their students for a decline in their religious faithfulness. Empirical work that praises the effectiveness of such schools while devaluing those values that make them distinctive may offer them a trade of a mess of pottage for their birthright.

2. This review has suggested that at least some of the organizational features of schools or of the educational system are properly viewed as derived from a conception of the central moral purposes of schooling. It is often thought that particular moral purposes require certain forms of social organization. For example, I have suggested the outline of a liberal argument for cooperative learning. Likewise, advocates of strong democracy argue that teaching deliberative competence requires forms of school governance that are themselves participatory and that include student participation. Those who believe that a democratic polity depends on the transmission of a common intellectual culture may emphasize the role of the intellectually competent. In short, forms of community organization are properly viewed as implications of the community's central moral ideals and, especially, of their visions of moral education. To treat them as though they were to be decided largely as a consequence of the effects of these forms of community on test scores is to misunderstand how forms of social organization reasonably occur.

3. The presumption that forms of social organization should be decided primarily in terms of their consequences for standardized test scores begs some questions of political philosophy. It treats questions of rights in an uncritically consequentialist manner. One of the central claims of deontological liberalism is that the right is prior to the good. This means that the basic structures of society are to be seen as the products of an agreement between individuals about the character of fair social arrangements. It also means that such institutions are not to be determined by pointing to their consequences. I have suggested that liberals are likely to object that many forms of communitarianism have a consequentialist view of rights where rights are seen as contingent on their connection to the particular vision of the good that organizes the community. They will object that thinking about rights in this way inevitably threatens the liberty of dissenters. Insofar as the structural characteristics of schools and the forms of authority that they express involve various rights and liberties, to treat their effects on test scores as a central fact in their determination is to propose an overly consequentialist form of reasoning about them.

None of this means that studies seeking to link the structural characteristics of schools to achievement are inappropriate or irrelevant to reflection on schooling. What it does mean is that the relevance of such work needs to be assessed within a broader conceptual framework that treats the results of such research as one factor, among many, that is relevant to the question of school organization and in which the values that form the basis of the moral aspirations of an educational community are central. That we uncritically allow test scores to play a large normative role in these deliberations may be a measure of the extent to which we have lost any vision of the moral purposes of schooling in a liberal democratic society and of our incapacity to engage in serious public philosophy.

CONCLUSIONS

In what precedes I have been most intent on describing the structure of alternative views. Although the discerning reader has no doubt noted where my sympathies lie, the arguments I have developed for various views and the weaknesses I have noted have been designed to illuminate their differences and points of tension. They have not been meant to lead to a particular conclusion. Nor am I going to try to argue a position in any comprehensive way. That would make this already overlong paper a mere preface to a longer piece. Instead, I wish to "stake out" a position and give a few suggestions as to how I would develop it.

But first, what are the central themes? One is that human development requires "thick" cultures. Whether or not persons are by nature political animals, they are social animals. Despite much educational mythology to the contrary, their growth is not some unfolding of what is naturally within. It is highly dependent on initiation into practices and intellectual and moral traditions, into those social resources that we call culture, or into what Wittgenstein (1953) called forms of life. Thus, much depends on the quality of the social resources available to people and on the way in which these resources are made available to the young. Education depends on social capital.

But we are also a society in which there is much disagreement about the nature of a good life. We come from diverse religious, ethnic, national, and intellectual traditions. Much of our politics is rooted in this fact. Our politics has an elaborate set of rights and of checks and balances. Many of these are intended to keep us from ganging up on one another democratically or otherwise. Freedom of conscience is a central value in our polity.

The danger in this kind of politics as a way of operating in public schools is that it can serve to deny to children initiation into thick communities. When the fact of our diversity dominates educational policy, we are apt to produce a curriculum from which everything controversial, and thus everything important and interesting, has been expunged. We are likely to provide institutions that serve only narrowly conceived instrumental purposes. The human relations in such institutions will not be governed by shared assumptions about what constitutes a good education for a good life. There will be no such shared assumptions. Instead, human relations will be governed by the legalistic enforcement of rights that turn out not to be rooted in a coherent conception of education and are often, in practice, understood by students as means for avoiding the "imposition" of an education they wish to avoid (see Strike & Serow, 1978). Some of the richest resources in our society will be excluded from such schools. The "liberal cafeteria" of cultural goods will be restricted to cognitive fast food, and students will face their choices armed with untutored or even misshaped preferences that are unlikely to lead them to lives that are full and satisfying. The politics of disagreement is likely to produce public schools that have a thin and educationally incoherent culture.

This, at least, is the kind of assessment that communitarians might give of public schools. They are thus likely to see educational reform as requiring a movement toward thick communities for children to be nurtured in. But this is not one solution, for there are two different strategies that might be pursued. The first is to make those forms of local community that are still real and viable in our society more central in the lives of children. Regardless of the details of the fiscal and administrative arrangements for such schools, this means that the private functions of schooling will increase at the expense of the public ones. They will emphasize the pursuit of values not shared by the larger society. For such schools, the crucial difficulty will be their care for the public sphere. The second solution is to attempt to strengthen the center, to create a thicker democratic culture. For this view, the difficulty is to respect diversity and freedom of conscience. The first strategy emphasizes the liberal strain in our liberal democratic tradition; the second emphasizes the democratic strain. The first seeks autonomy or freedom of conscience, the right to pursue one's own vision; the second seeks the democratic *polis*. One ought not to think of these as sharply mutually exclusive. They have much in common. They are best seen as different emphases in a common liberal democratic tradition rooted in a belief in human equality and dignity. But it is likewise a mistake to believe that these different emphases are not real, that they do not require real choices, or that they can be blended into some happy synthesis. There are real issues to debate and real choices to be made.

I think of myself as a liberal with strong communitarian sympathies. I am a liberal because I believe that freedom is central. Part of respecting the dignity of human beings is to permit them to lead their lives in ways that seem satisfying to them, to pursue their own projects, and to live in concert with the requirements of their own consciences. Conversely, the greatest violence that one can do to people is to prevent them from living according to the dictates of their consciences. Although I consider myself to be a civic-minded fellow and much in me resonates the ideals of democratic participation, I find myself unable to recommend that the power of the state be brought to bear to make such ideals the operating philosophy of public schools. Although I value community and I believe that liberals should value community, I believe that the identification of community with state is the greatest danger to liberty. When the form of community is the democratic *polis*, the danger is more insidious because it appeals to so much that is noble and to so much that is a part of our democratic tradition. Nonetheless, the democratic *polis* is a threat to liberty, especially to freedom of conscience. I would not choose a social order in which the Amish cannot live with integrity.

At the same time, I have some strong communitarian sympathies. In my judgment, schools that are "just cafeterias"—that offer to students armed merely with cultural coherence a smorgasbord of cultural goods to choose among according to the dictates of their current desires, but where adults share no common educational commitments beyond the requirements of liberal justice, where students reflect the valuational incoherence of the adults, and where the relationships between adults and children are governed more by rules than by common commitment and mutual respect—are not healthy places for children. They deprive children both of affective nurturance and of ethical coherence. Both are required for development. A liberalism that produces such institutions as Grant describes in *The World We Created at Hamilton High* deserves the approbation that has been cast at it.

However, I believe that liberalism need not be construed in such a way. As I have suggested, liberalism has no deeply rooted quarrel with the importance of community in human life. Its quarrel is with the merger of community and state, with the *polis*. Thus, liberalism has a preference for local community and for pluralism. An education that is genuinely liberal thus will seek to nurture the initiation of children into local communities.

At the same time, liberal aspirations are not adequately served merely by the absorption of children into various local communities. Such communities untempered are likely to frustrate the development of autonomy and to violate transgenerational neutrality. Bethany School is not a liberal school.

Autonomy and transgenerational neutrality are served by an education that subjects the values and moral traditions that form local community to criticism and rational appraisal. A curriculum that succeeds here must, at a minimum, acquaint students with the disciplines. They are required for reflective distance from local community. It must also provide for dialogue. Alternative lives and alternative ideas must be represented by other people, and a liberal education must provide the chance to talk with them. Thus, genuinely liberal education has two phases: The first seeks to develop an appreciation of various goods and facility within a moral tradition by emphasizing immersion in local communities. The second seeks to serve autonomy and rationality by promoting academic study and undominated dialogue. A sense of justice will be promoted in both phases.

This vision involves the following considerations:

1. An adequate appreciation of some human goods requires initiation into the communities associated with the practices in which these goods are pursued and in which the excellences required for their pursuit can be learned. Because the standards of appraisal and an understanding of the goods of the practice are often internal to the practice and cannot be adequately grasped by the novice, while the current desires of children are a desideratum in a choice of the practices they will engage in, they cannot be the sole or determining factor.

2. The capacity for moral reflection requires the initiation into some sustained moral tradition(s) that contains adequately sophisticated cognitive resources to make moral reflection possible. Moral reflection, like other forms of reflection, can occur only against the background of some set of shared assumptions.

3. Autonomy is an achievement. It requires social resources that enable one to identify, achieve some psychic distance from (see Bricker, 1988), and appraise those initially formative assumptions that one received from initiation into one's primary communities. Academic disciplines are uniquely suited for this role. Likewise, the appraisal of one's own traditions requires critical interaction with those held by others. Such interaction is best accomplished in undominated dialogue with those who hold alternative views.

4. The acquisition of a sense of justice requires both phases of education. Initiation into communities associated with various practices and moral traditions provides the kinds of human associations that allow people to form the attachments that are the substratum of a sense of justice. Disciplines, especially the humanities, provide the cognitive background required to understand liberal democratic societies and institutions and to participate intelligently in their deliberations. Undominated dialogue puts students into contact with others who are different from themselves and other members of their group in a setting and process that is conducive to mutual understanding, to the development of attachments to others that do not depend on membership in a primary group, and to the de-

velopment of those intellectual virtues on which deliberative as well as democratic processes depend.

Schools that meet these requirements will not satisfy those whose conception of education is dominated by some vision of a democratic *polis*, but they offer much that the advocates of this vision approve. They provide for learning in coherent and deep communities, although these communities need not be the civic community. They provide for friendship, although that friendship need not be civic friendship. Both academic learning and dialogical competence are highly valued, although they are valued because they promote autonomy, justice, and the renewal and reformulation of particular traditions, not because they are required by the democratic *polis*. Although such schools might not promote the democratic *polis*, they would be greatly different from the morally chaotic and purposeless institutions that currently dominate the lives of children.

NOTES

[1] The ideas that scientific reasoning is democratic in its character and that the diffusion of the disposition and capacity for scientific reasoning is central to the development of democratic society were central commitments of the progressive education movement in the earlier part of this century (Dewey, 1920). These commitments turn on the beliefs that the essence of science is the scientific method and that the scientific method can be learned and practiced by everyone. Some contemporary philosophies of science, such as that of Kuhn (1970), reject the notion of something called the scientific method and emphasize that the ability to do science depends on the initiation of individuals into a sophisticated conceptual tradition. Science is done within the confines of a guild. Such views suggest that science is far more elitist in its character than Dewey would have allowed (for discussion, see Strike, 1981).

[2] There is some irony in the fact that liberalism seems to support a curriculum that is quite different than the liberal arts curriculum with its emphasis on a core of largely humanistic learning. Such a conception of the liberal arts education commonly results from a particular conception of the nature of the good life.

[3] Just as the welfare of the spotted owl can be seen as a barometer of ecological damage, the welfare of the Amish—or other groups that, although willing to treat outsiders justly, have no interest in participating with them in any form of *polis* and that, by common standards, are likely to be seen as having unusual beliefs and customs—is a good barometer of liberal tolerance.

[4] Consider the problem from a different perspective. Some educational goals or aspirations should be viewed as requirements of each school in a liberal democratic society. Others might be seen as implying requirements of the educational system in aggregate, but not as generating expectations for any particular school. For example, the duties to create democratic character or develop a sense of justice are affirmative obligations of each school in a democratic society, public or private. However, the duty to tolerate or encourage reasonable diversity among the citizens of a democratic society is better thought of as a requirement of the educational system. It need not demand that any particular school have any particular educational aim. It is consistent with, and may necessitate, some singularity of purpose of particular schools and some diversification between individual

schools. It seems likely that those views that have expansive perspectives of democratic obligations that apply to each and every school, public or private, in an educational system will also function to diminish the diversity of the overall educational system.

REFERENCES

Ackerman B. A. (1980). *Social justice in the liberal state*. New Haven, CT: Yale University Press.

Adler, M. J. (1982). *The Paideia proposal*. New York: Macmillan.

Adler, M. (1983a). Understanding the U.S.A. *Journal of Teacher Education, 34*(6), 35–37.

Adler, M. J. (1983b). *Paideia problems and possibilities*. New York: Macmillan.

Aiken, W., & La Follette, H. (Eds). (1980). *Whose child? Children's rights, parental authority, and state power*. New York: Littlefield, Adams.

Apple, M. (1982a). Reproduction and contradiction in education: An introduction. In M. Apple (Ed.), *Cultural and economic reproduction in education* (pp. 1–31). London: Routledge & Kegan Paul.

Apple, M. (1982b). *Education and power*. London: Routledge & Kegan Paul.

Aristotle. (1941). Politics. In R. McKeon (Ed.), *The basic works of Aristotle* (pp. 1127–1316). New York: Random House.

Aronowitz, S., & Giroux, H. A. (1985). *Education under siege*. South Hadley, MA: Bergin & Garvey.

Baer, R. (1980). A critique of the use of values clarification in environmental education. *Journal of Environmental Education, 12*(1), 13–16.

Barber, B. R. (1984). *Strong democracy: Participatory politics for a new age*. Berkeley: University of California Press.

Bellah, R. N., Madsen, R., Sullivan, W. M., Swidler, A., & Tipton, S. M. (1985). *Habits of the heart*. New York: Harper & Row.

Benn, S. I., & Peters, R. S. (1959). *Social principles and the democratic state*. Boston: Allen & Unwin.

Benne, K. D. (1985). The learning community. In E. E. Roberston (Ed.), *Philosophy of education 1984* (pp. 27–32). Normal, IL: Philosophy of Education Society.

Bennett, W. J. (1984). *To reclaim a legacy: A report on the humanities in higher education*. Washington, DC: National Endowment for the Humanities.

Bentham, J., & Mill, J. S. (1961). *The utilitarians*. Garden City, NY: Doubleday.

Berlin, I. (1969). *Four essays on liberty*. Oxford, UK: Oxford University Press.

Beyer, L. E. (1988). Can schools further democratic practices? *Theory Into Practice, 27*, 262–269.

Bilow, S. (1990). Future persons and the justification of education. In R. Page (Ed.), *Philosophy of education 1988* (pp. 320–330). Normal, IL: Philosophy of Education Society.

Bloom, A. D. (1987). *The closing of the American mind*. New York: Simon & Schuster.

Bowles, S., & Gintis, H. (1976). *Schooling in capitalist America*. New York: Basic Books.

Bowles, S., & Gintis, H. (1986). *Democracy and capitalism: Property, community, and the contradictions of modern social thought*. New York: Basic Books.

Boyer, E. L. (1983). *High school. A report on secondary education in America*. New York: Harper & Row.

Bricker, D. C. (1989). *Classroom life as civic education*. New York: Teachers College Press.
Buchanan, A. E. (1982). *Marx and justice: The radical critique of liberalism*. Totowa, NJ: Rowan and Littlefield.
Buchanan, A. E. (1989). Assessing the communitarian critique of liberalism. *Ethics, 99*, 852–882.
Bull, B. (1989). Liberalism and parenthood. In J. Giarelli (Ed.), *Philosophy of education 1988* (pp. 358–368). Normal, IL: Philosophy of Education Society.
Burbules, N. (1988). Ideology-critique and the philosophy of education. In B. Arnstine & D. Arnstine (Eds.), *Philosophy of education 1987* (pp. 187–196). Normal, IL: Philosophy of Education Society.
Butts, R. (1980). *The revival of civic learning: A rationale for citizenship education in American schools*. Bloomington, IN: Phi Delta Kappa Educational Foundation.
Butts, R. (1982). The revival of civic learning requires a prescribed curriculum. *Liberal Education, 68*, 377–401.
Butts, R. (1983). Teacher education and the revival of civic learning: A reprise of yesteryear's theme. *Journal of Teacher Education, 34*(6), 48–49.
Callan, E. (1988). *Autonomy and schooling*. Kingston, Canada: McGill-Queen's University Press.
Carnoy, M., & Levin, H. M. (1985). *Schooling and work in the democratic state*. Stanford, CA: Stanford University Press.
Chubb, J. (1988). Why the current wave of school reform will fail. *The Public Interest, 90*, 28–49.
Chubb, J., & Moe, T. (1990). *Politics, markets and American schools*. Washington, DC: Brookings Institute.
Coleman, J. S. (1974). *Youth: Transition to adulthood* (Report of the Panel on Youth of the President's Science Advisory Committee). Chicago: University of Chicago Press.
Coleman, J. S. (1981). Private schools, public schools, and the public interest. *The Public Interest, 64*, 19–30.
Coleman, J. S., & Hoffer, T. (1987). *Public and private high schools: The impact of communities*. New York: Basic Books.
Cooley, C. (1909). *Social organizations*. New York: Charles Scribner.
Coons, J. E., & Sugarman, S. D. (1978). *Education by choice: The case for family control*. Berkeley: University of California Press.
Counts, G. (1932). *Dare the schools build a new social order?* New York: Arno Press.
Crittendon, B. (1988). *Parents, the state and the right to educate*. Carlton, Victoria, Australia: Melbourne University Press.
Dahl, R. (1972). *Democracy in the United States*. Chicago: Rand McNally.
Dewey, J. (1916). *Democracy and education: An introduction to the philosophy of education*. New York: Macmillan.
Dewey, J. (1920). *Reconstruction in philosophy*. New York: H. Holt & Co.
Dewey, J. (1922). *Human nature and conduct: An introduction to social psychology*. New York: H. Holt & Co.
Dewey, J. (1927). *The public and its problems*. New York: H. Holt & Co.
Dewey, J. (1930). *Individualism old and new*. New York: Minton, Balch & Co.
Dewey, J. (1939). *Logic, the theory of inquiry*. New York: H. Holt & Co.
Dewey, J. (1963). *Liberalism and social action*. New York: Capricorn.
Durkheim, E. (1961). *Moral education*. New York: The Free Press.

Dworkin, R. M. (1977). *Taking rights seriously*. Cambridge, MA: Harvard University Press.

Dworkin, R. M. (1984). Liberalism. In M. J. Sandel, *Liberalism and its critics* (pp. 60–79). New York: New York University Press.

Feinberg, W. (1990). The moral responsibility of public schools. In J. I. Goodlad, R. Soder, & K. A. Sorotnik (Eds.), *The moral dimensions of teaching* (pp. 155–187). San Francisco: Jossey-Bass.

Friedman, M. (1962). *Capitalism and freedom*. Chicago: University of Chicago Press.

Gilligan, C. (1982). *In a different voice: Psychological theory and women's development*. Cambridge, MA: Harvard University Press.

Giroux, H. (1986). Authority, intellectuals, and the politics of practical learning. *Teachers College Record, 88*, 22–40.

Good, T., & Brophy, J. (1986). School effects. In M. Wittrock (Ed.), *Handbook of research in teaching* (pp. 570–602). New York: Macmillan.

Goodlad, J. I. (1984). *A place called school: Prospects for the future*. New York: McGraw-Hill.

Gough, J. W. (1950). *John Locke's political philosophy*. Oxford, England: Clarendon Press.

Grant, G. (1988). *The world we created at Hamilton High*. Cambridge, MA: Harvard University Press.

Green, T. F. (1971). *The activities of teaching*. New York: McGraw-Hill.

Green, T. (1984). *The formation of conscience in an age of technology*. Syracuse, NY: The John Dewey Society.

Greene, M. (1984). Excellence: Meanings and multiplicity. *Teachers College Record, 86*, 287–297.

Greene, M. (1988). *The dialectic of freedom*. New York: Teachers College Press.

Gutmann, A. (1980). Children, paternalism, and education: A liberal argument. *Philosophy and Public Affairs, 9*, 338–358.

Gutmann, A. (1987). *Democratic education*. Princeton, NJ: Princeton University Press.

Gutmann, A. (1989). Undemocratic education. In N. Rosenblum (Ed.), *Liberalism and moral life* (pp. 71–88). Cambridge, MA: Harvard University Press.

Habermas, J. (1979). *Communication and the evolution of society* (T. McCarthy, Trans.). Boston: Beacon Press.

Habermas, J. (1984). *The theory of communicative action. Vol. 1: Reason and the rationalization of society*. Boston: Beacon Press.

Hauerwas, S. (1977). *Truthfulness and tragedy: Further investigations into Christian ethics*. Notre Dame, IN: University of Notre Dame Press.

Hayek, F. A. von. (1960). *The constitution of liberty*. Chicago: University of Chicago Press.

Hegel, G. W. F. (1967). *Philosophy of right* (T. M. Knox, Trans.). New York: Oxford University Press.

Hegel, G. W. F. (1977). *Phenomenology of spirit* (A. V. Miller, Trans.). Oxford, England: Clarendon Press.

Hirsch, E. D., Jr. (1987). *Cultural literacy: What every literate American needs to know*. Boston: Houghton Mifflin.

Hobbes, T. (1968). *Leviathan*. New York: Collier Books.

Hutchins, R. (1953). *The conflict in education in a democratic society*. New York: Harper & Row.

Kant, I. (1956). *Critique of practical reason* (L. W. Beck, Trans.). Indianapolis: Bobbs-Merrill.

Kohlberg, L. (1963). The development of children's orientation toward a moral order: 1. Sequence in the development of moral thought. *Vita Humana, 6*, 11–33.

Kohlberg, L. (1969). Stage and sequence: The cognitive development approach to socialization. In D. A. Goslin (Ed.), *Handbook of socialization theory and research* (pp. 347–480). Chicago: Rand McNally.

Kohlberg, L. (1971a). Education for justice. A modern statement of the Socratic view. In L. Kohlberg, *The philosophy of moral development* (pp. 29–48). New York: Harper & Row.

Kohlberg, L. (1971b). From is to ought: How to commit the naturalistic falacy and get away with it in the study of moral development. In L. Kohlberg, *The philosophy of moral development* (pp. 101–189). New York: Harper & Row.

Kohlberg, L. (1980). High school democracy and education for a just society. In R. Mosher (Ed.), *Moral education: A first generation of research and development* (pp. 20–57). New York: Praeger.

Kristol, I. (1976). Moral and ethical development in a democratic society. In D. Purpel & K. Ryan (Eds.), *Moral education . . . It comes with the territory* (pp. 370–383). Berkeley, CA: McCutchan.

Kuhn, T. (1970). *The structure of scientific revolutions*. Chicago: University of Chicago Press.

Lee, G. C. (Ed.). (1961). *Crusade against ignorance: Thomas Jefferson on education*. New York: Teachers College Press.

Lemon v. Kurtzman, 403 U.S. 602, 91 S.Ct. 2105 (1971).

Lightfoot, S. L. (1983). *The good high school: Portraits of character and culture*. New York: Basic Books.

Locke, J. (1946). *A letter concerning toleration*. Oxford, England: Basil Blackwood.

Locke, J. (1960). Second treatise. In J. Locke, *Two treatises of government*. New York: Cambridge University Press.

Locke, J. (1964). *John Locke on education* (P. Gay, Ed.). New York: Teachers College Press.

Lockwood, A. (1976). A critical view of values clarification. In D. Purpel & K. Ryan (Eds.), *Moral education . . . It comes with the territory* (pp. 152–170). Berkeley, CA: McCutchan.

Lukes, S. (1973). *Individualism*. Oxford, England: Basil Blackwell.

MacIntyre, A. (1981). *After virtue*. Notre Dame, IN: Notre Dame University Press.

MacIntyre, A. (1988). *Whose justice? Which rationality?* Notre Dame, IN: Notre Dame University Press.

Mansbridge, J. M. (1990). Hard decisions. *Report from the Institute for Philosophy & Public Policy, 10*(1), 2–4.

Matthews, D. (1984). The public in practice and theory. *Public Administration Review, 44*, 120–125.

Mill, J. S. (1956). *On liberty*. New York: Bobbs-Merrill.

Miller, R. (1984). *Analyzing Marx: Morality, power and history*. Princeton, NJ: Princeton University Press.

Mitscerlich, A., & Mitscerlich, M. (1975). *The inability to mourn: Principles of collective behavior*. New York: Grove Press.

Mozart v. Hawkins County Public Schools, 647 F. Supp. 1194 (E.D. Tenn. 1986).

Nagel, T. (1986). *The view from nowhere*. New York: Oxford University Press.

Nash, R. J., & Griffin, R. S. (1987). Repairing the public-private split: Excellence, character and civic virtue. *Teachers College Record, 88*, 549–566.

National Commission on Excellence in Education. (1983). *A nation at risk: The imperative for educational reform*. Washington, DC: The Commission.
Neill, A. S. (1960). *Summerhill: A radical approach to child rearing*. New York: Hart Publishing.
Noddings, N. (1984). *Caring: A feminine approach to ethics and moral education*. Berkeley: University of California Press.
Nozick, R. (1974). *Anarchy, state and utopia*. New York: Basic Books.
Pepperell, K. (1990). Democracy and schooling: An essential contested relationship. In R. Page (Ed.), *Philosophy of education 1988* (pp. 226–238). Normal, IL: Philosophy of Education Society.
Peskin, A. (1986). *God's choice: The total world of a fundamentalist Christian school*. Chicago: University of Chicago Press.
Piaget, J. (1932). *The moral judgment of the child*. London: Kegan Paul, Trench, Trubner & Co.
Pierce v. Society of the Sisters of the Holy Names of Jesus and Mary, 268 U.S. 510, 45 S.Ct. 571 (1925).
Pincoffs, E. (1986). *Quandries and virtues*. Lawrence: University of Kansas Press.
Plato. (1962). *The Republic of Plato* (F. M. Cornford, Trans.). New York: Oxford University Press.
Prakash, M. S. (1984). In pursuit of wholeness: Moral development, the ethics of care and the virtue of *Philia*. In E. E. Robertson (Ed.), *Philosophy of education 1984* (pp. 64–74). Normal, IL: Philosophy of Education Society.
Pratte, R. (1988). *The civic imperative: Examining the need for civic education*. New York: Teachers College Press.
Preskill, S. (1990). Strong democracy, the ethic of caring and civic education. In R. Page (Ed.), *Philosophy of education 1988* (pp. 217–225). Normal, IL: Philosophy of Education Society.
Raths, L. E., Harmin, M., & Simon, S. B. (1966). *Values and teaching*. Columbus, OH: Charles E. Merrill.
Rawls, J. (1971). *A theory of justice*. Cambridge, MA: Harvard University Press.
Rawls, J. (1985). Justice as fairness; political, not metaphysical. *Philosophy and Public Affairs, 14*, 223–251.
Rawls, J. (1988). The priority of right and ideas of the good. *Philosophy and Public Affairs, 17*, 251–276.
Raywid, M. (1988). Community and schools: A prolegomenon. *Teachers College Record, 90*, 197–210.
Rogers, C. R. (1983). *Freedom to learn for the 80's: A view of what education might become*. Columbus, OH: Charles E. Merrill.
Rousseau, J. J. (1968). *The social contract*. Baltimore: Penguin Books.
Rowan, B. (1990). Commitment and control: Alternative strategies for the organizational design of schools. *Review of Research in Education, 16*, 353–389.
Rutter, M. (1979). *Fifteen thousand hours: Secondary schools and their effects on children*. Cambridge, MA: Harvard University Press.
Sandel, M. J. (1982). *Liberalism and the limits of justice*. New York: Cambridge University Press.
Sandel, M. J. (1988). Religious liberty: Freedom of conscience or freedom of choice? In *Proceedings of the National Symposium on the First Amendment, Religious Liberty Clauses and American Public Life* (pp. 24–42). Washington, DC: Williamsburg Charles Foundation.
Schrag, F. (1978). From childhood to adulthood: Assigning rights and responsi-

bilities. In K. Strike & K. Egan (Eds.), *Ethics and educational policy* (pp. 61–78). London: Routledge & Kegan Paul.
Schwandt, T. A. (1989). Recapturing moral discourse in evaluation. *Educational Research, 18*(8), 11–16.
Sichel, B. (1988). *Moral education: Character, community, and ideals*. Philadelphia: Temple University Press.
Snook, I. A. (1972). *Concepts of indoctrination*. London: Routledge & Kegan Paul.
Stout, J. (1988). *Ethics after Babel*. Boston: Beacon Press.
Stoutland, F. (1990). Self and society in the claims of individualism. *Studies in Philosophy and Education, 10*, 105–138.
Strike, K. A. (1981). *Liberty and learning*. Oxford, England: M. Robertson.
Strike, K. (1982). *Educational policy and the just society*. Urbana: University of Illinois Press.
Strike, K. A. (1989). *Liberal justice and the Marxist critique of education*. New York: Routledge.
Strike, K. (1990). Are secular ethical languages religiously neutral? *The Journal of Law and Politics, 6*, 469–502.
Strike, K. (in press). Liberal justice: Aspirations and limitations. In D. Verstagen (Ed.), *Annual yearbook of the American Education Finance Association*.
Strike, K. A., & Serow, R. (1978). How tolerant are high school students? *Educational Forum, 42*, 327, 336.
Sullivan, W. M. (1982). *Reconstructing public philosophy*. Berkeley: University of California Press.
Taylor, C. (1984). Hegel: History and politics. In M. J. Sandel (Ed.), *Liberalism and its critics* (pp. 177–200). New York: New York University Press.
Taylor, C. (1989). *Sources of the self: Sources of modern identity*. Cambridge, MA: Harvard University Press.
Taylor, P. W. (1964–1965). Moral virtue and responsibility for character. *Analysis, 25*(1), 17–23.
Tocqueville, A. de. (1969). *Democracy in America*. Garden City, NY: Doubleday.
Tucker, R. C. (1978). *The Marx-Engels reader* (2nd ed.). New York: W. W. Norton.
Walzer, M. (1983). *Spheres of justice*. New York: Basic Books.
White, J. P. (1973). *Towards a compulsory curriculum*. London: Routledge & Kegan Paul.
White, J. P. (1982). *The aims of education restated*. London: Routledge & Kegan Paul.
White, P. (1983). *Beyond domination: An essay in the political philosophy of education*. London: Routledge & Kegan Paul.
Wigginton, E. (1985). *Sometimes a shining moment: Twenty years teaching in a high school classroom*. Garden City, NY: Anchor/Doubleday.
Will, G. F. (1983). *Statecraft as soulcraft: What government does*. New York: Simon & Schuster.
Williams, B. (1985). *Ethics and the limits of philosophy*. Cambridge, MA: Harvard University Press.
Willis, P. E. (1977). *Learning to labour*. Farnborough, England: Saxon House.
Wisconsin v. Yoder, 406 U.S. 205 (1972).
Wittgenstein, L. (1953). *Philosophical investigations*. Oxford, England: Basil Blackwell.
Wolff, R. (1975). *Reading Rawls: Critical studies on Rawls' A Theory of Justice*. New York: Basic Books.

Wood, A. W. (1981). *Karl Marx*. London: Routledge & Kegan Paul.

Worsfold, V. (1987). Competing conceptions of community. In N. C. Burbules (Ed.), *Philosophy of education 1986* (pp. 287–298). Normal, IL: Philosophy of Education Society.

Wringe, C. (1981). *Children's rights: A philosophical study*. London: Routledge & Kegan Paul.

Wringe, C. (1984). *Democracy, schooling and political education*. London: George Allen & Unwin.